The Editor

ROBERT S. LEVINE is Professor of English at the University of Maryland, College Park. He is the author of *Conspiracy and Romance: Studies in Brockden Brown, Cooper, Hawthorne, and Melville* and *Martin Delany, Frederick Douglass, and the Politics of Representative Identity*, and the editor of *The Cambridge Companion to Herman Melville, Martin R. Delany: A Documentary Reader*, and several other volumes.

A NORTON CRITICAL EDITION

Nathaniel Hawthorne

THE HOUSE OF THE SEVEN GABLES

AUTHORITATIVE TEXT
CONTEXTS
CRITICISM

Edited by

ROBERT S. LEVINE

UNIVERSITY OF MARYLAND, COLLEGE PARK

W. W. NORTON & COMPANY • *New York* • *London*

W. W. Norton & Company has been independent since its founding in 1923, when William Warder Norton and Mary D. Herter Norton first published lectures delivered at the People's Institute, the adult education division of New York City's Cooper Union. The Nortons soon expanded their program beyond the Institute, publishing books by celebrated academics from America and abroad. By mid-century, the two major pillars of Norton's publishing program—trade books and college texts—were firmly established. In the 1950s, the Norton family transferred control of the company to its employees, and today—with a staff of four hundred and a comparable number of trade, college, and professional titles published each year—W. W. Norton & Company stands as the largest and oldest publishing house owned wholly by its employees.

The text of this book is composed in Fairfield Medium
with the display set in Bernhard Modern.
Composition by PennSet, Inc.

Manufacturing by the Courier Companies—Westford Division.
Production manager: Benjamin Reynolds.

Library of Congress Cataloging-in-Publication Data
Hawthorne, Nathaniel, 1804–1864.
    The house of the seven gables : authoritative text, contents, criticism / Nathaniel Hawthorne ; edited by Robert S. Levine.
        p. cm. — (A Norton critical edition)
    Includes bibliographical references.

    ISBN 0-393-92476-9 (pbk.)

    1. Haunted houses—Fiction. 2. Salem (Mass.)—Fiction. 3. Hawthorne, Nathaniel, 1804–1864. House of the seven gables. I. Levine, Robert S. (Robert Steven), 1953– II. Title. III. Series.

PS1861.A2L485 2005
813'.3—dc22
                                                        2005051294

W. W. Norton & Company, Inc., 500 Fifth Avenue, New York, N.Y. 10110-0017
www.wwnorton.com

W. W. Norton & Company Ltd., Castle House,
75/76 Wells Street, London W1T 3QT

1 2 3 4 5 6 7 8 9 0

Contents

Introduction

In March 1850, after years of toiling in semiobscurity as a writer of tales and sketches, the forty-five-year-old Nathaniel Hawthorne published his first novel, *The Scarlet Letter*, to great acclaim and good (albeit modest) sales of around six thousand copies. Writing the novel after the loss of his civil service job at the Salem Custom House and the death of his mother, Hawthorne tapped into what Herman Melville termed his "great power of blackness" to produce a tale so intensely concentrated in its tragic tone and vision that, as Hawthorne proudly reported to his friend Horatio Bridge, its conclusion gave his wife, Sophia, "a grievous headache." Eager to build on the success of *The Scarlet Letter*, Hawthorne's publisher James T. Fields urged him to get to work on a second novel, and Hawthorne readily complied, beginning the writing in September 1850. He completed *The House of the Seven Gables* within five months, and it was published in April 1851. Sophia Hawthorne much preferred the conclusion of her husband's second novel—or at least it made her happier. "There is unspeakable grace and beauty in the conclusion," she declared, "throwing back upon the sterner tragedy of the commencement an ethereal light, and a dear home-loveliness and satisfaction."[1] Hawthorne, too, appeared to prefer the "home-loveliness" of his second novel to the putative gloom of his first, remarking to Bridge that the novel is "as good as anything that I can hope to write" and asserting to his friend (and reviewer) Evert Duyckinck that the novel is a "more natural and healthy product of my mind." Whereas some reviewers of *The Scarlet Letter* were disturbed by its darkness, reviewers and readers of *The House of the Seven Gables* were nearly unanimous in celebrating the novel for its literary mastery, grace, and cheerful perspective on life's possibilities. As Henry T. Tuckerman rhapsodized about the novel in his June 1851 essay-review in the *Southern Literary Messenger*: "The natural refinements of the human heart, the holiness of a ministry of disinterested affection, the gracefulness of the

---

1. Herman Melville, "Hawthorne and His Mosses," in Melville, *The Piazza Tales and Other Prose Pieces, 1839–1860*, ed. Harrison Hayford et al. (1987), 243; Hawthorne to Horatio Bridge, February 4, 1850, in Hawthorne, *The Letters, 1843–1853*, ed. Thomas Woodson et al. (1985), 311; Julian Hawthorne, *Nathaniel Hawthorne and His Wife*, 2 vols., 3rd ed. (1885), I:383.

homeliest services when irradiated by cheerfulness and benevolence, are illustrated with singular beauty." Hawthorne thought
Tuckerman got things just right, and he wrote Tuckerman immediately upon reading his "beautiful article": "I felt that you saw into
my books and understood what I meant." Hawthorne's readers, too,
seemed to appreciate *The House of the Seven Gables* even more
than *The Scarlet Letter*, for in its first year of publication it outsold
The Scarlet Letter by over seven hundred copies.[2]

Though this overview of Hawthorne's relatively late emergence as
a novelist tells a happy story of burgeoning authorial confidence
and success, it also looks forward to problems to come for the reputation of *The House of the Seven Gables*. True, in the first year after its publication, the novel was received more enthusiastically
than *The Scarlet Letter*, but over their initial ten years in print *The
Scarlet Letter* would outsell *The House of the Seven Gables* by approximately two thousand copies (13,500 to 11,550). While *The
Scarlet Letter* would quickly become known as Hawthorne's master-
piece, *The House of the Seven Gables* would be viewed with suspicion as a novel that suffers for its dogged determination to provide
readers with uplift and good cheer. Critics have been especially
hard on the very conclusion that had moved Sophia to celebrate
her husband's artistry, with some regarding it not only as
Hawthorne's sell-out to his middle-class readership but also as a
sign of his blindness to the more complex interrogation of property
rights and class that had informed the bulk of the novel. I will return to the problem of the ending (without ruining the suspense for
new readers). But first it would be useful to reconsider the question
of the novel's supposed normalcy, a virtual tenet of criticism of *The
House of the Seven Gables* for the past hundred years or so that has
helped keep the novel in the shadows of *The Scarlet Letter*. *The
House of the Seven Gables* may be much stranger than its critical
reputation suggests.

To recover a sense of that strangeness, we should consider
Hawthorne's own comments on the novel in a letter to Fields of
November 1850. While explaining to Fields that he aspired toward
a realism commensurate with the detailed "minuteness of a Dutch
picture," he confessed to his difficulty in working as a realist, and
consequently asserted his rights as a romancer to depart from strict
verisimilitude. But even as he declared those rights, he recognized

2. Hawthorne to Bridge, March 15, 1851, in *Letters, 1843–1853*, 406; Hawthorne to E. A.
Duyckinck, April 27, 1851, in *Letters, 1843–1853*, 421; Henry T. Tuckerman,
"Nathaniel Hawthorne," *Southern Literary Messenger* 17 (June 1851), 348; Hawthorne
to H. T. Tuckerman, June 20, 1851, in *Letters, 1843–1853*, 452. See also Duyckinck,
p. 323 herein, and Tuckerman, p. 327 herein. For sales figures, see the Introduction to
Nathaniel Hawthorne, *The House of the Seven Gables*, ed. William Charvat et al. (1965),
xx.

the risks. "Sometimes, when tired of it," he stated to Fields of his romance in progress, "it strikes me that the whole is an absurdity, from beginning to end; but the fact is, in writing a romance, a man is always—or always ought to be—careering on the utmost verge of a precipitous absurdity, and the skill lies in coming as close as possible, without actually tumbling over."[3] Voicing his frustrations at getting things right, Hawthorne in this letter offers an artistic manifesto of sorts, asserting what he as a writer "ought" to do and is in fact trying to do: take the creative risks that could result in either a wonderfully illuminating new work of art, or a disaster. The image of Hawthorne as a risk taker and even as an experimental novelist attempting to plumb the limits of romance poses a challenge to the talk of normalcy, good cheer, and prudential artistry that has surrounded the critical discussion of *The House of the Seven Gables*. Choosing a method that involves "careering on the utmost verge of a precipitous absurdity," Hawthorne is trying to do nothing less than comprehend the realities of the increasingly fragmented modern world of the antebellum United States through the mode of romance.

Hawthorne grounds the world of *The House of the Seven Gables* in the known "realistic" world of Salem in the 1840s or very early 1850s in relation to its historical past, particularly the Salem witch crisis of 1692. In doing so, he presents his readers with a cast of characters, melodramatic plot, and worldview suggestive of a temperament radically at odds with the conventional values and perspectives of his reading public. Consider the novel's main characters. In Hepzibah we have a prideful, scowling old woman who has spent much of her life waiting for her brother to be released from prison. In the old man Clifford we have a repressed sensualist and possible murderer who is taken to the extremes of cosmic exhilaration by the simple act of sipping a cup of coffee. What sort of hero and heroine are these? More conventionally, there are Holgrave and Phoebe, but in Holgrave we have an enthusiast of the arts and social reform who seems at a sadistic remove from the lives that he observes, judges, and sometimes represents; and in Phoebe we have an angel of the house who emerges out of thin air (or from a country carriage) and soon exerts an eerie redemptive dominance over the domestic order of the House of the Seven Gables. The grasping hypocrite Judge Pyncheon seems an obvious villain, though much of what we know about him comes to us through rumor, and the most telling knowledge about this honored politician is communicated by a fly. In the novel's characterizations and plot, there is an obsession with the corporeal weight of

---

3. Hawthorne to J. T. Fields, letter of November 3, 1850, in *Letters, 1843–1853*, 371.

history that speaks in an undertone similar to the hissing appre-
hended by Walt Whitman's persona in "Out of the Cradle Endlessly
Rocking" (1859): "death, death, death, death, death."[4] Though
Hawthorne appears to resolve the novel's unconventionalities and
gloom, over the course of the novel he also presents a less than redemptive vision of what he terms the "Now" of the social world:
evanescent, confused, elusive, and lacking in transcendental cer-
tainties and meanings. As he remarks rather "unhealthily" on Clifford's conception of the present moment: "he has only this
visionary and impalpable Now, which, if you once look closely at it,
is nothing."[5] However normal and pleasing *The House of the Seven
Gables* is by reputation, the novel has a close literary kinship with
Poe's perverse and death-ridden "The Fall of the House of Usher"
(p. 260 herein).

That said, there is a crucial difference between Poe's "The Fall of
the House of Usher" and Hawthorne's *The House of the Seven
Gables*, even beyond the matter of their respective endings. In Poe's
short story, the narrator is disconcertingly vague in describing the
social world. But in *The House of the Seven Gables* Hawthorne engages fully and concretely the new cultural developments of the antebellum period—its technologies, politics, and ideologies. As
Hawthorne's November 1850 letter to Fields suggests, he worried
over the possible incongruities of Dutch realism and his own version of romance, and he expressed similar concerns to Fields in a
letter written on the day in January 1851 when he completed the
draft of the novel: "It has undoubtedly one disadvantage, in being
brought so close to the present time; whereby its romantic improb-
abilities become more glaring."[6] Hawthorne's confession here, at
the precise moment at which he is preparing to deliver the manuscript to Fields, can again be read as an assertion of aesthetic vision
and method akin to his wish to "career" on the brink of precipitous
absurdities. In *The House of the Seven Gables*, Hawthorne *chooses*
to work as a fictionalist in a mode that may appear to be inappropriate to his interest in social reality but, on second glance, is peculiarly well suited to a social reality with its own phantasmagoric
character. For Hawthorne, romance best conveys the reigning reality of his modern world.

As a romancer, Hawthorne used his second novel to investigate
his social world with a latitude and freedom far more telling than
documentary realism. In the Gothic romance tradition established
by British writers such as Horace Walpole and Ann Radcliffe, he

---

4. Walt Whitman, "Out of the Cradle Endlessly Rocking," in Whitman, *Leaves of Grass,* ed.
   Scully Bradley and Harold W. Blodgett (1973), 253.
5. Hawthorne, *The House of the Seven Gables,* p. 107 herein.
6. Hawthorne to J. T. Fields, letter of January 27, 1851, in *Letters, 1843–1853,* 386.

explores the sometimes hidden connections between genealogy and property. Given his interest in blood and ownership, to what extent is he also commenting on contemporary debates on race and slavery? It is difficult to say, though it is also difficult not to notice the parallels that Hawthorne develops between the genealogical history of the Pyncheon fowls and that of the Pyncheons. His close attention to Chanticleer's racial pride, as analogized to Judge Pyncheon's (and vice-versa), is a shrewd demystification of the racial (and highly racist) thinking of the day. David Anthony argues (p. 438 herein) that Hawthorne uses romance to make race and property fluid and highly provisional categories. Whatever his intentions in adopting such a perspective on race, Hawthorne in *The House of the Seven Gables* participates in the cultural work of antislavery writers such as William Wells Brown and Harriet Beecher Stowe, who similarly raised questions about the accepted "truths" of genealogical histories, race, and property rights.

Hawthorne's methods and perspective in the novel do not come without their contradictions and paradoxes. For his entire adult life Hawthorne remained aligned with the Democratic Party, the party that time and again sought the expedient way of keeping the slave South in its fold. In view of this biographical fact, how are we to interpret a novel that questions the "truths" of racial genealogies and property rights while, in its happy ending and its blithe unconcern for nonwhite characters, seems to ignore the very implications of its unmaskings? Hawthorne complained to his publisher, William D. Ticknor, about the "d——d mob of scribbling women" in an infamous letter of 1855.[7] Given Hawthorne's longstanding distrust of some (but not all) women writers, what are we to make of a novel that, with its interest in the gendered interiors of a house, seems as domestic and sentimental as any of the writings that his letter had implicitly criticized? Hawthorne clearly was fascinated by new technologies of communication and representation. To what extent does he succeed in using the older and somewhat traditional mode of romance to convey his own views on technology? These are just some of the conflicts and questions that have helped make criticism on the novel particularly lively over the past several decades.

The primary and secondary materials in this Norton Critical Edition of *The House of the Seven Gables* are intended to help readers participate in these debates by providing materials on the novel's more compelling contexts, by offering an overview of the novel's critical history, and by reprinting a number of the recent critical essays that have reenergized critical discussion of the novel. The materials in the Contexts section are grouped into four distinct categories.

---

7. Hawthorne to W. D. Ticknor, letter of January 19, 1855, in Hawthorne, *The Letters, 1853–1856*, ed. Thomas Woodson et al. (1988), 303.

The History section presents readers with selections from a number of the primary texts that Hawthorne drew on for his representation of Salem history. The section Hawthorne and the Literary Sketch will enable readers to see how a mode of writing central to his earlier career remained central to his career as a novelist. Hawthorne's novel is about a house, and in antebellum culture the house had all sorts of associations, whether as a figure of the body, of the genealogical house (and thus of racial descent), or of the republican middle class. The insides and outsides of houses were also at the center of contemporary ideological debates on gender and separate spheres. The documents in the Houses section will provide readers with a fuller grasp of the discursive overlaps and implications of these varied ways of thinking about the house during the antebellum period. Finally, the selections in the Daguerreotypy and Other Technologies section will help readers better understand the centrality of technology to Hawthorne's second novel, especially the newly invented form of photography, daguerreotypy, which made its way from France to the United States in 1839. That same year Hawthorne wrote his fiancée Sophia Peabody about daguerreotypy: "I wish there was something in the intellectual world analogous to the Daguerrotype [sic] (is that the name of it?) in the visible— something which should print off our deepest, and subtlest, and delicatest thoughts and feelings, as minutely and accurately as the above-mentioned instrument paints the various aspects of nature."[8] In *The House of the Seven Gables*, Hawthorne engaged daguerreotypy and other technologies from a variety of perspectives, including that of the romancer anxious about competing with the new technologies that were capturing the public's attention. The section Daguerreotypy and Other Technologies includes five texts on daguerreotypy, plus additional selections on other key technological developments that Hawthorne represents in his novel: mesmerism (hypnotism), the railroad, and the prison.

In the tradition of the Norton Critical Editions, this edition of *The House of the Seven Gables* offers an extensive section on the critical response to *The House of the Seven Gables* from the time of its publication to the present day. As readers of the articles in the Criticism section will note, the question of the novel's ending has for years been central to critical discussions of the novel, as has the question of the novel's health or normalcy. (See, for example, Catharine Sedgwick's letter of 1851 [p. 320 herein], which offers a dissenting perspective on the matter of the novel's good cheer.) The Criticism section includes nine contemporary responses, a sampling of major critical works written from 1879 to 1979, and eight

8. Hawthorne to Sophia Peabody, letter of December 11, 1839, in Hawthorne, *The Letters, 1813–1843*, ed. Thomas Woodson et al. (1984), 384.

influential essays published since 1981. A number of recent critics have emphasized that, rather than providing a fictional bromide for troubled times, *The House of the Seven Gables* addressed some of the most vexed political and cultural issues of the day: social class, property rights, race, the consequences of the new media, and so on. Though some critics continue to complain about it, there is an increasing critical consensus that *The House of the Seven Gables* is not so easily reduced to its ending.

And yet the ending will no doubt remain central to critical debate on the novel. In the spirit and tradition of romance (and with all of the pleasures of Shakespearean romance), Hawthorne concludes *The House of the Seven Gables* on an affirmative note. But in celebrating the end to the long cycle of violence and retribution chronicled in the novel, Hawthorne provides the seemingly marginal Uncle Venner with an important place in the novel's happy (re)construction of family. Hawthorne's disposition of Uncle Venner raises questions about what sort of "family" he is constructing in this supposedly conventional resolution. Why is it that Hawthorne leaves us not with two individuals choosing to live together happily ever after but with five? Stranger than most readers care to admit, the conclusion is just one "precipitous absurdity" among many that help give *The House of the Seven Gables* its meaning and its power.

A Note on the Text and Annotations

The text of *The House of the Seven Gables* is that of the Centenary Edition of the Works of Nathaniel Hawthorne, a publication of the Ohio State University Center for Textual Studies and the Ohio State University Press. Published in 1965, the Centenary text of *The House of the Seven Gables*, edited by William Charvat et al., provides what its editors argue is the version of the novel that is closest to Hawthorne's intentions. Since 1965, the Centenary has been accepted by most scholars as the best available text of *The House of the Seven Gables*. Because Hawthorne's manuscript of the novel survives, the editors of the Centenary text were able to collate the manuscript against the edition first published by Ticknor, Reed, and Fields on April 9, 1851 (and against numerous other editions as well), and to draw informed conclusions about the variants between the manuscript and the published versions. Unfortunately, the proof sheets from the April 1851 printing do not survive, so we can never be absolutely certain about which changes from manuscript to book were made by Hawthorne and which by an editor (or by printers who may have made errors). We do know that Hawthorne never complained about the Ticknor, Reed, and Fields text, which went into several reprintings. In 1883 Houghton, Mifflin, and Company brought out the first of its several printings of *The House of the Seven Gables* in their popular Riverside Edition. The Riverside emerged as the most widely used text until the publication of the Centenary in 1965. It is important to note that Hawthorne's contemporary readers and reviewers responded to the text established by Ticknor, Reed, and Fields in 1851; that critics such as William Dean Howells and F. O. Matthiessen responded to the text established by Houghton, Mifflin in 1883; and that neither is exactly the same as the Centenary. The editors of the Centenary *The House of the Seven Gables* provide several sections in their edition that will be of use to those interested in textual history, including a comprehensive listing of the variants between the manuscript and the first book publication.

The footnotes in this Norton Critical Edition aspire to offer basic information in a nonintrusive manner about such matters as Hawthorne's many literary and historical allusions; some effort has also been made to use the footnotes to guide the reader to the appropriate material in the Contexts sections. The materials in the Contexts sections are also annotated. With the exception of the footnotes to the works reprinted in "Selections from Classic Studies" and "Recent Criticism, 1981–Present," all of the footnotes have been provided by the editor. In the final two sections, the footnotes (with the exception of the initial source note) belong to the respective authors, unless otherwise indicated.

Acknowledgments

I am pleased to acknowledge the individuals who have helped me complete this project. I am indebted to Marcy Dinius for sharing sections of her book in progress on daguerreotypy and antebellum literature and for leading me to the image that is on the cover of this volume. My thanks to Christopher Hale for offering crucial help with the editing of the primary documents, and I am also pleased to thank Neil Fraistat and Ivy Goodman for their help along the way. I am grateful to David Anthony, Amy Lang, and Rick Millington for aiding and abetting in the adaptation of their essays and chapters for this Norton Critical Edition. For helping me gain access to some of the rarer documents in this edition, my thanks to the librarians at the Library of Congress's Rare Book Room. I am delighted to acknowledge my indebtedness to my editor at Norton, Carol Bemis, who throughout the project has been a model of collegiality and professionalism; and I am grateful as well to Brian B. Baker for his skillful work on the final phases of production.

Despite her serious illness, Gillian Brown graciously helped me adapt her chapter for this edition. I am honored to dedicate this Norton Critical Edition of *The House of the Seven Gables* to the memory of Gillian Brown, an extraordinary scholar, teacher, and colleague.

The Text of
THE HOUSE OF THE
SEVEN GABLES

Preface

When a writer calls his work a Romance, it need hardly be observed that he wishes to claim a certain latitude, both as to its fashion and material, which he would not have felt himself entitled to assume, had he professed to be writing a Novel. The latter form of composition is presumed to aim at a very minute fidelity, not merely to the possible, but to the probable and ordinary course of man's experience. The former—while, as a work of art, it must rigidly subject itself to laws, and while it sins unpardonably, so far as it may swerve aside from the truth of the human heart—has fairly a right to present that truth under circumstances, to a great extent, of the writer's own choosing or creation. If he think fit, also, he may so manage his atmospherical medium as to bring out or mellow the lights and deepen and enrich the shadows of the picture. He will be wise, no doubt, to make a very moderate use of the privileges here stated, and, especially, to mingle the Marvellous rather as a slight, delicate, and evanescent flavor, than as any portion of the actual substance of the dish offered to the Public. He can hardly be said, however, to commit a literary crime, even if he disregard this caution.

In the present work, the Author has proposed to himself (but with what success, fortunately, it is not for him to judge) to keep undeviatingly within his immunities. The point of view in which this Tale comes under the Romantic definition, lies in the attempt to connect a by-gone time with the very Present that is flitting away from us. It is a Legend, prolonging itself, from an epoch now gray in the distance, down into our own broad daylight, and bringing along with it some of its legendary mist, which the Reader, according to his pleasure, may either disregard, or allow it to float almost imperceptibly about the characters and events, for the sake of a picturesque effect. The narrative, it may be, is woven of so humble a texture as to require this advantage, and, at the same time, to render it the more difficult of attainment.

Many writers lay very great stress upon some definite moral purpose, at which they profess to aim their works. Not to be deficient, in this particular, the Author has provided himself with a moral;— the truth, namely, that the wrong-doing of one generation lives into the successive ones, and, divesting itself of every temporary advantage, becomes a pure and uncontrollable mischief;—and he would feel it a singular gratification, if this Romance might effectually convince mankind (or, indeed, any one man) of the folly of tumbling down an avalanche of ill-gotten gold, or real estate, on the heads of an unfortunate posterity, thereby to maim and crush them, until the accumulated mass shall be scattered abroad in its original atoms. In good faith, however, he is not sufficiently imaginative to flatter himself with the slightest hope of this kind. When romances do really teach anything, or produce any effective operation, it is usually through a far more subtle process than the ostensible one. The Author has considered it hardly worth his while, therefore, re-lentlessly to impale the story with its moral, as with an iron rod—or rather, as by sticking a pin through a butterfly—thus at once de-priving it of life, and causing it to stiffen in an ungainly and unnat-ural attitude. A high truth, indeed, fairly, finely, and skilfully wrought out, brightening at every step, and crowning the final de-velopement of a work of fiction, may add an artistic glory, but is never any truer, and seldom any more evident, at the last page than at the first.

The Reader may perhaps choose to assign an actual locality[1] to the imaginary events of this narrative. If permitted by the historical connection, (which, though slight, was essential to his plan,) the Author would very willingly have avoided anything of this nature. Not to speak of other objections, it exposes the Romance to an in-flexible and exceedingly dangerous species of criticism, by bringing his fancy-pictures almost into positive contact with the realities of the moment. It has been no part of his object, however, to describe local manners, nor in any way to meddle with the characteristics of a community for whom he cherishes a proper respect and a natural regard. He trusts not to be considered as unpardonably offending, by laying out a street that infringes upon nobody's private rights, and appropriating a lot of land which had no visible owner, and building a house, of materials long in use for constructing castles in the air. The personages of the Tale—though they give themselves out to be of ancient stability and considerable prominence—are re-ally of the Author's own making, or, at all events, of his own mixing; their virtues can shed no lustre, nor their defects redound, in the remotest degree, to the discredit of the venerable town of which they profess to be inhabitants. He would be glad, therefore, if—especially in the quarter to which he alludes—the book may be read strictly as a Romance, having a great deal more to do with the clouds overhead, than with any portion of the actual soil of the County of Essex.[2]

Lenox, January 27, 1851.

---

1. Hawthorne's readers would have recognized the locale as based on Salem, Massachu-setts.
2. In northeastern Massachusetts and includes Salem.

The House of the Seven Gables

I. The Old Pyncheon Family

Half-way down a by-street of one of our New England towns, stands a rusty wooden house, with seven acutely peaked gables facing towards various points of the compass, and a huge, clustered chimney in the midst.[3] The street is Pyncheon-street; the house is the old Pyncheon-house; and an elm-tree of wide circumference, rooted before the door, is familiar to every town-born child by the title of the Pyncheon-elm. On my occasional visits to the town aforesaid, I seldom fail to turn down Pyncheon-street, for the sake of passing through the shadow of these two antiquities; the great elm-tree, and the weather-beaten edifice.

The aspect of the venerable mansion has always affected me like a human countenance,[4] bearing the traces not merely of outward storm and sunshine, but expressive also of the long lapse of mortal life, and accompanying vicissitudes, that have passed within. Were these to be worthily recounted, they would form a narrative of no small interest and instruction, and possessing, moreover, a certain remarkable unity, which might almost seem the result of artistic arrangement. But the story would include a chain of events, extending over the better part of two centuries, and, written out with reasonable amplitude, would fill a bigger folio volume, or a longer series of duodecimos,[5] than could prudently be appropriated to the annals of all New England, during a similar period. It consequently becomes imperative to make short work with most of the traditionary lore of which the old Pyncheon-house, otherwise known as the House of the Seven Gables, has been the theme. With a brief sketch, therefore, of the circumstances amid which the foundation of the house was laid, and a rapid glimpse at its quaint exterior, as it grew black in the prevalent east-wind—pointing, too, here and

---

3. If Hawthorne had an actual house in mind, it would have been the five-gabled house in Salem, Massachusetts, owned by his cousin Susan Ingersoll, which, he had learned in 1840, formerly had seven gables.
4. See the opening of Edgar Allan Poe's "The Fall of the House of Usher" (p. 260 herein).
5. Books made from sheets that have been folded to make twelve pages. "Folio": book made from sheets that have been folded in half to make two pages.

there, at some spot of more verdant mossiness on its roof and walls—we shall commence the real action of our tale at an epoch not very remote from the present day. Still, there will be a connection with the long past—a reference to forgotten events and personages, and to manners, feelings, and opinions, almost or wholly obsolete—which, if adequately translated to the reader, would serve to illustrate how much of old material goes to make up the freshest novelty of human life. Hence, too, might be drawn a weighty lesson from the little regarded truth, that the act of the passing generation is the germ which may and must produce good or evil fruit, in a far distant time; that, together with the seed of the merely temporary crop, which mortals term expediency, they inevitably sow the acorns of a more enduring growth, which may darkly overshadow their posterity.

The House of the Seven Gables, antique as it now looks, was not the first habitation erected by civilized man, on precisely the same spot of ground. Pyncheon-street formerly bore the humbler appellation of Maule's Lane, from the name of the original occupant of the soil, before whose cottage-door it was a cow-path. A natural spring of soft and pleasant water—a rare treasure on the sea-girt peninsula, where the Puritan settlement was made—had early induced Matthew Maule[6] to build a hut, shaggy with thatch, at this point, although somewhat too remote from what was then the centre of the village. In the growth of the town, however, after some thirty or forty years, the site covered by this rude hovel had become exceedingly desirable in the eyes of a prominent and powerful personage, who asserted plausible claims to the proprietorship of this, and a large adjacent tract of land, on the strength of a grant from the legislature. Colonel Pyncheon, the claimant, as we gather from whatever traits of him are preserved, was characterized by an iron energy of purpose. Matthew Maule, on the other hand, though an obscure man, was stubborn in the defence of what he considered his right; and, for several years, he succeeded in protecting the acre or two of earth which, with his own toil, he had hewn out of the primeval forest, to be his garden-ground and homestead. No written record of this dispute is known to be in existence. Our acquaintance with the whole subject is derived chiefly from tradition. It would be bold, therefore, and possibly unjust, to venture a decisive opinion as to its merits; although it appears to have been at least a matter of doubt, whether Colonel Pyncheon's claim were not unduly stretched, in order to make it cover the small metes and bounds of Matthew Maule. What greatly strengthens such a suspi-

---

6. A possible source for this Maule is Thomas Maule (1645–1724), a Quaker who challenged Puritan authority in the late seventeenth century. See Thomas Maule, p. 230 herein.

cion is the fact, that this controversy between two ill-matched an-
tagonists—at a period, moreover, laud it as we may, when personal
influence had far more weight than now—remained for years unde-
cided, and came to a close only with the death of the party occupying the disputed soil. The mode of his death, too, affects the mind
differently, in our day, from what it did a century and a half ago. It
was a death that blasted with strange horror the humble name of
the dweller in the cottage, and made it seem almost a religious act
to drive the plough over the little area of his habitation, and obliterate his place and memory from among men.

Old Matthew Maule, in a word, was executed for the crime of
witchcraft. He was one of the martyrs to that terrible delusion[7]
which should teach us, among its other morals, that the influential
classes, and those who take upon themselves to be leaders of the
people, are fully liable to all the passionate error that has ever characterized the maddest mob. Clergymen, judges, statesmen—the
wisest, calmest, holiest persons of their day—stood in the inner circle roundabout the gallows, loudest to applaud the work of blood,
latest to confess themselves miserably deceived. If any one part of
their proceedings can be said to deserve less blame than another, it
was the singular indiscrimination with which they persecuted, not
merely the poor and aged, as in former judicial massacres, but people of all ranks; their own equals, brethren, and wives. Amid the
disorder of such various ruin, it is not strange that a man of incon-
siderable note, like Maule, should have trodden the martyr's path to
the hill of execution, almost unremarked in the throng of his fel-
low-sufferers. But, in after days, when the frenzy of that hideous
epoch had subsided, it was remembered how loudly Colonel Pyncheon had joined in the general cry, to purge the land from witchcraft; nor did it fail to be whispered, that there was an invidious
acrimony in the zeal with which he had sought the condemnation
of Matthew Maule. It was well known, that the victim had recognized the bitterness of personal enmity in his persecutor's conduct
towards him, and that he declared himself hunted to death for his
spoil. At the moment of execution—with the halter about his neck,
and while Colonel Pyncheon sat on horseback, grimly gazing at the
scene—Maule had addressed him from the scaffold, and uttered a
prophecy, of which history, as well as fireside tradition, has preserved the very words.—"God," said the dying man, pointing his
finger with a ghastly look at the undismayed countenance of his enemy, "God will give him blood to drink!"[8]

---

7. I.e., the Salem witchcraft crisis of 1692, which resulted in the execution of nineteen
   people as witches. Hawthorne's great-great-grandfather, John Hathorne (1641–1717),
   was one of the judges.
8. According to early historians of the witchcraft crisis, Sarah Good (1653–1692) spoke
   these words to one of her accusers, the Reverend Nicholas Noyes, just before her exe-

After the reputed wizard's death, his humble homestead had fallen an easy spoil into Colonel Pyncheon's grasp. When it was understood, however, that the Colonel intended to erect a family-mansion—spacious, ponderously framed of oaken timber, and calculated to endure for many generations of his posterity—over the spot first covered by the log-built hut of Matthew Maule, there was much shaking of the head among the village-gossips. Without absolutely expressing a doubt whether the stalwart Puritan had acted as a man of conscience and integrity, throughout the proceedings which have been sketched, they nevertheless hinted that he was about to build his house over an unquiet grave. His home would include the home of the dead and buried wizard, and would thus afford the ghost of the latter a kind of privilege to haunt its new apartments, and the chambers into which future bridegrooms were to lead their brides, and where children of the Pyncheon blood were to be born. The terror and ugliness of Maule's crime, and the wretchedness of his punishment, would darken the freshly plastered walls, and infect them early with the scent of an old and melancholy house. Why, then—while so much of the soil around him was bestrewn with the virgin forest-leaves—why should Colonel Pyncheon prefer a site that had already been accurst?

But the Puritan soldier and magistrate was not a man to be turned aside from his well-considered scheme, either by dread of the wizard's ghost, or by flimsy sentimentalities of any kind, however specious. Had he been told of a bad air, it might have moved him somewhat; but he was ready to encounter an evil spirit, on his own ground. Endowed with common-sense, as massive and hard as blocks of granite, fastened together by stern rigidity of purpose, as with iron clamps, he followed out his original design, probably without so much as imagining an objection to it. On the score of delicacy, or any scrupulousness which a finer sensibility might have taught him, the Colonel, like most of his breed and generation, was impenetrable. He therefore dug his cellar, and laid the deep foundations of his mansion, on the square of earth whence Matthew Maule, forty years before, had first swept away the fallen leaves. It was a curious, and, as some people thought, an ominous fact, that, very soon after the workmen began their operations, the spring of water, above-mentioned, entirely lost the deliciousness of its pristine quality. Whether its sources were disturbed by the depth of the new cellar, or whatever subtler cause might lurk at the bottom, it is certain that the water of Maule's Well, as it continued to be called,

---

cution (see Robert Calef, p. 230 herein). Good's curse had its source in Revelation 16:6: "For they have shed the blood of saints and prophets, and thou hast given them blood to drink."

grew hard and brackish. Even such we find it now; and any old woman of the neighborhood will certify, that it is productive of intestinal mischief to those who quench their thirst there.

The reader may deem it singular, that the head-carpenter of the new edifice was no other than the son of the very man, from whose dead gripe the property of the soil had been wrested. Not improbably, he was the best workman of his time; or, perhaps, the Colonel thought it expedient, or was impelled by some better feeling, thus openly to cast aside all animosity against the race of his fallen antagonist. Nor was it out of keeping with the general coarseness and matter-of-fact character of the age, that the son should be willing to earn an honest penny—or rather, a weighty amount of sterling pounds—from the purse of his father's deadly enemy. At all events, Thomas Maule became the architect of the House of the Seven Gables, and performed his duty so faithfully, that the timber framework, fastened by his hands, still holds together.[9]

Thus the great house was built. Familiar as it stands in the writer's recollection—for it has been an object of curiosity with him from boyhood, both as a specimen of the best and stateliest architecture of a long-past epoch, and as the scene of events more full of human interest, perhaps, than those of a gray, feudal castle—familiar as it stands, in its rusty old-age, it is therefore only the more difficult to imagine the bright novelty with which it first caught the sunshine. The impression of its actual state, at this distance of a hundred and sixty years, darkens inevitably through the picture which we would fain give of its appearance, on the morning when the Puritan magnate bade all the town to be his guests. A ceremony of consecration, festive, as well as religious, was now to be performed. A prayer and discourse from the Reverend Mr. Higginson,[1] and the outpouring of a psalm from the general throat of the community, was to be made acceptable to the grosser sense by ale, cider, wine, and brandy, in copious effusion, and, as some authorities aver, by an ox roasted whole, or, at least, by the weight and substance of an ox, in more manageable joints and sirloins. The carcass of a deer, shot within twenty miles, had supplied material for the vast circumference of a pasty. A cod-fish of sixty pounds, caught in the bay, had been dissolved into the rich liquid of a chowder. The chimney of the new house, in short, belching forth its kitchen-smoke, impregnated the whole air with the scent of meats, fowls, and fishes, spicily concocted with odoriferous herbs, and

---

9. The historical Thomas Maule was an architect who designed Salem's first Quaker church in 1688. Hawthorne called attention to his source in Thomas Maule by naming Matthew Maule's son Thomas.

1. John Higginson (1616–1708), pastor of the First Church in Salem in 1660. As recounted in Joseph B. Felt's *Annals of Salem* (1845–49), Thomas Maule was ordered whipped after accusing Higginson of preaching lies. See Felt, p. 232 herein.

onions in abundance. The mere smell of such festivity, making its way to everybody's nostrils, was at once an invitation and an appetite.

Maule's Lane—or Pyncheon-street, as it were now more decorous to call it—was thronged, at the appointed hour, as with a congregation on its way to church. All, as they approached, looked upward at the imposing edifice, which was henceforth to assume its rank among the habitations of mankind. There it rose, a little withdrawn from the line of the street, but in pride, not modesty. Its whole visible exterior was ornamented with quaint figures, conceived in the grotesqueness of a Gothic fancy, and drawn or stamped in the glittering plaster, composed of lime, pebbles, and bits of glass, with which the wood-work of the walls was overspread. On every side, the seven gables pointed sharply towards the sky, and presented the aspect of a whole sisterhood of edifices, breathing through the spiracles[2] of one great chimney. The many lattices, with their small, diamond-shaped panes, admitted the sunlight into hall and chamber; while, nevertheless, the second story, projecting far over the base, and itself retiring beneath the third, threw a shadow and thoughtful gloom into the lower rooms. Carved globes of wood were affixed under the jutting stories. Little, spiral rods of iron beautified each of the seven peaks. On the triangular portion of the gable that fronted next the street, was a dial, put up that very morning, and on which the sun was still marking the passage of the first bright hour in a history, that was not destined to be all so bright. All around were scattered shavings, chips, shingles, and broken halves of bricks; these—together with the lately turned earth, on which the grass had not begun to grow—contributed to the impression of strangeness and novelty, proper to a house that had yet its place to make among men's daily interests.

The principal entrance, which had almost the breadth of a church-door, was in the angle between the two front gables, and was covered by an open porch, with benches beneath its shelter. Under this arched door-way, scraping their feet on the unworn threshold, now trod the clergymen, the elders, the magistrates, the deacons, and whatever of aristocracy there was in town or county. Thither, too, thronged the plebeian classes, as freely as their betters, and in larger number. Just within the entrance, however, stood two serving-men, pointing some of the guests to the neighborhood of the kitchen, and ushering others into the statelier rooms; hospitable alike to all, but still with a scrutinizing regard to the high or low degree of each. Velvet garments, sombre, but rich, stiffly plaited ruffs and bands, embroidered gloves, venerable beards, the

2. Air holes.

mien and countenance of authority, made it easy to distinguish the gentleman of worship, at that period, from the tradesman, with his plodding air, or the laborer in his leathern jerkin,[3] stealing awe-stricken into the house which he had perhaps helped to build.

One inauspicious circumstance there was, which awakened a hardly concealed displeasure in the breasts of a few of the more punctilious visitors. The founder of this stately mansion—a gentleman noted for the square and ponderous courtesy of his demeanor—ought surely to have stood in his own hall, and to have offered the first welcome to so many eminent personages as here presented themselves, in honor of his solemn festival. He was as yet invisible; the most favored of the guests had not beheld him. This sluggishness on Colonel Pyncheon's part became still more unaccountable, when the second dignitary of the province made his appearance, and found no more ceremonious a reception. The Lieutenant Governor, although his visit was one of the anticipated glories of the day, had alighted from his horse, and assisted his lady from her side-saddle, and crossed the Colonel's threshold, without other greeting than that of the principal domestic.

This person—a gray-headed man of quiet and most respectful deportment—found it necessary to explain that his master still remained in his study, or private apartment; on entering which, an hour before, he had expressed a wish on no account to be disturbed.

"Do not you see, fellow," said the high-sheriff of the county, taking the servant aside, "that this is no less a man than the Lieutenant Governor? Summon Colonel Pyncheon at once! I know that he received letters from England, this morning; and, in the perusal and consideration of them, an hour may have passed away, without his noticing it. But he will be ill-pleased, I judge, if you suffer him to neglect the courtesy due to one of our chief rulers, and who may be said to represent King William,[4] in the absence of the Governor himself. Call your master instantly!"

"Nay, please your worship," answered the man, in much perplexity, but with a backwardness that strikingly indicated the hard and severe character of Colonel Pyncheon's domestic rule, "my master's orders were exceedingly strict; and, as your worship knows, he permits of no discretion in the obedience of those who owe him service. Let who list open yonder door! I dare not, though the Governor's own voice should bid me do it!"

"Pooh, pooh, Master High Sheriff!" cried the Lieutenant Governor, who had overheard the foregoing discussion, and felt himself

---

3. Short jacket, typically without sleeves.
4. William III (1650–1702), king of England from 1689 to 1702.

high enough in station to play a little with his dignity.—"I will take the matter into my own hands. It is time that the good Colonel came forth to greet his friends; else we shall be apt to suspect that he has taken a sip too much of his Canary wine,[5] in his extreme deliberation which cask it were best to broach, in honor of the day! But since he is so much behindhand, I will give him a remembrancer myself!"

Accordingly—with such a tramp of his ponderous riding-boots as might of itself have been audible in the remotest of the seven gables—he advanced to the door, which the servant pointed out, and made its new panels re-echo with a loud, free knock. Then, looking round with a smile to the spectators, he awaited a response. As none came, however, he knocked again, but with the same, unsatisfactory result as at first. And, now, being a trifle choleric in his temperament, the Lieutenant Governor uplifted the heavy-hilt of his sword, wherewith he so beat and banged upon the door, that, as some of the bystanders whispered, the racket might have disturbed the dead. Be that as it might, it seemed to produce no awakening effect on Colonel Pyncheon. When the sound subsided, the silence through the house was deep, dreary, and oppressive; notwithstanding that the tongues of many of the guests had already been loosened by a surreptitious cup or two of wine or spirits.

"Strange, forsooth!—very strange!" cried the Lieutenant Governor, whose smile was changed to a frown. "But, seeing that our host sets us the good example of forgetting ceremony, I shall likewise throw it aside, and make free to intrude on his privacy!"

He tried the door, which yielded to his hand, and was flung wide open by a sudden gust of wind that passed, as with a loud sigh, from the outermost portal through all the passages and apartments of the new house. It rustled the silken garments of the ladies, and waved the long curls of the gentlemen's wigs, and shook the window-hangings and the curtains of the bed-chambers; causing everywhere a singular stir, which yet was more like a hush. A shadow of awe and half-fearful anticipation—nobody knew wherefore, nor of what—had all at once fallen over the company.

They thronged, however, to the now open door, pressing the Lieutenant Governor, in the eagerness of their curiosity, into the room in advance of them. At the first glimpse, they beheld nothing extraordinary; a handsomely furnished room of moderate size, somewhat darkened by curtains; books arranged on shelves; a large map on the wall, and likewise a portrait of Colonel Pyncheon, beneath which sat the original Colonel himself, in an oaken elbow-chair, with a pen in his hand. Letters, parchments, and blank

5. A sweet white wine imported from the Canary Islands off the northwest coast of Africa.

sheets of paper were on the table before him. He appeared to gaze at the curious crowd, in front of which stood the Lieutenant Governor; and there was a frown on his dark and massive countenance, as if sternly resentful of the boldness that had impelled them into his private retirement.

A little boy—the Colonel's grandchild, and the only human being that ever dared to be familiar with him—now made his way among the guests and ran towards the seated figure; then pausing half-way, he began to shriek with terror. The company—tremulous as the leaves of a tree, when all are shaking together—drew nearer, and perceived that there was an unnatural distortion in the fixedness of Colonel Pyncheon's stare; that there was blood on his ruff, and that his hoary beard was saturated with it. It was too late to give assistance. The iron-hearted Puritan—the relentless persecutor—the grasping and strong-willed man—was dead! Dead, in his new house! There is a tradition—only worth alluding to, as lending a tinge of superstitious awe to a scene, perhaps gloomy enough without it—that a voice spoke loudly among the guests, the tones of which were like those of old Matthew Maule, the executed wizard:—"God hath given him blood to drink!"

Thus early had that one guest—the only guest who is certain, at one time or another, to find his way into every human dwelling—thus early had Death stept across the threshold of the House of the Seven Gables!

Colonel Pyncheon's sudden and mysterious end made a vast deal of noise in its day. There were many rumors, some of which have vaguely drifted down to the present time, how that appearances indicated violence; that there were the marks of fingers on his throat, and the print of a bloody hand on his plaited ruff; and that his peaked beard was dishevelled, as if it had been fiercely clutched and pulled. It was averred, likewise, that the lattice-window, near the Colonel's chair, was open, and that, only a few minutes before the fatal occurrence, the figure of a man had been seen clambering over the garden-fence, in the rear of the house. But it were folly to lay any stress on stories of this kind, which are sure to spring up around such an event as that now related, and which, as in the present case, sometimes prolong themselves for ages afterwards, like the toadstools that indicate where the fallen and buried trunk of a tree has long since mouldered into the earth. For our own part, we allow them just as little credence as to that other fable of the skeleton hand, which the Lieutenant Governor was said to have seen at the Colonel's throat, but which vanished away, as he advanced farther into the room. Certain it is, however, that there was a great consultation and dispute of doctors over the dead body. One—John Swinnerton by name—who appears to have been a man of eminence, upheld it, if we have rightly understood his terms of art, to be a case of apoplexy.[6] His professional brethren, each for himself, adopted various hypotheses, more or less plausible, but all dressed out in a perplexing mystery of phrase, which, if it do not show a bewilderment of mind in these erudite physicians, certainly causes it in the unlearned peruser of their opinions. The coroner's jury sat upon the corpse, and, like sensible men, returned an unassailable verdict of "Sudden Death!"

It is indeed difficult to imagine that there could have been a serious suspicion of murder, or the slightest grounds for implicating any particular individual as the perpetrator. The rank, wealth, and eminent character of the deceased, must have ensured the strictest scrutiny into every ambiguous circumstance. As none such is on record, it is safe to assume that none existed. Tradition—which sometimes brings down truth that history has let slip, but is oftener the wild babble of the time, such as was formerly spoken at the fireside, and now congeals in newspapers—tradition is responsible for all contrary averments. In Colonel Pyncheon's funeral sermon, which was printed and is still extant, the Reverend Mr. Higginson enumerates, among the many felicities of his distinguished parishioner's earthly career, the happy seasonableness of his death. His duties all performed,—the highest prosperity attained,—his race and future generations fixed on a stable basis, and with a stately roof to shelter them, for centuries to come,—what other upward step remained for this good man to take, save the final step from earth to the golden gate of Heaven! The pious clergyman surely would not have uttered words like these, had he in the least suspected that the Colonel had been thrust into the other world with the clutch of violence upon his throat.

The family of Colonel Pyncheon, at the epoch of his death, seemed destined to as fortunate a permanence as can anywise consist with the inherent instability of human affairs. It might fairly be anticipated that the progress of time would rather increase and ripen their prosperity, than wear away and destroy it. For, not only had his son and heir come into immediate enjoyment of a rich estate, but there was a claim, through an Indian deed, confirmed by a subsequent grant of the General Court,[7] to a vast, and as yet unexplored and unmeasured tract of eastern lands. These possessions—

---

6. Term used to describe a stroke or cerebral hemorrhage. In Hawthorne's time, it also referred more generally to sudden death from such conditions as a pulmonary hemorrhage, in which blood would appear in the mouth of the deceased. Swinnerton (1635–1690): Salem physician who died before the Salem witch crisis of 1692. Hawthorne may have included him in this scene because of his connection to Thomas Maule, for in 1693 Swinnerton's stepson married one of Maule's daughters.

7. I.e., the Massachusetts colonial legislature.

for as such they might almost certainly be reckoned—comprised the greater part of what is now known as Waldo County, in the State of Maine, and were more extensive than many a dukedom, or even a reigning prince's territory, on European soil.[8] When the pathless forest, that still covered this wild principality, should give place—as it inevitably must, though perhaps not till ages hence—to the golden fertility of human culture, it would be the source of incalculable wealth to the Pyncheon blood. Had the Colonel survived only a few weeks longer, it is probable that his great political influence, and powerful connections, at home and abroad, would have consummated all that was necessary to render the claim available. But, in spite of good Mr. Higginson's congratulatory eloquence, this appeared to be the one thing which Colonel Pyncheon, provident and sagacious as he was, had allowed to go at loose ends. So far as the prospective territory was concerned, he unquestionably died too soon. His son lacked not merely the father's eminent position, but the talent and force of character to achieve it; he could therefore effect nothing by dint of political interest; and the bare justice or legality of the claim was not so apparent, after the Colonel's decease, as it had been pronounced in his lifetime. Some connecting link had slipt out of the evidence, and could not anywhere be found.

Efforts, it is true, were made by the Pyncheons, not only then, but, at various periods, for nearly a hundred years afterwards, to obtain what they stubbornly persisted in deeming their right. But, in course of time, the territory was partly re-granted to more favored individuals, and partly cleared and occupied by actual settlers. These last, if they ever heard of the Pyncheon title, would have laughed at the idea of any man's asserting a right—on the strength of mouldy parchments, signed with the faded autographs of governors and legislators, long dead and forgotten—to the lands which they or their fathers had wrested from the wild hand of Nature, by their own sturdy toil. This impalpable claim, therefore, resulted in nothing more solid than to cherish, from generation to generation, an absurd delusion of family importance, which all along characterized the Pyncheons. It caused the poorest member of the race to feel as if he inherited a kind of nobility, and might yet come into the possession of princely wealth to support it. In the better specimens of the breed, this peculiarity threw an ideal grace over the hard material of human life, without stealing away any truly valuable quality. In the baser sort, its effect was to increase the liability to sluggishness and dependence, and induce the victim

---

8. Some of Hawthorne's relatives on his mother's side clung to the idea that a lost Indian deed would reveal their ownership of thousands of acres in Maine.

of a shadowy hope to remit all self-effort, while awaiting the realization of his dreams. Years and years after their claim had passed out of the public memory, the Pyncheons were accustomed to consult the Colonel's ancient map, which had been projected while Waldo County was still an unbroken wilderness. Where the old land-surveyor had put down woods, lakes, and rivers, they marked out the cleared spaces, and dotted the villages and towns, and calculated the progressively increasing value of the territory, as if there were yet a prospect of its ultimately forming a princedom for themselves.

In almost every generation, nevertheless, there happened to be some one descendant of the family, gifted with a portion of the hard, keen sense, and practical energy, that had so remarkably distinguished the original founder. His character, indeed, might be traced all the way down, as distinctly as if the Colonel himself, a little diluted, had been gifted with a sort of intermittent immortality on earth. At two or three epochs, when the fortunes of the family were low, this representative of hereditary qualities had made his appearance, and caused the traditionary gossips of the town to whisper among themselves:—"Here is the old Pyncheon come again! Now the Seven Gables will be new-shingled!" From father to son, they clung to the ancestral house, with singular tenacity of home-attachment. For various reasons, however, and from impressions often too vaguely founded to be put on paper, the writer cherishes the belief that many, if not most, of the successive proprietors of this estate, were troubled with doubts as to their moral right to hold it. Of their legal tenure, there could be no question; but old Matthew Maule, it is to be feared, trode downward from his own age to a far later one, planting a heavy footstep, all the way, on the conscience of a Pyncheon. If so, we are left to dispose of the awful query, whether each inheritor of the property—conscious of wrong, and failing to rectify it—did not commit anew the great guilt of his ancestor, and incur all its original responsibilities. And supposing such to be the case, would it not be a far truer mode of expression to say, of the Pyncheon family, that they inherited a great misfortune, than the reverse?[9]

We have already hinted, that it is not our purpose to trace down the history of the Pyncheon family, in its unbroken connection with the House of the Seven Gables; nor to show, as in a magic picture, how the rustiness and infirmity of age gathered over the venerable house itself. As regards its interior life, a large, dim looking-glass used to hang in one of the rooms, and was fabled to contain within

---

9. For Hawthorne's similar reflection in a notebook entry of October 23, 1849, see p. 239 herein.

its depths all the shapes that had ever been reflected there; the old
Colonel himself, and his many descendants, some in the garb of
antique babyhood, and others in the bloom of feminine beauty, or
manly prime, or saddened with the wrinkles of frosty age. Had we
the secret of that mirror, we would gladly sit down before it, and
transfer its revelations to our page. But there was a story, for which it
is difficult to conceive any foundation, that the posterity of Matthew
Maule had some connection with the mystery of the looking-
glass, and that—by what appears to have been a sort of mesmeric
process[1]—they could make its inner region all alive with the departed
Pyncheons; not as they had shown themselves to the world, nor in
their better and happier hours, but as doing over again some deed
of sin, or in the crisis of life's bitterest sorrow. The popular imagination, indeed, long kept itself busy with the affair of the old Puritan Pyncheon and the wizard Maule; the curse, which the latter
flung from his scaffold, was remembered, with the very important
addition, that it had become a part of the Pyncheon inheritance. If
one of the family did but gurgle in his throat, a bystander would
be likely enough to whisper, between jest and earnest—"He has
Maule's blood to drink!"—The sudden death of a Pyncheon, about
a hundred years ago, with circumstances very similar to what have
been related of the Colonel's exit, was held as giving additional
probability to the received opinion on this topic. It was considered,
moreover, an ugly and ominous circumstance, that Colonel Pyncheon's picture—in obedience, it was said, to a provision of his
will—remained affixed to the wall of the room in which he died.
Those stern, immitigable features seemed to symbolize an evil influence, and so darkly to mingle the shadow of their presence with
the sunshine of the passing hour, that no good thoughts or purposes could ever spring up and blossom there. To the thoughtful
mind, there will be no tinge of superstition in what we figuratively
express, by affirming that the ghost of a dead progenitor—perhaps
as a portion of his own punishment—is often doomed to become
the Evil Genius[2] of his family.

The Pyncheons, in brief, lived along, for the better part of two
centuries, with perhaps less of outward vicissitude than has attended most other New England families, during the same period
of time. Possessing very distinctive traits of their own, they nevertheless took the general characteristics of the little community in
which they dwelt; a town noted for its frugal, discreet, well-ordered,
and home-loving inhabitants, as well as for the somewhat confined

1. A reference to mesmerism, or hypnotism, developed by the Austrian physician Franz Anton Mesmer (1734–1815). See also Charles Poyen, p. 304 herein, and Hawthorne,
   p. 307 herein.
2. Something like a genie, or attending spirit, in this case having evil intent.

scope of its sympathies; but in which, be it said, there are odder individuals, and, now and then, stranger occurrences, than one meets
with almost anywhere else. During the revolution, the Pyncheon of
that epoch, adopting the royal side, became a refugee, but re-
pented, and made his re-appearance, just at the point of time to
preserve the House of the Seven Gables from confiscation.[3] For the
last seventy years, the most noted event in the Pyncheon annals
had been likewise the heaviest calamity that ever befell the race; no
less than the violent death—for so it was adjudged—of one member of the family, by the criminal act of another. Certain circumstances, attending this fatal occurrence, had brought the deed
irresistibly home to a nephew of the deceased Pyncheon. The
young man was tried and convicted of the crime; but either the cir-
cumstantial nature of the evidence, and possibly some lurking
doubt in the breast of the Executive, or, lastly—an argument of
greater weight in a republic, than it could have been under a
monarchy—the high respectability and political influence of the
criminal's connections, had availed to mitigate his doom from
death to perpetual imprisonment. This sad affair had chanced
about thirty years before the action of our story commences. Latterly, there were rumors (which few believed, and only one or two
felt greatly interested in) that this long-buried man was likely, for
some reason or other, to be summoned forth from his living tomb.

It is essential to say a few words respecting the victim of this now
almost forgotten murder. He was an old bachelor, and possessed of
great wealth, in addition to the house and real estate which constituted what remained of the ancient Pyncheon property. Being of an
eccentric and melancholy turn of mind, and greatly given to rum-
maging old records and hearkening to old traditions, he had
brought himself, it is averred, to the conclusion, that Matthew
Maule, the wizard, had been foully wronged out of his homestead,
if not out of his life. Such being the case, and he, the old bachelor,
in possession of the ill-gotten spoil—with the black stain of blood
sunken deep into it, and still to be scented by conscientious nostrils—the question occurred, whether it were not imperative upon
him, even at this late hour, to make restitution to Maule's posterity.
To a man living so much in the past, and so little in the present, as
the secluded and antiquarian old bachelor, a century and a half
seemed not so vast a period as to obviate the propriety of substituting right for wrong. It was the belief of those who knew him best,
that he would positively have taken the very singular step of giving
up the House of the Seven Gables to the representative of Matthew

3. In the immediate wake of the American Revolution, the property of many of the Loyal-
   ists who supported the British side during the American Revolution was confiscated by
   the victorious patriots.

Maule, but for the unspeakable tumult which a suspicion of the old gentleman's project awakened among his Pyncheon relatives. Their exertions had the effect of suspending his purpose; but it was feared that he would perform, after death, by the operation of his last will, what he had so hardly been prevented from doing, in his proper lifetime. But there is no one thing which men so rarely do, whatever the provocation or inducement, as to bequeath patrimonial property away from their own blood. They may love other individuals far better than their relatives; they may even cherish dislike, or positive hatred, to the latter; but yet, in view of death, the strong prejudice of propinquity revives, and impels the testator to send down his estate in the line marked out by custom, so immemorial, that it looks like nature. In all the Pyncheons, this feeling had the energy of disease. It was too powerful for the conscientious scruples of the old bachelor; at whose death, accordingly, the mansion-house, together with most of his other riches, passed into the possession of his next legal representative.

This was a nephew; the cousin of the miserable young man who had been convicted of the uncle's murder. The new heir, up to the period of his accession, was reckoned rather a dissipated youth, but had at once reformed, and made himself an exceedingly respectable member of society. In fact, he showed more of the Pyncheon quality, and had won higher eminence in the world, than any of his race since the time of the original Puritan. Applying himself, in earlier manhood, to the study of the law, and having a natural tendency towards office, he had attained, many years ago, to a judicial situation in some inferior court, which gave him, for life, the very desirable and imposing title of Judge. Later, he had engaged in politics, and served a part of two terms in Congress, besides making a considerable figure in both branches of the state legislature. Judge Pyncheon[4] was unquestionably an honor to his race. He had built himself a country-seat, within a few miles of his native town, and there spent such portions of his time as could be spared from public service, in the display of every grace and virtue—as a newspaper phrased it, on the eve of an election—befitting the christian, the good citizen, the horticulturist, and the gentleman!

There were few of the Pyncheons left, to sun themselves in the glow of the Judge's prosperity. In respect to natural increase, the breed had not thriven; it appeared rather to be dying out. The only

---

4. Shortly after publication of *House*, members of a Pynchon family of Massachusetts complained that Hawthorne had smeared one of their ancestors in his characterization of Judge Pynchon. But Hawthorne, who did not know that Pynchon, most likely modeled his character on Charles Upham (1802–1875), the Salem Whig who had been chiefly responsible for removing the Democrat Hawthorne from his Custom House job in Salem following the election of the Whig president Zachary Taylor. See the discussion of Upham in the History section (p. 235 herein).

members of the family, known to be extant, were, first, the Judge himself, and a single surviving son, who was now travelling in Europe; next, the thirty-years' prisoner, already alluded to, and a sister of the latter, who occupied, in an extremely retired manner, the House of the Seven Gables, in which she had a life-estate by the will of the old bachelor. She was understood to be wretchedly poor, and seemed to make it her choice to remain so; inasmuch as her affluent cousin, the Judge, had repeatedly offered her all the comforts of life, either in the old mansion or his own modern residence. The last and youngest Pyncheon was a little country-girl of seventeen, the daughter of another of the Judge's cousins, who had married a young woman of no family or property, and died early, and in poor circumstances. His widow had recently taken another husband.

As for Matthew Maule's posterity, it was supposed now to be extinct. For a very long period after the witchcraft delusion, however, the Maules had continued to inhabit the town, where their progenitor had suffered so unjust a death. To all appearance, they were a quiet, honest, well-meaning race of people, cherishing no malice against individuals or the public, for the wrong which had been done them; or if, at their own fireside, they transmitted, from father to child, any hostile recollection of the wizard's fate, and their lost patrimony, it was never acted upon, nor openly expressed. Nor would it have been singular, had they ceased to remember that the House of the Seven Gables was resting its heavy frame-work on a foundation that was rightfully their own. There is something so massive, stable, and almost irresistibly imposing, in the exterior presentment of established rank and great possessions, that their very existence seems to give them a right to exist; at least, so excellent a counterfeit of right, that few poor and humble men have moral force enough to question it, even in their secret minds. Such is the case now, after so many ancient prejudices have been overthrown; and it was far more so in ante-revolutionary days, when the aristocracy could venture to be proud, and the low were content to be abased. Thus the Maules, at all events, kept their resentments within their own breasts. They were generally poverty-stricken; always plebeian and obscure; working with unsuccessful diligence at handicrafts; laboring on the wharves, or following the sea, as sailors before the mast; living here and there about the town, in hired tenements, and coming finally to the alms house, as the natural home of their old age. At last, after creeping, as it were, for such a length of time, along the utmost verge of the opaque puddle of obscurity, they had taken that downright plunge, which, sooner or later, is the destiny of all families, whether princely or plebeian. For thirty years past, neither town-record, nor grave-stone, nor the directory, nor the knowledge or memory of man, bore any trace of Matthew Maule's descendants. His blood might possibly exist elsewhere; here, where its lowly current could be traced so far back, it had ceased to keep an onward course.

So long as any of the race were to be found, they had been marked out from other men—not strikingly, nor as with a sharp line, but with an effect that was felt, rather than spoken of—by an hereditary character of reserve. Their companions, or those who endeavored to become such, grew conscious of a circle roundabout the Maules, within the sanctity or the spell of which—in spite of an exterior of sufficient frankness and good-fellowship—it was impossible for any man to step. It was this indefinable peculiarity, perhaps, that, by insulating them from human aid, kept them always so unfortunate in life. It certainly operated to prolong, in their case, and to confirm to them, as their only inheritance, those feelings of repugnance and superstitious terror with which the people of the town, even after awakening from their frenzy, continued to regard the memory of the reputed witches. The mantle, or rather, the ragged cloak of old Matthew Maule, had fallen upon his children. They were half-believed to inherit mysterious attributes; the family eye was said to possess strange power. Among other good-for-nothing properties and privileges, one was especially assigned them, of exercising an influence over people's dreams. The Pyncheons, if all stories were true, haughtily as they bore themselves in the noonday streets of their native town, were no better than bond-servants to these plebeian Maules, on entering the topsyturvy commonwealth of sleep. Modern psychology, it may be, will endeavor to reduce these alleged necromancies within a system, instead of rejecting them as altogether fabulous.

A descriptive paragraph or two, treating of the seven-gabled mansion in its more recent aspect, will bring this preliminary chapter to a close. The street, in which it upreared its venerable peaks, has long ceased to be a fashionable quarter of the town; so that, though the old edifice was surrounded by habitations of modern date, they were mostly small, built entirely of wood, and typical of the most plodding uniformity of common life. Doubtless, however, the whole story of human existence may be latent in each of them, but with no picturesqueness, externally, that can attract the imagination or sympathy to seek it there. But as for the old structure of our story, its white-oak frame, and its boards, shingles, and crumbling plaster, and even the huge, clustered chimney in the midst, seemed to constitute only the least and meanest part of its reality. So much of mankind's varied experience had passed there—so much had been suffered, and something, too, enjoyed—that the very timbers were oozy, as with the moisture of a heart. It was itself like a great human heart, with a life of its own, and full of rich and sombre reminiscences.

The deep projection of the second story gave the house such a meditative look, that you could not pass it without the idea that it had secrets to keep, and an eventful history to moralize upon. In front, just on the edge of the unpaved sidewalk, grew the Pyncheon-elm, which, in reference to such trees as one usually meets with, might well be termed gigantic. It had been planted by a great-grandson of the first Pyncheon, and, though now fourscore years of age, or perhaps nearer a hundred, was still in its strong and broad maturity, throwing its shadow from side to side of the street, overtopping the seven gables, and sweeping the whole black roof with its pendent foliage. It gave beauty to the old edifice, and seemed to make it a part of nature. The street having been widened, about forty years ago, the front gable was now precisely on a line with it. On either side extended a ruinous wooden fence, of open lattice-work, through which could be seen a grassy yard, and, especially in the angles of the building, an enormous fertility of burdocks,[5] with leaves, it is hardly an exaggeration to say, two or three feet long. Behind the house, there appeared to be a garden, which undoubtedly had once been extensive, but was now infringed upon by other enclosures, or shut in by habitations and outbuildings that stood on another street. It would be an omission, trifling, indeed, but unpardonable, were we to forget the green moss that had long since gathered over the projections of the windows, and on the slopes of the roof; nor must we fail to direct the reader's eye to a crop, not of weeds, but flower-shrubs, which were growing aloft in the air not a great way from the chimney, in the nook between two of the gables. They were called Alice's Posies. The tradition was, that a certain Alice Pyncheon had flung up the seeds, in sport, and that the dust of the street and the decay of the roof gradually formed a kind of soil for them, out of which they grew, when Alice had long been in her grave. However the flowers might have come there, it was both sad and sweet to observe how Nature adopted to herself this desolate, decaying, gusty, rusty, old house of the Pyncheon family; and how the ever-returning Summer did her best to gladden it with tender beauty, and grew melancholy in the effort.

There is one other feature, very essential to be noticed, but which, we greatly fear, may damage any picturesque and romantic impression, which we have been willing to throw over our sketch of this respectable edifice. In the front gable, under the impending brow of the second story, and contiguous to the street, was a shopdoor, divided horizontally in the midst, and with a window for its

5. A type of weed.

upper segment, such as is often seen in dwellings of a somewhat ancient date. This same shop-door had been a subject of no slight mortification to the present occupant of the august Pyncheon-house, as well as to some of her predecessors. The matter is disagreeably delicate to handle; but, since the reader must needs be let into the secret, he will please to understand, that, about a century ago, the head of the Pyncheons found himself involved in serious financial difficulties. The fellow (gentleman as he styled himself) can hardly have been other than a spurious interloper; for, instead of seeking office from the King or the royal Governor, or urging his hereditary claim to eastern lands, he bethought himself of no better avenue to wealth, than by cutting a shop-door through the side of his ancestral residence. It was the custom of the time, indeed, for merchants to store their goods, and transact business, in their own dwellings. But there was something pitifully small in this old Pyncheon's mode of setting about his commercial operations; it was whispered, that, with his own hands, all beruffled as they were, he used to give change for a shilling, and would turn a half-penny twice over, to make sure that it was a good one. Beyond all question, he had the blood of a petty huckster[6] in his veins, through whatever channel it may have found its way there.

Immediately on his death, the shop-door had been locked, bolted, and barred, and, down to the period of our story, had probably never once been opened. The old counter, shelves, and other fixtures of the little shop, remained just as he had left them. It used to be affirmed, that the dead shopkeeper, in a white wig, a faded velvet coat, an apron at his waist, and his ruffles carefully turned back from his wrists, might be seen through the chinks of the shutters, any night of the year, ransacking his till, or poring over the dingy pages of his day-book. From the look of unutterable woe upon his face, it appeared to be his doom to spend eternity in a vain effort to make his accounts balance.

And now—in a very humble way, as will be seen—we proceed to open our narrative.

II. The Little Shop-Window

It still lacked half-an-hour of sunrise, when Miss Hepzibah Pyncheon—we will not say awoke; it being doubtful whether the poor lady had so much as closed her eyes, during the brief night of midsummer—but, at all events, arose from her solitary pillow, and began what it would be mockery to term the adornment of her

6. Pedlar who hawks goods.

person. Far from us be the indecorum of assisting, even in imagination, at a maiden lady's toilet! Our story must therefore await Miss
Hepzibah at the threshold of her chamber; only presuming, meanwhile, to note some of the heavy sighs that labored from her
bosom, with little restraint as to their lugubrious depth and volume
of sound, inasmuch as they could be audible to nobody, save a disembodied listener like ourself. The old maid was alone in the old
house. Alone, except for a certain respectable and orderly young
man, an artist in the daguerreotype line,[7] who, for about three
months back, had been a lodger in a remote gable—quite a house
by itself, indeed—with locks, bolts, and oaken bars, on all the intervening doors. Inaudible, consequently, were poor Miss Hepzibah's gusty sighs. Inaudible, the creaking joints of her stiffened
knees, as she knelt down by the bedside. And inaudible, too, by
mortal ear, but heard with all-comprehending love and pity, in the
farthest Heaven, that almost agony of prayer—now whispered, now
a groan, now a struggling silence—wherewith she besought the Divine assistance through the day! Evidently, this is to be a day of
more than ordinary trial to Miss Hepzibah, who, for above a quarter of a century gone-by, has dwelt in strict seclusion; taking no
part in the business of life, and just as little in its intercourse and
pleasures. Not with such fervor prays the torpid recluse, looking
forward to the cold, sunless, stagnant calm of a day that is to be
like innumerable yesterdays!

The maiden lady's devotions are concluded. Will she now issue
forth over the threshold of our story? Not yet, by many moments.
First, every drawer in the tall, old-fashioned bureau is to be
opened, with difficulty, and with a succession of spasmodic jerks;
then, all must close again, with the same fidgety reluctance. There
is a rustling of stiff silks; a tread of backward and forward footsteps,
to-and-fro, across the chamber. We suspect Miss Hepzibah, moreover, of taking a step upward into a chair, in order to give heedful
regard to her appearance, on all sides, and at full length, in the
oval, dingy-framed toilet-glass, that hangs above her table. Truly!
Well, indeed! Who would have thought it! Is all this precious time
to be lavished on the matutinal[8] repair and beautifying of an elderly
person, who never goes abroad—whom nobody ever visits—and
from whom, when she shall have done her utmost, it were the best
charity to turn one's eyes another way!

Now, she is almost ready. Let us pardon her one other pause; for

---

7. Daguerreotypes were images produced by the photographic process developed in France
   by Louis Jacques Mandé Daguerre (1789–1851). A plate treated with silver, nitric acid,
   and iodine was exposed to sunlight; the image was then developed with heated mercury.
   Daguerreotypy was in vogue in the United States during the 1840s and 1850s. For a
   fuller discussion, see p. 293 herein; and Alan Trachtenberg, p. 418 herein.
8. Morning.

it is given to the sole sentiment, or we might better say—heightened and rendered intense, as it has been, by sorrow and seclusion—to the strong passion of her life. We heard the turning of a key in a small lock; she has opened a secret drawer of an escritoir, and is probably looking at a certain miniature, done in Malbone's most perfect style, and representing a face worthy of no less delicate a pencil.[9] It was once our good fortune to see this picture. It is the likeness of a young man, in a silken dressing-gown of an old fashion, the soft richness of which is well adapted to the countenance of reverie, with its full, tender lips, and beautiful eyes, that seem to indicate not so much capacity of thought, as gentle and voluptuous emotion. Of the possessor of such features we should have a right to ask nothing, except that he would take the rude world easily, and make himself happy in it. Can it have been an early lover of Miss Hepzibah? No; she never had a lover—poor thing, how could she?—nor ever knew, by her own experience, what love technically means. And yet, her undying faith and trust, her fresh remembrance, and continual devotedness towards the original of that miniature, have been the only substance for her heart to feed upon.

She seems to have put aside the miniature, and is standing again before the toilet-glass. There are tears to be wiped off. A few more footsteps to-and-fro; and here, at last—with another pitiful sigh, like a gust of chill, damp wind out of a long-closed vault, the door of which has accidentally been set ajar—here comes Miss Hepzibah Pyncheon! Forth she steps into the dusky, time-darkened passage; a tall figure, clad in black silk, with a long and shrunken waist, feeling her way towards the stairs like a near-sighted person, as in truth she is.

The sun, meanwhile, if not already above the horizon, was ascending nearer and nearer to its verge. A few clouds, floating high upward, caught some of the earliest light, and threw down its golden gleam on the windows of all the houses in the street; not forgetting the House of the Seven Gables, which—many such sunrises as it had witnessed—looked cheerfully at the present one. The reflected radiance served to show, pretty distinctly, the aspect and arrangement of the room which Hepzibah entered, after descending the stairs. It was a low-studded-room,[1] with a beam across the ceiling, panelled with dark wood, and having a large chimney-piece, set round with pictured tiles, but now closed by an iron fireboard, through which ran the funnel of a modern stove. There was a

---

9. Fine-haired paintbrush (archaic). "Escritoir": writing desk. Edward Greene Malbone (1777–1807), American painter based in Boston, was celebrated for his miniature portraits, many of which were done on ivory.
1. I.e., a room with a low ceiling.

carpet on the floor, originally of rich texture, but so worn and
faded, in these latter years, that its once brilliant figure had quite
vanished into one indistinguishable hue. In the way of furniture,
there were two tables; one, constructed with perplexing intricacy,
and exhibiting as many feet as a centipede; the other, most delicately wrought, with four long and slender legs, so apparently frail,
that it was almost incredible what a length of time the ancient tea-
table had stood upon them. Half-a-dozen chairs stood about the
room, straight and stiff, and so ingeniously contrived for the discomfort of the human person, that they were irksome even to sight,
and conveyed the ugliest possible idea of the state of society to
which they could have been adapted. One exception there was,
however, in a very antique elbow-chair, with a high back, carved
elaborately in oak, and a roomy depth within its arms, that made
up, by its spacious comprehensiveness, for the lack of any of those
artistic curves which abound in a modern chair.

As for ornamental articles of furniture, we recollect but two, if
such they may be called. One was a map of the Pyncheon territory
at the eastward, not engraved, but the handiwork of some skilful
old draftsman, and grotesquely illuminated with pictures of Indians
and wild beasts, among which was seen a lion; the natural history
of the region being as little known as its geography, which was put
down most fantastically awry. The other adornment was the portrait
of old Colonel Pyncheon, at two thirds length, representing the
stern features of a Puritanic-looking personage, in a scull-cap, with
a laced band and a grizzly beard; holding a Bible with one hand,
and in the other uplifting an iron sword-hilt. The latter object, being more successfully depicted by the artist, stood out in far greater
prominence than the sacred volume. Face to face with this picture,
on entering the apartment, Miss Hepzibah Pyncheon came to a
pause; regarding it with a singular scowl—a strange contortion of
the brow—which, by people who did not know her, would probably
have been interpreted as an expression of bitter anger and ill-will.
But it was no such thing. She, in fact, felt a reverence for the pictured visage, of which only a far-descended and time-stricken virgin
could be susceptible; and this forbidding scowl was the innocent
result of her near-sightedness, and an effort so to concentrate her
powers of vision, as to substitute a firm outline of the object, instead of a vague one.

We must linger, a moment, on this unfortunate expression of
poor Hepzibah's brow. Her scowl—as the world, or such part of it
as sometimes caught a transitory glimpse of her at the window,
wickedly persisted in calling it—her scowl had done Miss Hepzibah
a very ill-office, in establishing her character as an ill-tempered old
maid; nor does it appear improbable, that, by often gazing at herself

in a dim looking-glass, and perpetually encountering her own frown within its ghostly sphere, she had been led to interpret the expression almost as unjustly as the world did.—"How miserably cross I look!"—she must often have whispered to herself;—and ultimately have fancied herself so, by a sense of inevitable doom. But her heart never frowned. It was naturally tender, sensitive, and full of little tremors and palpitations; all of which weaknesses it retained, while her visage was growing so perversely stern, and even fierce. Nor had Hepzibah ever any hardihood, except what came from the very warmest nook in her affections.

All this time, however, we are loitering faint-heartedly on the threshold of our story. In very truth, we have an invincible reluctance to disclose what Miss Hepzibah Pyncheon was about to do.

It has already been observed, that, in the basement story of the gable fronting on the street, an unworthy ancestor, nearly a century ago, had fitted up a shop. Ever since the old gentleman retired from trade, and fell asleep under his coffin-lid, not only the shop-door, but the inner arrangements, had been suffered to remain unchanged; while the dust of ages gathered inch-deep over the shelves and counter, and partly filled an old pair of scales, as if it were of value enough to be weighed.—It treasured itself up, too, in the half-open till, where there still lingered a base sixpence, worth neither more nor less than the hereditary pride which had here been put to shame. Such had been the state and condition of the little shop, in old Hepzibah's childhood, when she and her brother used to play at hide-and-seek in its forsaken precincts. So it had remained, until within a few days past.

But now, though the shop-window was still closely curtained from the public gaze, a remarkable change had taken place in its interior. The rich and heavy festoons of cobweb, which it had cost a long ancestral succession of spiders their life's labor to spin and weave, had been carefully brushed away from the ceiling. The counter, shelves, and floor had all been scoured, and the latter was overstrewn with fresh blue sand. The brown scales, too, had evidently undergone rigid discipline, in an unavailing effort to rub off the rust, which, alas! had eaten through and through their substance. Neither was the little old shop any longer empty of merchantable goods. A curious eye, privileged to take an account of stock and investigate behind the counter, would have discovered a barrel—yea, two or three barrels and half-ditto—one containing flour, another apples, and a third, perhaps, Indian meal.[2] There was likewise a square box of pine-wood, full of soap in bars; also,

2. Cornmeal. "Half-ditto": another half of the same. Hawthorne probably learned this term from his custom-house work in Boston and Salem.

another of the same size, in which were tallow-candles, ten to the pound. A small stock of brown sugar, some white beans and split peas, and a few other commodities of low price, and such as are constantly in demand, made up the bulkier portion of the merchandize. It might have been taken for a ghostly or phantasmagoric reflection of the old shopkeeper Pyncheon's shabbily provided shelves; save that some of the articles were of a description and outward form, which could hardly have been known in his day. For instance, there was a glass pickle-jar, filled with fragments of Gibraltar-rock;[3] not, indeed, splinters of the veritable stone foundation of the famous fortress, but bits of delectable candy, neatly done up in white paper. Jim Crow,[4] moreover, was seen executing his world-renowned dance, in gingerbread. A party of leaden dragoons were galloping along one of the shelves, in equipments and uniform of modern cut; and there were some sugar figures, with no strong resemblance to the humanity of any epoch, but less unsatisfactorily representing our own fashions, than those of a hundred years ago. Another phenomenon, still more strikingly modern, was a package of lucifer-matches, which, in old times, would have been thought actually to borrow their instantaneous flame from the nether fires of Tophet.[5]

In short, to bring the matter at once to a point, it was incontrovertibly evident that somebody had taken the shop and fixtures of the long retired and forgotten Mr. Pyncheon, and was about to renew the enterprise of that departed worthy, with a different set of customers. Who could this bold adventurer be? And, of all places in the world, why had he chosen the House of the Seven Gables as the scene of his commercial speculations?

We return to the elderly maiden. She at length withdrew her eyes from the dark countenance of the Colonel's portrait, heaved a sigh—indeed, her breast was a very cave of Æolus,[6] that morning—and stept across the room on tiptoe, as is the customary gait of elderly women. Passing through an intervening passage, she opened a door that communicated with the shop, just now so elaborately described. Owing to the projection of the upper story—and, still more, to the thick shadow of the Pyncheon-elm, which stood almost directly in front of the gable—the twilight, here, was still as much akin to night as morning. Another heavy sigh from Miss Hepzibah! After a moment's pause on the threshold, peering towards the window with her near-sighted scowl, as if frowning down some

---

3. A rock candy named after the British fortress at the southern tip of Spain.
4. The stereotypical image of a gaily dancing black man, derived from the blackface impersonations popularized in the minstrel shows of the 1840s and 1850s.
5. A place likened to hell. Tophet was a site of child sacrifice to Moloch in a valley near ancient Jerusalem. "Lucifer-matches": matches lit by friction.
6. The mythological god of the winds, who kept his winds confined to a cave.

bitter enemy, she suddenly projected herself into the shop. The haste, and, as it were, the galvanic impulse[7] of the movement, were really quite startling.

Nervously—in a sort of frenzy, we might almost say—she began to busy herself in arranging some children's playthings and other little wares, on the shelves and at the shop-window. In the aspect of this dark-arrayed, pale-faced, ladylike, old figure, there was a deeply tragic character that contrasted irreconcilably with the ludicrous pettiness of her employment. It seemed a queer anomaly, that so gaunt and dismal a personage should take a toy in hand;—a miracle, that the toy did not vanish in her grasp;—a miserably absurd idea, that she should go on perplexing her stiff and sombre intellect with the question how to tempt little boys into her premises! Yet such is undoubtedly her object! Now, she places a gingerbread elephant against the window, but with so tremulous a touch that it tumbles upon the floor, with the dismemberment of three legs and its trunk; it has ceased to be an elephant, and has become a few bits of musty gingerbread. There, again, she has upset a tumbler of marbles, all of which roll different ways, and each individual marble, devil-directed, into the most difficult obscurity that it can find. Heaven help our poor old Hepzibah, and forgive us for taking a ludicrous view of her position! As her rigid and rusty frame goes down upon its hands and knees, in quest of the absconding marbles, we positively feel so much the more inclined to shed tears of sympathy, from the very fact that we must needs turn aside and laugh at her! For here—and if we fail to impress it suitably upon the reader, it is our own fault, not that of the theme—here is one of the truest points of melancholy interest that occur in ordinary life. It was the final term of what called itself old gentility. A lady—who had fed herself from childhood with the shadowy food of aristocratic reminiscences, and whose religion it was, that a lady's hand soils itself irremediably by doing aught for bread—this born lady, after sixty years of narrowing means, is fain to step down from her pedestal of imaginary rank. Poverty, treading closely at her heels for a lifetime, has come up with her at last. She must earn her own food, or starve! And we have stolen upon Miss Hepzibah Pyncheon, too irreverently, at the instant of time when the patrician lady is to be transformed into the plebeian woman.

In this republican country, amid the fluctuating waves of our social life, somebody is always at the drowning-point. The tragedy is enacted with as continual a repetition as that of a popular drama on a holiday, and, nevertheless, is felt as deeply, perhaps, as when an hereditary noble sinks below his order. More deeply; since, with

7. An electrical current, named after the Italian scientist Luigi Galvini (1737–1798), who observed a connection between such current and muscle contraction.

us, rank is the grosser substance of wealth and a splendid establishment, and has no spiritual existence after the death of these,
but dies hopelessly along with them. And, therefore, since we have
been unfortunate enough to introduce our heroine at so inauspicious a juncture, we would entreat for a mood of due solemnity in
the spectators of her fate. Let us behold, in poor Hepzibah, the immemorial lady—two hundred years old, on this side of the water,
and thrice as many, on the other—with her antique portraits, pedi-
grees, coats of arms, records, and traditions, and her claim, as joint
heiress, to that princely territory at the eastward, no longer a
wilderness, but a populous fertility—born, too, in Pyncheon-street,
under the Pyncheon-elm, and in the Pyncheon-house, where she
has spent all her days—reduced now, in that very house, to be the
hucksteress of a cent-shop!

This business of setting up a petty shop is almost the only resource of women, in circumstances at all similar to those of our unfortunate recluse. With her near-sightedness, and those tremulous
fingers of hers, at once inflexible and delicate, she could not be a
seamstress; although her sampler, of fifty years gone-by, exhibited
some of the most recondite specimens of ornamental needlework. A
school for little children had been often in her thoughts; and, at
one time, she had begun a review of her early studies in the New
England primer, with a view to prepare herself for the office of in-
structress. But the love of children had never been quickened in
Hepzibah's heart, and was now torpid, if not extinct; she watched
the little people of the neighborhood, from her chamber-window,
and doubted whether she could tolerate a more intimate acquaintance with them. Besides, in our day, the very A. B. C. has become
a science, greatly too abstruse to be any longer taught by pointing a
pin from letter to letter. A modern child could teach old Hepzibah
more than old Hepzibah could teach the child. So—with many a
cold, deep heartquake at the idea of at last coming into sordid contact with the world, from which she had so long kept aloof, while
every added day of seclusion had rolled another stone against the
cavern-door of her hermitage—the poor thing bethought herself of
the ancient shop-window, the rusty scales, and dusty till. She might
have held back a little longer; but another circumstance, not yet
hinted at, had somewhat hastened her decision. Her humble preparations, therefore, were duly made, and the enterprise was now to be
commenced. Nor was she entitled to complain of any remarkable
singularity in her fate; for, in the town of her nativity, we might point
to several little shops of a similar description; some of them in
houses as ancient as that of the seven gables; and one or two, it may
be, where a decayed gentlewoman stands behind the counter, as
grim an image of family-pride as Miss Hepzibah Pyncheon herself.

It was overpoweringly ridiculous—we must honestly confess it—the deportment of the maiden lady, while setting her shop in order for the public eye. She stole on tiptoe to the window, as cautiously as if she conceived some bloody-minded villain to be watching behind the elm-tree, with intent to take her life. Stretching out her long, lank arm, she put a paper of pearl-buttons, a jewsharp,[8] or whatever the small article might be, in its destined place, and straightway vanished back into the dusk, as if the world need never hope for another glimpse of her. It might have been fancied, indeed, that she expected to minister to the wants of the community, unseen, like a disembodied divinity, or enchantress, holding forth her bargains to the reverential and awe-stricken purchaser, in an invisible hand. But Hepzibah had no such flattering dream. She was well aware that she must ultimately come forward, and stand revealed in her proper individuality; but, like other sensitive persons, she could not bear to be observed in the gradual process, and chose rather to flash forth on the world's astonished gaze, at once.

The inevitable moment was not much longer to be delayed. The sunshine might now be seen stealing down the front of the opposite house, from the windows of which came a reflected gleam, struggling through the boughs of the elm-tree, and enlightening the interior of the shop, more distinctly than heretofore. The town appeared to be waking-up. A baker's cart had already rattled through the street, chasing away the latest vestige of night's sanctity with the jingle-jangle of its dissonant bells. A milkman was distributing the contents of his cans from door to door; and the harsh peal of a fisherman's conch-shell was heard far off, around the corner. None of these tokens escaped Hepzibah's notice. The moment had arrived. To delay longer, would be only to lengthen out her misery. Nothing remained, except to take down the bar from the shop-door, leaving the entrance free—more than free—welcome, as if all were household friends—to every passer-by, whose eyes might be attracted by the commodities at the window. This last act Hepzibah now performed, letting the bar fall, with what smote upon her excited nerves as a most astounding clatter. Then—as if the only barrier betwixt herself and the world had been thrown down, and a flood of evil consequences would come tumbling through the gap—she fled into the inner parlor, threw herself into the ancestral elbow-chair, and wept.

Our miserable old Hepzibah! It is a heavy annoyance to a writer, who endeavors to represent nature, its various attitudes and circumstances, in a reasonably correct outline and true coloring, that

---

8. A small musical instrument consisting of a lyre-shaped metal frame and metal tongue, which is plucked while the instrument is held in the teeth.

so much of the mean and ludicrous should be hopelessly mixed up with the purest pathos which life anywhere supplies to him. What tragic dignity, for example, can be wrought into a scene like this! How can we elevate our history of retribution for the sin of long ago, when, as one of our most prominent figures, we are compelled to introduce—not a young and lovely woman, nor even the stately remains of beauty, storm-shattered by affliction—but a gaunt, sallow, rusty-jointed maiden, in a long-waisted silk-gown, and with the strange horror of a turban on her head! Her visage is not even ugly. It is redeemed from insignificance only by the contraction of her eyebrows into a near-sighted scowl. And, finally, her great life-trial seems to be, that, after sixty years of idleness, she finds it convenient to earn comfortable bread by setting up a shop, in a small way. Nevertheless, if we look through all the heroic fortunes of mankind, we shall find this same entanglement of something mean and trivial with whatever is noblest in joy or sorrow. Life is made up of marble and mud. And, without all the deeper trust in a comprehensive sympathy above us, we might hence be led to suspect the insult of a sneer, as well as an immitigable frown, on the iron countenance of fate. What is called poetic insight is the gift of discerning, in this sphere of strangely mingled elements, the beauty and the majesty which are compelled to assume a garb so sordid.

III. The First Customer

Miss Hepzibah Pyncheon sat in the oaken elbow-chair, with her hands over her face, giving way to that heavy downsinking of the heart which most persons have experienced, when the image of Hope itself seems ponderously moulded of lead, on the eve of an enterprise, at once doubtful and momentous. She was suddenly startled by the tinkling alarum—high, sharp, and irregular—of a little bell. The maiden lady arose upon her feet, as pale as a ghost at cockcrow;[9] for she was an enslaved spirit, and this the talisman to which she owed obedience. This little bell—to speak in plainer terms—being fastened over the shop-door, was so contrived as to vibrate by means of a steel-spring, and thus convey notice to the inner regions of the house, when any customer should cross the threshold. Its ugly and spiteful little din, (heard now for the first time, perhaps, since Hepzibah's periwigged predecessor had retired from trade,) at once set every nerve of her body in responsive and tumultuous vibration. The crisis was upon her! Her first customer was at the door!

9. An allusion to the medieval-based folk legend that ghosts turn even paler at the sound of a crowing cock.

Without giving herself time for a second thought, she rushed into the shop, pale, wild, desperate in gesture and expression, scowling portentously, and looking far better qualified to do fierce battle with a housebreaker than to stand smiling behind the counter, bartering small wares for a copper recompense. Any ordinary customer, indeed, would have turned his back, and fled. And yet there was nothing fierce in Hepzibah's poor old heart; nor had she, at the moment, a single bitter thought against the world at large, or one individual man or woman. She wished them all well, but wished, too, that she herself were done with them, and in her quiet grave.

The applicant, by this time, stood within the door-way. Coming freshly, as he did, out of the morning light, he appeared to have brought some of its cheery influences into the shop along with him. It was a slender young man, not more than one or two and twenty years old, with rather a grave and thoughtful expression, for his years, but likewise a springy alacrity and vigor. These qualities were not only perceptible, physically, in his make and motions, but made themselves felt, almost immediately, in his character. A brown beard, not too silken in its texture, fringed his chin, but as yet without completely hiding it; he wore a short moustache, too; and his dark, high-featured countenance looked all the better for these natural ornaments. As for his dress, it was of the simplest kind; a summer sack[1] of cheap and ordinary material, thin checkered pantaloons, and a straw hat, by no means of the finest braid. Oak-hall[2] might have supplied his entire equipment. He was chiefly marked as a gentleman—if such, indeed, he made any claim to be—by the rather remarkable whiteness and nicety of his clean linen.

He met the scowl of old Hepzibah without apparent alarm, as having heretofore encountered it, and found it harmless.

"So, my dear Miss Pyncheon," said the Daguerreotypist—for it was that sole other occupant of the seven-gabled mansion—"I am glad to see that you have not shrunk from your good purpose. I merely look in, to offer my best wishes, and to ask if I can assist you any further in your preparations?"

People in difficulty and distress, or in any manner at odds with the world, can endure a vast amount of harsh treatment, and perhaps be only the stronger for it; whereas, they give way at once before the simplest expression of what they perceive to be genuine sympathy. So it proved with poor Hepzibah; for when she saw the young man's smile—looking so much the brighter on a thoughtful face—and heard his kindly tone, she broke first into an hysteric giggle, and then began to sob.

---

1. A loose-fitting jacket or shirt made of sackcloth.
2. A Boston store that sold relatively inexpensive, ready-made clothes.

"Ah, Mr. Holgrave," cried she, as soon as she could speak, "I never can go through with it! Never, never, never! I wish I were dead, and in the old family-tomb, with all my forefathers! With my father, and my mother, and my sister! Yes;—and with my brother, who had far better find me there than here! The world is too chill and hard—and I am too old, and too feeble, and too hopeless!"

"Oh, believe me, Miss Hepzibah," said the young man quietly, "these feelings will not trouble you any longer, after you are once fairly in the midst of your enterprise. They are unavoidable at this moment, standing, as you do, on the outer verge of your long seclusion, and peopling the world with ugly shapes, which you will soon find to be as unreal as the giants and ogres of a child's story-book. I find nothing so singular in life, as that everything appears to lose its substance, the instant one actually grapples with it. So it will be with what you think so terrible."

"But I am a woman!" said Hepzibah piteously. "I was going to say, a lady,—but I consider that as past."

"Well; no matter if it be past!" answered the artist, a strange gleam of half-hidden sarcasm flashing through the kindliness of his manner. "Let it go! You are the better without it. I speak frankly, my dear Miss Pyncheon:—for are we not friends? I look upon this as one of the fortunate days of your life. It ends an epoch, and begins one. Hitherto, the life-blood has been gradually chilling in your veins, as you sat aloof, within your circle of gentility, while the rest of the world was fighting out its battle with one kind of necessity or another. Henceforth, you will at least have the sense of healthy and natural effort for a purpose, and of lending your strength—be it great or small—to the united struggle of mankind. This is success—all the success that anybody meets with!"

"It is natural enough, Mr. Holgrave, that you should have ideas like these," rejoined Hepzibah, drawing up her gaunt figure with slightly offended dignity.—"You are a man—a young man—and brought up, I suppose, as almost everybody is, now-a-days, with a view to seeking your fortune. But I was born a lady, and have always lived one—no matter in what narrowness of means, always a lady!"

"But I was not born a gentleman; neither have I lived like one," said Holgrave, slightly smiling; "so, my dear Madam, you will hardly expect me to sympathize with sensibilities of this kind; though— unless I deceive myself—I have some imperfect comprehension of them. These names of gentleman and lady had a meaning, in the past history of the world, and conferred privileges, desirable, or otherwise, on those entitled to bear them. In the present—and still more in the future condition of society—they imply, not privilege, but restriction."

"These are new notions," said the old gentlewoman, shaking her head. "I shall never understand them; neither do I wish it."

"We will cease to speak of them, then," replied the artist, with a friendlier smile than his last one; "and I will leave you to feel whether it is not better to be a true woman, than a lady. Do you really think, Miss Hepzibah, that any lady of your family has ever done a more heroic thing, since this house was built, than you are performing in it to-day? Never;—and if the Pyncheons had always acted so nobly, I doubt whether the old wizard Maule's anathema, of which you told me once, would have had much weight with Providence against them."

"Ah!—no, no!" said Hepzibah, not displeased at this allusion to the sombre dignity of an inherited curse. "If old Maule's ghost, or a descendant of his, could see me behind the counter to-day, he would call it the fulfilment of his worst wishes. But I thank you for your kindness, Mr. Holgrave, and will do my utmost to be a good shopkeeper!"

"Pray do," said Holgrave, "and let me have the pleasure of being your first customer. I am about taking a walk to the sea-shore, before going to my rooms, where I misuse Heaven's blessed sunshine by tracing out human features, through its agency.[3] A few of those biscuits, dipt in sea-water, will be just what I need for breakfast. What is the price of half-a-dozen?"

"Let me be a lady a moment longer," replied Hepzibah, with a manner of antique stateliness, to which a melancholy smile lent a kind of grace. She put the biscuits into his hand, but rejected the compensation.—"A Pyncheon must not, at all events, under her forefathers' roof, receive money for a morsel of bread, from her only friend!"

Holgrave took his departure, leaving her, for the moment, with spirits not quite so much depressed. Soon, however, they had subsided nearly to their former dead-level. With a beating heart, she listened to the footsteps of early passengers, which now began to be frequent along the street. Once or twice, they seemed to linger; these strangers, or neighbors, as the case might be, were looking at the display of toys and petty commodities in Hepzibah's shop-window. She was doubly tortured;—in part, with a sense of overwhelming shame, that strange and unloving eyes should have the privilege of gazing;—and, partly, because the idea occurred to her, with ridiculous importunity, that the window was not arranged so skilfully, nor nearly to so much advantage, as it might have been. It seemed as if the whole fortune or failure of her shop might depend

3. A reference to the process of making a daguerreotype (see n. 7, p. 24).

on the display of a different set of articles, or substituting a fairer apple for one which appeared to be specked. So she made the change, and straightway fancied that everything was spoiled by it; not recognizing that it was the nervousness of the juncture, and her own native squeamishness, as an old maid, that wrought all the seeming mischief.

Anon, there was an encounter, just at the door-step, betwixt two laboring men, as their rough voices denoted them to be. After some slight talk about their own affairs, one of them chanced to notice the shop-window, and directed the other's attention to it.

"See here!" cried he. "What do you think of this? Trade seems to be looking up, in Pyncheon-street!"

"Well, well, this is a sight, to be sure!" exclaimed the other. "In the old Pyncheon-house, and underneath the Pyncheon-elm! Who would have thought it! Old Maid Pyncheon is setting up a cent-shop!"

"Will she make it go, think you, Dixey?" said his friend. "I don't call it a very good stand. There's another shop, just round the corner."

"Make it go!" cried Dixey, with a most contemptuous expression, as if the very idea were impossible to be conceived. "Not a bit of it! Why, her face—I've seen it; for I dug her garden for her, one year— her face is enough to frighten the Old Nick[4] himself, if he had ever so great a mind to trade with her. People can't stand it, I tell you! She scowls dreadfully, reason or none, out of pure ugliness of temper!"

"Well; that's not so much matter," remarked the other man. "These sour-tempered folks are mostly handy at business, and know pretty well what they are about. But, as you say, I don't think she'll do much. This business of keeping cent-shops is overdone, like all other kinds of trade, handicraft, and bodily labor. I know it, to my cost! My wife kept a cent-shop, three months, and lost five dollars on her outlay!"

"Poor business!" responded Dixey, in a tone as if he were shaking his head.—"Poor business!"

For some reason or other, not very easy to analyze, there had hardly been so bitter a pang in all her previous misery about the matter, as what thrilled Hepzibah's heart, on overhearing the above conversation. The testimony in regard to her scowl was frightfully important; it seemed to hold up her image, wholly relieved from the false light of her self-partialities, and so hideous that she dared not look at it. She was absurdly hurt, moreover, by the slight and idle effect that her setting-up shop—an event of such breathless inter-

4. The Devil.

est to herself—appeared to have upon the public, of which these two men were the nearest representatives. A glance; a passing word or two; a coarse laugh;—and she was doubtless forgotten, before they turned the corner! They cared nothing for her dignity, and just as little for her degradation. Then, also, the augury of ill-success, uttered from the sure wisdom of experience, fell upon her half-dead hope, like a clod into a grave. The man's wife had already tried the same experiment, and failed! How could the born lady—the recluse of half-a-lifetime, utterly unpractised in the world, at sixty years of age—how could she ever dream of succeeding, when the hard, vulgar, keen, busy, hackneyed New England woman had lost five dollars on her little outlay? Success presented itself as an impossibility, and the hope of it as a wild hallucination.

Some malevolent spirit, doing his utmost to drive Hepzibah mad, unrolled before her imagination a kind of panorama, representing the great thoroughfare of a city, all astir with customers. So many and so magnificent shops as there were! Groceries, toy-shops, dry-goods stores, with their immense panes of plate-glass, their gorgeous fixtures, their vast and complete assortments of merchandize, in which fortunes had been invested; and those noble mirrors at the farther end of each establishment, doubling all this wealth by a brightly burnished vista of unrealities! On one side of the street, this splendid bazaar, with a multitude of perfumed and glossy salesmen, smirking, smiling, bowing, and measuring out the goods! On the other, the dusky old House of the Seven Gables, with the antiquated shop-window under its projecting story, and Hepzibah herself in a gown of rusty black silk, behind the counter, scowling at the world as it went by! This mighty contrast thrust itself forward as a fair expression of the odds against which she was to begin her struggle for a subsistence. Success? Preposterous! She would never think of it again! The house might just as well be buried in an eternal fog, while all other houses had the sunshine on them; for not a foot would ever cross the threshold, nor a hand so much as try the door!

But, at this instant, the shop-bell, right over her head, tinkled as if it were bewitched. The old gentlewoman's heart seemed to be attached to the same steel-spring; for it went through a series of sharp jerks, in unison with the sound. The door was thrust open, although no human form was perceptible on the other side of the half-window. Hepzibah, nevertheless, stood at a gaze, with her hands clasped, looking very much as if she had summoned up an evil spirit, and were afraid, yet resolved, to hazard the encounter.

"Heaven help me!" she groaned mentally. "Now is my hour of need!"

The door, which moved with difficulty on its creaking and rusty hinges, being forced quite open, a square and sturdy little urchin became apparent, with cheeks as red as an apple. He was clad rather shabbily, (but, as it seemed, more owing to his mother's carelessness than his father's poverty,) in a blue apron, very wide and short trowsers, shoes somewhat out at the toes, and a chip-hat,[5] with the frizzles of his curly hair sticking through its crevices. A book and a small slate, under his arm, indicated that he was on his way to school. He stared at Hepzibah, a moment, as an elder customer than himself would have been likely enough to do; not knowing what to make of the tragic attitude and queer scowl, wherewith she regarded him.

"Well, child!" said she, taking heart at sight of a personage so little formidable.—"Well, my child, what did you wish for?"

"That Jim Crow there, in the window!" answered the urchin, holding out a cent, and pointing to the gingerbread figure that had attracted his notice, as he loitered along to school.—"The one that has not a broken foot!"

So Hepzibah put forth her lank arm, and taking the effigy from the shop-window, delivered it to her first customer.

"No matter for the money!" said she, giving him a little push towards the door—for her old gentility was contumaciously squeamish at sight of the copper-coin; and, besides, it seemed such pitiful meanness to take the child's pocket-money, in exchange for a bit of stale gingerbread.—"No matter for the cent! You are welcome to Jim Crow!"

The child—staring with round eyes at this instance of liberality, wholly unprecedented in his large experience of cent-shops—took the man of gingerbread, and quitted the premises. No sooner had he reached the sidewalk (little cannibal that he was!) than Jim Crow's head was in his mouth. As he had not been careful to shut the door, Hepzibah was at the pains of closing it after him, with a pettish ejaculation or two about the troublesomeness of young people, and particularly of small boys. She had just placed another representative of the renowned Jim Crow at the window, when again the shop-bell tinkled clamorously; and again the door being thrust open, with its characteristic jerk and jar, disclosed the same sturdy little urchin who, precisely two minutes ago, had made his exit. The crumbs and discoloration of the cannibal-feast, as yet hardly consummated, were exceedingly visible about his mouth!

"What is it now, child?" asked the maiden lady, rather impatiently.—"Did you come back to shut the door?"

"No!" answered the urchin, pointing to the figure that had just been put up.—"I want that other Jim Crow!"

---

5. An inexpensive hat made of straw or palm leaves.

"Well, here it is for you," said Hepzibah, reaching it down; but, recognizing that this pertinacious customer would not quit her on any other terms, so long as she had a gingerbread figure in her shop, she partly drew back her extended hand—"Where is the cent?"

The little boy had the cent ready, but, like a true-born Yankee, would have preferred the better bargain to the worse. Looking somewhat chagrined, he put the coin into Hepzibah's hand, and departed, sending the second Jim Crow in quest of the former one. The new shopkeeper dropt the first solid result of her commercial enterprise into the till. It was done! The sordid stain of that copper-coin could never be washed away from her palm. The little school-boy, aided by the impish figure of the negro dancer, had wrought an irreparable ruin. The structure of ancient aristocracy had been demolished by him, even as if his childish gripe had torn down the seven-gabled mansion! Now let Hepzibah turn the old Pyncheon portraits with their faces to the wall, and take the map of her eastern-territory to kindle the kitchen-fire, and blow up the flame with the empty breath of her ancestral traditions! What had she to do with ancestry? Nothing;—no more than with posterity! No lady, now, but simply Hepzibah Pyncheon, a forlorn old maid, and keeper of a cent-shop!

Nevertheless—even while she paraded these ideas somewhat ostentatiously through her mind—it is altogether surprising what a calmness had come over her. The anxiety and misgivings which had tormented her, whether asleep or in melancholy day-dreams, ever since her project began to take an aspect of solidity, had now vanished quite away. She felt the novelty of her position, indeed, but no longer with disturbance or affright. Now and then, there came a thrill of almost youthful enjoyment. It was the invigorating breath of a fresh outward atmosphere, after the long torpor and monotonous seclusion of her life. So wholesome is effort! So miraculous the strength that we do not know of! The healthiest glow, that Hepzibah had known for years, had come now, in the dreaded crisis, when, for the first time, she had put forth her hand to help herself. That little circlet of the schoolboy's copper-coin—dim and lustreless though it was, with the small services which it had been doing, here and there about the world—had proved a talisman, fragrant with good, and deserving to be set in gold and worn next her heart. It was as potent, and perhaps endowed with the same kind of efficacy, as a galvanic ring![6] Hepzibah, at all events, was indebted to its subtile operation, both in body and spirit; so much the more, as it inspired her with energy to get some breakfast, at which—still the better to keep up her courage—she allowed herself an extra spoonful in her infusion of black tea.

6. A ring of metals believed to generate a health-producing electrical field for the wearer (see also n. 7, p. 29).

Her introductory day of shopkeeping did not run on, however, without many and serious interruptions of this mood of cheerful vigor. As a general rule, Providence seldom vouchsafes to mortals any more than just that degree of encouragement, which suffices to keep them at a reasonably full exertion of their powers. In the case of our old gentlewoman, after the excitement of new effort had subsided, the despondency of her whole life threatened, ever and anon, to return. It was like the heavy mass of clouds, which we may often see obscuring the sky, and making a gray twilight everywhere, until, towards nightfall, it yields temporarily to a glimpse of sunshine. But, always, the envious cloud strives to gather again across the streak of celestial azure.

Customers came in, as the forenoon advanced, but rather slowly; in some cases, too, it must be owned, with little satisfaction either to themselves or Miss Hepzibah; nor on the whole, with an aggregate of very rich emolument to the till. A little girl, sent by her mother to match a skein of cotton-thread, of a peculiar hue, took one that the near-sighted old lady pronounced extremely like, but soon came running back, with a blunt and cross message, that it would not do, and, besides, was very rotten! Then there was a pale, care-wrinkled woman, not old, but haggard, and already with streaks of gray among her hair, like silver ribbons; one of those women, naturally delicate, whom you at once recognize as worn to death by a brute—probably, a drunken brute—of a husband, and at least nine children. She wanted a few pounds of flour, and offered the money, which the decayed gentlewoman silently rejected, and gave the poor soul better measure than if she had taken it. Shortly afterwards, a man in a blue cotton-frock, much soiled, came in and bought a pipe; filling the whole shop, meanwhile, with the hot odor of strong drink, not only exhaled in the torrid atmosphere of his breath, but oozing out of his entire system, like an inflammable gas. It was impressed on Hepzibah's mind, that this was the husband of the care-wrinkled woman. He asked for a paper of tobacco; and, as she had neglected to provide herself with the article, her brutal customer dashed down his newly-bought pipe, and left the shop, muttering some unintelligible words, which had the tone and bitterness of a curse. Hereupon, Hepzibah threw up her eyes, unintentionally scowling in the face of Providence!

No less than five persons, during the forenoon, inquired for ginger-beer, or root-beer, or any drink of a similar brewage, and, obtaining nothing of the kind, went off in an exceedingly bad humor. Three of them left the door open; and the other two pulled it so spitefully, in going out, that the little bell played the very deuce with Hepzibah's nerves. A round, bustling, fire-ruddy housewife, of the neighborhood, burst breathless into the shop, fiercely demanding yeast; and when the poor gentlewoman, with her cold shyness of manner, gave her hot customer to understand that she did not keep the article, this very capable housewife took upon herself to administer a regular rebuke.

"A cent-shop, and no yeast!" quoth she. "That will never do! Who ever heard of such a thing? Your loaf will never rise, no more than mine will to-day. You had better shut up shop at once!"

"Well," said Hepzibah, heaving a deep sigh, "perhaps I had!"

Several times, moreover, besides the above instance, her ladylike sensibilities were seriously infringed upon by the familiar, if not rude tone with which people addressed her. They evidently considered themselves not merely her equals, but her patrons and superiors. Now, Hepzibah had unconsciously flattered herself with the idea, that there would be a gleam or halo of some kind or other, about her person, which would ensure an obeisance to her sterling gentility, or, at least, a tacit recognition of it. On the other hand, nothing tortured her more intolerably than when this recognition was too prominently expressed. To one or two rather officious offers of sympathy, her responses were little short of acrimonious; and, we regret to say, Hepzibah was thrown into a positively unchristian state of mind by the suspicion that one of her customers was drawn to the shop, not by any real need of the article which she pretended to seek, but by a wicked wish to stare at her. The vulgar creature was determined to see for herself what sort of a figure a mildewed piece of aristocracy—after wasting all the bloom and much of the decline of her life, apart from the world—would cut behind a counter. In this particular case—however mechanical and innocuous it might be, at other times—Hepzibah's contortion of brow served her in good stead.

"I never was so frightened in my life!" said the curious customer in describing the incident to one of her acquaintances. "She's a real old vixen, take my word of it. She says little, to be sure;—but if you could only see the mischief in her eye!"

On the whole, therefore, her new experience led our decayed gentlewoman to very disagreeable conclusions as to the temper and manners of what she termed the lower classes, whom, heretofore, she had looked down upon with a gentle and pitying complacence, as herself occupying a sphere of unquestionable superiority. But, unfortunately, she had likewise to struggle against a bitter emotion, of a directly opposite kind; a sentiment of virulence, we mean, towards the idle aristocracy to which it had so recently been her pride to belong. When a lady, in a delicate and costly summer garb, with a floating veil and gracefully swaying gown, and, altogether, an ethereal lightness that made you look at her beautifully slippered feet, to see whether she trod on the dust or floated in the air—when such a vision happened to pass through this retired street, leaving it tenderly and delusively fragrant with her passage, as if a boquet of tea-roses had been borne along—then, again, it is to be feared, old Hepzibah's scowl could no longer vindicate itself entirely on the plea of near-sightedness.

"For what end," thought she, giving vent to that feeling of hostility, which is the only real abasement of the poor, in presence of the rich, "for what good end, in the wisdom of Providence, does that woman live! Must the whole world toil, that the palms of her hands may be kept white and delicate?"

Then, ashamed and penitent, she hid her face.

"May God forgive me!" said she.

Doubtless, God did forgive her. But, taking the inward and outward history of the first half-day into consideration, Hepzibah began to fear that the shop would prove her ruin, in a moral and religious point of view, without contributing very essentially towards even her temporal welfare.

IV. A Day behind the Counter

Towards noon, Hepzibah saw an elderly gentleman, large and portly, and of remarkably dignified demeanor, passing slowly along, on the opposite side of the white and dusty street. On coming within the shadow of the Pyncheon-elm, he stopt, and (taking off his hat, meanwhile, to wipe the perspiration from his brow) seemed to scrutinize, with especial interest, the dilapidated and rusty-visaged House of the Seven Gables. He himself, in a very different style, was as well worth looking at as the house. No better model need be sought, nor could have been found, of a very high order of respectability, which by some indescribable magic, not merely expressed itself in his looks and gestures, but even governed the fashion of his garments, and rendered them all proper and essential to the man. Without appearing to differ, in any tangible way, from other people's clothes, there was yet a wide and rich gravity about them, that must have been a characteristic of the wearer, since it could not be defined as pertaining either to the cut or material. His gold-headed cane, too—a serviceable staff, of dark, polished wood—had similar traits, and, had it chosen to take a walk by itself, would have been recognized anywhere as a tolerably adequate representative of its master. This character—which showed itself so strikingly in everything about him, and the effect of which we seek to convey to the reader—went no deeper than his station, habits of life, and external circumstances. One perceived him to be a person-age of mark, influence, and authority; and, especially, you could feel just as certain that he was opulent, as if he had exhibited his bank account—or as if you had seen him touching the twigs of the Pyncheon-elm, and, Midas-like, transmuting them to gold.

In his youth, he had probably been considered a handsome man; at his present age, his brow was too heavy, his temples too bare, his remaining hair too gray, his eye too cold, his lips too closely com-pressed, to bear any relation to mere personal beauty. He would have made a good and massive portrait; better now, perhaps, than at any previous period of his life, although his look might grow pos-itively harsh, in the process of being fixed upon the canvass. The artist would have found it desirable to study his face, and prove its capacity for varied expression; to darken it with a frown—to kindle it up with a smile.

While the elderly gentleman stood looking at the Pyncheon-house, both the frown and the smile passed successively over his countenance. His eye rested on the shop-window, and putting up a pair of gold-bowed spectacles, which he held in his hand, he minutely surveyed Hepzibah's little arrangement of toys and com-modities. At first, it seemed not to please him—nay, to cause him exceeding displeasure—and yet, the very next moment, he smiled. While the latter expression was yet on his lips, he caught a glimpse of Hepzibah, who had involuntarily bent forward to the window; and then the smile changed from acrid and disagreeable, to the sunniest complaisancy and benevolence. He bowed, with a happy mixture of dignity and courteous kindliness, and pursued his way.

"There he is!" said Hepzibah to herself, gulping down a very bit-ter emotion, and, since she could not rid herself of it, trying to drive it back into her heart.—"What does he think of it, I wonder? Does it please him? Ah!—he is looking back!"

The gentleman had paused in the street, and turned himself half about, still with his eyes fixed on the shop-window. In fact, he wheeled wholly round, and commenced a step or two, as if design-ing to enter the shop; but, as it chanced, his purpose was antici-pated by Hepzibah's first customer, the little cannibal of Jim Crow, who, staring up at the window, was irresistibly attracted by an ele-phant of gingerbread. What a grand appetite had this small urchin!—two Jim Crows, immediately after breakfast!—and now an elephant, as a preliminary whet before dinner! By the time this lat-ter purchase was completed, the elderly gentleman had resumed his way, and turned the street-corner.

"Take it as you like, Cousin Jaffrey!" muttered the maiden lady, as she drew back after cautiously thrusting out her head, and looking up and down the street. "Take it as you like! You have seen my little shop-window! Well!—what have you to say?—is not the Pyncheon-house my own, while I'm alive?"

After this incident, Hepzibah retreated to the back parlor, where she at first caught up a half-finished stocking, and began knitting at it with nervous and irregular jerks; but quickly finding herself at odds with the stitches, she threw it aside, and walked hurriedly about the room. At length, she paused before the portrait of the stern old Puritan, her ancestor, and the founder of the house. In one sense, this picture had almost faded into the canvass, and hidden itself behind the duskiness of age; in another, she could not but fancy that it had been growing more prominent, and strikingly expressive, ever since her earliest familiarity with it, as a child. For, while the physical outline and substance were darkening away from the beholder's eye, the bold, hard, and, at the same time, indirect character of the man seemed to be brought out in a kind of spiritual relief. Such an effect may occasionally be observed in pictures of antique date. They acquire a look which an artist (if he have anything like the complaisancy of artists, now-a-days) would never dream of presenting to a patron as his own characteristic expression, but which, nevertheless, we at once recognize as reflecting the unlovely truth of a human soul. In such cases, the painter's deep conception of his subject's inward traits has wrought itself into the essence of the picture, and is seen, after the superficial coloring has been rubbed off by time.

While gazing at the portrait, Hepzibah trembled under its eye. Her hereditary reverence made her afraid to judge the character of the original so harshly, as a perception of the truth compelled her to do. But still she gazed, because the face of the picture enabled her—at least, she fancied so—to read more accurately, and to a greater depth, the face which she had just seen in the street.

"This is the very man!" murmured she to herself. "Let Jaffrey Pyncheon smile as he will, there is that look beneath! Put on him a scull-cap, and a band, and a black cloak, and a Bible in one hand and a sword in the other—then let Jaffrey smile as he might—nobody would doubt that it was the old Pyncheon come again! He has proved himself the very man to build up a new house! Perhaps, too, to draw down a new curse!"

Thus did Hepzibah bewilder herself with these fantasies of the old time. She had dwelt too much alone—too long in the Pyncheon-house—until her very brain was impregnated with the dry-rot of its timbers. She needed a walk along the noonday street, to keep her sane.

By the spell of contrast, another portrait rose up before her, painted with more daring flattery than any artist would have ventured upon, but yet so delicately touched that the likeness re-

mained perfect. Malbone's miniature, though from the same original, was far inferior to Hepzibah's air-drawn picture, at which affection and sorrowful remembrance wrought together. Soft, mildly
and cheerfully contemplative, with full, red lips, just on the verge
of a smile, which the eyes seemed to herald by a gentle kindling-up
of their orbs! Feminine traits, moulded inseparably with those of
the other sex! The miniature, likewise, had this last peculiarity; so
that you inevitably thought of the original as resembling his
mother; and she, a lovely and loveable woman, with perhaps some
beautiful infirmity of character, that made it all the pleasanter to
know, and easier to love her.

"Yes," thought Hepzibah, with grief of which it was only the more
tolerable portion that welled up from her heart to her eyelids, "they
persecuted his mother in him! He never was a Pyncheon!"

But here the shop-bell rang; it was like a sound from a remote
distance—so far had Hepzibah descended into the sepulchral
depths of her reminiscences. On entering the shop, she found an
old man there, a humble resident of Pyncheon-street, and whom,
for a great many years past, she had suffered to be a kind of familiar of the house. He was an immemorial personage, who seemed always to have had a white head and wrinkles, and never to have
possessed but a single tooth, and that a half-decayed one, in the
front of the upper jaw. Well advanced as Hepzibah was, she could
not remember when Uncle Venner, as the neighborhood called
him, had not gone up and down the street, stooping a little and
drawing his feet heavily over the gravel or pavement. But still there
was something tough and vigorous about him, that not only kept
him in daily breath, but enabled him to fill a place which would
else have been vacant, in the apparently crowded world. To go of
errands, with his slow and shuffling gait, which made you doubt
how he ever was to arrive anywhere; to saw a small household's foot
or two of firewood, or knock to pieces an old barrel, or split up a
pine board, for kindling-stuff; in summer, to dig the few yards of
garden-ground, appertaining to a low-rented tenement, and share
the produce of his labor at the halves;[7] in winter, to shovel away the
snow from the sidewalk, or open paths to the wood-shed, or along
the clothes-line;—such were some of the essential offices which
Uncle Venner performed among at least a score of families. Within
that circle, he claimed the same sort of privilege, and probably felt
as much warmth of interest, as a clergyman does in the range of his
parishioners. Not that he laid claim to the tithe pig;[8] but, as an
analogous mode of reverence, he went his rounds, every morning,

7. To share the work in exchange for a half-share of the crop.
8. A pig that is donated as part of a parishioner's pledge to donate one-tenth (a tithe) of the
family income to a church.

to gather up the crumbs of the table and overflowings of the dinner-pot, as food for a pig of his own.

In his younger days—for, after all, there was a dim tradition that he had been, not young, but younger—Uncle Venner was commonly regarded as rather deficient, than otherwise, in his wits. In truth, he had virtually pleaded guilty to the charge, by scarcely aiming at such success as other men seek, and by taking only that humble and modest part in the intercourse of life, which belongs to the alleged deficiency. But, now, in his extreme old age—whether it were, that his long and hard experience had actually brightened him, or that his decaying judgement rendered him less capable of fairly measuring himself—the venerable man made pretensions to no little wisdom, and really enjoyed the credit of it. There was likewise, at times, a vein of something like poetry in him; it was the moss or wall-flower of his mind in its small dilapidation, and gave a charm to what might have been vulgar and common-place, in his earlier and middle life. Hepzibah had a regard for him, because his name was ancient in the town, and had formerly been respectable. It was a still better reason for awarding him a species of familiar reverence, that Uncle Venner was himself the most ancient existence, whether of man or thing, in Pyncheon-street; except the House of the Seven Gables, and perhaps the elm that overshadowed it.

This patriarch now presented himself before Hepzibah, clad in an old blue coat, which had a fashionable air, and must have accrued to him from the cast-off wardrobe of some dashing clerk. As for his trowsers, they were of tow-cloth,[9] very short in the legs, and bagging down strangely in the rear, but yet having a suitableness to his figure, which his other garment entirely lacked. His hat had relation to no other part of his dress, and but very little to the head that wore it. Thus Uncle Venner was a miscellaneous old gentleman, partly himself, but, in good measure, somebody else; patched together, too, of different epochs; an epitome of times and fashions.

"So, you have really begun trade," said he—"really begun trade! Well, I'm glad to see it. Young people should never live idle in the world, nor old ones neither, unless when the rheumatize gets hold of them. It has given me warning already; and in two or three years longer, I shall think of putting aside business, and retiring to my farm. That's yonder—the great brick house, you know—the workhouse,[1] most folks call it; but I mean to do my work first, and go there to be idle and enjoy myself. And I'm glad to see you beginning to do your work, Miss Hepzibah!"

9. Coarse cloth made from the less desirable flax fibers.
1. Institution that cares for the poor, usually run by church organizations.

"Thank you, Uncle Venner," said Hepzibah smiling; for she always felt kindly towards the simple and talkative old man. Had he been an old woman, she might probably have repelled the freedom which she now took in good part.—"It is time for me to begin work, indeed! Or, to speak the truth, I have but just begun, when I ought to be giving it up."

"Oh, never say that, Miss Hepzibah," answered the old man. "You are a young woman yet. Why, I hardly thought myself younger than I am now—it seems so little while ago—since I used to see you playing about the door of the old house, quite a small child! Oftener, though, you used to be sitting at the threshold and looking gravely into the street; for you had always a grave kind of way with you—a grown-up air, when you were only the height of my knee. It seems as if I saw you now; and your grandfather, with his red cloak, and his white wig, and his cocked hat, and his cane, coming out of the house, and stepping so grandly up the street! Those old gentlemen, that grew up before the revolution, used to put on grand airs. In my young days, the great man of the town was commonly called King, and his wife—not Queen, to be sure—but Lady. Now-a-days, a man would not dare to be called King; and if he feels himself a little above common folks, he only stoops so much the lower to them. I met your cousin, the Judge, ten minutes ago; and, in my old tow-cloth trowsers, as you see, the Judge raised his hat to me, I do believe! At any rate, the Judge bowed and smiled!"

"Yes," said Hepzibah, with something bitter stealing unawares into her tone; "my Cousin Jaffrey is thought to have a very pleasant smile!"

"And so he has!" replied Uncle Venner. "And that's rather remarkable, in a Pyncheon; for—begging your pardon, Miss Hepzibah—they never had the name of being an easy and agreeable set of folks. There was no getting close to them. But, now, Miss Hepzibah, if an old man may be bold to ask, why don't Judge Pyncheon, with his great means, step forward, and tell his cousin to shut up her little shop at once? It's for your credit to be doing something; but it's not for the Judge's credit to let you!"

"We won't talk of this, if you please, Uncle Venner," said Hepzibah coldly. "I ought to say, however, that, if I choose to earn bread for myself, it is not Judge Pyncheon's fault. Neither will he deserve the blame," added she more kindly, remembering Uncle Venner's privileges of age and humble familiarity, "if I should, by-and-by, find it convenient to retire with you to your farm."

"And it's no bad place neither, that farm of mine!" cried the old man cheerily, as if there were something positively delightful in the prospect.—"No bad place is the great brick farm-house, especially for them that will find a good many old cronies there, as will be my

case. I quite long to be among them, sometimes, of the winter
evenings; for it is but dull business for a lonesome elderly man, like
me, to be nodding, by the hour together, with no company but his
air-tight stove. Summer or winter, there's a great deal to be said in
favor of my farm! And, take it in the autumn, what can be pleasanter than to spend a whole day, on the sunny side of a barn or a
wood-pile, chatting with somebody as old as one's self; or perhaps
idling away the time with a natural-born simpleton, who knows
how to be idle, because even our busy Yankees have never found
out how to put him to any use? Upon my word, Miss Hepzibah, I
doubt whether I've ever been so comfortable as I mean to be at my
farm, which most folks call the work-house. But you—you're a
young woman yet—you never need go there! Something still better
will turn up for you. I'm sure of it!"

Hepzibah fancied that there was something peculiar in her venerable friend's look and tone; insomuch that she gazed into his face
with considerable earnestness, endeavoring to discover what secret
meaning, if any, might be lurking there. Individuals, whose affairs
have reached an utterly desperate crisis, almost invariably keep
themselves alive with hopes, so much the more airily magnificent,
as they have the less of solid matter within their grasp, whereof to
mould any judicious and moderate expectation of good. Thus, all
the while Hepzibah was projecting the scheme of her little shop,
she had cherished an unacknowledged idea that some harlequin-
trick[2] of fortune would intervene, in her favor. For example, an uncle
—who had sailed for India, fifty years before, and never been heard
of since—might yet return, and adopt her to be the comfort of his
very extreme and decrepit age, and adorn her with pearls, diamonds, and oriental shawls and turbans, and make her the ultimate
heiress of his unreckonable riches. Or the member of parliament,
now at the head of the English branch of the family—with which
the elder stock, on this side of the Atlantic, had held little or no intercourse for the last two centuries—this eminent gentleman might
invite Hepzibah to quit the ruinous House of the Seven Gables,
and come over to dwell with her kindred, at Pyncheon Hall. But,
for reasons the most imperative, she could not yield to his request.
It was more probable, therefore, that the descendants of a Pyncheon who had emigrated to Virginia, in some past generation, and
become a great planter there—hearing of Hepzibah's destitution,
and impelled by the splendid generosity of character, with which
their Virginian mixture must have enriched the New England
blood—would send her a remittance of a thousand dollars, with a
hint of repeating the favor, annually. Or—and, surely, anything so

2. A clown's magic trick.

undeniably just could not be beyond the limits of reasonable anticipation—the great claim to the heritage of Waldo County might finally be decided in favor of the Pyncheons; so that, instead of
keeping a cent-shop, Hepzibah would build a palace, and look
down from its highest tower on hill, dale, forest, field, and town, as
her own share of the ancestral territory!

These were some of the fantasies which she had long dreamed
about; and, aided by these, Uncle Venner's casual attempt at encouragement kindled a strange festal glory in the poor, bare, melancholy chambers of her brain, as if that inner world were suddenly
lighted up with gas. But either he knew nothing of her castles in
the air—as how should he?—or else her earnest scowl disturbed his
recollection, as it might a more courageous man's. Instead of pursuing any weightier topic, Uncle Venner was pleased to favor Hepzibah with some sage counsel in her shop-keeping capacity.

"Give no credit!"—these were some of his golden maxims—
"Never take paper-money! Look well to your change! Ring the silver
on the four-pound weight! Shove back all English half-pence and
base copper-tokens,[3] such as are very plenty about town! At your
leisure hours, knit children's woollen socks and mittens! Brew your
own yeast, and make your own ginger-beer!"

And while Hepzibah was doing her utmost to digest the hard little pellets of his already uttered wisdom, he gave vent to his final,
and what he declared to be his all-important advice, as follows:—

"Put on a bright face for your customers, and smile pleasantly as
you hand them what they ask for! A stale article, if you dip it in a
good, warm, sunny smile, will go off better than a fresh one that
you've scowled upon!"

To this last apothegm, poor Hepzibah responded with a sigh, so
deep and heavy that it almost rustled Uncle Venner quite away, like
a withered leaf, as he was, before an autumnal gale. Recovering
himself, however, he bent forward, and, with a good deal of feeling
in his ancient visage, beckoned her nearer to him.

"When do you expect him home?" whispered he.

"Whom do you mean?" asked Hepzibah, turning pale.

"Ah!—You don't love to talk about it," said Uncle Venner. "Well,
well, we'll say no more, though there's word of it, all over town. I
remember him, Miss Hepzibah, before he could run alone!"

During the remainder of the day, poor Hepzibah acquitted
herself even less creditably, as a shopkeeper, than in her earlier efforts. She appeared to be walking in a dream; or, more truly, the
vivid life and reality, assumed by her emotions, made all outward
occurrences unsubstantial, like the teasing phantasms of a half-

---

3. Tokens used by merchants as IOUs when short of coins.

conscious slumber. She still responded, mechanically, to the frequent summons of the shop-bell, and, at the demand of her customers, went prying with vague eyes about the shop; proffering them one article after another, and thrusting aside—perversely, as most of them supposed—the identical thing they asked for. There is sad confusion, indeed, when the spirit thus flits away into the past, or into the more awful future, or, in any manner, steps across the spaceless boundary betwixt its own region and the actual world; where the body remains to guide itself, as best it may, with little more than the mechanism of animal life. It is like death, without death's quiet privilege; its freedom from mortal care. Worst of all, when the actual duties are comprised in such petty details as now vexed the brooding soul of the old gentlewoman. As the animosity of fate would have it, there was a great influx of custom, in the course of the afternoon. Hepzibah blundered to-and-fro about her small place of business, committing the most unheard of errors; now stringing up twelve, and now seven tallow-candles, instead of ten to the pound; selling ginger for Scotch snuff, pins for needles, and needles for pins; misreckoning her change, sometimes to the public detriment, and much oftener to her own; and thus she went on, doing her utmost to bring chaos back again, until, at the close of the day's labor, to her inexplicable astonishment, she found the money-drawer almost destitute of coin. After all her painful traffic, the whole proceeds were perhaps half-a-dozen coppers, and a questionable ninepence, which ultimately proved to be copper likewise.

At this price, or at whatever price, she rejoiced that the day had reached its end. Never before had she had such a sense of the intolerable length of time that creeps between dawn and sunset, and of the miserable irksomeness of having aught to do, and of the better wisdom that it would be, to lie down at once, in sullen resignation, and let life, and its toils and vexations, trample over one's prostrate body, as they may! Hepzibah's final operation was with the little devourer of Jim Crow and the elephant, who now proposed to eat a camel. In her bewilderment, she offered him first a wooden dragoon, and next a handfull of marbles; neither of which being adapted to his else omnivorous appetite, she hastily held out her whole remaining stock of natural history, in gingerbread, and huddled the small customer out of the shop. She then muffled the bell in an unfinished stocking, and put up the oaken bar across the door.

During the latter process, an omnibus[4] came to a standstill under the branches of the elm-tree. Hepzibah's heart was in her mouth. Remote and dusky, and with no sunshine on all the intervening

4. Horse-drawn passenger carriage.

space, was that region of the Past, whence her only guest might be expected to arrive! Was she to meet him now?

Somebody, at all events, was passing from the farthest interior of the omnibus, towards its entrance. A gentleman alighted; but it was only to offer his hand to a young girl, whose slender figure, nowise needing such assistance, now lightly descended the steps, and made an airy little jump from the final one to the sidewalk. She rewarded her cavalier with a smile, the cheery glow of which was seen reflected on his own face, as he re-entered the vehicle. The girl then turned towards the House of the Seven Gables; to the door of which, meanwhile—not the shop-door, but the antique-portal—the omnibus-man had carried a light trunk and a bandbox. First giving a sharp rap of the old iron knocker, he left his passenger and her luggage at the door-step, and departed.

"Who can it be?" thought Hepzibah, who had been screwing her visual organs into the acutest focus of which they were capable. "The girl must have mistaken the house!"

She stole softly into the hall, and, herself invisible, gazed through the dusty side-lights of the portal at the young, blooming, and very cheerful face, which presented itself for admittance into the gloomy old mansion. It was a face to which almost any door would have opened of its own accord.

The young girl, so fresh, so unconventional, and yet so orderly and obedient to common rules, as you at once recognized her to be, was widely in contrast, at that moment, with everything about her. The sordid and ugly luxuriance of gigantic weeds, that grew in the angle of the house, and the heavy projection that overshadowed her, and the time-worn frame-work of the door;—none of these things belonged to her sphere. But—even as a ray of sunshine, fall into what dismal place it may, instantaneously creates for itself a propriety in being there—so did it seem altogether fit that the girl should be standing at the threshold. It was no less evidently proper, that the door should swing open to admit her. The maiden lady herself, sternly inhospitable in her first purposes, soon began to feel that the bolt ought to be shoved back, and the rusty key be turned in the reluctant lock.

"Can it be Phoebe?"[5] questioned she within herself. "It must be little Phoebe; for it can be nobody else—and there is a look of her father about her, too! But what does she want here? And how like a country-cousin, to come down upon a poor body in this way, without so much as a day's notice, or asking whether she would be welcome! Well; she must have a night's lodging, I suppose; and to-morrow the child shall go back to her mother."

---

5. One of Hawthorne's affectionate names for his wife, Sophia.

Phoebe, it must be understood, was that one little offshoot of the Pyncheon race to whom we have already referred, as a native of a rural part of New England, where the old fashions and feelings of relationship are still partially kept up. In her own circle, it was regarded as by no means improper for kinsfolk to visit one another, without invitation, or preliminary and ceremonious warning. Yet, in consideration of Miss Hepzibah's recluse way of life, a letter had actually been written and despatched, conveying information of Phoebe's projected visit. This epistle, for three or four days past, had been in the pocket of the penny-postman, who, happening to have no other business in Pyncheon-street, had not yet made it convenient to call at the House of the Seven Gables.

"No!—she can stay only one night," said Hepzibah, unbolting the door. "If Clifford were to find her here, it might disturb him!"

V. May and November

Phoebe Pyncheon slept, on the night of her arrival, in a chamber that looked down on the garden of the old house. It fronted towards the east, so that, at a very seasonable hour, a glow of crimson light came flooding through the window, and bathed the dingy ceiling and paper-hangings in its own hue. There were curtains to Phoebe's bed; a dark, antique canopy and ponderous festoons, of a stuff which had been rich, and even magnificent, in its time; but which now brooded over the girl like a cloud, making a night in that one corner, while elsewhere it was beginning to be day. The morning-light, however, soon stole into the aperture at the foot of the bed, betwixt those faded curtains. Finding the new guest there—with a bloom on her cheeks, like the morning's own, and a gentle stir of departing slumber in her limbs, as when an early breeze moves the foliage—the Dawn kissed her brow. It was the caress which a dewy maiden—such as the Dawn is, immortally—gives to her sleeping sister, partly from the impulse of irresistible fondness, and partly as a pretty hint, that it is time now to unclose her eyes.

At the touch of those lips of light, Phoebe quietly awoke, and, for a moment, did not recognize where she was, nor how those heavy curtains chanced to be festooned around her. Nothing, indeed, was absolutely plain to her, except that it was now early morning, and that, whatever might happen next, it was proper, first of all, to get up and say her prayers. She was the more inclined to devotion, from the grim aspect of the chamber and its furniture, especially the tall, stiff chairs; one of which stood close by her bedside, and looked as if some old-fashioned personage had been sitting there;

all night, and had vanished only just in season to escape discovery.

When Phoebe was quite dressed, she peeped out of the window, and saw a rose-bush in the garden. Being a very tall one, and of luxurious growth, it had been propt up against the side of the house, and was literally covered with a rare and very beautiful species of white rose. A large portion of them, as the girl afterwards discovered, had blight or mildew at their hearts; but, viewed at a fair distance, the whole rose-bush looked as if it had been brought from Eden, that very summer, together with the mould in which it grew. The truth was, nevertheless, that it had been planted by Alice Pyncheon—she was Phoebe's great-great-grand-aunt—in soil which, reckoning only its cultivation as a garden-plat, was now unctuous with nearly two hundred years of vegetable decay. Growing as they did, however, out of the old earth, the flowers still sent a fresh and sweet incense up to their Creator; nor could it have been the less pure and acceptable, because Phoebe's young breath mingled with it, as the fragrance floated past the window. Hastening down the creaking and carpetless staircase, she found her way into the garden, gathered some of the most perfect of the roses, and brought them to her chamber.

Little Phoebe was one of those persons who possess, as their exclusive patrimony, the gift of practical arrangement. It is a kind of natural magic, that enables these favored ones to bring out the hidden capabilities of things around them; and particularly to give a look of comfort and habitableness to any place which, for however brief a period, may happen to be their home. A wild hut of underbrush, tossed together by wayfarers through the primitive forest, would acquire the home aspect by one night's lodging of such a woman, and would retain it, long after her quiet figure had disappeared into the surrounding shade. No less a portion of such homely witchcraft was requisite, to reclaim, as it were, Phoebe's waste, cheerless, and dusky chamber, which had been untenanted so long—except by spiders, and mice, and rats, and ghosts—that it was all overgrown with the desolation, which watches to obliterate every trace of man's happier hours. What was precisely Phoebe's process, we find it impossible to say. She appeared to have no preliminary design, but gave a touch here, and another there; brought some articles of furniture to light, and dragged others into the shadow; looped up or let down a window-curtain; and, in the course of half-an-hour, had fully succeeded in throwing a kindly and hospitable smile over the apartment. No longer ago than the night before, it had resembled nothing so much as the old maid's heart; for there was neither sunshine nor household-fire in one nor the other, and, save for ghosts, and ghostly reminiscences, not a guest, for many years gone-by, had entered the heart or the chamber.

There was still another peculiarity of this inscrutable charm. The bed-chamber, no doubt, was a chamber of very great and varied experience, as a scene of human life; the joy of bridal nights had throbbed itself away here; new immortals had first drawn earthly breath here; and here old people had died. But—whether it were the white roses, or whatever the subtle influence might be—a person of delicate instinct would have known, at once, that it was now a maiden's bed-chamber, and had been purified of all former evil and sorrow by her sweet breath and happy thoughts. Her dreams of the past night, being such cheerful ones, had exorcised the gloom, and now haunted the chamber in its stead.

After arranging matters to her satisfaction, Phoebe emerged from her chamber, with a purpose to descend again into the garden. Besides the rose-bush, she had observed several other species of flowers, growing there in a wilderness of neglect, and obstructing one another's developement (as is often the parallel case in human society) by their uneducated entanglement and confusion. At the head of the stairs, however, she met Hepzibah, who, it being still early, invited her into a room which she would probably have called her boudoir, had her education embraced any such French phrase. It was strewn about with a few old books, and a work-basket, and a dusty writing-desk, and had, on one side, a large, black article of furniture, of very strange appearance, which the old gentlewoman told Phoebe was a harpsichord. It looked more like a coffin than anything else; and, indeed—not having been played upon, or opened, for years—there must have been a vast deal of dead music in it, stifled for want of air. Human finger was hardly known to have touched its chords, since the days of Alice Pyncheon, who had learned the sweet accomplishment of melody, in Europe.

Hepzibah bade her young guest sit down, and, herself taking a chair near by, looked as earnestly at Phoebe's trim little figure as if she expected to see right into its springs and motive secrets.

"Cousin Phoebe," said she, at last, "I really can't see my way clear to keep you with me."

These words, however, had not the inhospitable bluntness with which they may strike the reader; for the two relatives, in a talk before bedtime, had arrived at a certain degree of mutual understanding. Hepzibah knew enough to enable her to appreciate the circumstances (resulting from the second marriage of the girl's mother) which made it desirable for Phoebe to establish herself in another home. Nor did she misinterpret Phoebe's character, and the genial activity pervading it—one of the most valuable traits of the true New England woman—which had impelled her forth, as might be said, to seek her fortune, but with a self-respecting purpose to confer as much benefit as she could anywise receive. As one of her nearest kindred, she had naturally betaken herself to Hepzibah, with no idea of forcing herself on her cousin's protection, but only for a visit of a week or two, which might be indefinitely extended, should it prove for the happiness of both.

To Hepzibah's blunt observation, therefore, Phoebe replied as frankly, and more cheerfully.

"Dear Cousin, I cannot tell how it will be," said she. "But I really think we may suit one another, much better than you suppose."

"You are a nice girl—I see it plainly," continued Hepzibah; "and it is not any question, as to that point, which makes me hesitate. But, Phoebe, this house of mine is but a melancholy place for a young person to be in. It lets in the wind and rain—and the snow, too, in the garret and upper chambers, in winter-time—but it never lets in the sunshine! And as for myself, you see what I am;—a dismal and lonesome old woman (for I begin to call myself old, Phoebe) whose temper, I am afraid, is none of the best, and whose spirits are as bad as can be! I cannot make your life pleasant, Cousin Phoebe; neither can I so much as give you bread to eat."

"You will find me a cheerful little body," answered Phoebe smiling, and yet with a kind of gentle dignity; "and I mean to earn my bread. You know, I have not been brought up a Pyncheon. A girl learns many things in a New England village."

"Ah, Phoebe," said Hepzibah sighing, "your knowledge would do but little for you here! And then it is a wretched thought, that you should fling away your young days in a place like this. Those cheeks would not be so rosy, after a month or two. Look at my face!"—and, indeed, the contrast was very striking—"you see how pale I am! It is my idea that the dust and continual decay of these old houses are unwholesome for the lungs."

"There is the garden—the flowers to be taken care of," observed Phoebe. "I should keep myself healthy with exercise in the open air."

"And, after all, child," exclaimed Hepzibah, suddenly rising, as if to dismiss the subject, "it is not for me to say who shall be a guest, or inhabitant of the old Pyncheon-house! Its master is coming!"

"Do you mean Judge Pyncheon?" asked Phoebe in surprise.

"Judge Pyncheon!" answered her cousin angrily. "He will hardly cross the threshold, while I live. No, no! But, Phoebe, you shall see the face of him I speak of!"

She went in quest of the miniature already described, and returned with it in her hand. Giving it to Phoebe, she watched her features narrowly, and with a certain jealousy as to the mode in which the girl would show herself affected by the picture.

"How do you like the face?" asked Hepzibah.

"It is handsome—it is very beautiful!" said Phoebe admiringly. "It is as sweet a face as a man's can be, or ought to be. It has something of a child's expression—and yet not childish—only, one feels so very kindly towards him! He ought never to suffer anything. One would bear much, for the sake of sparing him toil or sorrow. Who is it, Cousin Hepzibah?"

"Did you never hear," whispered her cousin, bending towards her, "of Clifford Pyncheon?"

"Never! I thought there were no Pyncheons left, except yourself and our Cousin Jaffrey," answered Phoebe. "And, yet, I seem to have heard the name of Clifford Pyncheon. Yes!—from my father, or my mother—but has he not been a long while dead?"

"Well, well, child, perhaps he has!" said Hepzibah, with a sad, hollow laugh. "But, in old houses like this, you know, dead people are very apt to come back again! We shall see! And, Cousin Phoebe—since, after all that I have said, your courage does not fail you—we will not part so soon. You are welcome, my child, for the present, to such a home as your kinswoman can offer you."

With this measured, but not exactly cold assurance of a hospitable purpose, Hepzibah kissed her cheek.

They now went below stairs, where Phoebe—not so much assuming the office as attracting it to herself, by the magnetism of innate fitness—took the most active part in preparing breakfast. The mistress of the house, meanwhile, as is usual with persons of her stiff and unmalleable cast, stood mostly aside; willing to lend her aid, yet conscious that her natural inaptitude would be likely to impede the business in hand. Phoebe, and the fire that boiled the teakettle, were equally bright, cheerful, and efficient, in their respective offices. Hepzibah gazed forth from her habitual sluggishness, the necessary result of long solitude, as from another sphere. She could not help being interested, however, and even amused, at the readiness with which her new inmate adapted herself to the circumstances, and brought the house, moreover, and all its rusty old appliances, into a suitableness for her purposes. Whatever she did, too, was done without conscious effort, and with frequent outbreaks of song which were exceedingly pleasant to the ear. This natural tunefulness made Phoebe seem like a bird in a shadowy tree; or conveyed the idea that the stream of life warbled through her heart, as a brook sometimes warbles through a pleasant little dell. It betokened the cheeriness of an active temperament, finding joy in its activity, and therefore rendering it beautiful; it was a New England trait—the stern old stuff of Puritanism, with a gold thread in the web.

Hepzibah brought out some old silver spoons, with the family crest upon them, and a China tea-set, painted over with grotesque figures of man, bird, and beast, in as grotesque a landscape. These

pictured people were odd humorists, in a world of their own; a
world of vivid brilliancy, so far as color went, and still unfaded, although the tea-pot and small cups were as ancient as the custom itself of tea-drinking.

"Your great, great, great, great grandmother had these cups,
when she was married," said Hepzibah to Phoebe. "She was a Davenport,[6] of a good family. They were almost the first tea-cups ever
seen in the colony; and if one of them were to be broken, my heart
would break with it. But it is nonsense to speak so, about a brittle
tea-cup, when I remember what my heart has gone through without breaking!"

The cups—not having been used, perhaps, since Hepzibah's
youth—had contracted no small burthen of dust, which Phoebe
washed away with so much care and delicacy, as to satisfy even the
proprietor of this invaluable China.

"What a nice little housewife you are!" exclaimed the latter smiling, and, at the same time, frowning so prodigiously that the smile
was sunshine under a thunder-cloud.—"Do you do other things as
well? Are you as good at your book as you are at washing tea-cups?"

"Not quite, I am afraid," said Phoebe, laughing at the form of
Hepzibah's question.—"But I was schoolmistress for the little children, in our district, last summer, and might have been so still."

"Ah; 'tis all very well!" observed the maiden lady, drawing herself
up.—"But these things must have come to you with your mother's
blood. I never knew a Pyncheon that had any turn for them!"

It is very queer, but not the less true, that people are generally
quite as vain, or even more so, of their deficiencies, than of their
available gifts; as was Hepzibah of this native inapplicability, so to
speak, of the Pyncheons to any useful purpose. She regarded it as
an hereditary trait; and so, perhaps, it was, but, unfortunately, a
morbid one, such as is often generated in families that remain long
above the surface of society.

Before they left the breakfast-table, the shop-bell rang sharply;
and Hepzibah set down the remnant of her final cup of tea, with a
look of sallow despair that was truly piteous to behold. In cases of
distasteful occupation, the second day is generally worse than the
first; we return to the rack, with all the soreness of the preceding
torture in our limbs. At all events, Hepzibah had fully satisfied herself of the impossibility of ever becoming wonted to this peevishly
obstreperous little bell. Ring as often as it might, the sound always
smote upon her nervous system rudely and suddenly. And especially
now, while, with her crested tea-spoons and antique China, she was

6. A descendant of John Davenport (1597–1670), pastor of the church at New Haven from
    1638 to 1667.

flattering herself with ideas of gentility, she felt an unspeakable dis-
inclination to confront a customer.

"Do not trouble yourself, dear Cousin!" cried Phoebe, starting
lightly up. "I am shopkeeper to-day."

"You, child!" exclaimed Hepzibah. "What can a little country-girl
know of such matters?"

"Oh, I have done all the shopping for the family, at our village-
store," said Phoebe. "And I have had a table at a fancy-fair, and
made better sales than anybody. These things are not to be learnt;
they depend upon a knack that comes, I suppose," added she smiling, "with one's mother's blood. You shall see that I am as nice a little saleswoman, as I am a housewife!"

The old gentlewoman stole behind Phoebe, and peeped from the
passage-way into the shop, to note how she would manage her undertaking. It was a case of some intricacy. A very ancient woman, in
a white, short gown, and a green petticoat, with a string of gold
beads about her neck, and what looked like a night-cap on her
head, had brought a quantity of yarn to barter for the commodities
of the shop. She was probably the very last person in town, who
still kept the time-honored spinning-wheel in constant revolution.
It was worth while to hear the croaking and hollow tones of the old
lady and the pleasant voice of Phoebe, mingling in one twisted
thread of talk; and still better, to contrast their figures—so light and
bloomy—so decrepit and dusky—with only the counter betwixt
them, in one sense, but more than threescore years, in another. As
for the bargain, it was wrinkled slyness and craft, pitted against native truth and sagacity.

"Was not that well done?" asked Phoebe laughing, when the customer was gone.

"Nicely done, indeed, child!" answered Hepzibah. "I could not
have gone through with it nearly so well. As you say, it must be a
knack that belongs to you on the mother's side."

It is a very genuine admiration, that with which persons, too shy,
or too aukward, to take a due part in the bustling world, regard the
real actors in life's stirring scenes;—so genuine, in fact, that the
former are usually fain to make it palatable to their self-love, by assuming that these active and forcible qualities are incompatible
with others, which they choose to deem higher and more important. Thus, Hepzibah was well content to acknowledge Phoebe's
vastly superior gifts as a shopkeeper; she listened, with compliant
ear, to her suggestion of various methods whereby the influx of
trade might be increased, and rendered profitable, without a hazardous outlay of capital. She consented that the village-maiden
should manufacture yeast, both liquid and in cakes; and should
brew a certain kind of beer, nectareous to the palate, and of rare

stomachic virtues; and, moreover, should bake and exhibit for sale some little spice-cakes, which whosoever tasted, would longingly desire to taste again. All such proofs of a ready mind, and skilful handiwork, were highly acceptable to the aristocratic hucksteress, so long as she could murmur to herself, with a grim smile, and a half-natural sigh, and a sentiment of mixed wonder, pity, and growing affection:—

"What a nice little body she is! If she could only be a lady, too!— but that's impossible! Phoebe is no Pyncheon. She takes everything from her mother!"

As to Phoebe's not being a lady, or whether she were a lady or no, it was a point perhaps difficult to decide, but which could hardly have come up for judgement at all, in any fair and healthy mind. Out of New England, it would be impossible to meet with a person, combining so many ladylike attributes with so many others, that form no necessary, if compatible, part of the character. She shocked no canon of taste; she was admirably in keeping with herself, and never jarred against surrounding circumstances. Her figure, to be sure—so small as to be almost childlike, and so elastic that motion seemed as easy, or easier to it than rest—would hardly have suited one's idea of a countess. Neither did her face—with the brown ringlets on either side, and the slightly piquant nose, and the wholesome bloom, and the clear shade of tan, and the half-a-dozen freckles, friendly remembrancers of the April sun and breeze— precisely give us a right to call her beautiful. But there was both lustre and depth, in her eyes. She was very pretty; as graceful as a bird, and graceful much in the same way; as pleasant, about the house, as a gleam of sunshine falling on the floor through a shadow of twinkling leaves, or as a ray of firelight that dances on the wall, while evening is drawing nigh. Instead of discussing her claim to rank among ladies, it would be preferable to regard Phoebe as the example of feminine grace and availability combined, in a state of society, if there were any such, where ladies did not exist. There, it should be woman's office to move in the midst of practical affairs, and to gild them all—the very homeliest, were it even the scouring of pots and kettles—with an atmosphere of loveliness and joy.

Such was the sphere of Phoebe. To find the born and educated lady, on the other hand, we need look no farther than Hepzibah, our forlorn old maid, in her rustling and rusty silks, with her deeply cherished and ridiculous consciousness of long descent, her shadowy claims to princely territory; and, in the way of accomplishment, her recollections, it may be, of having formerly thrummed on a harpsichord, and walked a minuet, and worked an antique tapestry-stitch on her sampler. It was a fair parallel between new Plebeianism and old Gentility!

It really seemed as if the battered visage of the House of the Seven Gables, black and heavy-browed as it still certainly looked, must have shown a kind of cheerfulness glimmering through its dusky windows, as Phoebe passed to-and-fro in the interior. Otherwise, it is impossible to explain how the people of the neighborhood so soon became aware of the girl's presence. There was a great run of custom, setting steadily in from about ten o'clock until towards noon—relaxing, somewhat, at dinner-time—but re-commencing in the afternoon, and finally dying away, a half-an-hour or so before the long day's sunset. One of the staunchest patrons was little Ned Higgins, the devourer of Jim Crow and the elephant, who, to-day, had signalized his omnivorous prowess by swallowing two dromedaries and a locomotive. Phoebe laughed, as she summed up her aggregate of sales, upon the slate; while Hepzibah, first drawing on a pair of silk gloves, reckoned over the sordid accumulation of copper-coin, not without silver intermixed, that had jingled into the till.

"We must renew our stock, Cousin Hepzibah!" cried the little saleswoman. "The gingerbread figures are all gone, and so are those Dutch wooden milk-maids, and most of our other playthings. There has been constant inquiry for cheap raisins, and a great cry for whistles, and trumpets, and jewsharps, and at least a dozen little boys have asked for molasses-candy. And we must contrive to get a peck of russet-apples, late in the season as it is. But, dear Cousin, what an enormous heap of copper! Positively a copper-mountain!"

"Well done! Well done! Well done!" quoth Uncle Venner, who had taken occasion to shuffle in and out of the shop, several times in the course of the day. "Here's a girl that will never end her days at my farm! Bless my eyes, what a brisk little soul!"

"Yes!—Phoebe is a nice girl," said Hepzibah, with a scowl of austere approbation. "But, Uncle Venner, you have known the family a great many years. Can you tell me whether there ever was a Pyncheon whom she takes after?"

"I don't believe there ever was," answered the venerable man. "At any rate, it never was my luck to see her like among them, nor—for that matter—anywhere else. I've seen a great deal of the world, not only in people's kitchens and backyards, but at the street-corners, and on the wharves, and in other places where my business calls me; and I'm free to say, Miss Hepzibah, that I never knew a human creature do her work so much like one of God's angels, as this child Phoebe does!"

Uncle Venner's eulogium, if it appear rather too high-strained for the person and occasion, had nevertheless a sense in which it was both subtle and true. There was a spiritual quality in Phoebe's activity. The life of the long and busy day—spent in occupations that might so easily have taken a squalid and ugly aspect—had been made pleasant, and even lovely, by the spontaneous grace with which these homely duties seemed to bloom out of her character; so that labor, while she dealt with it, had the easy and flexible charm of play. Angels do not toil, but let their good works grow out of them; and so did Phoebe.

The two relatives—the young maid and the old one—found time, before nightfall, in the intervals of trade, to make rapid advances towards affection and confidence. A recluse, like Hepzibah, usually displays remarkable frankness, and at least temporary affability, on being absolutely cornered, and brought to the point of personal intercourse;—like the angel whom Jacob wrestled with, she is ready to bless you, when once overcome.[7]

The old gentlewoman took a dreary and proud satisfaction, in leading Phoebe from room to room of the house, and recounting the traditions with which, as we may say, the walls were lugubriously frescoed. She showed the indentations, made by the Lieutenant Governor's sword-hilt, in the door-panels of the apartment where old Colonel Pyncheon, a dead host, had received his affrighted visitors with an awful frown. The dusky terror of that frown, Hepzibah observed, was thought to be lingering ever since in the passage-way. She bade Phoebe step into one of the tall chairs, and inspect the ancient map of the Pyncheon territory, at the eastward. In a tract of land, on which she laid her finger, there existed a silver-mine, the locality of which was precisely pointed out in some memoranda of Colonel Pyncheon himself, but only to be made known when the family-claim should be recognized by government. Thus, it was for the interest of all New England that the Pyncheons should have justice done them. She told, too, how that there was undoubtedly an immense treasure of English guineas, hidden somewhere about the house, or in the cellar, or possibly in the garden.

"If you should happen to find it, Phoebe," said Hepzibah, glancing aside at her, with a grim, yet kindly smile, "we will tie up the shop-bell for good and all!"

"Yes, dear Cousin," answered Phoebe; "but, in the meantime, I hear somebody ringing it!"

When the customer was gone, Hepzibah talked rather vaguely, and at great length, about a certain Alice Pyncheon, who had been exceedingly beautiful and accomplished, in her lifetime, a hundred years ago. The fragrance of her rich and delightful character still lingered about the place where she had lived, as a dried rosebud

---

7. In Genesis 32:24–32, Jacob wrestles with an angel who eventually blesses him and gives him the new name of Israel.

scents the drawer where it has withered and perished. This lovely Alice had met with some great and mysterious calamity, and had grown thin and white, and gradually faded out of the world. But, even now, she was supposed to haunt the House of the Seven Gables, and, a great many times, especially when one of the Pyncheons was to die, she had been heard playing sadly and beautifully on the harpsichord. One of these tunes, just as it sounded from her spiritual touch, had been written down by an amateur of music; it was so exquisitely mournful that nobody, to this day, could bear to hear it played, unless when a great sorrow had made them know the still profounder sweetness of it.

"Was it the same harpsichord that you showed me?" inquired Phoebe.

"The very same," said Hepzibah. "It was Alice Pyncheon's harpsichord. When I was learning music, my father would never let me open it. So, as I could only play on my teacher's instrument, I have forgotten all my music, long ago."

Leaving these antique themes, the old lady began to talk about the Daguerreotypist, whom, as he seemed to be a well-meaning and orderly young man, and in narrow circumstances, she had permitted to take up his residence in one of the seven gables. But, on seeing more of Mr. Holgrave, she hardly knew what to make of him. He had the strangest companions imaginable;—men with long beards, and dressed in linen blouses, and other such new-fangled and ill-fitting garments;—reformers, temperance-lecturers, and all manner of cross-looking philanthropists;—community-men and come-outers, as Hepzibah believed, who acknowledged no law and ate no solid food, but lived on the scent of other people's cookery, and turned up their noses at the fare.[8] As for the Daguerreotypist, she had read a paragraph in a penny-paper, the other day, accusing him of making a speech, full of wild and disorganizing matter, at a meeting of his banditti-like associates. For her own part, she had reason to believe that he practised animal-magnetism,[9] and, if such things were in fashion now-a-days, should be apt to suspect him of studying the Black Art, up there in his lonesome chamber.

"But, dear Cousin," said Phoebe, "if the young man is so dangerous, why do you let him stay? If he does nothing worse, he may set the house on fire!"

"Why, sometimes," answered Hepzibah, "I have seriously made it a question, whether I ought not to send him away. But, with all his

8. References to a mélange of antebellum reform movements. "Temperance-lecturers" called for individuals to abstain from alcoholic beverages. "Community-men" developed utopian groups, such as Brook Farm in Roxbury, Massachusetts. "Come-outers" encouraged people to leave established churches and other traditional institutions to undertake social reform.
9. Term used interchangeably with *mesmerism* (hypnotism; see n. 1, p. 17).

oddities, he is a quiet kind of a person, and has such a way of taking hold of one's mind, that, without exactly liking him, (for I don't
know enough of the young man,) I should be sorry to lose sight of
him entirely. A woman clings to slight acquaintances, when she
lives so much alone as I do."

"But if Mr. Holgrave is a lawless person!" remonstrated Phoebe,
a part of whose essence it was, to keep within the limits of law.

"Oh," said Hepzibah carelessly—for, formal as she was, still, in
her life's experience, she had gnashed her teeth against human
law—"I suppose he has a law of his own!"

VI. Maule's Well

After an early tea, the little country-girl strayed into the garden.
The enclosure had formerly been very extensive, but was now contracted within small compass, and hemmed about, partly by high
wooden fences, and partly by the outbuildings of houses that stood
on another street. In its centre was a grass-plat,[1] surrounding a ruinous little structure, which showed just enough of its original design to indicate that it had once been a summer-house. A hop-vine,
springing from last year's root, was beginning to clamber over it,
but would be long in covering the roof with its green mantle. Three
of the seven gables either fronted, or looked sideways, with a dark
solemnity of aspect, down into the garden.

The black, rich soil had fed itself with the decay of a long period
of time; such as fallen leaves, the petals of flowers, and the stalks
and seed-vessels of vagrant and lawless plants, more useful after
their death, than ever while flaunting in the sun. The evil of these
departed years would naturally have sprung up again, in such rank
weeds (symbolic of the transmitted vices of society) as are always
prone to root themselves about human dwellings. Phoebe saw,
however, that their growth must have been checked by a degree of
careful labor, bestowed daily and systematically on the garden. The
white double-rosebush had evidently been propt up anew against
the house, since the commencement of the season; and a pear-tree
and three damson-trees,[2] which, except a row of currant-bushes,
constituted the only varieties of fruit, bore marks of the recent am-
putation of several superfluous or defective limbs. There were also
a few species of antique and hereditary flowers, in no very flourishing condition, but scrupulously weeded; as if some person, either
out of love or curiosity, had been anxious to bring them to such perfection as they were capable of attaining. The remainder of the

1. Plot of land.
2. Plum trees.

garden presented a well-selected assortment of esculent[3] vegetables, in a praiseworthy state of advancement. Summer-squashes, almost in their golden-blossom; cucumbers, now evincing a tendency to spread away from the main-stock, and ramble far and wide; two or three rows of string-beans, and as many more, that were about to festoon themselves on poles; tomatoes, occupying a site so sheltered and sunny, that the plants were already gigantic, and promised an early and abundant harvest.

Phoebe wondered whose care and toil it could have been, that had planted these vegetables, and kept the soil so clean and orderly. Not, surely, her Cousin Hepzibah's, who had no taste nor spirits for the ladylike employment of cultivating flowers, and—with her recluse habits, and tendency to shelter herself within the dismal shadow of the house—would hardly have come forth, under the speck of open sky, to weed and hoe, among the fraternity of beans and squashes.

It being her first day of complete estrangement from rural objects, Phoebe found an unexpected charm in this little nook of grass, and foliage, and aristocratic flowers, and plebeian vegetables. The eye of Heaven seemed to look down into it, pleasantly, and with a peculiar smile; as if glad to perceive that Nature, elsewhere overwhelmed, and driven out of the dusty town, had here been able to retain a breathing-place. The spot acquired a somewhat wilder grace, and yet a very gentle one, from the fact that a pair of robins had built their nest in the pear-tree, and were making themselves exceedingly busy and happy, in the dark intricacy of its boughs. Bees, too—strange to say—had thought it worth their while to come hither, possibly from the range of hives beside some farmhouse, miles away. How many aerial voyages might they have made, in quest of honey, or honey-laden, betwixt dawn and sunset! Yet, late as it now was, there still arose a pleasant hum out of one or two of the squash-blossoms, in the depths of which these bees were plying their golden labor. There was one other object in the garden, which Nature might fairly claim as her inalienable property, in spite of whatever man could do to render it his own. This was a fountain, set round with a rim of old, mossy stones, and paved, in its bed, with what appeared to be a sort of mosaic-work of variously colored pebbles. The play and slight agitation of the water, in its upward gush, wrought magically with these variegated pebbles, and made a continually shifting apparition of quaint figures, vanishing too suddenly to be definable. Thence, welling over the rim of moss-grown stones, the water stole away under the fence, through what we regret to call a gutter, rather than a channel.

3. Edible.

Nor must we forget to mention a hen-coop, of very reverend antiquity, that stood in the farther corner of the garden, not a great way from the fountain. It now contained only Chanticleer,[4] his two wives, and a solitary chicken. All of them were pure specimens of a breed which had been transmitted down as an heirloom in the Pyncheon family, and were said, while in their prime, to have attained almost the size of turkeys, and, on the score of delicate flesh, to be fit for a prince's table. In proof of the authenticity of this legendary renown, Hepzibah could have exhibited the shell of a great egg, which an ostrich need hardly have been ashamed of. Be that as it might, the hens were now scarcely larger than pigeons, and had a queer, rusty, withered aspect, and a gouty kind of movement, and a sleepy and melancholy tone throughout all the variations of their clucking and cackling. It was evident that the race had degenerated, like many a noble race besides, in consequence of too strict a watchfulness to keep it pure. These feathered people had existed too long, in their distinct variety; a fact of which the present representatives, judging by their lugubrious deportment, seemed to be aware. They kept themselves alive, unquestionably, and laid now and then an egg, and hatched a chicken, not for any pleasure of their own, but that the world might not absolutely lose what had once been so admirable a breed of fowls. The distinguishing mark of the hens was a crest, of lamentably scanty growth, in these latter days, but so oddly and wickedly analogous to Hepzibah's turban, that Phoebe—to the poignant distress of her conscience, but inevitably—was led to fancy a general resemblance betwixt these forlorn bipeds and her respectable relative.

The girl ran into the house to get some crumbs of bread, cold potatoes, and other such scraps as were suitable to the accommodating appetite of fowls. Returning, she gave a peculiar call, which they seemed to recognize. The chicken crept through the pales of the coop, and ran with some show of liveliness to her feet; while Chanticleer and the ladies of his household regarded her with queer, sidelong glances, and then croaked one to another, as if communicating their sage opinions of her character. So wise as well as antique was their aspect, as to give color to the idea, not merely that they were the descendants of a time-honored race, but that they had existed, in their individual capacity, ever since the House of the Seven Gables was founded, and were somehow mixed up with its destiny. They were a species of tutelary sprite, or Banshee;[5]

4. Conventional name for the cock or rooster in medieval beast fables. Among the best known of Chanticleers is the cock in "The Nun's Priest's Tale" in Chaucer's *Canterbury Tales* (1386–1400).
5. In Irish folklore, a female spirit whose wails, when heard by members of a family, portend that someone in that family is about to die. "Tutelary sprite": guardian spirit.

although winged and feathered differently from most other guardian-angels.

"Here, you odd little chicken!" cried Phoebe. "Here are some nice crumbs for you!"

The chicken, hereupon, though almost as venerable in appearance as its mother—possessing, indeed, the whole antiquity of its progenitors, in miniature—mustered vivacity enough to flutter upward and alight on Phoebe's shoulder.

"That little fowl pays you a high compliment!" said a voice behind Phoebe.

Turning quickly, she was surprised at sight of a young man, who had found access into the garden by a door, opening out of another gable than that whence she had emerged. He held a hoe in his hand, and, while Phoebe was gone in quest of the crumbs, had begun to busy himself with drawing up fresh earth about the roots of the tomatoes.

"The chicken really treats you like an old acquaintance," continued he, in a quiet way, while a smile made his face pleasanter than Phoebe at first fancied it.—"Those venerable personages in the coop, too, seem very affably disposed. You are lucky to be in their good graces so soon! They have known me much longer, but never honor me with any familiarity, though hardly a day passes without my bringing them food. Miss Hepzibah, I suppose, will interweave the fact with her other traditions, and set it down that the fowls know you to be a Pyncheon!"

"The secret is," said Phoebe smiling, "that I have learned how to talk with hens and chickens."

"Ah; but these hens," answered the young man, "these hens of aristocratic lineage would scorn to understand the vulgar language of a barn-door fowl. I prefer to think—and so would Miss Hepzibah—that they recognize the family tone. For you are a Pyncheon?"

"My name is Phoebe Pyncheon," said the girl, with a manner of some reserve; for she was aware that her new acquaintance could be no other than the Daguerreotypist, of whose lawless propensities the old maid had given her a disagreeable idea. "I did not know that my Cousin Hepzibah's garden was under another person's care."

"Yes," said Holgrave, "I dig, and hoe, and weed, in this black old earth, for the sake of refreshing myself with what little nature and simplicity may be left in it, after men have so long sown and reaped here. I turn up the earth by way of pastime. My sober occupation, so far as I have any, is with a lighter material. In short, I make pictures out of sunshine;[6] and, not to be too much dazzled with my

---

6. Daguerreotypy.

own trade, I have prevailed with Miss Hepzibah to let me lodge in one of these dusky gables. It is like a bandage over one's eyes, to come into it. But would you like to see a specimen of my productions?"

"A daguerreotype likeness, do you mean?" asked Phoebe, with less reserve; for, in spite of prejudice, her own youthfulness sprang forward to meet his. "I don't much like pictures of that sort—they are so hard and stern; besides dodging away from the eye, and trying to escape altogether. They are conscious of looking very unamiable, I suppose, and therefore hate to be seen."

"If you would permit me," said the artist, looking at Phoebe, "I should like to try whether the daguerreotype can bring out disagreeable traits on a perfectly amiable face. But there certainly is truth in what you have said. Most of my likenesses do look unamiable; but the very sufficient reason, I fancy, is, because the originals are so. There is a wonderful insight in heaven's broad and simple sunshine. While we give it credit only for depicting the merest surface, it actually brings out the secret character with a truth that no painter would ever venture upon, even could he detect it. There is at least no flattery in my humble line of art. Now, here is a likeness which I have taken, over and over again, and still with no better result. Yet the original wears, to common eyes, a very different expression. It would gratify me to have your judgement on this character."

He exhibited a daguerreotype miniature, in a morocco[7] case. Phoebe merely glanced at it, and gave it back.

"I know the face," she replied; "for its stern eye has been following me about, all day. It is my Puritan ancestor, who hangs yonder in the parlor. To be sure, you have found some way of copying the portrait without its black velvet cap and gray beard, and have given him a modern coat and satin cravat, instead of his cloak and band. I don't think him improved by your alterations."

"You would have seen other differences, had you looked a little longer," said Holgrave, laughing, yet apparently much struck.—"I can assure you that this is a modern face, and one which you will very probably meet. Now, the remarkable point is, that the original wears, to the world's eye—and, for aught I know, to his most intimate friends—an exceedingly pleasant countenance, indicative of benevolence, openness of heart, sunny good humor, and other praiseworthy qualities of that cast. The sun, as you see, tells quite another story, and will not be coaxed out of it, after half-a-dozen patient attempts on my part. Here we have the man, sly, subtle, hard, imperious, and, withal, cold as ice. Look at that eye! Would

---

7. A type of leather.

you like to be at its mercy? At that mouth! Could it ever smile? And yet, if you could only see the benign smile of the original! It is so much the more unfortunate, as he is a public character of some eminence, and the likeness was intended to be engraved."

"Well; I don't wish to see it any more," observed Phoebe, turning away her eyes. "It is certainly very like the old portrait. But my Cousin Hepzibah has another picture; a miniature. If the original is still in the world, I think he might defy the sun to make him look stern and hard."

"You have seen that picture, then?" exclaimed the artist, with an expression of much interest.—"I never did, but have a great curiosity to do so. And you judge favorably of the face?"

"There never was a sweeter one," said Phoebe. "It is almost too soft and gentle for a man's."

"Is there nothing wild in the eye?" continued Holgrave, so earnestly that it embarrassed Phoebe, as did also the quiet freedom with which he presumed on their so recent acquaintance. "Is there nothing dark or sinister, anywhere? Could you not conceive the original to have been guilty of a great crime?"

"It is nonsense," said Phoebe, a little impatiently, "for us to talk about a picture which you have never seen. You mistake it for some other. A crime, indeed! Since you are a friend of my Cousin Hepzibah's, you should ask her to show you the picture."

"It will suit my purpose still better, to see the original," replied the Daguerreotypist coolly. "As to his character, we need not discuss its points—they have already been settled by a competent tribunal, or one which called itself competent.—But, stay! Do not go yet, if you please! I have a proposition to make you."

Phoebe was on the point of retreating, but turned back, with some hesitation; for she did not exactly comprehend his manner, although, on better observation, its feature seemed rather to be lack of ceremony, than any approach to offensive rudeness. There was an odd kind of authority, too, in what he now proceeded to say; rather as if the garden were his own, than a place to which he was admitted merely by Hepzibah's courtesy.

"If agreeable to you," he observed, "it would give me pleasure to turn over these flowers, and those ancient and respectable fowls, to your care. Coming fresh from country-air and occupations, you will soon feel the need of some such out-of-door employment. My own sphere does not so much lie among flowers. You can trim and tend them, therefore, as you please; and I will ask only the least trifle of a blossom, now and then, in exchange for all the good, honest kitchen-vegetables with which I propose to enrich Miss Hepzibah's table. So, we will be fellow-laborers, somewhat on the community-system."

Silently, and rather surprised at her own compliance, Phoebe accordingly betook herself to weeding a flower-bed, but busied herself still more with cogitations respecting this young man, with whom she so unexpectedly found herself on terms approaching to familiarity. She did not altogether like him. His character perplexed the little country-girl, as it might a more practised observer; for, while the tone of his conversation had generally been playful, the impression left on her mind was that of gravity, and, except as his youth modified it, almost sternness. She rebelled, as it were, against a certain magnetic element in the artist's nature, which he exercised towards her, possibly without being conscious of it.

After a little while, the twilight, deepened by the shadows of the fruit-trees and the surrounding buildings, threw an obscurity over the garden.

"There," said Holgrave; "it is time to give over work! That last stroke of the hoe has cut off a bean-stalk. Good night, Miss Phoebe Pyncheon! Any bright day, if you will put one of those rosebuds in your hair, and come to my rooms in Central-street, I will seize the purest ray of sunshine, and make a picture of the flower and its wearer."

He retired towards his own solitary gable, but turned his head, on reaching the door, and called to Phoebe, with a tone which certainly had laughter in it, yet which seemed to be more than half in earnest.

"Be careful not to drink at Maule's Well!" said he. "Neither drink nor bathe your face in it!"

"Maule's Well!" answered Phoebe. "Is that it, with the rim of mossy stones? I have no thought of drinking there—but why not?"

"Oh," rejoined the Daguerreotypist, "because, like an old lady's cup of tea, it is water bewitched!"[8]

He vanished; and Phoebe, lingering a moment, saw a glimmering light, and then the steady beam of a lamp, in a chamber of the gable. On returning into Hepzibah's department of the house, she found the low-studded parlor so dim and dusky, that her eyes could not penetrate the interior. She was indistinctly aware, however, that the gaunt figure of the old gentlewoman was sitting in one of the straight-backed chairs, a little withdrawn from the window, the faint gleam of which showed the blanched paleness of her cheek, turned sideway towards a corner.

"Shall I light a lamp, Cousin Hepzibah?" she asked.

"Do, if you please, my dear child," answered Hepzibah. "But put it on the table in the corner of the passage. My eyes are weak; and I can seldom bear the lamplight on them."

8. Colloquial term for a highly diluted beverage, such as weak tea.

What an instrument is the human voice! How wonderfully responsive to every emotion of the human soul! In Hepzibah's tone, at that moment, there was a certain rich depth and moisture, as if the words, common-place as they were, had been steeped in the warmth of her heart. Again, while lighting the lamp in the kitchen, Phoebe fancied that her cousin spoke to her.

"In a moment, Cousin!" answered the girl. "These matches just glimmer, and go out."

But, instead of a response from Hepzibah, she seemed to hear the murmur of an unknown voice. It was strangely indistinct, however, and less like articulate words than an unshaped sound, such as would be the utterance of feeling and sympathy, rather than of the intellect. So vague was it, that its impression or echo, in Phoebe's mind, was that of unreality. She concluded that she must have mistaken some other sound for that of the human voice; or else that it was altogether in her fancy.

She set the lighted lamp in the passage, and again entered the parlor. Hepzibah's form, though its sable outline mingled with the dusk, was now less imperfectly visible. In the remoter parts of the room, however, its walls being so ill adapted to reflect light, there was nearly the same obscurity as before.

"Cousin," said Phoebe, "did you speak to me just now?"

"No, child!" replied Hepzibah.

Fewer words than before, but with the same mysterious music in them! Mellow, melancholy, yet not mournful, the tone seemed to gush up out of the deep well of Hepzibah's heart, all steeped in its profoundest emotion. There was a tremor in it, too, that—as all strong feeling is electric—partly communicated itself to Phoebe. The girl sat silently for a moment. But soon, her senses being very acute, she became conscious of an irregular respiration in an obscure corner of the room. Her physical organization, moreover, being at once delicate and healthy, gave her a perception, operating with almost the effect of a spiritual medium, that somebody was near at hand.

"My dear Cousin," asked she, overcoming an indefinable reluctance, "is there not some one in the room with us?"

"Phoebe, my dear little girl," said Hepzibah, after a moment's pause, "you were up betimes, and have been busy all day. Pray go to bed; for I am sure you must need rest. I will sit in the parlor, awhile, and collect my thoughts. It has been my custom for more years, child, than you have lived!"

While thus dismissing her, the maiden lady stept forward, kissed Phoebe, and pressed her to her heart, which beat against the girl's bosom with a strong, high, and tumultuous swell. How came there to be so much love in this desolate old heart, that it could afford to well over thus abundantly!

"Good night, Cousin," said Phoebe, strangely affected by Hepzibah's manner. "If you begin to love me, I am glad!"

She retired to her chamber, but did not soon fall asleep, nor then very profoundly. At some uncertain period in the depths of night, and, as it were, through the thin veil of a dream, she was conscious of a footstep mounting the stairs, heavily, but not with force and decision. The voice of Hepzibah, with a hush through it, was going up along with the footsteps; and, again, responsive to her cousin's voice, Phoebe heard that strange, vague murmur, which might be likened to an indistinct shadow of human utterance.

VII. The Guest

When Phoebe awoke—which she did with the early twittering of the conjugal couple of robins, in the pear-tree—she heard movements below stairs, and hastening down, found Hepzibah already in the kitchen. She stood by a window, holding a book in close contiguity to her nose; as if with the hope of gaining an olfactory acquaintance with its contents, since her imperfect vision made it not very easy to read them. If any volume could have manifested its essential wisdom, in the mode suggested, it would certainly have been the one now in Hepzibah's hand; and the kitchen, in such an event, would forthwith have steamed with the fragrance of venison, turkeys, capons, larded partridges, puddings, cakes, and Christmas pies, in all manner of elaborate mixture and concoction. It was a Cookery Book, full of innumerable old fashions of English dishes, and illustrated with engravings, which represented the arrangements of the table, at such banquets as it might have befitted a nobleman to give, in the great hall of his castle. And, amid these rich and potent devices of the culinary art, (not one of which, probably, had been tested, within the memory of any man's grandfather,) poor Hepzibah was seeking for some nimble little tidbit, which, with what skill she had, and such materials as were at hand, she might toss up for breakfast!

Soon, with a deep sigh, she put aside the savory volume, and inquired of Phoebe whether old Speckle, as she called one of the hens, had laid an egg, the preceding day. Phoebe ran to see, but returned without the expected treasure in her hand. At that instant, however, the blast of a fishdealer's conch[9] was heard, announcing his approach along the street. With energetic raps at the shop-window, Hepzibah summoned the man in, and made purchase of what he warranted as the finest mackerel in his cart, and as fat a

9. Mollusk shell used as a horn.

one as ever he felt with his finger, so early in the season. Request-
ing Phoebe to roast some coffee—which she casually observed was
the real Mocha,[1] and so long kept that each of the small berries
ought to be worth its weight in gold—the maiden lady heaped fuel
into the vast receptacle of the ancient fireplace, in such quantity as
soon to drive the lingering dusk out of the kitchen. The country-
girl, willing to give her utmost assistance, proposed to make an
Indian cake,[2] after her mother's peculiar method, of easy manufacture, and which she could vouch for as possessing a richness, and,
if rightly prepared, a delicacy, unequalled by any other mode of
breakfast-cake. Hepzibah gladly assenting, the kitchen was soon
the scene of savory preparation. Perchance, amid their proper element of smoke, which eddied forth from the ill-constructed chimney, the ghosts of departed cook-maids looked wonderingly on, or
peeped down the great breadth of the flue, despising the simplicity
of the projected meal, yet ineffectually pining to thrust their shadowy hands into each inchoate dish. The half-starved rats, at any
rate, stole visibly out of their hiding-places, and sat on their hind-
legs, snuffing the fumy atmosphere, and wistfully awaiting an opportunity to nibble.

Hepzibah had no natural turn for cookery, and, to say the truth,
had fairly incurred her present meagerness by often choosing to go
without her dinner, rather than be attendant on the rotation of the
spit or ebullition of the pot. Her zeal over the fire, therefore, was
quite an heroic test of sentiment. It was touching, and positively
worthy of tears, (if Phoebe, the only spectator, except the rats and
ghosts aforesaid, had not been better employed than in shedding
them,) to see her rake out a bed of fresh and glowing coals, and
proceed to broil the mackerel. Her usually pale cheeks were all
a-blaze with heat and hurry. She watched the fish with as much
tender care, and minuteness of attention, as if—we know not how
to express it otherwise—as if her own heart were on the gridiron,
and her immortal happiness were involved in its being done precisely to a turn!

Life, within doors, has few pleasanter prospects than a neatly
arranged and well-provisioned breakfast-table. We come to it
freshly, in the dewy youth of the day, and when our spiritual and
sensual elements are in better accord than at a later period; so that
the material delights of the morning meal are capable of being fully
enjoyed, without any very grievous reproaches, whether gastric or
conscientious, for yielding even a trifle overmuch to the animal department of our nature. The thoughts, too, that run around the ring

1. A fine coffee originally from the seaport town of Mocha, South Yemen.
2. Cornbread.

of familiar guests, have a piquancy and mirthfulness, and often-times a vivid truth, which more rarely find their way into the elaborate intercourse of dinner. Hepzibah's small and ancient table, supported on its slender and graceful legs, and covered with a cloth of the richest damask, looked worthy to be the scene and centre of one of the cheerfullest of parties. The vapor of the broiled fish arose like incense from the shrine of a barbarian idol; while the fragrance of the Mocha might have gratified the nostrils of a tutelary Lar,[3] or whatever power has scope over a modern breakfast-table. Phoebe's Indian cakes were the sweetest offering of all—in their hue, befitting the rustic altars of the innocent and golden age—or, so brightly yellow were they, resembling some of the bread which was changed to glistening gold, when Midas[4] tried to eat it. The butter must not be forgotten—butter which Phoebe herself had churned, in her own rural home, and brought it to her cousin as a propitiatory gift—smelling of clover-blossoms, and diffusing the charm of pastoral scenery through the dark-panelled parlor. All this, with the quaint gorgeousness of the old China cups and saucers, and the crested spoons, and a silver cream-jug (Hepzibah's only other article of plate, and shaped like the rudest porringer[5]) set out a board, at which the stateliest of old Colonel Pyncheon's guests need not have scorned to take his place. But the Puritan's face scowled down out of the picture, as if nothing on the table pleased his appetite.

By way of contributing what grace she could, Phoebe gathered some roses and a few other flowers, possessing either scent or beauty, and arranged them in a glass-pitcher, which, having long ago lost its handle, was so much the fitter for a flower-vase. The early sunshine—as fresh as that which peeped into Eve's bower, while she and Adam sat at breakfast there—came twinkling through the branches of the pear-tree, and fell quite across the table. All was now ready. There were chairs and plates for three. A chair and plate for Hepzibah—the same for Phoebe:—but what other guest did her cousin look for?

Throughout this preparation, there had been a constant tremor in Hepzibah's frame; an agitation so powerful, that Phoebe could see the quivering of her gaunt shadow, as thrown by the firelight on the kitchen-wall, or by the sunshine on the parlor-floor. Its manifestations were so various, and agreed so little with one another, that the girl knew not what to make of it. Sometimes, it seemed an

3. A Roman deity of the home.
4. In Greek mythology, when King Midas obtained his wish that all he touched would turn to gold, he found it impossible to eat. See Hawthorne's "The Golden Touch" in his *Wonder-Book for Girls and Boys* (1851).
5. A low dish or bowl for porridge, soups, and similar foods.

ecstacy of delight and happiness. At such moments, Hepzibah would fling out her arms, and enfold Phoebe in them, and kiss her cheek, as tenderly as ever her mother had; she appeared to do so by an inevitable impulse, and as if her bosom were oppressed with tenderness, of which she must needs pour out a little, in order to gain breathing-room. The next moment, without any visible cause for the change, her unwonted joy shrank back, appalled, as it were, and clothed itself in mourning; or it ran and hid itself, so to speak, in the dungeon of her heart, where it had long lain chained; while a cold, spectral sorrow took the place of the imprisoned joy, that was afraid to be enfranchised—a sorrow as black as that was bright. She often broke into a little, nervous, hysteric laugh, more touching than any tears could be; and forthwith, as if to try which was the most touching, a gust of tears would follow; or perhaps the laughter and tears came both at once, and surrounded our poor Hepzibah, in a moral sense, with a kind of pale, dim rainbow. Towards Phoebe, as we have said, she was affectionate—far tenderer than ever before, in their brief acquaintance, except for that one kiss, on the preceding night—yet with a continually recurring pettishness and irritability. She would speak sharply to her; then, throwing aside all the starched reserve of her ordinary manner, ask pardon, and, the next instant, renew the just forgiven injury.

At last, when their mutual labor was all finished, she took Phoebe's hand in her own trembling one.

"Bear with me, my dear child," she cried, "for truly my heart is full to the brim! Bear with me; for I love you, Phoebe, though I speak so roughly! Think nothing of it, dearest child! By-and-by, I shall be kind, and only kind!"

"My dearest Cousin, cannot you tell me what has happened?" asked Phoebe, with a sunny and tearful sympathy. "What is it that moves you so?"

"Hush! hush! He is coming!" whispered Hepzibah, hastily wiping her eyes. "Let him see you first, Phoebe; for you are young and rosy, and cannot help letting a smile break out, whether or no. He always liked bright faces! And mine is old, now, and the tears are hardly dry on it. He never could abide tears. There; draw the curtain a little, so that the shadow may fall across his side of the table! But let there be a good deal of sunshine, too; for he never was fond of gloom, as some people are. He has had but little sunshine in his life—poor Clifford—and, Oh, what a black shadow! Poor, poor, Clifford!"

Thus murmuring, in an undertone, as if speaking rather to her own heart than to Phoebe, the old gentlewoman stept on tiptoe about the room, making such arrangements as suggested themselves at the crisis.

Meanwhile, there was a step in the passage-way, above-stairs. Phoebe recognized it as the same which had passed upward, as through her dream, in the night-time. The approaching guest, whoever it might be, appeared to pause at the head of the staircase; he paused, twice or thrice, in the descent; he paused again at the foot. Each time, the delay seemed to be without purpose, but rather from a forgetfulness of the purpose which had set him in motion, or as if the person's feet came involuntarily to a standstill, because the motive power was too feeble to sustain his progress. Finally, he made a long pause at the threshold of the parlor. He took hold of the knob of the door; then loosened his grasp, without opening it. Hepzibah, her hands convulsively clasped, stood gazing at the entrance.

"Dear Cousin Hepzibah, pray don't look so!" said Phoebe trembling; for her cousin's emotion, and this mysteriously reluctant step, made her feel as if a ghost were coming into the room.—"You really frighten me! Is something awful going to happen?"

"Hush!" whispered Hepzibah. "Be cheerful! Whatever may happen, be nothing but cheerful!"

The final pause at the threshold proved so long, that Hepzibah, unable to endure the suspense, rushed forward, threw open the door, and led in the stranger by the hand. At the first glance, Phoebe saw an elderly personage, in an old-fashioned dressing-gown of faded damask, and wearing his gray, or almost white hair, of an unusual length. It quite overshadowed his forehead, except when he thrust it back, and stared vaguely about the room. After a very brief inspection of his face, it was easy to conceive that his footstep must necessarily be such an one as that which—slowly, and with as indefinite an aim as a child's first journey across a floor—had just brought him hitherward. Yet there were no tokens that his physical strength might not have sufficed for a free and determined gait. It was the spirit of the man, that could not walk. The expression of his countenance—while, notwithstanding, it had the light of reason in it—seemed to waver, and glimmer, and nearly to die away, and feebly to recover itself again. It was like a flame which we see twinkling among half-extinguished embers; we gaze at it, more intently than if it were a positive blaze, gushing vividly upward—more intently, but with a certain impatience, as if it ought either to kindle itself into satisfactory splendor, or be at once extinguished.

For an instant after entering the room, the guest stood still, retaining Hepzibah's hand, instinctively, as a child does that of the grown person who guides it. He saw Phoebe, however, and caught an illumination from her youthful and pleasant aspect, which, indeed, threw a cheerfulness about the parlor, like the circle of reflected brilliancy around the glass vase of flowers that was standing in the sunshine. He made a salutation, or, to speak nearer the truth, an ill-defined, abortive attempt at courtesy. Imperfect as it was, however, it conveyed an idea, or, at least, gave a hint, of indescribable grace, such as no practised art of external manners could have attained. It was too slight to seize upon, at the instant, yet, as recollected afterwards, seemed to transfigure the whole man.

"Dear Clifford," said Hepzibah, in the tone with which one soothes a wayward infant, "this is our Cousin Phoebe—little Phoebe Pyncheon—Arthur's only child, you know! She has come from the country to stay with us awhile; for our old house has grown to be very lonely now."

"Phoebe?—Phoebe Pyncheon!—Phoebe?" repeated the guest, with a strange, sluggish, ill-defined utterance.—"Arthur's child! Ah, I forget! No matter! She is very welcome!"

"Come, dear Clifford, take this chair," said Hepzibah, leading him to his place.—"Pray, Phoebe, lower the curtain a very little more. Now let us begin breakfast!"

The guest seated himself in the place assigned him, and looked strangely around. He was evidently trying to grapple with the present scene, and bring it home to his mind with a more satisfactory distinctness. He desired to be certain, at least, that he was here, in the low-studded, cross-beamed, oaken-panelled parlor, and not in some other spot, which had stereotyped itself[6] into his senses. But the effort was too great to be sustained with more than a fragmentary success. Continually, as we may express it, he faded away out of his place; or, in other words, his mind and consciousness took their departure, leaving his wasted, gray, and melancholy figure—a substantial emptiness, a material ghost—to occupy his seat at table. Again, after a blank moment, there would be a flickering taper-gleam[7] in his eyeballs. It betokened that his spiritual part had returned, and was doing its best to kindle the heart's household-fire, and light up intellectual lamps in the dark and ruinous mansion, where it was doomed to be a forlorn inhabitant.

At one of these moments of less torpid, yet still imperfect animation, Phoebe became convinced of what she had at first rejected as too extravagant and startling an idea. She saw that the person before her must have been the original of the beautiful miniature in her Cousin Hepzibah's possession. Indeed, with a feminine eye for costume, she had at once identified the damask dressing-gown, which enveloped him, as the same in figure, material, and fashion, with that so elaborately represented in the picture. This old, faded

---

6. Imprinted itself; an allusion to a printing process using cast metal forms.
7. Glow from a small candle (taper).

garment, with all its pristine brilliancy extinct, seemed, in some indescribable way, to translate the wearer's untold misfortune, and
make it perceptible to the beholder's eye. It was the better to be discerned, by this exterior type, how worn and old were the soul's
more immediate garments; that form and countenance, the beauty
and grace of which had almost transcended the skill of the most exquisite of artists. It could the more adequately be known, that the
soul of the man must have suffered some miserable wrong from its
earthly experience. There he seemed to sit, with a dim veil of decay
and ruin betwixt him and the world, but through which, at flitting
intervals, might be caught the same expression, so refined, so softly
imaginative, which Malbone—venturing a happy touch, with suspended breath—had imparted to the miniature! There had been
something so innately characteristic in this look, that all the dusky
years, and the burthen of unfit calamity which had fallen upon
him, did not suffice utterly to destroy it.

Hepzibah had now poured out a cup of deliciously fragrant coffee, and presented it to her guest. As his eyes met hers, he seemed
bewildered and disquieted.

"Is this you, Hepzibah?" he murmured sadly; then, more apart,
and perhaps unconscious that he was overheard.—"How changed!
How changed! And is she angry with me? Why does she bend her
brow so!"

Poor Hepzibah! It was that wretched scowl, which time, and her
near-sightedness, and the fret of inward discomfort, had rendered
so habitual, that any vehemence of mood invariably evoked it. But,
at the indistinct murmur of his words, her whole face grew tender,
and even lovely, with sorrowful affection; the harshness of her features disappeared, as it were, behind the warm and misty glow.

"Angry!" she repeated. "Angry with you, Clifford!"

Her tone, as she uttered this exclamation, had a plaintive and really exquisite melody thrilling through it, yet without subduing a
certain something which an obtuse auditor might still have mistaken for asperity. It was as if some transcendent musician should
draw a soul-thrilling sweetness out of a cracked instrument, which
makes its physical imperfection heard in the midst of ethereal harmony. So deep was the sensibility that found an organ in Hepzibah's voice!

"There is nothing but love here, Clifford," she added—"nothing
but love! You are at home!"

The guest responded to her tone by a smile, which did not half
light up his face. Feeble as it was, however, and gone in a moment,
it had a charm of wonderful beauty. It was followed by a coarser expression; or one that had the effect of coarseness on the fine mould
and outline of his countenance, because there was nothing intel-

lectual to temper it. It was a look of appetite. He ate food with what might almost be termed voracity, and seemed to forget himself, Hepzibah, the young girl, and everything else around him, in the sensual enjoyment which the bountifully spread table afforded. In his natural system, though high-wrought and delicately refined, a sensibility to the delights of the palate was probably inherent. It would have been kept in check, however, and even converted into an accomplishment, and one of the thousand modes of intellectual culture, had his more ethereal characteristics retained their vigor. But, as it existed now, the effect was painful, and made Phoebe droop her eyes.

In a little while, the guest became sensible of the fragrance of the yet untasted coffee. He quaffed it eagerly. The subtle essence acted on him like a charmed draught, and caused the opaque substance of his animal being to grow transparent, or, at least, translucent; so that a spiritual gleam was transmitted through it, with a clearer lustre than hitherto.

"More, more!" he cried, with nervous haste in his utterance, as if anxious to retain his grasp of what sought to escape him.—"This is what I need! Give me more!"

Under this delicate and powerful influence, he sat more erect, and looked out from his eyes with a glance that took note of what it rested on. It was not so much, that his expression grew more intellectual; this, though it had its share, was not the most peculiar effect. Neither was what we call the moral nature so forcibly awakened, as to present itself in remarkable prominence. But a certain fine temper of being was now—not brought out in full relief, but changeably and imperfectly betrayed—of which it was the function to deal with all beautiful and enjoyable things. In a character where it should exist as the chief attribute, it would bestow on its possessor an exquisite taste, and an enviable susceptibility of happiness. Beauty would be his life; his aspirations would all tend towards it; and, allowing his frame and physical organs to be in consonance, his own developments would likewise be beautiful. Such a man should have nothing to do with sorrow; nothing with strife; nothing with the martyrdom which, in an infinite variety of shapes, awaits those who have the heart, and will, and conscience, to fight a battle with the world. To these heroic tempers, such martyrdom is the richest meed in the world's gift. To the individual before us, it could only be a grief, intense in due proportion with the severity of the infliction. He had no right to be a martyr; and, beholding him so fit to be happy, and so feeble for all other purposes, a generous, strong, and noble spirit would, methinks, have been ready to sacrifice what little enjoyment it might have planned for itself—it would have flung down the hopes, so paltry in its regard—if thereby the wintry blasts of our rude sphere might come tempered to such a man.

Not to speak it harshly or scornfully, it seemed Clifford's nature to be a Sybarite.[8] It was perceptible, even there, in the dark, old parlor, in the inevitable polarity with which his eyes were attracted towards the quivering play of sunbeams through the shadowy foliage. It was seen in his appreciating notice of the vase of flowers, the scent of which he inhaled with a zest, almost peculiar to a physical organization so refined that spiritual ingredients are moulded in with it. It was betrayed in the unconscious smile with which he regarded Phoebe, whose fresh and maidenly figure was both sunshine and flowers, their essence, in a prettier and more agreeable mode of manifestation. Not less evident was this love and necessity for the Beautiful, in the instinctive caution with which, even so soon, his eyes turned away from his hostess, and wandered to any quarter, rather than come back. It was Hepzibah's misfortune; not Clifford's fault. How could he—so yellow as she was, so wrinkled, so sad of mien, with that odd uncouthness of a turban on her head, and that most perverse of scowls contorting her brow—how could he love to gaze at her! But, did he owe her no affection for so much as she had silently given? He owed her nothing. A nature like Clifford's can contract no debts of that kind. It is—we say it without censure, nor in diminution of the claim which it indefeasibly possesses on beings of another mould—it is always selfish in its essence; and we must give it leave to be so, and heap up our heroic and disinterested love upon it, so much the more, without a recompense. Poor Hepzibah knew this truth, or, at least, acted on the instinct of it. So long estranged from what was lovely, as Clifford had been, she rejoiced—rejoiced, though with a present sigh, and a secret purpose to shed tears in her own chamber—that he had brighter objects now before his eyes, than her aged and uncomely features. They never possessed a charm; and if they had, the canker of her grief for him would long since have destroyed it.

The guest leaned back in his chair. Mingled in his countenance with a dreamy delight, there was a troubled look of effort and unrest. He was seeking to make himself more fully sensible of the scene around him; or perhaps, dreading it to be a dream, or a play of imagination, was vexing the fair moment with a struggle for some added brilliancy and more durable illusion.

"How pleasant!—How delightful!" he murmured, but not as if addressing any one. "Will it last? How balmy the atmosphere,

---

8. Sensualist; derived from Sybaris, an ancient Greek city in southern Italy known for its inhabitants' devotion to pleasure and luxury.

through that open window! An open window! How beautiful that play of sunshine! Those flowers, how very fragrant! That young girl's face, how cheerful, how blooming; a flower with the dew on it, and sunbeams in the dew-drops! Ah; this must be all a dream! A dream! A dream! But it has quite hidden the four stone-walls!"

Then his face darkened, as if the shadow of a cavern or a dungeon had come over it; there was no more light in its expression than might have come through the iron grates of a prison-window—still lessening, too, as if he were sinking farther into the depths. Phoebe (being of that quickness and activity of temperament that she seldom long refrained from taking a part, and generally a good one, in what was going forward) now felt herself moved to address the stranger.

"Here is a new kind of rose, which I found, this morning, in the garden," said she, choosing a small crimson one from among the flowers in the vase. "There will be but five or six on the bush, this season. This is the most perfect of them all; not a speck of blight or mildew in it. And how sweet it is!—sweet like no other rose! One can never forget that scent!"

"Ah!—let me see!—let me hold it!" cried the guest, eagerly seizing the flower, which, by the spell peculiar to remembered odors, brought innumerable associations along with the fragrance that it exhaled.—"Thank you! This has done me good. I remember how I used to prize this flower—long ago, I suppose, very long ago!—or was it only yesterday? It makes me feel young again! Am I young? Either this remembrance is singularly distinct, or this consciousness strangely dim! But how kind of the fair young girl! Thank you! Thank you!"

The favorable excitement, derived from this little crimson rose, afforded Clifford the brightest moment which he enjoyed at the breakfast-table. It might have lasted longer, but that his eyes happened, soon afterwards, to rest on the face of the old Puritan, who, out of his dingy frame and lustreless canvass, was looking down on the scene like a ghost, and a most ill-tempered and ungenial one. The guest made an impatient gesture of the hand, and addressed Hepzibah with what might easily be recognized as the licensed irritability of a petted member of the family.

"Hepzibah!—Hepzibah!" cried he, with no little force and distinctness. "Why do you keep that odious picture on the wall? Yes, yes!—that is precisely your taste! I have told you, a thousand times, that it was the evil genius of the house!—my evil genius particularly! Take it down at once!"

"Dear Clifford," said Hepzibah sadly, "you know it cannot be!"

"Then, at all events," continued he, still speaking with some energy, "pray cover it with a crimson curtain, broad enough to hang in folds, and with a golden border and tassels! I cannot bear it! It must not stare me in the face!"

"Yes, dear Clifford, the picture shall be covered," said Hepzibah soothingly. "There is a crimson curtain in a trunk above-stairs—a little faded and moth-eaten, I'm afraid—but Phoebe and I will do wonders with it."

"This very day, remember!" said he; and then added, in a low, self-communing voice,—"Why should we live in this dismal house at all? Why not go to the south of France?—to Italy?—Paris, Naples, Venice, Rome? Hepzibah will say, we have not the means. A droll idea, that!"

He smiled to himself, and threw a glance of fine, sarcastic meaning towards Hepzibah.

But the several moods of feeling, faintly as they were marked, through which he had passed, occurring in so brief an interval of time, had evidently wearied the stranger. He was probably accustomed to a sad monotony of life, not so much flowing in a stream, however sluggish, as stagnating in a pool around his feet. A slumberous veil diffused itself over his countenance, and had an effect, morally speaking, on its naturally delicate and elegant outline, like that which a brooding mist, with no sunshine in it, throws over the features of a landscape. He appeared to become grosser; almost cloddish. If aught of interest or beauty—even ruined beauty—had heretofore been visible in this man, the beholder might now begin to doubt it, and to accuse his own imagination of deluding him with whatever grace had flickered over that visage, and whatever exquisite lustre had gleamed in those filmy eyes.

Before he had quite sunken away, however, the sharp and peevish tinkle of the shop-bell made itself audible. Striking most disagreeably on Clifford's auditory organs and the characteristic sensibility of his nerves, it caused him to start upright out of his chair.

"Good Heavens, Hepzibah, what horrible disturbance have we now in the house?" cried he, wreaking his resentful impatience—as a matter of course, and a custom of old—on the one person in the world that loved him. "I have never heard such a hateful clamor! Why do you permit it? In the name of all dissonance, what can it be?"

It was very remarkable into what prominent relief—even as if a dim picture should leap suddenly from its canvass—Clifford's character was thrown by this apparently trifling annoyance. The secret was, that an individual of his temper can always be pricked more acutely through his sense of the beautiful and harmonious, than through his heart. It is even possible—for similar cases have often happened—that if Clifford, in his foregoing life, had enjoyed the means of cultivating his taste to its utmost perfectibility, that subtle attribute might, before this period, have completely eaten out or filed away his affections. Shall we venture to pronounce, therefore, that his long and black calamity may not have had a redeeming drop of mercy, at the bottom?

"Dear Clifford, I wish I could keep the sound from your ears," said Hepzibah patiently, but reddening with a painful suffusion of shame. "It is very disagreeable even to me. But, do you know, Clifford, I have something to tell you? This ugly noise—pray run, Phoebe, and see who is there!—this naughty little tinkle is nothing but our shop-bell!"

"Shop-bell!" repeated Clifford, with a bewildered stare.

"Yes; our shop-bell!" said Hepzibah; a certain natural dignity, mingled with deep emotion, now asserting itself in her manner. "For you must know, dearest Clifford, that we are very poor. And there was no resource, but either to accept assistance from a hand that I would push aside, (and so would you!) were it to offer bread when we were dying for it—no help, save from him, or else to earn our subsistence with my own hands! Alone, I might have been content to starve. But you were to be given back to me! Do you think, then, dear Clifford," added she, with a wretched smile, "that I have brought an irretrievable disgrace on the old house, by opening a little shop in the front gable? Our great, great-grandfather did the same, when there was far less need! Are you ashamed of me?"

"Shame! Disgrace! Do you speak these words to me, Hepzibah?" said Clifford, not angrily, however; for when a man's spirit has been thoroughly crushed, he may be peevish at small offences, but never resentful of great ones. So he spoke with only a grieved emotion.— "It was not kind to say so, Hepzibah! What shame can befall me now?"

And then the unnerved man—he that had been born for enjoyment, but had met a doom so very wretched—burst into a woman's passion of tears. It was but of brief continuance, however; soon leaving him in a quiescent, and, to judge by his countenance, not an uncomfortable state. From this mood, too, he partially rallied, for an instant, and looked at Hepzibah with a smile, the keen, half-derisory purport of which was a puzzle to her.

"Are we so very poor, Hepzibah?" said he.

Finally, his chair being deep and softly cushioned, Clifford fell asleep. Hearing the more regular rise and fall of his breath— (which, however, even then, instead of being strong and full, had a feeble kind of tremor, corresponding with the lack of vigor in his character)—hearing these tokens of settled slumber, Hepzibah seized the opportunity to peruse his face, more attentively than she had yet dared to do. Her heart melted away in tears; her profoundest spirit sent forth a moaning voice, low, gentle, but inexpressibly sad. In this depth of grief and pity, she felt that there was no irreverence in gazing at his altered, aged, faded, ruined face. But, no sooner was she a little relieved, than her conscience smote her for gazing curiously at him, now that he was so changed; and, turning hastily away, Hepzibah let down the curtain over the sunny window, and left Clifford to slumber there.

VIII. The Pyncheon of To-day

Phoebe, on entering the shop, beheld there the already familiar face of the little devourer—if we can reckon his mighty deeds aright—of Jim Crow, the elephant, the camel, the dromedaries, and the locomotive. Having expended his private fortune, on the two preceding days, in the purchase of the above unheard-of luxuries, the young gentleman's present errand was on the part of his mother, in quest of three eggs and half-a-pound of raisins. These articles Phoebe accordingly supplied, and—as a mark of gratitude for his previous patronage, and a slight, superadded morsel, after breakfast—put likewise into his hand a whale! The great fish—reversing his experience with the prophet of Nineveh[9]—immediately began his progress down the same red pathway of fate, whither so varied a caravan had preceded him. This remarkable urchin, in truth, was the very emblem of old Father Time, both in respect of his all-devouring appetite for men and things, and because he, as well as Time, after engulfing thus much of creation, looked almost as youthful as if he had been just that moment made.

After partly closing the door, the child turned back, and mumbled something to Phoebe which, as the whale was but half-disposed of, she could not perfectly understand.

"What did you say, my little fellow?" asked she.

"Mother wants to know," repeated Ned Higgins, more distinctly, "how Old Maid Pyncheon's brother does? Folks say he has got home!"

"My Cousin Hepzibah's brother!" exclaimed Phoebe, surprised at this sudden explanation of the relationship between Hepzibah and her guest.—"Her brother! And where can he have been!"

The little boy only put his thumb to his broad snub-nose, with that look of shrewdness which a child, spending much of his time in the street, so soon learns to throw over his features, however unintelligent in themselves. Then, as Phoebe continued to gaze at him without answering his mother's message, he took his departure.

9. Jonah, who is swallowed by a whale soon after he refuses God's command to denounce the sinners of Nineveh; see Jonah 1:1–17.

As the child went down the steps, a gentleman ascended them, and made his entrance into the shop. It was the portly, and, had it possessed the advantage of a little more height, would have been the stately figure of a man considerably in the decline of life, dressed in a black suit of some thin stuff, resembling broadcloth as closely as possible. A gold-headed cane of rare, oriental wood, added materially to the high respectability of his aspect; as did also a white neckcloth of the utmost snowy purity, and the conscientious polish of his boots. His dark, square countenance, with its almost shaggy depth of eyebrows, was naturally impressive, and would perhaps have been rather stern, had not the gentleman considerately taken upon himself to mitigate the harsh effect by a look of exceeding good-humor and benevolence. Owing, however, to a somewhat massive accumulation of animal substance about the lower region of his face, the look was perhaps unctuous, rather than spiritual, and had, so to speak, a kind of fleshly effulgence, not altogether so satisfactory as he doubtless intended it to be. A susceptible observer, at any rate, might have regarded it as affording very little evidence of the genuine benignity of soul, whereof it purported to be the outward reflection. And if the observer chanced to be ill-natured, as well as acute and susceptible, he would probably suspect, that the smile on the gentleman's face was a good deal akin to the shine on his boots, and that each must have cost him and his boot-black, respectively, a good deal of hard labor to bring out and preserve them.

As the stranger entered the little shop—where the projection of the second story and the thick foliage of the elm-tree, as well as the commodities at the window, created a sort of gray medium—his smile grew as intense as if he had set his heart on counteracting the whole gloom of the atmosphere (besides any moral gloom pertaining to Hepzibah and her inmates) by the unassisted light of his countenance. On perceiving a young rosebud of a girl, instead of the gaunt presence of the old maid, a look of surprise was manifest. He at first knit his brows; then smiled with more unctuous benignity than ever.

"Ah, I see how it is!" said he, in a deep voice—a voice which, had it come from the throat of an uncultivated man, would have been gruff, but, by dint of careful training, was now sufficiently agreeable—"I was not aware that Miss Hepzibah Pyncheon had commenced business under such favorable auspices. You are her assistant, I suppose?"

"I certainly am," answered Phoebe, and added, with a little air of ladylike assumption—(for, civil as the gentleman was, he evidently took her to be a young person serving for wages)—"I am a cousin of Miss Hepzibah, on a visit to her."

"Her cousin?—and from the country? Pray pardon me, then," said the gentleman, bowing and smiling as Phoebe never had been bowed to nor smiled on before.—"In that case, we must be better acquainted; for, unless I am sadly mistaken, you are my own little kinswoman likewise! Let me see—Mary?—Dolly?—Phoebe?—yes, Phoebe is the name! Is it possible that you are Phoebe Pyncheon, only child of my dear cousin and classmate, Arthur? Ah, I see your father now, about your mouth! Yes; yes; we must be better acquainted! I am your kinsman, my dear. Surely you must have heard of Judge Pyncheon?"

As Phoebe courtesied in reply, the Judge bent forward, with the pardonable and even praiseworthy purpose—considering the nearness of blood and the difference of age—of bestowing on his young relative a kiss of acknowledged kindred and natural affection. Unfortunately, (without design, or only with such instinctive design as gives no account of itself to the intellect,) Phoebe, just at the critical moment, drew back; so that her highly respectable kinsman, with his body bent over the counter, and his lips protruded, was betrayed into the rather absurd predicament of kissing the empty air. It was a modern parallel to the case of Ixion embracing a cloud,[1] and was so much the more ridiculous, as the Judge prided himself on eschewing all airy matter, and never mistaking a shadow for a substance. The truth was—and it is Phoebe's only excuse—that, although Judge Pyncheon's glowing benignity might not be absolutely unpleasant to the feminine beholder, with the width of a street or even an ordinary sized room interposed between, yet it became quite too intense, when this dark, full-fed physiognomy (so roughly bearded, too, that no razor could ever make it smooth) sought to bring itself into actual contact with the object of its regards. The man, the sex, somehow or other, was entirely too prominent in the Judge's demonstrations of that sort. Phoebe's eyes sank, and, without knowing why, she felt herself blushing deeply under his look. Yet she had been kissed before, and without any particular squeamishness, by perhaps half-a-dozen different cousins, younger, as well as older, than this dark-browed, grisly bearded, white-neckclothed, and unctuously benevolent Judge! Then why not by him?

On raising her eyes, Phoebe was startled by the change in Judge Pyncheon's face. It was quite as striking, allowing for the difference of scale, as that betwixt a landscape under a broad sunshine, and just before a thunder-storm; not that it had the passionate intensity of the latter aspect, but was cold, hard, immitigable, like a day-long brooding cloud.

1. Seeking to thwart Ixion's seduction of his wife, Zeus created an image of Hera made from clouds. Zeus later punished the mortal by fixing him to an eternally revolving wheel.

"Dear me, what is to be done now?" thought the country-girl to herself.—"He looks as if there were nothing softer in him than a rock, nor milder than the east-wind! I meant no harm! Since he is really my cousin, I would have let him kiss me, if I could!"

Then, all at once, it struck Phoebe, that this very Judge Pyncheon was the original of the miniature, which the Daguerreotypist had shown her in the garden, and that the hard, stern, relentless look, now on his face, was the same that the sun had so inflexibly persisted in bringing out. Was it, therefore, no momentary mood, but, however skilfully concealed, the settled temper of his life? And not merely so, but was it hereditary in him, and transmitted down as a precious heirloom from that bearded ancestor, in whose picture both the expression, and, to a singular degree, the features of the modern Judge, were shown as by a kind of prophecy? A deeper philosopher than Phoebe might have found something very terrible in this idea. It implied that the weaknesses and defects, the bad passions, the mean tendencies, and the moral diseases which lead to crime, are handed down from one generation to another, by a far surer process of transmission than human law has been able to establish, in respect to the riches and honors which it seeks to entail upon posterity.

But, as it happened, scarcely had Phoebe's eyes rested again on the Judge's countenance, than all its ugly sternness vanished; and she found herself quite overpowered by the sultry, dog-day heat, as it were, of benevolence, which this excellent man diffused out of his great heart into the surrounding atmosphere;—very much like a serpent, which, as a preliminary to fascination, is said to fill the air with his peculiar odor.

"I like that, Cousin Phoebe!" cried he, with an emphatic nod of approbation.—"I like it much, my little cousin! You are a good child, and know how to take care of yourself. A young girl—especially if she be a very pretty one—can never be too chary of her lips."

"Indeed, Sir," said Phoebe, trying to laugh the matter off, "I did not mean to be unkind."

Nevertheless, whether or no it were entirely owing to the inauspicious commencement of their acquaintance, she still acted under a certain reserve, which was by no means customary to her frank and genial nature. The fantasy would not quit her, that the original Puritan, of whom she had heard so many sombre traditions—the progenitor of the whole race of New England Pyncheons, the founder of the House of the Seven Gables, and who had died so strangely in it—had now stept into the shop. In these days of off-hand equipment, the matter was easily enough arranged. On his arrival from the other world, he had merely found it necessary to spend a quarter-of-an-hour at a barber's, who had trimmed down the Puritan's full beard into a pair of grizzled whiskers; then, patronizing a ready-made clothing establishment, he had exchanged his velvet doublet[2] and sable cloak, with the richly worked band under his chin, for a white collar and cravat, coat, vest, and pantaloons; and, lastly, putting aside his steel-hilted broadsword to take up a gold-headed cane, the Colonel Pyncheon, of two centuries ago, steps forward as the Judge, of the passing moment!

Of course, Phoebe was far too sensible a girl to entertain this idea in any other way than as matter for a smile. Possibly, also, could the two personages have stood together before her eye, many points of difference would have been perceptible, and perhaps only a general resemblance. The long lapse of intervening years, in a climate so unlike that which had fostered the ancestral Englishman, must inevitably have wrought important changes in the physical system of his descendant. The Judge's volume of muscle could hardly be the same as the Colonel's; there was undoubtedly less beef in him. Though looked upon as a weighty man among his contemporaries, in respect of animal substance; and as favored with a remarkable degree of fundamental developement, well adapting him for the judicial bench, we conceive that the modern Judge Pyncheon, if weighed in the same balance with his ancestor, would have required at least an old-fashioned fifty-six,[3] to keep the scale in equilibrio. Then the Judge's face had lost the ruddy English hue, that showed its warmth through all the duskiness of the Colonel's weather-beaten cheek, and had taken a sallow shade, the established complexion of his countrymen. If we mistake not, moreover, a certain quality of nervousness had become more or less manifest, even in so solid a specimen of Puritan descent, as the gentleman now under discussion. As one of its effects, it bestowed on his countenance a quicker mobility than the old Englishman's had possessed, and keener vivacity, but at the expense of a sturdier something, on which these acute endowments seemed to act like dissolving acids. This process, for aught we know, may belong to the great system of human progress, which, with every ascending footstep, as it diminishes the necessity for animal force, may be destined gradually to spiritualize us by refining away our grosser attributes of body. If so, Judge Pyncheon could endure a century or two more of such refinement, as well as most other men.

The similarity, intellectual and moral, between the Judge and his ancestor, appears to have been at least as strong as the resemblance of mien and feature would afford reason to anticipate. In old

2. Close-fitting outer garment worn in the seventeenth century.
3. As a former custom-house officer, Hawthorne would have known that the standard weight of a bushel of wheat was approximately fifty-six pounds.

Colonel Pyncheon's funeral discourse, the clergyman absolutely canonized his deceased parishioner, and opening, as it were, a vista through the roof of the church, and thence through the firmament above, showed him seated, harp in hand, among the crowned choristers of the spiritual world. On his tombstone, too, the record is highly eulogistic; nor does history, so far as he holds a place upon its page, assail the consistency and uprightness of his character. So also, as regards the Judge Pyncheon of to-day, neither clergyman, nor legal critic, nor inscriber of tombstones, nor historian of general or local politics, would venture a word against this eminent person's sincerity as a christian, or respectability as a man, or integrity as a judge, or courage and faithfulness as the often-tried representative of his political party. But, besides these cold, formal, and empty words of the chisel that inscribes, the voice that speaks, and the pen that writes for the public eye and for distant time—and which inevitably lose much of their truth and freedom by the fatal consciousness of so doing—there were traditions about the ancestor, and private diurnal gossip about the Judge, remarkably accordant in their testimony. It is often instructive to take the woman's, the private and domestic view, of a public man; nor can anything be more curious than the vast discrepancy between portraits intended for engraving, and the pencil-sketches that pass from hand to hand, behind the original's back.

For example, tradition affirmed that the Puritan had been greedy of wealth; the Judge, too, with all the show of liberal expenditure, was said to be as close-fisted as if his gripe were of iron. The ancestor had clothed himself in a grim assumption of kindliness, a rough heartiness of word and manner, which most people took to be the genuine warmth of nature, making its way through the thick and inflexible hide of a manly character. His descendant, in compliance with the requirements of a nicer age, had etherealized this rude benevolence into that broad benignity of smile, wherewith he shone like a noonday sun along the streets, or glowed like a household fire, in the drawing-rooms of his private acquaintance. The Puritan—if not belied by some singular stories, murmured, even at this day, under the narrator's breath—had fallen into certain transgressions to which men of his great animal developement, whatever their faith or principles, must continue liable, until they put off impurity, along with the gross earthly substance that involves it. We must not stain our page with any contemporary scandal, to a similar purport, that may have been whispered against the Judge. The Puritan, again, an autocrat in his own household, had worn out three wives, and, merely by the remorseless weight and hardness of his character in the conjugal relation, had sent them, one after another, broken hearted, to their graves. Here, the parallel, in some sort, fails. The Judge had wedded but a single wife, and lost her in the third or fourth year of their marriage. There was a fable, however—for such we choose to consider it, though, not impossibly, typical of Judge Pyncheon's marital deportment—that the lady got her death-blow in the honey-moon, and never smiled again, because her husband compelled her to serve him with coffee, every morning, at his bedside, in token of fealty to her liege-lord and master.

But it is too fruitful a subject, this of hereditary resemblances,— the frequent recurrence of which, in a direct line, is truly unaccountable, when we consider how large an accumulation of ancestry lies behind every man, at the distance of one or two centuries. We shall only add, therefore, that the Puritan—so, at least, says chimney-corner tradition, which often preserves traits of character with marvellous fidelity—was bold, imperious, relentless, crafty; laying his purposes deep, and following them out with an inveteracy of pursuit that knew neither rest nor conscience; trampling on the weak, and, when essential to his ends, doing his utmost to beat down the strong. Whether the Judge in any degree resembled him, the farther progress of our narrative may show.

Scarcely any of the items in the above-drawn parallel occurred to Phoebe, whose country-birth and residence, in truth, had left her pitifully ignorant of most of the family traditions, which lingered, like cobwebs and incrustations of smoke, about the rooms and chimney-corners of the House of the Seven Gables. Yet there was a circumstance, very trifling in itself, which impressed her with an odd degree of horror. She had heard of the anathema flung by Maule, the executed wizard, against Colonel Pyncheon and his posterity—that God would give them blood to drink—and likewise of the popular notion, that this miraculous blood might now and then be heard gurgling in their throats. The latter scandal (as became a person of sense, and, more especially, a member of the Pyncheon family) Phoebe had set down for the absurdity which it unquestionably was. But ancient superstitions, after being steeped in human hearts, and embodied in human breath, and passing from lip to ear in manifold repetition, through a series of generations, become imbued with an effect of homely truth. The smoke of the domestic hearth has scented them, through and through. By long transmission among household facts, they grow to look like them, and have such a familiar way of making themselves at home, that their influence is usually greater than we suspect. Thus it happened, that when Phoebe heard a certain noise in Judge Pyncheon's throat—rather habitual with him, not altogether voluntary, yet indicative of nothing, unless it were a slight bronchial complaint, or, as some people hinted, an apoplectic symptom—when the girl heard this queer and aukward ingurgitation, (which the writer never did hear, and therefore cannot describe,) she, very foolishly, started, and clasped her hands.

Of course, it was exceedingly ridiculous in Phoebe to be discomposed by such a trifle, and still more unpardonable to show her discomposure to the individual most concerned in it. But the incident chimed in so oddly with her previous fancies about the Colonel and the Judge, that, for the moment, it seemed quite to mingle their identity.

"What is the matter with you, young woman?" said Judge Pyncheon, giving her one of his harsh looks. "Are you afraid of anything?"

"Oh, nothing, Sir, nothing in the world!" answered Phoebe, with a little laugh of vexation at herself.—"But perhaps you wish to speak with my Cousin Hepzibah. Shall I call her?"

"Stay a moment, if you please!" said the Judge, again beaming sunshine out of his face.—"You seem to be a little nervous, this morning. The town air, Cousin Phoebe, does not agree with your good, wholesome country-habits. Or, has anything happened to disturb you?—anything remarkable in Cousin Hepzibah's family? An arrival, eh? I thought so! No wonder you are out of sorts, my little cousin. To be an inmate with such a guest may well startle an innocent young girl!"

"You quite puzzle me, Sir," replied Phoebe, gazing inquiringly at the Judge. "There is no frightful guest in the house, but only a poor, gentle, childlike man, whom I believe to be Cousin Hepzibah's brother. I am afraid (but you, Sir, will know better than I) that he is not quite in his sound senses; but so mild and quiet, he seems to be, that a mother might trust her baby with him; and I think he would play with the baby as if he were only a few years older than itself. He startle me! Oh, no indeed!"

"I rejoice to hear so favorable and so ingenuous an account of my Cousin Clifford," said the benevolent Judge. "Many years ago, when we were boys and young men together, I had a great affection for him, and still feel a tender interest in all his concerns. You say, Cousin Phoebe, he appears to be weak-minded. Heaven grant him at least enough of intellect to repent of his past sins!"

"Nobody, I fancy," observed Phoebe, "can have fewer to repent of."

"And is it possible, my dear," rejoined the Judge, with a commiserating look, "that you have never heard of Clifford Pyncheon?— that you know nothing of his history? Well; it is all right; and your mother has shown a very proper regard for the good name of the family with which she connected herself. Believe the best you can of this unfortunate person, and hope the best! It is a rule which christians should always follow, in their judgements of one another; and especially is it right and wise among near relatives, whose characters have necessarily a degree of mutual dependence. But is Clifford in the parlor? I will just step in and see!"

"Perhaps, Sir, I had better call my Cousin Hepzibah," said Phoebe; hardly knowing, however, whether she ought to obstruct the entrance of so affectionate a kinsman, into the private regions of the house.—"Her brother seemed to be just falling asleep, after breakfast; and I am sure she would not like him to be disturbed. Pray, Sir, let me give her notice!"

But the Judge showed a singular determination to enter unannounced; and as Phoebe, with the vivacity of a person whose movements unconsciously answer to her thoughts, had stept towards the door, he used little or no ceremony in putting her aside.

"No, no, Miss Phoebe!" said Judge Pyncheon, in a voice as deep as a thunder-growl, and with a frown as black as the cloud whence it issues. "Stay you here! I know the house, and know my Cousin Hepzibah, and know her brother Clifford likewise!—nor need my little country-cousin put herself to the trouble of announcing me!"—in these latter words, by-the-by, there were symptoms of a change from his sudden harshness into his previous benignity of manner—"I am at home here, Phoebe, you must recollect, and you are the stranger. I will just step in, therefore, and see for myself how Clifford is, and assure him and Hepzibah of my kindly feelings and best wishes. It is right, at this juncture, that they should both hear from my own lips how much I desire to serve them. Ha! Here is Hepzibah herself!"

Such was the case. The vibrations of the Judge's voice had reached the old gentlewoman in the parlor, where she sat, with face averted, waiting on her brother's slumber. She now issued forth, as would appear, to defend the entrance, looking, we must needs say, amazingly like the dragon which, in fairy tales, is wont to be the guardian over an enchanted beauty. The habitual scowl of her brow was, undeniably, too fierce, at this moment, to pass itself off on the innocent score of near-sightedness; and it was bent on Judge Pyncheon in a way that seemed to confound, if not alarm him—so inadequately had he estimated the moral force of a deeply grounded antipathy. She made a repelling gesture with her hand, and stood, a perfect picture of Prohibition, at full length, in the dark frame of the door-way. But we must betray Hepzibah's secret, and confess, that the native timorousness of her character even now developed itself, in a quick tremor, which, to her own perception, set each of her joints at variance with its fellow.

Possibly, the Judge was aware how little true hardihood lay

behind Hepzibah's formidable front. At any rate, being a gentleman of sturdy nerves, he soon recovered himself, and failed not to approach his cousin with outstretched hand; adopting the sensible precaution, however, to cover his advance with a smile, so broad and sultry, that, had it been only half as warm as it looked, a trellis of grapes might at once have turned purple under its summer-like exposure. It may have been his purpose, indeed, to melt poor Hepzibah, on the spot, as if she were a figure of yellow wax.

"Hepzibah, my beloved Cousin, I am rejoiced!" exclaimed the Judge, most emphatically. "Now, at length, you have something to live for. Yes; and all of us, let me say, your friends and kindred, have more to live for than we had yesterday. I have lost no time in hastening to offer any assistance in my power towards making Clifford comfortable. He belongs to us all. I know how much he requires—how much he used to require—with his delicate taste, and his love of the beautiful. Anything in my house—pictures, books, wine, luxuries of the table—he may command them all! It would afford me a most heartfelt gratification to see him! Shall I step in, this moment?"

"No," replied Hepzibah, her voice quivering too painfully to allow of many words. "He cannot see visitors!"

"A visitor, my dear Cousin?—do you call me so?" cried the Judge, whose sensibility, it seems, was hurt by the coldness of the phrase. "Nay, then, let me be Clifford's host, and your own likewise. Come at once to my house! The country-air, and all the conveniences—I may say, luxuries—that I have gathered about me, will do wonders for him. And you and I, dear Hepzibah, will consult together, and watch together, and labor together, to make our dear Clifford happy. Come! Why should we make more words about what is both a duty and a pleasure, on my part? Come to me at once!"

On hearing these so hospitable offers, and such generous recognition of the claims of kindred, Phoebe felt very much in the mood of running up to Judge Pyncheon, and giving him, of her own accord, the kiss from which she had so recently shrunk away. It was quite otherwise with Hepzibah; the Judge's smile seemed to operate on her acerbity of heart like sunshine upon vinegar, making it ten times sourer than ever.

"Clifford," said she—still too agitated to utter more than an abrupt sentence—"Clifford has a home here!"

"May Heaven forgive you, Hepzibah," said Judge Pyncheon—reverently lifting his eyes towards that high court of equity to which he appealed—"if you suffer any ancient prejudice or animosity to weigh with you, in this matter! I stand here, with an open heart, willing and anxious to receive yourself and Clifford into it. Do not refuse my good offices—my earnest propositions for your welfare! They are such, in all respects, as it behoves your nearest kinsman to make. It will be a heavy responsibility, Cousin, if you confine your brother to this dismal house and stifled air, when the delightful freedom of my country-seat is at his command."

"It would never suit Clifford," said Hepzibah, as briefly as before.

"Woman," broke forth the Judge, giving way to his resentment, "what is the meaning of all this? Have you other resources? Nay; I suspected as much! Take care, Hepzibah, take care! Clifford is on the brink of as black a ruin as ever befell him yet! But why do I talk with you, woman as you are! Make way! I must see Clifford!"

Hepzibah spread out her gaunt figure across the door, and seemed really to increase in bulk; looking the more terrible, also, because there was so much terror and agitation in her heart. But Judge Pyncheon's evident purpose of forcing a passage was interrupted by a voice from the inner room; a weak, tremulous, wailing voice, indicating helpless alarm, with no more energy for self-defence than belongs to a frightened infant.

"Hepzibah, Hepzibah," cried the voice, "go down on your knees to him! Kiss his feet! Entreat him not to come in! Oh, let him have mercy on me! Mercy!—mercy!"

For the instant, it appeared doubtful whether it were not the Judge's resolute purpose to set Hepzibah aside, and step across the threshold into the parlor, whence issued that broken and miserable murmur of entreaty. It was not pity that restrained him; for, at the first sound of the enfeebled voice, a red fire kindled in his eyes; and he made a quick pace forward, with something inexpressibly fierce and grim, darkening forth, as it were, out of the whole man. To know Judge Pyncheon, was to see him at that moment. After such a revelation, let him smile with what sultriness he would, he could much sooner turn grapes purple, or pumpkins yellow, than melt the iron-branded impression out of the beholder's memory. And it rendered his aspect not the less, but more frightful, that it seemed not to express wrath or hatred, but a certain hot fellness[4] of purpose, which annihilated everything but itself.

Yet, after all, are we not slandering an excellent and amiable man? Look at the Judge now! He is apparently conscious of having erred, in too energetically pressing his deeds of loving-kindness on persons unable to appreciate them. He will await their better mood, and hold himself as ready to assist them, then, as at this moment. As he draws back from the door, an all-comprehensive benignity blazes from his visage, indicating that he gathers Hepzibah, little Phoebe, and the invisible Clifford, all three, together with the whole world besides, into his immense heart, and gives them a warm bath in its flood of affection.

4. Deadliness.

"You do me great wrong, dear Cousin Hepzibah," said he, first kindly offering her his hand, and then drawing on his glove preparatory to departure. "Very great wrong! But I forgive it, and will study to make you think better of me. Of course, our poor Clifford being in so unhappy a state of mind, I cannot think of urging an interview at present. But I shall watch over his welfare, as if he were my own beloved brother; nor do I at all despair, my dear Cousin, of constraining both him and you to acknowledge your injustice. When that shall happen, I desire no other revenge than your acceptance of the best offices in my power to do you."

With a bow to Hepzibah, and a degree of paternal benevolence in his parting nod to Phoebe, the Judge left the shop, and went smiling along the street. As is customary with the rich, when they aim at the honors of a republic, he apologized, as it were, to the people, for his wealth, prosperity, and elevated station, by a free and hearty manner towards those who knew him; putting off the more of his dignity, in due proportion with the humbleness of the man whom he saluted; and thereby proving a haughty consciousness of his advantages, as irrefragably as if he had marched forth, preceded by a troop of lackeys to clear the way. On this particular forenoon, so excessive was the warmth of Judge Pyncheon's kindly aspect, that (such, at least, was the rumor about town) an extra passage of the water-carts was found essential, in order to lay the dust occasioned by so much extra sunshine!

No sooner had he disappeared, than Hepzibah grew deadly white, and staggering towards Phoebe, let her head fall on the young girl's shoulder.

"Oh, Phoebe," murmured she, "that man has been the horror of my life! Shall I never, never have the courage—will my voice never cease from trembling long enough—to let me tell him what he is!"

"Is he so very wicked?" asked Phoebe. "Yet his offers were surely kind!"

"Do not speak of them—he has a heart of iron!" rejoined Hepzibah.—"Go now, and talk to Clifford! Amuse, and keep him quiet! It would disturb him wretchedly, to see me so agitated as I am. There, go, dear child, and I will try to look after the shop!"

Phoebe went, accordingly, but perplexed herself, meanwhile, with queries as to the purport of the scene which she had just witnessed, and also whether judges, clergymen, and other characters of that eminent stamp and respectability, could really, in any single instance, be otherwise than just and upright men. A doubt of this nature has a most disturbing influence, and, if shown to be a fact, comes with fearful and startling effect, on minds of the trim, orderly, and limit-loving class, in which we find our little country-girl. Dispositions more boldly speculative may derive a stern enjoyment from the discovery, since there must be evil in the world, that a high man is as likely to grasp his share of it, as a low one. A wider scope of view, and a deeper insight, may see rank, dignity, and station, all proved illusory, so far as regards their claim to human reverence, and yet not feel as if the universe were thereby tumbled headlong into chaos. But Phoebe, in order to keep the universe in its old place, was fain to smother, in some degree, her own intuitions as to Judge Pyncheon's character. And as for her cousin's testimony in disparagement of it, she concluded that Hepzibah's judgement was embittered by one of those family feuds, which render hatred the more deadly, by the dead and corrupted love that they intermingle with its native poison.

IX. Clifford and Phoebe

Truly was there something high, generous, and noble, in the native composition of our poor old Hepzibah! Or else—and it was quite as probably the case—she had been enriched by poverty, developed by sorrow, elevated by the strong and solitary affection of her life, and thus endowed with heroism, which never could have characterized her in what are called happier circumstances. Through dreary years, Hepzibah had looked forward—for the most part, despairingly, never with any confidence of hope, but always with the feeling that it was her brightest possibility—to the very position in which she now found herself. In her own behalf, she had asked nothing of Providence, but the opportunity of devoting herself to this brother whom she had so loved—so admired for what he was, or might have been—and to whom she had kept her faith, alone of all the world, wholly, unfaulteringly, at every instant, and throughout life. And here, in his late decline, the lost one had come back out of his long and strange misfortune, and was thrown on her sympathy, as it seemed, not merely for the bread of his physical existence, but for everything that should keep him morally alive. She had responded to the call! She had come forward—our poor, gaunt Hepzibah, in her rusty silks, with her rigid joints, and the sad perversity of her scowl—ready to do her utmost, and with affection enough, if that were all, to do a hundred times as much!— There could be few more tearful sights—and Heaven forgive us, if a smile insist on mingling with our conception of it!—few sights with truer pathos in them, than Hepzibah presented, on that first afternoon.

How patiently did she endeavor to wrap Clifford up in her great, warm love, and make it all the world to him, so that he should retain no torturing sense of the coldness and dreariness, without!

Her little efforts to amuse him! How pitiful, yet magnanimous, they were!

Remembering his early love of poetry and fiction, she unlocked a bookcase, and took down several books that had been excellent reading, in their day. There was a volume of Pope, with the Rape of the Lock in it, and another of the Tatler, and an odd one of Dryden's Miscellanies, all with tarnished gilding on their covers, and thoughts of tarnished brilliancy, inside.[5] They had no success with Clifford. These, and all such writers of society, whose new works glow like the rich texture of a just-woven carpet, must be content to relinquish their charm, for every reader, after an age or two, and could hardly be supposed to retain any portion of it for a mind, that had utterly lost its estimate of modes and manners. Hepzibah then took up Rasselas, and began to read of the Happy Valley,[6] with a vague idea that some secret of a contented life had there been elaborated, which might at least serve Clifford and herself for this one day. But the Happy Valley had a cloud over it. Hepzibah troubled her auditor, moreover, by innumerable sins of emphasis, which he seemed to detect without any reference to the meaning; nor, in fact, did he appear to take much note of the sense of what she read, but evidently felt the tedium of the lecture without harvesting its profit. His sister's voice, too, naturally harsh, had, in the course of her sorrowful lifetime, contracted a kind of croak, which, when it once gets into the human throat, is as ineradicable as sin. In both sexes, occasionally, this life-long croak, accompanying each word of joy or sorrow, is one of the symptoms of a settled melancholy; and wherever it occurs, the whole history of misfortune is conveyed in its slightest accent. The effect is as if the voice had been dyed black; or—if we must use a more moderate simile—this miserable croak, running through all the variations of the voice, is like a black silken thread, on which the crystal beads of speech are strung, and whence they take their hue. Such voices have put on mourning for dead hopes; and they ought to die and be buried along with them!

Discerning that Clifford was not gladdened by her efforts, Hepzibah searched about the house for the means of more exhilarating pastime. At one time, her eyes chanced to rest on Alice Pyncheon's

5. References to major works of British literature from the late seventeenth and early eighteenth centuries. Alexander Pope (1688–1744) published his mock-heroic poem *The Rape of the Lock* in 1714. Richard Steele (1672–1729) and Joseph Addison (1672–1719) wrote the sketches and essays making up the influential periodicals the *Tatler* (1709–11) and the *Spectator* (1711–12). John Dryden (1631–1700) published the first of his four volumes of miscellanies (collections of poems, essays, and other literary writings) in 1684.

6. In *The History of Rasselas, Prince of Abissinia* (1759), Samuel Johnson (1709–1784) writes of a young man who leaves the mythical Happy Valley to enter the world of sorrow and hardship.

harpsichord. It was a moment of great peril; for—despite the traditionary awe that had gathered over this instrument of music, and
the dirges which spiritual fingers were said to play on it—the devoted sister had solemn thoughts of thrumming on its chords for
Clifford's benefit, and accompanying the performance with her
voice. Poor Clifford! Poor Hepzibah! Poor harpsichord! All three
would have been miserable together. By some good agency—
possibly, by the unrecognized interposition of the long-buried Alice,
herself—the threatening calamity was averted.

But the worst of all—the hardest stroke of fate for Hepzibah to
endure, and perhaps for Clifford too—was his invincible distaste
for her appearance. Her features, never the most agreeable, and
now harsh with age and grief, and resentment against the world for
his sake; her dress, and especially her turban; the queer and quaint
manners, which had unconsciously grown upon her in solitude;—
such being the poor gentlewoman's outward characteristics, it is no
great marvel, although the mournfullest of pities, that the instinctive lover of the Beautiful was fain to turn away his eyes! There was
no help for it. It would be the latest impulse to die within him. In
his last extremity, the expiring breath stealing faintly through Clifford's lips, he would doubtless press Hepzibah's hand, in fervent
recognition of all her lavished love, and close his eyes—but not so
much to die, as to be constrained to look no longer on her face!
Poor Hepzibah! She took counsel with herself what might be done,
and thought of putting ribbons on her turban, but, by the instant
rush of several guardian angels, was withheld from an experiment,
that could hardly have proved less than fatal to the beloved object
of her anxiety.[7]

To be brief, besides Hepzibah's disadvantages of person, there
was an uncouthness pervading all her deeds; a clumsy something,
that could but ill adapt itself for use, and not at all for ornament.
She was a grief to Clifford, and she knew it. In this extremity, the
antiquated virgin turned to Phoebe. No grovelling jealousy was in
her heart. Had it pleased Heaven to crown the heroic fidelity of her
life by making her personally the medium of Clifford's happiness, it
would have rewarded her for all the past, by a joy with no bright
tints, indeed, but deep and true, and worth a thousand gayer ecsta-
cies. This could not be. She therefore turned to Phoebe, and re-
signed the task into the young girl's hands. The latter took it up,
cheerfully, as she did everything, but with no sense of a mission to
perform, and succeeding all the better for that same simplicity.

By the involuntary effect of a genial temperament, Phoebe soon

---

7. An allusion to the moment in *The Rape of the Lock* (I.146–47) when the sylphs watching over Belinda, the elegant woman of high society, tend to her hair.

grew to be absolutely essential to the daily comfort, if not the daily life, of her two forlorn companions. The grime and sordidness of the House of the Seven Gables seemed to have vanished, since her appearance there; the gnawing tooth of the dry-rot was stayed, among the old timbers of its skeleton-frame; the dust had ceased to settle down so densely from the antique ceilings, upon the floors and furniture of the rooms below;—or, at any rate, there was a little housewife, as light-footed as the breeze that sweeps a garden-walk, gliding hither and thither, to brush it all away. The shadows of gloomy events, that haunted the else lonely and desolate apartments; the heavy, breathless scent which Death had left in more than one of the bed-chambers, ever since his visits of long ago;—these were less powerful than the purifying influence, scattered throughout the atmosphere of the household by the presence of one, youthful, fresh, and thoroughly wholesome heart. There was no morbidness in Phoebe; if there had been, the old Pyncheon-house was the very locality to ripen it into incurable disease. But, now, her spirit resembled, in its potency, a minute quantity of attar of rose[8] in one of Hepzibah's huge, iron-bound trunks, diffusing its fragrance through the various articles of linen and wrought-lace, kerchiefs, caps, stockings, folded dresses, gloves, and whatever else was treasured there. As every article in the great trunk was the sweeter for the rose-scent, so did all the thoughts and emotions of Hepzibah and Clifford, sombre as they might seem, acquire a subtle attribute of happiness from Phoebe's intermixture with them. Her activity of body, intellect, and heart, impelled her continually to perform the ordinary little toils that offered themselves around her, and to think the thought, proper for the moment, and to sympathize—now with the twittering gaiety of the robins in the pear-tree—and now, to such depth as she could, with Hepzibah's dark anxiety, or the vague moan of her brother. This facile adaptation was at once the symptom of perfect health, and its best preservative.

A nature like Phoebe's has invariably its due influence, but is seldom regarded with due honor. Its spiritual force, however, may be partially estimated by the fact of her having found a place for herself, amid circumstances so stern, as those which surrounded the mistress of the house; and also by the effect which she produced on a character of so much more mass than her own. For the gaunt, bony frame and limbs of Hepzibah, as compared with the tiny light-someness of Phoebe's figure, were perhaps in some fit proportion with the moral weight and substance, respectively, of the woman and the girl.

8. Perfume made from rose petals.

To the guest—to Hepzibah's brother—or Cousin Clifford, as Phoebe now began to call him—she was especially necessary. Not that he could ever be said to converse with her, or often manifest, in any other very definite mode, his sense of a charm in her society. But, if she were a long while absent, he became pettish and nervously restless, pacing the room to-and-fro, with the uncertainty that characterized all his movements; or else would sit broodingly in his great chair, resting his head on his hands, and evincing life only by an electric sparkle of ill-humor, whenever Hepzibah endeavored to arouse him. Phoebe's presence, and the contiguity of her fresh life to his blighted one, was usually all that he required. Indeed, such was the native gush and play of her spirit, that she was seldom perfectly quiet and undemonstrative, any more than a fountain ever ceases to dimple and warble with its flow. She possessed the gift of song, and that too so naturally, that you would as little think of inquiring whence she had caught it, or what master had taught her, as of asking the same questions about a bird, in whose small strain of music we recognize the voice of the Creator, as distinctly as in the loudest accents of His thunder. So long as Phoebe sang, she might stray at her own will about the house. Clifford was content, whether the sweet, airy homeliness of her tones came down from the upper chambers, or along the passage-way from the shop, or was sprinkled through the foliage of the pear-tree, inward from the garden, with the twinkling sunbeams. He would sit quietly, with a gentle pleasure gleaming over his face, brighter now, and now a little dimmer, as the song happened to float near him, or was more remotely heard. It pleased him best, however, when she sat on a low footstool at his knee.

It is perhaps remarkable, considering her temperament, that Phoebe oftener chose a strain of pathos than of gaiety. But the young and happy are not ill-pleased to temper their life with a transparent shadow. The deepest pathos of Phoebe's voice and song, moreover, came sifted through the golden texture of a cheery spirit, and was somehow so interfused with the quality thence acquired, that one's heart felt all the lighter for having wept at it. Broad mirth, in the sacred presence of dark misfortune, would have jarred harshly and irreverently with the solemn symphony, that rolled its undertone through Hepzibah's and her brother's life. Therefore it was well that Phoebe so often chose sad themes, and not amiss that they ceased to be so sad, while she was singing them.

Becoming habituated to her companionship, Clifford readily showed how capable of imbibing pleasant tints, and gleams of cheerful light from all quarters, his nature must originally have been. He grew youthful, while she sat by him. A beauty—not precisely real, even in its utmost manifestation, and which a painter would have watched long to seize, and fix upon his canvass, and, after all, in vain—beauty, nevertheless, that was not a mere dream, would sometimes play upon and illuminate his face. It did more than to illuminate; it transfigured him with an expression that could only be interpreted as the glow of an exquisite and happy spirit. That gray hair, and those furrows—with their record of infinite sorrow, so deeply written across his brow, and so compressed, as with a futile effort to crowd in all the tale, that the whole inscription was made illegible—these, for the moment, vanished. An eye, at once tender and acute, might have beheld in the man some shadow of what he was meant to be. Anon, as age came stealing, like a sad twilight, back over his figure, you would have felt tempted to hold an argument with Destiny, and affirm, that either this being should not have been made mortal, or mortal existence should have been tempered to his qualities. There seemed no necessity for his having drawn breath, at all;—the world never wanted him;—but, as he had breathed, it ought always to have been the balmiest of summer air. The same perplexity will invariably haunt us with regard to natures, that tend to feed exclusively upon the Beautiful, let their earthly fate be as lenient as it may.

Phoebe, it is probable, had but a very imperfect comprehension of the character, over which she had thrown so beneficent a spell. Nor was it necessary. The fire upon the hearth can gladden a whole semi-circle of faces roundabout it, but need not know the individuality of one among them all. Indeed, there was something too fine and delicate in Clifford's traits, to be perfectly appreciated by one whose sphere lay so much in the Actual as Phoebe's did. For Clifford, however, the reality, and simplicity, and thorough homeliness of the girl's nature, were as powerful a charm as any that she possessed. Beauty, it is true, and beauty almost perfect in its own style, was indispensable. Had Phoebe been coarse in feature, shaped clumsily, of a harsh voice, and uncouthly mannered, she might have been rich with all good gifts, beneath this unfortunate exterior; and still, so long as she wore the guise of woman, she would have shocked Clifford and depressed him by her lack of beauty. But nothing more beautiful—nothing prettier, at least—was ever made, than Phoebe. And, therefore, to this man—whose whole poor and impalpable enjoyment of existence, heretofore, and until both his heart and fancy died within him, had been a dream—whose images of women had more and more lost their warmth and substance, and been frozen, like the pictures of secluded artists, into the chillest ideality—to him, this little figure of the cheeriest household-life was just what he required, to bring him back into the breathing world. Persons who have wandered, or been expelled, out of the common track of things, even were it for a better system, desire nothing so much as to be led back. They shiver in their loneliness, be it on a mountain-top or in a dungeon. Now, Phoebe's presence made a home about her—that very sphere which the outcast, the prisoner, the potentate, the wretch beneath mankind, the wretch aside from it, or the wretch above it, instinctively pines after—a home! She was real! Holding her hand, you felt something; a tender something; a substance, and a warm one; and so long as you should feel its grasp, soft as it was, you might be certain that your place was good in the whole sympathetic chain of human nature. The world was no longer a delusion.

By looking a little farther in this direction, we might suggest an explanation of an often suggested mystery. Why are poets so apt to choose their mates, not for any similarity of poetic endowment, but for qualities which might make the happiness of the rudest handicraftsman, as well as that of the ideal craftsman of the spirit? Because, probably, at his highest elevation, the poet needs no human intercourse; but he finds it dreary to descend, and be a stranger.

There was something very beautiful in the relation that grew up between this pair; so closely and constantly linked together, yet with such a waste of gloomy and mysterious years from his birthday to hers. On Clifford's part, it was the feeling of a man naturally endowed with the liveliest sensibility to feminine influence, but who had never quaffed the cup of passionate love, and knew that it was now too late. He knew it, with the instinctive delicacy that had survived his intellectual decay. Thus, his sentiment for Phoebe, without being paternal, was not less chaste than if she had been his daughter. He was a man, it is true, and recognized her as a woman. She was his only representative of womankind. He took unfailing note of every charm that appertained to her sex, and saw the ripeness of her lips, and the virginal development of her bosom. All her little, womanly ways, budding out of her like blossoms on a young fruit-tree, had their effect on him, and sometimes caused his very heart to tingle with the keenest thrills of pleasure. At such moments—for the effect was seldom more than momentary—the half-torpid man would be full of harmonious life, just as a long-silent harp is full of sound, when the musician's fingers sweep across it. But, after all, it seemed rather a perception, or a sympathy, than a sentiment belonging to himself as an individual. He read Phoebe, as he would a sweet and simple story; he listened to her, as if she were a verse of household poetry, which God, in requital of his bleak and dismal lot, had permitted some angel, that most pitied him, to warble through the house. She was not an actual fact for him, but the interpretation of all that he had lacked on earth, brought warmly home to his conception; so that this mere symbol or lifelike picture had almost the comfort of reality.

But we strive in vain to put the idea into words. No adequate expression of the beauty and profound pathos, with which it impresses us, is attainable. This being, made only for happiness, and heretofore so miserably failing to be happy—his tendencies so hideously thwarted, that, some unknown time ago, the delicate springs of his character, never morally or intellectually strong, had given way, and he was now imbecile—this poor, forlorn voyager from the Islands of the Blest,[9] in a frail bark, on a tempestuous sea, had been flung, by the last mountain-wave of his shipwreck, into a quiet harbor. There, as he lay more than half-lifeless on the strand, the fragrance of an earthly rosebud had come to his nostrils, and, as odors will, had summoned up reminiscences or visions of all the living and breathing beauty, amid which he should have had his home. With his native susceptibility of happy influences, he inhales the slight, ethereal rapture into his soul, and expires!

And how did Phoebe regard Clifford? The girl's was not one of those natures which are most attracted by what is strange and exceptional in human character. The path, which would best have suited her, was the well-worn track of ordinary life; the companions, in whom she would most have delighted, were such as one encounters at every turn. The mystery which enveloped Clifford, so far as it affected her at all, was an annoyance, rather than the piquant charm which many women might have found in it. Still, her native kindliness was brought strongly into play, not by what was darkly picturesque in his situation, nor so much even by the finer grace of his character, as by the simple appeal of a heart so forlorn as his, to one so full of genuine sympathy as hers. She gave him an affectionate regard, because he needed so much love, and seemed to have received so little. With a ready tact, the result of ever-active and wholesome sensibility, she discerned what was good for him, and did it. Whatever was morbid in his mind and experience, she ignored, and thereby kept their intercourse healthy by the incautious, but, as it were, heaven-directed freedom of her whole conduct. The sick in mind, and perhaps in body, are rendered more darkly and hopelessly so, by the manifold reflection of their disease, mirrored back from all quarters, in the deportment of those about them; they are compelled to inhale the poison of their own breath,

9. According to Greek myth, islands at the western end of the world where nymphs called the Hesperides guarded a tree with golden apples. The site was also known as Elysium, a mythical place for those exempted from death.

in infinite repetition. But Phoebe afforded her poor patient a supply of purer air. She impregnated it, too, not with a wild-flower
scent—for wildness was no trait of hers—but with the perfume of
garden-roses, pinks, and other blossoms of much sweetness, which
nature and man have consented together in making grow, from
summer to summer, and from century to century. Such a flower
was Phoebe, in her relation with Clifford, and such the delight that
he inhaled from her.

Yet, it must be said, her petals sometimes drooped a little, in consequence of the heavy atmosphere about her. She grew more
thoughtful than heretofore. Looking aside at Clifford's face, and
seeing the dim, unsatisfactory elegance, and the intellect almost
quenched, she would try to inquire what had been his life. Was he
always thus? Had this veil been over him from his birth?—this veil,
under which far more of his spirit was hidden than revealed, and
through which he so imperfectly discerned the actual world—or
was its gray texture woven of some dark calamity? Phoebe loved no
riddles, and would have been glad to escape the perplexity of this
one. Nevertheless, there was so far a good result of her meditations
on Clifford's character, that, when her involuntary conjectures, together with the tendency of every strange circumstance to tell its
own story, had gradually taught her the fact, it had no terrible effect upon her. Let the world have done him what vast wrong it
might, she knew Cousin Clifford too well—or fancied so—ever to
shudder at the touch of his thin, delicate fingers.

Within a few days after the appearance of this remarkable inmate, the routine of life had established itself with a good deal of
uniformity in the old house of our narrative. In the morning, very
shortly after breakfast, it was Clifford's custom to fall asleep in his
chair; nor, unless accidentally disturbed, would he emerge from a
dense cloud of slumber, or the thinner mists that flitted to-and-fro,
until well towards noonday. These hours of drowsyhead were the
season of the old gentlewoman's attendance on her brother, while
Phoebe took charge of the shop; an arrangement which the public
speedily understood, and envinced their decided preference of the
younger shopwoman by the multiplicity of their calls, during her
administration of affairs. Dinner over, Hepzibah took her knitting-
work—a long stocking of gray yarn, for her brother's winter-wear—
and with a sigh, and a scowl of affectionate farewell to Clifford,
and a gesture enjoining watchfulness on Phoebe, went to take her
seat behind the counter. It was now the young girl's turn to be
the nurse, the guardian, the playmate—or whatever is the fitter
phrase—of the gray haired man.

X. The Pyncheon-Garden

Clifford, except for Phoebe's more active instigation, would ordinarily have yielded to the torpor which had crept through all his modes of being, and which sluggishly counselled him to sit in his morning chair, till eventide. But the girl seldom failed to propose a removal to the garden, where Uncle Venner and the Daguerreotypist had made such repairs on the roof of the ruinous arbor, or summer-house, that it was now a sufficient shelter from sunshine and casual showers. The hop-vine, too, had begun to grow luxuriantly over the sides of the little edifice, and made an interior of verdant seclusion, with innumerable peeps and glimpses into the wider solitude of the garden.

Here, sometimes, in this green play-place of flickering light, Phoebe read to Clifford. Her acquaintance, the artist, who appeared to have a literary turn, had supplied her with works of fiction, in pamphlet-form, and a few volumes of poetry, in altogether a different style and taste from those which Hepzibah selected for his amusement. Small thanks were due to the books, however, if the girl's readings were in any degree more successful than her elderly cousin's. Phoebe's voice had always a pretty music in it, and could either enliven Clifford, by its sparkle and gaiety of tone, or soothe him by a continued flow of pebbly and brook-like cadences. But the fictions—in which the country-girl, unused to works of that nature, often became deeply absorbed—interested her strange auditor very little, or not at all. Pictures of life, scenes of passion or sentiment, wit, humor, and pathos, were all thrown away, or worse than thrown away, on Clifford; either because he lacked an experience by which to test their truth, or because his own griefs were a touchstone of reality that few feigned emotions could withstand. When Phoebe broke into a peal of merry laughter at what she read, he would now and then laugh for sympathy, but oftener respond with a troubled, questioning look. If a tear—a maiden's sunshiny tear, over imaginary woe—dropt upon some melancholy page, Clifford either took it as a token of actual calamity, or else grew peevish, and angrily motioned her to close the volume. And wisely, too! Is not the world sad enough, in genuine earnest, without making a pastime of mock-sorrows?

With poetry, it was rather better. He delighted in the swell and subsidence of the rhythm, and the happily recurring rhyme. Nor was Clifford incapable of feeling the sentiment of poetry—not perhaps where it was highest or deepest—but where it was most flitting and ethereal. It was impossible to foretell in what exquisite verse the awakening spell might lurk; but, on raising her eyes from the page to Clifford's face, Phoebe would be made aware, by the light breaking through it, that a more delicate intelligence than her own had caught a lambent[1] flame from what she read. One glow of this kind, however, was often the precursor of gloom, for many hours afterward, because, when the glow left him, he seemed conscious of a missing sense and power, and groped about for them, as if a blind man should go seeking his lost eyesight.

It pleased him more, and was better for his inward welfare, that Phoebe should talk, and make passing occurrences vivid to his mind by her accompanying description and remarks. The life of the garden offered topics enough for such discourse as suited Clifford best. He never failed to inquire what flowers had bloomed, since yesterday. His feeling for flowers was very exquisite, and seemed not so much a taste, as an emotion; he was fond of sitting with one in his hand, intently observing it, and looking from its petals into Phoebe's face, as if the garden-flower were the sister of the household-maiden. Not merely was there a delight in the flower's perfume, or pleasure in its beautiful form, and the delicacy or brightness of its hue; but Clifford's enjoyment was accompanied with a perception of life, character, and individuality, that made him love these blossoms of the garden, as if they were endowed with sentiment and intelligence. This affection and sympathy for flowers is almost exclusively a woman's trait. Men, if endowed with it by nature, soon lose, forget, and learn to despise it, in their contact with coarser things than flowers. Clifford, too, had long forgotten it, but found it again, now, as he slowly revived from the chill torpor of his life.

It is wonderful how many pleasant incidents continually came to pass in that secluded garden-spot, when once Phoebe had set herself to look for them. She had seen or heard a bee there, on the first day of her acquaintance with the place. And often—almost continually, indeed—since then, the bees kept coming thither, Heaven knows why, or by what pertinacious desire for far-fetched sweets; when, no doubt, there were broad clover-fields, and all kinds of garden-growth, much nearer home than this. Thither the bees came, however, and plunged into the squash-blossoms, as if there were no other squash-vines within a long day's flight, or as if the soil of Hepzibah's garden gave its productions just the very quality which these laborious little wizards wanted, in order to impart the Hymettus[2] odor to their whole hive of New England honey. When Clifford heard their sunny, buzzing murmur, in the heart of the great, yellow blossoms, he looked about him with a joyful sense of

1. Softly radiant.
2. A mountain in Greece famed for its bees and honey.

warmth, and blue sky, and green grass, and of God's free air in the whole height from earth to heaven. After all, there need be no question why the bees came to that one green nook, in the dusty town. God sent them thither to gladden our poor Clifford! They brought the rich summer with them, in requital of a little honey.

When the bean-vines began to flower on the poles, there was one particular variety which bore a vivid scarlet blossom. The Daguerreotypist had found these beans in a garret, over one of the seven gables, treasured up in an old chest of drawers by some horticultural Pyncheon of days gone-by, who doubtless meant to sow them, the next summer, but was himself first sown in Death's garden-ground.[3] By way of testing whether there was still a living germ in such ancient seeds, Holgrave had planted some of them; and the result of his experiment was a splendid row of bean-vines, clambering early to the full height of the poles, and arraying them, from top to bottom, in a spiral profusion of red blossoms. And, ever since the unfolding of the first bud, a multitude of humming-birds had been attracted thither. At times, it seemed as if, for every one of the hundred blossoms, there was one of these tiniest fowls of the air, a thumb's bigness of burnished plumage, hovering and vibrating about the bean-poles. It was with indescribable interest, and even more than childish delight, that Clifford watched the humming-birds. He used to thrust his head softly out of the arbor, to see them the better; all the while, too, motioning Phoebe to be quiet, and snatching glimpses of the smile upon her face, so as to heap his enjoyment up the higher with her sympathy. He had not merely grown young; he was a child again.

Hepzibah, whenever she happened to witness one of these fits of miniature enthusiasm, would shake her head, with a strange mingling of the mother and sister, and of pleasure and sadness, in her aspect. She said that it had always been thus with Clifford, when the humming-birds came—always, from his babyhood—and that his delight in them had been one of the earliest tokens by which he showed his love for beautiful things. And it was a wonderful coincidence, the good lady thought, that the artist should have planted these scarlet-flowering beans—which the humming-birds sought, far and wide, and which had not grown in the Pyncheon-garden before, for forty years—on the very summer of Clifford's return.

Then would the tears stand in poor Hepzibah's eyes, or overflow them with a too abundant gush, so that she was fain to betake herself into some corner, lest Clifford should espy her agitation. Indeed, all the enjoyments of this period were provocative of tears.

3. A playful allusion to *The Scarlet Letter*. Holgrave finds and sows the beans in ways that parallel Hawthorne's account in "The Custom-House" of finding and making use of Surveyor Pue's manuscript.

Coming so late as it did, it was a kind of Indian summer,[4] with a mist in its balmiest sunshine, and decay and death in its gaudiest delight. The more Clifford seemed to taste the happiness of a child, the sadder was the difference to be recognized. With a mysterious and terrible Past, which had annihilated his memory, and a blank Future before him, he had only this visionary and impalpable Now, which, if you once look closely at it, is nothing. He himself, as was perceptible by many symptoms, lay darkly behind his pleasure, and knew it to be a baby-play, which he was to toy and trifle with, instead of thoroughly believing. Clifford saw, it may be, in the mirror of his deeper consciousness, that he was an example and representative of that great chaos of people, whom an inexplicable Providence is continually putting at cross-purposes with the world; breaking what seems its own promise in their nature; withholding their proper food, and setting poison before them for a banquet; and thus—when it might so easily, as one would think, have been adjusted otherwise—making their existence a strangeness, a solitude, and torment. All his life long, he had been learning how to be wretched, as one learns a foreign tongue; and now, with the lesson thoroughly at heart, he could with difficulty comprehend his little, airy happiness. Frequently, there was a dim shadow of doubt in his eyes.—"Take my hand, Phoebe," he would say, "and pinch it hard with your little fingers! Give me a rose, that I may press its thorns, and prove myself awake, by the sharp touch of pain!"—Evidently, he desired this prick of a trifling anguish, in order to assure himself, by that quality which he best knew to be real, that the garden, and the seven weather-beaten gables, and Hepzibah's scowl and Phoebe's smile, were real, likewise. Without this signet in his flesh, he could have attributed no more substance to them, than to the empty confusion of imaginary scenes with which he had fed his spirit, until even that poor sustenance was exhausted.

The author needs great faith in his reader's sympathy; else he must hesitate to give details so minute, and incidents apparently so trifling, as are essential to make up the idea of this garden-life. It was the Eden of a thunder-smitten Adam, who had fled for refuge thither out of the same dreary and perilous wilderness, into which the original Adam was expelled.

One of the available means of amusement, of which Phoebe made the most, in Clifford's behalf, was that feathered society, the hens, a breed of whom, as we have already said, was an immemorial heirloom in the Pyncheon family. In compliance with a whim of Clifford, as it troubled him to see them in confinement, they had been set at liberty, and now roamed at will about the garden; doing

4. A period of unseasonably mild weather in late fall or early winter.

some little mischief, but hindered from escape by buildings, on three sides, and the difficult peaks of a wooden fence, on the other. They spent much of their abundant leisure on the margin of Maule's Well, which was haunted by a kind of snail, evidently a tidbit to their palates; and the brackish water itself, however nauseous to the rest of the world, was so greatly esteemed by these fowls, that they might be seen tasting, turning up their heads, and smacking their bills, with precisely the air of wine-bibbers[5] round a probationary cask. Their generally quiet, yet often brisk, and constantly diversified talk, one to another, or sometimes in soliloquy— as they scratched worms out of the rich, black soil, or pecked at such plants as suited their taste—had such a domestic tone, that it was almost a wonder why you could not establish a regular interchange of ideas about household matters, human and gallinaceous.[6] All hens are well-worth studying, for the piquancy and rich variety of their manners; but by no possibility can there have been other fowls, of such odd appearance and deportment as these ancestral ones. They probably embodied the traditionary peculiarities of their whole line of progenitors, derived through an unbroken succession of eggs; or else this individual Chanticleer and his two wives had grown to be humorists, and a little crack-brained withal, on account of their solitary way of life, and out of sympathy for Hepzibah, their lady-patroness.

Queerly indeed they looked! Chanticleer himself, though stalking on two stilt-like legs, with the dignity of interminable descent in all his gestures, was hardly bigger than an ordinary partridge; his two wives were about the size of quails; and as for the one chicken, it looked small enough to be still in the egg, and, at the same time, sufficiently old, withered, wizened, and experienced, to have been the founder of the antiquated race. Instead of being the youngest of the family, it rather seemed to have aggregated into itself the ages, not only of these living specimens of the breed, but of all its fore-fathers and fore-mothers, whose united excellencies and oddities were squeezed into its little body. Its mother evidently regarded it as the one chicken of the world, and as necessary, in fact, to the world's continuance, or, at any rate, to the equilibrium of the present system of affairs, whether in church or state. No lesser sense of the infant fowl's importance could have justified, even in a mother's eyes, the perseverance with which she watched over its safety, ruffling her small person to twice its proper size, and flying in everybody's face that so much as looked towards her hopeful progeny. No lower estimate could have vindicated the indefatigable zeal with which she scratched, and her unscrupulousness in digging up the

5. Habitual drinkers of wine.
6. Pertaining to domestic fowls.

choicest flower or vegetable, for the sake of the fat earth-worm at its root. Her nervous cluck, when the chicken happened to be hidden in the long grass or under the squash-leaves; her gentle croak of satisfaction, while sure of it beneath her wing; her note of ill-concealed fear and obstreperous defiance, when she saw her arch-enemy, a neighbor's cat, on the top of the high fence;—one or other of these sounds was to be heard at almost every moment of the day. By degrees, the observer came to feel nearly as much interest in this chicken of illustrious race, as the mother-hen did.

Phoebe, after getting well acquainted with the old hen, was sometimes permitted to take the chicken in her hand, which was quite capable of grasping its cubic inch or two of body. While she curiously examined its hereditary marks—the peculiar speckle of its plumage, the funny tuft on its head, and a knob on each of its legs—the little biped, as she insisted, kept giving her a sagacious wink. The Daguerreotypist once whispered her, that these marks betokened the oddities of the Pyncheon family, and that the chicken itself was a symbol of the life of the old house; embodying its interpretation, likewise, although an unintelligible one, as such clues generally are. It was a feathered riddle; a mystery hatched out of an egg, and just as mysterious as if the egg had been addle![7]

The second of Chanticleer's two wives, ever since Phoebe's arrival, had been in a state of heavy despondency, caused, as it afterwards appeared, by her inability to lay an egg. One day, however, by her self-important gait, the sideway turn of her head, and the cock of her eye, as she pried into one and another nook of the garden—croaking to herself, all the while, with inexpressible complacency—it was made evident that this identical hen, much as mankind undervalued her, carried something about her person, the worth of which was not to be estimated either in gold or precious stones. Shortly after, there was a prodigious cackling and gratulation[8] of Chanticleer and all his family, including the wizened chicken, who appeared to understand the matter, quite as well as did his sire, his mother, or his aunt. That afternoon, Phoebe found a diminutive egg—not in the regular nest—it was far too precious to be trusted there—but cunningly hidden under the currant-bushes, on some dry stalks of last year's grass. Hepzibah, on learning the fact, took possession of the egg and appropriated it to Clifford's breakfast, on account of a certain delicacy of flavor, for which, as she affirmed, these eggs had always been famous. Thus unscrupulously did the old gentlewoman sacrifice the continuance, perhaps, of an ancient feathered race, with no better end than to supply her brother with

7. Spoiled.
8. Congratulations.

a dainty that hardly filled the bowl of a teaspoon! It must have been in reference to this outrage, that Chanticleer, the next day, accompanied by the bereaved mother of the egg, took his post in front of Phoebe and Clifford, and delivered himself of a harangue that might have proved as long as his own pedigree, but for a fit of merriment on Phoebe's part. Hereupon, the offended fowl stalked away on his long stilts, and utterly withdrew his notice from Phoebe and the rest of human nature; until she made her peace with an offering of spice-cake, which, next to snails, was the delicacy most in favor with his aristocratic taste.

We linger too long, no doubt, beside this paltry rivulet of life that flowed through the garden of the Pyncheon-house. But we deem it pardonable to record these mean incidents, and poor delights, because they proved so greatly to Clifford's benefit. They had the earth-smell in them, and contributed to give him health and substance. Some of his occupations wrought less desirably upon him. He had a singular propensity, for example, to hang over Maule's Well, and look at the constantly shifting phantasmagoria of figures, produced by the agitation of the water over the mosaic-work of colored pebbles, at the bottom. He said that faces looked upward to him there—beautiful faces, arrayed in bewitching smiles—each momentary face so fair and rosy, and every smile so sunny, that he felt wronged at its departure, until the same flitting witchcraft made a new one. But sometimes he would suddenly cry out—"The dark face gazes at me!"—and be miserable, the whole day afterwards. Phoebe, when she hung over the fountain by Clifford's side, could see nothing of all this—neither the beauty nor the ugliness—but only the colored pebbles, looking as if the gush of the water shook and disarranged them. And the dark face, that so troubled Clifford, was no more than the shadow, thrown from a branch of one of the damson-trees,[9] and breaking the inner light of Maule's Well. The truth was, however, that his fancy—reviving faster than his will and judgement, and always stronger than they—created shapes of loveliness that were symbolic of his native character, and now and then a stern and dreadful shape, that typified his fate.

On Sundays, after Phoebe had been at church—for the girl had a church-going conscience, and would hardly have been at ease, had she missed either prayer, singing, sermon, or benediction—after church-time, therefore, there was ordinarily a sober little festival in the garden. In addition to Clifford, Hepzibah, and Phoebe, two guests made up the company. One was the artist, Holgrave, who, in spite of his consociation with reformers, and his other queer and questionable traits, continued to hold an elevated place in Hep-

9. Variety of plum tree.

zibah's regard. The other, we are almost ashamed to say, was the
venerable Uncle Venner, in a clean shirt, and a broadcloth coat,
more respectable than his ordinary wear; inasmuch as it was neatly
patched on each elbow, and might be called an entire garment, except for a slight inequality in the length of its skirts. Clifford, on
several occasions, had seemed to enjoy the old man's intercourse,
for the sake of his mellow, cheerful vein, which was like the sweet
flavor of a frost-bitten apple, such as one picks up under the tree,
in December. A man, at the very lowest point of the social scale,
was easier and more agreeable for the fallen gentleman to encounter, than a person at any of the intermediate degrees; and,
moreover, as Clifford's young manhood had been lost, he was fond
of feeling himself comparatively youthful, now, in apposition with
the patriarchal age of Uncle Venner. In fact, it was sometimes observable, that Clifford half wilfully hid from himself the consciousness of being stricken in years, and cherished visions of an earthly
future still before him; visions, however, too indistinctly drawn to
be followed by disappointment—though, doubtless, by depression—when any casual incident or recollection made him sensible
of the withered leaf.

So this oddly composed little social party used to assemble under
the ruinous arbor. Hepzibah—stately as ever, at heart, and yielding
not an inch of her old gentility, but resting upon it so much the
more, as justifying a princesslike condescension—exhibited a not
ungraceful hospitality. She talked kindly to the vagrant artist, and
took sage counsel, lady as she was, with the wood-sawyer, the messenger of everybody's petty errands, the patched philosopher. And
Uncle Venner, who had studied the world at street-corners, and at
other posts equally well adapted for just observation, was as ready
to give out his wisdom as a town-pump to give water.

"Miss Hepzibah, Ma'am," said he once, after they had all been
cheerful together, "I really enjoy these quiet little meetings, of a
Sabbath afternoon. They are very much like what I expect to have,
after I retire to my farm!"

"Uncle Venner," observed Clifford, in a drowsy, inward tone, "is
always talking about his farm. But I have a better scheme for him,
by-and-by. We shall see!"

"Ah, Mr. Clifford Pyncheon," said the man of patches, "you may
scheme for me as much as you please; but I'm not going to give up
this one scheme of my own, even if I never bring it really to pass. It
does seem to me that men make a wonderful mistake in trying to
heap up property upon property. If I had done so, I should feel as if
Providence was not bound to take care of me; and, at all events, the
city wouldn't be! I'm one of those people who think that Infinity is
big enough for us all—and Eternity long enough!"

"Why, so they are, Uncle Venner," remarked Phoebe after a pause; for she had been trying to fathom the profundity and appositeness of this concluding apothegm. "But, for this short life of ours, one would like a house and a moderate garden-spot of one's own."

"It appears to me," said the Daguerreotypist smiling, "that Uncle Venner has the principles of Fourier[1] at the bottom of his wisdom; only they have not quite so much distinctness, in his mind, as in that of the systematizing Frenchman."

"Come, Phoebe," said Hepzibah, "it is time to bring the currants."

And then, while the yellow richness of the declining sunshine still fell into the open space of the garden, Phoebe brought out a loaf of bread, and a China bowl of currants, freshly gathered from the bushes, and crushed with sugar. These, with water—but not from the fountain of ill-omen, close at hand—constituted all the entertainment. Meanwhile, Holgrave took some pains to establish an intercourse with Clifford; actuated, it might seem, entirely by an impulse of kindliness, in order that the present hour might be cheerfuller than most which the poor recluse had spent, or was destined yet to spend. Nevertheless, in the artist's deep, thoughtful, all-observant eyes, there was now-and-then an expression, not sinister, but questionable; as if he had some other interest in the scene than a stranger, a youthful and unconnected adventurer, might be supposed to have. With great mobility of outward mood, however, he applied himself to the task of enlivening the party, and with so much success, that even dark-hued Hepzibah threw off one tint of melancholy, and made what shift she could with the remaining portion. Phoebe said to herself—"How pleasant he can be!" As for Uncle Venner, as a mark of friendship and approbation, he readily consented to afford the young man his countenance in the way of his profession—not metaphorically, be it understood—but literally, by allowing a daguerreotype of his face, so familiar to the town, to be exhibited at the entrance of Holgrave's studio.

Clifford, as the company partook of their little banquet, grew to be the gayest of them all. Either it was one of those up-quivering flashes of the spirit, to which minds in an abnormal state are liable; or else the artist had subtly touched some chord that made musical vibration. Indeed, what with the pleasant summer-evening, and the

---

1. The French social theorist Charles Fourier (1772–1837) sought to reorganize society into communitarian subunits housed in buildings that he termed "phalansteries." His ideas, based on mystical concepts of social and natural harmony and on pre-Marxist notions of class conflict, had an important influence on American socialistic thinking during the 1840s and were taken up at Brook Farm shortly after Hawthorne left the experimental community in 1841. In *The Blithedale Romance*, Hawthorne questions some of Fourier's more radical notions, such as his encouragement of the free expression of sexual passion.

sympathy of this little circle of not unkindly souls, it was perhaps natural that a character so susceptible as Clifford's should become animated, and show itself readily responsive to what was said around him. But he gave out his own thoughts, likewise, with an airy and fanciful glow; so that they glistened, as it were, through the arbor, and made their escape among the interstices of the foliage. He had been as cheerful, no doubt, while alone with Phoebe, but never with such tokens of acute, although partial intelligence.

But, as the sunlight left the peaks of the seven gables, so did the excitement fade out of Clifford's eyes. He gazed vaguely and mournfully about him, as if he missed something precious, and missed it the more drearily for not knowing precisely what it was.

"I want my happiness!" at last he murmured hoarsely and indistinctly, hardly shaping out the words. "Many, many years have I waited for it! It is late! It is late! I want my happiness!"

Alas, poor Clifford! You are old, and worn with troubles that ought never to have befallen you. You are partly crazy, and partly imbecile; a ruin, a failure, as almost everybody is—though some in less degree, or less perceptibly, than their fellows. Fate has no happiness in store for you; unless your quiet home in the old family residence, with the faithful Hepzibah, and your long summer-afternoons with Phoebe, and these Sabbath festivals with Uncle Venner and the Daguerreotypist, deserve to be called happiness! Why not? If not the thing itself, it is marvellously like it, and the more so for that ethereal and intangible quality, which causes it all to vanish, at too close an introspection. Take it, therefore, while you may. Murmur not—question not—but make the most of it!

XI. The Arched Window

From the inertness, or what we may term the vegetative character of his ordinary mood, Clifford would perhaps have been content to spend one day after another, interminably—or, at least throughout the summer-time—in just the kind of life described in the preceding pages. Fancying, however, that it might be for his benefit occasionally to diversify the scene, Phoebe sometimes suggested that he should look out upon the life of the street. For this purpose, they used to mount the staircase together, to the second story of the house, where, at the termination of a wide entry, there was an arched window of uncommonly large dimensions, shaded by a pair of curtains. It opened above the porch, where there had formerly been a balcony, the balustrade of which had long since gone to decay, and been removed. At this arched window, throwing it open, but keeping himself in comparative obscurity by means of the curtain, Clifford had an opportunity of witnessing such a portion of the great world's movement, as might be supposed to roll through one of the retired streets of a not very populous city. But he and Phoebe made a sight as well worth seeing as any that the city could exhibit. The pale, gray, childish, aged, melancholy, yet often simply cheerful, and sometimes delicately intelligent, aspect of Clifford, peering from behind the faded crimson of the curtain—watching the monotony of every-day occurrences with a kind of inconsequential interest and earnestness—and, at every petty throb of his sensibility, turning for sympathy to the eyes of the bright young girl!

If once he were fairly seated at the window, even Pyncheon-street would hardly be so dull and lonely but that, somewhere or other along its extent, Clifford might discover matter to occupy his eye, and titillate, if not engross, his observation. Things, familiar to the youngest child that had begun its outlook at existence, seemed strange to him. A cab; an omnibus, with its populous interior, dropping here-and-there a passenger, and picking up another, and thus typifying that vast rolling vehicle, the world, the end of whose journey is everywhere, and nowhere;—these objects he followed eagerly with his eyes, but forgot them, before the dust, raised by the horses and wheels, had settled along their track. As regarded novelties, (among which, cabs and omnibusses were to be reckoned,) his mind appeared to have lost its proper gripe and retentiveness. Twice or thrice, for example, during the sunny hours of the day, a water-cart went along by the Pyncheon-house, leaving a broad wake of moistened earth, instead of the white dust that had risen at a lady's lightest footfall; it was like a summer-shower, which the city-authorities had caught and tamed, and compelled it into the commonest routine of their convenience. With the water-cart Clifford could never grow familiar; it always affected him with just the same surprise as at first. His mind took an apparently sharp impression from it, but lost the recollection of this perambulatory shower, before its next re-appearance, as completely as did the street itself, along which the heat so quickly strewed white dust again. It was the same with the railroad. Clifford could hear the obstreperous howl of the steam-devil, and, by leaning a little way from the arched window, could catch a glimpse of the trains of cars, flashing a brief transit across the extremity of the street. The idea of terrible energy, thus forced upon him, was new at every recurrence, and seemed to affect him as disagreeably, and with almost as much surprise, the hundredth time as the first.

Nothing gives a sadder sense of decay, than this loss or suspension of the power to deal with unaccustomed things and to keep up with the swiftness of the passing moment. It can merely be a suspended animation; for, were the power actually to perish, there would be little use of immortality. We are less than ghosts, for the time being, whenever this calamity befalls us.

Clifford was indeed the most inveterate of conservatives. All the antique fashions of the street were dear to him; even such as were characterized by a rudeness that would naturally have annoyed his fastidious senses. He loved the old rumbling and jolting carts, the former track of which he still found in his long-buried remembrance, as the observer of to-day finds the wheel-tracks of ancient vehicles, in Herculaneum.[2] The butcher's cart, with its snowy canopy, was an acceptable object; so was the fish-cart, heralded by its horn; so, likewise, was the countryman's cart of vegetables, plodding from door to door, with long pauses of the patient horse, while his owner drove a trade in turnips, carrots, summer-squashes, string-beans, green peas, and new potatoes, with half the housewives of the neighborhood. The baker's cart, with the harsh music of its bells, had a pleasant effect on Clifford, because, as few things else did, it jingled the very dissonance of yore. One afternoon, a scissor-grinder chanced to set his wheel a-going, under the Pyncheon-elm, and just in front of the arched window. Children came running with their mothers' scissors, or the carving-knife, or the paternal razor, or anything else that lacked an edge, (except, indeed, poor Clifford's wits,) that the grinder might apply the article to his magic wheel, and give it back as good as new. Round went the busily revolving machinery, kept in motion by the scissor-grinder's foot, and wore away the hard steel against the hard stone, whence issued an intense and spiteful prolongation of a hiss, as fierce as those emitted by Satan and his compeers in Pandemonium,[3] though squeezed into smaller compass. It was an ugly, little, venomous serpent of a noise, as ever did petty violence to human ears. But Clifford listened with rapturous delight. The sound, however disagreeable, had very brisk life in it, and, together with the circle of curious children, watching the revolutions of the wheel, appeared to give him a more vivid sense of active, bustling, and sunshiny existence, than he had attained in almost any other way. Nevertheless, its charm lay chiefly in the past; for the scissor-grinder's wheel had hissed in his childish ears.

He sometimes made doleful complaint, that there were no stage-coaches, now-a-days. And he asked, in an injured tone, what had become of all those old square-top chaises, with wings sticking out

---

2. A city in southern Italy destroyed along with Pompeii by the eruption of Mount Vesuvius in 79 C.E. The city was discovered in the early decades of the eighteenth century, and excavations were ongoing during the nineteenth century.
3. The capital of Hell, as described by John Milton (1608–1674) in Book X of *Paradise Lost* (1667). Hawthorne alludes to the moment when, just as Satan boasts of his victory over Adam and Eve, God transforms Satan and his fellow fallen angels into snakes, and "dreadful was the din / Of hissing through the hall" (X.521–22).

on either side, that used to be drawn by a plough-horse, and driven by a farmer's wife and daughter, peddling whortle-berries and black-berries about the town. Their disappearance made him doubt, he said, whether the berries had not left off growing in the broad pastures, and along the shady country-lanes.

But anything that appealed to the sense of beauty, in however humble a way, did not require to be recommended by these old associations. This was observable, when one of those Italian boys (who are rather a modern feature of our streets) came along, with his barrel-organ,[4] and stopt under the wide and cool shadows of the elm. With his quick professional eye, he took note of the two faces watching him from the arched window, and, opening his instrument, began to scatter its melodies abroad. He had a monkey on his shoulder, dressed in a highland plaid;[5] and, to complete the sum of splendid attractions wherewith he presented himself to the public, there was a company of little figures, whose sphere and habitation was in the mahogany case of his organ, and whose principle of life was the music, which the Italian made it his business to grind out. In all their variety of occupation—the cobbler, the blacksmith, the soldier, the lady with her fan, the toper[6] with his bottle, the milk-maid sitting by her cow—this fortunate little society might truly be said to enjoy a harmonious existence, and to make life literally a dance. The Italian turned a crank; and, behold! every one of these small individuals started into the most curious vivacity. The cobbler wrought upon a shoe; the blacksmith hammered his iron; the soldier waved his glittering blade; the lady raised a tiny breeze with her fan; the jolly toper swigged lustily at his bottle; a scholar opened his book, with eager thirst for knowledge, and turned his head to-and-fro along the page; the milk-maid energetically drained her cow; and a miser counted gold into his strong-box;—all at the same turning of a crank. Yes; and moved by the self-same impulse, a lover saluted his mistress on her lips! Possibly, some cynic, at once merry and bitter, had desired to signify, in this pantomimic scene, that we mortals, whatever our business or amusement— however serious, however trifling—all dance to one identical tune, and, in spite of our ridiculous activity, bring nothing finally to pass. For the most remarkable aspect of the affair was, that, at the cessation of the music, everybody was petrified at once, from the most extravagant life into a dead torpor. Neither was the cobbler's shoe finished, nor the blacksmith's iron shaped out; nor was there a drop less of brandy in the toper's bottle, nor a drop more of milk in the milk-maid's pail, nor one additional coin in the miser's strong-box;

4. A portable organ played by turning a crank.
5. Patterned cloth worn by Scottish highlanders.
6. Drunkard.

nor was the scholar a page deeper in his book. All were precisely in the same condition as before they made themselves so ridiculous by their haste to toil, to enjoy, to accumulate gold, and to become wise. Saddest of all, moreover, the lover was none the happier for the maiden's granted kiss! But, rather than swallow this last too acrid ingredient, we reject the whole moral of the show.

The monkey, meanwhile, with a thick tail curling out into preposterous prolixity from beneath his tartans, took his station at the Italian's feet. He turned a wrinkled and abominable little visage to every passer-by, and to the circle of children that soon gathered round, and to Hepzibah's shop-door, and upward to the arched window, whence Phoebe and Clifford were looking down. Every moment, also, he took off his highland bonnet, and performed a bow and scrape. Sometimes, moreover, he made personal application to individuals, holding out his small black palm, and otherwise plainly signifying his excessive desire for whatever filthy lucre might happen to be in anybody's pocket. The mean and low, yet strangely man-like expression of his wilted countenance; the prying and crafty glance, that showed him ready to gripe at every miserable advantage; his enormous tail, (too enormous to be decently concealed under his gabardine,) and the deviltry of nature which it betokened;—take this monkey just as he was, in short, and you could desire no better image of the Mammon[7] of copper-coin, symbolizing the grossest form of the love of money. Neither was there any possibility of satisfying the covetous little devil. Phoebe threw down a whole handfull of cents, which he picked up with joyless eagerness, handed them over to the Italian for safe-keeping, and immediately re-commenced a series of pantomimic petitions for more.

Doubtless, more than one New-Englander—or let him be of what country he might, it is as likely to be the case—passed by, and threw a look at the monkey, and went on, without imagining how nearly his own moral condition was here exemplified. Clifford, however, was a being of another order. He had taken childish delight in the music, and smiled, too, at the figures which it set in motion. But, after looking awhile at the long-tailed imp, he was so shocked by his horrible ugliness, spiritual as well as physical, that he actually began to shed tears; a weakness which men of merely delicate endowments—and destitute of the fiercer, deeper, and more tragic power of laughter—can hardly avoid, when the worst and meanest aspect of life happens to be presented to them.

7. The personification of greed. In a notebook entry of October 11, 1845, an important source for this passage, Hawthorne similarly described an organ-grinder's monkey he had observed in Boston: "With his tail and all, he might be taken for the Mammon of copper coin—a symbol of covetousness of small gains, the lowest form of the love of money" (*The American Notebooks* [1972], 271). "Gabardine": a long, loose coat with a twill weave.

Pyncheon-street was sometimes enlivened by spectacles of more imposing pretensions than the above, and which brought the multitude along with them. With a shivering repugnance at the idea of personal contact with the world, a powerful impulse still seized on Clifford, whenever the rush and roar of the human tide grew strongly audible to him. This was made evident, one day, when a political procession, with hundreds of flaunting banners, and drums, fifes, clarions, and cymbals, reverberating between the rows of buildings, marched all through town, and trailed its length of trampling footsteps, and most infrequent uproar, past the ordinarily quiet House of the Seven Gables. As a mere object of sight, nothing is more deficient in picturesque features than a procession, seen in its passage through narrow streets. The spectator feels it to be fool's play, when he can distinguish the tedious common-place of each man's visage, with the perspiration and weary self-importance on it, and the very cut of his pantaloons, and the stiffness or laxity of his shirt-collar, and the dust on the back of his black coat. In order to become majestic, it should be viewed from some vantage-point, as it rolls its slow and long array through the centre of a wide plain, or the stateliest public square of a city; for then, by its remoteness, it melts all the petty personalities, of which it is made up, into one broad mass of existence—one great life—one collected body of mankind, with a vast, homogeneous spirit animating it. But, on the other hand, if an impressible person, standing alone over the brink of one of these processions, should behold it, not in its atoms, but in its aggregate—as a mighty river of life, massive in its tide, and black with mystery, and, out of its depths, calling to the kindred depth within him—then the contiguity would add to the effect. It might so fascinate him, that he would hardly be restrained from plunging into the surging stream of human sympathies.

So it proved with Clifford. He shuddered; he grew pale, he threw an appealing look at Hepzibah and Phoebe, who were with him at the window. They comprehended nothing of his emotions, and supposed him merely disturbed by the unaccustomed tumult. At last, with tremulous limbs, he started up, set his foot on the window-sill, and, in an instant more, would have been in the unguarded balcony. As it was, the whole procession might have seen him, a wild, haggard figure, his gray locks floating in the wind that waved their banners; a lonely being, estranged from his race, but now feeling himself man again, by virtue of the irrepressible instinct that possessed him. Had Clifford attained the balcony, he would probably have leaped into the street; but whether impelled by the species of terror, that sometimes urges its victim over the very precipice which he shrinks from, or by a natural magnetism, tending towards the great centre of humanity—it were not easy to decide. Both impulses might have wrought on him at once.

But his companions, affrighted by his gesture—which was that of a man hurried away, in spite of himself—seized Clifford's garment and held him back. Hepzibah shrieked. Phoebe, to whom all extravagance was a horror, burst into sobs and tears.

"Clifford, Clifford, are you crazy?" cried his sister.

"I hardly know, Hepzibah!" said Clifford, drawing a long breath. "Fear nothing—it is over now—but had I taken that plunge, and survived it, methinks it would have made me another man!"

Possibly, in some sense, Clifford may have been right. He needed a shock; or perhaps he required to take a deep, deep plunge into the ocean of human life, and to sink down and be covered by its profoundness, and then to emerge, sobered, invigorated, restored to the world and to himself. Perhaps, again, he required nothing less than the great final remedy—death!

A similar yearning to renew the broken links of brotherhood with his kind sometimes showed itself in a milder form; and once it was made beautiful by the religion that lay even deeper than itself. In the incident now to be sketched, there was a touching recognition, on Clifford's part, of God's care and love towards him—towards this poor, forsaken man, who, if any mortal could, might have been pardoned for regarding himself as thrown aside, forgotten, and left to be the sport of some fiend, whose playfulness was an ecstacy of mischief.

It was the Sabbath morning; one of those bright, calm Sabbaths, with its own hallowed atmosphere, when Heaven seems to diffuse itself over the earth's face in a solemn smile, no less sweet than solemn. On such a Sabbath morn, were we pure enough to be its medium, we should be conscious of the earth's natural worship ascending through our frames, on whatever spot of ground we stood. The church-bells, with various tones, but all in harmony, were calling out, and responding to one another—"It is the Sabbath!—The Sabbath!—Yea; the Sabbath!"—and over the whole city, the bells scattered the blessed sounds, now slowly, now with livelier joy, now one bell alone, now all the bells together, crying earnestly—"It is the Sabbath!"—and flinging their accents afar off, to melt into the air, and pervade it with the holy word. The air, with God's sweetest and tenderest sunshine in it, was meet for mankind to breathe into their hearts, and send it forth again as the utterance of prayer.

Clifford sat at the window, with Hepzibah, watching the neighbors as they stept into the street. All of them, however unspiritual on other days, were transfigured by the Sabbath influence; so that their very garments—whether it were an old man's decent coat, well-brushed for the thousandth time, or a little boy's first sack and trowsers, finished yesterday by his mother's needle—had somewhat of the quality of ascension-robes.[8] Forth, likewise, from the portal of the old house, stept Phoebe, putting up her small, green sun-shade, and throwing upward a glance and smile of parting kindness to the faces at the arched window. In her aspect, there was a famil-iar gladness, and a holiness that you could play with, and yet rever-ence it as much as ever. She was like a prayer, offered up in the homeliest beauty of one's mother-tongue. Fresh was Phoebe, more-over, and airy and sweet in her apparel; as if nothing that she wore—neither her gown, nor her small straw bonnet, nor her little kerchief, any more than her snowy stockings—had ever been put on, before; or, if worn, were all the fresher for it, and with a fra-grance as if they had lain among the rosebuds.

The girl waved her hand to Hepzibah and Clifford, and went up the street; a Religion in herself, warm, simple, true, with a sub-stance that could walk on earth, and a spirit that was capable of Heaven.

"Hepzibah," asked Clifford, after watching Phoebe to the corner, "do you never go to church?"

"No, Clifford," she replied—"not these many, many years!"

"Were I to be there," he rejoined, "it seems to me that I could pray once more, when so many human souls were praying all around me!"

She looked into Clifford's face, and beheld there a soft, natural effusion; for his heart gushed out, as it were, and ran over at his eyes, in delightful reverence for God, and kindly affection for his human brethren. The emotion communicated itself to Hepzibah. She yearned to take him by the hand, and go and kneel down, they two together—both so long separate from the world, and, as she now recognized, scarcely friends with Him above—to kneel down among the people, and be reconciled to God and man at once.

"Dear brother," said she, earnestly, "let us go! We belong nowhere. We have not a foot of space, in any church, to kneel upon; but let us go to some place of worship, even if we stand in the broad aisle. Poor and forsaken as we are, some pew-door[9] will be opened to us!"

So Hepzibah and her brother made themselves ready—as ready as they could, in the best of their old-fashioned garments, which had hung on pegs, or been laid away in trunks, so long that the dampness and mouldy smell of the past was on them—made them-selves ready, in their faded bettermost, to go to church. They de-scended the staircase together, gaunt, sallow Hepzibah, and pale, emaciated, age-stricken Clifford! They pulled open the front-door,

8. Special robes for symbolically following Jesus Christ's ascent to heaven.
9. Some churches charged fees for entrance into pews or enclosed seats.

and stept across the threshold, and felt, both of them, as if they were standing in the presence of the whole world, and with mankind's great and terrible eye on them alone. The eye of their Father seemed to be withdrawn, and gave them no encouragement. The warm, sunny air of the street made them shiver. Their hearts quaked within them, at the idea of taking one step further.

"It cannot be, Hepzibah!—it is too late," said Clifford with deep sadness.—"We are ghosts! We have no right among human beings—no right anywhere, but in this old house, which has a curse on it, and which therefore we are doomed to haunt. And, besides," he continued, with a fastidious sensibility, inalienably characteristic of the man, "it would not be fit nor beautiful, to go! It is an ugly thought, that I should be frightful to my fellow-beings, and that children would cling to their mothers' gowns, at sight of me!"

They shrank back into the dusky passage-way, and closed the door. But, going up the staircase again, they found the whole interior of the house tenfold more dismal, and the air closer and heavier, for the glimpse and breath of freedom which they had just snatched. They could not flee; their jailor had but left the door ajar, in mockery, and stood behind it, to watch them stealing out. At the threshold, they felt his pitiless gripe upon them. For, what other dungeon is so dark as one's own heart! What jailor so inexorable as one's self!

But it would be no fair picture of Clifford's state of mind, were we to represent him as continually or prevailingly wretched. On the contrary, there was no other man in the city, we are bold to affirm, of so much as half his years, who enjoyed so many lightsome and griefless moments, as himself. He had no burthen of care upon him; there were none of those questions and contingencies with the future to be settled, which wear away all other lives, and render them not worth having by the very process of providing for their support. In this respect, he was a child; a child for the whole term of his existence, be it long or short. Indeed, his life seemed to be standing still at a period little in advance of childhood, and to cluster all its reminiscences about that epoch; just as, after the torpor of a heavy blow, the sufferer's reviving consciousness goes back to a moment considerably behind the accident that stupefied him. He sometimes told Phoebe and Hepzibah his dreams, in which he invariably played the part of a child, or a very young man. So vivid were they, in his relation of them, that he once held a dispute with his sister as to the particular figure or print of a chintz morning-dress, which he had seen their mother wear, in the dream of the preceding night. Hepzibah, piquing herself on a woman's accuracy in such matters, held it to be slightly different from what Clifford described; but, producing the very gown from an old trunk, it proved to be identical with his remembrance of it. Had Clifford, every time that he emerged out of dreams so lifelike, undergone the torture of transformation from a boy into an old and broken man, the daily recurrence of the shock would have been too much to bear. It would have caused an acute agony to thrill, from the morning twilight, all the day through, until bedtime, and even then would have mingled a dull, inscrutable pain, and pallid hue of misfortune, with the visionary bloom and adolescence of his slumber. But the nightly moonshine interwove itself with the morning mist, and enveloped him as in a robe, which he hugged about his person, and seldom let realities pierce through; he was not often quite awake, but slept open-eyed, and perhaps fancied himself most dreaming, then.

Thus, lingering always so near his childhood, he had sympathies with children, and kept his heart the fresher thereby, like a reservoir into which rivulets come pouring, not far from the fountain-head. Though prevented, by a subtle sense of propriety, from desiring to associate with them, he loved few things better than to look out of the arched window, and see a little girl, driving her hoop along the sidewalk, or schoolboys at a game of ball. Their voices, also, were very pleasant to him, heard at a distance, all swarming and intermingling together, as flies do in a sunny room.

Clifford would doubtless have been glad to share their sports. One afternoon, he was seized with an irresistible desire to blow soap-bubbles; an amusement, as Hepzibah told Phoebe apart, that had been a favorite one with her brother, when they were both children. Behold him, therefore, at the arched window, with an earthen pipe in his mouth! Behold him, with his gray hair, and a wan, unreal smile over his countenance, where still hovered a beautiful grace, which his worst enemy must have acknowledged to be spiritual and immortal, since it had survived so long! Behold him, scattering airy spheres abroad, from the window into the street! Little, impalpable worlds, were those soap-bubbles, with the big world depicted, in hues bright as imagination, on the nothing of their surface. It was curious to see how the passers-by regarded these brilliant fantasies, as they came floating down, and made the dull atmosphere imaginative, about them. Some stopt to gaze, and perhaps carried a pleasant recollection of the bubbles, onward, as far as the street-corner; some looked angrily upward, as if poor Clifford wronged them, by setting an image of beauty afloat so near their dusty pathway. A great many put out their fingers, or their walking-sticks, to touch withal, and were perversely gratified, no doubt, when the bubble, with all its pictured earth and sky scene, vanished as if it had never been.

At length, just as an elderly gentleman of very dignified presence happened to be passing, a large bubble sailed majestically down, and burst right against his nose! He looked up—at first with a stern, keen glance, which penetrated at once into the obscurity behind the arched window—then with a smile, which might be conceived as diffusing a dog-day sultriness for the space of several yards about him.

"Aha, Cousin Clifford!" cried Judge Pyncheon. "What! Still blowing soap-bubbles!"

The tone seemed as if meant to be kind and soothing, but yet had a bitterness of sarcasm in it. As for Clifford, an absolute palsy of fear came over him. Apart from any definite cause of dread, which his past experience might have given him, he felt that native and original horror of the excellent Judge, which is proper to a weak, delicate, and apprehensive character, in the presence of massive strength. Strength is incomprehensible by weakness, and therefore the more terrible. There is no greater bugbear[1] than a strong-willed relative, in the circle of his own connections.

XII. The Daguerreotypist

It must not be supposed that the life of a personage, naturally so active as Phoebe, could be wholly confined within the precincts of the old Pyncheon-house. Clifford's demands upon her time were usually satisfied, in those long days, considerably earlier than sunset. Quiet as his daily existence seemed, it nevertheless drained all the resources by which he lived. It was not physical exercise that over-wearied him; for—except that he sometimes wrought a little with a hoe, or paced the garden-walk, or, in rainy weather, traversed a large, unoccupied room—it was his tendency to remain only too quiescent, as regarded any toil of the limbs and muscles. But either there was a smouldering fire within him, that consumed his vital energy, or the monotony, that would have dragged itself with benumbing effect over a mind differently situated, was no monotony to Clifford. Possibly, he was in a state of second growth and recovery, and was constantly assimilating nutriment for his spirit and intellect from sights, sounds, and events, which passed as a perfect void to persons more practised with the world. As all is activity and vicissitude to the new mind of a child, so might it be, likewise, to a mind that had undergone a kind of new creation, after its long-suspended life.

Be the cause what it might, Clifford commonly retired to rest, thoroughly exhausted, while the sunbeams were still melting

---

1. A source of fear, typically overstated or imaginary.

through his window-curtains, or were thrown with late lustre on the chamber-wall. And while he thus slept early, as other children do, and dreamed of childhood, Phoebe was free to follow her own tastes for the remainder of the day and evening.

This was a freedom essential to the health even of a character so little susceptible of morbid influences as that of Phoebe. The old house, as we have already said, had both the dry-rot and the damp-rot in its walls; it was not good to breathe no other atmosphere than that. Hepzibah, though she had her valuable and redeeming traits, had grown to be a kind of lunatic, by imprisoning herself so long in one place, with no other company than a single series of ideas, and but one affection, and one bitter sense of wrong. Clifford, the reader may perhaps imagine, was too inert to operate morally on his fellow-creatures, however intimate and exclusive their relations with him. But the sympathy or magnetism among human beings is more subtle and universal, than we think; it exists, indeed, among different classes of organized life, and vibrates from one to another. A flower, for instance, as Phoebe herself observed, always began to droop sooner in Clifford's hand, or Hepzibah's, than in her own; and by the same law, converting her whole daily life into a flower-fragrance for these two sickly spirits, the blooming girl must inevitably droop and fade, much sooner than if worn on a younger and happier breast. Unless she had now and then indulged her brisk impulses, and breathed rural air in a suburban walk, or ocean-breezes along the shore—had occasionally obeyed the impulse of nature, in New England girls, by attending a metaphysical or philosophical lecture, or viewing a seven-mile panorama,[2] or listening to a concert—had gone shopping about the city, ransacking entire depots of splendid merchandize, and bringing home a ribbon—had enjoyed, likewise, a little time to read the Bible in her chamber, and had stolen a little more, to think of her mother and her native place—unless for such moral medicines as the above, we should soon have beheld our poor Phoebe grow thin, and put on a bleached, unwholesome aspect, and assume strange, shy ways, prophetic of old-maidenhood and a cheerless future.

Even as it was, a change grew visible; a change partly to be regretted, although whatever charm it infringed upon was repaired by another, perhaps more precious. She was not so constantly gay, but had her moods of thought, which Clifford, on the whole, liked better than her former phase of unmingled cheerfulness; because now she understood him better and more delicately, and sometimes even interpreted him to himself. Her eyes looked larger, and darker,

2. A series of pictures on a canvas that was unrolled for viewers. The panorama was a popular form of entertainment during the antebellum period.

and deeper; so deep, at some silent moments, that they seemed like Artesian wells,[3] down, down, into the infinite. She was less girlish than when we first beheld her, alighting from the omnibus; less girlish, but more a woman!

The only youthful mind, with which Phoebe had an opportunity of frequent intercourse, was that of the Daguerreotypist. Inevitably, by the pressure of the seclusion about them, they had been brought into habits of some familiarity. Had they met under different circumstances, neither of these young persons would have been likely to bestow much thought upon the other; unless, indeed, their extreme dissimilarity should have proved a principle of mutual attraction. Both, it is true, were characters proper to New England life, and possessing a common ground, therefore, in their more external developments; but as unlike, in their respective interiors, as if their native climes had been at world-wide distance. During the early part of their acquaintance, Phoebe had held back rather more than was customary with her frank and simple manners, from Holgrave's not very marked advances. Nor was she yet satisfied that she knew him well, although they almost daily met and talked together in a kind, friendly, and what seemed to be a familiar way.

The artist, in a desultory manner, had imparted to Phoebe something of his history. Young as he was, and had his career terminated at the point already attained, there had been enough of incident to fill, very creditably, an autobiographic volume. A romance on the plan of Gil Blas,[4] adapted to American society and manners, would cease to be a romance. The experience of many individuals among us, who think it hardly worth the telling, would equal the vicissitudes of the Spaniard's earlier life; while their ultimate success, or the point whither they tend, may be incomparably higher than any that a novelist would imagine for his hero. Holgrave, as he told Phoebe, somewhat proudly, could not boast of his origin, unless as being exceedingly humble, nor of his education, except that it had been the scantiest possible, and obtained by a few winter-months' attendance at a district-school. Left early to his own guidance, he had begun to be self-dependent while yet a boy; and it was a condition aptly suited to his natural force of will. Though now but twenty-two years old, (lacking some months, which are years, in such a life,) he had already been, first, a country-schoolmaster; next, a salesman in a country-store; and, either at the same time or afterwards, the political-editor of a country-newspaper. He had subsequently travelled New England and the middle states as a pedler, in the employment of a Connecticut manufactory of

3. Wells in which the water rises through the buildup of pressure.
4. The French picaresque novel *Gil Blas de Santillane* (1715–35), by Alain René Lesage (1668–1747), chronicles the adventures of an adaptable and crafty Spanish hero.

Cologne water and other essences. In an episodical way, he had studied and practised dentistry, and with very flattering success, especially in many of the factory-towns along our inland-streams. As a supernumerary official, of some kind or other, aboard a packet-ship,[5] he had visited Europe, and found means, before his return, to see Italy, and part of France and Germany. At a later period, he had spent some months in a community of Fourierists.[6] Still more recently, he had been a public lecturer on Mesmerism, for which science (as he assured Phoebe, and, indeed, satisfactorily proved by putting Chanticleer, who happened to be scratching, near by, to sleep) he had very remarkable endowments.

His present phase, as a Daguerreotypist, was of no more importance in his own view, nor likely to be more permanent, than any of the preceding ones. It had been taken up with the careless alacrity of an adventurer, who had his bread to earn; it would be thrown aside as carelessly, whenever he should choose to earn his bread by some other equally digressive means. But what was most remarkable, and perhaps showed a more than common poise in the young man, was the fact, that, amid all these personal vicissitudes, he had never lost his identity. Homeless as he had been—continually changing his whereabout, and therefore responsible neither to public opinion nor to individuals—putting off one exterior, and snatching up another, to be soon shifted for a third—he had never violated the innermost man, but had carried his conscience along with him. It was impossible to know Holgrave, without recognizing this to be the fact. Hepzibah had seen it. Phoebe soon saw it, likewise, and gave him the sort of confidence which such a certainty inspires. She was startled, however, and sometimes repelled—not by any doubt of his integrity to whatever law he acknowledged—but by a sense that his law differed from her own. He made her uneasy, and seemed to unsettle everything around her, by his lack of reverence for what was fixed; unless, at a moment's warning, it could establish its right to hold its ground.

Then, moreover, she scarcely thought him affectionate in his nature. He was too calm and cool an observer. Phoebe felt his eye, often; his heart, seldom or never. He took a certain kind of interest in Hepzibah and her brother, and Phoebe herself; he studied them attentively, and allowed no slightest circumstance of their individualities to escape him; he was ready to do them whatever good he might;—but, after all, he never exactly made common cause with them, nor gave any reliable evidence that he loved them better, in proportion as he knew them more. In his relations with them, he

5. A ship carrying mail and passengers along a fixed route.
6. In 1841, Hawthorne had spent seven months at Brook Farm, which was influenced by Fourierism (see n. 1, p. 112).

seemed to be in quest of mental food; not heart-sustenance. Phoebe could not conceive what interested him so much in her friends and herself, intellectually, since he cared nothing for them, or comparatively so little, as objects of human affection.

Always, in his interviews with Phoebe, the artist made especial inquiry as to the welfare of Clifford, whom, except at the Sunday festival, he seldom saw.

"Does he still seem happy?" he asked, one day.

"As happy as a child," answered Phoebe, "but—like a child, too—very easily disturbed."

"How disturbed?" inquired Holgrave.—"By things without?—or by thoughts within?"

"I cannot see his thoughts!—How should I?" replied Phoebe, with simple piquancy.—"Very often, his humor changes without any reason that can be guessed at, just as a cloud comes over the sun. Latterly, since I have begun to know him better, I feel it to be not quite right to look closely into his moods. He has had such a great sorrow, that his heart is made all solemn and sacred by it. When he is cheerful—when the sun shines into his mind—then I venture to peep in, just as far as the light reaches, but no farther. It is holy ground where the shadow falls!"

"How prettily you express this sentiment!" said the artist. "I can understand the feeling, without possessing it. Had I your opportunities, no scruples would prevent me from fathoming Clifford to the full depth of my plummet-line!"[7]

"How strange that you should wish it!" remarked Phoebe involuntarily. "What is Cousin Clifford to you?"

"Oh, nothing, of course, nothing!" answered Holgrave with a smile. "Only this is such an odd and incomprehensible world! The more I look at it, the more it puzzles me; and I begin to suspect that a man's bewilderment is the measure of his wisdom. Men and women, and children, too, are such strange creatures, that one never can be certain that he really knows them; nor ever guess what they have been, from what he sees them to be, now. Judge Pyncheon! Clifford! What a complex riddle—a complexity of complexities—do they present! It requires intuitive sympathy, like a young girl's, to solve it. A mere observer, like myself, (who never have any intuitions, and am, at best, only subtile and acute,) is pretty certain to go astray."

The artist now turned the conversation to themes less dark than that which they had touched upon. Phoebe and he were young together; nor had Holgrave, in his premature experience of life, wasted entirely that beautiful spirit of youth, which, gushing forth

7. Weighted line used to measure nautical depths.

from one small heart and fancy, may diffuse itself over the universe, making it all as bright as on the first day of creation. Man's own youth is the world's youth; at least, he feels as if it were, and imagines that the earth's granite substance is something not yet hardened, and which he can mould into whatever shape he likes. So it was with Holgrave. He could talk sagely about the world's old age, but never actually believed in what he said; he was a young man still, and therefore looked upon the world—that gray-bearded and wrinkled profligate, decrepit, without being venerable—as a tender stripling, capable of being improved into all that it ought to be, but scarcely yet had shown the remotest promise of becoming. He had that sense, or inward prophecy—which a young man had better never have been born, than not to have, and a mature man had better die at once, than utterly to relinquish—that we are not doomed to creep on forever in the old, bad way, but that, this very now, there are the harbingers abroad of a golden era, to be accomplished in his own lifetime. It seemed to Holgrave—as doubtless it has seemed to the hopeful of every century, since the epoch of Adam's grandchildren—that in this age, more than ever before, the moss-grown and rotten Past is to be torn down, and lifeless institutions to be thrust out of the way, and their dead corpses buried, and everything to begin anew.

As to the main point—may we never live to doubt it!—as to the better centuries that are coming, the artist was surely right. His error lay, in supposing that this age, more than any past or future one, is destined to see the tattered garments of Antiquity exchanged for a new suit, instead of gradually renewing themselves by patchwork; in applying his own little life-span as the measure of an interminable achievement; and, more than all, in fancying that it mattered anything to the great end in view, whether he himself should contend for it or against it. Yet it was well for him to think so. This enthusiasm, infusing itself through the calmness of his character, and thus taking an aspect of settled thought and wisdom, would serve to keep his youth pure, and make his aspirations high. And when, with the years settling down more weightily upon him, his early faith should be modified by inevitable experience, it would be with no harsh and sudden revolution of his sentiments. He would still have faith in man's brightening destiny, and perhaps love him all the better, as he should recognize his helplessness in his own behalf; and the haughty faith, with which he began life, would be well bartered for a far humbler one, at its close, in discerning that man's best-directed effort accomplishes a kind of dream, while God is the sole worker of realities.

Holgrave had read very little, and that little, in passing through the thoroughfare of life, where the mystic language of his books was necessarily mixed up with the babble of the multitude; so that both one and the other were apt to lose any sense, that might have been properly their own. He considered himself a thinker, and was certainly of a thoughtful turn, but, with his own path to discover, had perhaps hardly yet reached the point where an educated man begins to think. The true value of his character lay in that deep consciousness of inward strength, which made all his past vicissitudes seem merely like a change of garments; in that enthusiasm, so quiet that he scarcely knew of its existence, but which gave a warmth to everything that he laid his hand on; in that personal ambition, hidden—from his own as well as other eyes—among his more generous impulses, but in which lurked a certain efficacy, that might solidify him from a theorist into the champion of some practicable cause. Altogether, in his culture and want of culture; in his crude, wild, and misty philosophy, and the practical experience that counteracted some of its tendencies; in his magnanimous zeal for man's welfare, and his recklessness of whatever the ages had established in man's behalf; in his faith, and in his infidelity; in what he had, and in what he lacked—the artist might fitly enough stand forth as the representative of many compeers in his native land.

His career it would be difficult to prefigure. There appeared to be qualities in Holgrave, such as, in a country where everything is free to the hand that can grasp it, could hardly fail to put some of the world's prizes within his reach. But these matters are delightfully uncertain. At almost every step in life, we meet with young men of just about Holgrave's age, for whom we anticipate wonderful things, but of whom, even after much and careful inquiry, we never happen to hear another word. The effervescence of youth and passion, and the fresh gloss of the intellect and imagination, endow them with a false brilliancy, which makes fools of themselves and other people. Like certain chintzes, calicoes, and ginghams, they show finely in their first newness, but cannot stand the sun and rain, and assume a very sober aspect after washing-day.

But our business is with Holgrave, as we find him on this particular afternoon, and in the arbor of the Pyncheon-garden. In that point of view, it was a pleasant sight to behold this young man, with so much faith in himself, and so fair an appearance of admirable powers—so little harmed, too, by the many tests that had tried his metal—it was pleasant to see him in his kindly intercourse with Phoebe. Her thought had scarcely done him justice, when it pronounced him cold; or if so, he had grown warmer, now. Without such purpose, on her part, and unconsciously on his, she made the House of the Seven Gables like a home to him, and the garden a familiar precinct. With the insight on which he prided himself, he fancied that he could look through Phoebe, and all around her, and could read her off like a page of a child's story-book. But these transparent natures are often deceptive in their depth; those pebbles at the bottom of the fountain are farther from us than we think. Thus the artist, whatever he might judge of Phoebe's capacity, was beguiled, by some silent charm of hers, to talk freely of what he dreamed of doing in the world. He poured himself out as to another self. Very possibly, he forgot Phoebe while he talked to her, and was moved only by the inevitable tendency of thought, when rendered sympathetic by enthusiasm and emotion, to flow into the first safe reservoir which it finds. But, had you peeped at them through the chinks of the garden-fence, the young man's earnestness and heightened color might have led you to suppose that he was making love to the young girl!

At length, something was said by Holgrave, that made it apposite for Phoebe to inquire what had first brought him acquainted with her Cousin Hepzibah, and why he now chose to lodge in the desolate old Pyncheon-house. Without directly answering her, he turned from the Future, which had heretofore been the theme of his discourse, and began to speak of the influences of the Past. One subject, indeed, is but the reverberation of the other.

"Shall we never, never get rid of this Past!" cried he, keeping up the earnest tone of his preceding conversation.—"It lies upon the Present like a giant's dead body! In fact, the case is just as if a young giant were compelled to waste all his strength in carrying about the corpse of the old giant, his grandfather, who died a long while ago, and only needs to be decently buried. Just think, a moment; and it will startle you to see what slaves we are to by-gone times—to Death, if we give the matter the right word!"

"But I do not see it," observed Phoebe.

"For example, then," continued Holgrave, "a Dead Man, if he happen to have made a will, disposes of wealth no longer his own; or, if he die intestate,[8] it is distributed in accordance with the notions of men much longer dead than he. A Dead Man sits on all our judgement-seats; and living judges do but search out and repeat his decisions. We read in Dead Men's books! We laugh at Dead Men's jokes, and cry at Dead Men's pathos! We are sick of Dead Men's diseases, physical and moral, and die of the same remedies with which dead doctors killed their patients! We worship the living Deity, according to Dead Men's forms and creeds! Whatever we seek to do, of our own free motion, a Dead Man's icy hand obstructs us! Turn our eyes to what point we may, a Dead Man's white, immitigable face encounters them, and freezes our very heart! And we must be dead ourselves, before we can begin to have our proper in-

8. Without a will.

fluence on our own world, which will then be no longer our world, but the world of another generation, with which we shall have no shadow of a right to interfere. I ought to have said, too, that we live in Dead Men's houses; as, for instance, in this of the seven gables!"[9]

"And why not," said Phoebe, "so long as we can be comfortable in them?"

"But we shall live to see the day, I trust," went on the artist, "when no man shall build his house for posterity. Why should he? He might just as reasonably order a durable suit of clothes— leather, or gutta percha,[1] or whatever else lasts longest—so that his great-grandchildren should have the benefit of them, and cut precisely the same figure in the world that he himself does. If each generation were allowed and expected to build its own houses, that single change, comparatively unimportant in itself, would imply almost every reform which society is now suffering for. I doubt whether even our public edifices—our capitols, state-houses, court-houses, city-halls, and churches—ought to be built of such permanent materials as stone or brick. It were better that they should crumble to ruin, once in twenty years, or thereabouts, as a hint to the people to examine into and reform the institutions which they symbolize."

"How you hate everything old!" said Phoebe in dismay.—"It makes me dizzy to think of such a shifting world!"

"I certainly love nothing mouldy," answered Holgrave. "Now this old Pyncheon-house! Is it a wholesome place to live in, with its black shingles, and the green moss that shows how damp they are?—its dark, low-studded rooms?—its grime and sordidness, which are the crystallization on its walls of the human breath, that has been drawn and exhaled here, in discontent and anguish? The house ought to be purified with fire—purified till only its ashes remain!"

"Then why do you live in it?" asked Phoebe, a little piqued.

"Oh, I am pursuing my studies here; not in books, however!" replied Holgrave. "The house, in my view, is expressive of that odious and abominable Past, with all its bad influences, against which I have just been declaiming. I dwell in it for awhile, that I may know the better how to hate it. By-the-by, did you ever hear the story of Maule, the wizard, and what happened between him and your immeasurably great-grandfather?"

"Yes indeed!" said Phoebe. "I heard it long ago from my father, and two or three times from my Cousin Hepzibah, in the month that I have been here. She seems to think that all the calamities of

9. See Hawthorne's notebook entry of 1844 (p. 239 herein). Similar ideas were voiced by Ralph Waldo Emerson (1803–1882) in "The American Scholar" (1837).
1. Rubbery substance extracted from tropical trees.

the Pyncheons began from that quarrel with the wizard, as you call him. And you, Mr. Holgrave, look as if you thought so too! How singular, that you should believe what is so very absurd, when you reject many things that are a great deal worthier of credit!"

"I do believe it," said the artist seriously—"not as a superstition, however—but as proved by unquestionable facts, and as exemplifying a theory. Now, see! Under those seven gables, at which we now look up—and which old Colonel Pyncheon meant to be the home of his descendants, in prosperity and happiness, down to an epoch far beyond the present—under that roof, through a portion of three centuries, there has been perpetual remorse of conscience, a constantly defeated hope, strife amongst kindred, various misery, a strange form of death, dark suspicion, unspeakable disgrace,—all, or most of which calamity, I have the means of tracing to the old Puritan's inordinate desire to plant and endow a family. To plant a family! This idea is at the bottom of most of the wrong and mischief which men do. The truth is, that, once in every half-century, at longest, a family should be merged into the great, obscure mass of humanity, and forget all about its ancestors. Human blood, in order to keep its freshness, should run in hidden streams, as the water of an aqueduct is conveyed in subterranean pipes. In the family-existence of these Pyncheons, for instance—forgive me, Phoebe; but I cannot think of you as one of them—in their brief, New England pedigree, there has been time enough to infect them all with one kind of lunacy or another!"

"You speak very unceremoniously of my kindred," said Phoebe, debating with herself whether she ought to take offence.

"I speak true thoughts to a true mind!" answered Holgrave, with a vehemence which Phoebe had not before witnessed in him. "The truth is as I say! Furthermore, the original perpetrator and father of this mischief appears to have perpetuated himself, and still walks the street—at least, his very image, in mind and body—with the fairest prospect of transmitting to posterity as rich, and as wretched, an inheritance as he has received! Do you remember the daguerreotype, and its resemblance to the old portrait?"

"How strangely in earnest you are," exclaimed Phoebe, looking at him with surprise and perplexity, half-alarmed, and partly inclined to laugh. "You talk of the lunacy of the Pyncheons! Is it contagious?"

"I understand you!" said the artist, coloring and laughing. "I believe I am a little mad! This subject has taken hold of my mind with the strangest tenacity of clutch, since I have lodged in yonder old gable. As one method of throwing it off, I have put an incident of the Pyncheon family-history, with which I happen to be acquainted, into the form of a legend, and mean to publish it in a magazine."

"Do you write for the magazines?" inquired Phoebe.

"Is it possible you did not know it?" cried Holgrave.—"Well; such is literary fame! Yes, Miss Phoebe Pyncheon, among the multitude of my marvellous gifts, I have that of writing stories; and my name has figured, I can assure you, on the covers of Graham and Godey, making as respectable an appearance, for aught I could see, as any of the canonized bead-roll[2] with which it was associated. In the humorous line, I am thought to have a very pretty way with me; and as for pathos, I am as provocative of tears as an onion! But shall I read you my story?"

"Yes; if it is not very long," said Phoebe—and added, laughingly—"nor very dull!"

As this latter point was one which the Daguerreotypist could not decide for himself, he forthwith produced his roll of manuscript, and, while the late sunbeams gilded the seven gables, began to read.

XIII. Alice Pyncheon

There was a message brought, one day, from the worshipful Gervayse Pyncheon to young Matthew Maule, the carpenter, desiring his immediate presence at the House of the Seven Gables.

"And what does your master want with me?" said the carpenter to Mr. Pyncheon's black servant. "Does the house need any repair? Well it may, by this time; and no blame to my father who built it, neither! I was reading the old Colonel's tombstone, no longer ago than last Sabbath; and reckoning from that date, the house has stood seven-and-thirty years. No wonder if there should be a job to do on the roof!"

"Don't know what Massa wants!" answered Scipio.[3] "The house is a berry good house, and old Colonel Pyncheon think so too, I reckon;—else why the old man haunt it so, and frighten a poor nigger, as he does?"

"Well, well, friend Scipio, let your master know that I'm coming," said the carpenter with a laugh. "For a fair, workmanlike job, he'll find me his man. And so the house is haunted, is it? It will take a tighter workman than I am, to keep the spirits out of the seven gables. Even if the Colonel would be quit," he added, muttering to himself, "my old grandfather, the wizard, will be pretty sure to stick to the Pyncheons, as long as their walls hold together!"

---

2. A list of saints. *Graham's Magazine* (1826–58) and *Godey's Lady's Book* (1830–98) were popular magazines based in Philadelphia. In 1844 Hawthorne published a story in each magazine.

3. A conventional name for black slaves and literary characters, derived from the Roman general Scipio Africanus Major (ca. 237–183 B.C.E.).

"What's that you mutter to yourself, Matthew Maule?" asked Scipio. "And what for do you look so black at me?"

"No matter, darkey!" said the carpenter. "Do you think nobody is to look black but yourself? Go tell your master I'm coming; and if you happen to see Mistress Alice, his daughter, give Matthew Maule's humble respects to her. She has brought a fair face from Italy—fair, and gentle, and proud—has that same Alice Pyncheon!"

"He talk of Mistress Alice!" cried Scipio, as he returned from his errand. "The low carpenter-man! He no business so much as to look at her a great way off!"

This young Matthew Maule, the carpenter, it must be observed, was a person little understood, and not very generally liked, in the town where he resided; not that anything could be alleged against his integrity, or his skill and diligence in the handicraft which he exercised. The aversion (as it might justly be called) with which many persons regarded him, was partly the result of his own character and deportment, and partly an inheritance.

He was the grandson of a former Matthew Maule; one of the early settlers of the town, and who had been a famous and terrible wizard, in his day. This old reprobate was one of the sufferers, when Cotton Mather, and his brother ministers, and the learned judges, and other wise men, and Sir William Phips, the sagacious Governor, made such laudable efforts to weaken the great Enemy of souls, by sending a multitude of his adherents up the rocky pathway of Gallows-Hill.[4] Since those days, no doubt, it had grown to be suspected, that, in consequence of an unfortunate overdoing of a work praiseworthy in itself, the proceedings against the witches had proved far less acceptable to the Beneficent Father, than to that very Arch-Enemy, whom they were intended to distress and utterly overwhelm. It is not the less certain, however, that awe and terror brooded over the memories of those who died for this horrible crime of witchcraft. Their graves, in the crevices of the rocks, were supposed to be incapable of retaining the occupants, who had been so hastily thrust into them. Old Matthew Maule, especially, was known to have as little hesitation or difficulty in rising out of his grave, as an ordinary man in getting out of bed, and was as often seen at midnight, as living people at noonday. This pestilent wizard (in whom his just punishment seemed to have wrought no

---

4. The site in Salem where persons convicted of witchcraft were executed and buried. Hawthorne's narrator in "Alice Doane's Appeal" (p. 241 herein) tells his story on Gallows Hill. Mather (1663–1728), a Puritan minister, did not participate in the Salem witch trials of 1692, but he defended the Salem authorities in his 1692 *Wonders of the Invisible World* (see Robert Calef, p. 230 herein). Phips (1651–1695), the royal governor of Massachusetts in 1692, initially supported the witch trials. But when his wife was accused of witchcraft, he closed down the court on October 29, 1692. "Enemy of souls": Satan.

manner of amends) had an inveterate habit of haunting a certain mansion, styled the House of the Seven Gables, against the owner of which he pretended to hold an unsettled claim for ground-rent. The ghost, it appears—with the pertinacity which was one of his distinguishing characteristics, while alive—insisted that he was the rightful proprietor of the site upon which the house stood. His terms were, that either the aforesaid ground-rent, from the day when the cellar began to be dug, should be paid down, or the mansion itself given up; else he, the ghostly creditor, would have his finger in all the affairs of the Pyncheons, and make everything go wrong with them, though it should be a thousand years after his death. It was a wild story, perhaps, but seemed not altogether so incredible, to those who could remember what an inflexibly obstinate old fellow this wizard Maule had been!

Now, the wizard's grandson, the young Matthew Maule of our story, was popularly supposed to have inherited some of his ancestor's questionable traits. It is wonderful how many absurdities were promulgated in reference to the young man. He was fabled, for example, to have a strange power of getting into people's dreams, and regulating matters there according to his own fancy, pretty much like the stage-manager of a theatre. There was a great deal of talk among the neighbors, particularly the petticoated ones, about what they called the witchcraft of Maule's eye. Some said, that he could look into people's minds; others, that, by the marvellous power of this eye, he could draw people into his own mind, or send them, if he pleased, to do errands to his grandfather, in the spiritual world; others again, that it was what is termed an Evil Eye, and possessed the valuable faculty of blighting corn, and drying children into mummies with the heart-burn. But, after all, what worked most to the young carpenter's disadvantage was, first, the reserve and sternness of his natural disposition, and next, the fact of his not being a church-communicant, and the suspicion of his holding heretical tenets in matters of religion and polity.

After receiving Mr. Pyncheon's message, the carpenter merely tarried to finish a small job, which he happened to have in hand, and then took his way towards the House of the Seven Gables. This noted edifice, though its style might be getting a little out of fashion, was still as respectable a family residence as that of any gentleman in town. The present owner, Gervayse Pyncheon, was said to have contracted a dislike to the house, in consequence of a shock to his sensibility, in early childhood, from the sudden death of his grandfather. In the very act of running to climb Colonel Pyncheon's knee, the boy had discovered the old Puritan to be a corpse! On arriving at manhood, Mr. Pyncheon had visited England, where he married a lady of fortune, and had subsequently spent many years, partly in the mother-country, and partly in various cities, on the continent of Europe. During this period, the family-mansion had been consigned to the charge of a kinsman, who was allowed to make it his home, for the time being, in consideration of keeping the premises in thorough repair. So faithfully had this contract been fulfilled, that now, as the carpenter approached the house, his practised eye could detect nothing to criticize in its condition. The peaks of the seven gables rose up sharply; the shingled roof looked thoroughly water-tight; and the glittering plaster-work entirely covered the exterior walls, and sparkled in the October sun, as if it had been new only a week ago.

The house had that pleasant aspect of life, which is like the cheery expression of comfortable activity, in the human countenance. You could see at once that there was the stir of a large family within it. A huge load of oak-wood was passing through the gateway, towards the outbuildings in the rear; the fat cook, or probably it might be the housekeeper, stood at the side-door, bargaining for some turkeys and poultry, which a countryman had brought for sale. Now and then, a maid-servant, neatly dressed, and now the shining, sable face of a slave,[5] might be seen bustling across the windows, in the lower part of the house. At an open window of a room in the second story, hanging over some pots of beautiful and delicate flowers—exotics, but which had never known a more genial sunshine than that of the New England autumn—was the figure of a young lady, an exotic, like the flowers, and beautiful and delicate as they. Her presence imparted an indescribable grace and faint witchery to the whole edifice. In other respects, it was a substantial, jolly-looking mansion, and seemed fit to be the residence of a patriarch, who might establish his own head-quarters in the front gable, and assign one of the remainder to each of his six children; while the great chimney, in the centre, should symbolize the old fellow's hospitable heart, which kept them all warm, and made a great whole of the seven smaller ones.

There was a vertical sun-dial on the front gable; and as the carpenter passed beneath it, he looked up and noted the hour.

"Three o'clock!" said he to himself. "My father told me, that dial was put up only an hour before the old Colonel's death. How truly it has kept time, these seven-and-thirty years past! The shadow creeps and creeps, and is always looking over the shoulder of the sunshine!"

It might have befitted a craftsman, like Matthew Maule, on being sent for to a gentleman's house, to go to the back-door, where ser-

---

5. Slavery was effectively abolished in Massachusetts in 1783 through a series of court rulings.

vants and work-people were usually admitted; or at least to the
side-entrance, where the better class of tradesmen made application. But the carpenter had a great deal of pride and stiffness in his
nature; and at this moment, moreover, his heart was bitter with
the sense of hereditary wrong, because he considered the great
Pyncheon-house to be standing on soil which should have been his
own. On this very site, beside a spring of delicious water, his grandfather had felled the pine-trees and built a cottage, in which children had been born to him; and it was only from a dead man's
stiffened fingers, that Colonel Pyncheon had wrested away the title-
deeds. So young Maule went straight to the principal entrance,
beneath a portal of carved oak, and gave such a peal of the iron
knocker, that you would have imagined the stern old wizard himself
to be standing at the threshold.

Black Scipio answered the summons in a prodigious hurry, but
showed the whites of his eyes, in amazement, on beholding only
the carpenter.

"Lord-a-mercy, what a great man he be, this carpenter fellow!"
mumbled Scipio, down in his throat. "Anybody think he beat on the
door with his biggest hammer!"

"Here I am!" said Maule sternly. "Show me the way to your master's parlor!"

As he stept into the house, a note of sweet and melancholy music trilled and vibrated along the passage-way, proceeding from one
of the rooms above-stairs. It was the harpsichord which Alice Pyncheon had brought with her from beyond the sea. The fair Alice bestowed most of her maiden leisure between flowers and music,
although the former were apt to droop, and the melodies were often sad. She was of foreign education, and could not take kindly to
the New England modes of life, in which nothing beautiful had
ever been developed.

As Mr. Pyncheon had been impatiently awaiting Maule's arrival,
black Scipio, of course, lost no time in ushering the carpenter into
his master's presence. The room, in which this gentleman sat, was
a parlor of moderate size, looking out upon the garden of the
house, and having its windows partly shadowed by the foliage of
fruit-trees. It was Mr. Pyncheon's peculiar apartment, and was provided with furniture, in an elegant and costly style, principally from
Paris; the floor (which was unusual, at that day) being covered with
a carpet, so skilfully and richly wrought, that it seemed to glow as
with living flowers. In one corner stood a marble woman, to whom
her own beauty was the sole and sufficient garment. Some pictures—that looked old, and had a mellow tinge, diffused through
all their artful splendor—hung on the walls. Near the fire-place was
a large and very beautiful cabinet of ebony, inlaid with ivory; a

piece of antique furniture, which Mr. Pyncheon had bought in Venice, and which he used as the treasure-place for medals, ancient coins, and whatever small and valuable curiosities he had picked up, on his travels. Through all this variety of decoration, however, the room showed its original characteristics; its low stud, its cross-beam, its chimney-piece, with the old-fashioned Dutch tiles;[6] so that it was the emblem of a mind, industriously stored with foreign ideas, and elaborated into artificial refinement, but neither larger, nor, in its proper self, more elegant, than before.

There were two objects that appeared rather out of place in this very handsomely furnished room. One was a large map, or surveyor's plan of a tract of land, which looked as if it had been drawn a good many years ago, and was now dingy with smoke, and soiled, here and there, with the touch of fingers. The other was a portrait of a stern old man, in a Puritan garb, painted roughly, but with a bold effect, and a remarkably strong expression of character.

At a small table, before a fire of English sea-coal,[7] sat Mr. Pyncheon, sipping coffee, which had grown to be a very favorite beverage with him, in France. He was a middle-aged and really handsome man, with a wig flowing down upon his shoulders; his coat was of blue velvet, with lace on the borders and at the buttonholes; and the firelight glistened on the spacious breadth of his waistcoat, which was flowered all over with gold. On the entrance of Scipio, ushering in the carpenter, Mr. Pyncheon turned partly round, but resumed his former position, and proceeded deliberately to finish his cup of coffee, without immediate notice of the guest whom he had summoned to his presence. It was not that he intended any rudeness, or improper neglect—which, indeed, he would have blushed to be guilty of—but it never occurred to him that a person in Maule's station had a claim on his courtesy, or would trouble himself about it, one way or the other.

The carpenter, however, stept at once to the hearth, and turned himself about, so as to look Mr. Pyncheon in the face.

"You sent for me!" said he. "Be pleased to explain your business, that I may go back to my own affairs!"

"Ah! excuse me," said Mr. Pyncheon quietly.—"I did not mean to tax your time without a recompense. Your name, I think, is Maule—Thomas or Matthew Maule[8]—a son or grandson of the builder of this house?"

---

6. Decorative tiles from the Netherlands popular with the wealthy.
7. A relatively scarce and much more expensive coal than the charcoal, wood, and peat used by most others in New England.
8. The mistaken reference to "Thomas" further helps link Matthew Maule to the historical Thomas Maule.

"Matthew Maule," replied the carpenter—"son of him who built the house—grandson of the rightful proprietor of the soil!"

"I know the dispute to which you allude," observed Mr. Pyncheon, with undisturbed equanimity. "I am well aware, that my grandfather was compelled to resort to a suit at law, in order to establish his claim to the foundation-site of this edifice. We will not, if you please, renew the discussion. The matter was settled at the time, and by the competent authorities—equitably, it is to be presumed—and, at all events, irrevocably. Yet, singularly enough, there is an incidental reference to this very subject in what I am now about to say to you. And this same inveterate grudge—excuse me, I mean no offence—this irritability, which you have just shown, is not entirely aside from the matter."

"If you can find anything for your purpose, Mr. Pyncheon," said the carpenter, "in a man's natural resentment for the wrongs done to his blood, you are welcome to it!"

"I take you at your word, Goodman[9] Maule," said the owner of the seven gables, with a smile, "and will proceed to suggest a mode in which your hereditary resentments—justifiable, or otherwise—may have had a bearing on my affairs. You have heard, I suppose, that the Pyncheon family, ever since my grandfather's days, have been prosecuting a still unsettled claim to a very large extent of territory at the eastward?"

"Often," replied Maule—and it is said that a smile came over his face—"very often—from my father!"

"This claim," continued Mr. Pyncheon, after pausing a moment, as if to consider what the carpenter's smile might mean, "appeared to be on the very verge of a settlement and full allowance, at the period of my grandfather's decease. It was well known, to those in his confidence, that he anticipated neither difficulty nor delay. Now, Colonel Pyncheon, I need hardly say, was a practical man, well acquainted with public and private business, and not at all the person to cherish ill-founded hopes, or to attempt the following out of an impracticable scheme. It is obvious to conclude, therefore, that he had grounds—not apparent to his heirs—for his confident anticipation of success in the matter of this eastern claim. In a word, I believe—and my legal advisers coincide in the belief, which, moreover, is authorized, to a certain extent, by the family-traditions—that my grandfather was in possession of some deed, or other document, essential to this claim, but which has since disappeared."

"Very likely," said Matthew Maule—and again, it is said, there was a dark smile on his face—"but what can a poor carpenter have to do with the grand affairs of the Pyncheon family?"

9. Term indicating nongentleman, or common, status.

"Perhaps nothing," returned Mr. Pyncheon—"possibly, much!"

Here ensued a great many words between Matthew Maule and the proprietor of the seven gables, on the subject which the latter had thus broached. It seems (although Mr. Pyncheon had some hesitation in referring to stories, so exceedingly absurd in their aspect) that the popular belief pointed to some mysterious connection and dependence, existing between the family of the Maules, and these vast, unrealized possessions of the Pyncheons. It was an ordinary saying, that the old wizard, hanged though he was, had obtained the best end of the bargain, in his contest with Colonel Pyncheon; inasmuch as he had got possession of the great eastern claim, in exchange for an acre or two of garden-ground. A very aged woman, recently dead, had often used the metaphorical expression, in her fireside-talk, that miles and miles of the Pyncheon lands had been shovelled into Maule's grave; which, by-the-by, was but a very shallow nook, between two rocks, near the summit of Gallows-Hill. Again, when the lawyers were making inquiry for the missing document, it was a by-word, that it would never be found, unless in the wizard's skeleton-hand. So much weight had the shrewd lawyers assigned to these fables, that—(but Mr. Pyncheon did not see fit to inform the carpenter of the fact)—they had secretly caused the wizard's grave to be searched. Nothing was discovered, however, except that, unaccountably, the right hand of the skeleton was gone.

Now, what was unquestionably important, a portion of these popular rumors could be traced, though rather doubtfully and indistinctly, to chance words and obscure hints of the executed wizard's son, and the father of this present Matthew Maule. And here Mr. Pyncheon could bring an item of his own personal evidence into play. Though but a child, at the time, he either remembered or fancied, that Matthew's father had had some job to perform, on the day before, or possibly the very morning, of the Colonel's decease, in the private room where he and the carpenter were at this moment talking. Certain papers belonging to Colonel Pyncheon, as his grandson distinctly recollected, had been spread out on the table.

Matthew Maule understood the insinuated suspicion.

"My father," he said—but still there was that dark smile, making a riddle of his countenance—"my father was an honester man than the bloody old Colonel! Not to get his rights back again, would he have carried off one of those papers!"

"I shall not bandy words with you," observed the foreign-bred Mr. Pyncheon, with haughty composure. "Nor will it become me to resent any rudeness towards either my grandfather or myself. A gentleman, before seeking intercourse with a person of your station and habits, will first consider whether the urgency of the end may compensate for the disagreeableness of the means. It does so, in the present instance."

He then renewed the conversation, and made great pecuniary offers to the carpenter, in case the latter should give information leading to the discovery of the lost document, and the consequent success of the eastern claim. For a long time, Matthew Maule is said to have turned a cold ear to these propositions. At last, however, with a strange kind of laugh, he inquired whether Mr. Pyncheon would make over to him the old wizard's homestead-ground, together with the House of the Seven Gables, now standing on it, in requital of the documentary evidence, so urgently required.

The wild, chimney-corner legend (which, without copying all its extravagances, my narrative essentially follows) here gives an account of some very strange behavior on the part of Colonel Pyncheon's portrait. This picture, it must be understood, was supposed to be so intimately connected with the fate of the house, and so magically built into its walls, that, if once it should be removed, that very instant, the whole edifice would come thundering down, in a heap of dusty ruin. All through the foregoing conversation between Mr. Pyncheon and the carpenter, the portrait had been frowning, clenching its fist, and giving many such proofs of excessive discomposure, but without attracting the notice of either of the two colloquists. And finally, at Matthew Maule's audacious suggestion of a transfer of the seven-gabled structure, the ghostly portrait is averred to have lost all patience, and to have shown itself on the point of descending bodily from its frame. But such incredible incidents are merely to be mentioned aside.

"Give up this house!" exclaimed Mr. Pyncheon, in amazement at the proposal. "Were I to do so, my grandfather would not rest quiet in his grave!"

"He never has, if all stories are true," remarked the carpenter, composedly. "But that matter concerns his grandson, more than it does Matthew Maule. I have no other terms to propose."

Impossible as he at first thought it, to comply with Maule's conditions, still, on a second glance, Mr. Pyncheon was of opinion that they might at least be made matter of discussion. He himself had no personal attachment for the house, nor any pleasant associations connected with his childish residence in it. On the contrary, after seven-and-thirty years, the presence of his dead grandfather seemed still to pervade it, as on that morning when the affrighted boy had beheld him, with so ghastly an aspect, stiffening in his chair. His long abode in foreign parts, moreover, and familiarity with many of the castles and ancestral halls of England, and the marble palaces of Italy, had caused him to look contemptuously at the House of the Seven Gables, whether in point of splendor or convenience. It was a mansion exceedingly inadequate to the style of living, which it would be incumbent on Mr. Pyncheon to support, after realizing his territorial rights. His steward might deign to occupy it, but never, certainly, the great landed proprietor himself. In the event of success, indeed, it was his purpose to return to England; nor, to say the truth, would he recently have quitted that more congenial home, had not his own fortune, as well as his deceased wife's, begun to give symptoms of exhaustion. The eastern claim once fairly settled, and put upon the firm basis of actual possession, Mr. Pyncheon's property—to be measured by miles, not acres—would be worth an earldom, and would reasonably entitle him to solicit, or enable him to purchase, that elevated dignity from the British monarch. Lord Pyncheon!—or the Earl of Waldo!—how could such a magnate be expected to contract his grandeur within the pitiful compass of seven shingled gables?

In short, on an enlarged view of the business, the carpenter's terms appeared so ridiculously easy, that Mr. Pyncheon could scarcely forbear laughing in his face. He was quite ashamed, after the foregoing reflections, to propose any diminution of so moderate a recompense for the immense service to be rendered.

"I consent to your proposition, Maule!" cried he. "Put me in possession of the document, essential to establish my rights, and the House of the Seven Gables is your own!"

According to some versions of the story, a regular contract to the above effect was drawn up by a lawyer, and signed and sealed in the presence of witnesses. Others say, that Matthew Maule was contented with a private, written agreement, in which Mr. Pyncheon pledged his honor and integrity to the fulfilment of the terms concluded upon. The gentleman then ordered wine, which he and the carpenter drank together, in confirmation of their bargain. During the whole preceding discussion and subsequent formalities, the old Puritan's portrait seems to have persisted in its shadowy gestures of disapproval, but without effect; except that, as Mr. Pyncheon set down the emptied glass, he thought he beheld his grandfather frown.

"This Sherry is too potent a wine for me;—it has affected my brain already," he observed, after a somewhat startled look at the picture.—"On returning to Europe, I shall confine myself to the more delicate vintages of Italy and France, the best of which will not bear transportation."

"My Lord Pyncheon may drink what wine he will, and wherever he pleases!" replied the carpenter, as if he had been privy to Mr. Pyncheon's ambitious projects. "But first, Sir, if you desire tidings of this lost document, I must crave the favor of a little talk with your fair daughter Alice!"

"You are mad, Maule!" exclaimed Mr. Pyncheon haughtily; and now, at last, there was anger mixed up with his pride.—"What can my daughter have to do with a business like this?"

Indeed, at this new demand on the carpenter's part, the proprietor of the seven gables was even more thunderstruck, than at the cool proposition to surrender his house. There was, at least, an assignable motive for the first stipulation; there appeared to be none whatever, for the last. Nevertheless, Matthew Maule sturdily insisted on the young lady being summoned, and even gave her father to understand, in a mysterious kind of explanation—which made the matter considerably darker than it looked before—that the only chance of acquiring the requisite knowledge was through the clear, crystal medium of a pure and virgin intelligence, like that of the fair Alice. Not to encumber our story with Mr. Pyncheon's scruples, whether of conscience, pride, or fatherly affection, he at length ordered his daughter to be called. He well knew that she was in her chamber, and engaged in no occupation that could not readily be laid aside; for, as it happened, ever since Alice's name had been spoken, both her father and the carpenter had heard the sad and sweet music of her harpsichord, and the airier melancholy of her accompanying voice.

So Alice Pyncheon was summoned, and appeared. A portrait of this young lady, painted by a Venetian artist and left by her father in England, is said to have fallen into the hands of the present Duke of Devonshire, and to be now preserved at Chatsworth;[1] not on account of any associations with the original, but for its value as a picture, and the high character of beauty, in the countenance. If ever there was a lady born, and set apart from the world's vulgar mass by a certain gentle and cold stateliness, it was this very Alice Pyncheon. Yet there was the womanly mixture in her;—the tenderness, or, at least, the tender capabilities. For the sake of that redeeming quality, a man of generous nature would have forgiven all her pride, and have been content, almost, to lie down in her path, and let Alice set her slender foot upon his heart. All that he would have required, was simply the acknowledgement that he was indeed a man, and a fellow-being, moulded of the same elements as she.

As Alice came into the room, her eyes fell upon the carpenter, who was standing near its centre, clad in a green, woollen jacket, a pair of loose breeches, open at the knees, and with a long pocket for his rule, the end of which protruded; it was as proper a mark of the artizan's calling, as Mr. Pyncheon's full-dress sword, of that gentleman's aristocratic pretensions. A glow of artistic approval

---

1. The seat of the dukes of Devonshire, in Derbyshire, famed for its great art collections. William Cavendish (1790–1858), sixth duke of Devonshire, remained committed to maintaining those collections.

brightened over Alice Pyncheon's face; she was struck with admiration—which she made no attempt to conceal—of the remarkable
comeliness, strength, and energy of Maule's figure. But that admiring glance (which most other men, perhaps, would have cherished
as a sweet recollection, all through life) the carpenter never for-
gave. It must have been the devil himself that made Maule so subtile in his perception.

"Does the girl look at me as if I were a brute beast!" thought he,
setting his teeth. "She shall know whether I have a human spirit;
and the worse for her, if it prove stronger than her own!"

"My father, you sent for me," said Alice, in her sweet and harp-
like voice. "But, if you have business with this young man, pray let
me go again. You know I do not love this room, in spite of that
Claude,[2] with which you try to bring back sunny recollections."

"Stay a moment, young lady, if you please!" said Matthew Maule.
"My business with your father is over. With yourself, it is now to
begin!"

Alice looked towards her father, in surprise and inquiry.

"Yes, Alice," said Mr. Pyncheon, with some disturbance and confusion. "This young man—his name is Matthew Maule—professes,
so far as I can understand him, to be able to discover, through your
means, a certain paper or parchment, which was missing long before your birth. The importance of the document in question renders it advisable to neglect no possible, even if improbable, method
of regaining it. You will therefore oblige me, my dear Alice, by answering this person's inquiries, and complying with his lawful and
reasonable requests, so far as they may appear to have the aforesaid
object in view. As I shall remain in the room, you need apprehend
no rude nor unbecoming deportment, on the young man's part;
and, at your slightest wish, of course, the investigation, or whatever
we may call it, shall immediately be broken off."

"Mistress Alice Pyncheon," remarked Matthew Maule, with the
utmost deference, but yet a half-hidden sarcasm in his look and
tone, "will no doubt feel herself quite safe in her father's presence,
and under his all-sufficient protection."

"I certainly shall entertain no manner of apprehension, with my
father at hand," said Alice, with maidenly dignity. "Neither do I
conceive that a lady, while true to herself, can have aught to fear
from whomsoever, or in any circumstances!"

Poor Alice! By what unhappy impulse did she thus put herself at
once on terms of defiance against a strength which she could not
estimate?

"Then, Mistress Alice," said Matthew Maule, handing a chair—

2. A painting by the French landscape painter Claude Lorrain (1600–1682).

gracefully enough, for a craftsman—"will it please you only to sit down, and do me the favor (though altogether beyond a poor carpenter's deserts) to fix your eyes on mine!"

Alice complied. She was very proud. Setting aside all advantages of rank, this fair girl deemed herself conscious of a power—combined of beauty, high, unsullied purity, and the preservative force of womanhood—that could make her sphere impenetrable, unless betrayed by treachery within. She instinctively knew, it may be, that some sinister or evil potency was now striving to pass her barriers; nor would she decline the contest. So Alice put woman's might against man's might; a match not often equal, on the part of woman.

Her father, meanwhile, had turned away, and seemed absorbed in the contemplation of a landscape by Claude, where a shadowy and sun-streaked vista penetrated so remotely into an ancient wood, that it would have been no wonder if his fancy had lost itself in the picture's bewildering depths. But, in truth, the picture was no more to him, at that moment, than the blank wall against which it hung. His mind was haunted with the many and strange tales which he had heard, attributing mysterious, if not supernatural endowments to these Maules, as well the grandson, here present, as his two immediate ancestors. Mr. Pyncheon's long residence abroad, and intercourse with men of wit and fashion—courtiers, worldlings, and free thinkers—had done much towards obliterating the grim, Puritan superstitions, which no man of New England birth, at that early period, could entirely escape. But, on the other hand, had not a whole community believed Maule's grandfather to be a wizard? Had not the crime been proved? Had not the wizard died for it? Had he not bequeathed a legacy of hatred against the Pyncheons to this only grandson, who, as it appeared, was now about to exercise a subtle influence over the daughter of his enemy's house? Might not this influence be the same that was called witchcraft?

Turning half around, he caught a glimpse of Maule's figure in the looking-glass. At some paces from Alice, with his arms uplifted in the air, the carpenter made a gesture, as if directing downward a slow, ponderous, and invisible weight upon the maiden.

"Stay, Maule!" exclaimed Mr. Pyncheon, stepping forward. "I forbid your proceeding farther!"

"Pray, my dear father, do not interrupt the young man!" said Alice, without changing her position. "His efforts, I assure you, will prove very harmless."

Again, Mr. Pyncheon turned his eyes towards the Claude. It was then his daughter's will, in opposition to his own, that the experiment should be fully tried. Henceforth, therefore, he did but consent, not urge it. And was it not for her sake, far more than for his

own, that he desired its success? That lost parchment once restored, the beautiful Alice Pyncheon, with the rich dowry which
he could then bestow, might wed an English duke, or a German
reigning-prince, instead of some New England clergyman or
lawyer! At the thought, the ambitious father almost consented, in
his heart, that, if the devil's power were needed to the accomplishment of this great object, Maule might evoke him! Alice's own purity would be her safe-guard.

With his mind full of imaginary magnificence, Mr. Pyncheon
heard a half-uttered exclamation from his daughter. It was very
faint and low; so indistinct, that there seemed but half a will to
shape out the words, and too undefined a purport, to be intelligible.
Yet it was a call for help!—his conscience never doubted it!—and,
little more than a whisper to his ear, it was a dismal shriek, and
long re-echoed so, in the region round his heart! But, this time, the
father did not turn.

After a farther interval, Maule spoke.

"Behold your daughter!" said he.

Mr. Pyncheon came hastily forward. The carpenter was standing
erect in front of Alice's chair, and pointing his finger towards the
maiden with an expression of triumphant power, the limits of which
could not be defined; as, indeed, its scope stretched vaguely towards the unseen and the infinite. Alice sat in an attitude of profound repose, with the long, brown lashes drooping over her eyes.

"There she is!" said the carpenter. "Speak to her!"

"Alice! My daughter!" exclaimed Mr. Pyncheon. "My own Alice!"
She did not stir.

"Louder!" said Maule smiling.

"Alice! Awake!" cried her father. "It troubles me to see you thus!
Awake!"

He spoke loudly, with terror in his voice, and close to that delicate ear which had always been so sensitive to every discord. But
the sound evidently reached her not. It is indescribable what a
sense of remote, dim, unattainable distance, betwixt himself and
Alice, was impressed on the father by this impossibility of reaching
her with his voice.

"Best touch her!" said Matthew Maule. "Shake the girl, and
roughly too! My hands are hardened with too much use of axe, saw,
and plane; else I might help you!"

Mr. Pyncheon took her hand, and pressed it with the earnestness
of startled emotion. He kissed her, with so great a heart-throb in
the kiss, that he thought she must needs feel it. Then, in a gust of
anger at her insensibility, he shook her maiden form, with a violence which, the next moment, it affrighted him to remember. He
withdrew his encircling arms; and Alice—whose figure, though flex-

ible, had been wholly impassive—relapsed into the same attitude as
before these attempts to arouse her. Maule having shifted his position, her face was turned towards him, slightly, but with what
seemed to be a reference of her very slumber to his guidance.

Then, it was a strange sight to behold, how the man of conven-
tionalities shook the powder out of his periwig; how the reserved
and stately gentleman forgot his dignity; how the gold-embroidered
waistcoat flickered and glistened in the firelight, with the convul-
sion of rage, terror, and sorrow, in the human heart that was beating under it!

"Villain!" cried Mr. Pyncheon, shaking his clenched fist at
Maule. "You and the fiend together have robbed me of my daugh-
ter! Give her back—spawn of the old wizard!—or you shall climb
Gallows-Hill in your grandfather's footsteps!"

"Softly, Mr. Pyncheon!" said the carpenter with scornful composure.—"Softly, an' it please your worship; else you will spoil those
rich lace-ruffles, at your wrists! Is it my crime, if you have sold your
daughter for the mere hope of getting a sheet of yellow parchment
into your clutch? There sits Mistress Alice, quietly asleep! Now let
Matthew Maule try whether she be as proud, as the carpenter
found her awhile since!"

He spoke; and Alice responded, with a soft, subdued, inward ac-
quiescence, and a bending of her form towards him, like the flame
of a torch, when it indicates a gentle draft of air. He beckoned with
his hand; and, rising from her chair—blindly, but undoubtingly, as
tending to her sure and inevitable centre—the proud Alice approached him. He waved her back; and, retreating, Alice sank again
into her seat!

"She is mine!" said Matthew Maule. "Mine, by the right of the
strongest spirit!"

In the further progress of the legend, there is a long, grotesque,
and occasionally awe-striking account of the carpenter's incanta-
tions (if so they are to be called) with a view of discovering the lost
document. It appears to have been his object to convert the mind
of Alice into a kind of telescopic medium, through which Mr. Pyncheon and himself might obtain a glimpse into the spiritual world.
He succeeded, accordingly, in holding an imperfect sort of intercourse, at one remove, with the departed personages, in whose custody the so much valued secret had been carried beyond the
precincts of earth. During her trance, Alice described three figures,
as being present to her spiritualized perception. One was an aged,
dignified, stern-looking gentleman, clad, as for a solemn festival, in
grave and costly attire, but with a great blood-stain on his richly
wrought band;—the second, an aged man, meanly dressed, with a
dark and malign countenance, and a broken halter about his

neck;—the third, a person not so advanced in life as the former two, but beyond the middle-age, wearing a coarse woollen tunic and leather-breeches, and with a carpenter's rule sticking out of his side-pocket. These three visionary characters possessed a mutual knowledge of the missing document. One of them, in truth—it was he with the blood-stain on his band—seemed, unless his gestures were misunderstood, to hold the parchment in his immediate keeping, but was prevented, by his two partners in the mystery, from disburthening himself of the trust. Finally, when he showed a purpose of shouting forth the secret, loudly enough to be heard from his own sphere into that of mortals, his companions struggled with him, and pressed their hands over his mouth; and forthwith—whether that he were choked by it, or that the secret itself was of a crimson hue—there was a fresh flow of blood upon his band. Upon this, the two meanly-dressed figures mocked and jeered at the much-abashed old dignitary, and pointed their fingers at the stain!

At this juncture, Maule turned to Mr. Pyncheon.

"It will never be allowed!" said he. "The custody of this secret, that would so enrich his heirs, makes part of your grandfather's retribution. He must choke with it, until it is no longer of any value. And keep you the House of the Seven Gables! It is too dear bought an inheritance, and too heavy, with the curse upon it, to be shifted yet awhile from the Colonel's posterity!"

Mr. Pyncheon tried to speak, but—what with fear and passion—could make only a gurgling murmur in his throat. The carpenter smiled.

"Aha, worshipful Sir! So, you have old Maule's blood to drink!" said he jeeringly.

"Fiend in man's shape, why dost thou keep dominion over my child?" cried Mr. Pyncheon, when his choked utterance could make way.—"Give me back my daughter! Then go thy ways; and may we never meet again!"

"Your daughter!" said Matthew Maule. "Why, she is fairly mine! Nevertheless, not to be too hard with fair Mistress Alice, I will leave her in your keeping; but I do not warrant you, that she shall never have occasion to remember Maule, the carpenter."

He waved his hands with an upward motion; and, after a few repetitions of similar gestures, the beautiful Alice Pyncheon awoke from her strange trance. She awoke, without the slightest recollection of her visionary experience; but as one losing herself in a momentary reverie, and returning to the consciousness of actual life, in almost as brief an interval as the down-sinking flame of the hearth should quiver again up the chimney. On recognizing Matthew Maule, she assumed an air of somewhat cold, but gentle dignity; the rather, as there was a certain peculiar smile on the carpenter's visage, that stirred the native pride of the fair Alice. So ended, for that time, the quest for the lost title-deed of the Pyncheon territory at the eastward; nor, though often subsequently renewed, has it ever yet befallen a Pyncheon to set his eye upon that parchment.

But alas, for the beautiful, the gentle, yet too haughty Alice! A power, that she little dreamed of, had laid its grasp upon her maiden soul. A will, most unlike her own, constrained her to do its grotesque and fantastic bidding. Her father, as it proved, had martyred his poor child to an inordinate desire for measuring his land by miles, instead of acres. And, therefore, while Alice Pyncheon lived, she was Maule's slave, in a bondage more humiliating, a thousand-fold, than that which binds its chain around the body. Seated by his humble fireside, Maule had but to wave his hand; and, wherever the proud lady chanced to be—whether in her chamber, or entertaining her father's stately guests, or worshipping at church—whatever her place or occupation, her spirit passed from beneath her own control, and bowed itself to Maule. "Alice, laugh!"—the carpenter, beside his hearth, would say; or perhaps intensely will it, without a spoken word. And, even were it prayer-time, or at a funeral, Alice must break into wild laughter. "Alice, be sad!"—and, at the instant, down would come her tears, quenching all the mirth of those around her, like sudden rain upon a bonfire. "Alice, dance!"—and dance she would, not in such court-like measures as she had learned abroad, but some high-paced jig, or hop-skip rigadoon, befitting the brisk lasses at a rustic merry-making. It seemed to be Maule's impulse, not to ruin Alice, nor to visit her with any black or gigantic mischief, which would have crowned her sorrow with the grace of tragedy, but to wreak a low, ungenerous scorn upon her. Thus all the dignity of life was lost. She felt herself too much abased, and longed to change natures with some worm!

One evening, at a bridal party—(but not her own; for, so lost from self-control, she would have deemed it sin to marry)—poor Alice was beckoned forth by her unseen despot, and constrained, in her gossamer white dress and satin slippers, to hasten along the street to the mean dwelling of a laboring-man. There was laughter and good cheer, within; for Matthew Maule, that night, was to wed the laborer's daughter, and had summoned proud Alice Pyncheon to wait upon his bride. And so she did; and when the twain were one, Alice awoke out of her enchanted sleep. Yet, no longer proud—humbly, and with a smile, all steeped in sadness—she kissed Maule's wife, and went her way. It was an inclement night; the southeast wind drove the mingled snow and rain into her thinly sheltered bosom; her satin slippers were wet through and through, as she trod the muddy sidewalks. The next day, a cold; soon, a settled cough; anon, a hectic cheek, a wasted form, that sat beside the harpsichord, and filled the house with music! Music, in which a strain of the heavenly choristers was echoed! Oh, joy! For Alice had borne her last humiliation! Oh, greater joy! For Alice was penitent of her one earthly sin, and proud no more!

The Pyncheons made a great funeral for Alice. The kith and kin were there, and the whole respectability of the town besides. But, last in the procession, came Matthew Maule, gnashing his teeth, as if he would have bitten his own heart in twain; the darkest and wofullest man that ever walked behind a corpse. He meant to humble Alice, not to kill her;—but he had taken a woman's delicate soul into his rude gripe, to play with;—and she was dead!

XIV. Phoebe's Good Bye

Holgrave, plunging into his tale with the energy and absorption natural to a young author, had given a good deal of action to the parts capable of being developed and exemplified in that manner. He now observed that a certain remarkable drowsiness (wholly unlike that with which the reader possibly feels himself affected) had been flung over the senses of his auditress. It was the effect, unquestionably, of the mystic gesticulations, by which he had sought to bring bodily before Phoebe's perception the figure of the mesmerizing carpenter. With the lids drooping over her eyes—now lifted, for an instant, and drawn down again, as with leaden weights—she leaned slightly towards him, and seemed almost to regulate her breath by his. Holgrave gazed at her, as he rolled up his manuscript, and recognized an incipient stage of that curious psychological condition, which, as he had himself told Phoebe, he possessed more than an ordinary faculty of producing. A veil was beginning to be muffled about her, in which she could behold only him, and live only in his thoughts and emotions. His glance, as he fastened it on the young girl, grew involuntarily more concentrated; in his attitude, there was the consciousness of power, investing his hardly mature figure with a dignity that did not belong to its physical manifestation. It was evident, that, with but one wave of his hand and a corresponding effort of his will, he could complete his mastery over Phoebe's yet free and virgin spirit; he could establish an influence over this good, pure, and simple child, as dangerous, and perhaps as disastrous, as that which the carpenter of his legend had acquired and exercised over the ill-fated Alice.[3]

To a disposition like Holgrave's, at once speculative and active,

---

3. In a letter of October 18, 1841 (p. 307 herein), Hawthorne used similar language in warning his future wife, Sophia Peabody, about the dangers of mesmerism.

there is no temptation so great as the opportunity of acquiring empire over the human spirit; nor any idea more seductive to a young
man, than to become the arbiter of a young girl's destiny. Let us,
therefore—whatever his defects of nature and education, and in
spite of his scorn for creeds and institutions—concede to the Daguerreotypist the rare and high quality of reverence for another's
individuality. Let us allow him integrity, also, forever after to be
confided in; since he forbade himself to twine that one link more,
which might have rendered his spell over Phoebe indissoluble.

He made a slight gesture upward, with his hand.

"You really mortify me, my dear Miss Phoebe!" he exclaimed,
smiling half sarcastically at her. "My poor story, it is but too evident, will never do for Godey or Graham! Only think of your falling
asleep, at what I hoped the newspaper critics would pronounce a
most brilliant, powerful, imaginative, pathetic, and original winding
up! Well; the manuscript must serve to light lamps with;—if, indeed, being so imbued with my gentle dulness, it is any longer capable of flame!"

"Me asleep! How can you say so?" answered Phoebe, as unconscious of the crisis through which she had passed, as an infant of
the precipice to the verge of which it has rolled. "No, no! I consider
myself as having been very attentive; and though I don't remember
the incidents quite distinctly, yet I have an impression of a vast deal
of trouble and calamity—so, no doubt, the story will prove exceedingly attractive."

By this time, the sun had gone down, and was tinting the clouds
towards the zenith with those bright hues, which are not seen there
until some time after sunset, and when the horizon has quite lost
its richer brilliancy. The moon, too, which had long been climbing
overhead, and unobtrusively melting its disk into the azure—like an
ambitious demagogue, who hides his aspiring purpose by assuming
the prevalent hue of popular sentiment—now began to shine out,
broad and oval, in its middle pathway. These silvery beams were already powerful enough to change the character of the lingering
daylight. They softened and embellished the aspect of the old
house; although the shadows fell deeper into the angles of its many
gables, and lay brooding under the projecting story, and within the
half-open door. With the lapse of every moment, the garden grew
more picturesque; the fruit-trees, shrubbery, and flower-bushes had
a dark obscurity among them. The common-place characteristics—
which, at noontide, it seemed to have taken a century of sordid life
to accumulate—were now transfigured by a charm of romance. A
hundred mysterious years were whispering among the leaves,
whenever the slight sea-breeze found its way thither, and stirred
them. Through the foliage that roofed the little summer-house, the

moonlight flickered to-and-fro, and fell, silvery white, on the dark floor, the table, and the circular bench, with a continual shift and play, according as the chinks and wayward crevices among the twigs admitted or shut out the glimmer.

So sweetly cool was the atmosphere, after all the feverish day, that the summer Eve might be fancied as sprinkling dews and liquid moonlight, with a dash of icy temper in them, out of a silver vase. Here and there, a few drops of this freshness were scattered on a human heart, and gave it youth again, and sympathy with the eternal youth of nature. The artist chanced to be one, on whom the reviving influence fell. It made him feel—what he sometimes almost forgot, thrust so early, as he had been, into the rude struggle of man with man—how youthful he still was.

"It seems to me," he observed, "that I never watched the coming of so beautiful an eve, and never felt anything so very much like happiness as at this moment. After all, what a good world we live in! How good, and beautiful! How young it is, too, with nothing really rotten or age-worn in it! This old house, for example, which sometimes has positively oppressed my breath with its smell of decaying timber! And this garden, where the black mould always clings to my spade, as if I were a sexton, delving in a grave-yard! Could I keep the feeling that now possesses me, the garden would every day be virgin soil, with the earth's first freshness in the flavor of its beans and squashes; and the house!—it would be like a bower in Eden, blossoming with the earliest roses that God ever made. Moonlight, and the sentiment in man's heart, responsive to it, is the greatest of renovators and reformers. And all other reform and renovation, I suppose, will prove to be no better than moonshine!"

"I have been happier than I am now—at least, much gayer," said Phoebe thoughtfully. "Yet I am sensible of a great charm in this brightening moonlight; and I love to watch how the day, tired as it is, lags away reluctantly, and hates to be called yesterday, so soon. I never cared much about moonlight before. What is there, I wonder, so beautiful in it, to-night?"

"And you have never felt it before?" inquired the artist, looking earnestly at the girl, through the twilight.

"Never," answered Phoebe; "and life does not look the same, now that I have felt it so. It seems as if I had looked at everything, hitherto, in broad daylight, or else in the ruddy light of a cheerful fire, glimmering and dancing through a room. Ah, poor me!" she added, with a half-melancholy laugh. "I shall never be so merry as before I knew Cousin Hepzibah and poor Cousin Clifford. I have grown a great deal older, in this little time. Older, and, I hope, wiser, and—not exactly sadder—but, certainly, with not half so much lightness in my spirits! I have given them my sunshine, and have been glad to give it; but, of course, I cannot both give and keep it. They are welcome, notwithstanding!"

"You have lost nothing, Phoebe, worth keeping, nor which it was possible to keep," said Holgrave, after a pause. "Our first youth is of no value; for we are never conscious of it, until after it is gone. But sometimes—always, I suspect, unless one is exceedingly unfortunate—there comes a sense of second youth, gushing out of the heart's joy at being in love; or, possibly, it may come to crown some other grand festival in life, if any other such there be. This bemoaning of one's self (as you do now) over the first, careless, shallow gaiety of youth departed, and this profound happiness at youth regained—so much deeper and richer than that we lost—are essential to the soul's development. In some cases, the two states come almost simultaneously, and mingle the sadness and the rapture in one mysterious emotion."

"I hardly think I understand you," said Phoebe.

"No wonder," replied Holgrave, smiling; "for I have told you a secret which I hardly began to know, before I found myself giving it utterance. Remember it, however; and when the truth becomes clear to you, then think of this moonlight scene!"

"It is entirely moonlight now; except only a little flush of faint crimson, upward from the west, between those buildings," remarked Phoebe. "I must go in. Cousin Hepzibah is not quick at figures, and will give herself a headache over the day's accounts, unless I help her."

But Holgrave detained her a little longer.

"Miss Hepzibah tells me," observed he, "that you return to the country, in a few days."

"Yes; but only for a little while," answered Phoebe; "for I look upon this as my present home. I go to make a few arrangements, and to take a more deliberate leave of my mother and friends. It is pleasant to live where one is much desired, and very useful; and I think I may have the satisfaction of feeling myself so, here."

"You surely may, and more than you imagine," said the artist. "Whatever health, comfort, and natural life, exists in the house, is embodied in your person. These blessings came along with you, and will vanish when you leave the threshold. Miss Hepzibah, by secluding herself from society, has lost all true relation with it, and is in fact dead; although she galvanizes herself into a semblance of life, and stands behind her counter, afflicting the world with a greatly-to-be-deprecated scowl. Your poor Cousin Clifford is another dead and long-buried person, on whom the Governor and Council have wrought a necromantic miracle. I should not wonder if he were to crumble away, some morning, after you are gone, and nothing be seen of him more, except a heap of dust. Miss Hepzibah, at any rate, will lose what little flexibility she has. They both exist by you!"

"I should be very sorry to think so," answered Phoebe, gravely. "But it is true that my small abilities were precisely what they needed; and I have a real interest in their welfare—an odd kind of motherly sentiment—which I wish you would not laugh at! And let me tell you frankly, Mr. Holgrave, I am sometimes puzzled to know whether you wish them well or ill."

"Undoubtedly," said the Daguerreotypist, "I do feel an interest in this antiquated, poverty-stricken, old maiden lady; and this de-graded and shattered gentleman—this abortive lover of the Beauti-ful. A kindly interest too, helpless old children that they are! But you have no conception what a different kind of heart mine is from your own. It is not my impulse—as regards these two individuals—either to help or hinder; but to look on, to analyze, to explain mat-ters to myself, and to comprehend the drama which, for almost two hundred years, has been dragging its slow length over the ground, where you and I now tread. If permitted to witness the close, I doubt not to derive a moral satisfaction from it, go matters how they may. There is a conviction within me, that the end draws nigh. But, though Providence sent you hither to help, and sends me only as a privileged and meet spectator, I pledge myself to lend these un-fortunate beings whatever aid I can!"

"I wish you would speak more plainly," cried Phoebe, perplexed and displeased;—"and, above all, that you would feel more like a christian and a human being! How is it possible to see people in distress, without desiring, more than anything else, to help and comfort them? You talk as if this old house were a theatre; and you seem to look at Hepzibah's and Clifford's misfortunes, and those of generations before them, as a tragedy, such as I have seen acted in the hall of a country-hotel; only the present one appears to be played exclusively for your amusement! I do not like this. The play costs the performers too much—and the audience is too cold-hearted!"

"You are severe!" said Holgrave, compelled to recognize a degree of truth in this piquant sketch of his own mood.

"And then," continued Phoebe, "what can you mean by your con-viction, which you tell me of, that the end is drawing near? Do you know of any new trouble hanging over my poor relatives? If so, tell me at once, and I will not leave them!"

"Forgive me, Phoebe!" said the Daguerreotypist, holding out his hand, to which the girl was constrained to yield her own. "I am somewhat of a mystic, it must be confessed. The tendency is in my blood, together with the faculty of mesmerism, which might have brought me to Gallows-Hill, in the good old times of witchcraft.

Believe me, if I were really aware of any secret, the disclosure of which would benefit your friends—who are my own friends, likewise—you should learn it, before we part. But I have no such knowledge."

"You hold something back!" said Phoebe.

"Nothing—no secrets, but my own," answered Holgrave. "I can perceive, indeed, that Judge Pyncheon still keeps his eye on Clifford, in whose ruin he had so large a share. His motives and intentions, however, are a mystery to me. He is a determined and relentless man, with the genuine character of an inquisitor; and had he any object to gain by putting Clifford to the rack, I verily believe that he would wrench his joints from their sockets in order to accomplish it. But, so wealthy and eminent as he is—so powerful in his own strength, and in the support of society on all sides— what can Judge Pyncheon have to hope or fear from the imbecile, branded, half-torpid Clifford?"

"Yet," urged Phoebe, "you did speak as if misfortune were impending!"

"Oh, that was because I am morbid!" replied the artist. "My mind has a twist aside, like almost everybody's mind, except your own. Moreover, it is so strange to find myself an inmate of this old Pyncheon-house, and sitting in this old garden—(hark, how Maule's Well is murmuring!)—that, were it only for this one circumstance, I cannot help fancying that Destiny is arranging its fifth act for a catastrophe."

"There!" cried Phoebe with renewed vexation; for she was by nature as hostile to mystery, as the sunshine to a dark corner. "You puzzle me more than ever!"

"Then let us part friends!" said Holgrave, pressing her hand. "Or, if not friends, let us part before you entirely hate me. You, who love everybody else in the world!"

"Good bye, then," said Phoebe frankly. "I do not mean to be angry a great while, and should be sorry to have you think so. There has Cousin Hepzibah been standing in the shadow of the door-way, this quarter-of-an-hour past! She thinks I stay too long in the damp garden. So, good night, and good bye!"

On the second morning thereafter, Phoebe might have been seen, in her straw bonnet, with a shawl on one arm and a little carpet-bag on the other, bidding adieu to Hepzibah and Cousin Clifford. She was to take a seat in the next train of cars, which would transport her to within half-a-dozen miles of her country village.

The tears were in Phoebe's eyes; a smile, dewy with affectionate regret, was glimmering around her pleasant mouth. She wondered how it came to pass, that her life of a few weeks, here in this heavy-hearted old mansion, had taken such hold of her, and so melted into her associations, as now to seem a more important centre-point of remembrance than all which had gone before. How had Hepzibah—grim, silent, and irresponsive to her overflow of cordial sentiment—contrived to win so much love? And Clifford—in his abortive decay, with the mystery of fearful crime upon him, and the close prison-atmosphere yet lurking in his breath—how had he transformed himself into the simplest child, whom Phoebe felt bound to watch over, and be, as it were, the Providence of his un-considered hours! Everything, at that instant of farewell, stood out prominently to her view. Look where she would, lay her hand on what she might, the object responded to her consciousness; as if a moist human heart were in it.

She peeped from the window into the garden, and felt herself more regretful at leaving this spot of black earth, vitiated with such an age-long growth of weeds, than joyful at the idea of again scent-ing her pine-forests and fresh clover-fields. She called Chanticleer, his two wives, and the venerable chicken, and threw them some crumbs of bread from the breakfast-table. These being hastily gob-bled up, the chicken spread its wings, and alighted close by Phoebe on the window-sill, where it looked gravely into her face and vented its emotions in a croak. Phoebe bade it be a good old chicken, dur-ing her absence, and promised to bring it a little bag of buckwheat.

"Ah, Phoebe," remarked Hepzibah, "you do not smile so naturally as when you came to us! Then, the smile chose to shine out;—now, you choose it should. It is well that you are going back, for a little while, into your native air! There has been too much weight on your spirits. The house is too gloomy and lonesome; the shop is full of vexations; and as for me, I have no faculty of making things look brighter than they are. Dear Clifford has been your only comfort!"

"Come hither, Phoebe!" suddenly cried her Cousin Clifford, who had said very little, all the morning.—"Close!—closer!—and look me in the face!"

Phoebe put one of her small hands on each elbow of his chair, and leaned her face towards him, so that he might peruse it as carefully as he would. It is probable that the latent emotions of this parting hour had revived, in some degree, his bedimmed and enfee-bled faculties. At any rate, Phoebe soon felt that, if not the pro-found insight of a seer, yet a more than feminine delicacy of appreciation was making her heart the subject of its regard. A mo-ment before, she had known nothing which she would have sought to hide. Now, as if some secret were hinted to her own conscious-ness through the medium of another's perception, she was fain to let her eyelids droop beneath Clifford's gaze. A blush, too—the redder, because she strove hard to keep it down—ascended higher and higher, in a tide of fitful progress, until even her brow was all suffused with it.

"It is enough, Phoebe!" said Clifford, with a melancholy smile. "When I first saw you, you were the prettiest little maiden in the world; and now you have deepened into beauty! Girlhood has passed into womanhood; the bud is a bloom! Go, now! I feel lonelier than I did."

Phoebe took leave of the desolate couple, and passed through the shop, twinkling her eyelids to shake off a dew-drop; for—considering how brief her absence was to be, and therefore the folly of being cast down about it—she would not so far acknowledge her tears as to dry them with her handkerchief. On the door-step, she met the little urchin, whose marvellous feats of gastronomy have been recorded in the earlier pages of our narrative. She took from the window some specimen or other of natural history—her eyes being too dim with moisture to inform her accurately whether it was a rabbit or a hippopotamus—put it into the child's hand, as a parting gift, and went her way. Old Uncle Venner was just coming out of his door, with a wood-horse and saw on his shoulder; and, trudging along the street, he scrupled not to keep company with Phoebe, so far as their paths lay together; nor, in spite of his patched coat and rusty beaver,[4] and the curious fashion of his tow-cloth trowsers, could she find it in her heart to outwalk him.

"We shall miss you, next Sabbath afternoon," observed the street-philosopher. "It is unaccountable how little while it takes some folks to grow just as natural to a man as his own breath; and, begging your pardon, Miss Phoebe, (though there can be no offence in an old man's saying it,) that's just what you've grown, to me! My years have been a great many, and your life is but just beginning; and yet, you are somehow as familiar to me as if I had found you at my mother's door, and you had blossomed, like a running vine, all along my pathway since. Come back soon, or I shall be gone to my farm; for I begin to find these wood-sawing jobs a little too tough for my back-ache."

"Very soon, Uncle Venner," replied Phoebe.

"And let it be all the sooner, Phoebe, for the sake of those poor souls yonder," continued her companion. "They can never do without you, now—never, Phoebe, never!—no more than if one of God's angels had been living with them, and making their dismal house pleasant and comfortable. Don't it seem to you they'd be in a sad case, if, some pleasant summer morning like this, the angel should spread his wings, and fly to the place he came from? Well;

4. A top hat made with beaver fur or an imitation.

just so they feel, now that you're going home by the railroad! They can't bear it, Miss Phoebe; so be sure to come back!"

"I am no angel, Uncle Venner," said Phoebe, smiling, as she offered him her hand at the street-corner. "But, I suppose, people never feel so much like angels as when they are doing what little good they may. So I shall certainly come back!"

Thus parted the old man and the rosy girl; and Phoebe took the wings of the morning, and was soon flitting almost as rapidly away, as if endowed with the aerial locomotion of the angels, to whom Uncle Venner had so graciously compared her.

XV. The Scowl and Smile

Several days passed over the seven gables, heavily and drearily enough. In fact (not to attribute the whole gloom of sky and earth to the one inauspicious circumstance of Phoebe's departure) an easterly storm had set in, and indefatigably applied itself to the task of making the black roof and walls of the old house look more cheerless than ever before. Yet was the outside not half so cheerless as the interior. Poor Clifford was cut off, at once, from all his scanty resources of enjoyment. Phoebe was not there; nor did the sunshine fall upon the floor. The garden, with its muddy walks and the chill, dripping foliage of its summer-house, was an image to be shuddered at. Nothing flourished in the cold, moist, pitiless atmosphere, drifting with the brackish scud of sea-breezes, except the moss along the joints of the shingle-roof, and the great bunch of weeds, that had lately been suffering from drought, in the angle between the two front gables.

As for Hepzibah, she seemed not merely possessed with the east-wind, but to be, in her very person, only another phase of this gray and sullen spell of weather; the East-Wind itself, grim and disconsolate, in a rusty black silk-gown, and with a turban of cloud-wreaths on its head! The custom of the shop fell off, because a story got abroad that she soured her small beer and other damageable commodities, by scowling on them. It is perhaps true, that the public had something reasonably to complain of in her deportment; but towards Clifford she was neither ill-tempered nor unkind, nor felt less warmth of heart than always, had it been possible to make it reach him. The inutility of her best efforts, however, palsied the poor old gentlewoman. She could do little else than sit silently in a corner of the room, where the wet pear-tree branches, sweeping across the small windows, created a noonday dusk, which Hepzibah unconsciously darkened with her wo-begone aspect. It was no fault of Hepzibah's. Everything—even the old chairs and tables, that had known what weather was, for three or four such lifetimes as her own—looked as damp and chill as if the present were their worst experience. The picture of the Puritan Colonel shivered on the wall. The house itself shivered, from every attic of its seven gables, down to the great kitchen-fireplace, which served all the better as an emblem of the mansion's heart, because, though built for warmth, it was now so comfortless and empty.

Hepzibah attempted to enliven matters by a fire in the parlor. But the storm-demon kept watch above, and, whenever a flame was kindled, drove the smoke back again, choking the chimney's sooty throat with its own breath. Nevertheless, during four days of this miserable storm, Clifford wrapt himself in an old cloak, and occupied his customary chair. On the morning of the fifth, when summoned to breakfast, he responded only by a broken-hearted murmur, expressive of a determination not to leave his bed. His sister made no attempt to change his purpose. In fact, entirely as she loved him, Hepzibah could hardly have borne any longer the wretched duty—so impracticable by her few and rigid faculties—of seeking pastime for a still sensitive, but ruined mind, critical, and fastidious, without force or volition. It was, at least, something short of positive despair, that, to-day, she might sit shivering alone, and not suffer continually a new grief, and unreasonable pang of remorse, at every fitful sigh of her fellow-sufferer.

But Clifford, it seemed, though he did not make his appearance below stairs, had, after all, bestirred himself in quest of amusement. In the course of the forenoon, Hepzibah heard a note of music, which (there being no other tuneful contrivance in the House of the Seven Gables) she knew must proceed from Alice Pyncheon's harpsichord. She was aware that Clifford, in his youth, had possessed a cultivated taste for music, and a considerable degree of skill in its practice. It was difficult, however, to conceive of his retaining an accomplishment to which daily exercise is so essential, in the measure indicated by the sweet, airy, and delicate, though most melancholy strain, that now stole upon her ear. Nor was it less marvellous, that the long silent instrument should be capable of so much melody. Hepzibah involuntarily thought of the ghostly harmonies, prelusive of death in the family, which were attributed to the legendary Alice. But it was, perhaps, proof of the agency of other than spiritual fingers, that, after a few touches, the chords seemed to snap asunder with their own vibrations, and the music ceased.

But a harsher sound succeeded to the mysterious notes; nor was the easterly day fated to pass without an event, sufficient in itself to poison, for Hepzibah and Clifford, the balmiest air that ever brought the humming-birds along with it. The final echoes of Alice

Pyncheon's performance, (or Clifford's, if his we must consider it,) were driven away by no less vulgar a dissonance than the ringing of the shop-bell. A foot was heard scraping itself on the threshold, and thence somewhat ponderously stepping on the floor. Hepzibah delayed, a moment, while muffling herself in a faded shawl, which had been her defensive armor in a forty years' warfare against the east-wind. A characteristic sound, however—neither a cough nor a hem, but a kind of rumbling and reverberating spasm in somebody's capacious depth of chest—impelled her to hurry forward, with that aspect of fierce faint-heartedness, so common to women in cases of perilous emergency. Few of her sex, on such occasions, have ever looked so terrible as our poor scowling Hepzibah. But the visitor quietly closed the shop-door behind him, stood up his umbrella against the counter, and turned a visage of composed benignity, to meet the alarm and anger which his appearance had excited.

Hepzibah's presentiment had not deceived her. It was no other than Judge Pyncheon, who, after in vain trying the front-door, had now effected his entrance into the shop.

"How do you do, Cousin Hepzibah?—and how does this most inclement weather affect our poor Clifford?" began the Judge; and wonderful it seemed, indeed, that the easterly storm was not put to shame, or, at any rate, a little mollified, by the genial benevolence of his smile. "I could not rest without calling to ask, once more, whether I can in any manner promote his comfort, or your own!"

"You can do nothing," said Hepzibah, controlling her agitation as well as she could. "I devote myself to Clifford. He has every comfort which his situation admits of."

"But, allow me to suggest, dear Cousin," rejoined the Judge, "you err—in all affection and kindness, no doubt, and with the very best intentions—but you do err, nevertheless, in keeping your brother so secluded. Why insulate him thus from all sympathy and kindness? Clifford, alas! has had too much of solitude. Now let him try society—the society, that is to say, of kindred and old friends. Let me, for instance, but see Clifford; and I will answer for the good effect of the interview."

"You cannot see him," answered Hepzibah. "Clifford has kept his bed since yesterday."

"What! How! Is he ill?" exclaimed Judge Pyncheon, starting with what seemed to be angry alarm; for the very frown of the old Puritan darkened through the room as he spoke. "Nay, then, I must and will see him! What if he should die?"

"He is in no danger of death," said Hepzibah—and added, with bitterness that she could repress no longer, "None;—unless he shall be persecuted to death, now, by the same man who long ago attempted it!"

"Cousin Hepzibah," said the Judge, with an impressive earnestness of manner, which grew even to tearful pathos as he proceeded, "is it possible that you do not perceive how unjust, how unkind, how unchristian, is this constant, this long-continued bitterness against me, for a part which I was constrained by duty and conscience, by the force of law, and at my own peril, to act? What did I do, in detriment to Clifford, which it was possible to leave undone? How could you, his sister—if, for your never-ending sorrow, as it has been for mine, you had known what I did—have shown greater tenderness? And do you think, Cousin, that it has cost me no pang?—that it has left no anguish in my bosom, from that day to this, amidst all the prosperity with which Heaven has blessed me?—or that I do not now rejoice, when it is deemed consistent with the dues of public justice and the welfare of society, that this dear kinsman, this early friend, this nature so delicately and beautifully constituted—so unfortunate, let us pronounce him, and forbear to say, so guilty—that our own Clifford, in fine, should be given back to life and its possibilities of enjoyment? Ah, you little know me, Cousin Hepzibah! You little know this heart! It now throbs at the thought of meeting him! There lives not the human being—(except yourself; and you not more than I)—who has shed so many tears for Clifford's calamity! You behold some of them now. There is none who would so delight to promote his happiness! Try me, Hepzibah!—try me, Cousin!—try the man whom you have treated as your enemy and Clifford's!—try Jaffrey Pyncheon, and you shall find him true, to the heart's core!"

"In the name of Heaven," cried Hepzibah, provoked only to intenser indignation by this outgush of the inestimable tenderness of a stern nature—"in God's name, whom you insult—and whose power I could almost question, since He hears you utter so many false words, without palsying your tongue—give over, I beseech you, this loathsome pretence of affection for your victim! You hate him! Say so, like a man! You cherish, at this moment, some black purpose against him, in your heart! Speak it out, at once!—or, if you hope so to promote it better, hide it, till you can triumph in its success. But never speak again of your love for my poor brother! I cannot bear it! It will drive me beyond a woman's decency! It will drive me mad! Forbear! Not another word! It will make me spurn at you!"

For once, Hepzibah's wrath had given her courage. She had spoken. But, after all, was this unconquerable distrust of Judge Pyncheon's integrity—and this utter denial, apparently, of his claim to stand in the ring of human sympathies—were they founded in any just perception of his character, or merely the offspring of a woman's unreasoning prejudice, deduced from nothing?

The Judge, beyond all question, was a man of eminent respectability. The church acknowledged it; the state acknowledged
it. It was denied by nobody. In all the very extensive sphere of those
who knew him, whether in his public or private capacities, there
was not an individual—except Hepzibah, and some lawless mystic
like the Daguerreotypist, and possibly a few political opponents—
who would have dreamed of seriously disputing his claim to a high
and honorable place in the world's regard. Nor, we must do him the
further justice to say, did Judge Pyncheon himself, probably, entertain many or very frequent doubts, that his enviable reputation
accorded with his deserts. His conscience, therefore—usually considered the surest witness to a man's integrity—his conscience,
unless, it might be for the little space of five minutes in the twenty-
four hours, or, now and then, some black day in the whole year's
circle—his conscience bore an accordant testimony with the
world's laudatory voice. And yet, strong as this evidence may seem
to be, we should hesitate to peril our own conscience on the assertion, that the Judge and the consenting world were right, and that
poor Hepzibah, with her solitary prejudice, was wrong. Hidden
from mankind—forgotten by himself, or buried so deeply under a
sculptured and ornamented pile of ostentatious deeds, that his
daily life could take no note of it—there may have lurked some evil
and unsightly thing. Nay; we could almost venture to say farther,
that a daily guilt might have been acted by him, continually renewed, and reddening forth afresh, like the miraculous blood-stain
of a murder, without his necessarily, and at every moment, being
aware of it.

Men of strong minds, great force of character, and a hard texture
of the sensibilities, are very capable of falling into mistakes of this
kind. They are ordinarily men to whom forms are of paramount importance. Their field of action lies among the external phenomena
of life. They possess vast ability in grasping, and arranging, and appropriating to themselves, the big, heavy, solid unrealities, such as
gold, landed estate, offices of trust and emolument, and public
honors. With these materials, and with deeds of goodly aspect,
done in the public eye, an individual of this class builds up, as it
were, a tall and stately edifice, which, in the view of other people,
and ultimately in his own view, is no other than the man's character, or the man himself. Behold, therefore, a palace! Its splendid
halls and suites of spacious apartments are floored with a mosaic-
work of costly marbles; its windows, the whole height of each room,
admit the sunshine through the most transparent of plate-glass; its
high cornices are gilded, and its ceilings gorgeously painted; and a
lofty dome—through which, from the central pavement, you may
gaze up to the sky, as with no obstructing medium between—sur-

mounts the whole. With what fairer and nobler emblem could any man desire to shadow forth his character? Ah; but in some low and obscure nook—some narrow closet on the ground floor, shut, locked, and bolted, and the key flung away—or beneath the marble pavement, in a stagnant water-puddle, with the richest pattern of mosaic-work above—may lie a corpse, half-decayed, and still decaying, and diffusing its death-scent all through the palace! The inhabitant will not be conscious of it; for it has long been his daily breath! Neither will the visitors; for they smell only the rich odors which the master sedulously scatters through the palace, and the incense which they bring, and delight to burn before him! Now and then, perchance, comes in a seer, before whose sadly gifted eye the whole structure melts into thin air, leaving only the hidden nook, the bolted closet, with the cobwebs festooned over its forgotten door, or the deadly hole under the pavement, and the decaying corpse within. Here, then, we are to seek the true emblem of the man's character, and of the deed that gives whatever reality it possesses, to his life. And, beneath the show of a marble palace, that pool of stagnant water, foul with many impurities, and perhaps tinged with blood—that secret abomination, above which, possibly, he may say his prayers, without remembering it—is this man's miserable soul!

To apply this train of remark somewhat more closely to Judge Pyncheon! We might say (without, in the least, imputing crime to a personage of his eminent respectability) that there was enough of splendid rubbish in his life to cover up and paralyze a more active and subtle conscience than the Judge was ever troubled with. The purity of his judicial character, while on the bench; the faithfulness of his public service in subsequent capacities; his devotedness to his party, and the rigid consistency with which he had adhered to its principles, or, at all events, kept pace with its organized movements; his remarkable zeal as president of a Bible society; his unimpeachable integrity as treasurer of a Widow's and Orphan's fund; his benefits to horticulture, by producing two much-esteemed varieties of the pear, and to agriculture, through the agency of the famous Pyncheon-bull; the cleanliness of his moral deportment, for a great many years past; the severity with which he had frowned upon, and finally cast off, an expensive and dissipated son, delaying forgiveness until within the final quarter of an hour of the young man's life; his prayers at morning and eventide, and graces at mealtime; his efforts in furtherance of the temperance-cause; his confining himself, since the last attack of the gout, to five diurnal glasses of old Sherry wine; the snowy whiteness of his linen, the polish of his boots, the handsomeness of his gold-headed cane, the square and roomy fashion of his coat, and the fineness of its material, and, in general, the studied propriety of his dress and equipment; the scrupulousness with which he paid public notice, in the street, by a bow, a lifting of the hat, a nod, or a motion of the hand, to all and sundry his acquaintances, rich or poor, the smile of broad benevolence wherewith he made it a point to gladden the whole world;—what room could possibly be found for darker traits, in a portrait made up of lineaments like these! This proper face was what he beheld in the looking-glass. This admirably arranged life was what he was conscious of, in the progress of every day. Then, might not he claim to be its result and sum, and say to himself and the community—"Behold Judge Pyncheon, there"?

And, allowing that, many, many years ago, in his early and reck-less youth, he had committed some one wrong act—or that, even now, the inevitable force of circumstances should occasionally make him do one questionable deed, among a thousand praisewor-thy, or, at least, blameless ones—would you characterize the Judge by that one necessary deed, and that half-forgotten act, and let it overshadow the fair aspect of a lifetime! What is there so ponder-ous in evil, that a thumb's bigness of it should outweigh the mass of things not evil, which were heaped into the other scale! This scale and balance system is a favorite one with people of Judge Pyn-cheon's brotherhood. A hard, cold man, thus unfortunately situ-ated, seldom or never looking inward, and resolutely taking his idea of himself from what purports to be his image, as reflected in the mirror of public opinion, can scarcely arrive at true self-knowledge, except through loss of property and reputation. Sickness will not al-ways help him to it; not always the death-hour!

But our affair, now, is with Judge Pyncheon, as he stood con-fronting the fierce outbreak of Hepzibah's wrath. Without premedi-tation, to her own surprise, and indeed terror, she had given vent, for once, to the inveteracy of her resentment, cherished against this kinsman, for thirty years.

Thus far, the Judge's countenance had expressed mild forbear-ance—grave and almost gentle deprecation of his cousin's unbe-coming violence—free and christianlike forgiveness of the wrong inflicted by her words. But, when those words were irrevocably spo-ken, his look assumed sternness, the sense of power, and immitiga-ble resolve; and this with so natural and imperceptible a change, that it seemed as if the iron man had stood there from the first, and the meek man not at all. The effect was as when the light vapory clouds, with their soft coloring, suddenly vanish from the stony brow of a precipitous mountain, and leave there the frown which you at once feel to be eternal. Hepzibah almost adopted the insane belief, that it was her old Puritan ancestor, and not the modern Judge, on whom she had just been wreaking the bitterness of her heart. Never did a man show stronger proof of the lineage attributed to him, than Judge Pyncheon, at this crisis, by his unmistakeable resemblance to the picture in the inner room.

"Cousin Hepzibah," said he, very calmly, "it is time to have done with this."

"With all my heart!" answered she. "Then why do you persecute us any longer? Leave poor Clifford and me in peace. Neither of us desires anything better!"

"It is my purpose to see Clifford before I leave this house," continued the Judge. "Do not act like a madwoman, Hepzibah! I am his only friend, and an all-powerful one. Has it never occurred to you—are you so blind as not to have seen—that, without not merely my consent, but my efforts, my representations, the exertion of my whole influence, political, official, personal—Clifford would never have been what you call free? Did you think his release a triumph over me? Not so, my good Cousin; not so, by any means! The farthest possible from that! No; but it was the accomplishment of a purpose long entertained on my part. I set him free!"

"You!" answered Hepzibah. "I never will believe it! He owed his dungeon to you; his freedom, to God's providence!"

"I set him free!" re-affirmed Judge Pyncheon, with the calmest composure. "And I come hither now to decide whether he shall retain his freedom. It will depend upon himself. For this purpose, I must see him."

"Never!—it would drive him mad!" exclaimed Hepzibah, but with an irresoluteness, sufficiently perceptible to the keen eye of the Judge; for, without the slightest faith in his good intentions, she knew not whether there was most to dread in yielding, or resistance. "And why should you wish to see this wretched, broken man, who retains hardly a fraction of his intellect, and will hide even that from an eye which has no love in it?"

"He shall see love enough in mine, if that be all!" said the Judge, with well-grounded confidence in the benignity of his aspect. "But, Cousin Hepzibah, you confess a great deal, and very much to the purpose. Now, listen, and I will frankly explain my reasons for insisting on this interview. At the death, thirty years since, of our Uncle Jaffrey, it was found—I know not whether the circumstance ever attracted much of your attention, among the sadder interests that clustered round that event—but it was found that his visible estate, of every kind, fell far short of any estimate ever made of it. He was supposed to be immensely rich. Nobody doubted that he stood among the weightiest men of his day. It was one of his eccentricities, however—and not altogether a folly, neither—to conceal the amount of his property by making distant and foreign investments, perhaps under other names than his own, and by various means, familiar enough to capitalists, but unnecessary here to be specified. By Uncle Jaffrey's last will and testament, as you are aware, his entire property was bequeathed to me, with the single exception of a life-interest, to yourself, in this old family-mansion, and the strip of patrimonial estate, remaining attached to it."

"And do you seek to deprive us of that?" asked Hepzibah, unable to restrain her bitter contempt. "Is this your price for ceasing to persecute poor Clifford?"

"Certainly not, my dear Cousin!" answered the Judge, smiling benevolently. "On the contrary, as you must do me the justice to own, I have constantly expressed my readiness to double or treble your resources, whenever you should make up your mind to accept any kindness of that nature, at the hands of your kinsman. No, no! But here lies the gist of the matter. Of my Uncle's unquestionably great estate, as I have said, not the half—no, not one third, as I am fully convinced—was apparent after his death. Now, I have the best possible reasons for believing, that your brother Clifford can give me a clue to the recovery of the remainder!"

"Clifford?—Clifford know of any hidden wealth?—Clifford have it in his power to make you rich?" cried the old gentlewoman, affected with a sense of something like ridicule, at the idea. "Impossible! You deceive yourself! It is really a thing to laugh at!"

"It is as certain as that I stand here!" said Judge Pyncheon, striking his gold-headed cane on the floor, and at the same time stamping his foot, as if to express his conviction the more forcibly by the whole emphasis of his substantial person.—"Clifford told me so himself!"

"No, no!" exclaimed Hepzibah incredulously. "You are dreaming, Cousin Jaffrey!"

"I do not belong to the dreaming class of men," said the Judge quietly. "Some months before my Uncle's death, Clifford boasted to me of the possession of the secret of incalculable wealth. His purpose was to taunt me, and excite my curiosity. I know it well. But, from a pretty distinct recollection of the particulars of our conversation, I am thoroughly convinced that there was truth in what he said. Clifford, at this moment, if he chooses—and choose he must—can inform me where to find the schedule, the documents, the evidences, in whatever shape they exist, of the vast amount of Uncle Jaffrey's missing property. He has the secret. His boast was no idle word. It had a directness, an emphasis, a particularity, that showed a backbone of solid meaning within the mystery of his expression."

"But what could have been Clifford's object," asked Hepzibah, "in concealing it so long?"

"It was one of the bad impulses of our fallen nature," replied the

Judge, turning up his eyes. "He looked upon me as his enemy. He considered me as the cause of his overwhelming disgrace, his imminent peril of death, his irretrievable ruin. There was no great probability, therefore, of his volunteering information, out of his dungeon, that should elevate me still higher on the ladder of prosperity. But the moment has now come, when he must give up his secret."

"And what if he should refuse?" inquired Hepzibah. "Or—as I steadfastly believe—what if he has no knowledge of this wealth?"

"My dear Cousin," said Judge Pyncheon, with a quietude which he had the power of making more formidable than any violence, "since your brother's return, I have taken the precaution (a highly proper one in the near kinsman and natural guardian of an individual so situated) to have his deportment and habits constantly and carefully overlooked. Your neighbors have been eye-witnesses to whatever has passed in the garden. The butcher, the baker, the fishmonger, some of the customers of your shop, and many a prying old woman, have told me several of the secrets of your interior. A still larger circle—I myself among the rest—can testify to his extravagances, at the arched window. Thousands beheld him, a week or two ago, on the point of flinging himself thence into the street. From all this testimony, I am led to apprehend—reluctantly, and with deep grief—that Clifford's misfortunes have so affected his intellect, never very strong, that he cannot safely remain at large. The alternative, you must be aware—and its adoption will depend entirely on the decision which I am now about to make—the alternative is his confinement, probably for the remainder of his life, in a public asylum for persons in his unfortunate state of mind."

"You cannot mean it!" shrieked Hepzibah.

"Should my Cousin Clifford," continued Judge Pyncheon, wholly undisturbed, "from mere malice, and hatred of one whose interests ought naturally to be dear to him—a mode of passion that, as often as any other, indicates mental disease—should he refuse me the information, so important to myself, and which he assuredly possesses, I shall consider it the one needed jot of evidence, to satisfy my mind of his insanity. And, once sure of the course pointed out by conscience, you know me too well, Cousin Hepzibah, to entertain a doubt that I shall pursue it."

"Oh, Jaffrey—Cousin Jaffrey," cried Hepzibah, mournfully, not passionately—"it is you that are diseased in mind, not Clifford! You have forgotten that a woman was your mother!—that you have had sisters, brothers, children of your own!—or that there ever was affection between man and man, or pity from one man to another, in this miserable world! Else, how could you have dreamed of this? You are not young, Cousin Jaffrey—no, nor middle-aged—but already an old man. The hair is white upon your head! How many years have you to live? Are you not rich enough for that little time? Shall you be hungry?—shall you lack clothes, or a roof to shelter you, between this point and the grave? No; but, with the half of what you now possess, you could revel in costly food and wines, and build a house twice as splendid as you now inhabit, and make a far greater show to the world—and yet leave riches to your only son, to make him bless the hour of your death! Then why should you do this cruel, cruel thing?—so mad a thing, that I know not whether to call it wicked! Alas, Cousin Jaffrey, this hard and grasping spirit has run in our blood, these two hundred years! You are but doing over again, in another shape, what your ancestor before you did, and sending down to your posterity the curse inherited from him!"

"Talk sense, Hepzibah, for Heaven's sake!" exclaimed the Judge, with the impatience natural to a reasonable man, on hearing anything so utterly absurd as the above, in a discussion about matters of business. "I have told you my determination. I am not apt to change. Clifford must give up his secret, or take the consequences. And let him decide quickly; for I have several affairs to attend to, this morning, and an important dinner-engagement with some political friends."

"Clifford has no secret!" answered Hepzibah. "And God will not let you do the thing you meditate!"

"We shall see!" said the unmoved Judge. "Meanwhile, choose whether you will summon Clifford, and allow this business to be amicably settled by an interview between two kinsmen; or drive me to harsher measures, which I should be most happy to feel myself justified in avoiding. The responsibility is altogether on your part."

"You are stronger than I," said Hepzibah, after a brief consideration; "and you have no pity in your strength. Clifford is not now insane; but the interview, which you insist upon, may go far to make him so. Nevertheless, knowing you as I do, I believe it to be my best course to allow you to judge for yourself as to the improbability of his possessing any valuable secret. I will call Clifford. Be merciful in your dealings with him!—be far more merciful than your heart bids you be!—for God is looking at you, Jaffrey Pyncheon!"

The Judge followed his cousin from the shop, where the foregoing conversation had passed, into the parlor, and flung himself heavily into the great, ancestral chair. Many a former Pyncheon had found repose in its capacious arms;—rosy children, after their sports, young men, dreamy with love, grown men, weary with cares, old men, burthened with winters;—they had mused, and slumbered, and departed, to a yet profounder sleep. It had been a long tradition, though a doubtful one, that this was the very chair,

seated in which, the earliest of the Judge's New England forefathers—he whose picture still hung upon the wall—had given a
dead man's silent and stern reception to the throng of distinguished
guests. From that hour of evil omen, until the present, it may be—
though we know not the secret of his heart—but it may be, that no
wearier and sadder man had ever sunk into the chair, than this
same Judge Pyncheon, whom we have just beheld so immitigably
hard and resolute. Surely, it must have been at no slight cost, that
he had thus fortified his soul with iron! Such calmness is a might-
ier effort than the violence of weaker men. And there was yet a
heavy task for him to do! Was it a little matter—a trifle, to be prepared for in a single moment, and to be rested from, in another moment—that he must now, after thirty years, encounter a kinsman
risen from a living tomb, and wrench a secret from him, or else
consign him to a living tomb again?

"Did you speak?" asked Hepzibah, looking in from the threshold
of the parlor; for she imagined that the Judge had uttered some
sound, which she was anxious to interpret as a relenting impulse. "I
thought you called me back!"

"No, no!" gruffly answered Judge Pyncheon, with a harsh frown,
while his brow grew almost a black purple, in the shadow of the
room. "Why should I call you back? Time flies! Bid Clifford come
to me!"

The Judge had taken his watch from his vest-pocket, and now
held it in his hand, measuring the interval which was to ensue before the appearance of Clifford.

XVI. Clifford's Chamber

Never had the old house appeared so dismal to poor Hepzibah, as
when she departed on that wretched errand. There was a strange
aspect in it. As she trode along the foot-worn passages, and opened
one crazy door after another, and ascended the creaking staircase,
she gazed wistfully and fearfully around. It would have been no
marvel, to her excited mind, if, behind or beside her, there had
been the rustle of dead people's garments, or pale visages awaiting
her on the landing place above. Her nerves were set all ajar by the
scene of passion and terror, through which she had just struggled.
Her colloquy with Judge Pyncheon, who so perfectly represented
the person and attributes of the founder of the family, had called
back the dreary past. It weighed upon her heart. Whatever she had
heard from legendary aunts and grandmothers, concerning the
good or evil fortunes of the Pyncheons—stories, which had heretofore been kept warm in her remembrance by the chimney-corner

glow, that was associated with them—now recurred to her, sombre, ghastly, cold, like most passages of family history, when brooded over in melancholy mood. The whole seemed little else but a series of calamity, reproducing itself in successive generations, with one general hue, and varying in little save the outline. But Hepzibah now felt as if the Judge, and Clifford, and herself—they three together—were on the point of adding another incident to the annals of the house, with a bolder relief of wrong and sorrow, which would cause it to stand out from all the rest. Thus it is, that the grief of the passing moment takes upon itself an individuality, and a character of climax, which it is destined to lose, after awhile, and to fade into the dark gray tissue, common to the grave or glad events of many years ago. It is but for a moment, comparatively, that anything looks strange or startling;—a truth, that has the bitter and the sweet in it!

But Hepzibah could not rid herself of the sense of something unprecedented, at that instant passing, and soon to be accomplished. Her nerves were in a shake. Instinctively, she paused before the arched window, and looked out upon the street, in order to seize its permanent objects with her mental grasp, and thus to steady herself from the reel and vibration which affected her more immediate sphere. It brought her up, as we may say, with a kind of shock, when she beheld everything under the same appearance as the day before, and numberless preceding days, except for the difference between sunshine and sullen storm. Her eyes travelled along the street, from door-step to door-step, noting the wet sidewalks, with here and there a puddle in hollows that had been imperceptible, until filled with water. She screwed her dim optics to their acutest point in the hope of making out, with greater distinctness, a certain window, where she half saw, half guessed, that a tailor's seamstress was sitting at her work. Hepzibah flung herself upon that unknown woman's companionship, even thus far off. Then she was attracted by a chaise rapidly passing, and watched its moist and glistening top, and its splashing wheels, until it had turned the corner, and refused to carry any further her idly trifling, because appalled and overburthened, mind. When the vehicle had disappeared, she allowed herself still another loitering moment; for the patched figure of good Uncle Venner was now visible, coming slowly from the head of the street downward, with a rheumatic limp, because the east-wind had got into his joints. Hepzibah wished that he would pass yet more slowly, and befriend her shivering solitude, a little longer. Anything that would take her out of the grievous present, and interpose human beings betwixt herself and what was nearest to her—whatever would defer, for an instant, the inevitable errand on which she was bound—all such impediments were welcome. Next to the lightest heart, the heaviest is apt to be most playful.

Hepzibah had little hardihood for her own proper pain, and far less for what she must inflict on Clifford. Of so slight a nature, and so shattered by his previous calamities, it could not well be short of utter ruin, to bring him face to face with the hard, relentless man, who had been his Evil Destiny through life. Even had there been no bitter recollections, nor any hostile interest now at stake between them, the mere natural repugnance of the more sensitive system to the massive, weighty, and unimpressible one, must in itself have been disastrous to the former. It would be like flinging a porcelain vase, with already a crack in it, against a granite column. Never before had Hepzibah so adequately estimated the powerful character of her Cousin Jaffrey;—powerful by intellect, energy of will, the long habit of acting among men, and, as she believed, by his unscrupulous pursuit of selfish ends through evil means. It did but increase the difficulty, that Judge Pyncheon was under a delusion as to the secret which he supposed Clifford to possess. Men of his strength of purpose, and customary sagacity, if they chance to adopt a mistaken opinion in practical matters, so wedge it and fasten it among things known to be true, that to wrench it out of their minds is hardly less difficult than pulling up an oak. Thus, as the Judge required an impossibility of Clifford, the latter, as he could not perform it, must needs perish. For what, in the grasp of a man like this, was to become of Clifford's soft, poetic nature, that never should have had a task more stubborn than to set a life of beautiful enjoyment to the flow and rhythm of musical cadences! Indeed, what had become of it, already? Broken! Blighted! All but annihilated! Soon to be wholly so!

For a moment, the thought crossed Hepzibah's mind, whether Clifford might not really have such knowledge of their deceased uncle's vanished estate, as the Judge imputed to him. She remembered some vague intimations, on her brother's part, which—if the supposition were not essentially preposterous—might have been so interpreted. There had been schemes of travel and residence abroad, day-dreams of brilliant life at home, and splendid castles in the air, which it would have required boundless wealth to build and realize. Had this wealth been in her power, how gladly would Hepzibah have bestowed it all upon her iron-hearted kinsman, to buy for Clifford the freedom and seclusion of the desolate old house! But she believed that her brother's schemes were as destitute of actual substance and purpose, as a child's pictures of its future life, while sitting in a little chair by its mother's knee. Clifford had none but shadowy gold at his command; and it was not the stuff to satisfy Judge Pyncheon!

Was there no help in their extremity? It seemed strange that there should be none, with a city roundabout her. It would be so

easy to throw up the window and send forth a shriek, at the strange
agony of which, everybody would come hastening to the rescue,
well understanding it to be the cry of a human soul, at some dreadful crisis! But how wild, how almost laughable the fatality—and yet
how continually it comes to pass, thought Hepzibah, in this dull
delirium of a world—that whosoever, and with however kindly a
purpose, should come to help, they would be sure to help the
strongest side! Might and wrong combined, like iron magnetized,
are endowed with irresistible attraction. There would be Judge Pyncheon; a person eminent in the public view, of high station and
great wealth, a philanthropist, a member of Congress and of the
church, and intimately associated with whatever else bestows good
name; so imposing, in these advantageous lights, that Hepzibah
herself could hardly help shrinking from her own conclusions as to
his hollow integrity! The Judge, on one side! And who, on the
other? The guilty Clifford! Once, a by-word! Now, an indistinctly
remembered ignominy!

Nevertheless, in spite of this perception that the Judge would
draw all human aid to his own behalf, Hepzibah was so unaccustomed to act for herself, that the least word of counsel would have
swayed her to any mode of action. Little Phoebe Pyncheon would
at once have lighted up the whole scene, if not by any available suggestion, yet simply by the warm vivacity of her character. The idea
of the artist occurred to Hepzibah. Young and unknown, mere vagrant adventurer as he was, she had been conscious of a force in
Holgrave, which might well adapt him to be the champion of a crisis. With this thought in her mind, she unbolted a door, cobwebbed
and long disused, but which had served as a former medium of
communication between her own part of the house, and the gable
where the wandering Daguerreotypist had now established his temporary home. He was not there. A book, face downward on the
table, a roll of manuscript, a half-written sheet, a newspaper, some
tools of his present occupation, and several rejected daguerreotypes, conveyed an impression as if he were close at hand. But, at
this period of the day, as Hepzibah might have anticipated, the
artist was at his public rooms. With an impulse of idle curiosity,
that flickered among her heavy thoughts, she looked at one of the
daguerreotypes, and beheld Judge Pyncheon frowning at her! Fate
stared her in the face. She turned back from her fruitless quest,
with a heart-sinking sense of disappointment. In all her years of
seclusion, she had never felt, as now, what it was to be alone. It
seemed as if the house stood in a desert, or, by some spell, was
made invisible to those who dwelt around, or passed beside it; so
that any mode of misfortune, miserable accident, or crime, might
happen in it, without the possibility of aid. In her grief and

wounded pride, Hepzibah had spent her life in divesting herself of
friends;—she had wilfully cast off the support which God has ordained His creatures to need from one another;—and it was now
her punishment, that Clifford and herself would fall the easier victims to their kindred enemy.

Returning to the arched window, she lifted her eyes—scowling,
poor, dim-sighted Hepzibah, in the face of Heaven!—and strove
hard to send up a prayer through the dense, gray pavement of
clouds. Those mists had gathered, as if to symbolize a great, brooding mass of human trouble, doubt, confusion, and chill indifference, between earth and the better regions. Her faith was too weak;
the prayer too heavy to be thus uplifted. It fell back, a lump of lead,
upon her heart. It smote her with the wretched conviction, that
Providence intermeddled not in these petty wrongs of one individual to his fellow, nor had any balm for these little agonies of a solitary soul, but shed its justice, and its mercy, in a broad, sunlike
sweep, over half the universe at once. Its vastness made it nothing.
But Hepzibah did not see, that, just as there comes a warm sunbeam into every cottage-window, so comes a love-beam of God's
care and pity, for every separate need.

At last, finding no other pretext for deferring the torture that she
was to inflict on Clifford, her reluctance to which was the true
cause of her loitering at the window, her search for the artist, and
even her abortive prayer—dreading also to hear the stern voice of
Judge Pyncheon from below stairs, chiding her delay—she crept
slowly, a pale, grief-stricken figure, a dismal shape of woman, with
almost torpid limbs, slowly to her brother's door, and knocked.

There was no reply!

And how should there have been! Her hand, tremulous with the
shrinking purpose which directed it, had smitten so feebly against
the door that the sound could hardly have gone inward. She
knocked again. Still, no response! Nor was it to be wondered at.
She had struck with the entire force of her heart's vibration, communicating by some subtle magnetism her own terror to the summons. Clifford would turn his face to the pillow, and cover his head
beneath the bed-clothes, like a startled child at midnight. She
knocked a third time, three regular strokes, gentle, but perfectly
distinct, and with meaning in them; for, modulate it with what cautious art we will, the hand cannot help playing some tune of what
we feel, upon the senseless wood.

Clifford returned no answer.

"Clifford! Dear brother!" said Hepzibah. "Shall I come in?"

A silence!

Two or three times, and more, Hepzibah repeated his name, without result; till, thinking her brother's sleep unwontedly profound,

she undid the door, and entering, found the chamber vacant. How could he have come forth, and when, without her knowledge? Was it possible that, in spite of the stormy day, and worn out with the irksomeness within doors, he had betaken himself to his customary haunt, in the garden, and was now shivering under the cheerless shelter of the summer-house? She hastily threw up a window, thrust forth her turbaned head and the half of her gaunt figure, and searched the whole garden through, as completely as her dim vision would allow. She could see the interior of the summer-house, and its circular seat, kept moist by the droppings of the roof. It had no occupant. Clifford was not thereabouts; unless, indeed, he had crept for concealment—(as, for a moment, Hepzibah fancied might be the case)—into a great, wet mass of tangled and broad-leaved shadow, where the squash-vines were clambering tumultuously upon an old wooden frame-work, set casually aslant against the fence. This could not be, however; he was not there; for, while Hepzibah was looking, a strange Grimalkin[5] stole forth from the very spot, and picked his way across the garden. Twice, he paused to snuff the air, and then anew directed his course towards the parlor-window. Whether it was only on account of the stealthy, prying manner common to the race, or that this cat seemed to have more than ordinary mischief in his thoughts, the old gentlewoman, in spite of her much perplexity, felt an impulse to drive the animal away, and accordingly flung down a window-stick. The cat stared up at her, like a detected thief or murderer, and, the next instant, took to flight. No other living creature was visible in the garden. Chanticleer and his family had either not left their roost, disheartened by the interminable rain, or had done the next wisest thing, by seasonably returning to it. Hepzibah closed the window.

But where was Clifford? Could it be, that, aware of the presence of his Evil Destiny, he had crept silently down the staircase, while the Judge and Hepzibah stood talking in the shop, and had softly undone the fastenings of the outer door, and made his escape into the street? With that thought, she seemed to behold his gray, wrinkled, yet childlike aspect, in the old-fashioned garments which he wore about the house; a figure such as one sometimes imagines himself to be, with the world's eye upon him, in a troubled dream. This figure of her wretched brother would go wandering through the city, attracting all eyes, and everybody's wonder and repugnance, like a ghost, the more to be shuddered at because visible at noontide. To incur the ridicule of the younger crowd, that knew him not; the harsher scorn and indignation of a few old men, who might recall his once familiar features! To be the sport of boys,

5. A cat, typically an old female cat.

who, when old enough to run about the streets, have no more reverence for what is beautiful and holy, nor pity for what is sad—no more sense of sacred misery, sanctifying the human shape in which it embodies itself—than if Satan were the father of them all! Goaded by their taunts, their loud, shrill cries, and cruel laughter—insulted by the filth of the public ways, which they would fling upon him—or, as it might well be, distracted by the mere strangeness of his situation, though nobody should afflict him with so much as a thoughtless word—what wonder if Clifford were to break into some wild extravagance, which was certain to be interpreted as lunacy? Thus Judge Pyncheon's fiendish scheme would be ready accomplished to his hands!

Then Hepzibah reflected that the town was almost completely water-girdled. The wharves stretched out towards the centre of the harbor, and, in this inclement weather, were deserted by the ordinary throng of merchants, laborers, and sea-faring men; each wharf a solitude, with the vessels moored stem and stern, along its misty length. Should her brother's aimless footsteps stray thitherward, and he but bend, one moment, over the deep, black tide, would he not bethink himself that here was the sure refuge within his reach, and that, with a single step, or the slightest overbalance of his body, he might be forever beyond his kinsman's gripe? Oh, the temptation! To make of his ponderous sorrow a security! To sink, with its leaden weight upon him, and never rise again!

The horror of this last conception was too much for Hepzibah. Even Jaffrey Pyncheon must help her now! She hastened down the staircase, shrieking as she went.

"Clifford is gone!" she cried. "I cannot find my brother! Help, Jaffrey Pyncheon! Some harm will happen to him!"

She threw open the parlor-door. But, what with the shade of branches across the windows, and the smoke-blackened ceiling, and the dark oak-panelling of the walls, there was hardly so much daylight in the room that Hepzibah's imperfect sight could accurately distinguish the Judge's figure. She was certain, however, that she saw him sitting in the ancestral arm-chair, near the centre of the floor, with his face somewhat averted, and looking towards a window. So firm and quiet is the nervous system of such men as Judge Pyncheon, that he had perhaps stirred not more than once since her departure, but, in the hard composure of his temperament, retained the position into which accident had thrown him.

"I tell you, Jaffrey," cried Hepzibah impatiently, as she turned from the parlor-door to search other rooms, "my brother is not in his chamber! You must help me seek him!"

But Judge Pyncheon was not the man to let himself be startled from an easy-chair, with haste ill-befitting either the dignity of his character or his broad personal basis, by the alarm of an hysteric woman. Yet, considering his own interest in the matter, he might have bestirred himself with a little more alacrity!

"Do you hear me, Jaffrey Pyncheon?" screamed Hepzibah, as she again approached the parlor-door, after an ineffectual search elsewhere. "Clifford is gone!"

At this instant, on the threshold of the parlor, emerging from within, appeared Clifford himself! His face was preternaturally pale; so deadly white, indeed, that, through all the glimmering indistinctness of the passage-way, Hepzibah could discern his features, as if a light fell on them alone. Their vivid and wild expression seemed likewise sufficient to illuminate them; it was an expression of scorn and mockery, coinciding with the emotions indicated by his gesture. As Clifford stood on the threshold, partly turning back, he pointed his finger within the parlor, and shook it slowly, as though he would have summoned not Hepzibah alone, but the whole world, to gaze at some object inconceivably ridiculous. This action, so ill-timed and extravagant—accompanied, too, with a look that showed more like joy than any other kind of excitement—compelled Hepzibah to dread that her stern kinsman's ominous visit had driven her poor brother to absolute insanity. Nor could she otherwise account for the Judge's quiescent mood, than by supposing him craftily on the watch, while Clifford developed these symptoms of a distracted mind.

"Be quiet, Clifford!" whispered his sister, raising her hand to impress caution. "Oh, for Heaven's sake, be quiet!"

"Let him be quiet!—What can he do better?" answered Clifford, with a still wilder gesture, pointing into the room which he had just quitted. "As for us, Hepzibah, we can dance now!—we can sing, laugh, play, do what we will! The weight is gone, Hepzibah; it is gone off this weary old world; and we may be as light-hearted as little Phoebe herself!"

And, in accordance with his words, he began to laugh, still pointing his finger at the object, invisible to Hepzibah, within the parlor. She was seized with a sudden intuition of some horrible thing. She thrust herself past Clifford, and disappeared into the room, but almost immediately returned, with a cry choking in her throat. Gazing at her brother, with an affrighted glance of inquiry, she beheld him all in a tremor and a quake, from head to foot; while, amid these commoted elements of passion or alarm, still flickered his gusty mirth.

"My God, what is to become of us!" gasped Hepzibah.

"Come!" said Clifford, in a tone of brief decision, most unlike what was usual with him. "We stay here too long! Let us leave the old house to our Cousin Jaffrey! He will take good care of it!"

Hepzibah now noticed that Clifford had on a cloak—a garment of long ago—in which he had constantly muffled himself during these days of easterly storm. He beckoned with his hand, and intimated, so far as she could comprehend him, his purpose that they should go together from the house. There are chaotic, blind, or drunken moments, in the lives of persons who lack real force of character—moments of test, in which courage would most assert itself—but where these individuals, if left to themselves, stagger aimlessly along, or follow implicitly whatever guidance may befall them, even if it be a child's. No matter how preposterous or insane, a purpose is a god-send to them. Hepzibah had reached this point. Unaccustomed to action or responsibility—full of horror at what she had seen, and afraid to inquire, or almost to imagine, how it had come to pass—affrighted at the fatality which seemed to pursue her brother—stupefied by the dim, thick, stifling atmosphere of dread, which filled the house as with a death-smell, and obliterated all definiteness of thought—she yielded without a question, and on the instant, to the will which Clifford expressed. For herself, she was like a person in a dream, when the will always sleeps. Clifford, ordinarily so destitute of this faculty, had found it in the tension of the crisis.

"Why do you delay so?" cried he sharply. "Put on your cloak and hood, or whatever it pleases you to wear! No matter what;—you cannot look beautiful nor brilliant, my poor Hepzibah! Take your purse, with money in it, and come along!"

Hepzibah obeyed these instructions, as if nothing else were to be done or thought of. She began to wonder, it is true, why she did not wake up, and at what still more intolerable pitch of dizzy trouble her spirit would struggle out of the maze, and make her conscious that nothing of all this had actually happened. Of course, it was not real; no such black, easterly day as this had yet begun to be; Judge Pyncheon had not talked with her; Clifford had not laughed, pointed, beckoned her away with him; but she had merely been afflicted—as lonely sleepers often are—with a great deal of unreasonable misery in a morning dream!

"Now—now—I shall certainly awake!" thought Hepzibah, as she went to-and-fro, making her little preparations. "I can bear it no longer! I must wake up now!"

But it came not, that awakening moment! It came not, even when, just before they left the house, Clifford stole to the parlor-door, and made a parting obeisance to the sole occupant of the room.

"What an absurd figure the old fellow cuts now!" whispered he to Hepzibah. "Just when he fancied he had me completely under his thumb! Come, come; make haste; or he will start up like Giant

Despair in pursuit of Christian and Hopeful, and catch us yet!"[6]

As they passed into the street, Clifford directed Hepzibah's attention to something on one of the posts of the front-door. It was merely the initials of his own name, which, with somewhat of his characteristic grace about the forms of the letters, he had cut there, when a boy. The brother and sister departed, and left Judge Pyncheon sitting in the old home of his forefathers, all by himself; so heavy and lumpish that we can liken him to nothing better than a defunct nightmare, which had perished in the midst of its wickedness, and left its flabby corpse on the breast of the tormented one, to be gotten rid of as it might!

XVII. The Flight of Two Owls

Summer as it was, the east-wind set poor Hepzibah's few remaining teeth chattering in her head, as she and Clifford faced it, on their way up Pyncheon-street, and towards the centre of the town. Not merely was it the shiver which this pitiless blast brought to her frame, (although her feet and hands, especially, had never seemed so death-a-cold as now,) but there was a moral sensation, mingling itself with the physical chill, and causing her to shake more in spirit than in body. The world's broad, bleak atmosphere was all so comfortless! Such, indeed, is the impression which it makes on every new adventurer, even if he plunge into it while the warmest tide of life is bubbling through his veins. What then must it have been to Hepzibah and Clifford—so time-stricken as they were, yet so like children in their inexperience—as they left the door-step, and passed from beneath the wide shelter of the Pyncheon-elm! They were wandering all abroad, on precisely such a pilgrimage as a child often meditates, to the world's end, with perhaps a sixpence and a biscuit in his pocket. In Hepzibah's mind, there was the wretched consciousness of being adrift. She had lost the faculty of self-guidance, but, in view of the difficulties around her, felt it hardly worth an effort to regain it, and was, moreover, incapable of making one.

As they proceeded on their strange expedition, she now and then cast a look sidelong at Clifford, and could not but observe that he was possessed and swayed by a powerful excitement. It was this, indeed, that gave him the control which he had at once, and so irresistibly, established over her movements. It not a little resembled the exhilaration of wine. Or it might more fancifully be compared to a joyous piece of music, played with wild vivacity, but upon a dis-

6. A reference to John Bunyan's *Pilgrim's Progress* (1678), a Puritan allegory of the Christian soul's journey to salvation. In Part I, Christian and Hopeful escape from Giant Despair's dungeon with the help of the key Promise.

ordered instrument. As the cracked, jarring note might always be heard, and as it jarred loudest amid the loftiest exultation of the melody, so was there a continual quake through Clifford, causing him most to quiver while he wore a triumphant smile, and seemed almost under a necessity to skip in his gait.

They met few people abroad, even on passing from the retired neighborhood of the House of the Seven Gables into what was ordinarily the more thronged and busier portion of the town. Glistening sidewalks, with little pools of rain, here and there, along their unequal surface; umbrellas, displayed ostentatiously in the shop-windows, as if the life of trade had concentred itself in that one article; wet leaves of the horse-chestnut or elm-trees, torn off untimely by the blast, and scattered along the public-way; an unsightly accumulation of mud in the middle of the street, which perversely grew the more unclean for its long and laborious washing;—these were the more definable points of a very sombre picture. In the way of movement, and human life, there was the hasty rattle of a cab or coach, its driver protected by a water-proof cap over his head and shoulders; the forlorn figure of an old man, who seemed to have crept out of some subterranean sewer, and was stooping along the kennel, and poking the wet rubbish with a stick, in quest of rusty nails; a merchant or two, at the door of the post-office, together with an editor, and a miscellaneous politician, awaiting a dilatory mail; a few visages of retired sea-captains at the window of an Insurance Office,[7] looking out vacantly at the vacant street, blaspheming at the weather, and fretting at the dearth as well of public news as local gossip. What a treasure-trove to these venerable quidnuncs,[8] could they have guessed the secret which Hepzibah and Clifford were carrying along with them! But their two figures attracted hardly so much notice as that of a young girl, who passed, at the same instant, and happened to raise her skirt a trifle too high above her ancles. Had it been a sunny and cheerful day, they could hardly have gone through the streets without making themselves obnoxious to remark. Now, probably, they were felt to be in keeping with the dismal and bitter weather, and therefore did not stand out in strong relief, as if the sun were shining on them, but melted into the gray gloom, and were forgotten as soon as gone.

Poor Hepzibah! Could she have understood this fact, it would have brought her some little comfort; for, to all her other troubles—strange to say!—there was added the womanish and old-maidenlike misery, arising from a sense of unseemliness in her attire. Thus, she was fain to shrink deeper into herself, as it were,

7. Marine insurance offices were popular gathering places for sailors, sea captains, and merchants; there were around six such offices in Salem in 1850.
8. Gossips, busybodies.

as if in the hope of making people suppose that here was only a cloak and hood, threadbare and wofully faded, taking an airing in the midst of the storm, without any wearer!

As they went on, the feeling of indistinctness and unreality kept dimly hovering roundabout her, and so diffusing itself into her system that one of her hands was hardly palpable to the touch of the other. Any certainty would have been preferable to this. She whispered to herself, again and again—'Am I awake?—Am I awake?'—and sometimes exposed her face to the chill spatter of the wind, for the sake of its rude assurance, that she was. Whether it were Clifford's purpose, or only chance had led them thither, they now found themselves passing beneath the arched entrance of a large structure of gray stone. Within, there was a spacious breadth, and an airy height from floor to roof, now partially filled with smoke and steam, which eddied voluminously upward, and formed a mimic cloud-region over their heads. A train of cars was just ready for a start; the locomotive was fretting and fuming, like a steed impatient for a headlong rush; and the bell rang out its hasty peal, so well expressing the brief summons which life vouchsafes to us, in its hurried career. Without question or delay—with the irresistible decision, if not rather to be called recklessness, which had so strangely taken possession of him, and through him of Hepzibah—Clifford impelled her towards the cars, and assisted her to enter. The signal was given; the engine puffed forth its short, quick breaths; the train began its movement; and, along with a hundred other passengers, these two unwonted travellers sped onward like the wind.

At last, therefore, and after so long estrangement from everything that the world acted or enjoyed, they had been drawn into the great current of human life, and were swept away with it, as by the suction of fate itself.

Still haunted with the idea that not one of the past incidents, inclusive of Judge Pyncheon's visit, could be real, the recluse of the seven gables murmured in her brother's ear:—

"Clifford! Clifford! Is not this a dream?"

"A dream, Hepzibah!" repeated he, almost laughing in her face. "On the contrary, I have never been awake before!"

Meanwhile, looking from the window, they could see the world racing past them. At one moment, they were rattling through a solitude;—the next, a village had grown up around them;—a few breaths more, and it had vanished, as if swallowed by an earthquake. The spires of meeting-houses seemed set adrift from their foundations; the broad-based hills glided away. Everything was unfixed from its age-long rest, and moving at whirlwind speed in a direction opposite to their own.

Within the car, there was the usual interior life of the railroad, offering little to the observation of other passengers, but full of novelty for this pair of strangely enfranchised prisoners. It was novelty enough, indeed, that there were fifty human beings in close relation with them, under one long and narrow roof, and drawn onward by the same mighty influence that had taken their two selves into its grasp. It seemed marvellous how all these people could remain so quietly in their seats, while so much noisy strength was at work in their behalf. Some, with tickets in their hats, (long travellers these, before whom lay a hundred miles of railroad,) had plunged into the English scenery and adventures of pamphlet-novels, and were keeping company with dukes and earls. Others, whose briefer span forbade their devoting themselves to studies so abstruse, beguiled the little tedium of the way with penny-papers. A party of girls, and one young man, on opposite sides of the car, found huge amusement in a game of ball. They tossed it to-and-fro, with peals of laughter that might be measured by mile-lengths; for, faster than the nimble ball could fly, the merry players fled unconsciously along, leaving the trail of their mirth afar behind, and ending their game under another sky than had witnessed its commencement. Boys, with apples, cakes, candy, and rolls of variously tinctured lozenges—merchandize that reminded Hepzibah of her deserted shop—appeared at each momentary stopping-place, doing up their business in a hurry, or breaking it short off, lest the market should ravish them away with it. New people continually entered. Old acquaintances—for such they soon grew to be, in this rapid current of affairs—continually departed. Here and there, amid the rumble and the tumult, sat one asleep. Sleep; sport; business; graver or lighter study;—and the common and inevitable movement onward! It was life itself![9]

Clifford's naturally poignant sympathies were all aroused. He caught the color of what was passing about him, and threw it back more vividly than he received it, but mixed, nevertheless, with a lurid and portentous hue. Hepzibah, on the other hand, felt herself more apart from humankind than even in the seclusion which she had just quitted.

"You are not happy, Hepzibah!" said Clifford apart, in a tone of reproach. "You are thinking of that dismal old house, and of Cousin Jaffrey"—here came the quake through him—"and of Cousin Jaffrey sitting there, all by himself! Take my advice—follow my example—and let such things slip aside. Here we are, in the world, Hepzibah!—in the midst of life!—in the throng of our fellow-

9. This passage draws on Hawthorne's journal entry of May 5, 1850 (p. 312 herein).

beings! Let you and I be happy! As happy as that youth, and those pretty girls, at their game of ball!"

"Happy!" thought Hepzibah, bitterly conscious, at the word, of her dull and heavy heart, with the frozen pain in it. "Happy! He is mad already; and, if I could once feel myself broad awake, I should go mad too!"

If a fixed idea be madness, she was perhaps not remote from it. Fast and far as they had rattled and clattered along the iron track, they might just as well, as regarded Hepzibah's mental images, have been passing up and down Pyncheon-street. With miles and miles of varied scenery between, there was no scene for her, save the seven old gable-peaks, with their moss, and the tuft of weeds in one of the angles, and the shop-window, and a customer shaking the door, and compelling the little bell to jingle fiercely, but without disturbing Judge Pyncheon! This one old house was everywhere! It transported its great, lumbering bulk, with more than railroad speed, and set itself phlegmatically down on whatever spot she glanced at. The quality of Hepzibah's mind was too unmalleable to take new impressions so readily as Clifford's. He had a winged nature; she was rather of the vegetable kind, and could hardly be kept long alive, if drawn up by the roots. Thus it happened, that the relation heretofore existing between her brother and herself was changed. At home, she was his guardian; here, Clifford had become hers, and seemed to comprehend whatever belonged to their new position, with a singular rapidity of intelligence. He had been startled into manhood and intellectual vigor; or, at least, into a condition that resembled them, though it might be both diseased and transitory.

The conductor now applied for their tickets; and Clifford, who had made himself the purse-bearer, put a bank-note into his hand, as he had observed others do.

"For the lady and yourself?" asked the conductor. "And how far?"

"As far as that will carry us," said Clifford. "It is no great matter. We are riding for pleasure, merely!"

"You choose a strange day for it, Sir!" remarked a gimlet-eyed[1] old gentleman, on the other side of the car, looking at Clifford and his companion as if curious to make them out.—"The best chance of pleasure in an easterly rain, I take it, is in a man's own house, with a nice little fire in the chimney."

"I cannot precisely agree with you," said Clifford, courteously bowing to the old gentleman, and at once taking up the clue of conversation which the latter had proffered.—"It had just occurred to me, on the contrary, that this admirable invention of the rail-

---

1. Eyes with a piercing look. (A gimlet punches holes in leather.)

road[2]—with the vast and inevitable improvements to be looked for, both as to speed and convenience—is destined to do away with those stale ideas of home and fireside, and substitute something better."

"In the name of common sense," asked the old gentleman, rather testily, "what can be better for a man than his own parlor and chimney-corner?"

"These things have not the merit which many good people attribute to them," replied Clifford. "They may be said, in few and pithy words, to have ill-served a poor purpose! My impression is, that our wonderfully increased, and still increasing, facilities of locomotion are destined to bring us round again to the nomadic state. You are aware, my dear Sir—you must have observed it, in your own experience—that all human progress is in a circle; or, to use a more accurate and beautiful figure, in an ascending spiral curve. While we fancy ourselves going straight forward, and attaining, at every step, an entirely new position of affairs, we do actually return to something long ago tried and abandoned, but which we now find etherealized, refined, and perfected to its ideal. The past is but a coarse and sensual prophecy of the present and the future. To apply this truth to the topic now under discussion! In the early epochs of our race, men dwelt in temporary huts, or bowers of branches, as easily constructed as a bird's nest, and which they built—if it should be called building, when such sweet homes of a summer-solstice rather grew, than were made with hands—which Nature, we will say, assisted them to rear, where fruit abounded, where fish and game were plentiful, or, most especially, where the sense of beauty was to be gratified by a lovelier shade than elsewhere, and a more exquisite arrangement of lake, wood, and hill. This life possessed a charm, which, ever since man quitted it, has vanished from existence. And it typified something better than itself. It had its drawbacks; such as hunger and thirst, inclement weather, hot sunshine, and weary and foot-blistering marches over barren and ugly tracts, that lay between the sites desirable for their fertility and beauty. But, in our ascending spiral, we escape all this. These railroads— could but the whistle be made musical, and the rumble and the jar got rid of—are positively the greatest blessing that the ages have wrought out for us. They give us wings; they annihilate the toil and dust of pilgrimage; they spiritualize travel! Transition being so facile, what can be any man's inducement to tarry in one spot? Why, therefore, should he build a more cumbrous habitation than can readily be carried off with him? Why should he make himself a prisoner for life in brick, and stone, and old worm-eaten timber,

2. Railroads were developed in the United States in the late 1820s and 1830s.

when he may just as easily dwell, in one sense, nowhere—in a better sense, wherever the fit and beautiful shall offer him a home?"[3]

Clifford's countenance glowed, as he divulged this theory; a youthful character shone out from within, converting the wrinkles and pallid duskiness of age into an almost transparent mask. The merry girls let their ball drop upon the floor, and gazed at him. They said to themselves, perhaps, that, before his hair was gray and the crow's feet tracked his temples, this now decaying man must have stamped the impress of his features on many a woman's heart. But, alas, no woman's eye had seen his face, while it was beautiful!

"I should scarcely call it an improved state of things," observed Clifford's new acquaintance, "to live everywhere, and nowhere!"

"Would you not?" exclaimed Clifford, with singular energy. "It is as clear to me as sunshine—were there any in the sky—that the greatest possible stumbling-blocks in the path of human happiness and improvement, are these heaps of bricks, and stones, consolidated with mortar, or hewn timber, fastened together with spike-nails, which men painfully contrive for their own torment, and call them house and home! The soul needs air; a wide sweep and frequent change of it. Morbid influences, in a thousand-fold variety, gather about hearths, and pollute the life of households. There is no such unwholesome atmosphere as that of an old home, rendered poisonous by one's defunct forefathers and relatives! I speak of what I know! There is a certain house within my familiar recollection—one of those peaked-gable, (there are seven of them,) projecting-storied edifices, such as you occasionally see, in our elder towns—a rusty, crazy, creaky, dry-rotted, damp-rotted, dingy, dark, and miserable old dungeon, with an arched window over the porch, and a little shop-door on one side, and a great, melancholy elm before it. Now, Sir, whenever my thoughts recur to this seven-gabled mansion—(the fact is so very curious that I must needs mention it)—immediately, I have a vision or image of an elderly man, of remarkably stern countenance, sitting in an oaken elbow-chair, dead, stone-dead, with an ugly flow of blood upon his shirt-bosom. Dead, but with open eyes! He taints the whole house, as I remember it. I could never flourish there, nor be happy, nor do nor enjoy what God meant me to do and enjoy!"

His face darkened, and seemed to contract, and shrivel itself up, and wither into age.

"Never, Sir!" he repeated. "I could never draw cheerful breath there!"

"I should think not," said the old gentleman, eyeing Clifford

---

3. In Hawthorne's sketch "The Celestial Rail-road" (1843), the narrator ironically voices similar sentiments.

earnestly and rather apprehensively. "I should conceive not, Sir, with that notion in your head!"

"Surely not," continued Clifford; "and it were a relief to me, if that house could be torn down, or burnt up, and so the earth be rid of it, and grass be sown abundantly over its foundation. Not that I should ever visit its site again! For, Sir, the farther I get away from it, the more does the joy, the lightsome freshness, the heart-leap, the intellectual dance, the youth, in short—yes, my youth, my youth!—the more does it come back to me. No longer ago than this morning, I was old. I remember looking in the glass, and wondering at my own gray hair, and the wrinkles, many and deep, right across my brow, and the furrows down my cheeks, and the prodigious trampling of crow's feet about my temples! It was too soon! I could not bear it! Age had no right to come! I had not lived! But now do I look old? If so, my aspect belies me strangely; for—a great weight being off my mind—I feel in the very hey-day of my youth, with the world and my best days before me!"

"I trust you may find it so," said the old gentleman, who seemed rather embarrassed, and desirous of avoiding the observation which Clifford's wild talk drew on them both. "You have my best wishes for it!"

"For Heaven's sake, dear Clifford, be quiet!" whispered his sister. "They think you mad!"

"Be quiet yourself, Hepzibah!" returned her brother. "No matter what they think! I am not mad. For the first time in thirty years, my thoughts gush up and find words ready for them. I must talk, and I will!"

He turned again towards the old gentleman, and renewed the conversation.

"Yes, my dear Sir," said he, "it is my firm belief and hope, that these terms of roof and hearth-stone, which have so long been held to embody something sacred, are soon to pass out of men's daily use, and be forgotten. Just imagine, for a moment, how much of human evil will crumble away, with this one change! What we call real estate—the solid ground to build a house on—is the broad foundation on which nearly all the guilt of this world rests. A man will commit almost any wrong—he will heap up an immense pile of wickedness, as hard as granite, and which will weigh as heavily upon his soul, to eternal ages—only to build a great, gloomy, dark-chambered mansion, for himself to die in, and for his posterity to be miserable in. He lays his own dead corpse beneath the under-pinning, as one may say, and hangs his frowning picture on the wall, and, after thus converting himself into an Evil Destiny, expects his remotest great-grandchildren to be happy there! I do not speak wildly. I have just such a house in my mind's eye!"

"Then, Sir," said the old gentleman, getting anxious to drop the subject, "you are not to blame for leaving it."

"Within the lifetime of the child already born," Clifford went on, "all this will be done away. The world is growing too ethereal and spiritual to bear these enormities a great while longer. To me— though, for a considerable period of time, I have lived chiefly in re- tirement, and know less of such things than most men—even to me, the harbingers of a better era are unmistakeable. Mesmerism, now! Will that effect nothing, think you, towards purging away the grossness out of human life?"

"All a humbug!" growled the old gentleman.

"These rapping spirits[4] that little Phoebe told us of, the other day," said Clifford. "What are these but the messengers of the spir- itual world, knocking at the door of substance? And it shall be flung wide open!"

"A humbug, again!" cried the old gentleman, growing more and more testy at these glimpses of Clifford's metaphysics.—"I should like to rap, with a good stick, on the empty pates of the dolts who circulate such nonsense!"

"Then there is electricity;—the demon, the angel, the mighty physical power, the all-pervading intelligence!" exclaimed Clifford. "Is that a humbug, too? Is it a fact—or have I dreamt it—that, by means of electricity, the world of matter has become a great nerve, vibrating thousands of miles in a breathless point of time? Rather, the round globe is a vast head, a brain, instinct with intelligence! Or, shall we say, it is itself a thought, nothing but thought, and no longer the substance which we deemed it?"

"If you mean the telegraph,"[5] said the old gentleman, glancing his eye towards its wire, alongside the rail-track, "it is an excellent thing;—that is, of course, if the speculators in cotton and politics don't get possession of it. A great thing indeed, Sir; particularly as regards the detection of bank-robbers and murderers!"

"I don't quite like it, in that point of view," replied Clifford. "A bank-robber—and what you call a murderer, likewise—has his rights, which men of enlightened humanity and conscience should regard in so much the more liberal spirit, because the bulk of soci- ety is prone to controvert their existence. An almost spiritual medium, like the electric telegraph, should be consecrated to high, deep, joyful, and holy missions. Lovers, day by day—hour by hour, if so often moved to do it—might send their heart-throbs from

4. Communications from the spirit world. In western New York in 1848, the sisters Katie and Maggie Fox achieved notoriety for their alleged ability to serve as mediums for the dead, who supposedly passed along their communications through the sisters' rappings on tables.
5. Pioneered by Samuel F. B. Morse (1791–1872), who popularized the new technology during the 1830s.

Maine to Florida, with some such words as these—'I love you forever!'—'My heart runs over with love!'—'I love you more than I
can!'—and, again, at the next message—'I have lived an hour
longer, and love you twice as much!' Or, when a good man has departed, his distant friend should be conscious of an electric thrill,
as from the world of happy spirits, telling him—'Your dear friend is
in bliss!' Or, to an absent husband, should come tidings thus—'An
immortal being, of whom you are the father, has this moment come
from God!'—and immediately its little voice would seem to have
reached so far, and to be echoing in his heart. But for these poor
rogues, the bank-robbers—who, after all, are about as honest as
nine people in ten, except that they disregard certain formalities,
and prefer to transact business at midnight, rather than 'Change-
hours[6]—and for these murderers, as you phrase it, who are often
excusable in the motives of their deed, and deserve to be ranked
among public benefactors, if we consider only its result—for unfortunate individuals like these, I really cannot applaud the enlistment
of an immaterial and miraculous power in the universal world-hunt
at their heels!"

"You can't, hey?" cried the old gentleman, with a hard look.

"Positively, no!" answered Clifford. "It puts them too miserably at
disadvantage. For example, Sir, in a dark, low, cross-beamed, panelled room of an old house, let us suppose a dead man, sitting in an
arm-chair, with a blood-stain on his shirt-bosom—and let us add to
our hypothesis another man, issuing from the house which he feels
to be over-filled with the dead man's presence—and let us lastly
imagine him fleeing, Heaven knows whither, at the speed of a hurricane, by railroad! Now, Sir,—if the fugitive alight in some distant
town, and find all the people babbling about that self-same dead
man, whom he has fled so far to avoid the sight and thought of—
will you not allow that his natural rights have been infringed? He
has been deprived of his city of refuge, and, in my humble opinion,
has suffered infinite wrong!"

"You are a strange man, Sir!" said the old gentleman, bringing his
gimlet-eye to a point on Clifford, as if determined to bore right into
him.—"I can't see through you!"

"No, I'll be bound you can't!" cried Clifford laughing. "And yet,
my dear Sir, I am as transparent as the water of Maule's Well! But,
come, Hepzibah! We have flown far enough for once. Let us alight,
as the birds do, and perch ourselves on the nearest twig, and consult whither we shall fly next!"

Just then, as it happened, the train reached a solitary way-

6. The hours during which Boston's Merchant's Exchange was open for the trading of
   stocks and bonds.

station. Taking advantage of the brief pause, Clifford left the car, and drew Hepzibah along with him. A moment afterwards, the train—with all the life of its interior, amid which Clifford had made himself so conspicuous an object—was gliding away in the distance, and rapidly lessening to a point, which, in another moment, vanished. The world had fled away from these two wanderers. They gazed drearily about them. At a little distance stood a wooden church, black with age, and in a dismal state of ruin and decay, with broken windows, a great rift through the main-body of the edifice, and a rafter dangling from the top of the square tower. Farther off was a farm-house in the old style, as venerably black as the church, with a roof sloping downward from the three-story peak to within a man's height of the ground. It seemed uninhabited. There were the relics of a wood-pile, indeed, near the door, but with grass sprouting up among the chips and scattered logs. The small raindrops came down aslant; the wind was not turbulent, but sullen, and full of chilly moisture.[7]

Clifford shivered from head to foot. The wild effervescence of his mood—which had so readily supplied thoughts, fantasies, and a strange aptitude of words, and impelled him to talk from the mere necessity of giving vent to this bubbling up-gush of ideas—had entirely subsided. A powerful excitement had given him energy and vivacity. Its operation over, he forthwith began to sink.

"You must take the lead now, Hepzibah!" murmured he, with a torpid and reluctant utterance. "Do with me as you will!"

She knelt down upon the platform where they were standing, and lifted her clasped hands to the sky. The dull, gray weight of clouds made it invisible; but it was no hour for disbelief;—no juncture this, to question that there was a sky above, and an Almighty Father looking down from it!

"Oh, God!"—ejaculated poor, gaunt Hepzibah—then paused a moment, to consider what her prayer should be—"Oh, God—our Father—are we not thy children? Have mercy on us!"

XVIII. Governor Pyncheon

Judge Pyncheon, while his two relatives have fled away with such ill-considered haste, still sits in the old parlor, keeping house, as the familiar phrase is, in the absence of its ordinary occupants. To him, and to the venerable House of the Seven Gables, does our story now betake itself, like an owl, bewildered in the daylight, and hastening back to his hollow tree.

---

7. For this passage Hawthorne again drew on his notebook entry of May 5, 1850; see n. 9, p. 181.

The Judge has not shifted his position for a long while, now. He has not stirred hand or foot—nor withdrawn his eyes, so much as a hair's breadth, from their fixed gaze towards the corner of the room—since the footsteps of Hepzibah and Clifford creaked along the passage, and the outer door was closed cautiously behind their exit. He holds his watch in his left hand, but clutched in such a manner that you cannot see the dial-plate. How profound a fit of meditation! Or, supposing him asleep, how infantile a quietude of conscience, and what wholesome order in the gastric region, are betokened by slumber so entirely undisturbed with starts, cramp, twitches, muttered dream-talk, trumpet-blasts through the nasal organ, or any, the slightest, irregularity of breath! You must hold your own breath, to satisfy yourself whether he breathes at all. It is quite inaudible. You hear the ticking of his watch; his breath you do not hear. A most refreshing slumber, doubtless! And yet the Judge cannot be asleep. His eyes are open! A veteran politician, such as he, would never fall asleep with wide-open eyes; lest some enemy or mischief-maker, taking him thus at unawares, should peep through these windows into his consciousness, and make strange discoveries among the reminiscences, projects, hopes, apprehensions, weaknesses, and strong points, which he has heretofore shared with nobody. A cautious man is proverbially said to sleep with one eye open. That may be wisdom. But not with both; for this were heedlessness! No, no! Judge Pyncheon cannot be asleep.

It is odd, however, that a gentleman so burthened with engagements—and noted, too, for punctuality—should linger thus in an old, lonely mansion, which he has never seemed very fond of visiting. The oaken chair, to be sure, may tempt him with its roominess. It is, indeed, a spacious, and—allowing for the rude age that fashioned it—a moderately easy seat, with capacity enough, at all events, and offering no restraint to the Judge's breadth of beam. A bigger man might find ample accommodation in it. His ancestor, now pictured upon the wall, with all his English beef about him, used hardly to present a front extending from elbow to elbow of this chair, or a base that would cover its whole cushion. But there are better chairs than this—mahogany, black walnut, rosewood, spring-seated and damask-cushioned, with varied slopes, and innumerable artifices to make them easy, and obviate the irksomeness of too tame an ease;—a score of such might be at Judge Pyncheon's service. Yes; in a score of drawing-rooms, he would be more than welcome. Mamma would advance to meet him, with outstretched hand; the virgin daughter, elderly as he has now got to be—an old widower, as he smilingly describes himself—would shake up the cushion for the Judge, and do her pretty little utmost to make him comfortable. For the Judge is a prosperous man. He cherishes his schemes, moreover, like other people, and reasonably brighter than most others; or did so, at least, as he lay abed, this morning, in an agreeable half-drowse, planning the business of the day, and speculating on the probabilities of the next fifteen years. With his firm health, and the little inroad that age has made upon him, fifteen years, or twenty—yes, or perhaps five-and-twenty!—are no more than he may fairly call his own. Five-and-twenty years for the enjoyment of his real estate in town and country, his railroad, bank, and insurance shares, his United States stock, his wealth, in short, however invested, now in possession, or soon to be acquired; together with the public honors that have fallen upon him, and the weightier ones that are yet to fall! It is good! It is excellent! It is enough!

Still lingering in the old chair! If the Judge has a little time to throw away, why does not he visit the Insurance Office, as is his frequent custom, and sit awhile in one of their leathern-cushioned arm-chairs, listening to the gossip of the day, and dropping some deeply designed chance-word, which will be certain to become the gossip of tomorrow? And have not the Bank Directors a meeting, at which it was the Judge's purpose to be present, and his office to preside? Indeed they have; and the hour is noted on a card, which is, or ought to be, in Judge Pyncheon's right vest-pocket. Let him go thither, and loll at ease upon his money-bags! He has lounged long enough in the old chair.

This was to have been such a busy day! In the first place, the interview with Clifford. Half-an-hour, by the Judge's reckoning, was to suffice for that; it would probably be less, but—taking into consideration that Hepzibah was first to be dealt with, and that these women are apt to make many words where a few would do much better—it might be safest to allow half-an-hour. Half-an-hour? Why, Judge, it is already two hours, by your own undeviatingly accurate chronometer![8] Glance your eye down at it, and see. Ah; he will not give himself the trouble either to bend his head, or elevate his hand, so as to bring the faithful timekeeper within his range of vision. Time, all at once, appears to have become a matter of no moment with the Judge!

And has he forgotten all the other items of his memoranda? Clifford's affair arranged, he was to meet a State-street broker, who has undertaken to procure a heavy per-centage, and the best of paper, for a few loose thousands which the Judge happens to have by him, uninvested. The wrinkled note-shaver[9] will have taken his railroad trip in vain. Half-an-hour later, in the street next to this, there was

---

8. Timepiece with an ability to determine longitude, and thus generally used at sea.
9. Loan agent seeking high interest payments.

to be an auction of real estate, including a portion of the old Pyncheon property, originally belonging to Maule's garden-ground. It has been alienated from the Pyncheons, these fourscore years; but the Judge had kept it in his eye, and had set his heart on the reannexing it to the small demesne[1] still left around the seven gables;—and now, during this odd fit of oblivion, the fatal hammer must have fallen, and transferred our ancient patrimony to some alien possessor! Possibly, indeed, the sale may have been postponed till fairer weather. If so, will the Judge make it convenient to be present, and favor the auctioneer with his bid, on the proximate occasion?

The next affair was to buy a horse for his own driving. The one, heretofore his favorite, stumbled, this very morning, on the road to town, and must be at once discarded. Judge Pyncheon's neck is too precious to be risked on such a contingency as a stumbling steed. Should all the above business be seasonably got through with, he might attend the meeting of a charitable society; the very name of which, however, in the multiplicity of his benevolence, is quite forgotten; so that this engagement may pass unfulfilled, and no great harm done. And if he have time, amid the press of more urgent matters, he must take measures for the renewal of Mrs. Pyncheon's tombstone, which, the sexton tells him, has fallen on its marble face, and is cracked quite in twain. She was a praiseworthy woman enough, thinks the Judge, in spite of her nervousness, and the tears that she was so oozy with, and her foolish behavior about the coffee; and as she took her departure so seasonably, he will not grudge the second tombstone. It is better, at least, than if she had never needed any! The next item on his list was to give orders for some fruit-trees, of a rare variety, to be deliverable at his country-seat, in the ensuing autumn. Yes; buy them, by all means; and may the peaches be luscious in your mouth, Judge Pyncheon! After this, comes something more important. A committee of his political party has besought him for a hundred or two of dollars, in addition to his previous disbursements, towards carrying on the fall-campaign. The Judge is a patriot; the fate of the country is staked on the November election; and besides, as will be shadowed forth in another paragraph, he has no trifling stake of his own, in the same great game. He will do what the committee asks; nay, he will be liberal beyond their expectations; they shall have a check for five hundred dollars, and more anon, if it be needed. What next? A decayed widow, whose husband was Judge Pyncheon's early friend, has laid her case of destitution before him, in a very moving letter. She and her fair daughter have scarcely bread to eat. He partly

1. Domain; land held by the owner of an estate.

intends to call on her, to-day—perhaps so—perhaps not—accordingly as he may happen to have leisure, and a small bank-note.

Another business, which, however, he puts no great weight on—(it is well, you know, to be heedful, but not over anxious, as respects one's personal health)—another business, then, was to consult his family-physician. About what, for Heaven's sake? Why, it is rather difficult to describe the symptoms. A mere dimness of sight and dizziness of brain, was it?—or a disagreeable choking, or stifling, or gurgling, or bubbling, in the region of the thorax, as the anatomists say?—or was it a pretty severe throbbing and kicking of the heart, rather creditable to him than otherwise, as showing that the organ had not been left out of the Judge's physical contrivance? No matter what it was. The Doctor, probably, would smile at the statement of such trifles to his professional ear; the Judge would smile, in his turn; and meeting one another's eyes, they would enjoy a hearty laugh, together! But, a fig for medical advice! The Judge will never need it.

Pray, pray, Judge Pyncheon, look at your watch, now! What, not a glance? It is within ten minutes of the dinner-hour! It surely cannot have slipt your memory, that the dinner of to-day is to be the most important, in its consequences, of all the dinners you ever ate. Yes; precisely the most important; although, in the course of your some-what eminent career, you have been placed high towards the head of the table, at splendid banquets, and have poured out your festive eloquence to ears yet echoing with Webster's mighty organ-tones.[2] No public dinner this, however. It is merely a gathering of some dozen or so of friends from several districts of the State; men of dis-tinguished character and influence, assembling, almost casually, at the house of a common friend, likewise distinguished, who will make them welcome to a little better than his ordinary fare. Nothing in the way of French cookery, but an excellent dinner, nevertheless! Real turtle, we understand, and salmon, tautog, canvass-backs,[3] pig, English mutton, good roast-beef, or dainties of that serious kind, fit for substantial country-gentlemen, as these honorable persons mostly are. The delicacies of the season, in short, and flavored by a brand of old Madeira[4] which has been the pride of many seasons. It is the Juno brand; a glorious wine, fra-grant, and full of gentle might; a bottled-up happiness, put by for use; a golden liquid, worth more than liquid gold; so rare and ad-mirable, that veteran wine-bibbers count it among their epochs to

2. A reference to the Massachusetts senator Daniel Webster (1782–1852), who was renowned for his oratory.
3. North American wild ducks. "Tautog": a blackfish found along the North Atlantic coast.
4. A fortified white wine from the Portuguese Madeira islands.

have tasted it! It drives away the heart-ache, and substitutes no head-ache! Could the Judge but quaff a glass, it might enable him to shake off the unaccountable lethargy, which—(for the ten intervening minutes, and five to boot, are already past)—has made him such a laggard at this momentous dinner. It would all but revive a dead man! Would you like to sip it now, Judge Pyncheon?

Alas, this dinner! Have you really forgotten its true object? Then let us whisper it, that you may start at once out of the oaken chair, which really seems to be enchanted, like the one in Comus, or that in which Moll Pitcher[5] imprisoned your own grandfather. But ambition is a talisman more powerful than witchcraft. Start up, then, and hurrying through the streets, burst in upon the company, that they may begin before the fish is spoiled! They wait for you; and it is little for your interest that they should wait. These gentlemen—need you be told it?—have assembled, not without purpose, from every quarter of the State. They are practised politicians, every man of them, and skilled to adjust those preliminary measures, which steal from the people, without its knowledge, the power of choosing its own rulers. The popular voice, at the next gubernatorial election, though loud as thunder, will be really but an echo of what these gentlemen shall speak, under their breath, at your friend's festive board. They meet to decide upon their candidate. This little knot of subtle schemers will control the Convention, and, through it, dictate to the party. And what worthier candidate—more wise and learned, more noted for philanthropic liberality, truer to safe principles, tried oftener by public trusts, more spotless in private character, with a larger stake in the common welfare, and deeper grounded, by hereditary descent, in the faith and practice of the Puritans—what man can be presented for the suffrage of the people, so eminently combining all these claims to the chief-rulership, as Judge Pyncheon here before us?

Make haste, then! Do your part! The meed for which you have toiled, and fought, and climbed, and crept, is ready for your grasp! Be present at this dinner!—drink a glass or two of that noble wine!—make your pledges in as low a whisper as you will!—and you rise up from table, virtually governor of the glorious old State! Governor Pyncheon of Massachusetts!

And is there no potent and exhilarating cordial in a certainty like this? It has been the grand purpose of half your lifetime to attain it. Now, when there needs little more than to signify your acceptance, why do you sit so lumpishly in your great-great-grandfather's oaken

---

5. A well-known fortune-teller and clairvoyant of Lynn, Massachusetts (d. 1813). In John Milton's masque *Comus* (1634), Comus, the Roman god of drinking, imprisons a lady in an enchanted chair to test her virtue.

chair, as if preferring it to the gubernatorial one? We have all heard of King Log;[6] but, in these jostling times, one of that royal kindred will hardly win the race for an elective chief-magistracy!

Well; it is absolutely too late for dinner. Turtle, salmon, tautog, woodcock, boiled turkey, Southdown mutton, pig, roast-beef, have vanished, or exist only in fragments, with lukewarm potatoes, and gravies crusted over with cold fat. The Judge, had he done nothing else, would have achieved wonders with his knife and fork. It was he, you know, of whom it used to be said, in reference to his ogre-like appetite, that his Creator made him a great animal, but that the dinner-hour made him a great beast. Persons of his large sensual endowments must claim indulgence, at their feeding-time. But, for once, the Judge is entirely too late for dinner. Too late, we fear, even to join the party at their wine! The guests are warm and merry; they have given up the Judge; and, concluding that the Free Soilers[7] have him, they will fix upon another candidate. Were our friend now to stalk in among them, with that wide-open stare, at once wild and stolid, his ungenial presence would be apt to change their cheer. Neither would it be seemly in Judge Pyncheon, generally so scrupulous in his attire, to show himself at a dinner-table with that crimson stain upon his shirt-bosom. By-the-by, how came it there? It is an ugly sight, at any rate; and the wisest way for the Judge is to button his coat closely over his breast, and, taking his horse and chaise from the livery-stable, to make all speed to his own house. There, after a glass of brandy and water, and a mutton-chop, a beef-steak, a broiled fowl, or some such hasty little dinner and supper, all in one, he had better spend the evening by the fire-side. He must toast his slippers a long while, in order to get rid of the chilliness, which the air of this vile old house has sent curdling through his veins.

Up, therefore, Judge Pyncheon, up! You have lost a day. But to-morrow will be here anon. Will you rise, betimes, and make the most of it? Tomorrow! Tomorrow! Tomorrow![8] We, that are alive, may rise betimes tomorrow. As for him that has died to-day, his morrow will be the resurrection-morn.

Meanwhile the twilight is glooming upward out of the corners of the room. The shadows of the tall furniture grow deeper, and at

6. An allusion to the Aesop fable in which Jupiter responds to frogs' complaints about having a silent log as their king by sending them a more lively stork, which subsequently
eats them.
7. Emerging in response to the war with Mexico (1846–48), the Free Soil political party
fought against the extension of slavery into the new territories.
8. An ironic allusion to one of Macbeth's famous speeches: "To-morrow, and to-morrow,
and to-morrow / Creeps in this petty pace from day to day / To the last syllable of
recorded time, / And all our yesterdays have lighted fools / The way to dusty death. Out,
out brief candle!" (Shakespeare, *Macbeth* [ca. 1606], V.iv.19–23).

first become more definite; then, spreading wider, they lose their distinctness of outline in the dark, gray tide of oblivion, as it were, that creeps slowly over the various objects, and the one human figure sitting in the midst of them. The gloom has not entered from without; it has brooded here all day, and now, taking its own inevitable time, will possess itself of everything. The Judge's face, indeed, rigid, and singularly white, refuses to melt into this universal solvent. Fainter and fainter grows the light. It is as if another double-handfull of darkness had been scattered through the air. Now it is no longer gray, but sable. There is still a faint appearance at the window; neither a glow, nor a gleam, nor a glimmer—any phrase of light would express something far brighter than this doubtful perception, or sense, rather, that there is a window there. Has it yet vanished? No!—yes!—not quite! And there is still the swarthy whiteness—we shall venture to marry these ill-agreeing words—the swarthy whiteness of Judge Pyncheon's face. The features are all gone; there is only the paleness of them left. And how looks it now? There is no window! There is no face! An infinite, inscrutable blackness has annihilated sight! Where is our universe? All crumbled away from us; and we, adrift in chaos, may hearken to the gusts of homeless wind, that go sighing and murmuring about, in quest of what was once a world!

Is there no other sound? One other, and a fearful one. It is the ticking of the Judge's watch, which, ever since Hepzibah left the room in search of Clifford, he has been holding in his hand. Be the cause what it may, this little, quiet, never-ceasing throb of Time's pulse, repeating its small strokes with such busy regularity, in Judge Pyncheon's motionless hand, has an effect of terror, which we do not find in any other accompaniment of the scene.

But, listen! That puff of the breeze was louder; it had a tone unlike the dreary and sullen one, which has bemoaned itself, and afflicted all mankind with miserable sympathy, for five days past. The wind has veered about! It now comes boisterously from the northwest, and, taking hold of the aged frame-work of the seven gables, gives it a shake, like a wrestler that would try strength with his antagonist. Another, and another sturdy tustle with the blast! The old house creaks again, and makes a vociferous, but somewhat unintelligible bellowing in its sooty throat—(the big flue, we mean, of its wide chimney)—partly in complaint at the rude wind, but rather, as befits their century-and-a-half of hostile intimacy, in tough defiance. A rumbling kind of a bluster roars behind the fire-board. A door has slammed above-stairs. A window, perhaps, has been left open, or else is driven in by an unruly gust. It is not to be conceived, beforehand, what wonderful wind-instruments are these old timber-mansions, and how haunted with the strangest noises, which immediately begin to sing, and sigh, and sob, and shriek— and to smite with sledge-hammers, airy, but ponderous, in some distant chamber—and to tread along the entries as with stately footsteps, and rustle up and down the staircase, as with silks mirac- ulously stiff—whenever the gale catches the house with a window open, and gets fairly into it. Would that we were not an attendant spirit, here! It is too awful! This clamor of the wind through the lonely house; the Judge's quietude, as he sits invisible; and that per- tinacious ticking of his watch!

As regards Judge Pyncheon's invisibility, however, that matter will soon be remedied. The north-west wind has swept the sky clear. The window is distinctly seen. Through its panes, moreover, we dimly catch the sweep of the dark, clustering foliage, outside, flut- tering with a constant irregularity of movement, and letting in a peep of starlight, now here, now there. Oftener than any other ob- ject, these glimpses illuminate the Judge's face. But here comes more effectual light. Observe that silvery dance upon the upper branches of the pear-tree, and now a little lower, and now on the whole mass of boughs, while, through their shifting intricacies, the moonbeams fall aslant into the room. They play over the Judge's figure, and show that he has not stirred throughout the hours of darkness. They follow the shadows, in changeful sport, across his unchanging features. They gleam upon his watch. His grasp con- ceals the dial-plate; but we know that the faithful hands have met; for one of the city-clocks tells midnight.

A man of sturdy understanding, like Judge Pyncheon, cares no more for twelve o'clock at night, than for the corresponding hour of noon. However just the parallel, drawn in some of the preceding pages, between his Puritan ancestor and himself, it fails in this point. The Pyncheon of two centuries ago, in common with most of his contemporaries, professed his full belief in spiritual ministra- tions, although reckoning them chiefly of a malignant character. The Pyncheon of to-night, who sits in yonder chair, believes in no such nonsense. Such, at least, was his creed, some few hours since. His hair will not bristle, therefore, at the stories which—in times when chimney-corners had benches in them, where old people sat poking into the ashes of the past, and raking out traditions, like live coals—used to be told about this very room of his ancestral house. In fact, these tales are too absurd to bristle even childhood's hair. What sense, meaning, or moral, for example, such as even ghost- stories should be susceptible of, can be traced in the ridiculous legend, that, at midnight, all the dead Pyncheons are bound to assemble in this parlor! And, pray, for what? Why, to see whether the portrait of their ancestor still keeps its place upon the wall, in compliance with his testamentary directions![9] Is it worth while to come out of their graves for that?

We are tempted to make a little sport with the idea. Ghost-stories are hardly to be treated seriously, any longer. The family-party of the defunct Pyncheons, we presume, goes off in this wise.

First comes the ancestor himself, in his black cloak, steeple-hat, and trunk-breeches, girt about the waist with a leathern belt, in which hangs his steel-hilted sword; he has a long staff in his hand, such as gentlemen in advanced life used to carry, as much for the dignity of the thing, as for the support to be derived from it. He looks up at the portrait; a thing of no substance, gazing at its own painted image! All is safe. The picture is still there. The purpose of his brain has been kept sacred, thus long after the man himself has sprouted up in grave-yard grass. See; he lifts his ineffectual hand, and tries the frame. All safe! But, is that a smile?—is it not, rather, a frown of deadly import, that darkens over the shadow of his features? The stout Colonel is dissatisfied! So decided is his look of discontent as to impart additional distinctness to his features; through which, nevertheless, the moonlight passes, and flickers on the wall beyond. Something has strangely vexed the ancestor! With a grim shake of the head, he turns away. Here come other Pyncheons, the whole tribe, in their half-a-dozen generations, jostling and elbowing one another, to reach the picture. We behold aged men and grandames, a clergyman, with the Puritanic stiffness still in his garb and mien, and a red-coated officer of the Old French War;[1] and there comes the shopkeeping Pyncheon of a century ago, with the ruffles turned back from his wrists; and there the periwigged and brocaded gentleman of the artist's legend, with the beautiful and pensive Alice, who brings no pride, out of her virgin grave. All try the picture-frame. What do these ghostly people seek? A mother lifts her child that his little hands may touch it! There is evidently a mystery about the picture, that perplexes these poor Pyncheons when they ought to be at rest. In a corner, meanwhile, stands the figure of an elderly man, in a leather jerkin and breeches, with a carpenter's rule sticking out of his side-pocket; he points his finger at the bearded Colonel and his descendants, nodding, jeering, mocking, and finally bursting into obstreperous, though inaudible laughter.

Indulging our fancy in this freak, we have partly lost the power of restraint and guidance. We distinguish an unlooked-for figure in our visionary scene. Among those ancestral people, there is a young man, dressed in the very fashion of to-day; he wears a dark frock-

9. The directions, or instructions, written into a last will.
1. The French and Indian War (1754–63) was the final major war between England and France for dominance in North America.

coat, almost destitute of skirts, gray pantaloons, gaiter-boots of patent leather, and has a finely wrought gold chain across his breast, and a little silver-headed whalebone-stick in his hand. Were we to meet this figure at noonday, we should greet him as young Jaffrey Pyncheon, the Judge's only surviving child, who has been spending the last two years in foreign travel. If still in life, how comes his shadow hither? If dead, what a misfortune! The old Pyncheon property, together with the great estate, acquired by this young man's father, would devolve on whom? On poor, foolish Clifford, gaunt Hepzibah, and rustic little Phoebe! But another, and a greater marvel greets us! Can we believe our eyes? A stout, elderly gentleman has made his appearance; he has an aspect of eminent respectability, wears a black coat and pantaloons, of roomy width, and might be pronounced scrupulously neat in his attire, but for a broad crimson-stain, across his snowy neckcloth and down his shirt-bosom. Is it the Judge, or no? How can it be Judge Pyncheon? We discern his figure, as plainly as the flickering moonbeams can show us anything, still seated in the oaken chair! Be the apparition whose it may, it advances to the picture, seems to seize the frame, tries to peep behind it, and turns away, with a frown as black as the ancestral one.

The fantastic scene, just hinted at, must by no means be considered as forming an actual portion of our story. We were betrayed into this brief extravagance by the quiver of the moonbeams; they dance hand-in-hand with shadows, and are reflected in the looking-glass, which, you are aware, is always a kind of window or door-way into the spiritual world. We needed relief, moreover, from our too long and exclusive contemplation of that figure in the chair. This wild wind, too, has tossed our thoughts into strange confusion, but without tearing them away from their one determined centre. Yonder leaden Judge sits immoveably upon our soul. Will he never stir again? We shall go mad, unless he stirs! You may the better estimate his quietude by the fearlessness of a little mouse, which sits on its hind-legs, in a streak of moonlight, close by Judge Pyncheon's foot, and seems to meditate a journey of exploration over this great, black bulk. Ha! What has startled the nimble little mouse? It is the visage of Grimalkin, outside of the window, where he appears to have posted himself for a deliberate watch. This Grimalkin has a very ugly look. Is it a cat watching for a mouse, or the Devil for a human soul? Would we could scare him from the window!

Thank Heaven, the night is well-nigh past! The moonbeams have no longer so silvery a gleam, nor contrast so strongly with the blackness of the shadows among which they fall. They are paler, now; the shadows look gray, not black. The boisterous wind is hushed. What is the hour? Ah! The watch has at last ceased to tick;

for the Judge's forgetful fingers neglected to wind it up, as usual, at ten o'clock, being half-an-hour, or so, before his ordinary bed-time;—and it has run down, for the first time in five years. But the great world-clock of Time still keeps its beat. The dreary night—for, Oh, how dreary seems its haunted waste, behind us!—gives place to a fresh, transparent, cloudless morn. Blessed, blessed radiance! The day-beam—even what little of it finds its way into this always dusky parlor—seems part of the universal benediction, annulling evil, and rendering all goodness possible, and happiness attainable. Will Judge Pyncheon now rise up from his chair? Will he go forth, and receive the early sunbeams on his brow? Will he begin this new day—which God has smiled upon, and blessed, and given to mankind—will he begin it with better purposes than the many that have been spent amiss? Or are all the deep-laid schemes of yester-day as stubborn in his heart, and as busy in his brain, as ever?

In this latter case, there is much to do. Will the Judge still insist with Hepzibah on the interview with Clifford? Will he buy a safe, elderly gentleman's horse? Will he persuade the purchaser of the old Pyncheon property to relinquish the bargain, in his favor? Will he see his family-physician, and obtain a medicine that shall pre-serve him, to be an honor and blessing to his race, until the utmost term of patriarchal longevity? Will Judge Pyncheon, above all, make due apologies to that company of honorable friends, and satisfy them that his absence from the festive board was unavoidable, and so fully retrieve himself in their good opinion, that he shall yet be Governor of Massachusetts? And, all these great purposes accom-plished, will he walk the streets again, with that dog-day smile of elaborate benevolence, sultry enough to tempt flies to come and buzz in it? Or will he—after the tomblike seclusion of the past day and night—go forth a humbled and repentant man, sorrowful, gen-tle, seeking no profit, shrinking from worldly honor, hardly daring to love God, but bold to love his fellow-man, and to do him what good he may? Will he bear about with him—no odious grin of feigned benignity, insolent in its pretence, and loathsome in its falsehood—but the tender sadness of a contrite heart, broken, at last, beneath its own weight of sin? For it is our belief, whatever show of honor he may have piled upon it, that there was heavy sin at the base of this man's being.

Rise up, Judge Pyncheon! The morning sunshine glimmers through the foliage, and, beautiful and holy as it is, shuns not to kindle up your face. Rise up, thou subtile, worldly, selfish, iron-hearted hypocrite, and make thy choice, whether still to be subtile, worldly, selfish, iron-hearted, and hypocritical, or to tear these sins out of thy nature, though they bring the life-blood with them! The Avenger is upon thee! Rise up, before it be too late!

What! Thou art not stirred by this last appeal? No; not a jot! And there we see a fly—one of your common house-flies, such as are always buzzing on the window-pane—which has smelt out Governor Pyncheon, and alights now on his forehead, now on his chin, and now, Heaven help us, is creeping over the bridge of his nose, towards the would-be chief-magistrate's wide-open eyes! Canst thou not brush the fly away? Art thou too sluggish? Thou man, that hadst so many busy projects, yesterday! Art thou too weak, that wast so powerful? Not brush away a fly! Nay, then, we give thee up!

And, hark! the shop-bell rings. After hours like these latter ones, through which we have borne our heavy tale, it is good to be made sensible that there is a living world, and that even this old, lonely mansion retains some manner of connection with it. We breathe more freely, emerging from Judge Pyncheon's presence into the street before the seven gables.

XIX. Alice's Posies

Uncle Venner, trundling a wheelbarrow, was the earliest person stirring in the neighborhood, the day after the storm.

Pyncheon-street, in front of the House of the Seven Gables, was a far pleasanter scene than a by-lane, confined by shabby fences, and bordered with wooden dwellings of the meaner class, could reasonably be expected to present. Nature made sweet amends, that morning, for the five unkindly days which had preceded it. It would have been enough to live for, merely to look up at the wide benediction of the sky, or as much of it as was visible between the houses, genial once more with sunshine. Every object was agreeable, whether to be gazed at in the breadth, or examined more minutely. Such, for example, were the well-washed pebbles and gravel of the sidewalk; even the sky-reflecting pools in the centre of the street; and the grass, now freshly verdant, that crept along the base of the fences, on the other side of which, if one peeped over, was seen the multifarious growth of gardens. Vegetable productions, of whatever kind, seemed more than negatively happy, in the juicy warmth and abundance of their life. The Pyncheon-elm, throughout its great circumference, was all alive, and full of the morning sun and a sweetly tempered little breeze, which lingered within this verdant sphere, and set a thousand leafy tongues a-whispering all at once. This aged tree appeared to have suffered nothing from the gale. It had kept its boughs unshattered, and its full complement of leaves, and the whole in perfect verdure, except a single branch, that, by the earlier change with which the elm-tree sometimes prophesies the autumn, had been transmuted to bright gold. It was like the golden branch, that gained Æneas and the Sibyl admittance into Hades.[2]

This one mystic branch hung down before the main-entrance of the seven gables, so nigh the ground, that any passer-by might have stood on tiptoe and plucked it off. Presented at the door, it would have been a symbol of his right to enter, and be made acquainted with all the secrets of the house. So little faith is due to external appearance, that there was really an inviting aspect over the venerable edifice, conveying an idea that its history must be a decorous and happy one, and such as would be delightful for a fireside-tale. Its windows gleamed cheerfully in the slanting sunlight. The lines and tufts of green moss, here and there, seemed pledges of familiarity and sisterhood with Nature; as if this human dwelling-place, being of such old date, had established its prescriptive title among primeval oaks, and whatever other objects, by virtue of their long continuance, have acquired a gracious right to be. A person of imaginative temperament, while passing by the house, would turn, once and again, and peruse it well,—its many peaks, consenting together in the clustered chimney; the deep projection over its base-ment story; the arched window, imparting a look, if not of grandeur, yet of antique gentility, to the broken portal over which it opened; the luxuriance of gigantic burdocks, near the threshold;—he would note all these characteristics, and be conscious of something deeper than he saw. He would conceive the mansion to have been the residence of the stubborn old Puritan, Integrity, who, dying in some forgotten generation, had left a blessing in all its rooms and chambers, the efficacy of which was to be seen in the religion, hon-esty, moderate competence, or upright poverty, and solid happiness, of his descendants, to this day.

One object, above all others, would take root in the imaginative observer's memory. It was the great tuft of flowers—weeds, you would have called them, only a week ago—the tuft of crimson-spotted flowers, in the angle between the two front gables. The old people used to give them the name of Alice's Posies, in remem-brance of fair Alice Pyncheon, who was believed to have brought their seeds from Italy. They were flaunting in rich beauty and full bloom, to-day, and seemed, as it were, a mystic expression that something within the house was consummated.

It was but little after sunrise, when Uncle Venner made his ap-pearance, as aforesaid, impelling a wheelbarrow along the street. He was going his matutinal rounds to collect cabbage-leaves, turnip-tops, potato-skins, and the miscellaneous refuse of the

---

2. An allusion to the moment in Book VI of Virgil's *Aeneid* (ca. 19 B.C.E.) when Aeneas, the founder of Rome, is directed by the sibyl of Cumae to pluck a sacred golden bough for protection during their journey through the underworld.

dinner-pot, which the thrifty housewives of the neighborhood were accustomed to put aside, as fit only to feed a pig. Uncle Venner's pig was fed entirely and kept in prime order on these eleemosynary[3] contributions; insomuch that the patched philosopher used to promise that, before retiring to his farm, he would make a feast of the portly grunter, and invite all his neighbors to partake of the joints and spare-ribs which they had helped to fatten. Miss Hepzibah Pyncheon's house-keeping had so greatly improved, since Clifford became a member of the family, that her share of the banquet would have been no lean one; and Uncle Venner, accordingly, was a good deal disappointed not to find the large earthen pan, full of fragmentary eatables, that ordinarily awaited his coming, at the back-doorstep of the seven gables.

"I never knew Miss Hepzibah so forgetful before," said the patriarch to himself. "She must have had a dinner, yesterday—no question of that! She always has one, now-a-days. So where's the pot-liquor[4] and potato-skins, I ask? Shall I knock, and see if she's stirring yet? No, no—'twon't do! If little Phoebe was about the house, I should not mind knocking; but Miss Hepzibah, likely as not, would scowl down at me, out of the window, and look cross, even if she felt pleasantly. So I'll come back at noon."

With these reflections, the old man was shutting the gate of the little back-yard. Creaking on its hinges, however, like every other gate and door about the premises, the sound reached the ears of the occupant of the northern gable; one of the windows of which had a side-view towards the gate.

"Good morning, Uncle Venner!" said the Daguerreotypist, leaning out of the window.—"Do you hear nobody stirring?"

"Not a soul!" said the man of patches. "But that's no wonder. 'Tis barely half-an-hour past sunrise, yet. But I'm really glad to see you, Mr. Holgrave! There's a strange, lonesome look about this side of the house; so that my heart misgave me, somehow or other, and I felt as if there was nobody alive in it. The front of the house looks a good deal cheerier; and Alice's Posies are blooming there beautifully; and if I were a young man, Mr. Holgrave, my sweetheart should have one of those flowers in her bosom, though I risked my neck climbing for it! Well!—and did the wind keep you awake, last night?"

"It did indeed!" answered the artist smiling. "If I were a believer in ghosts—and I don't quite know whether I am, or not—I should have concluded that all the old Pyncheons were running riot in the lower rooms; especially in Miss Hepzibah's part of the house. But it is very quiet, now."

---

3. Charitable.
4. The broth produced by cooking meats or vegetables in a pot.

"Yes; Miss Hepzibah will be apt to oversleep herself, after being disturbed, all night, with the racket," said Uncle Venner. "But it would be odd, now—wouldn't it?—if the Judge had taken both his cousins into the country along with him. I saw him go into the shop, yesterday."

"At what hour?" inquired Holgrave.

"Oh, along in the forenoon," said the old man. "Well, well; I must go my rounds, and so must my wheelbarrow. But I'll be back here at dinner-time; for my pig likes a dinner as well as a breakfast. No meal-time, and no sort of victuals, ever seems to come amiss to my pig. Good morning to you! And, Mr. Holgrave, if I were a young man, like you, I'd get one of Alice's Posies, and keep it in water till Phoebe comes back."

"I have heard," said the Daguerreotypist, as he drew in his head, "that the water of Maule's Well suits those flowers best."

Here the conversation ceased, and Uncle Venner went on his way. For half-an-hour longer, nothing disturbed the repose of the seven gables, nor was there any visitor, except a carrier-boy, who, as he passed the front-doorstep, threw down one of his newspapers; for Hepzibah, of late, had regularly taken it in. After awhile, there came a fat woman, making prodigious speed, and stumbling as she ran up the steps of the shop-door. Her face glowed with fire-heat; and, it being a pretty warm morning, she bubbled and hissed, as it were, as if all a-fry with chimney-warmth, and summer-warmth, and the warmth of her own corpulent velocity. She tried the shop-door; it was fast. She tried it again, with so angry a jar that the bell tinkled angrily back at her.

"The deuce take Old Maid Pyncheon!" muttered the irascible housewife. "Think of her pretending to set up a cent-shop, and then lying abed till noon! These are what she calls gentlefolk's airs, I suppose! But I'll either start her ladyship, or break the door down!"

She shook it accordingly; and the bell, having a spiteful little temper of its own, rang obstreperously, making its remonstrances heard—not, indeed, by the ears for which they were intended—but by a good lady on the opposite side of the street. She opened her window, and addressed the impatient applicant.

"You'll find nobody there, Mrs. Gubbins."

"But I must and will find somebody here!" cried Mrs. Gubbins, inflicting another outrage on the bell. "I want a half-pound of pork, to fry some first-rate flounders for Mr. Gubbins's breakfast; and, lady or not, Old Maid Pyncheon shall get up and serve me with it!"

"But do hear reason, Mrs. Gubbins!" responded the lady oppo-site.—"She, and her brother too, have both gone to their cousin, Judge Pyncheon's, at his country-seat. There's not a soul in the

house but that young daguerreotype-man, that sleeps in the north-
gable. I saw old Hepzibah and Clifford go away, yesterday; and a
queer couple of ducks they were, paddling through the mud-
puddles! They're gone, I'll assure you."

"And how do you know they're gone to the Judge's?" asked Mrs.
Gubbins.—"He's a rich man; and there's been a quarrel between
him and Hepzibah, this many a day, because he won't give her a living. That's the main reason of her setting up a cent-shop."

"I know that well enough," said the neighbor. "But they're gone—
that's one thing certain. And who but a blood-relation, that couldn't
help himself, I ask you, would take in that awful-tempered Old
Maid, and that dreadful Clifford? That's it, you may be sure!"

Mrs. Gubbins took her departure, still brimming over with hot
wrath against the absent Hepzibah. For another half-hour, or perhaps considerably more, there was almost as much quiet on the
outside of the house, as within. The elm, however, made a pleasant,
cheerful, sunny sigh, responsive to the breeze that was elsewhere
imperceptible; a swarm of insects buzzed merrily under its drooping
shadow, and became specks of light, whenever they darted into the
sunshine; a locust sang, once or twice, in some inscrutable seclusion of the tree; and a solitary little bird, with plumage of pale gold,
came and hovered about Alice's Posies.

At last, our small acquaintance Ned Higgins trudged up the
street, on his way to school; and happening, for the first time in a
fortnight, to be the possessor of a cent, he could by no means get
past the shop-door of the seven gables. But it would not open.
Again and again, however, and half-a-dozen other agains, with the
inexorable pertinacity of a child, intent upon some object important
to itself, did he renew his efforts for admittance. He had doubtless
set his heart upon an elephant; or, possibly, with Hamlet, he meant
to eat a crocodile.[5] In response to his more violent attacks, the bell
gave now-and-then a moderate tinkle, but could not be stirred into
clamor by any exertion of the little fellow's childish and tiptoe
strength. Holding by the door-handle, he peeped through a crevice
of the curtain, and saw that the inner door, communicating with
the passage towards the parlor, was closed.

"Miss Pyncheon!" screamed the child, rapping on the window-
pane. "I want an elephant!"

There being no answer to several repetitions of the summons,
Ned began to grow impatient; and his little pot of passion quickly
boiling over, he picked up a stone, with a naughty purpose to fling

---

5. A reference to the grief-stricken Hamlet's jeering at the overly demonstrative Laertes after he leaps into Ophelia's grave: " 'Swounds, show me what thou'd do. / Woo't weep?
woo't fight? woo't tear thyself? / Woo't drink up esill [vinegar]? eat a crocodile?" (Shakespeare, *Hamlet* [1604], V.i.261–63).

it through the window; at the same time blubbering and sputtering
with wrath. A man, one of two who happened to be passing by,
caught the urchin's arm.

"What's the trouble, old gentleman?" he asked.

"I want old Hepzibah, or Phoebe, or any of them!" answered
Ned, sobbing. "They won't open the door; and I can't get my
elephant!"

"Go to school, you little scamp!" said the man. "There's another
cent-shop round the corner. 'Tis very strange, Dixey," added he to
his companion, "what's become of all these Pyncheons! Smith, the
livery-stable keeper, tells me Judge Pyncheon put his horse up, yesterday, to stand till after dinner, and has not taken him away, yet.
And one of the Judge's hired men has been in, this morning, to
make inquiry about him. He's a kind of person, they say, that seldom breaks his habits, or stays out o'nights."

"Oh, he'll turn up safe enough!" said Dixey. "And as for Old Maid
Pyncheon, take my word for it, she has run in debt, and gone off
from her creditors. I foretold, you remember, the first morning she
set up shop, that her devilish scowl would frighten away customers.
They couldn't stand it!"

"I never thought she'd make it go," remarked his friend. "This
business of cent-shops is overdone among the women-folks. My
wife tried it, and lost five dollars on her outlay!"

"Poor business!" said Dixey, shaking his head. "Poor business!"

In the course of the morning, there were various other attempts
to open a communication with the supposed inhabitants of this
silent and impenetrable mansion. The man of root-beer came, in
his neatly painted wagon, with a couple of dozen full bottles, to be
exchanged for empty ones; the baker, with a lot of crackers which
Hepzibah had ordered for her retail-custom; the butcher, with a
nice tidbit which he fancied she would be eager to secure for Clifford. Had any observer of these proceedings been aware of the fearful secret, hidden within the house, it would have affected him
with a singular shape and modification of horror, to see the current
of human life making this small eddy hereabouts;—whirling sticks,
straws, and all such trifles, round and round, right over the black
depth where a dead corpse lay unseen.

The butcher was so much in earnest with his sweetbread of
lamb, or whatever the dainty might be, that he tried every accessi-
ble door of the seven gables, and at length came round again to the
shop, where he ordinarily found admittance.

"It's a nice article, and I know the old lady would jump at it," said
he to himself.—"She can't be gone away! In fifteen years that I
have driven my cart through Pyncheon-street, I've never known her
to be away from home; though, often enough, to be sure, a man

might knock all day without bringing her to the door. But that was when she'd only herself to provide for."

Peeping through the same crevice of the curtain where, only a little while before, the urchin of elephantine appetite had peeped, the butcher beheld the inner door, not closed, as the child had seen it, but ajar, and almost wide open. However it might have happened, it was the fact. Through the passage-way there was a dark vista into the lighter, but still obscure, interior of the parlor. It appeared to the butcher that he could pretty clearly discern what seemed to be the stalwart legs, clad in black pantaloons, of a man sitting in a large oaken chair, the back of which concealed all the remainder of his figure. This contemptuous tranquillity on the part of an occupant of the house, in response to the butcher's indefatigable efforts to attract notice, so piqued the man of flesh that he determined to withdraw.

"So," thought he, "there sits Old Maid Pyncheon's bloody brother, while I've been giving myself all this trouble! Why, if a hog hadn't more manners, I'd stick him! I call it demeaning a man's business to trade with such people; and from this time forth, if they want a sausage or an ounce of liver, they shall run after the cart for it!"

He tossed the tidbit angrily into his cart, and drove off in a pet.

Not a great while afterwards, there was a sound of music turning the corner, and approaching down the street, with several intervals of silence, and then a renewed and nearer outbreak of brisk melody. A mob of children was seen moving onward, or stopping, in unison with the sound, which appeared to proceed from the centre of the throng; so that they were loosely bound together by slender strains of harmony, and drawn along captive; with ever and anon an accession of some little fellow in an apron and straw hat, capering forth from door or gateway. Arriving under the shadow of the Pyncheon-elm, it proved to be the Italian boy, who, with his monkey and show of puppets, had once before played his hurdy-gurdy beneath the arched window. The pleasant face of Phoebe—and doubtless, too, the liberal recompense which she had flung him—still dwelt in his remembrance. His expressive features kindled up, as he recognized the spot where this trifling incident of his erratic life had chanced. He entered the neglected yard, (now wilder than ever, with its growth of hogweed and burdock,) stationed himself on the door-step of the main-entrance, and opening his show-box, began to play. Each individual of the automatic community forthwith set to work, according to his or her proper vocation; the monkey, taking off his highland bonnet, bowed and scraped to the bystanders, most obsequiously, with ever an observant eye to pick up a stray cent; and the young foreigner himself, as he turned the crank of his ma-

chine, glanced upward to the arched window, expectant of a presence that would make his music the livelier and sweeter. The
throng of children stood near; some on the sidewalk; some within
the yard; two or three establishing themselves on the very door-
step; and one squatting on the threshold. Meanwhile, the locust
kept singing, in the great, old Pyncheon-elm.

"I don't hear anybody in the house," said one of the children to
another. "The monkey won't pick up anything here."

"There is somebody at home," affirmed the urchin on the threshold. "I heard a step!"

Still the young Italian's eye turned sidelong upward; and it really
seemed as if the touch of genuine, though slight and almost playful
emotion, communicated a juicier sweetness to the dry, mechanical
process of his minstrelsy. These wanderers are readily responsive to
any natural kindness—be it no more than a smile, or a word, itself
not understood, but only a warmth in it—which befalls them on
the roadside of life. They remember these things, because they are
the little enchantments which, for the instant—for the space that
reflects a landscape in a soap-bubble—build up a home about
them. Therefore, the Italian boy would not be discouraged by the
heavy silence, with which the old house seemed resolute to clog the
vivacity of his instrument. He persisted in his melodious appeals;
he still looked upward, trusting that his dark, alien countenance
would soon be brightened by Phoebe's sunny aspect. Neither could
he be willing to depart without again beholding Clifford, whose
sensibility, like Phoebe's smile, had talked a kind of heart's language
to the foreigner. He repeated all his music, over and over again, until his auditors were getting weary. So were the little wooden-people
in his show-box, and the monkey most of all. There was no response, save the singing of the locust.

"No children live in this house," said a schoolboy, at last. "Nobody lives here but an old maid and an old man. You'll get nothing
here! Why don't you go along?"

"You fool, you, why do you tell him?" whispered a shrewd little
Yankee, caring nothing for the music, but a good deal for the cheap
rate at which it was had. "Let him play as long as he likes. If there's
nobody to pay him, that's his own look-out!"

Once more, however, the Italian ran over his round of melodies.
To the common observer—who could understand nothing of the
case, except the music and the sunshine on the hither side of
the door—it might have been amusing to watch the pertinacity of
the street-performer. Will he succeed at last? Will that stubborn
door be suddenly flung open? Will a group of joyous children, the
young ones of the house, come dancing, shouting, laughing, into
the open air, and cluster round the show-box, looking with eager

merriment at the puppets, and tossing each a copper for long-tailed Mammon, the monkey, to pick up?

But, to us, who know the inner heart of the seven gables, as well as its exterior face, there is a ghastly effect in this repetition of light popular tunes at its door-step. It would be an ugly business, indeed, if Judge Pyncheon (who would not have cared a fig for Paganini's fiddle,[6] in his most harmonious mood) should make his appearance at the door, with a bloody shirt-bosom, and a grim frown on his swarthily white visage, and motion the foreign vagabond away! Was ever before such a grinding-out of jigs and waltzes, where nobody was in the cue to dance? Yes; very often. This contrast, or intermingling of tragedy with mirth, happens daily, hourly, momently. The gloomy and desolate old house, deserted of life, and with awful Death sitting sternly in its solitude, was the emblem of many a human heart, which, nevertheless, is compelled to hear the trill and echo of the world's gaiety around it.

Before the conclusion of the Italian's performance, a couple of men happened to be passing, on their way to dinner.

"I say, you young French fellow!" called out one of them,—"come away from that door-step, and go somewhere else with your nonsense! The Pyncheon family live there; and they are in great trouble, just about this time. They don't feel musical to-day. It is reported, all over town, that Judge Pyncheon, who owns the house, has been murdered; and the City Marshal is going to look into the matter. So be off with you at once!"

As the Italian shouldered his hurdy-gurdy, he saw on the door-step a card, which had been covered, all the morning, by the newspaper that the carrier had flung upon it, but was now shuffled into sight. He picked it up, and perceiving something written in pencil, gave it to the man to read. In fact, it was an engraved card of Judge Pyncheon's, with certain pencilled memoranda on the back, referring to various businesses which it had been his purpose to transact during the preceding day. It formed a prospective epitome of the day's history; only that affairs had not turned out altogether in accordance with the programme. The card must have been lost from the Judge's vest-pocket, in his preliminary attempt to gain access by the main-entrance of the house. Though well-soaked with rain, it was still partially legible.

"Look here, Dixey!" cried the man. "This has something to do with Judge Pyncheon. See;—here's his name printed on it; and here, I suppose, is some of his handwriting."

"Let's go to the City Marshal with it!" said Dixey. "It may give him just the clue he wants. After all," whispered he in his compan-

---

6. The Italian violinist Nicolò Paganini (1784–1840) was acclaimed for his virtuosity.

ion's ear, "it would be no wonder if the Judge has gone into that door, and never come out again! A certain cousin of his may have been at his old tricks. And Old Maid Pyncheon having got herself in debt by the cent-shop—and the Judge's pocket-book being well-filled—and bad blood amongst them already! Put all these things together, and see what they make!"

"Hush, hush!" whispered the other. "It seems like a sin to be the first to speak of such a thing. But I think, with you, that we had better go to the City Marshal."

"Yes, yes!" said Dixey. "Well!—I always said there was something devilish in that woman's scowl!"

The men wheeled about, accordingly, and retraced their steps up the street. The Italian, also, made the best of his way off, with a parting glance up at the arched window. As for the children, they took to their heels, with one accord, and scampered, as if some giant or ogre were in pursuit; until, at a good distance from the house, they stopt as suddenly and simultaneously as they had set out. Their susceptible nerves took an indefinite alarm from what they had overheard. Looking back at the grotesque peaks and shadowy angles of the old mansion, they fancied a gloom diffused about it, which no brightness of the sunshine could dispel. An imaginary Hepzibah scowled and shook her finger at them, from several windows at the same moment. An imaginary Clifford—for (and it would have deeply wounded him to know it) he had always been a horror to these small people—stood behind the unreal Hepzibah, making awful gestures, in a faded dressing-gown. Children are even more apt, if possible, than grown people, to catch the contagion of a panic terror. For the rest of the day, the more timid went whole streets about, for the sake of avoiding the seven gables; while the bolder signalized their hardihood by challenging their comrades to race past the mansion, at full speed.

It could not have been more than half-an-hour after the disappearance of the Italian boy, with his unseasonable melodies, when a cab drove down the street. It stopt beneath the Pyncheon-elm; the cabman took a trunk, a canvass-bag, and a bandbox, from the top of his vehicle, and deposited them on the door-step of the old house; a straw bonnet, and then the pretty figure of a young girl, came into view from the interior of the cab. It was Phoebe! Though not altogether so blooming as when she first tript into our story—for, in the few intervening weeks, her experiences had made her graver, more womanly, and deeper-eyed, in token of a heart that had begun to suspect its depths—still there was the quiet glow of natural sunshine over her. Neither had she forfeited her proper gift of making things look real, rather than fantastic, within her sphere. Yet we feel it to be a questionable venture, even for Phoebe, at this juncture, to cross the threshold of the seven gables. Is her healthful presence potent enough to chase away the crowd of pale, hideous, and sinful phantoms, that have gained admittance there, since her departure? Or will she, likewise, fade, sicken, sadden, and grow into deformity, and be only another pallid phantom, to glide noiselessly up and down the stairs, and affright children, as she pauses at the window?

At least, we would gladly forewarn the unsuspecting girl, that there is nothing in human shape or substance to receive her, unless it be the figure of Judge Pyncheon, who—wretched spectacle that he is, and frightful in our remembrance, since our night-long vigil with him!—still keeps his place in the oaken chair.

Phoebe first tried the shop-door. It did not yield to her hand; and the white curtain, drawn across the window which formed the upper section of the door, struck her quick perceptive faculty as something unusual. Without making another effort to enter here, she betook herself to the great portal, under the arched window. Finding it fastened, she knocked. A reverberation came from the emptiness within. She knocked again, and a third time, and, listening intently, fancied that the floor creaked, as if Hepzibah were coming, with her ordinary tiptoe movement, to admit her. But so dead a silence ensued upon this imaginary sound, that she began to question whether she might not have mistaken the house, familiar as she thought herself with its exterior.

Her notice was now attracted by a child's voice, at some distance. It appeared to call her name. Looking in the direction whence it proceeded, Phoebe saw little Ned Higgins, a good way down the street, stamping, shaking his head violently, making deprecatory gestures with both hands, and shouting to her at mouth-wide screech.

"No, no, Phoebe!" he screamed. "Don't you go in! There's something wicked there! Don't—don't—don't go in!"

But, as the little personage could not be induced to approach near enough to explain himself, Phoebe concluded that he had been frightened, on some of his visits to the shop, by her Cousin Hepzibah; for the good lady's manifestations, in truth, ran about an equal chance of scaring children out of their wits, or compelling them to unseemly laughter. Still, she felt the more, for this incident, how unaccountably silent and impenetrable the house had become. As her next resort, Phoebe made her way into the garden, where, on so warm and bright a day as the present, she had little doubt of finding Clifford, and perhaps Hepzibah also, idling away the noontide in the shadow of the arbor. Immediately on her entering the garden-gate, the family of hens half ran, half flew, to meet her; while a strange Grimalkin, which was prowling under the parlor-window, took to his heels, clambered hastily over the fence, and vanished. The arbor was vacant, and its floor, table, and circular bench, were still damp, and bestrewn with twigs, and the disarray of the past storm. The growth of the garden seemed to have got quite out of bounds; the weeds had taken advantage of Phoebe's absence, and the long-continued rain, to run rampant over the flowers and kitchen-vegetables. Maule's Well had overflowed its stone-border, and made a pool of formidable breadth, in that corner of the garden.

The impression of the whole scene was that of a spot, where no human foot had left its print, for many preceding days—probably, not since Phoebe's departure—for she saw a side-comb of her own under the table of the arbor, where it must have fallen, on the last afternoon when she and Clifford sat there.

The girl knew that her two relatives were capable of far greater oddities, than that of shutting themselves up in their old house, as they appeared now to have done. Nevertheless, with indistinct misgivings of something amiss, and apprehensions to which she could not give shape, she approached the door that formed the customary communication between the house and garden. It was secured within, like the two which she had already tried. She knocked, however; and, immediately, as if the application had been expected, the door was drawn open, by a considerable exertion of some unseen person's strength, not widely, but far enough to afford her a sidelong entrance. As Hepzibah, in order not to expose herself to inspection from without, invariably opened a door in this manner, Phoebe necessarily concluded that it was her cousin who now admitted her.

Without hesitation, therefore, she stept across the threshold, and had no sooner entered, than the door closed behind her.

XX. The Flower of Eden

Phoebe, coming so suddenly from the sunny daylight, was altogether bedimmed in such density of shadow as lurked in most of the passages of the old house. She was not at first aware by whom she had been admitted. Before her eyes had adapted themselves to the obscurity, a hand grasped her own, with a firm, but gentle and warm pressure, thus imparting a welcome which caused her heart to leap and thrill with an undefinable shiver of enjoyment. She felt herself drawn along, not towards the parlor, but into a large and unoccupied apartment, which had formerly been the grand reception-room of the seven gables. The sunshine came freely into all the uncurtained windows of this room, and fell upon the dusty floor; so that Phoebe now clearly saw—what, indeed, had been no secret, after the encounter of a warm hand with hers—that it was not Hepzibah nor Clifford, but Holgrave, to whom she owed her reception. The subtle, intuitive communication, or, rather, the vague and formless impression of something to be told, had made her yield unresistingly to his impulse. Without taking away her hand, she looked eagerly in his face, not quick to forebode evil, but unavoidably conscious that the state of the family had changed, since her departure, and therefore anxious for an explanation.

The artist looked paler than ordinary; there was a thoughtful and severe contraction of his forehead, tracing a deep, vertical line between the eyebrows. His smile, however, was full of genuine warmth, and had in it a joy, by far the most vivid expression that Phoebe had ever witnessed, shining out of the New England reserve with which Holgrave habitually masked whatever lay near his heart. It was the look wherewith a man, brooding alone over some fearful object, in a dreary forest or illimitable desert, would recognize the familiar aspect of his dearest friend, bringing up all the peaceful ideas that belong to home, and the gentle current of everyday affairs. And yet, as he felt the necessity of responding to her look of inquiry, the smile disappeared.

"I ought not to rejoice that you have come, Phoebe!" said he. "We meet at a strange moment!"

"What has happened?" she exclaimed. "Why is the house so deserted? Where are Hepzibah and Clifford?"

"Gone! I cannot imagine where they are!" answered Holgrave. "We are alone in the house!"

"Hepzibah and Clifford gone?" cried Phoebe. "It is not possible! And why have you brought me into this room, instead of the parlor? Ah, something terrible has happened! I must run and see!"

"No, no, Phoebe!" said Holgrave, holding her back. "It is as I have told you. They are gone, and I know not whither. A terrible event has indeed happened, but not to them, nor, as I undoubtingly believe, through any agency of theirs. If I read your character rightly, Phoebe," he continued, fixing his eyes on hers with stern anxiety, intermixed with tenderness, "gentle as you are, and seeming to have your sphere among common things, you yet possess remarkable strength. You have wonderful poise, and a faculty which, when tested, will prove itself capable of dealing with matters that fall far out of the ordinary rule."

"Oh, no, I am very weak!" replied Phoebe trembling. "But tell me what has happened!"

"You are strong!" persisted Holgrave. "You must be both strong and wise; for I am all astray, and need your counsel. It may be, you can suggest the one right thing to do!"

"Tell me!—tell me!" said Phoebe, all in a tremble. "It oppresses—it terrifies me—this mystery! Anything else, I can bear!"

The artist hesitated. Notwithstanding what he had just said, and most sincerely, in regard to the self-balancing power with which Phoebe impressed him, it still seemed almost wicked to bring the awful secret of yesterday to her knowledge. It was like dragging a hideous shape of death into the cleanly and cheerful space before a household fire, where it would present all the uglier aspect, amid the decorousness of everything about it. Yet it could not be concealed from her; she must needs know it.

"Phoebe," said he, "do you remember this?"

He put into her hand a daguerreotype; the same that he had shown her at their first interview, in the garden, and which so strikingly brought out the hard and relentless traits of the original.

"What has this to do with Hepzibah and Clifford?" asked Phoebe, with impatient surprise that Holgrave should so trifle with her, at such a moment. "It is Judge Pyncheon! You have shown it to me before!"

"But here is the same face, taken within this half-hour," said the artist, presenting her with another miniature. "I had just finished it, when I heard you at the door."

"This is death!" shuddered Phoebe, turning very pale. "Judge Pyncheon dead!"

"Such as there represented," said Holgrave, "he sits in the next room. The Judge is dead, and Clifford and Hepzibah have vanished! I know no more. All beyond is conjecture. On returning to my solitary chamber, last evening, I noticed no light, either in the parlor, or Hepzibah's room, or Clifford's;—no stir nor footstep about the house. This morning, there was the same deathlike quiet. From my window, I overheard the testimony of a neighbor, that your relatives were seen leaving the house, in the midst of yesterday's storm. A rumor reached me, too, of Judge Pyncheon being missed. A feeling which I cannot describe—an indefinite sense of some catastrophe, or consummation—impelled me to make my way into this part of the house, where I discovered what you see. As a point of evidence that may be useful to Clifford—and also as a memorial valuable to myself; for, Phoebe, there are hereditary reasons that connect me strangely with that man's fate—I used the means at my disposal to preserve this pictorial record of Judge Pyncheon's death."

Even in her agitation, Phoebe could not help remarking the calmness of Holgrave's demeanor. He appeared, it is true, to feel the whole awfulness of the Judge's death, yet had received the fact into his mind without any mixture of surprise, but as an event preordained, happening inevitably, and so fitting itself into past occurrences, that it could almost have been prophesied.

"Why have not you thrown open the doors, and called in witnesses?" inquired she, with a painful shudder. "It is terrible to be here alone!"

"But Clifford!" suggested the artist. "Clifford and Hepzibah! We must consider what is best to be done in their behalf. It is a wretched fatality, that they should have disappeared. Their flight will throw the worst coloring over this event, of which it is susceptible. Yet how easy is the explanation, to those who know them! Bewildered and terror-stricken by the similarity of this death to a former one, which was attended with such disastrous consequences to Clifford, they have had no idea but of removing themselves from the scene. How miserably unfortunate! Had Hepzibah but shrieked aloud—had Clifford flung wide the door, and proclaimed Judge Pyncheon's death—it would have been, however awful in itself, an event fruitful of good consequences to them. As I view it, it would have gone far towards obliterating the black stain on Clifford's character."

"And how," asked Phoebe, "could any good come from what is so very dreadful?"

"Because," said the artist, "if the matter can be fairly considered, and candidly interpreted, it must be evident that Judge Pyncheon could not have come unfairly to his end. This mode of death has been an idiosyncrasy with his family, for generations past; not often occurring, indeed, but—when it does occur—usually attacking individuals of about the Judge's time of life, and generally in the tension of some mental crisis, or perhaps in an access of wrath. Old Maule's prophecy was probably founded on a knowledge of this physical predisposition in the Pyncheon race. Now, there is a minute and almost exact similarity in the appearances, connected with the death that occurred yesterday, and those recorded of the death of Clifford's uncle, thirty years ago. It is true, there was a certain arrangement of circumstances, unnecessary to be recounted, which made it possible—nay, as men look at these things, probable, or even certain—that old Jaffrey Pyncheon came to a violent death, and by Clifford's hands."

"Whence came those circumstances?" exclaimed Phoebe—"he being innocent, as we know him to be!"

"They were arranged," said Holgrave—"at least, such has long been my conviction—they were arranged, after the uncle's death, and before it was made public, by the man who sits in yonder parlor. His own death, so like that former one, yet attended with none of those suspicious circumstances, seems the stroke of God upon him, at once a punishment for his wickedness, and making plain the innocence of Clifford. But this flight—it distorts everything! He may be in concealment, near at hand. Could we but bring him back, before the discovery of the Judge's death, the evil might be rectified."

"We must not hide this thing, a moment longer!" said Phoebe. "It is dreadful to keep it so closely in our hearts. Clifford is innocent. God will make it manifest! Let us throw open the doors, and call all the neighborhood to see the truth!"

"You are right, Phoebe," rejoined Holgrave. "Doubtless, you are right."

Yet the artist did not feel the horror, which was proper to Phoebe's sweet and order-loving character, at thus finding herself at issue with society, and brought in contact with an event that transcended ordinary rules. Neither was he in haste, like her, to betake himself within the precincts of common life. On the contrary, he gathered a wild enjoyment—as it were, a flower of strange beauty, growing in a desolate spot, and blossoming in the wind—such a flower of momentary happiness he gathered from his present position. It separated Phoebe and himself from the world, and bound them to each other, by their exclusive knowledge of Judge Pyncheon's mysterious death, and the counsel which they were forced to hold respecting it. The secret, so long as it should continue such, kept them within the circle of a spell, a solitude in the midst of men, a remoteness as entire as that of an island in mid-ocean; —once divulged, the ocean would flow betwixt them, standing on its widely sundered shores. Meanwhile, all the circumstances of their situation seemed to draw them together; they were like two children who go hand in hand, pressing closely to one another's side, through a shadow-haunted passage. The image of awful Death, which filled the house, held them united by his stiffened grasp.

These influences hastened the development of emotions, that might not otherwise have flowered so soon. Possibly, indeed, it had been Holgrave's purpose to let them die in their undeveloped germs.

"Why do we delay so?" asked Phoebe. "This secret takes away my breath! Let us throw open the doors!"

"In all our lives, there can never come another moment like this!" said Holgrave. "Phoebe, is it all terror?—nothing but terror? Are you conscious of no joy, as I am, that has made this the only point of life, worth living for?"

"It seems a sin," replied Phoebe trembling, "to think of joy, at such a time!"

"Could you but know, Phoebe, how it was with me, the hour before you came!" exclaimed the artist. "A dark, cold, miserable hour! The presence of yonder dead man threw a great black shadow over everything; he made the universe, so far as my perception could reach, a scene of guilt, and of retribution more dreadful than the guilt. The sense of it took away my youth. I never hoped to feel young again! The world looked strange, wild, evil, hostile;—my past life, so lonesome and dreary; my future, a shapeless gloom, which I must mould into gloomy shapes! But, Phoebe, you crossed the threshold; and hope, warmth, and joy, came in with you! The black moment became at once a blissful one. It must not pass without the spoken word. I love you!"

"How can you love a simple girl, like me?" asked Phoebe, compelled by his earnestness to speak. "You have many, many thoughts, with which I should try in vain to sympathize. And I—I, too—I have tendencies with which you would sympathize as little. That is less matter. But I have not scope enough to make you happy."

"You are my only possibility of happiness!" answered Holgrave. "I have no faith in it, except as you bestow it on me!"

"And then—I am afraid!" continued Phoebe, shrinking towards Holgrave, even while she told him so frankly the doubts with which he affected her. "You will lead me out of my own quiet path. You will make me strive to follow you, where it is pathless. I cannot do so. It is not my nature. I shall sink down, and perish!"

"Ah, Phoebe!" exclaimed Holgrave, with almost a sigh, and a smile that was burthened with thought. "It will be far otherwise than as you forebode. The world owes all its onward impulse to men ill at ease. The happy man inevitably confines himself within ancient limits. I have a presentiment, that, hereafter, it will be my lot to set out trees, to make fences—perhaps, even, in due time, to build a house for another generation—in a word, to conform myself to laws, and the peaceful practice of society. Your poise will be more powerful than any oscillating tendency of mine."

"I would not have it so!" said Phoebe earnestly.

"Do you love me?" asked Holgrave. "If we love one another, the moment has room for nothing more. Let us pause upon it, and be satisfied. Do you love me, Phoebe?"

"You look into my heart," replied she, letting her eyes droop. "You know I love you!"

And it was in this hour, so full of doubt and awe, that the one miracle was wrought, without which every human existence is a blank. The bliss, which makes all things true, beautiful, and holy, shone around this youth and maiden. They were conscious of nothing sad nor old. They transfigured the earth, and made it Eden again, and themselves the two first dwellers in it. The dead man, so close beside them, was forgotten. At such a crisis, there is no Death; for Immortality is revealed anew, and embraces everything in its hallowed atmosphere.

But how soon the heavy earth-dream settled down again!

"Hark!" whispered Phoebe. "Somebody is at the street-door!"

"Now let us meet the world!" said Holgrave. "No doubt, the rumor of Judge Pyncheon's visit to this house, and the flight of Hepzibah and Clifford, is about to lead to the investigation of the premises. We have no way but to meet it. Let us open the door at once!"

But, to their surprise, before they could reach the street-door—even before they quitted the room in which the foregoing interview had passed—they heard footsteps in the farther passage. The door, therefore, which they supposed to be securely locked—which Holgrave, indeed, had seen to be so, and at which Phoebe had vainly tried to enter—must have been opened from without. The sound of footsteps was not harsh, bold, decided, and intrusive, as the gait of strangers would naturally be, making authoritative entrance into a dwelling where they knew themselves unwelcome. It was feeble, as of persons either weak or weary; there was the mingled murmur of two voices, familiar to both the listeners.

"Can it be!" whispered Holgrave.

"It is they!" answered Phoebe. "Thank God!—thank God!"

And then, as if in sympathy with Phoebe's whispered ejaculation, they heard Hepzibah's voice, more distinctly.

"Thank God, my brother, we are at home!"

"Well!—Yes!—thank God!" responded Clifford. "A dreary home, Hepzibah! But you have done well to bring me hither! Stay! That parlor-door is open. I cannot pass by it! Let me go and rest me in the arbor, where I used—Oh, very long ago, it seems to me, after what has befallen us—where I used to be so happy with little Phoebe!"

But the house was not altogether so dreary as Clifford imagined it. They had not made many steps—in truth, they were lingering in the entry, with the listlessness of an accomplished purpose, uncertain what to do next—when Phoebe ran to meet them. On beholding her, Hepzibah burst into tears. With all her might, she had staggered onward beneath the burden of grief and responsibility, until now that it was safe to fling it down. Indeed, she had not energy to fling it down, but only ceased to uphold it, and suffered it to press her to the earth. Clifford appeared the stronger of the two.

"It is our own little Phoebe!—Ah! and Holgrave with her," exclaimed he, with a glance of keen and delicate insight, and a smile, beautiful, kind, but melancholy. "I thought of you both, as we came down the street, and beheld Alice's Posies in full bloom. And so the flower of Eden has bloomed, likewise, in this old, darksome house, to-day!"

XXI. The Departure

The sudden death of so prominent a member of the social world, as the Honorable Judge Jaffrey Pyncheon, created a sensation (at least, in the circles more immediately connected with the deceased) which had hardly quite subsided in a fortnight.

It may be remarked, however, that, of all the events which constitute a person's biography, there is scarcely one—none, certainly, of anything like a similar importance—to which the world so easily reconciles itself, as to his death. In most other cases and contingencies, the individual is present among us, mixed up with the daily revolution of affairs, and affording a definite point for observation. At his decease, there is only a vacancy, and a momentary eddy—very small, as compared with the apparent magnitude of the ingurgitated object—and a bubble or two, ascending out of the black depth, and bursting at the surface. As regarded Judge Pyncheon, it seemed probable, at first blush, that the mode of his final departure might give him a larger and longer posthumous vogue, than ordinarily attends the memory of a distinguished man. But when it came to be understood, on the highest professional authority, that the event was a natural, and—except for some unimportant particulars, denoting a slight idiosyncrasy—by no means an unusual form of death, the public, with its customary alacrity, proceeded to forget that he had ever lived. In short, the honorable Judge was beginning to be a stale subject, before half the county-newspapers had found time to put their columns in mourning, and publish his exceedingly eulogistic obituary.

Nevertheless, creeping darkly through the places which this excellent person had haunted in his lifetime, there was a hidden stream of private talk, such as it would have shocked all decency to speak loudly at the street-corners. It is very singular, how the fact of a man's death often seems to give people a truer idea of his character, whether for good or evil, than they have ever possessed while he was living and acting among them. Death is so genuine a fact that it excludes falsehood, or betrays its emptiness; it is a touchstone that proves the gold, and dishonors the baser metal.[7] Could the departed, whoever he may be, return in a week after his decease, he would almost invariably find himself at a higher or lower point than he had formerly occupied, on the scale of public appreciation. But the talk, or scandal, to which we now allude, had reference to matters of no less old a date than the supposed murder, thirty or forty years ago, of the late Judge Pyncheon's uncle. The medical opinion, with regard to his own recent and regretted de-

---

7. A black stone used to test for genuine gold.

cease, had almost entirely obviated the idea that a murder was committed, in the former case. Yet, as the record showed, there were circumstances irrefragably indicating that some person had gained access to old Jaffrey Pyncheon's private apartments, at or near the moment of his death. His desk and private drawers, in a room contiguous to his bed-chamber, had been ransacked; money and valuable articles were missing; there was a bloody handprint on the old man's linen; and, by a powerfully welded chain of deductive evidence, the guilt of the robbery and apparent murder had been fixed on Clifford, then residing with his uncle in the House of the Seven Gables.[8]

Whencesoever originating, there now arose a theory that undertook so to account for these circumstances as to exclude the idea of Clifford's agency. Many persons affirmed, that the history and elucidation of the facts, long so mysterious, had been obtained by the Daguerreotypist from one of those mesmerical seers, who, now-a-days, so strangely perplex the aspect of human affairs, and put everybody's natural vision to the blush, by the marvels which they see with their eyes shut.

According to this version of the story, Judge Pyncheon, exemplary as we have portrayed him in our narrative, was, in his youth, an apparently irreclaimable scapegrace. The brutish, the animal instincts, as is often the case, had been developed earlier than the intellectual qualities, and the force of character, for which he was afterwards remarkable. He had shown himself wild, dissipated, addicted to low pleasures, little short of ruffianly in his propensities, and recklessly expensive, with no other resources than the bounty of his uncle. This course of conduct had alienated the old bachelor's affection, once strongly fixed upon him. Now, it is averred— but whether on authority available in a court of justice, we do not pretend to have investigated—that the young man was tempted by the devil, one night, to search his uncle's private drawers, to which he had unsuspected means of access. While thus criminally occupied, he was startled by the opening of the chamber-door. There stood old Jaffrey Pyncheon, in his night-clothes! The surprise of such a discovery, his agitation, alarm, and horror, brought on the crisis of a disorder to which the old bachelor had an hereditary liability; he seemed to choke with blood, and fell upon the floor, striking his temple a heavy blow against the corner of a table. What was to be done? The old man was surely dead! Assistance would come too late! What a misfortune, indeed, should it come too soon; since

---

8. Hawthorne drew on details of the 1830 murder in Salem of Captain Joseph White (see Joseph Felt, p. 234 herein). In the murder of White, the murderers aspiring to the wealthy man's inheritance attempted to shape the circumstances so that guilt would fall on a nephew, but the nephew was quickly absolved of blame.

his reviving consciousness would bring the recollection of the igno-
minious offence, which he had beheld his nephew in the very act of
committing!

But he never did revive. With the cool hardihood, that always
pertained to him, the young man continued his search of the drawers, and found a will of recent date, in favor of Clifford—which he
destroyed—and an older one in his own favor, which he suffered to
remain. But, before retiring, Jaffrey bethought himself of the evidence, in these ransacked drawers, that some one had visited the
chamber with sinister purposes. Suspicion, unless averted, might
fix upon the real offender. In the very presence of the dead man,
therefore, he laid a scheme that should free himself at the expense
of Clifford, his rival, for whose character he had at once a contempt and a repugnance. It is not probable, be it said, that he acted
with any set purpose of involving Clifford in a charge of murder;
knowing that his uncle did not die by violence, it may not have occurred to him, in the hurry of the crisis, that such an inference
might be drawn. But, when the affair took this darker aspect, Jaffrey's previous steps had already pledged him to those which remained. So craftily had he arranged the circumstances, that, at
Clifford's trial, his cousin hardly found it necessary to swear to anything false, but only to withhold the one decisive explanation, by
refraining to state what he had himself done and witnessed.

Thus, Jaffrey Pyncheon's inward criminality, as regarded Clifford,
was indeed black and damnable; while its mere outward show and
positive commission was the smallest that could possibly consist
with so great a sin. This is just the sort of guilt that a man of eminent respectability finds it easiest to dispose of. It was suffered to
fade out of sight, or be reckoned a venial matter, in the Honorable
Judge Pyncheon's long subsequent survey of his own life. He shuffled it aside, among the forgotten and forgiven frailties of his youth,
and seldom thought of it again.

We leave the Judge to his repose. He could not be styled fortunate, at the hour of death. Unknowingly, he was a childless man,
while striving to add more wealth to his only child's inheritance.
Hardly a week after his decease, one of the Cunard steamers[9]
brought intelligence of the death, by cholera, of Judge Pyncheon's
son, just at the point of embarkation for his native land. By this
misfortune, Clifford became rich; so did Hepzibah; so did our little
village-maiden, and through her, that sworn foe of wealth and all
manner of conservatism—the wild reformer—Holgrave!

It was now far too late in Clifford's life for the good opinion of

---

9. Founded by Samuel Cunard (1787–1865) in 1839, Cunard steamships first crossed the
Atlantic between England and America in 1840.

society to be worth the trouble and anguish of a formal vindication. What he needed was the love of a very few; not the admiration, or even the respect, of the unknown many. The latter might probably have been won for him, had those, on whom the guardianship of his welfare had fallen, deemed it advisable to expose Clifford to a miserable resuscitation of past ideas, when the condition of whatever comfort he might expect lay in the calm of forgetfulness. After such wrong as he had suffered, there is no reparation. The pitiable mockery of it, which the world might have been ready enough to offer, coming so long after the agony had done its utmost work, would have been fit only to provoke bitterer laughter than poor Clifford was ever capable of. It is a truth (and it would be a very sad one, but for the higher hopes which it suggests) that no great mistake, whether acted or endured, in our mortal sphere, is ever really set right. Time, the continual vicissitude of circumstances, and the invariable inopportunity of death, render it impossible. If, after long lapse of years, the right seems to be in our power, we find no niche to set it in. The better remedy is for the sufferer to pass on, and leave what he once thought his irreparable ruin far behind him.

The shock of Judge Pyncheon's death had a permanently invigorating and ultimately beneficial effect on Clifford. That strong and ponderous man had been Clifford's nightmare. There was no free breath to be drawn, within the sphere of so malevolent an influence. The first effect of freedom, as we have witnessed in Clifford's aimless flight, was a tremulous exhilaration. Subsiding from it, he did not sink into his former intellectual apathy. He never, it is true, attained to nearly the full measure of what might have been his faculties. But he recovered enough of them partially to light up his character, to display some outline of the marvellous grace that was abortive in it, and to make him the object of no less deep, although less melancholy interest than heretofore. He was evidently happy. Could we pause to give another picture of his daily life, with all the appliances now at command to gratify his instinct for the Beautiful, the garden-scenes, that seemed so sweet to him, would look mean and trivial in comparison.

Very soon after their change of fortune, Clifford, Hepzibah, and little Phoebe, with the approval of the artist, concluded to remove from the dismal old House of the Seven Gables, and take up their abode, for the present, at the elegant country-seat of the late Judge Pyncheon. Chanticleer and his family had already been transported thither; where the two hens had forthwith begun an indefatigable process of egg-laying, with an evident design, as a matter of duty and conscience, to continue their illustrious breed under better auspices than for a century past. On the day set for their departure, the principal personages of our story, including good Uncle Venner, were assembled in the parlor.

"The country-house is certainly a very fine one, so far as the plan goes," observed Holgrave, as the party were discussing their future arrangements.—"But I wonder that the late Judge—being so opulent, and with a reasonable prospect of transmitting his wealth to descendants of his own—should not have felt the propriety of embodying so excellent a piece of domestic architecture in stone, rather than in wood. Then, every generation of the family might have altered the interior, to suit its own taste and convenience; while the exterior, through the lapse of years, might have been adding venerableness to its original beauty, and thus giving that impression of permanence, which I consider essential to the happiness of any one moment."

"Why," cried Phoebe, gazing into the artist's face with infinite amazement, "how wonderfully your ideas are changed! A house of stone, indeed! It is but two or three weeks ago, that you seemed to wish people to live in something as fragile and temporary as a bird's nest!"

"Ah, Phoebe, I told you how it would be!" said the artist, with a half-melancholy laugh. "You find me a conservative already! Little did I think ever to become one. It is especially unpardonable in this dwelling of so much hereditary misfortune, and under the eye of yonder portrait of a model-conservative, who, in that very character, rendered himself so long the Evil Destiny of his race."

"That picture!" said Clifford, seeming to shrink from its stern glance. "Whenever I look at it, there is an old, dreamy recollection haunting me, but keeping just beyond the grasp of my mind. Wealth, it seems to say!—boundless wealth!—unimaginable wealth! I could fancy, that, when I was a child, or a youth, that portrait had spoken, and told me a rich secret, or had held forth its hand, with the written record of hidden opulence. But those old matters are so dim with me, now-a-days! What could this dream have been!"

"Perhaps I can recall it," answered Holgrave.—"See! There are a hundred chances to one, that no person, unacquainted with the secret, would ever touch this spring."

"A secret spring!" cried Clifford. "Ah, I remember now! I did discover it, one summer afternoon, when I was idling and dreaming about the house, long, long ago. But the mystery escapes me."

The artist put his finger on the contrivance to which he had referred. In former days, the effect would probably have been, to cause the picture to start forward. But, in so long a period of concealment, the machinery had been eaten through with rust; so that, at Holgrave's pressure, the portrait, frame and all, tumbled suddenly from its position, and lay face downward on the floor. A recess in the wall was thus brought to light, in which lay an object so covered with a century's dust, that it could not immediately be recognized as a folded sheet of parchment. Holgrave opened it, and displayed an ancient deed, signed with the hieroglyphics of several Indian sagamores,[1] and conveying to Colonel Pyncheon and his heirs, forever, a vast extent of territory at the eastward.

"This is the very parchment, the attempt to recover which cost the beautiful Alice Pyncheon her happiness and life," said the artist, alluding to his legend. "It is what the Pyncheons sought in vain, while it was valuable; and now that they find the treasure, it has long been worthless."

"Poor Cousin Jaffrey! This is what deceived him," exclaimed Hepzibah. "When they were young together, Clifford probably made a kind of fairy-tale of this discovery. He was always dreaming hither and thither about the house, and lighting up its dark corners with beautiful stories. And poor Jaffrey, who took hold of everything as if it were real, thought my brother had found out his uncle's wealth. He died with this delusion in his mind!"

"But," said Phoebe, apart to Holgrave, "how came you to know the secret?"

"My dearest Phoebe," said Holgrave, "how will it please you to assume the name of Maule? As for the secret, it is the only inheritance that has come down to me from my ancestors. You should have known sooner, (only that I was afraid of frightening you away,) that, in this long drama of wrong and retribution, I represent the old wizard, and am probably as much of a wizard as ever he was. The son of the executed Matthew Maule, while building this house, took the opportunity to construct that recess, and hide away the Indian deed, on which depended the immense land-claim of the Pyncheons. Thus, they bartered their eastern-territory for Maule's garden-ground."

"And now," said Uncle Venner, "I suppose their whole claim is not worth one man's share in my farm yonder!"

"Uncle Venner," cried Phoebe, taking the patched philosopher's hand, "you must never talk any more about your farm! You shall never go there, as long as you live! There is a cottage in our new garden—the prettiest little, yellowish-brown cottage you ever saw; and the sweetest-looking place, for it looks just as if it were made of gingerbread—and we are going to fit it up and furnish it, on purpose for you. And you shall do nothing but what you choose, and shall be as happy as the day is long, and shall keep Cousin Clifford in spirits with the wisdom and pleasantness, which is always dropping from your lips!"

1. Chiefs or notable leaders among New England's Indians.

"Ah, my dear child," quoth good Uncle Venner, quite overcome, "if you were to speak to a young man as you do to an old one, his chance of keeping his heart, another minute, would not be worth one of the buttons on my waistcoat! And—soul alive!—that great sigh, which you made me heave, has burst off the very last of them! But never mind! It was the happiest sigh I ever did heave; and it seems as if I must have drawn in a gulp of heavenly breath, to make it with. Well, well, Miss Phoebe! They'll miss me in the gardens, hereabouts, and round by the back-doors; and Pyncheon-street, I'm afraid, will hardly look the same without old Uncle Venner, who re-members it with a mowing-field on one side, and the garden of the seven gables on the other. But either I must go to your country-seat, or you must come to my farm—that's one of two things cer-tain; and I leave you to choose which!"

"Oh, come with us, by all means, Uncle Venner!" said Clifford, who had a remarkable enjoyment of the old man's mellow, quiet, and simple spirit. "I want you always to be within five minutes' saunter of my chair. You are the only philosopher I ever knew of, whose wisdom has not a drop of bitter essence at the bottom!"

"Dear me!" cried Uncle Venner, beginning partly to realize what manner of man he was.—"And yet folks used to set me down among the simple ones, in my younger days! But I suppose I am like a Roxbury russet—a great deal the better, the longer I can be kept.[2] Yes; and my words of wisdom, that you and Phoebe tell me of, are like the golden dandelions, which never grow in the hot months, but may be seen glistening among the withered grass, and under the dry leaves, sometimes as late as December. And you are welcome, friends, to my mess of dandelions, if there were twice as many!"

A plain, but handsome, dark-green barouche[3] had now drawn up in front of the ruinous portal of the old mansion-house. The party came forth, and (with the exception of good Uncle Venner, who was to follow in a few days) proceeded to take their places. They were chatting and laughing very pleasantly together; and—as proves to be often the case, at moments when we ought to palpitate with sen-sibility—Clifford and Hepzibah bade a final farewell to the abode of their forefathers, with hardly more emotion than if they had made it their arrangement to return thither at tea-time. Several children were drawn to the spot, by so unusual a spectacle as the barouche and pair of gray horses. Recognizing little Ned Higgins among them, Hepzibah put her hand into her pocket, and presented the urchin, her earliest and staunchest customer, with silver enough to

2. A green winter apple that remains edible for a long period of time.
3. Four-wheeled carriage with two facing seats and a front seat for the driver.

people the Domdaniel cavern[4] of his interior with as various a procession of quadrupeds, as passed into the ark.

Two men were passing, just as the barouche drove off.

"Well, Dixey," said one of them, "what do you think of this? My wife kept a cent-shop, three months, and lost five dollars on her outlay. Old Maid Pyncheon has been in trade just about as long, and rides off in her carriage with a couple of hundred thousand—reckoning her share, and Clifford's, and Phoebe's—and some say twice as much! If you choose to call it luck, it is all very well; but if we are to take it as the will of Providence, why, I can't exactly fathom it!"

"Pretty good business!" quoth the sagacious Dixey. "Pretty good business!"

Maule's Well, all this time, though left in solitude, was throwing up a succession of kaleidoscopic pictures, in which a gifted eye might have seen fore-shadowed the coming fortunes of Hepzibah, and Clifford, and the descendant of the legendary wizard, and the village-maiden, over whom he had thrown love's web of sorcery. The Pyncheon-elm moreover, with what foliage the September gale had spared to it, whispered unintelligible prophecies. And wise Uncle Venner, passing slowly from the ruinous porch, seemed to hear a strain of music, and fancied that sweet Alice Pyncheon—after witnessing these deeds, this by-gone woe, and this present happiness, of her kindred mortals—had given one farewell touch of a spirit's joy upon her harpsichord, as she floated heavenward from the HOUSE OF THE SEVEN GABLES!

The End.

---

4. The underwater vault in Jacques Cazotte and Denis Chavis's *Continuation of the Arabian Nights* (1788–89) where a sorcerer meets with his apprentices.

CONTEXTS

History

Hawthorne drew on a number of sources for *The House of the Seven Gables*, the most important being texts about the Salem witch crisis of 1692. For Hawthorne, this historical event was particularly disturbing because it involved both the history of Massachusetts and the history of the Hawthorne family, as his great-great-grandfather John Hathorne was one of the presiding judges of the trials that led to the deaths of nineteen people. Hawthorne turned to numerous other historical sources as well, including the history of General Knox's land patent in Maine, the infamous murder in 1830 of Captain Joseph White of Salem, and the oft-stated beliefs on both the maternal and paternal sides of his family that the Mannings and Hawthornes, respectively, held claims to thousands of acres in Maine supposedly deeded to them during the seventeenth and eighteenth centuries. This section can present only a small sampling of the many historical texts, events, and memories that informed Hawthorne's conception of history in *The House of the Seven Gables*. The section begins with a selection from Thomas Maule, an ardent opponent of the Puritans who was the inspiration, at least in part, for Hawthorne's creation of Matthew Maule. Robert Calef's *More Wonders of the Invisible World* (1700) was the source for the malediction that Matthew Maule utters at Colonel Pyncheon; and Charles W. Upham's 1831 *Lectures on Witchcraft* was an important source for Hawthorne's own understanding of the witch trials. Published shortly before *The House of the Seven Gables*, Joseph Felt's *Annals of Salem* (1845–49) would have brought Thomas Maule to Hawthorne's attention and reminded him as well of the details of the 1830 murder of Captain White, details that Hawthorne used liberally in his account of the alleged murder of the bachelor Pyncheon. Finally, the selections from Hawthorne's notebooks reveal his thoughts on the Knox estate, aristocracy, and the weight of history on the present generation.

THOMAS MAULE

From Truth Held Forth and Maintained†

A possible source for the fictional Matthew Maule is the historical Thomas Maule (1645–1724), an architect and builder, who vigorously dissented from Salem's Puritan authorities. In 1669 he was ordered whipped for asserting that Salem's minister John Higginson (1616–1708) told lies; and in 1695 the General Court of Salem ruled that all copies of Maule's 1695 *Truth Held Forth and Maintained* should be confiscated. In that book, Maule focused specifically on what he regarded as the crimes committed by the Puritans of Boston and Salem during the witchcraft trials of 1692. The selection printed here gives a sense of Maule's flair for denunciation.

* * * [W]hat changeth the nature between black People, and white People? the colour of the skin doth not change the Nature. But some may say, *The Negroes in Barbadoes do not go to Church.* Indeed it so is, and what better are many for going to Church in *New-England*, where they that have been nearest related to the Church, have manifested themselves to be the further from God, as witness their puting four of the Lords Servants to death at *Boston*, which Church they then accounted the purest Church in the World; and if the sheding of innocent Blood be the mark of a pure Church, the *Church of Rome* is more pure than the church of *Boston*, of which I may hereafter more relate; so that it is not the going to Church in New-England, that causeth white People to differ in nature, from black people, which go not to Church in *Barbadoes.* And therefore Judges had need to consider all things aright, because they are expresly commanded, *To do no Unrighteousness in Judgment*, Lev.: 9, 15.

ROBERT CALEF

From More Wonders of the Invisible World‡

In 1693 the prominent Puritan minister Cotton Mather (1663–1728) published *Wonders of the Invisible World*, which defended the actions

† From *Truth Held Forth and Maintained* (New York: William Bradford, 1695), 189. The orthography has been modernized; the archaic spellings and punctuation have been maintained.

‡ From *More Wonders of the Invisible World*, (1700), rpt. in *The Witchcraft Delusion in New England: Its Rise, Progress, and Termination as Exhibited by Dr. Cotton Mather in*

of Salem's authorities during the 1692 witchcraft trials. The Boston merchant Robert Calef (1648–1719) wrote a scathing response, *More Wonders of the Invisible World*, accusing Mather of attempting to spread witchcraft scares in Boston itself. Unable to find a Boston publisher willing to print a book attacking Mather, Calef published *More Wonders* in London in 1700. (Mather's response, *Some Few Remarks upon a Scandalous Book*, appeared in Boston in 1701.) Calef was the first to report on the condemned "witch" Sarah Good's curse on her judge, which was an important source for Matthew Maule's similar curse in *The House of the Seven Gables* on his judge.

At the Tryal of *Sarah Good*,[1] one of the afflicted fell in a Fit, and after coming out of it, she cried out of the Prisoner, for stabbing her in the breast with a Knife, and that she had broken the Knife in stabbing of her, accordingly a piece of the blade of a Knife was found about her. Immediately information being given to the Court, a young Man was called, who produced a Haft[2] and part of the Blade, which the Court having viewed and compared, saw it to be the same. And upon inquiry the young Man affirmed, that yesterday he happened to brake that Knife, and that he cast away the upper part, this afflicted person being then present, the young Man was dismist, and she was bidden by the Court not to tell lyes; and was improved (after as she had been before) to give Evidence against the Prisoners.

At Execution, Mr. *Noyes*[3] urged *Sarah Good* to Confess, and told her she was a Witch, and she knew she was a Witch, to which she replied, you are a lyer; I am no more a Witch than you are a Wizard, and if you take away my Life, God will give you Blood to drink.

---

the *Wonders of the Invisible World* and by Mr. *Robert Calef in His More Wonders of the Invisible World*, 3 vols., ed. Samuel Gardner Drake (Roxbury, MA: W. E. Woodward, 1866), III.33–34. The archaic spelling has been retained, the orthography has been modernized, and Drake's notes have been cut. Drawing on Calef, Thomas Hutchinson (1711–1780), who was at the time the lieutenant governor of Massachusetts, also described this incident in his *The History of the Province of Massachusetts Bay*, 3 vols. (Boston, 1767), II.29–30, a text that Hawthorne knew well.
1. The impoverished Sarah Good (1653–1692), the mother of two young children, was regarded as a misfit by her Salem neighbors and had few defenders.
2. Handle.
3. Nicholas Noyes (1647–1717), minister of the church of Salem.

JOSEPH B. FELT

From Annals of Salem†

Joseph Barlow Felt (1789–1869) wrote a number of highly admired accounts of New England history. He published his best known work, *Annals of Salem*, in 1827, and brought out a revised and expanded version in 1845 and 1849. Hawthorne twice borrowed the 1827 edition from the Salem Athenæum during the 1830s, and he borrowed it again in 1849 (see Marion L. Kesselring, *Hawthorne's Reading: 1828–1850* [1949], 50). Felt's *Annals* provided Hawthorne with source material on Thomas Maule. It would have also reminded him of the famous White murder trial of 1830, which Hawthorne may have attended as a young man, and which he was to use as a source for Jaffrey Pyncheon's plot against Clifford in *The House of the Seven Gables*. The wealthy bachelor Captain Joseph White (1748–1830) of Salem was brutally murdered by one Richard Crowninshield Jr., who was hired to do the deed by Joseph Jenkins Knapp (1804–1831) and John Francis Knapp (1811–1830). The Knapp brothers hoped to be counted among the White heirs. To add to their possible wealth, and free themselves from suspicion, they attempted to pin the blame for the murder on one of White's nephews.

To the Citizens of Salem.

Among the endowments of our nature, are the affections and sympathies, which have a large share of their purest and happiest exercises in relation to the home of our birth or adoption. This is a wise provision of divine economy. It is well for the benefit of families, that every man should cherish a special regard for his own household. So it is well, that all should entertain a particular attachment to the place, where their domestic ties exist and their civil rights are secured. The operation of this principle is mostly experienced by those who are called to distant sections of their own or other countries. Seldom can any person so sunder the common bonds of humanity, as to feel alike in every clime. Justly has a departed genius doubted whether a man could be found,

> "Whose heart hath ne'er within him burned,
> As home his footsteps he hath turned,
> From wandering on a foreign strand."[1]

---

† From *Annals of Salem*, 2nd ed., 2 vols. (Salem: W. & S. B. Ives, 1845 [vol. 1], 1849 [vol. 2]), I.iii–iv; II.586–87, 590, 617, 465–67.

1. From Sir Walter Scott's *Lay of the Last Minstrel* (1805), canto 6, 1.4–6.

But this disposition, like every other of ours, was conferred for specific purposes, and is connected with appropriate responsibilities. Among these may be numbered the obligation to preserve the memorials of the community, which covers us with the shield of its protection. True, this is no monument of marble or brass, rising in classic proportions and communing with the clouds, so as to command the admiration of every passenger. But it speaks to us in clearer tones and with greater instruction and effect. It takes deeper hold on the susceptibilities of our spirits and engraves more lasting mementoes on the tablets of our hearts. Such is the intended object of this volume. As the production of mortal hands, it must have its imperfections. Still the author hopes that his labor is not altogether lost; that it will keep from oblivion, the deeds of our fathers, as well as of their descendants, and reflect no dishonor on the settlement, which the former selected, and the latter inherited, as an asylum of civil and religious liberty. * * *

* * *

1669, March 10. The Governor and Council send an address to Mr. Higginson and other ministers of the colony. It says, "We earnestly desiring you to be very diligent to catechize and instruct all the people (especially youth) under your charge in the orthodox principles of the Christian religion, and that not only in publick, but privately from house to house."

[1669], May 3. Thomas Maule is ordered to be whipped for saying that Mr. Higginson preached lies, and that his instruction was "the doctrine of devils." * * *

1692. Much trouble in the Village church about witchcraft, which continued for several years. So it was, to some extent, in the First church.

1695, Dec. 12. An order of General Court requires that all the copies of a book, entitled "Truth Held Forth," and edited by Thomas Maule, be searched for and seized. This work contained severe reflections on the government for their treatment of the Quakers.

* * *

From a book entitled "Truth held forth and maintained," published December 19, 1695, by Thomas Maule, and which was suppressed by order of General Court, we have a curious extract. "In the church of Salem, the women, in times of service, have their faces covered with a veil, which practice did not many years continue, and when this practice was laid aside, they had for the more order in their church to keep people from sleeping, a man that wholly tended with a short clubbed stick, having at one end a knop,[2] at the other a fox tail, with which he would stroke the

2. A decorative knob.

women's faces, that were drowsy to sleep, and with the other would knock unruly dogs and men that were asleep."

* * *

1830, Sept. 28. John Francis Knapp is hung at the north end of the Salem prison, in the yard.

[1830], Dec. 31. Joseph Jenkins Knapp, Jr., his brother, suffered the like punishment in the same place. More than 4,000 spectators witnessed each of their melancholy exits. As well known, their crime was conspiracy with Richard Crowninshield of Danvers, to murder Capt. Joseph White, one of our most noted and wealthy merchants, in his 82d year. The dreadful act, though previously intended at different times, was performed by Crowninshield in the night of April 6, for the price of $1,000. He entered the dwelling of his victim, proceeded to his chamber, where he was asleep, struck him on the head with a club and stabbed him several times near the heart. Having been imprisoned, and perceiving no prospect of escape from the demands of justice, he hung himself, June 15, in his cell. He left the subsequent warning. "May it (his own suicide) be the means of reforming many to virtue. Albeit they may meet with success at the commencement of vice, it is short lived, and, sooner or later, if they persist in it, they will meet with a fate similar to mine." Joseph J. Knapp, having married a relative of Capt. White, supposed, that by destroying his will and hastening him out of life, he should come to the possession of a large property. But he learned, too late, even before his apprehension, that his whole plan was futile; that he has 'sowed to the wind and must reap the whirlwind.' For weeks, stratagems were so laid, that public suspicion fell on a nephew, a principal heir of Capt. White. He keenly felt the neglect of former friends, but conscious innocence sustained him, until truth developed the mystery. The untimely end of three young men, and the inexpressible anguish of their connections, with whom many a heart deeply sympathized, was the incalculable price of hastening to be rich in a most unwarrantable way. Right motive and virtuous action lead to possessions, which alone can be enjoyed in peaceful reflection, present fruition and anticipation of the future.

CHARLES W. UPHAM

From Lectures on Witchcraft†

Charles Wentworth Upham (1802–1875) of Massachusetts was an influential historian, Unitarian clergyman, and politician. In 1831 he published *Lectures on Witchcraft*, an account of the Salem witch crisis of 1692, and he brought out a revised and expanded version, *Salem Witchcraft*, in 1867. In both versions Upham noted the often cruel role of Hawthorne's great-great-grandfather Judge John Hathorne in the trials themselves. But the main target of Upham's histories, as will be clear from the selection printed here, was the Puritan minister Cotton Mather, whom he regarded as particularly self-righteous and expedient. Hawthorne was influenced by Upham's 1831 history, and aspects of Upham's Mather came to inform Hawthorne's depiction of Colonel Pyncheon. Thus it is ironic that, as some of Hawthorne's contemporaries noted, aspects of Upham came to inform Hawthorne's depiction of Judge Pyncheon. In 1849, Upham wrote "Memorial of the Whigs of Salem in regard to Mr. Hawthorne," a document that purported to detail Hawthorne's failings as surveyor of the Salem custom house and that cemented his removal from office that same year. Hawthorne took the revenge of an author in creating a character based in part on what he regarded as Upham's own self-righteousness and expediency.

In the year 1692, special efforts were made to renew the power of the spirit of the gospel in many of the churches. The motives of those who acted in these measures were for the most part of the purest and holiest character. But there were not wanting individuals who were willing to abuse the opportunities offered by the general excitement and awakening thus produced. It was soon discerned by those ambitious of spiritual influence and domination, that their object could be most easily achieved by carrying the people to the greatest extreme of credulity, fanaticism, and superstition.

Opposition to prevailing vices, and attempts to reform society, were considered at that time in the light of a conflict with Satan himself, and he was thought to be the ablest minister who had the greatest power over the great enemy, who could most easily and effectually avert his blows and counteract his baleful influence. Dr Cotton Mather aspired to be considered the great champion of the church, and the most successful combatant against the prince of the power of the air. He seems to have longed for an opportunity to signalize himself in this particular kind of warfare; seized upon every occurrence that would admit of such a coloring to represent it as the result of diabolical agency; circulated in his numerous

† From *Lectures on Witchcraft, Comprising a History of the Delusion in Salem, in 1692* (Boston: Carter, Hendee, and Babcock, 1831), 105–8, 115–17.

publications as many tales of witchcraft as he could collect throughout New and Old England, and repeatedly endeavored to get up a delusion of this kind in Boston. He succeeded to some extent. An instance of witchcraft was brought about in that place by his management in 1688. There is some ground for suspicion that he was instrumental in causing the delusion in Salem; at any rate, he took a leading role in conducting it. And while there is evidence that he endeavored, after the delusion subsided, to escape the disgrace of having approved of the proceedings, and pretended to have been in some measure opposed to them, it can be too clearly shown that he was secretly and cunningly endeavoring to renew them during the next year in his own parish in Boston. I know nothing more artful and jesuitical than his attempts, to avoid the reproach of having been active in carrying on the delusion in Salem, and elsewhere, and, at the same time, to keep up such a degree of credulity and superstition in the minds of the people, as to render it easy to plunge them into it again at the first favorable moment.* * *

In addition to the designing exertions of ambitious ecclesiastics, and the benevolent and praiseworthy efforts of those whose only aim was to promote a real and thorough reformation of religion, all the passions of our nature stood ready to throw their concentrated energy into the excitement, (as they ever will do whatever may be its character,) so soon as it became sufficiently strong to encourage their action.

The whole force of popular superstition, all the fanatical propensities of the ignorant and deluded multitude united with the best feelings of our nature to heighten the fury of the storm. Piety was indignant at the supposed rebellion against the sovereignty of God, and was roused to an extreme of agitation and apprehension, in witnessing such a daring and fierce assault by the devil and his adherents upon the churches and the cause of the gospel. Virtue was shocked at the tremendous guilt of those who were believed to have entered the diabolical confederacy; while public order and security stood aghast, amidst the invisible, the supernatural, the infernal, and, apparently, the irresistible attacks that were making upon the foundations of society. In baleful combination with principles, good in themselves, thus urging the passions into wild operation, there were all the wicked and violent affections to which humanity is liable. Theological bitterness, personal animosities, local controversies, private feuds, long cherished grudges, and professional jealousies, rushed forward, and raised their discordant voices, to swell the horrible din; credulity rose with its monstrous and ever expanding form, on the ruins of truth, reason and the senses; malignity and cruelty rode triumphant through the storm, by whose fury every mild and gentle sentiment had been shipwrecked; and revenge, smiling in the mist of the tempest, welcomed its desolating wrath as it dashed the mangled objects of its hate along the shore.

It would indeed be worthy the attention of the metaphysician and moralist, to scrutinize this transaction thoroughly in all its periods and branches, to ascertain its causes and to mark its developments. There cannot be a doubt that much valuable instruction would thus be gathered respecting the elements of our nature, and of society.

NATHANIEL HAWTHORNE

From The American Notebooks†

Hawthorne regularly tried out ideas for his fiction in his journals. In these entries from 1837 to 1849, Hawthorne addressed the relationship of the past to the present. The specific concerns of these entries—land claims and patents, portraits and social class, hauntings and inheritance—all found their way into *The House of the Seven Gables*.

[Augusta (Maine), 12 August 1837]

Sunday, walked with Cilley[1] to see General Knox's old mansion— a large rusty-looking edifice of wood, with some grandeur in the architecture, standing on the banks of the river, close by the site of an old burial ground, and near where an ancient fort had been erected for defence against the French and Indians.[2] General Knox formerly owned a square of thirty miles in this part of the country; and he wished to settle it with a tenantry, after the fashion of English gentlemen. He would permit no edifices to be erected within a certain distance of his mansion. His patent covered, of course, the whole present town of Thomaston, together with Waldoboro'[3] and divers other flourishing commercial and country villages; and would have been of incalculable value, could it have remained unbroken to the present time. But the General lived in grand style, and received throngs of visiters [*sic*] from foreign parts; and was obliged to part

---

† From *The American Notebooks*, ed. Claude M. Simpson (Columbus: Ohio State University Press, 1972), 66–68, 154–55, 252, 293. Reprinted with permission of the Ohio State University Press.
1. A friend of Hawthorne's from Bowdoin College, Jonathan Cilley (1802–1838), at the time a congressman from Maine, was killed in a duel on February 24, 1838.
2. Henry Knox (1750–1806) rose to the rank of major general during the Revolutionary War and served as secretary of war in Washington's cabinet. He retired to Thomaston, Maine, in 1794.
3. Thomaston and Waldoboro are towns in southern Maine near the Atlantic coast, approximately twenty miles east of Bowdoin College.

with large tracts of his possessions, till now there is little left but the ruinous mansion, and the ground immediately around it. His tomb stands near the house, a spacious receptable, an iron door, at the end of a turf-covered mound, and surmounted by an obelisk of the Thomaston marble. * * * The house and its vicinity, and the whole tract covered by Knox's patent, may be taken as an illustration of what must be the result of American schemes of aristocracy. It is not forty years, since this house was built, and Knox was in his glory; but now the house is all in decay, while, within a stones [sic] throw of it, is a street of neat, smart, white edifices of one and two stories, oc-cupied chiefly by thriving mechanics. But towns have grown up, where Knox probably meant to have forests and parks. On the banks of the river, where he meant to have only one wharf, for his own west-India vessels and yacht, there are our two wharves, with stores, and a lime-kiln. Little appertains to the mansion, except the tomb, and the old burial ground, and the old fort. The descendants are all poor; and the inheritance was merely sufficient to make a dissipated and drunken fellow of the one of the old General's sons, who sur-vived to middle age.

*   *   *

[Salem, 22 August 1837]

In the cabinet of the Essex Historical Society,[4] old portraits.—Gov-ernor Leverett; a dark moustachioed face, the figure two-thirds length, clothed in a sort of frock coat; buttoned, and a broad sword-belt girded round the waist, and fastened with a large steel buckle; the hilt of the sword steel,—altogether very striking. Sir William Pepperell in English regimentals, coat, waistcoat, and breeches, all of red broadcloth, richly gold-embroidered; he holds a general's truncheon in his right hand, and extends the left towards the bat-teries erected against Louisbourg, in the country near which he is standing. Endicott, Pyncheon, and others, in scarlet robes, bands, &c.[5] Half a dozen or more family portraits of the Olivers,[6] some in plain dresses, brown, crimson, or claret; others with gorgeous gold-embroidered waistcoats, descending almost to the knees, so as to form the most conspicuous article of dress. Ladies, with lace ruf-

4. Located in Salem; now called the Essex Institute.
5. The subjects of the portraits are Governor John Leverett (1616–1679), governor of Massachusetts from 1673 to the time of his death; Sir William Pepperell (1696–1759), a British colonial official and acting governor of Massachusetts from 1756 to 1758; John Endicott (ca. 1589–1665), the notable Puritan leader who served as governor of the Massachusetts Bay Colony on several occasions; and William Pynchon (1590–1662), a Puritan and wealthy fur trader who was commissioned in 1636 to govern and settle what would become Springfield, Massachusetts.
6. A distinguished Massachusetts family. The best known political leader of the family, An-drew Oliver (1704–1774), a British loyalist, was responsible for enforcing the Stamp Act and became lieutenant governor of Massachusetts in 1771.

fles, the painting of which, in one of the pictures, cost five guineas. Peter Oliver,[7] who was crazy, used to fight with these family pictures in the old Mansion House; and the face and breast of one lady bear cuts and stabs inflicted by him. Miniatures in oil, with the paint peeling off, of stern, old, yellow faces. Oliver Cromwell,[8] apparently an old picture, half length or one third, in an oval frame, probably painted for some New England partisan. Some pictures that had been partly obliterated by scrubbing with sand. The dresses, embroidery, laces of the Oliver family are generally better done than the faces. Governor Leverett's gloves,—the glove-part of coarse leather, but round the wrist a deep three or four inch border of spangles and silver embroidery. Old drinking-glasses, with tall stalks. A black glass bottle, stamped with the name of Philip English,[9] with a broad bottom. The baby-linen, &c of Governor Bradford of Plymouth colony.[1] Old manuscript sermons, some written in short-hand, others in a hand that seems learnt from print.

Nothing gives a stronger idea of old worm-eaten aristocracy—of a family being crazy with age, and of its being time that it was extinct—than these black, dusty, faded, antique-dressed portraits, such as those of the Oliver family; the identical old white wig of an ancient minister producing somewhat the impression that his very scalp, or some other portion of his personal self, would do.

*   *   *

[Concord, c. 1844]

To represent the influence which Dead Men have among living affairs; for instance, a Dead Man controls the disposition of wealth; a Dead Man sits on the judgment-seat, and the living judges do but repeat his decisions; Dead Men's opinions in all things control the living truth; we believe in Dead Men's religion; we laugh at Dead Men's jokes; we cry at Dead Men's pathos; everywhere and in all matters, Dead Men tyrannize inexorably over us.

*   *   *

[Salem, 23 October 1849]

To inherit a great fortune. To inherit a great misfortune.

7. Peter Oliver (1713–1791), chief justice of the Massachusetts supreme court during the American Revolution, was impeached and left the country.
8. Oliver Cromwell (1599–1658), English Puritan revolutionary leader, was lord protector of England from 1653 to 1658.
9. English (1651–1736), born Philip L'Anglois, emigrated to Salem in 1670. During the Salem witch crisis, he and his wife, Mary, were both accused of being witches, perhaps because he was distrusted for his French origins. Though they were eventually acquitted, they lost most of their property.
1. From the early 1620s to the time of his death, with only a few years of interruption, William Bradford (1590–1657) served as governor of Plymouth.

Hawthorne and the
Literary Sketch

Canonized for such great historical tales as "My Kinsman, Major Molineaux" (1832) and "Young Goodman Brown" (1835), Hawthorne in his own time was also greatly admired for his literary sketches. As he complained in *The Scarlet Letter*'s prefatory "The Custom-House," he feared that he was fated to be best known as the author of "A Rill from the Town-Pump" (1835). Despite his evident embarrassment at having authored a sketch offering the first-person perspective of Salem's town pump, the fact is that Hawthorne wrote numerous sketches during the 1830s and 1840s. Influenced by the sketches of Joseph Addison and Richard Steele in the *Tatler* (1709–11) and the *Spectator* (1711–12), Hawthorne in such sketches as "Sights from a Steeple" (1831), "Little Annie's Ramble" (1835), and "Main-street" (1849) sought to align himself with his readers as shared observers of the contemporary scene. That perspective, as Kristie Hamilton argues in *America's Sketchbook: The Cultural Life of a Nineteenth-Century Literary Genre* (1998), helped make the sketches of Hawthorne and his contemporaries relatively modernistic, intent as the sketch writer was in engaging the quickly changing social landscape of the nineteenth-century United States. For the sketch writer, plot was relatively unimportant; tone, descriptiveness, and a strong rhetorical link with the widest possible reading audience were the most crucial components of the sketch (even if the point of the rhetorical link was to subvert the conventional values of that readership). To a certain extent, despite its interest in plot, from the moment the narrator takes his leisurely walk to the old Pyncheon House in chapter one of *The House of the Seven Gables*, the novel reads like a series of sketches. There are marked resemblances, for example, between Hawthorne's account of Hepzibah in chapter two of the novel and his account of the old man in the 1843 sketch "The Old Apple-Dealer." In addition to "The Old Apple-Dealer," this section includes Hawthorne's earlier sketch "Alice Doane's Appeal" (1835), which self-consciously engages the problem of how to present the historical to an audience consisting in large part of young women readers. When Holgrave tells his story of Alice Pyncheon, he faces the similar challenge of shaping history for what he conceives of as a somewhat bored and easily distracted reading public.

NATHANIEL HAWTHORNE

Alice Doane's Appeal†

On a pleasant afternoon of June, it was my good fortune to be the companion of two young ladies in a walk. The direction of our course being left to me, I led them neither to Legge's Hill, nor to the Cold Spring, nor to the rude shores and old batteries of the Neck, nor yet to Paradise;[1] though if the latter place were rightly named, my fair friends would have been at home there. We reached the outskirts of the town, and turning aside from a street of tanners and curriers,[2] began to ascend a hill, which at a distance, by its dark slope and the even line of its summit, resembled a green rampart along the road. It was less steep than its aspect threatened. The eminence formed part of an extensive tract of pasture land, and was traversed by cow paths in various directions; but, strange to tell, though the whole slope and summit were of a peculiarly deep green, scarce a blade of grass was visible from the base upward. This deceitful verdure was occasioned by a plentiful crop of 'wood-wax,'[3] which wears the same dark and glossy green throughout the summer, except at one short period, when it puts forth a profusion of yellow blossoms. At that season to a distant spectator, the hill appears absolutely overlaid with gold, or covered with a glory of sunshine, even beneath a clouded sky. But the curious wanderer on the hill will perceive that all the grass, and every thing that should nourish man or beast, has been destroyed by this vile and ineradicable weed: its tufted roots make the soil their own, and permit nothing else to vegetate among them; so that a physical curse may be said to have blasted the spot, where guilt and phrenzy consummated the most execrable scene, that our history blushes to record. For this was the field where superstition won her darkest triumph; the high place where our fathers set up their shame, to the mournful gaze of generations far remote. The dust of martyrs was beneath our feet. We stood on Gallows Hill.[4]

For my own part, I have often courted the historic influence of the spot. But it is singular, how few come on pilgrimage to this

† "Alice Doane's Appeal," in Hawthorne, *The Snow-Image and Uncollected Tales*, ed. J. Donald Crowley et al. (Columbus: Ohio State University Press, 1974), 266–80. Reprinted with permission of the Ohio State University Press. "Alice Doane's Appeal" was first published in *The Token and Atlantic Souvenir* (Boston: Charles Bowen, 1835) and was not reprinted during Hawthorne's lifetime.
1. Actual and colloquial names for various locales in Salem, Massachusetts.
2. Those who prepare tanned leather for use.
3. Weedy bushes.
4. The infamous hill in Salem where in 1692 approximately twenty of the people convicted as witches were executed and buried.

famous hill; how many spend their lives almost at its base, and never once obey the summons of the shadowy past, as it beckons them to the summit. Till a year or two since, this portion of our history had been very imperfectly written, and, as we are not a people of legend or tradition, it was not every citizen of our ancient town that could tell, within half a century, so much as the date of the witchcraft delusion. Recently, indeed, an historian has treated the subject in a manner that will keep his name alive, in the only desirable connection with the errors of our ancestry, by converting the hill of their disgrace into an honorable monument of his own antiquarian lore, and of that better wisdom, which draws the moral while it tells the tale.[5] But we are a people of the present and have no heartfelt interest in the olden time. Every fifth of November,[6] in commemoration of they know not what, or rather without an idea beyond the momentary blaze, the young men scare the town with bonfires on this haunted height, but never dream of paying funeral honors to those who died so wrongfully, and without a coffin or a prayer, were buried here.

Though with feminine susceptibility, my companions caught all the melancholy associations of the scene, yet these could but imperfectly overcome the gayety of girlish spirits. Their emotions came and went with quick vicissitude, and sometimes combined to form a peculiar and delicious excitement, the mirth brightening the gloom into a sunny shower of feeling, and a rainbow in the mind. My own more sombre mood was tinged by theirs. With now a merry word and next a sad one, we trod among the tangled weeds, and almost hoped that our feet would sink into the hollow of a witch's grave. Such vestiges were to be found within the memory of man, but have vanished now, and with them, I believe, all traces of the precise spot of the executions. On the long and broad ridge of the eminence, there is no very decided elevation of any one point, nor other prominent marks, except the decayed stumps of two trees, standing near each other, and here and there the rocky substance of the hill, peeping just above the wood-wax.

There are few such prospects of town and village, woodland and cultivated field, steeples and country seats, as we beheld from this unhappy spot. No blight had fallen on old Essex;[7] all was prosperity and riches, healthfully distributed. Before us lay our native town, extending from the foot of the hill to the harbor, level as a chess

---

5. Most likely a reference to Joseph B. Felt's *The Annals of Salem, from Its First Settlement* (1827), but Charles W. Upham's *Lectures on Witchcraft* (1831) is also a possibility.
6. Festive day marking the beginning of the year's final quarter. It is also Guy Fawkes Day, the traditional celebration of the failure of the English Catholic Guy Fawkes (1570–1606) and his associates to blow up the English Parliament and King James I on November 5, 1605.
7. The county in Massachusetts that includes Salem.

board, embraced by two arms of the sea, and filling the whole peninsula with a close assemblage of wooden roofs, overtopt by many a spire, and intermixed with frequent heaps of verdure, where trees threw up their shade from unseen trunks. Beyond, was the bay and its islands, almost the only objects, in a country unmarked by strong natural features, on which time and human toil had produced no change. Retaining these portions of the scene, and also the peaceful glory and tender gloom of the declining sun, we threw, in imagination, a veil of deep forest over the land, and pictured a few scattered villages, and this old town itself a village, as when the prince of hell bore sway there. The idea thus gained, of its former aspect, its quaint edifices standing far apart, with peaked roofs and projecting stories, and its single meeting house pointing up a tall spire in the midst; the vision, in short, of the town in 1692, served to introduce a wondrous tale of those old times.

I had brought the manuscript in my pocket. It was one of a series written years ago, when my pen, now sluggish and perhaps feeble, because I have not much to hope or fear, was driven by stronger external motives, and a more passionate impulse within, than I am fated to feel again. Three or four of these tales had appeared in the Token,[8] after a long time and various adventures, but had incumbered me with no troublesome notoriety, even in my birth place. One great heap had met a brighter destiny: they had fed the flames; thoughts meant to delight the world and endure for ages, had perished in a moment, and stirred not a single heart but mine. The story now to be introduced, and another, chanced to be in kinder custody at the time, and thus by no conspicuous merits of their own, escaped destruction.

The ladies, in consideration that I had never before intruded my performances on them, by any but the legitimate medium, through the press, consented to hear me read. I made them sit down on a moss-grown rock, close by the spot where we chose to believe that the death-tree had stood. After a little hesitation on my part, caused by a dread of renewing my acquaintance with fantasies that had lost their charm, in the ceaseless flux of mind, I began the tale, which opened darkly with the discovery of a murder.

A hundred years, and nearly half that time, have elapsed since the body of a murdered man was found, at about the distance of three miles, on the old road to Boston. He lay in a solitary spot, on the bank of a small lake, which the severe frost of December had covered with a sheet of ice. Beneath this, it seemed to have been

8. In 1829 Hawthorne submitted to the publisher Samuel G. Goodrich (1793–1860) a short collection of stories, *Provincial Tales of My Native Land*. Goodrich published some of the stories individually in his giftbook annual *The Token*.

the intention of the murderer to conceal his victim in a chill and watery grave, the ice being deeply hacked, perhaps with the weapon that had slain him, though its solidity was too stubborn for the patience of a man with blood upon his hand. The corpse therefore reclined on the earth, but was separated from the road by a thick growth of dwarf pines. There had been a slight fall of snow during the night, and as if Nature were shocked at the deed, and strove to hide it with her frozen tears, a little drifted heap had partly buried the body, and lay deepest over the pale dead face. An early traveller, whose dog had led him to the spot, ventured to uncover the features, but was affrighted by their expression. A look of evil and scornful triumph had hardened on them, and made death so life-like and so terrible, that the beholder at once took flight, as swiftly as if the stiffened corpse would rise up and follow.

I read on, and identified the body as that of a young man, a stranger in the country, but resident during several preceding months in the town which lay at our feet. The story described, at some length, the excitement caused by the murder, the unavailing quest after the perpetrator, the funeral ceremonies, and other common place matters, in the course of which, I brought forward the personages who were to move among the succeeding events. They were but three. A young man and his sister; the former characterized by a diseased imagination and morbid feelings; the latter, beautiful and virtuous, and instilling something of her own excellence into the wild heart of her brother, but not enough to cure the deep taint of his nature. The third person was a wizard; a small, gray, withered man, with fiendish ingenuity in devising evil, and superhuman power to execute it, but senseless as an idiot and feebler than a child, to all better purposes. The central scene of the story was an interview between this wretch and Leonard Doane, in the wizard's hut, situated beneath a range of rocks at some distance from the town. They sat beside a mouldering fire, while a tempest of wintry rain was beating on the roof. The young man spoke of the closeness of the tie which united him and Alice, the concentrated fervor of their affection from childhood upwards, their sense of lonely sufficiency to each other, because they only of their race had escaped death, in a night attack by the Indians. He related his discovery, or suspicion of a secret sympathy between his sister and Walter Brome, and told how a distempered jealousy had maddened him. In the following passage, I threw a glimmering light on the mystery of the tale.

'Searching,' continued Leonard, 'into the breast of Walter Brome, I at length found a cause why Alice must inevitably love him. For he was my very counterpart! I compared his mind by each individual portion, and as a whole, with mine. There was a resemblance from which I shrank with sickness, and loathing, and horror, as if my own features had come and stared upon me in a solitary place, or had met me in struggling through a crowd. Nay! the very same thoughts would often express themselves in the same words from our lips, proving a hateful sympathy in our secret souls. His education, indeed, in the cities of the old world, and mine in this rude wilderness, had wrought a superficial difference. The evil of his character, also, had been strengthened and rendered prominent by a reckless and ungoverned life, while mine had been softened and purified by the gentle and holy nature of Alice. But my soul had been conscious of the germ of all the fierce and deep passions, and of all the many varieties of wickedness, which accident had brought to their full maturity in him. Nor will I deny, that in the accursed one, I could see the withered blossom of every virtue, which by a happier culture, had been made to bring forth fruit in me. Now, here was a man, whom Alice might love with all the strength of sisterly affection, added to that impure passion which alone engrosses all the heart. The stranger would have more than the love which had been gathered to me from the many graves of our household—and I be desolate!'

Leonard Doane went on to describe the insane hatred that had kindled his heart into a volume of hellish flame. It appeared, indeed, that his jealousy had grounds, so far as that Walter Brome had actually sought the love of Alice, who also had betrayed an undefinable, but powerful interest in the unknown youth. The latter, in spite of his passion for Alice, seemed to return the loathful antipathy of her brother; the similarity of their dispositions made them like joint possessors of an individual nature, which could not become wholly the property of one, unless by the extinction of the other. At last, with the same devil in each bosom, they chanced to meet, they two on a lonely road. While Leonard spoke, the wizard had sat listening to what he already knew, yet with tokens of pleasurable interest, manifested by flashes of expression across his vacant features, by grisly smiles and by a word here and there, mysteriously filling up some void in the narrative. But when the young man told, how Walter Brome had taunted him with indubitable proofs of the shame of Alice, and before the triumphant sneer could vanish from his face, had died by her brother's hand, the wizard laughed aloud. Leonard started, but just then a gust of wind came down the chimney, forming itself into a close resemblance of the slow, unvaried laughter, by which he had been interrupted. 'I was deceived,' thought he; and thus pursued his fearful story.

'I trod out his accursed soul, and knew that he was dead; for my spirit bounded as if a chain had fallen from it and left me free. But the burst of exulting certainty soon fled, and was succeeded by a torpor over my brain and a dimness before my eyes, with the sensation of one who struggles through a dream. So I bent down over the body of Walter Brome, gazing into his face, and striving to make my soul glad with the thought, that he, in very truth, lay dead before me. I know not what space of time I had thus stood, nor how the vision came. But it seemed to me that the irrevocable years, since childhood had rolled back, and a scene, that had long been confused and broken in my memory, arrayed itself with all its first distinctness. Methought I stood a weeping infant by my father's hearth; by the cold and blood-stained hearth where he lay dead. I heard the childish wail of Alice, and my own cry arose with hers, as we beheld the features of our parent, fierce with the strife and distorted with the pain, in which his spirit had passed away. As I gazed, a cold wind whistled by, and waved my father's hair. Immediately, I stood again in the lonesome road, no more a sinless child, but a man of blood, whose tears were falling fast over the face of his dead enemy. But the delusion was not wholly gone; that face still wore a likeness of my father; and because my soul shrank from the fixed glare of the eyes, I bore the body to the lake, and would have buried it there. But before his icy sepulchre was hewn, I heard the voices of two travellers and fled.'

Such was the dreadful confession of Leonard Doane. And now tortured by the idea of his sister's guilt, yet sometimes yielding to a conviction of her purity; stung with remorse for the death of Walter Brome, and shuddering with a deeper sense of some unutterable crime, perpetrated, as he imagined, in madness or a dream; moved also by dark impulses, as if a fiend were whispering him to meditate violence against the life of Alice; he had sought this interview with the wizard, who, on certain conditions, had no power to withhold his aid in unravelling the mystery. The tale drew near its close.

The moon was bright on high; the blue firmament appeared to glow with an inherent brightness; the greater stars were burning in their spheres; the northern lights threw their mysterious glare far over the horizon; the few small clouds aloft were burthened with radiance; but the sky with all its variety of light, was scarcely so brilliant as the earth. The rain of the preceding night had frozen as it fell, and, by that simple magic, had wrought wonders. The trees were hung with diamonds and many-colored gems; the houses were overlaid with silver, and the streets paved with slippery brightness; a frigid glory was flung over all familiar things, from the cottage chimney to the steeple of the meeting house, that gleamed upward to the sky. This living world, where we sit by our firesides, or go forth to meet beings like ourselves, seemed rather the creation of wizard power, with so much of resemblance to known objects, that a man might shudder at the ghostly shape of his old beloved dwelling, and the shadow of a ghostly tree before his door. One looked to behold inhabitants suited to such a town, glittering in icy garments, with motionless features, cold, sparkling eyes, and just sensation enough in their frozen hearts to shiver at each other's presence.

By this fantastic piece of description, and more in the same style, I intended to throw a ghostly glimmer round the reader, so that his imagination might view the town through a medium that should take off its every day aspect, and make it a proper theatre for so wild a scene as the final one. Amid this unearthly show, the wretched brother and sister were represented as setting forth, at midnight, through the gleaming streets, and directing their steps to a grave yard, where all the dead had been laid, from the first corpse in that ancient town, to the murdered man who was buried three days before. As they went, they seemed to see the wizard gliding by their sides, or walking dimly on the path before them. But here I paused, and gazed into the faces of my two fair auditors, to judge whether, even on the hill where so many had been brought to death by wilder tales than this, I might venture to proceed. Their bright eyes were fixed on me; their lips apart. I took courage, and led the fated pair to a new made grave, where for a few moments, in the bright and silent midnight, they stood alone. But suddenly, there was a multitude of people among the graves.

Each family tomb had given up its inhabitants, who, one by one, through distant years, had been borne to its dark chamber, but now came forth and stood in a pale group together. There was the gray ancestor, the aged mother, and all their descendants, some withered and full of years, like themselves, and others in their prime; there, too, were the children who went prattling to the tomb, and there the maiden who yielded her early beauty to death's embrace, before passion had polluted it. Husbands and wives arose, who had lain many years side by side, and young mothers who had forgotten to kiss their first babes, though pillowed so long on their bosoms. Many had been buried in the habiliments of life, and still wore their ancient garb; some were old defenders of the infant colony, and gleamed forth in their steel caps and bright breast-plates, as if starting up at an Indian war-cry; other venerable shapes had been pastors of the church, famous among the New England clergy, and now leaned with hands clasped over their grave stones, ready to call the congregation to prayer. There stood the early settlers, those old illustrious ones, the heroes of tradition and fireside legends, the men of history whose features had been so long beneath the sod, that few alive could have remembered them. There, too, were faces of former townspeople, dimly recollected from childhood, and others, whom Leonard and Alice had wept in later years, but who now were most terrible of all, by their ghastly smile of recognition. All, in short, were there; the dead of other generations, whose moss-grown names could scarce be read upon their tomb stones, and their successors, whose graves were not yet green; all whom black funerals had followed slowly thither, now re-appeared where the mourners left them. Yet none but souls accursed were there, and fiends counterfeiting the likeness of departed saints.

The countenances of those venerable men, whose very features had been hallowed by lives of piety, were contorted now by intolerable pain or hellish passion, and now by an unearthly and derisive merriment. Had the pastors prayed, all saintlike as they seemed, it had been blasphemy. The chaste matrons, too, and the maidens with untasted lips, who had slept in their virgin graves apart from all other dust, now wore a look from which the two trembling mortals shrank, as if the unimaginable sin of twenty worlds were collected there. The faces of fond lovers, even of such as had pined into the tomb, because there their treasure was, were bent on one another with glances of hatred and smiles of bitter scorn, passions that are to devils, what love is to the blest. At times, the features of those, who had passed from a holy life to heaven, would vary to and fro, between their assumed aspect and the fiendish lineaments whence they had been transformed. The whole miserable multitude, both sinful souls and false spectres of good men, groaned horribly and gnashed their teeth, as they looked upward to the calm loveliness of the midnight sky, and beheld those homes of bliss where they must never dwell. Such was the apparition, though too shadowy for language to portray; for here would be the moonbeams on the ice, glittering through a warrior's breast-plate, and there the letters of a tomb stone, on the form that stood before it; and whenever a breeze went by, it swept the old men's hoary heads, the women's fearful beauty, and all the unreal throng, into one indistinguishable cloud together.

I dare not give the remainder of the scene, except in a very brief epitome. This company of devils and condemned souls had come on a holiday, to revel in the discovery of a complicated crime; as foul a one as ever was imagined in their dreadful abode. In the course of the tale, the reader had been permitted to discover, that all the incidents were results of the machinations of the wizard, who had cunningly devised that Walter Brome should tempt his unknown sister to guilt and shame, and himself perish by the hand of his twin-brother. I described the glee of the fiends, at this hideous conception, and their eagerness to know if it were consummated. The story concluded with the Appeal of Alice to the spectre of Walter Brome; his reply, absolving her from every stain; and the trembling awe with which ghost and devil fled, as from the sinless presence of an angel.

The sun had gone down. While I held my page of wonders in the fading light, and read how Alice and her brother were left alone among the graves, my voice mingled with the sigh of a summer wind, which passed over the hill top with the broad and hollow sound, as of the flight of unseen spirits. Not a word was spoken, till I added, that the wizard's grave was close beside us, and that the wood-wax had sprouted originally from his unhallowed bones. The ladies started; perhaps their cheeks might have grown pale, had not the crimson west been blushing on them; but after a moment they began to laugh, while the breeze took a livelier motion, as if responsive to their mirth. I kept an awful solemnity of visage, being indeed a little piqued, that a narrative which had good authority in our ancient superstitions, and would have brought even a church deacon to Gallows Hill, in old witch times, should now be considered too grotesque and extravagant, for timid maids to tremble at. Though it was past supper time, I detained them a while longer on the hill, and made a trial whether truth were more powerful than fiction.

We looked again towards the town, no longer arrayed in that icy splendor of earth, tree and edifice, beneath the glow of a wintry midnight, which, shining afar through the gloom of a century, had made it appear the very home of visions in visionary streets. An indistinctness had begun to creep over the mass of buildings and blend them with the intermingled tree tops, except where the roof of a statelier mansion, and the steeples and brick towers of churches, caught the brightness of some cloud that yet floated in the sunshine. Twilight over the landscape was congenial to the obscurity of time. With such eloquence as my share of feeling and fancy could supply, I called back hoar antiquity, and bade my companions imagine an ancient multitude of people, congregated on the hill side, spreading far below, clustering on the steep old roofs, and climbing the adjacent heights, wherever a glimpse of this spot might be obtained. I strove to realize and faintly communicate, the deep, unutterable loathing and horror, the indignation, the affrighted wonder, that wrinkled on every brow, and filled the universal heart. See! the whole crowd turns pale and shrinks within itself, as the virtuous emerge from yonder street. Keeping pace with that devoted company, I described them one by one; here tottered a woman in her dotage, knowing neither the crime imputed her, nor its punishment; there another, distracted by the universal madness, till feverish dreams were remembered as realities, and she almost believed her guilt. One, a proud man once, was so broken down by the intolerable hatred heaped upon him, that he seemed to hasten his steps, eager to hide himself in the grave hastily dug, at the foot of the gallows. As they went slowly on, a mother looked behind, and beheld her peaceful dwelling; she cast her eyes elsewhere, and groaned inwardly, yet with bitterest anguish; for there was her little son among the accusers. I watched the face of an ordained pastor, who walked onward to the same death; his lips moved in prayer, no narrow petition for himself alone, but embracing all, his fellow sufferers and the frenzied multitude; he looked to heaven and trod lightly up the hill.

Behind their victims came the afflicted, a guilty and miserable band; villains who had thus avenged themselves on their enemies, and viler wretches, whose cowardice had destroyed their friends; lunatics, whose ravings had chimed in with the madness of the land; and children, who had played a game that the imps of darkness might have envied them, since it disgraced an age, and dipped a people's hands in blood. In the rear of the procession rode a figure on horseback, so darkly conspicuous, so sternly triumphant, that my hearers mistook him for the visible presence of the fiend himself; but it was only his good friend, Cotton Mather,[9] proud of his well won dignity, as the representative of all the hateful features of his time; the one blood-thirsty man, in whom were concentrated those vices of spirit and errors of opinion, that sufficed to madden the whole surrounding multitude. And thus I marshalled them onward, the innocent who were to die, and the guilty who were to grow old in long remorse—tracing their every step, by rock, and shrub, and broken track, till their shadowy visages had circled round the hilltop, where we stood. I plunged into my imagination for a blacker horror, and a deeper woe, and pictured the scaffold——

But here my companions seized an arm on each side; their nerves were trembling; and sweeter victory still, I had reached the seldom trodden places of their hearts, and found the wellspring of their tears. And now the past had done all it could. We slowly descended, watching the lights as they twinkled gradually through the town, and listening to the distant mirth of boys at play, and to the voice of a young girl, warbling somewhere in the dusk, a pleasant

9. Like Robert Calef and Charles W. Upham, Hawthorne's narrator places principal blame for the Salem witch crisis on Cotton Mather, despite the fact that Mather did not participate in the actual trials.

sound to wanderers from old witch times. Yet ere we left the hill, we could not but regret, that there is nothing on its barren summit, no relic of old, nor lettered stone of later days, to assist the imagination in appealing to the heart. We build the memorial column on the height which our fathers made sacred with their blood, poured out in a holy cause. And here in dark, funereal stone, should rise another monument, sadly commemorative of the errors of an earlier race, and not to be cast down, while the human heart has one infirmity that may result in crime.

NATHANIEL HAWTHORNE

The Old Apple-Dealer†

The lover of the moral picturesque may sometimes find what he seeks in a character, which is, nevertheless, of too negative a description to be seized upon, and represented to the imaginative vision by word-painting. As an instance, I remember an old man who carries on a little trade of gingerbread and apples, at the depôt of one of our rail-roads. While awaiting the departure of the cars, my observation, flitting to and fro among the livelier characteristics of the scene, has often settled insensibly upon this almost hueless object. Thus, unconsciously to myself, and unsuspected by him, I have studied the old apple-dealer, until he has become a naturalized citizen of my inner world. How little would he imagine—poor, neglected, friendless, unappreciated, and with little that demands appreciation—that the mental eye of an utter stranger has so often reverted to his figure! Many a noble form—many a beautiful face— has flitted before me, and vanished like a shadow. It is a strange witchcraft, whereby this faded and featureless old apple-dealer has gained a settlement in my memory!

He is a small man with gray hair and gray stubble beard, and is invariably clad in a shabby surtout[1] of snuff-color, closely buttoned, and half-concealing a pair of gray pantaloons; the whole dress, though clean and entire, being evidently flimsy with much wear. His face, thin, withered, furrowed, and with features which even age has failed to render impressive, has a frost-bitten aspect. It is a moral frost, which no physical warmth or comfortableness could

† "The Old Apple-Dealer," in *Mosses from an Old Manse*, ed. J. Donald Crowley et al. (Columbus: Ohio State University Press, 1974), 439–46. Reprinted with permission of the Ohio State University Press. "The Old Apple-Dealer" first appeared in the January 1843 *Sargent's New Monthly Magazine of Literature, Fashion, and the Fine Arts*, and it was reprinted in the 1846 and 1854 editions of *Mosses from an Old Manse*.

1. Overcoat.

counteract. The summer sunshine may fling its white heat upon him, or the good fire of the depôt-room may make him the focus of its blaze, on a winter's day; but all in vain; for still the old man looks as if he were in a frosty atmosphere, with scarcely warmth enough to keep life in the region about his heart. It is a patient, long-suffering, quiet, hopeless, shivering aspect. He is not desperate—that, though its etymology implies no more, would be too positive an expression—but merely devoid of hope. As all his past life, probably, offers no spots of brightness to his memory, so he takes his present poverty and discomfort as entirely a matter of course; he thinks it the definition of existence, so far as himself is concerned, to be poor, cold, and uncomfortable. It may be added, that time has not thrown dignity, as a mantle, over the old man's figure; there is nothing venerable about him; you pity him without a scruple.

He sits on a bench in the depôt-room; and before him, on the floor, are deposited two baskets, of a capacity to contain his whole stock in trade. Across, from one basket to the other, extends a board, on which is displayed a plate of cakes and gingerbread, some russet and red cheeked apples, and a box containing variegated sticks of candy; together with that delectable condiment, known by children as Gibraltar rock, neatly done up in white paper. There is likewise a half-peck measure of cracked walnuts, and two or three tin half-pints or gills,[2] filled with the nut kernels, ready for purchasers. Such are the small commodities with which our old friend comes daily before the world, ministering to its petty needs and little freaks of appetite, and seeking thence the solid subsistence—so far as he may subsist—of his life.

A slight observer would speak of the old man's quietude. But, on closer scrutiny, you discover that there is a continual unrest within him, which somewhat resembles the fluttering action of the nerves, in a corpse from which life has recently departed. Though he never exhibits any violent action, and, indeed, might appear to be sitting quite still, yet you perceive, when his minuter peculiarities begin to be detected, that he is always making some little movement or other. He looks anxiously at his plate of cakes, or pyramid of apples, and slightly alters their arrangement, with an evident idea that a great deal depends on their being disposed exactly thus and so. Then, for a moment, he gazes out of the window; then he shivers, quietly, and folds his arms across his breast, as if to draw himself closer within himself, and thus keep a flicker of warmth in his lonesome heart. Now he turns again to his merchandise of cakes, apples, and candy, and discovers that this cake or that apple, or

2. Quarter pints.

yonder stick of red and white candy, has, somehow, got out of its
proper position. And is there not a walnut-kernel too many, or too
few, in one of those small tin measures? Again, the whole arrangement appears to be settled to his mind; but, in the course of a
minute or two, there will assuredly be something to set right. At
times, by an indescribable shadow upon his features—too quiet,
however, to be noticed, until you are familiar with his ordinary aspect—the expression of frost-bitten, patient despondency becomes
very touching. It seems as if, just at that instant, the suspicion occurred to him, that, in his chill decline of life, earning scanty bread
by selling cakes, apples, and candy, he is a very miserable old fellow.

But, if he think so, it is a mistake. He can never suffer the extreme of misery, because the tone of his whole being is too much
subdued for him to feel any thing acutely.

Occasionally, one of the passengers, to while away a tedious
interval, approaches the old man, inspects the articles upon his
board, and even peeps curiously into the two baskets. Another,
striding to and fro along the room, throws a look at the apples and
gingerbread, at every turn. A third, it may be, of a more sensitive
and delicate texture of being, glances shyly thitherward, cautious
not to excite expectations of a purchaser, while yet undetermined
whether to buy. But there appears to be no need of such a scrupulous regard to our old friend's feelings. True, he is conscious of the
remote possibility of selling a cake or an apple, but innumerable
disappointments have rendered him so far a philosopher, that, even
if the purchased article should be returned, he will consider it altogether in the ordinary train of events. He speaks to none, and
makes no sign of offering his wares to the public; not that he is de-
terred by pride, but by the certain conviction that such demonstrations would not increase his custom. Besides, this activity in
business would require an energy that never could have been a
characteristic of his almost passive disposition, even in youth.
Whenever an actual customer appears, the old man looks up with a
patient eye; if the price and the article are approved, he is ready to
make change; otherwise, his eyelids droop again, sadly enough, but
with no heavier despondency than before. He shivers, perhaps,
folds his lean arms around his lean body, and resumes the life-long,
frozen patience, in which consists his strength. Once in a while, a
schoolboy comes hastily up, places a cent or two upon the board,
and takes up a cake or a stick of candy, or a measure of walnuts, or
an apple as red cheeked as himself. There are no words as to the
price, that being as well known to the buyer as to the seller. The old
apple-dealer never speaks an unnecessary word; not that he is
sullen and morose; but there is none of the cheeriness and brisk-
ness in him, that stirs up people to talk.

Not seldom, he is greeted by some old neighbor, a man well-to-do in the world, who makes a civil, patronizing observation about the weather; and then by way of performing a charitable deed, begins to chaffer[3] for an apple. Our friend presumes not on any past acquaintance; he makes the briefest possible response to all general remarks, and shrinks quietly into himself again. After every diminution of his stock, he takes care to produce from the basket another cake, another stick of candy, another apple, or another measure of walnuts, to supply the place of the article sold. Two or three attempts—or, perchance, half a dozen—are requisite, before the board can be re-arranged to his satisfaction. If he have received a silver coin, he waits till the purchaser is out of sight, then examines it closely, and tries to bend it with his finger and thumb; finally, be puts it into his waistcoat pocket, with seemingly a gentle sigh. This sigh, so faint as to be hardly perceptible, and not expressive of any definite emotion, is the accompaniment and conclusion of all his actions. It is the symbol of the chillness and torpid melancholy of his old age, which only make themselves felt sensibly, when his repose is slightly disturbed.

Our man of gingerbread and apples is not a specimen of the 'needy man who has seen better days.' Doubtless, there have been better and brighter days in the far-off time of his youth; but none with so much sunshine of prosperity in them, that the chill, the depression, the narrowness of means, in his declining years, can have come upon him by surprise. His life has all been of a piece. His subdued and nerveless boyhood prefigured his abortive prime, which, likewise, contained within itself the prophecy and image of his lean and torpid age. He was perhaps a mechanic, who never came to be a master in his craft, or a petty tradesman, rubbing onward between passably-to-do and poverty. Possibly, he may look back to some brilliant epoch of his career, when there were a hundred or two of dollars to his credit, in the Savings Bank. Such must have been the extent of his better fortune—his little measure of this world's triumphs—all that he has known of success. A meek, downcast, humble, uncomplaining creature, he probably has never felt himself entitled to more than so much of the gifts of Providence. Is it not still something, that he has never held out his hand for charity, nor has yet been driven to that sad home and household of Earth's forlorn and broken-spirited children, the alms-house? He cherishes no quarrel, therefore, with his destiny, nor with the Author of it. All is as it should be.

If, indeed, he have been bereaved of a son—a bold, energetic, vigorous young man, on whom the father's feeble nature leaned, as

3. Bargain.

on a staff of strength—in that case, he may have felt a bitterness that could not otherwise have been generated in his heart. But, me-thinks, the joy of possessing such a son, and the agony of losing him, would have developed the old man's moral and intellectual na-ture to a much greater degree than we now find it. Intense grief appears to be as much out of keeping with his life, as fervid happiness.

To confess the truth, it is not the easiest matter in the world, to define and individualize a character like this which we are now handling. The portrait must be so generally negative, that the most delicate pencil is likely to spoil it by introducing some too positive tint. Every touch must be kept down or else you destroy the sub-dued tone, which is absolutely essential to the whole effect. Per-haps more may be done by contrast, than by direct description. For this purpose, I make use of another cake-and-candy merchant, who likewise infests the rail-road depôt. This latter worthy is a very smart and well-dressed boy, of ten years old or thereabouts, who skips briskly hither and thither, addressing the passengers in a pert voice, yet with somewhat of good breeding in his tone and pronun-ciation. Now he has caught my eye, and skips across the room with a pretty pertness, which I should like to correct with a box on the ear. "Any cake, sir?—any candy?"

No; none for me, my lad. I did but glance at your brisk figure, in order to catch a reflected light, and throw it upon your old rival yonder.

Again, in order to invest my conception of the old man with a more decided sense of reality, I look at him in the very moment of intensest bustle, on the arrival of the cars. The shriek of the engine, as it rushes into the car-house, is the utterance of the steam-fiend, whom man has subdued by magic spells, and compels to serve as a beast of burden. He has skimmed rivers in his headlong rush, dashed through forests, plunged into the hearts of mountains, and glanced from the city to the desert-place, and again to a far-off city, with a meteoric progress, seen, and out of sight, while his reverber-ating roar still fills the ear. The travellers swarm forth from the cars. All are full of the momentum which they have caught from their mode of conveyance. It seems as if the whole world, both morally and physically, were detached from its old standfasts, and set in rapid motion. And, in the midst of this terrible activity, there sits the old man of gingerbread, so subdued, so hopeless, so with-out a stake in life, and yet not positively miserable—there he sits, the forlorn old creature, one chill and sombre day after another, gathering scanty coppers for his cakes, apples and candy—there sits the old apple-dealer, in his threadbare suit of snuff-color and gray, and his grisly stubble-beard. See! he folds his lean arms around his lean figure, with that quiet sigh, and that scarcely perceptible shiver, which are the tokens of his inward state. I have him now. He and the steam-fiend are each other's antipodes; the latter is the type of all that go ahead—and the old man, the representative of that melancholy class who, by some sad witchcraft, are doomed never to share in the world's exulting progress. Thus the contrast between mankind and this desolate brother becomes picturesque, and even sublime.

And now farewell, old friend! Little do you suspect, that a student of human life has made your character the theme of more than one solitary and thoughtful hour. Many would say, that you have hardly individuality enough to be the object of your own self-love. How, then, can a stranger's eye detect any thing in your mind and heart, to study and to wonder at? Yet could I read but a tithe[4] of what is written there, it would be a volume of deeper and more comprehensive import than all that the wisest mortals have given to the world; for the soundless depths of the human soul, and of eternity, have an opening through your breast. God be praised, were it only for your sake, that the present shapes of human existence are not cast in iron, nor hewn in everlasting adamant,[5] but moulded of the vapors that vanish away while the essence flits upward to the infinite. There is a spiritual essence in this gray and lean old shape that shall flit upward too. Yes; doubtless there is a region, where the life-long shiver will pass away from his being, and that quiet sigh, which it has taken him so many years to breathe, will be brought to a close for good and all.

4. One-tenth.
5. Impenetrably hard substance, like a diamond.

Houses

This section offers a glimpse into the varied and sometimes conflicting conceptions of the house that Hawthorne drew on for his second novel. At the time that Hawthorne wrote *The House of the Seven Gables*, the house was a particularly rich figure in the culture. Health reformers such as William Andrus Alcott viewed the body as a kind of house in need of regular upkeep and care. The metaphor of the body as house extended well beyond the individual. The genealogical family itself had traditionally been viewed as a house (e.g., the House of Usher), and thus at a time of increasing debates on race, the figure of the genealogical house additionally brought to focus concerns about blood, history, and familial (and racial) identity. But even as the figure of the house had such metaphorical resonances, the house as an actual physical entity was at the center of much reformist and domestic writing of the period. Andrew Jackson Downing argued that the country house would contribute to the social health of the republic by elevating the morals of the burgeoning middle class. For Catharine Beecher, J. H. Agnew, and a host of other domestic writers, crucial to the middle-class home was the role of woman as its moral and spiritual center. Whereas Beecher and Agnew believed that woman's proper sphere was in the home, feminists such as Margaret Fuller posed a challenge to such a notion, accentuating the role of gender fluidity and free choice within and without the home.

WILLIAM ANDRUS ALCOTT

From The House I Live In†

The Bostonian William Andrus Alcott (1798–1859) published nearly a hundred books on physiological principles and health reform, preaching the values of temperance, vegetarianism, and education. In his widely reprinted *The House I Live in*, first published in 1834, he presented the human body as the house of the soul. Accordingly, he argued that it was of crucial importance that individuals understand and take care of their "houses."

*　*　*

† From *The House I Live in: or the Human Body*, 2nd ed. (Boston: Light & Stearns, 1837), 168–70, 172–74, 177–79, 184–85.

Chapter XIV.

APARTMENTS AND FURNITURE.

General Remarks. The External Ear. Chambers of the Nose. The Mouth, internally. The Salivary Glands. Passages to the Ear. The Chest. Cavity of the Lungs. The Food Pipe. The Stomach. The Intestines. Gall Bladder, &c. The Abdomen. The Apartment of the Circulation. Chambers of the Brain.

GENERAL REMARKS.—There are two kinds of apartments in the house of the soul. One of these is connected with outside doors; the other is not. Both are numerous, and both are important. I will begin with a description of the former; and occasionally speak, as I go along, of some of the latter.

In many houses a broad space or hall extends through from the door in front to the back side of the building. This space is not always either uniform or regular. Sometimes—and indeed usually—if the house has more than one story, it contains a stairway; and sometimes it includes a closet, or a room for other purposes. Doors also in the sides of this hall connect it with other apartments.

Now the house I live in is constructed very much on the same general plan, except that, as I told you in reference to the frame, there is no *square* work about it. The beauty of the internal parts of a common dwelling house depends very much on its straight lines, upright walls, and horizontal floors and ceilings; but the beauty of the habitation of the human soul consists, on the contrary, in curved lines. Not an apartment can be found, in good order, in which you can trace a single straight line.

But there is another difference which is still more essential. The same kind of covering which is applied to the house I live in, is also applied to form the covering—or perhaps you would say the lining—of the sides of the space or hall I have spoken of, as well as of its apartments; except that it is thinner, more neatly wrought, and without much pigment or paint. Whereas you know it is seldom, if ever, that you can see the inside of any part of a wooden house shingled or clap-boarded. We should laugh outright, to see the walls of a beautiful parlor or bed-room shingled.

There is one more essential and important difference. The rooms in many dwellings are often partly or wholly empty; or at least there is nothing in them except a small quantity of furniture and air. But except a few very small and not very important apartments, all the rooms of the house I live in are completely filled. Such a thing as empty space is hardly known there. The furniture, or whatever is in them, at all times completely fills them; for when anything is removed from them, their walls are accustomed to shrink accordingly; and when anything is introduced into them, these walls have the power of gradually yielding so as greatly to increase the capacity of the apartments.

* * *

CHAMBERS OF THE NOSE.— * * * Some kinds of head-ache probably have their seat in the hollows of the frontal or forehead bone, near the root of the nose. A very common disease in sheep, is known to be produced by worms in those hollows. The dull, heavy pain so often felt over the eyes, especially when we have what is commonly called a cold in the head, may be owing to a slight inflammation of the membranes of this cavity.

People ought to be careful about smelling things which give them much pain. Probably the use of most of our smelling bottles is injurious, in the end, to the delicate lining of all these "rooms" connected with the nose. Snuff certainly is, and so is the smoking of tobacco, cigars and opium—so common in some countries.

* * *

THE MOUTH, INTERNALLY.—The mouth, of itself, is one of the apartments of the human body, and a very curious apartment too. When I spoke of it as one of the doors, I referred principally to the aperture formed by a cleft of the lips, or the external mouth; and not to the *internal*, or more important part.

In this chamber—the entrance chamber of the front door—we find the teeth, the tongue, the palate, and several little glands. This entrance chamber is larger than the hall or space beyond it. Doors also open from it into several other apartments.

* * *

CAVITY OF THE LUNGS.— * * * The passage from the doorway at the top of the throat into the lungs, is at first considerably large, and may be both felt and seen at the top of the throat. It appears, at first view, to be a long bony tube, but it is not so. It is made of firm cartilage, almost as hard as bone. As soon, however, as it gets fairly within the cavity of the chest, it ceases to be cartilage, and becomes nothing more than common membrane.

The passage now divides into two, like the trunk of a tree when it divides into two branches. One of these smaller passages goes to the right side of the lungs, the other to the left. Soon each of these parts divide again; then those branches subdivide; and it is not long before the branches become as numerous as the limbs of the thickest tree top you ever saw; and indeed much more so. And what makes them appear thicker than they really are, is the ten thousand little cells, like innumerable small berries among the limbs of a tree or shrub, which are everywhere interspersed; for every one of the smallest passages, into which the larger passages lead, terminates in a little hollow cell. * * *

*   *   *

APARTMENT OF THE CIRCULATION.—This is a larger apartment than many would at first suppose. It must of course be large, to contain, as it does, twelve or fifteen quarts of blood. It is like the hollow channels of two great underground rivers, formed by the union of ten thousand thousand larger or smaller (but most of them very small) streams, running side by side with each other, but never intermingling their contents. As they have no communication with each other in their course, so they have no outlet—at least none of any considerable size.

To talk here about the circulation of blood, when my professed object is to describe a chamber, may to many seem out of place; but to me, it appears indispensable. For such is the irregularity of this circulatory apartment, that it is next to impossible to describe it, in any other way than by telling you something of its course and contents. But I will be very short.

You may first think of all these streams as if they were filled with blood; and afterward, as if emptied of that blood, and hollow. In the latter case, if a quantity of liquid, such as water, or melted wax, or even blood, were thrown into the cavities of the heart by means of a syringe, and if considerable effort were made, the liquid thrown in would soon run into all the large and small branches of this hollow river channel, or apartment, and fill it entirely; and the amount it would contain, as I have before intimated, would be in an adult equal to three or four gallons. Or to make it perfectly plain to all, it would be equal to a common sized pail full.

Thus you see that though the apartment of the circulation is strangely irregular, it is nevertheless a very spacious apartment; almost if not quite equal to the whole cavity of the chest, in which the lungs and heart are placed; and not much inferior in point of size, to the cavity below it, or that of the abdomen.

EDGAR ALLAN POE

The Fall of the House of Usher†

Edgar Allan Poe (1809–1849) first published "The Fall of the House of Usher" in the September 1839 issue of *Burton's Gentleman's Magazine*,

---

† From *The Complete Works of Edgar Allan Poe*, 17 vols., ed. James A. Harrison (New York: G. D. Sproul, 1902), III.273–97.

and it was reprinted in at least five different collections during Poe's lifetime. In all likelihood, Hawthorne knew the story and had mixed feelings about Poe. In a review of Hawthorne's *Twice-Told Tales* appearing in the May 1842 issue of *Graham's Magazine*, Poe declared that Hawthorne's tales "belong to the highest region of Art," but in a review of *Twice-Told Tales* and *Mosses from an Old Manse* appearing in the November 1847 *Godey's Lady's Book*, Poe remarked that Hawthorne is "peculiar and *not* original," and "infinitely too fond of allegory" (Edgar Allan Poe, *Essays and Reviews* [1984], 574, 587).

> Son cœur est un luth suspendu;
> Sitôt qu'on le touche il résonne.
> *De Béranger.*[1]

During the whole of a dull, dark, and soundless day in the autumn of the year, when the clouds hung oppressively low in the heavens, I had been passing alone, on horseback, through a singularly dreary tract of country; and at length found myself, as the shades of the evening drew on, within view of the melancholy House of Usher. I know not how it was—but, with the first glimpse of the building, a sense of insufferable gloom pervaded my spirit. I say insufferable; for the feeling was unrelieved by any of that half-pleasurable, because poetic, sentiment, with which the mind usually receives even the sternest natural images of the desolate or terrible. I looked upon the scene before me—upon the mere house, and the simple landscape features of the domain—upon the bleak walls— upon the vacant eye-like windows—upon a few rank sedges—and upon a few white trunks of decayed trees—with an utter depression of soul which I can compare to no earthly sensation more properly than to the after-dream of the reveller upon opium—the bitter lapse into everyday life—the hideous dropping off of the veil. There was an iciness, a sinking, a sickening of the heart—an unredeemed dreariness of thought which no goading of the imagination could torture into aught of the sublime. What was it—I paused to think— what was it that so unnerved me in the contemplation of the House of Usher? It was a mystery all insoluble; nor could I grapple with the shadowy fancies that crowded upon me as I pondered. I was forced to fall back upon the unsatisfactory conclusion, that while, beyond doubt, there *are* combinations of very simple natural objects which have the power of thus affecting us, still the analysis of this power lies among considerations beyond our depth. It was possible, I reflected, that a mere different arrangement of the particulars of the scene, of the details of the picture, would be sufficient to modify, or perhaps to annihilate its capacity for sorrowful impression; and,

---

1. "His heart is a suspended lute; / when touched, it resounds," from French poet Pierre-Jean de Béranger (1780–1857).

acting upon this idea, I reined my horse to the precipitous brink of a black and lurid tarn[2] that lay in unruffled lustre by the dwelling, and gazed down—but with a shudder even more thrilling than before— upon the remodelled and inverted images of the gray sedge, and the ghastly tree-stems, and the vacant and eye-like windows.

Nevertheless, in this mansion of gloom I now proposed to myself a sojourn of some weeks. Its proprietor, Roderick Usher, had been one of my boon companions in boyhood; but many years had elapsed since our last meeting. A letter, however, had lately reached me in a distant part of the country—a letter from him—which, in its wildly importunate nature, had admitted of no other than a personal reply. The MS. gave evidence of nervous agitation. The writer spoke of acute bodily illness—of a mental disorder which oppressed him—and of an earnest desire to see me, as his best, and indeed his only personal friend, with a view of attempting, by the cheerfulness of my society, some alleviation of his malady. It was the manner in which all this, and much more, was said—it was the apparent *heart* that went with his request—which allowed me no room for hesitation; and I accordingly obeyed forthwith what I still considered a very singular summons.

Although, as boys, we had been even intimate associates, yet I really knew little of my friend. His reserve had been always excessive and habitual. I was aware, however, that his very ancient family had been noted, time out of mind, for a peculiar sensibility of temperament, displaying itself, through long ages, in many works of exalted art, and manifested, of late, in repeated deeds of munificent yet unobtrusive charity, as well as in a passionate devotion to the intricacies, perhaps even more than to the orthodox and easily recognisable beauties, of musical science. I had learned, too, the very remarkable fact, that the stem of the Usher race, all time-honoured as it was, had put forth, at no period, any enduring branch; in other words, that the entire family lay in the direct line of descent, and had always, with very trifling and very temporary variation, so lain. It was this deficiency, I considered, while running over in thought the perfect keeping of the character of the premises with the accredited character of the people, and while speculating upon the possible influence which the one, in the long lapse of centuries, might have exercised upon the other—it was this deficiency, perhaps, of collateral issue, and the consequent undeviating transmission, from sire to son, of the patrimony with the name, which had, at length, so identified the two as to merge the original title of the estate in the quaint and equivocal appellation of the "House of Usher"—an appellation which seemed to include, in the minds of

2. Mountain lake.

the peasantry who used it, both the family and the family mansion.

I have said that the sole effect of my somewhat childish experiment—that of looking down within the tarn—had been to deepen
the first singular impression. There can be no doubt that the consciousness of the rapid increase of my superstition—for why should
I not so term it?—served mainly to accelerate the increase itself.
Such, I have long known, is the paradoxical law of all sentiments
having terror as a basis. And it might have been for this reason only,
that, when I again uplifted my eyes to the house itself, from its image in the pool, there grew in my mind a strange fancy—a fancy so
ridiculous, indeed, that I but mention it to show the vivid force of
the sensations which oppressed me. I had so worked upon my
imagination as really to believe that about the whole mansion and
domain there hung an atmosphere peculiar to themselves and their
immediate vicinity—an atmosphere which had no affinity with the
air of heaven, but which had reeked up from the decayed trees, and
the gray wall, and the silent tarn—a pestilent and mystic vapour,
dull, sluggish, faintly discernible, and leaden-hued.

Shaking off from my spirit what *must* have been a dream, I
scanned more narrowly the real aspect of the building. Its principal
feature seemed to be that of an excessive antiquity. The discoloration of ages had been great. Minute fungi overspread the whole
exterior, hanging in a fine tangled web-work from the eaves. Yet all
this was apart from any extraordinary dilapidation. No portion of
the masonry had fallen; and there appeared to be a wild inconsistency between its still perfect adaptation of parts, and the crumbling condition of the individual stones. In this there was much
that reminded me of the specious totality of old wood-work which
has rotted for long years in some neglected vault, with no disturbance from the breath of the external air. Beyond this indication of
extensive decay, however, the fabric gave little token of instability.
Perhaps the eye of a scrutinising observer might have discovered a
barely perceptible fissure, which, extending from the roof of the
building in front, made its way down the wall in a zigzag direction,
until it became lost in the sullen waters of the tarn.

Noticing these things, I rode over a short causeway to the house.
A servant in waiting took my horse, and I entered the Gothic archway of the hall. A valet, of stealthy step, thence conducted me, in
silence, through many dark and intricate passages in my progress to
the *studio* of his master. Much that I encountered on the way contributed, I know not how, to heighten the vague sentiments of
which I have already spoken. While the objects around me—while
the carvings of the ceilings, the sombre tapestries of the walls, the
ebon blackness of the floors, and the phantasmagoric armorial tro-
phies which rattled as I strode, were but matters to which, or to

such as which, I had been accustomed from my infancy—while I hesitated not to acknowledge how familiar was all this—I still wondered to find how unfamiliar were the fancies which ordinary images were stirring up. On one of the staircases, I met the physician of the family. His countenance, I thought, wore a mingled expression of low cunning and perplexity. He accosted me with trepidation and passed on. The valet now threw open a door and ushered me into the presence of his master.

The room in which I found myself was very large and lofty. The windows were long, narrow, and pointed, and at so vast a distance from the black oaken floor as to be altogether inaccessible from within. Feeble gleams of encrimsoned light made their way through the trellised panes, and served to render sufficiently distinct the more prominent objects around; the eye, however, struggled in vain to reach the remoter angles of the chamber, or the recesses of the vaulted and fretted ceiling. Dark draperies hung upon the walls. The general furniture was profuse, comfortless, antique, and tattered. Many books and musical instruments lay scattered about, but failed to give any vitality to the scene. I felt that I breathed an atmosphere of sorrow. An air of stern, deep, and irredeemable gloom hung over and pervaded all.

Upon my entrance, Usher arose from a sofa on which he had been lying at full length, and greeted me with a vivacious warmth which had much in it, I at first thought, of an overdone cordiality—of the constrained effort of the *ennuyé*[3] man of the world. A glance, however, at his countenance, convinced me of his perfect sincerity. We sat down; and for some moments, while he spoke not, I gazed upon him with a feeling half of pity, half of awe. Surely, man had never before so terribly altered, in so brief a period, as had Roderick Usher! It was with difficulty that I could bring myself to admit the identity of the wan being before me with the companion of my early boyhood. Yet the character of his face had been at all times remarkable. A cadaverousness of complexion; an eye large, liquid, and luminous beyond comparison; lips somewhat thin and very pallid, but of a surpassingly beautiful curve; a nose of a delicate Hebrew model, but with a breadth of nostril unusual in similar formations; a finely moulded chin, speaking, in its want of prominence, of a want of moral energy; hair of a more than web-like softness and tenuity; these features, with an inordinate expansion above the regions of the temple, made up altogether a countenance not easily to be forgotten. And now in the mere exaggeration of the prevailing character of these features, and of the expression they were wont to convey, lay so much of change that I doubted to

---

3. Bored (French).

whom I spoke. The now ghastly pallor of the skin, and the now miraculous lustre of the eye, above all things startled and even awed me. The silken hair, too, had been suffered to grow all unheeded, and as, in its wild gossamer texture, it floated rather than fell about the face, I could not, even with effort, connect its Arabesque[4] expression with any idea of simple humanity.

In the manner of my friend I was at once struck with an incoherence—an inconsistency; and I soon found this to arise from a series of feeble and futile struggles to overcome an habitual trepidancy—an excessive nervous agitation. For something of this nature I had indeed been prepared, no less by his letter, than by reminiscences of certain boyish traits, and by conclusions deduced from his peculiar physical conformation and temperament. His action was alternately vivacious and sullen. His voice varied rapidly from a tremulous indecision (when the animal spirits seemed utterly in abeyance) to that species of energetic concision—that abrupt, weighty, unhurried, and hollow-sounding enunciation—that leaden, self-balanced and perfectly modulated guttural utterance, which may be observed in the lost drunkard, or the irreclaimable eater of opium, during the periods of his most intense excitement.

It was thus that he spoke of the object of my visit, of his earnest desire to see me, and of the solace he expected me to afford him. He entered, at some length, into what he conceived to be the nature of his malady. It was, he said, a constitutional and a family evil, and one for which he despaired to find a remedy—a mere nervous affection, he immediately added, which would undoubtedly soon pass off. It displayed itself in a host of unnatural sensations. Some of these, as he detailed them, interested and bewildered me; although, perhaps, the terms, and the general manner of the narration had their weight. He suffered much from a morbid acuteness of the senses; the most insipid food was alone endurable; he could wear only garments of certain texture; the odours of all flowers were oppressive; his eyes were tortured by even a faint light; and there were but peculiar sounds, and these from stringed instruments, which did not inspire him with horror.

To an anomalous species of terror I found him a bounden slave. "I shall perish," said he, "I *must* perish in this deplorable folly. Thus, thus, and not otherwise, shall I be lost. I dread the events of the future, not in themselves, but in their results. I shudder at the thought of any, even the most trivial, incident, which may operate upon this intolerable agitation of soul. I have, indeed, no abhorrence of danger, except in its absolute effect—in terror. In this unnerved—in this pitiable condition—I feel that the period will

---

4. Unfamiliar or exotic; Poe used the word to describe some of his tales.

sooner or later arrive when I must abandon life and reason together, in some struggle with the grim phantasm, FEAR."

I learned, moreover, at intervals, and through broken and equivocal hints, another singular feature of his mental condition. He was enchained by certain superstitious impressions in regard to the dwelling which he tenanted, and whence, for many years, he had never ventured forth—in regard to an influence whose supposititious force was conveyed in terms too shadowy here to be re-stated—an influence which some peculiarities in the mere form and substance of his family mansion, had, by dint of long sufferance, he said, obtained over his spirit—an effect which the *physique* of the gray walls and turrets, and of the dim tarn into which they all looked down, had, at length, brought about upon the *morale* of his existence.

He admitted, however, although with hesitation, that much of the peculiar gloom which thus afflicted him could be traced to a more natural and far more palpable origin—to the severe and long-continued illness—indeed to the evidently approaching dissolution—of a tenderly beloved sister—his sole companion for long years—his last and only relative on earth. "Her decease," he said, with a bitterness which I can never forget, "would leave him (him the hopeless and the frail) the last of the ancient race of the Ushers." While he spoke, the lady Madeline (for so was she called) passed slowly through a remote portion of the apartment, and, without having noticed my presence, disappeared. I regarded her with an utter astonishment not unmingled with dread—and yet I found it impossible to account for such feelings. A sensation of stupor oppressed me, as my eyes followed her retreating steps. When a door, at length, closed upon her, my glance sought instinctively and eagerly the countenance of the brother—but he had buried his face in his hands, and I could only perceive that a far more than ordinary wanness had overspread the emaciated fingers through which trickled many passionate tears.

The disease of the lady Madeline had long baffled the skill of her physicians. A settled apathy, a gradual wasting away of the person, and frequent although transient affections of a partially cataleptical character,[5] were the unusual diagnosis. Hitherto she had steadily borne up against the pressure of her malady, and had not betaken herself finally to bed; but, on the closing in of the evening of my arrival at the house, she succumbed (as her brother told me at night with inexpressible agitation) to the prostrating power of the destroyer; and I learned that the glimpse I had obtained of her person would thus probably be the last I should obtain—that the lady, at least while living, would be seen by me no more.

5. A condition characterized by a loss of sensation and a kind of muscular paralysis.

For several days ensuing, her name was unmentioned by either Usher or myself: and during this period I was busied in earnest endeavours to alleviate the melancholy of my friend. We painted and read together; or I listened, as if in a dream, to the wild improvisations of his speaking guitar. And thus, as a closer and still closer intimacy admitted me more unreservedly into the recesses of his spirit, the more bitterly did I perceive the futility of all attempt at cheering a mind from which darkness, as if an inherent positive quality, poured forth upon all objects of the moral and physical universe, in one unceasing radiation of gloom.

I shall ever bear about me a memory of the many solemn hours I thus spent alone with the master of the House of Usher. Yet I should fail in any attempt to convey an idea of the exact character of the studies, or of the occupations, in which he involved me, or led me the way. An excited and highly distempered ideality threw a sulphureous lustre over all. His long improvised dirges will ring forever in my ears. Among other things, I hold painfully in mind a certain singular perversion and amplification of the wild air of the last waltz of Von Weber.[6] From the paintings over which his elaborate fancy brooded, and which grew, touch by touch, into vaguenesses at which I shuddered the more thrillingly, because I shuddered knowing not why;—from these paintings (vivid as their images now are before me) I would in vain endeavour to educe more than a small portion which should lie within the compass of merely written words. By the utter simplicity, by the nakedness of his designs, he arrested and overawed attention. If ever mortal painted an idea, that mortal was Roderick Usher. For me at least—in the circumstances then surrounding me—there arose out of the pure abstractions which the hypochondriac contrived to throw upon his canvas, an intensity of intolerable awe, no shadow of which felt I ever yet in the contemplation of the certainly glowing yet too concrete reveries of Fuseli.[7]

One of the phantasmagoric conceptions of my friend, partaking not so rigidly of the spirit of abstraction, may be shadowed forth, although feebly, in words. A small picture presented the interior of an immensely long and rectangular vault or tunnel, with low walls, smooth, white, and without interruption or device. Certain accessory points of the design served well to convey the idea that this excavation lay at an exceeding depth below the surface of the earth. No outlet was observed in any portion of its vast extent, and no torch, or other artificial source of light was discernible; yet a flood of intense rays rolled throughout, and bathed the whole in a ghastly and inappropriate splendour.

6. Carl Maria Friedrich Ernst von Weber (1786–1826), German composer. The "Last Waltz" was actually composed by Karl Gottlieb Reisinger (1798–1859).
7. Henry Fuseli (1741–1825), Swiss artist known for his paintings of the fantastic.

I have just spoken of that morbid condition of the auditory nerve which rendered all music intolerable to the sufferer, with the exception of certain effects of stringed instruments. It was, perhaps, the narrow limits to which he thus confined himself upon the guitar, which gave birth, in great measure, to the fantastic character of his performances. But the fervid *facility* of his *impromptus*[8] could not be so accounted for. They must have been, and were, in the notes, as well as in the words of his wild fantasias (for he not unfrequently accompanied himself with rhymed verbal improvisations), the result of that intense mental collectedness and concentration to which I have previously alluded as observable only in particular moments of the highest artificial excitement. The words of one of these rhapsodies I have easily remembered. I was, perhaps, the more forcibly impressed with it, as he gave it, because, in the under or mystic current of its meaning, I fancied that I perceived, and for the first time, a full consciousness on the part of Usher, of the tottering of his lofty reason upon her throne. The verses, which were entitled "The Haunted Palace,"[9] ran very nearly, if not accurately, thus:

I.

In the greenest of our valleys,
    By good angels tenanted,
Once a fair and stately palace—
    Radiant palace—reared its head.
In the monarch Thought's dominion—
    It stood there!
Never seraph spread a pinion
    Over fabric half so fair.

II.

Banners yellow, glorious, golden,
    On its roof did float and flow;
(This—all this—was in the olden
    Time long ago)
And every gentle air that dallied,
    In that sweet day,
Along the ramparts plumed and pallid,
    A winged odour went away.

III.

Wanderers in that happy valley
    Through two luminous windows saw

8. Musical works characterized by improvisation.
9. Poe had earlier published this poem separately in the April 1839 *American Museum*.

Spirits moving musically
   To a lute's well-tunèd law,
Round about a throne, where sitting
   (Porphyrogene!)[1]
In state his glory well befitting,
   The ruler of the realm was seen.

IV.

And all with pearl and ruby glowing
   Was the fair palace door,
Through which came flowing, flowing, flowing
   And sparkling evermore,
A troop of Echoes whose sweet duty
   Was but to sing,
In voices of surpassing beauty,
   The wit and wisdom of their king.

V.

But evil things, in robes of sorrow,
   Assailed the monarch's high estate;
(Ah, let us mourn, for never morrow
   Shall dawn upon him, desolate!)
And, round about his home, the glory
   That blushed and bloomed
Is but a dim-remembered story
   Of the old time entombed.

VI.

And travellers now within that valley,
   Through the red-litten windows, see
Vast forms that move fantastically
   To a discordant melody;
While, like a rapid ghastly river,
   Through the pale door,
A hideous throng rush out forever,
   And laugh—but smile no more.

I well remember that suggestions arising from this ballad, led us into a train of thought wherein there became manifest an opinion of Usher's which I mention not so much on account of its novelty, (for other men have thought thus,) as on account of the pertinacity with which he maintained it. This opinion, in its general form, was that of the sentience of all vegetable things. But, in his disordered fancy, the idea had assumed a more daring character, and trespassed, under certain conditions, upon the kingdom of inorganiza-

---

1. A word coined by Poe to suggest royalty.

tion. I lack words to express the full extent, or the earnest *abandon* of his persuasion. The belief, however, was connected (as I have previously hinted) with the gray stones of the home of his forefathers. The conditions of the sentience had been here, he imagined, fulfilled in the method of collocation of these stones—in the order of their arrangement, as well as in that of the many *fungi* which overspread them, and of the decayed trees which stood around—above all, in the long undisturbed endurance of this arrangement, and in its reduplication in the still waters of the tarn. Its evidence—the evidence of the sentience—was to be seen, he said, (and I here started as he spoke,) in the gradual yet certain condensation of an atmosphere of their own about the waters and the walls. The result was discoverable, he added, in that silent, yet importunate and terrible influence which for centuries had moulded the destinies of his family, and which made *him* what I now saw him—what he was. Such opinions need no comment, and I will make none.

Our books—the books which, for years, had formed no small portion of the mental existence of the invalid—were, as might be supposed, in strict keeping with this character of phantasm. We pored together over such works as the Ververt et Chartreuse of Gresset; the Belphegor of Machiavelli; the Heaven and Hell of Swedenborg; the Subterranean Voyage of Nicholas Klimm by Holberg; the Chiromancy of Robert Flud, of Jean D'Indaginé, and of De la Chambre; the Journey into the Blue Distance of Tieck; and the City of the Sun of Campanella. One favourite volume was a small octavo edition of the *Directorium Inquisitorum*, by the Dominican Eymeric de Gironne; and there were passages in Pomponius Mela, about the old African Satyrs and Ægipans, over which Usher would sit dreaming for hours.[2] His chief delight, however, was found in the perusal of an exceedingly rare and curious book in quarto Gothic—the manual of a forgotten church—the *Vigiliæ Mortuorum secundum Chorum Ecclesiæ Maguntinæ*.[3]

I could not help thinking of the wild ritual of this work, and of its probable influence upon the hypochondriac, when, one evening, having informed me abruptly that the lady Madeline was no more, he stated his intention of preserving her corpse for a fortnight, (previously to its final interment,) in one of the numerous vaults within the main walls of the building. The worldly reason, however, assigned for this singular proceeding, was one which I did not feel

---

2. A mèlange of works dealing with politics, the supernatural, and various pseudosciences. Among the best-known of the authors in Usher's collection are the Florentine political theorist Niccolò Machiavelli (1469–1527) and the Swedish philosopher and mystic Emmanuel Swedenborg (1688–1772). "Ægipans": forest gods.
3. *The Vigils of the Dead according to the Church of Mayence*, printed in Switzerland around 1500.

at liberty to dispute. The brother had been led to his resolution (so he told me) by consideration of the unusual character of the malady of the deceased, of certain obtrusive and eager inquiries on the part of her medical men, and of the remote and exposed situation of the burial-ground of the family. I will not deny that when I called to mind the sinister countenance of the person whom I met upon the staircase, on the day of my arrival at the house, I had no desire to oppose what I regarded as at best but a harmless, and by no means an unnatural, precaution.

At the request of Usher, I personally aided him in the arrangements for the temporary entombment. The body having been encoffined, we two alone bore it to its rest. The vault in which we placed it (and which had been so long unopened that our torches, half smothered in its oppressive atmosphere, gave us little opportunity for investigation) was small, damp, and entirely without means of admission for light; lying, at great depth, immediately beneath that portion of the building in which was my own sleeping apartment. It had been used, apparently, in remote feudal times, for the worst purposes of a donjon[4]-keep, and, in later days, as a place of deposit for powder, or some other highly combustible substance, as a portion of its floor, and the whole interior of a long archway through which we reached it, were carefully sheathed with copper. The door, of massive iron, had been, also, similarly protected. Its immense weight caused an unusually sharp grating sound, as it moved upon its hinges.

Having deposited our mournful burden upon tressels[5] within this region of horror, we partially turned aside the yet unscrewed lid of the coffin, and looked upon the face of the tenant. A striking similitude between the brother and sister now first arrested my attention; and Usher, divining, perhaps, my thoughts, murmured out some few words from which I learned that the deceased and himself had been twins, and that sympathies of a scarcely intelligible nature had always existed between them. Our glances, however, rested not long upon the dead—for we could not regard her unawed. The disease which had thus entombed the lady in the maturity of youth, had left, as usual in all maladies of a strictly cataleptical character, the mockery of a faint blush upon the bosom and the face, and that suspiciously lingering smile upon the lip which is so terrible in death. We replaced and screwed down the lid, and, having secured the door of iron, made our way, with toil, into the scarcely less gloomy apartments of the upper portion of the house.

And now, some days of bitter grief having elapsed, an observable

---

4. Dungeon (archaic).
5. I.e., trestles; braced supports.

change came over the features of the mental disorder of my friend. His ordinary manner had vanished. His ordinary occupations were neglected or forgotten. He roamed from chamber to chamber with hurried, unequal, and objectless step. The pallor of his countenance had assumed, if possible, a more ghastly hue—but the luminousness of his eye had utterly gone out. The once occasional huskiness of his tone was heard no more; and a tremulous quaver, as if of extreme terror, habitually characterized his utterance. There were times, indeed, when I thought his unceasingly agitated mind was labouring with some oppressive secret, to divulge which he struggled for the necessary courage. At times, again, I was obliged to resolve all into the mere inexplicable vagaries of madness, for I beheld him gazing upon vacancy for long hours, in an attitude of the profoundest attention, as if listening to some imaginary sound. It was no wonder that his condition terrified—that it infected me. I felt creeping upon me, by slow yet certain degrees, the wild influences of his own fantastic yet impressive superstitions.

It was, especially, upon retiring to bed late in the night of the seventh or eighth day after the placing of the lady Madeline within the donjon, that I experienced the full power of such feelings. Sleep came not near my couch—while the hours waned and waned away. I struggled to reason off the nervousness which had dominion over me. I endeavoured to believe that much, if not all of what I felt, was due to the bewildering influence of the gloomy furniture of the room—of the dark and tattered draperies, which, tortured into motion by the breath of a rising tempest, swayed fitfully to and fro upon the walls, and rustled uneasily about the decorations of the bed. But my efforts were fruitless. An irrepressible tremour gradually pervaded my frame; and, at length, there sat upon my very heart an incubus[6] of utterly causeless alarm. Shaking this off with a gasp and a struggle, I uplifted myself upon the pillows, and, peering earnestly within the intense darkness of the chamber, hearkened— I know not why, except that an instinctive spirit prompted me—to certain low and indefinite sounds which came, through the pauses of the storm, at long intervals, I knew not whence. Overpowered by an intense sentiment of horror, unaccountable yet unendurable, I threw on my clothes with haste (for I felt that I should sleep no more during the night), and endeavoured to arouse myself from the pitiable condition into which I had fallen, by pacing rapidly to and fro through the apartment.

I had taken but few turns in this manner, when a light step on an adjoining staircase arrested my attention. I presently recognised it as that of Usher. In an instant afterward he rapped, with a gentle

---

6. A demon or evil spirit that supposedly descends upon sleeping persons.

touch, at my door, and entered, bearing a lamp. His countenance was, as usual, cadaverously wan—but, moreover, there was a species of mad hilarity in his eyes—an evidently restrained *hysteria* in his whole demeanour. His air appalled me—but anything was preferable to the solitude which I had so long endured, and I even welcomed his presence as a relief.

"And you have not seen it?" he said abruptly, after having stared about him for some moments in silence—"you have not then seen it?—but, stay! you shall." Thus speaking, and having carefully shaded his lamp, he hurried to one of the casements, and threw it freely open to the storm.

The impetuous fury of the entering gust nearly lifted us from our feet. It was, indeed, a tempestuous yet sternly beautiful night, and one wildly singular in its terror and its beauty. A whirlwind had apparently collected its force in our vicinity; for there were frequent and violent alterations in the direction of the wind; and the exceeding density of the clouds (which hung so low as to press upon the turrets of the house) did not prevent our perceiving the life-like velocity with which they flew careering from all points against each other, without passing away into the distance. I say that even their exceeding density did not prevent our perceiving this—yet we had no glimpse of the moon or stars—nor was there any flashing forth of the lightning. But the under surfaces of the huge masses of agitated vapour, as well as all terrestrial objects immediately around us, were glowing in the unnatural light of a faintly luminous and distinctly visible gaseous exhalation which hung about and enshrouded the mansion.

"You must not—you shall not behold this!" said I, shudderingly, to Usher, as I led him, with a gentle violence, from the window to a seat. "These appearances, which bewilder you, are merely electrical phenomena not uncommon—or it may be that they have their ghastly origin in the rank miasma[7] of the tarn. Let us close this casement;—the air is chilling and dangerous to your frame. Here is one of your favourite romances. I will read, and you shall listen;— and so we will pass away this terrible night together."

The antique volume which I had taken up was the "Mad Trist" of Sir Launcelot Canning;[8] but I had called it a favourite of Usher's more in sad jest than in earnest; for, in truth, there is little in its uncouth and unimaginative prolixity which could have had interest for the lofty and spiritual ideality of my friend. It was, however, the only book immediately at hand; and I indulged a vague hope that the excitement which now agitated the hypochondriac, might find

7. Unwholesome gas.
8. A character and narrative invented by Poe.

relief (for the history of mental disorder is full of similar anomalies) even in the extremeness of the folly which I should read. Could I have judged, indeed, by the wild overstrained air of vivacity with which he hearkened, or apparently hearkened, to the words of the tale, I might well have congratulated myself upon the success of my design.

I had arrived at that well-known portion of the story where Ethelred, the hero of the Trist, having sought in vain for peaceable admission into the dwelling of the hermit, proceeds to make good an entrance by force. Here, it will be remembered, the words of the narrative run thus:

"And Ethelred, who was by nature of a doughty heart, and who was now mighty withal, on account of the powerfulness of the wine which he had drunken, waited no longer to hold parley with the hermit, who, in sooth, was of an obstinate and maliceful turn, but, feeling the rain upon his shoulders, and fearing the rising of the tempest, uplifted his mace outright, and, with blows, made quickly room in the plankings of the door for his gauntleted hand; and now pulling therewith sturdily, he so cracked, and ripped, and tore all asunder, that the noise of the dry and hollow-sounding wood alarumed and reverberated throughout the forest."

At the termination of this sentence I started, and for a moment, paused; for it appeared to me (although I at once concluded that my excited fancy had deceived me)—it appeared to me that, from some very remote portion of the mansion, there came, indistinctly, to my ears, what might have been, in its exact similarity of character, the echo (but a stifled and dull one certainly) of the very cracking and ripping sound which Sir Launcelot had so particularly described. It was, beyond doubt, the coincidence alone which had arrested my attention; for, amid the rattling of the sashes of the casements, and the ordinary commingled noises of the still increasing storm, the sound, in itself, had nothing, surely, which should have interested or disturbed me. I continued the story:

"But the good champion Ethelred, now entering within the door, was sore enraged and amazed to perceive no signal of the maliceful hermit; but, in the stead thereof, a dragon of a scaly and prodigious demeanour, and of a fiery tongue, which sate in guard before a palace of gold, with a floor of silver; and upon the wall there hung a shield of shining brass with this legend enwritten—

Who entereth herein, a conqueror hath bin;
Who slayeth the dragon, the shield he shall win;

And Ethelred uplifted his mace, and struck upon the head of the dragon, which fell before him, and gave up his pesty breath, with a shriek so horrid and harsh, and withal so piercing, that Ethelred had fain to close his ears with his hands against the dreadful noise of it, the like whereof was never before heard."

Here again I paused abruptly, and now with a feeling of wild amazement—for there could be no doubt whatever that, in this instance, I did actually hear (although from what direction it proceeded I found it impossible to say) a low and apparently distant, but harsh, protracted, and most unusual screaming or grating sound—the exact counterpart of what my fancy had already conjured up for the dragon's unnatural shriek as described by the romancer.

Oppressed, as I certainly was, upon the occurrence of the second and most extraordinary coincidence, by a thousand conflicting sensations, in which wonder and extreme terror were predominant, I still retained sufficient presence of mind to avoid exciting, by any observation, the sensitive nervousness of my companion. I was by no means certain that he had noticed the sounds in question; although, assuredly, a strange alteration had, during the last few minutes, taken place in his demeanour. From a position fronting my own, he had gradually brought round his chair, so as to sit with his face to the door of the chamber; and thus I could but partially perceive his features, although I saw that his lips trembled as if he were murmuring inaudibly. His head had dropped upon his breast—yet I knew that he was not asleep, from the wide and rigid opening of the eye as I caught a glance of it in profile. The motion of his body, too, was at variance with this idea—for he rocked from side to side with a gentle yet constant and uniform sway. Having rapidly taken notice of all this, I resumed the narrative of Sir Launcelot, which thus proceeded:

"And now, the champion, having escaped from the terrible fury of the dragon, bethinking himself of the brazen shield, and of the breaking up of the enchantment which was upon it, removed the carcass from out of the way before him, and approached valorously over the silver pavement of the castle to where the shield was upon the wall; which in sooth tarried not for his full coming, but fell down at his feet upon the silver floor, with a mighty great and terrible ringing sound."

No sooner had these syllables passed my lips, than—as if a shield of brass had indeed, at the moment, fallen heavily upon a floor of silver—I became aware of a distinct, hollow, metallic, and clangorous, yet apparently muffled reverberation. Completely unnerved, I leaped to my feet; but the measured rocking movement of Usher was undisturbed. I rushed to the chair in which he sat. His eyes were bent fixedly before him, and throughout his whole countenance there reigned a stony rigidity. But, as I placed my hand upon his shoulder, there came a strong shudder over his whole person; a sickly smile quivered about his lips; and I saw that he spoke in a low, hurried, and gibbering murmur, as if unconscious of my presence. Bending closely over him, I at length drank in the hideous import of his words.

"Not hear it?—yes, I hear it, and *have* heard it. Long—long—long—many minutes, many hours, many days, have I heard it—yet I dared not—oh, pity me, miserable wretch that I am!—I dared not—I *dared* not speak! *We have put her living in the tomb!* Said I not that my senses were acute? I *now* tell you that I heard her first feeble movements in the hollow coffin. I heard them—many, many days ago—yet I dared not—*I dared not speak!* And now—to-night—Ethelred—ha! ha!—the breaking of the hermit's door, and the death-cry of the dragon, and the clangour of the shield!—say, rather, the rending of her coffin, and the grating of the iron hinges of her prison, and her struggles within the coppered archway of the vault! Oh whither shall I fly? Will she not be here anon? Is she not hurrying to upbraid me for my haste? Have I not heard her footstep on the stair? Do I not distinguish that heavy and horrible beating of her heart? MADMAN!" here he sprang furiously to his feet, and shrieked out his syllables, as if in the effort he were giving up his soul—"MADMAN! I TELL YOU THAT SHE NOW STANDS WITHOUT THE DOOR!"

As if in the superhuman energy of his utterance there had been found the potency of a spell—the huge antique panels to which the speaker pointed, threw slowly back, upon the instant, their ponderous and ebony jaws. It was the work of the rushing gust—but then without those doors there DID stand the lofty and enshrouded figure of the lady Madeline of Usher. There was blood upon her white robes, and the evidence of some bitter struggle upon every portion of her emaciated frame. For a moment she remained trembling and reeling to and fro upon the threshold, then, with a low moaning cry, fell heavily inward upon the person of her brother, and in her violent and now final death-agonies, bore him to the floor a corpse, and a victim to the terrors he had anticipated.

From that chamber, and from that mansion, I fled aghast. The storm was still abroad in all its wrath as I found myself crossing the old causeway. Suddenly there shot along the path a wild light, and I turned to see whence a gleam so unusual could have issued; for the vast house and its shadows were alone behind me. The radiance was that of the full, setting, and blood-red moon which now shone vividly through that once barely-discernible fissure of which I have before spoken as extending from the roof of the building, in a zigzag direction, to the base. While I gazed, this fissure rapidly widened—there came a fierce breath of the whirlwind—the entire orb of the satellite burst at once upon my sight—my brain reeled as

I saw the mighty walls rushing asunder—there was a long tumultuous shouting sound like the voice of a thousand waters—and the
deep and dank tarn at my feet closed sullenly and silently over the
fragments of the "HOUSE OF USHER."

ANDREW JACKSON DOWNING

[American Country Houses]†

The New York landscape gardener, rural architect, and horticulturalist
Andrew Jackson Downing (1815–1852) was a prolific writer who
worked to present the single-family country home as the best possible
locale for developing republican virtue in the antebellum nation.
Among his most popular works were *A Treatise on the Theory and Practice of Landscape Gardening, Adapted to North America* (1841) and *The
Architecture of Country Houses* (1850).

There are three excellent reasons why my countrymen should
have good houses.

The first, is because a good house (and by this I mean a fitting,
tasteful, and significant dwelling) is a powerful means of civilization. A nation, whose rural population is content to live in mean
huts and miserable hovels, is certain to be behind its neighbors in
education, the arts, and all that makes up the external signs of
progress. With the perception of proportion, symmetry, order and
beauty, awakens the desire for possession, and with them comes
that refinement of manners which distinguishes a civilized from a
coarse and brutal people. So long as men are forced to dwell in log
huts and follow a hunter's life, we must not be surprised at lynch
law and the use of the bowie knife. But, when smiling lawns and
tasteful cottages begin to embellish a country, we know that order
and culture are established. And, as the first incentive towards this
change is awakened in the minds of most men by the perception of
beauty and superiority in external objects, it must follow that the
interest manifested in the Rural Architecture of a country like this,
has much to do with the progress of its civilization.

The second reason is, because the *individual home* has a great
social value for a people. Whatever new systems may be needed for
the regeneration of an old and enfeebled nation, we are persuaded
that, in America, not only is the distinct family the best social form,
but those elementary forces which give rise to the highest genius
and the finest character may, for the most part, be traced back to

† From *The Architecture of Country Houses* (New York: D. Appleton & Co., 1850), v–vi,
266–70.

the farm-house and the rural cottage. It is the solitude and freedom of the family home in the country which constantly preserves the purity of the nation, and invigorates its intellectual powers. The battle of life, carried on in cities, gives a sharper edge to the weapon of character, but its temper is, for the most part, fixed amid those communings with nature and the family, where individuality takes its most natural and strongest development.

The third reason is, because there is a moral influence in a country home—when, among an educated, truthful, and refined people, it is an echo of their character—which is more powerful than any mere oral teachings of virtue and morality. That family, whose religion lies away from its threshold, will show but slender results from the best teachings, compared with another where the family hearth is made a central point of the Beautiful and the Good. And much of that feverish unrest and want of balance between the desire and the fulfillment of life, is calmed and adjusted by the pursuit of tastes which result in making a little world of the family home, where truthfulness, beauty and order have the largest dominion.

The mere sentiment of home, with its thousand associations, has, like a strong anchor, saved many a man from shipwreck in the storms of life. How much the moral influence of that sentiment may be increased, by making the home all that it should be, and how much an attachment is strengthened by every external sign of beauty that awakens love in the young, are so well understood, that they need no demonstration here. All to which the heart can attach itself in youth, and the memory linger fondly over in riper years, contributes largely to our stock of happiness, and to the elevation of the moral character. For this reason, the condition of the family home—in this country where every man may have a home, should be raised, till it shall symbolize the best character and pursuits, and the dearest affections and enjoyments of social life.

*   *   *

* * * We see signs showing themselves, with the growing wealth of the country, of expenditure in domestic architecture quite unmeaning and unwise in a republic. Fortunes are rapidly accumulated in the United States, and the indulgence of one's taste and pride in the erection of a country-seat of great size and cost, is becoming a favourite mode of expending wealth. And yet these attempts at great establishment are always and inevitably, failures in America.

And why? Plainly, because they are contrary to the spirit of republican institutions; because the feelings upon which they are based can never take root, except in a government of hereditary rights: because they are wholly in contradiction to the spirit of our time and people.

In a country of hereditary rights, where the custom prevails of leaving the family home and estate to the eldest son, or to a single representative of the family, there is a meaning and purpose in the erection of great manorial halls and magnificent country-seats. The proprietor feels assured that it is always for his own family, genera- tion after generation, that this expenditure is made—that this great establishment, upon which such sums have been lavished, is to be the home of that family, and will bear its name, and stand as a monument of its wealth and power for ages. And this, in an aristoc- racy, consoles him for the enormous injustice of causing all his other descendants in each generation, to revolve as pale satellites round the eldest son, who represents all the wealth and power of the family.

In our republic, there is no law of primogeniture, there are no hereditary rights. The man of large wealth dies to-morrow, and his million, divided among all his children, leaves them each, but a few thousands. If he has been tempted to indulge in the luxury or pride of a great establishment, no one of his children is rich enough to hold it. Public opinion—the salutary operation of our institutions, frowns upon the attempt to continue the wealth and family estates in the hands of the family, by making one descendant rich at the ex- pense of the rest. And this home—this fine establishment which has been built in defiance of the spirit of the time and nation, must needs be abandoned by the family who built it; it must become the property of strangers, who, in their turn, will hold it but for one life-time.

We will not urge the difficulty, with our social habits, of main- taining an overgrown establishment, the personal drudgery it in- volves, the care and solicitude it requires, let the immediate fortune be what it may. It is only in an old country, where there is a large surplusage of domestic service, that domestic establishments of large size can be conducted with pleasure and ease to the propri- etor. Here, it is quite the contrary. A country-house, where the con- veniences are such that the establishment may be moderate, the living-rooms compact and well arranged, the facility of performing all household labors increased as much as possible, is the perfect villa for America.

But the main argument against the creation of large establish- ments is, that the whole theory is a mistake; that it is impossible, except for a day; that our laws render the attempt folly; and our in- stitutions finally grind it to powder.

There is something beautiful and touching in the associations that grow up in a home held sacred in the same family for genera- tions. A wealth of affection is kept alive in those old manor-houses and country halls of England, where, age after age, the descendants

of one family have lived, and loved, and suffered, and died,—
perhaps nobly and bravely too, sheltered by the same trees and
guarded by the same walls. It is quite natural that we, largely descended from this Anglo-Saxon stock, when we have fortunes to
spend, should fondly delude ourselves with the idea of realizing this
old and pleasing idyl of beautiful country life. But it is only an idyl,
or only a delusion to us. It belongs to the past, so far as we are concerned. It is no more to be re-animated in the republic of the new
world than the simple faith in the Virgin, which built the mighty
cathedrals of the middle ages. It could only be re-animated at the
sacrifice of the happiness of millions of free citizens.

But the true home still remains to us. Not, indeed, the feudal
castle, not the baronial hall, but the home of the individual man—
the home of that family of equal rights, which continually separates
and continually reforms itself in the new world—the republican
home, built by no robbery of the property of another class, maintained by no infringement of a brother's rights; the beautiful, rural,
unostentatious, moderate home of the country gentleman, large
enough to minister to all the wants, necessities, and luxuries of a
republican, and not too large or too luxurious to warp the life or
manners of his children.[1]

The just pride of a true American is not in a great hereditary
home, but in greater hereditary institutions. It is more to him that
all his children will be born under wise, and just, and equal laws,
than that one of them should come into the world with a great family estate. It is better, in his eyes, that it should be possible for the
humblest laborer to look forward to the possession of a future
country-house and home like his own, than to feel that a wide and
impassable gulf of misery separates him, the lord of the soil, from a
large class of his fellow beings born beneath him. Yes, the love of
home is one of the deepest feelings in our nature, and we believe
the happiness and virtue of a vast rural population to be centred in
it; but it must be a home built and loved, upon new world and not
the old world ideas and principles; a home in which humanity and
republicanism are stronger than family pride and aristocratic feeling; a home of the virtuous citizen, rather than of the mighty owner
of houses and lands.

---

1. Perhaps the true standard of the means to be expended in a country home is to be found
with us by the inquiry—Can the proprietor afford to leave it to one of his children?—or,
at the most, is it an expenditure that will not prove a serious loss, should they be compelled to part with it? * * * [Downing's note].

CATHARINE E. BEECHER

[American Housekeepers]†

The educator Catharine E. Beecher (1800–1878) was the best-known writer on domestic science of the antebellum period. Like her sister Harriet Beecher Stowe (1811–1896), she believed that women could play a crucial role in shaping U.S. culture by exerting their moral and spiritual authority from within the home. Unlike Stowe, however, she was opposed to political abolitionism and other forms of public activism. Beecher articulated her views on woman's domestic sphere in *A Treatise on Domestic Economy* (1841), which was frequently reprinted throughout the nineteenth century.

There is nothing, which has a more abiding influence on the happiness of a family, than the preservation of equable and cheerful temper and tones in the housekeeper. A woman who is habitually gentle, sympathizing, forbearing, and cheerful, carries an atmosphere about her, which imparts a soothing and sustaining influence, and renders it easier for all to do right, under her administration, than in any other situation.

The Writer has known families, where the mother's presence seemed the sunshine of the circle around her; imparting a cheering and vivifying power, scarcely realized, till it was withdrawn. Every one, without thinking of it, or knowing why it was so, experienced a peaceful and invigorating influence, as soon as they entered the sphere illumined by her smile and sustained by her cheering kindness and sympathy. On the contrary, many a good house-keeper, good in every respect but this, by wearing a countenance of anxiety and dissatisfaction, and by indulging in the frequent use of sharp and reprehensive tones, more than destroys all the comfort that otherwise would result from her system, neatness, and economy.

There is a secret, social sympathy, which every mind, to a greater or less degree, experiences with the feelings of those around, as they are manifested by the countenance and voice. A sorrowful, a discontented, or an angry, countenance, produces a silent sympathetic influence, imparting a sombre shade to the mind, while tones of anger or complaint still more effectually jar the spirits.

No person can maintain a quiet and cheerful frame of mind, while tones of discontent and displeasure are sounding on the ear. We may gradually accustom ourselves to the evil, till it is partially

† From *A Treatise on Domestic Economy, for the Use of Young Ladies at Home and at School* (Boston: Marsh, Capen, Lyon, and Webb, 1841), 134–38, 140–41.

diminished; but it always is an evil, which greatly interferes with the enjoyment of the family state. There are sometimes cases, where the entrance of the mistress of a family seems to awaken a slight apprehension, in every mind around, as if each felt in danger of a reproof, for something either perpetrated or neglected. A woman who should go around her house with a small stinging snapper, which she habitually applied to those she met, would be encountered with feelings very similar to those, experienced by the inmates of a family where the mistress often uses her countenance and voice to inflict similar penalties for duties neglected.

Yet there are many allowances to be made for housekeepers, who sometimes imperceptibly and unconsciously fall into such habits. A woman, who attempts to carry out any plans of system, order, and economy, and who has her feelings and habits conformed to certain rules, is constantly liable to have her plans crossed, and her taste violated, by the inexperience or inattention of those about her. And no housekeeper, whatever are her habits, can escape the frequent recurrence of negligence or mistake, which interferes with her plans. It is probable that there is no class or persons, in the world, who have such incessant trials of temper, and such temptation to be fretful, as American housekeepers. For a housekeeper's business is not like that of the other sex, limited to a particular department, for which previous preparation is made. It consists of ten thousand little disconnected items, which can never be so systematically arranged, that there is no daily jostling, somewhere. And in the best regulated families, it is not unfrequently the case, that some act of forgetfulness or carelessness, from some member, will disarrange the business of the whole day, so that every hour will bring renewed occasion for annoyance. And the more strongly a woman realizes the value of time, and the importance of system and order, the more will she be tempted to irritability and complaint.

The following considerations may aid in preparing a woman to meet such daily crosses with even a cheerful temper and tones.

In the first place, a woman, who has charge of a large household, should regard her duties as dignified, important, and difficult. The mind is so made, as to be elevated and cheered by a sense of far-reaching influence and usefulness. A woman, who feels that she is a cipher, and that it makes little difference how she performs her duties, has far less to sustain and invigorate her, than one who truly estimates the importance of her station. A man, who feels that the destinies of a nation are turning on the judgement and skill with which he plans and executes, has a pressure of motive, and an elevation of feeling, which are great safeguards from all that is low, trivial, and degrading.

So an American mother and housekeeper, who looks at her position in the aspect presented in the previous pages, and who rightly estimates the long train of influences which will pass down to hundreds, whose destinies, from generation to generation, will be modified by those decisions of her will, which regulated the temper, principles, and habits, of her family, must be elevated above petty temptations which would otherwise assail her.

Again, a housekeeper should feel that she really has great difficulties to meet and overcome. A person, who wrongly thinks that there is little danger, can never maintain so faithful a guard, as one who rightly estimates the temptations which beset her. Nor can one, who thinks that they are trifling difficulties which she has to encounter, and trivial temptations, to which she must yield, so much enjoy the just reward of conscious virtue and self-control, as one who takes an opposite view of the subject.

A third method, is, for a woman deliberately to calculate on having her best-arranged plans interfered with, very often; and to be in such a state of preparation that the evil will not come unawares. So complicated are the pursuits, and so diverse the habits of the various members of a family, that it is almost impossible for every one to avoid interfering with the plans and taste of a housekeeper, in some one point or another. It is therefore most wise, for a woman to keep the loins of her mind ever girt, to meet such collisions with a cheerful and quiet spirit.

Another important rule, is, to form all plans and arrangements in consistency with the means at command, and the character of those around. A woman who has a heedless husband, and young children, and incompetent domestics, ought not to make such plans, as one may properly form, who will not, in so many directions, meet embarrassment. She must aim at just so much as it is probable she can secure, and no more; and thus she will usually escape much temptation, and much of the irritation of disappointment.

The fifth, and a very important, consideration, is, that *system, economy*, and *neatness*, are valuable, only so far as they tend to promote comfort and the well-being of those affected. Some women seem to act under the impression, that these advantages *must* be secured, at all events, even if the comfort of the family be the sacrifice. True, it is very important that children grow up in habits of system, neatness, and order; and it is very desirable that the mother give them every incentive, both by precept and example: but it is still more important, that they grow up with amiable tempers, that they learn to meet the crosses of life with patience and cheerfulness; and nothing has a greater influence to secure this, than a mother's example. Whenever, therefore, a woman cannot carry her plans of neatness and order, without injury to her own temper, or to the temper of others, she ought to modify and reduce them, until she can.

The sixth method, relates to the government of the tones of voice. In many cases, when a woman's domestic arrangements are suddenly and seriously crossed, it is impossible not to feel some irritation. But it *is* always possible to refrain from angry tones. A woman can resolve, that, whatever happens, she will not speak, till she can do it in a calm and gentle manner. *Perfect silence* is a safe resort, when such control cannot be attained as enables a person to speak calmly; and this determination, persevered in, will eventually be crowned with success.

*   *   *

The last, and most important mode of securing placid and cheerful temper and tones, is, by a right view of the doctrine of a superintending Providence. All persons are too much in the habit of regarding the more important events of life as exclusively under the control of Perfect Wisdom. But the fall of a sparrow, or the loss of a hair, they do not feel to be equally the result of His directing agency. In consequence of this, Christian persons, who aim at perfect and cheerful submission to heavy afflictions, and who succeed, to the edification of all about them, are sometimes sadly deficient under petty crosses. If a beloved child is laid in the grave, even if its death resulted from the carelessness of a domestic, or a physician, the eye is turned from the subordinate agent, to the Supreme Guardian of all, and to Him they bow without murmur or complaint. But if a pudding is burnt, or a room badly swept, or an errand forgotten, then vexation and complaint are allowed, just as if these events were not appointed by Perfect Wisdom, as much as the sorer chastisement.

A woman, therefore, needs to cultivate the *habitual* feeling, that all the events of her nursery and kitchen are brought about by the permission of our Heavenly Father, and that fretfulness and complaint, in regard to these, is, in fact, complaining and disputing at the appointments of God, and are really as sinful, as unsubmissive murmurs amid the sorer chastisements of His hand. And a woman, who will daily cultivate this habit of referring all the events of her life to the wise and benevolent agency of a Heavenly Parent, will soon find it the perennial spring of abiding peace and content.

MARGARET FULLER

From The Great Lawsuit†

Essayist, translator, educator, and journalist, the Massachusetts intellectual Sarah Margaret Fuller (1810–1850) published "The Great
Lawsuit" in 1843; and in 1845 she published an expanded version of
her feminist argument in *Woman in the Nineteenth Century*. In the essay and book, Fuller challenged the notion, championed by Catharine
Beecher and many others, that woman's sphere was in the home as
mother and domestic. Fuller and Hawthorne were friendly during the
early 1840s, and she arguably helped inspire his characterizations
of Hester Prynne in *The Scarlet Letter* (1850) and Zenobia in *The
Blithedale Romance* (1852). In 1846 Fuller traveled to Europe, and
there took up the cause of the Roman revolutionaries. She had a child
out of wedlock with the Roman Giovanni Ossolli, whom she may have
subsequently married. Returning to the United States in April 1850,
Fuller and her family died in a shipwreck off Fire Island, New York. In
an April 1858 notebook entry, Hawthorne expressed his disillusionment
with Fuller, along with a begrudging admiration: "Margaret has not
left, in the hearts and minds of those who knew her, any deep witness
for her integrity and purity. She was a great humbug; of course with
much talent, and much moral reality, or else she could not have been
so great a humbug" (*The French and Italian Notebooks* [1980], 156).

* * * We have waited here long in the dust; we are tired and
hungry, but the triumphal procession must appear at last.

Of all its banners, none has been more steadily upheld, and under none has more valor and willingness for real sacrifices been
shown, than that of the champions of the enslaved African. And
this band it is, which, partly in consequence of a natural following
out of principles, partly because many women have been prominent
in that cause, makes, just now, the warmest appeal in behalf of
woman.

Though there has been a growing liberality on this point, yet society at large is not so prepared for the demands of this party, but
that they are, and will be for some time, coldly regarded as the Ja-
cobins[1] of their day.

"Is it not enough," cries the sorrowful trader, "that you have done
all you could to break up the national Union, and thus destroy the
prosperity of our country, but now you must be trying to break up
family union, to take my wife away from the cradle, and the kitchen

---

† From "The Great Lawsuit. Man *versus* Men. Woman *versus* Women," *The Dial: A Magazine for Literature, Philosophy, and Religion*, 4 (July 1843): 9–14.
1. Radical French revolutionaries of 1789–94.

hearth, to vote at polls, and preach from a pulpit? Of course, if she does such things, she cannot attend to those of her own sphere. She is happy enough as she is. She has more leisure than I have, every means of improvement, every indulgence."

"Have you asked her whether she was satisfied with these indulgences?"

"No, but I know she is. She is too amiable to wish what would make me unhappy, and too judicious to wish to step beyond the sphere of her sex. I will never consent to have our peace disturbed by any such discussions."

" 'Consent'—you? it is not consent from you that is in question, it is assent from your wife."

"Am I not the head of my house?"

"You are not the head of your wife. God has given her a mind of her own."

"I am the head and she the heart."

"God grant you play true to one another then. If the head represses no natural pulse of the heart, there can be no question as to your giving your consent. Both will be of one accord, and there needs but to present any question to get a full and true answer. There is no need of precaution, of indulgence, or consent. But our doubt is whether the heart consents with the head, or only acquiesces in its decree; and it is to ascertain the truth on this point, that we propose some liberating measures."

Thus vaguely are these questions proposed and discussed at present. But their being proposed at all implies much thought, and suggests more. Many women are considering within themselves what they need that they have not, and what they can have, if they find they need it. Many men are considering whether women are capable of being and having more than they are and have, and whether, if they are, it will be best to consent to improvement in their condition.

The numerous party, whose opinions are already labelled and adjusted too much to their mind to admit of any new light, strive, by lectures on some model-woman of bridal-like beauty and gentleness, by writing or lending little treatises, to mark out with due precision the limits of woman's sphere, and woman's mission, and to prevent other than the rightful shepherd from climbing the wall, or the flock from using any chance gap to run astray.

Without enrolling ourselves at once on either side, let us look upon the subject from that point of view which to-day offers. No better, it is to be feared, than a high house-top. A high hill-top, or at least a cathedral spire, would be desirable.

It is not surprising that it should be the Anti-Slavery party that pleads for woman, when we consider merely that she does not hold property on equal terms with men; so that, if a husband dies without a will, the wife, instead of stepping at once into his place as head of the family, inherits only a part of his fortune, as if she were a child, or ward only, not an equal partner.

We will not speak of the innumerable instances, in which profligate or idle men live upon the earnings of industrious wives; or if the wives leave them and take with them the children, to perform the double duty of mother and father, follow from place to place, and threaten to rob them of the children, if deprived of the rights of a husband, as they call them, planting themselves in their poor lodgings, frightening them into paying tribute by taking from them the children, running into debt at the expense of these otherwise so overtasked helots.[2] Though such instances abound, the public opinion of his own sex is against the man, and when cases of extreme tyranny are made known, there is private action in the wife's favor. But if woman be, indeed, the weaker party, she ought to have legal protection, which would make such oppression impossible.

And knowing that there exists, in the world of men, a tone of feeling towards women as towards slaves, such as is expressed in the common phrase, "Tell that to women and children;" that the infinite soul can only work through them in already ascertained limits; that the prerogative of reason, man's highest portion, is allotted to them in a much lower degree; that it is better for them to be engaged in active labor, which is to be furnished and directed by those better able to think, &c. &c.; we need not go further, for who can review the experience of last week, without recalling words which imply, whether in jest or earnest, these views, and views like these? Knowing this, can we wonder that many reformers think that measures are not likely to be taken in behalf of women, unless their wishes could be publicly represented by women?

That can never be necessary, cry the other side. All men are privately influenced by women; each has his wife, sister, or female friends, and is too much biassed by these relations to fail of representing their interests. And if this is not enough, let them propose and enforce their wishes with the pen. The beauty of home would be destroyed, the delicacy of the sex be violated, the dignity of halls of legislation destroyed, by an attempt to introduce them there. Such duties are inconsistent with those of a mother; and then we have ludicrous pictures of ladies in hysterics at the polls, and senate chambers filled with cradles.

But if, in reply, we admit as truth that woman seems destined by nature rather to the inner circle, we must add that the arrangements of civilized life have not been as yet such as to secure it to

2. Serfs or slaves.

her. Her circle, if the duller, is not the quieter. If kept from excitement, she is not from drudgery. Not only the Indian carries the bur-
dens of the camp, but the favorites of Louis the Fourteenth[3]
accompany him in his journeys, and the washerwoman stands at
her tub and carries home her work at all seasons, and in all states
of health.

As to the use of the pen, there was quite as much opposition to
woman's possessing herself of that help to free-agency as there is
now to her seizing on the rostrum or the desk; and she is likely to
draw, from a permission to plead her cause that way, opposite infer-
ences to what might be wished by those who now grant it.

As to the possibility of her filling, with grace and dignity, any
such position, we should think those who had seen the great
actresses, and heard the Quaker preachers of modern times,
would not doubt, that woman can express publicly the fulness of
thought and emotion, without losing any of the peculiar beauty of
her sex.

As to her home, she is not likely to leave it more than she now
does for balls, theatres, meetings for promoting missions, revival
meetings, and others to which she flies, in hope of an animation for
her existence, commensurate with what she sees enjoyed by men.
Governors of Ladies' Fairs are no less engrossed by such a charge,
than the Governor of the State by his; presidents of Washingtonian
societies,[4] no less away from home than presidents of conventions.
If men look straitly to it, they will find that, unless their own lives
are domestic, those of the women will not be. The female Greek, of
our day, is as much in the street as the male, to cry, What news? We
doubt not it was the same in Athens of old. The women, shut out
from the market-place, made up for it at the religious festivals. For
human beings are not so constituted, that they can live without expansion; and if they do not get it one way, must another, or perish.

And, as to men's representing women fairly, at present, while we
hear from men who owe to their wives not only all that is comfortable and graceful, but all that is wise in the arrangement of their
lives, the frequent remark, "You cannot reason with a woman,"
when from those of delicacy, nobleness, and poetic culture, the
contemptuous phrase, "Women and children," and that in no light
sally of the hour, but in works intended to give a permanent statement of the best experiences, when not one man in the million,
shall I say, no, not in the hundred million, can rise above the view
that woman was made *for man*, when such traits as these are daily
forced upon the attention, can we feel that man will always do jus-

---

3. King of France from 1643 to 1715, Louis XIV worked to create a court nobility dependent upon the king.
4. Temperance groups, which began meeting in the early 1840s.

tice to the interests of woman? Can we think that he takes a sufficiently discerning and religious view of her office and destiny, ever to do her justice, except when prompted by sentiment; accidentally or transiently, that is, for his sentiment will vary according to the relations in which he is placed. The lover, the poet, the artist, are likely to view her nobly. The father and the philosopher have some chance of liberality; the man of the world, the legislator for expediency, none.

Under these circumstances, without attaching importance in themselves to the changes demanded by the champions of woman, we hail them as signs of the times. We would have every arbitrary barrier thrown down. We would have every path laid open to woman as freely as to man. Were this done, and a slight temporary fermentation allowed to subside, we believe that the Divine would ascend into nature to a height unknown in the history of past ages, and nature, thus instructed, would regulate the spheres not only so as to avoid collisions but to bring forth ravishing harmony.

J. F. AGNEW

From Woman's Offices and Influence†

Founded in New York City in 1850, *Harper's New Monthly Magazine* grew to a circulation of two hundred thousand by 1860. J. F. Agnew, the author of this essay, is perhaps the relatively little known John Holmes Agnew (1804–1865), a publisher and editor who, during the 1840s, lived in New York City. In the magazine, the essay is attributed to "Prof. J. F. Agnew, University of Michigan."

Ours is an age of stirring life, an age of notions and novelties, of invention and enterprise, of steam-motives[1] and telegraph-wires. The ocean, for passage, has become a river. The air a medium for the flight, not only of birds, but of thoughts. Distance scarce any more lends enchantment to the view, for 'tis annihilated. The ends of the earth meet, and the watchmen on her walls see eye to eye. Even worlds long buried in the deep unknown are now revealed to human vision, and we almost penetrate the arcana of our own fair satellite, as she nightly looks down upon us in her beauty. And man would fain believe, too, in his wisdom, or his folly, that e'en the rappings of spirits are heard in this nether planet of ours.

---

† From "Woman's Offices and Influence," *Harper's New Monthly Magazine,* 30 (October 1851): 654–55. The essay directly precedes Herman Melville's "The Town-Ho's Story" (pp. 658–65), the only chapter from *Moby-Dick* that Melville published before the book itself.

1. Probably a printer's error for *steam-motors.*

But what of all this? Why, we live in this whirl of galvanic motion: we breathe this excited atmosphere: we revolve on this stirring sphere. And, think you, without feeling aught of its forces?

We have our being, too, amid the busy scenes of a new world, a free world, a forming world. Our geologic species is a conglomerate. Whether it shall be of rude, unshapen masses, or of polished gems, fit not only for the pillars of this republican edifice, but for its adornment also, will depend much on the present generation, more on the women of that generation.

Believing that woman not only takes impressions from the age, but emphatically makes them on it too, I select for my theme WOMAN'S OFFICES AND INFLUENCE.

To make home happy is one of the offices of woman. Home, blessed word. Thanks to our Saxon fathers for it. Not the name merely, but the realities it expresses. An English, an American home is a Bethlehem-star[2] in the horizon of earth's sorrows, the shadow of a great rock in a weary land.

> "There is a magic in that little word:
> It is a mystic circle that surrounds
> Comforts and virtues never known beyond
> The hallowed limit."[3]

> "The tabernacle of our earthly joys
> And sorrows, hopes and fears—this Home of ours
> Is it not pleasant?"[4]

Yes, home is the centre of all that is sweet in the sympathies, dear in the affections of the soul. There the kiss of love is impressed in its purity, the warm pressure of the hand knows no betrayal, the smile of joy plays no deceiver's part. All is candid, cordial, sincere. The faults and failings which belong to humanity fallen, are there covered by the mantle of charity, and the feeling of every member of the family is, "With all thy faults I love thee still."[5] * * *

Beautiful in the family is this spirit of cheerfulness; and surely it is an office of woman to cherish it. It can be wooed and won. Wherever woman goes, and especially at home, let it be as an halo of light around her head, and then shall she be a blessing to the circle in which she moves. Despondency is death, cheerfulness life. But remember that levity and boisterous mirth are no essential ingredients of this wholesome cordial. Its chief element is rather that

---

2. The star leading the wise men of the east to the birthplace of Jesus Christ (Matthew 2:1–7).
3. From "Hymn to the Penates (1797), 256–59, by Robert Southey (1774–1843).
4. From *The Dream of Life* (1843), 4:678–80, by John Moultrie (1794–1874).
5. From *The Task* (1785), 2:206, by William Cowper (1731–1800).

which Paul spake of when he said, "I have learned in whatsoever state I am, therewith to be content."[6]

Another office of woman is, *to check the utilitarianism, the money-loving spirit of the day.* There is something beside bread and water to be cared for in this probationary world of ours, inhabited by living *spirits.* And yet one is almost compelled to the conclusion that the whole race, at the present day, has given itself up to the worship of Mammon. * * *

Here is a wide field of influence for woman. You are the vestal virgins to watch the fires on the altar of the fine arts. Yours it is to check the sensuousness of man, to recall him from his ceaseless toil after the mammon of this life, his restless ambition to turn every thing to account in available funds, in bank-stocks, copper-stocks, railroad-stocks. Tell your sons and your sires that there are higher sources of joy. Point them away from earth's sordid gold to the brighter gems of literature. Direct their energies to the intellectual and moral advancement of their age. Help them to slake their quenchless thirst at the pure fountains of knowledge and religion.

There is a poetry of life worth cultivating. There are spiritual entities around us to which we are linked by ethereal chains. Let us not struggle to throw off those chains, but rather to bind them faster about us. And when you see a link broken, and others likely to drop, mend it.

Woman's office is it also *to soften political asperities in the other sex, and themselves to shun political publicity.* Not that woman need be ignorant of the great questions of the age; better be familiar with them. But let her not become absorbed in them: rather keep so aloof from exciting occasions as to be better qualified to form and express a deliberate and unbiased judgment on men and measures. Let her opinions be well matured, and always uttered with calmness and caution. When her dearest friends of the other sex seem embittered toward others, and in danger of forgetting the sweet charities of life amid the chafings of party rivalry, let her pour out the milk of human kindness into the cup of courtesy, and ask them to drink of it. When the waters are troubled and the billows roar, let her diffuse over them the oil of love to still the waters into a great calm. Surely this is an office higher, better far, than to be pressing on, as some would have her, into the busy bustle of out-door politics. Here is *influence*, and it is better than *power.*

Who that loves woman, that really admires her worth as *woman*, that thinks of her as the delicate, refined, tasteful, sensitive development of humanity, the incarnation of all that is lovely, gentle, modest, peaceful, and pure, the highest earthly manifestation of

6. Cf. St. Paul's Epistle to the Philippians 4:11.

God as *love*; who that remembers her as the "help-meet," can bear the thought of hurrying her out upon the theatre of politics, the platform of legislation?

"Woman's rights," they cry, and so loud the cry, that even woman's ambition has conquered her judgment and her delicacy, and she has gone forth, out of her appointed and fitting sphere, to be gazed on by a curious crowd, and perhaps to hear the plaudits of a noisy populace, *O tempora! O mores!*[7] Save us from such a race of women!

---

7. Alas for the times and the manners! (Latin).

Daguerreotypy and Other Technologies

Hawthorne's most modern work, *The House of the Seven Gables* draws on, and indeed can seem to be inspired by, the exciting technological developments of the period. Daguerreotypy, railroads, the telegraph, electricity, mesmerism, transatlantic travel on Cunard steamships, and even prisons are among the technologies that find their way into the novel. Daguerreotypy is at the novel's very center, which is not surprising given that daguerreotypy, like writing, was a form of representation. An early form of photography pioneered by the Parisian Louis Jacques Mandé Daguerre (1789–1851), daguerreotypy came to the United States in 1839 and was an instant sensation. This section includes five documents that chart the cultural excitement and concerns about this new photographic process, in which a photographic image was produced on a silver-coated copper plate treated with heated mercury.

Also making its way to the United States in the late 1830s, and central to *The House of the Seven Gables*, was the "science" of mesmerism, or hypnotisim, which had been pioneered by the Austrian physician Franz Anton Mesmer (1734–1815). As the mesmerist Charles Poyen's account of his 1836 New England tour suggests, mesmerists believed that their ability to control the mind of the hypnotized medium could bring about individual and social health. In a letter written to his fiancée, Sophia Peabody, five years after Poyen's visit, Hawthorne expressed his concerns about the intrusive methods of this science, though his depiction of Holgrave in *The House of the Seven Gables* reveals that he recognized the similarities between the storyteller and the mesmerist.

Selections on two other technologies conclude this section. Emphasizing solitude and labor, the new prisons of the Northeast, as documented by Gustave de Beaumont and Alexis de Tocqueville, were designed to exert a certain control over the mind of the imprisoned, not all that different from that of the mesmerist over the medium, bringing forth the social health that would allow the prisoner to return to society as a productive citizen. Such a citizen could then embrace yet another new technology of the period, the railroad, which had been introduced into the United States in the late 1820s. In the final piece of the section, Hawthorne reflects on his own railroad ride in ways that look forward to his representation of the railroad ride of the recently released Clifford, a character described in *The House of the Seven*

Gables as having "the close prison-atmosphere yet lurking in his breath" (156).

NATHANIEL PARKER WILLIS

From The Pencil of Nature: A New Discovery†

A magazine editor, essayist, travel writer, and overall man of letters, Nathaniel Parker Willis (1806–1867) emerged during the 1830s and 1840s as a celebrity in the New York literary scene. A controversial figure, he was scorned by many for his vanity. For example, his own sister, Sarah Payson Willis (1811–1872), who wrote under the name of Fanny Fern, depicted him as a malicious dandy in her popular autobiographical novel *Ruth Hall* (1855). In his 1839 essay on daguerreotypy published in his own New York weekly, *The Corsair*, Willis became one of the first in the United States to report on the new technology.

We know not how it is, but just as we are going to have something good in this world, up starts a mischief to mar it or to vilify it. There is not a real panacea, but has its rival. Engraving, set upon a firm basis, one would have thought might have been supreme. No such a thing—her illegitimate sister, Lithography,[1] sets up her claim, and by means of cheap publications, calls in the masses, who naturally prefer the inferior article; and here commences the democracy of art. Print shops have increased out of number—print auctions are every where; so that, if all the world do not become judges of art, it cannot be for lack of means to make them acquainted with it.

There is no breathing space—all is one great movement. Where are we going? Who can tell? The phantasmagoria of inventions passes rapidly before us—are we to see them no more?—are they to be obliterated? Is the hand of man to be altogether stayed in his work?—the wit active—the fingers idle? Wonderful wonder of wonders!! Vanish equa-tints and mezzotints[2]—as chimneys that consume their own smoke, devour yourselves. Steel engravers, copper engravers, and etchers, drink up your aquafortis,[3] and die! There is an end of your black art—"Othello's occupation's gone."[4] The real black art of true magic arises and cries avaunt. All nature shall

---

† From "The Pencil of Nature: A New Discovery," *The Corsair: A Gazette of Literature, Art, Dramatic Criticism, Fashion, and Novelty* 1 (April 13, 1839): 70–72.
1. A printing process that makes use of a flat stone or metallic substance.
2. Printing processes making use of copper or steel.
3. Acids used for printing as well as colloquial for strong drink.
4. From Shakespeare, *Othello* (1604), III.iii.373, spoken by Othello when the distressed black Moor is convinced by Iago of Desdemona's sexual profligacy.

paint herself—fields, rivers, trees, houses, plains, mountains, cities, shall all paint themselves at a bidding, and at a few moments' notice. Towns will not longer have any representatives but themselves. Invention says it. It has found out the one thing new under the sun; that, by virtue of the sun's patent, all nature, animate and inanimate, shall be henceforth its own painter, engraver, printer, and publisher. Here is a revolution in art; and, that we may not be behindhand in revolutions, for which we have so imitative a taste, no sooner does one start up in Paris, but we must have one in London too. And so Mr. Daguerre's invention is instantly rivalled by Mr. Fox Talbot's.[5] The Daguerroscope and the Photogenic revolutions are to keep you all down, ye painters, engravers, and, alas! the harmless race, the sketchers. All ye, before whose unsteady hands towers have toppled down upon the paper, and the pagodas of the East have bowed, hide your heads in holes and corners, and wait there till you are called for. The "mountain in labor" will no more produce a mouse;[6] it will produce itself, with all that is upon it. Ye artists of all denominations that have so vilified nature as her journeymen, see how she rises up against you, and takes the staff into her own hands. Your mistress now, with a vengeance, she will show you what she really is, and that the cloud is not "very like a whale."[7] * * *

Here, in truth, is a discovery launched upon the world, that must make a revolution in art. It is impossible, at first view, not to be amused at the sundry whimsical views the coming changes present. But, to speak more seriously, in what way, in what degree, will art be affected by it? Art is of two kinds, or more properly speaking, has two walks, the imaginative and the imitative; the latter may, indeed, greatly assist the former, but, in the *strictly* imitative, imagination may not enter but to do mischief. They may be considered therefore, as the two only proper walks. It must be evident that the higher, the imaginative, cannot immediately be affected by the new discovery—it is not tangible to its power—the poetry of the mind cannot be submitted to this material process; but there is a point of view in which it may be highly detrimental to genius, which, being but a power over materials, must collect with pains and labor, and acquire a *facility* of drawing. Now, it is manifest that, if the artist can lay up a store of objects without the (at first very tedious) process of correct drawing, both his mind and his hand will fail him; the mind will not readily supply what it does not know practi-

5. The Englishman William Henry Fox Talbot (1800–1877) began to develop the modern photographic process, involving the use of negatives, in the mid-1830s.
6. In the Aesop fable, a crowd of people anxiously watches a mountain that they believe is on the verge of exploding, only to see the emergence of a mouse.
7. An allusion to Shakespeare, *Hamlet* (1601), III.ii.367. Hamlet and then Polonius identify a cloud as looking first like a weasel and then like a whale.

cally and familiarly, and the hand must be crippled when brought
to execute what it has not previously supplied as a sketch. Who will
make elaborate drawings from statues or from life, if he can be supplied in a more perfect, a more true manner, and in the space of a
few minutes, either with the most simple or the most complicated
forms? How very few will apply themselves to a drudgery, the benefits of which are to be so remote, as an ultimate improvement, and
will forego for that hope, which genius may be most inclined
to doubt, immediate possession? But if genius could really be
schooled to severe discipline, the new discovery, by new and most
accurate forms, might greatly aid conception. If this view be correct, we may have fewer artists; but those few, who will "spurn delights and live laborious days,"[8] will arrive at an eminence which no
modern, and possibly no ancient master has reached.

ANONYMOUS

From Daguerreotypes†

For our own part we are unable to conceive any limits to the
progress of this art. On the contrary it tasks the imagination to conjecture what it will *not* accomplish. * * * Indeed, it will be impossible for a tree to bud and blossom, a flower to go to seed, or a
vegetable to sprout and come up, without executing at the same
time an exact photograph of the wonderful process on the skillfully
prepared plates of some agricultural, botanical, or horticultural
photographic society. A man cannot make a proposal, or a lady decline one—a steam-boiler cannot explode, or an ambitious river
overflow its banks—a gardener cannot elope with an heiress, or a
reverend bishop commit an indiscretion, but straightway, an officious daguerreotype will proclaim the whole affair to the world.
There will be no safety for rogues. Every apple-orchard, store-
house, and coat-pocket, will contain a self-regulating photographic
machine faithfully performing *its* functions, while the depredator is
executing *his*.

But we turn from contemplating the anticipated achievements of
the future, to dwell for a moment on the brilliant triumphs of the
past. For we are of the opinion that the daguerrian art has not received the attention which it deserves; and that its principles, when

---

8. An allusion to "Lycidas" (1638), a poem by John Milton (1608–1674) on the drowning
of his friend. Milton writes: "Fame is the spur that the clear spirit doth raise / (That last
infirmity of Noble mind) / To scorn delights and live laborious dayes" (lines 70–72).
† From "Daguerreotypes," *Littell's Living Age*, 20 (June 1846): 551–52. Founded in 1844
in Boston, *Littell's* was an eclectic journal focusing on literature and culture.

fully analyzed and developed, will fill an important place in some never-to-be-surpassed encyclopedia.

It is slowly accomplishing a great revolution in the morals of portrait painting. The flattery of countenance delineators, is notorious. No artist of eminence ever painted an ugly face, unless perchance, now and then a fancy sketch, or a copy of some antique, *so* antique that it is impossible ever to trace the original. Everybody who pays, must look handsome, intellectual, or interesting at least—on canvass. These abuses of the brush the photographic art is happily designed to correct. Your sun is no parasite. He pours his rays as freely and willingly into the cottage of the peasant, as into the palace of the peer; and he vouchsafes no brighter or purer light to the disdainful mistress than to her humble maid. Let it once become the *bon ton*[1] for plain-looking, homely, and ugly people to sit for likenesses that *are* likenesses—let a few hideous men and women of distinction consent to be daguerreotyped—in fine, let nature and art in their combined efforts be suffered to have fair play, and "it must follow as the night the day," that this moral revolution will be achieved. There are gratifying proofs that the custom is rapidly advancing into general favor; as any one may convince himself by examining the numerous daguerreotypes exposed to public view.

But of the advantages resulting from this novel art, the aid which it affords to the successful study of human nature, is among the most important. Daguerreotypes properly regarded, are the indices of human character. Lavater judged of men by their physiognomies; and in a voluminous treatise has developed the principles by which he was guided.[2] The photograph, we consider to be the grand climacteric of the science. Lord Chesterfield[3] assures his son that everybody has a weak point, which if you are fortunate enough to touch or irritate delivers him into your power at once. It has been said that the inhalation of exhilarating gas is a powerful artificial agent for disclosing these weaknesses of human nature. In reality, however, the sitting for a daguerreotype, far surpasses all other expedients. There is a peculiar and irresistible connection between one's weaknesses and his daguerreotype; and the latter as naturally attracts the former as the magnet the needle, or toasted cheese, the rat.

---

1. Good manner; the style (French).
2. Johann Kaspar Lavater (1741–1801), Swiss theologian, poet, and scientist. In his *Physiognomische Fragmente* (1775–1778), he attempted to develop a science of physiognomy, arguing that particular facial features revealed particular aspects of character.
3. Philip Dormer Stanhope, fourth earl of Chesterfield (1694–1773), English statesman and author who was best known for his conduct book, *Letters to His Son* (1774).

RALPH WALDO EMERSON

[Sea and Shore]†

Ralph Waldo Emerson (1803–1882) is best known for his philosophical essays, such as *Nature* (1836) and "The Over-Soul" (1841). But his notebooks and journals reveal an ongoing interest in technology and science. The entry printed here, from 1846, is one of a number on daguerreotypy.

Daguerrotype gives the sculpture of the face, but omits the expression, the painter aims at the expression & comes far short of Daguerre in the form and organism. But we must have sea and shore, the flowing & the fixed, in every work of art. On the sitter the effect of the Daguerrotypist is asinizing.

T. S. ARTHUR

The Daguerreotypist‡

Author of the best-selling temperance novel *Ten Nights in a Bar-room and What I Saw There* (1854), T. S. (Timothy Shay) Arthur (1809–1885) was one of the most widely read writers of the antebellum period. He wrote on a range of social reforms and developments from his home city of Philadelphia while editing various journals, including *Arthur's Home Magazine* (1853–85). His 1849 essay on daguerreotypy captured the excitement and wonder of the increasingly popular technology.

If our children and children's children to the third and fourth generation are not in possession of portraits of their ancestors, it will be no fault of the Daguerreotypists of the present day; for, verily, they are limning faces at a rate that promises soon to make every man's house a Daguerrean Gallery. From little Bess, the baby, up to great great grandpa', all must now have their likenesses; and even the sober Friend,[1] who heretofore rejected all the vanities of portrait-taking, is tempted to sit in the operator's chair, and quick as thought, his features are caught and fixed by a sunbeam. In our great cities, a Daguerreotypist is to be found in almost every

---

† Journal entry of May 1846, in *Emerson in His Journals*, ed. Joel Porte (Cambridge: Harvard University Press, 1982), 353.
‡ From "The Daguerreotypist," *Godey's Lady's Book*, 35 (May 1849): 352–55.
1. Quaker.

square; and there is scarcely a county in any state that has not one or more of these industrious individuals busy at work in catching "the shadow" ere the "substance fade." A few years ago it was not every man who could afford a likeness of himself, his wife or his children; these were luxuries known to those only who had money to spare; now it is hard to find the man who has not gone through the "operator's" hands from once to half-a-dozen times, or who has not the shadowy faces of his wife and children done up in purple morocco and velvet, together or singly, among his household treasures. Truly the sunbeam art is a most wonderful one, and the public feel it is a great benefit!

If a painter's studio is a place in which to get glimpses of human nature, how much more so the Daguerreotypist's operating-room, where dozens come daily, and are finished off in a sitting of half a minute. Scenes ludicrous, amusing or pathetic, are constantly occurring. People come for their portraits who have never seen the operation, and who have not the most distant conception of how the thing is done. Some, in taking their places in the chair, get so nervous that they tremble like aspens; and others, in the vain attempt to keep their features composed, distort them so much that they are frightened at their own image when it is placed in their hands.

Some months ago, a well-conditioned farmer from the interior of the state, arrived in Philadelphia, and after selling his produce and making sundry purchases, recollected that he had promised, on leaving home, that he would bring back his Daguerreotype. It was all a piece of nonsense, he had argued; but his argument was of no avail, for wife and daughters said that he must do as they wished, and so he had yielded an easy compliance. On inquiry, he was told that Root[2] was the man for him; so one bright morning he took his way down Chestnut street to the gallery of the far-famed Daguerreotypist. Mr. Root was at home, of course, and ready to accommodate the farmer, who, after looking at sundry portraits, asking prices and making his own remarks on all he saw, was invited to walk up into the operating-room.

"Where?" inquired the farmer, looking curious.

"Into the operating-room," replied Mr. Root, as he moved towards the door.

The farmer was not sure yet that he had heard correctly, but he did not like to ask again, so he followed on; but it sounded in his ears very much as if Mr. Root had said "operating"-room, and the only idea he had of "operations" was the cutting off of legs and

2. Marcus Aurelius Root (1808–1888), noted daguerreotypist and photographer based in Philadelphia and New York.

arms. However, up stairs he want, with his dog close behind him, and was soon introduced into a room in the third story.

"Now, sir," said Mr. Root—smiling, as the farmer thought, a little strangely—"we will see what we can do for you. Take a seat in that chair."

The farmer sat down, feeling a little uneasy, for he did not much like the appearance of things. Besides Mr. Root, there was another man in the room, and he felt that if any unfair play were attempted, they would prove too much for him. This idea, as it clearly presented itself, seemed so ridiculous that he tried to thrust it away, but he could not. There was a mysterious ticking in the room, for which he could not account. It was like the sound of a clock, and yet not like it. He glanced around, but could not perceive the source from whence it came. At one moment it seemed to be under the floor near his feet, then in the ceiling, and next in a far corner of the room.

As he took his place in the chair that had been pointed out, Mr. Root drew a singular-looking apparatus into the middle of the floor, and directed towards him the muzzle of what seemed a small brass cannon. At the same time, the other man placed his hand upon his head and drew it back into an iron clamp, the cold touch of which made the blood in his veins curdle to his very heart.

The farmer was a man who both took and read the newspapers, and through these he had become acquainted with many cases of "mysterious disappearance." Men with a few hundred dollars in their pockets—such as was then his own case—had been inveigled among robbers and murderers, and he might now be in one of their dens of iniquity. This fear once excited, every movement of the two men, who were acting in concert, but confirmed his suspicions. Their mysterious signs, their evident preparation to act together at a particular moment, all helped to excite still farther his alarm. It was more than human nature—at least the farmer's human nature—could stand; for, springing suddenly from the chair, he caught up his hat, and, escaping from the room, dashed down stairs as if a legion of evil spirits were after him, to the no small amusement of the two "operators," who, though they lost a customer, had a good joke to laugh over for a month.

The different impressions made upon sitters is curious enough. The most common is the illusion that the instrument exercises a kind of magnetic attraction, and many good ladies actually feel their eyes "drawn" towards the lens while the operation is in progress! Others perceive an impression as if a draft of cold air were blowing on their faces, while a few are affected with a pricking sensation, while the perspiration starts from every pore. A sense of suffocation is a common feeling among persons of delicate nerves and lively fancies, who find it next to impossible to sit still; and on leaving the chair, they catch their breath and pant as if they had been in a vacuum. No wonder so many Daguerreotypes have a strange, surprised look, or an air as if the original was ill at ease in his or her mind. Of course, these various impressions are all the result of an excited imagination and an *effort* to sit perfectly still and look composed. Forced ease is actual constraint, and must appear so. In Daguerreotype portraits this is particularly apparent.

* * * Not a great while ago, one of our Daguerreotypists observed in his rooms an old lady in deep mourning. She was a stranger, and was looking with evident eagerness along the walls at the various portraits that were exhibited as specimens of the art. All at once she uttered a low exclamation, and then sank half fainting upon a sofa. Water was brought to her, and after a little while she was restored to self-possession. She then stated that news of the death of her only daughter, a resident in the west, had been received by her a few days before. Remembering that a likeness had been taken a short time previous to her going to the west, the faint hope had crossed her mind that there might be a duplicate in the rooms of the Daguerreotypist. She had found it, and gazed once more into the almost speaking face of her child!

Another incident quite as touching occurred at the same establishment. A mother came with her first and only child, a bright little boy of four years, to sit for her likeness. The father was along, and, at his instance,[3] the child was placed on the mother's lap. The image of the little boy was beautiful, but the mother's picture was not good. It was then decided that the mother should sit alone, and that they would have the child taken when he was a few years older. As they were going away, the operator tried to persuade them to take the other picture also, the likeness of the child being such an admirable one. They hesitated, but finally concluded not to do so, saying that after he was a little older they would get his portrait taken; and so they went away. Three months afterwards the mother came again. She was in deep mourning. Her boy was dead. She had come in hopes that the picture of the child might still be in existence. But, alas! it was not so. Search was made among old and rejected plates in hopes that it might not have been rubbed out, but after looking for a day or two, the mother coming frequently during the time, the search was abandoned as hopeless. The shadow, fixed in a wonderful and mysterious manner by a ray of light, had faded also, and the only image of the child that remained for the mother was on the tablet of her memory.

It is often a matter of surprise to some that two portraits of the

---

3. Insistence.

same person by different Daguerreotypists should appear so unlike, it being supposed, at first thought, that nothing more than mechanical skill was required in the individual managing the instrument, and that it was only necessary for the image of the face to enter the lens and impress itself upon the chemically-prepared plate, to have a correct likeness; but this is an error. Unless the Daguerreotypist be an artist, or have the educated eye of an artist, he cannot take good pictures, except by the merest accident; for, unless the sitter be so placed as to throw the shadow on his face in a certain relation to his prominent features, a distortion will appear, and the picture, therefore, fail to give satisfaction. The painter can soften the shadows on the face of his sitter so as to make them only serve the purpose for which he uses them, but the Daguerreotype exercises no discrimination, and reflects the sitter just as he presents himself. It was owing to bad positions and bad management of light that the earlier Daguerreotypists made such strange-looking pictures of faces, one side of which would be a dark shadow and the other a white surface, in which features were scarcely distinguishable. But great improvements have taken place, and some establishments are turning out pictures of remarkable beauty and excellence.

In order to obtain a good picture, it is necessary to go to a Daguerreotypist who has the eye and taste of an artist, or who employs such a person in his establishment; and it is also necessary to dress in colors that do not reflect too much light. For a lady, a good dress is of some dark or figured material. White, pink or light blue must be avoided. Lace work, or a scarf or shawl sometimes adds much to the beauty of the picture. A gentleman should wear a dark vest and cravat. For children, a plaid or dark-striped or figured dress is preferred by most Daguerreotypists. Light dresses are in all cases to be avoided.

The strong shadows that appear in Daguerreotype portraits are a sad annoyance to many who, like Queen Elizabeth, see no such blemish on their faces when they consult their mirrors. "Can't you take me a likeness without these dark places?" asks a lady who sees, with surprise, a dirty mark under her nose, around her eyes, under her chin, or on the side of her cheek. "There is nothing like this on my face." "Why is my neck so black?" asks another; while another would like her picture well enough if the face were "not so smutty." A lady with a fair skin, upon which the sun has left some minute brown marks, which are almost hidden by the warm flush of health, is startled to find them faithfully recorded in her picture, and made so dark as to appear like serious blemishes. "What are these? There is nothing like them on my face?" she inquires, with a look of disappointment. The artist cannot tell her that her face is "freckled," and so makes some evasive excuse, and tries the experiment again;

but with no better success, for the all-discovering light will make no discrimination—the little black specks are still there, and the lady goes away with a poor conceit of the Daguerreotypist, who, though he could make the light work for him, could not force it to record anything but the truth.

FREDERICK DOUGLASS

[Our Photographic Process]†

Following the publication of his *Narrative* (1845), Frederick Douglass (1818–1895) emerged as the best known and most influential African American antislavery writer and lecturer. Accordingly, he was often the subject of photographs. In a lecture of December 3, 1861, at Boston's Tremont Temple, Douglass commented on the relatively new technology.

That Daguerre, has supplied a great want, is seen less in Eulogys bestowed upon his name, than in the rapidity and universality, with which his invention has been adopted. The smallest town now has its Daguerrian Gallery; and even at the cross roads—where stood but a solitary Blacksmith shop and what was once a country Tavern but now in the last stages of dilapidation—you will find the inevitable Daguerrian Gallery. Shaped like a baggage car, with a hot house window at the top—adorned with red curtains resting on gutterpurchia[1] springs and wooden wheels painted yellow. The farmer boy gets an iron shoe for his horse, and metallic picture for himself at the same time, and at the same price. * * *

Byron[2] says, a man always looks *dead*, when his Biography is written. The same is even more true when his picture is taken. There is ever something statue like about such men. See them when or where you will, and unless they are totally off guard, they are either serenely sitting, or rigidly standing in what they fancy their best attitude for a picture.

The stern serenity of our photographic processes, in tracing the features, and forms of men, might deter some of us from operation, but for that most kind natural Providence, by which, most men easily see in themselves points of beauty and excellence, which wholly ellude [*sic*] the observation of all others.

† From "Pictures and Progress: An Address Delivered in Boston, Massachusetts, on 3 December 1861," in *The Frederick Douglass Papers: Series One: Speeches, Debates, and Interviews. Volume 3: 1855–63* ed. John W. Blassingame et al. (New Haven: Yale University Press, 1985), 454–55.
1. I.e., gutta-percha, made from the gum of a sap tree.
2. The English romantic poet George Gordon Lord Byron (1788–1824).

CHARLES POYEN

[Animal Magnetism]†

In 1836 the French emigrant Charles Poyen (dates unknown) toured New England and performed mesmerical feats with subjects before public audiences. The performances were written up in the local newspapers and ignited widespread interest in the new "science." Influenced by the mesmerical theories of Franz Mesmer, Poyen also developed techniques derived from his observation earlier in the 1830s of vodoun practices on Caribbean sugar plantations. In the selection printed here, from his 1837 book on his New England tour, Poyen describes a well-publicized performance in Boston.

Animal Magnetism being * * * a science of observation, has not ceased to gain ground more and more rapidly, although violently and generally opposed, because the results of positive experiments proved stronger than all the arguments used against it. It is not advocated from "*a priori views*,"[1] or on the ground that it agrees with the religious or philosophical prejudices of man, &c. On the contrary, it apparently attacks and overturns all the received notions of the present generation, all that has been inculcated upon us by philosophy and education! It changes materially, in several points, the mental constitution of mankind. Far from being enthusiastically led into a belief in the reality of it, those who begin the investigation of its claims, are at first decided skeptics; they proceed with diffidence and care in their examination, and, in order to satisfy their mind fully, they do not resort to reasoning, but to repeated, sifted, and positive experiments.

Some will reply, that "*witchcraft*," which is now generally acknowledged to have been a gross and lamentable superstition, was likewise pretended to be founded on facts; that it was, for centuries, believed in by all classes of society, and countenanced even by a crowd of distinguished men, some of whom were the greatest geniuses of their time, &c. We answer, that witchcraft originated from an "*a priori notion*," from a mere article of faith, viz. the belief in the existence of the devil, and in his influence on human affairs. This belief had been handed down from the very beginning of society; it was deeply impressed on the public mind through education, religious doctrines, and social institutions; it had thus become a profound and powerful element of the mental constitution of

---

† From *Progress of Animal Magnetism in New England* (Boston: Weeks, Jordan & Co., 1837), 27–29, 78–82. Poyen's footnotes have been deleted.
1. Views existing in the mind prior to experience or observation.

mankind. The infernal agency being admitted as an indisputable truth, people were forcibly led into the most serious and absurd errors; every thing that appeared strange, was immediately attributed to the diabolical interference; even on some occasions, the public mind was so much engrossed and perverted by that superstition, that they mistook very plain, yea, common natural effects, for evident proofs of an intercourse existing between certain individuals and the evil spirit. Such was, to quote an instance, the witchcraft delusion in Salem, Massachusetts. * * * Now Animal Magnetism did not originate, like witchcraft, from any preconceived idea or popular notion; its claims are not founded on a mere article of faith; and those who have assented to a belief in its reality, had not within themselves, like the partisans of witchcraft, a cause of error. Animal Magnetism, I repeat, sprung from observation; Mesmer and all his disciples have claimed for it the title of natural science; they have constantly endeavored to combat superstition, and remove all remaining prejudices concerning the influence of spiritual agents, by contending and showing that the phenomena once attributed to the action of the devil, are the results of a peculiar modification of which the nervous organization of man is susceptible, when placed in certain circumstances.

*   *   *

I offer the following statement, merely as a specimen of some of the experiments which I usually perform, and that have already been seen by upwards of one hundred individuals of this city [Boston].

These experiments took place on Saturday evening, [February] 4th inst.[2] I put Miss Gleason to the magnetic sleep towards a quarter past seven o'clock. The operation did not last more than a minute and a half. At half past seven, some company which I expected, arrived, and found the lady on her rocking-chair, motionless, with her eyes closed, and exactly as a person delivered up to the natural sleep. Among the gentlemen present, were Dr. C. T. Jackson, Dr. H. Dewar, Messrs. Clark, H. K. Horton, Andrew Morse, Jr., well known by his ingenious and useful inventions in mechanics, Wilson Dana, a lawyer in Charlestown.[3]

Various attempts were made to awake Miss Gleason, but without success. Dr. Jackson examined the state of her eyes, and it was found that the lids were firmly closed, and resisted very much against the efforts which were made to open them. Being thus partially opened, the eye-balls were seen turned upward, and convulsed; the white of the eye, only, could be seen.

2. This account of Poyen's experiments on one Miss Gleason first appeared in the *Boston Courier* of February 10, 1837.
3. Boston-area professional elites, none of whom has achieved lasting notice.

Two gentlemen, in succession, shook her, spoke to her in a loud voice, and took her hand, but could not obtain a word from her. Then I approached and spoke to her, in a tone much lower, and she answered immediately the question I proposed to her.

Some time having elapsed in general conversation, a gentleman came to me, and asked me whether I could make the somnambulist talk with another person, and cause her to cease speaking by my will. I answered, that I thought I could.

Two handkerchiefs, folded up several times, were tied over Miss Gleason's eyes and face, down to the opening of the nostrils. It was agreed that a gentleman should stand behind the somnambulist's chair, in order to give the signal when to act. One of the gentlemen took the position, holding a pencil-case in his hand. The signals agreed upon were, that when the pencil was held horizontally, I could cause Miss Gleason to speak; when it was held vertically, I would cause her to stop speaking.

Dr. Jackson sat by Miss Gleason's right side, and I stood about one foot and a half distant from her left side, stooping, with both my hands leaning on my knees; my mouth was about on the level with the top of Miss Gleason's head.

Dr. Jackson began to talk, but obtained no answer. The pencil was placed on the horizontal line. Dr. Jackson put some other question—then Miss Gleason turned her head towards him, and answered his questions readily. The pencil was placed vertically, immediately the somnambulist ceased speaking. The pencil was held again horizontally, and she resumed the conversation. These experiments were made four or five times in succession, and always successfully. They were pronounced satisfactory by all the gentlemen. The bandages were removed; then I said aloud to the somnambulist, "Why have you spoken with Dr. Jackson, at times?" She answered—"Because you *told me to*." "Why did you cease to talk with him?" "Because you *told me to*." Now, it is a fact, that I did not move my lips once. None of those who were around, watching my motions, could discover any thing of the kind; neither did I touch the somnambulist; consequently, she was influenced by my will only. * * *

Some moments after this, Miss Gleason called me, and begged for some water. A tumbler was brought in; Dr. Jackson took it, and presented it to the somnambulist, even pressed it against her lip, but she took no notice of it. The tumbler was handed to me; I presented it to Miss Gleason, at some distance from her face, without speaking a word; then she stretched out her hand, grasped it, and drank part of the water. Dr. Dewar presented his hand to receive the tumbler; the somnambulist took no notice of him; he then took hold of the glass, and made considerable efforts to pull it, by force, from Miss Gleason's hand, but she resisted so strongly, that the gentleman was obliged to leave it off, for fear that she would break it, and hurt her fingers. Then I presented my hand, and willed her to give me the tumbler; she first put it to her lips, drank again two or three swallows, and *gave it back to me.*

These experiments, as well as the preceding, were declared satisfactory.

NATHANIEL HAWTHORNE

[Love Is the True Magnetism]†

Around the time that Charles Poyen helped popularize mesmerism in New England, Sophia Peabody (1809–1871), whom Hawthorne would marry in 1842, began to experience debilitating headaches. In search of a cure, she sought out regular mesmerical treatments with one Dr. Joseph Fiske of Salem, and then in 1840 turned to her friend Cornelia Park for similar treatments. Writing from the associative community of Brook Farm in West Roxbury, Massachusetts, Hawthorne, who had not known of Sophia's previous experiences with mesmerism, expressed his concerns.

Brook Farm, October 18th, Saturday [1841]

Most dear wife,[1] I received thy letter and note, last night, and was much gladdened by them; for never has my soul so yearned for thee as now. But, belovedest, my spirit is moved to talk to thee to day about these magnetic miracles, and to beseech thee to take no part in them. I am unwilling that a power should be exercised on thee, of which we know neither the origin nor the consequence, and the phenomena of which seem rather calculated to bewilder us, than to teach us any truths about the present or future state of being. If I possessed such a power over thee, I should not dare to exercise it; nor can I consent to its being exercised by another. Supposing that this power arises from the transfusion of one spirit into another, it seems to me that the sacredness of an individual is violated by it; there would be an intrusion into thy holy of holies—and the intruder would not be thy husband! Canst thou think, without a shrinking of thy soul, of any human being coming into closer communion with thee than I may?—than either nature or my own sense of right would permit me? *I* cannot. And, dearest, thou must remember, too, that thou art now a part of me, and that, by

† From *Love Letters of Nathaniel Hawthorne, 1839–1841*, 2 vols. (Chicago: The Society of the Dofobs, 1907), II.62–66.
1. At the time of this letter, Nathaniel Hawthorne and Sophia Peabody were engaged.

surrendering thyself to the influence of this magnetic lady, thou surrenderest more than thine own moral and spiritual being—allowing that the influence *is* a moral and spiritual one. And, sweetest, I really do not like the idea of being brought, through thy medium, into such an intimate relation with Mrs. Park!

Now, ownest wife, I have no faith whatever that people are raised to the seventh heaven, or to any heaven at all, or that they gain any insight into the mysteries of life beyond death, by means of this strange science. Without distrusting that the phenomena which thou tellest me of, and others as remarkable, have really occurred, I think that they are to be accounted for as the result of a physical and material, not of a spiritual, influence. *Opium* has produced many a brighter vision of heaven (and just as susceptible of proof) than those which thou recountest. They are dreams, my love—and such dreams as thy sweetest fancy, either waking or sleeping, could vastly improve upon. And what delusion can be more lamentable and mischievous, than to mistake the physical and material for the spiritual? What so miserable as to lose the soul's true, though hidden, knowledge and consciousness of heaven, in the mist of an earth-born vision? Thou shalt not do this. If thou wouldst know what heaven is, before thou comest thither hand in hand with thy husband, then retire into the depths of thine own spirit, and thou wilt find it there among holy thoughts and feelings; but do not degrade high Heaven and its inhabitants into any such symbols and forms as those which Miss Larned[2] describes—do not let an earthly effluence from Mrs. Park's corporeal system bewilder thee, and perhaps contaminate something spiritual and sacred. I should as soon think of seeking revelations of the future state in the rottenness of the grave—where so many do seek it.

Belovedest wife, I am sensible that these arguments of mine may appear to have little real weight; indeed, what I write does no sort of justice to what I think. But I care the less for this, because I know that my deep and earnest feeling upon the subject will weigh more with thee than all the arguments in the world. And thou wilt know that the view which I take of this matter is caused by no want of faith in mysteries, but from a deep reverence of the soul, and of the mysteries which it knows within itself, but never transmits to the earthly eye or ear. Keep thy imagination sane—that is one of the truest conditions of communion with Heaven.

Dearest, after these grave considerations, it seems hardly worth while to submit a merely external one; but as it occurs to me, I will write it. I cannot think, without invincible repugnance, of thy holy name being bruited abroad in connection with these magnetic phe-

2. A friend of Park's who was sometimes used as a medium.

nomena. Some (horrible thought!) would pronounce my Dove an imposter; the great majority would deem thee crazed; and even the few believers would feel a sort of interest in thee, which it would be anything but pleasant to excite. And what adequate motive can there be for exposing thyself to all this misconception? Thou wilt say, perhaps, that thy visions and experiences would never be known. But Miss Larned's are known to all who choose to listen.

October 19th. Monday.—Most beloved, what a preachment have I made to thee! I love thee, I love thee, I love thee, most infinitely. Love is the true magnetism. What carest thou for any other? Belovedest, it is probable that thou wilt see thy husband tomorrow. Art though magnificent? God bless thee. What a bright day is here; but the woods are fading now. It is time I were in the city, for the winter.

THINE OWNEST.

GUSTAVE DE BEAUMONT AND ALEXIS DE TOCQUEVILLE

From On the Penitentiary System in the United States†

From May 1831 to March 1832, the Frenchmen Gustave de Beaumont (1802–1866) and Alexis de Tocqueville (1805–1859) toured the United States, paying special attention to the new prisons created by the nation's social reformers. They were particularly interested in the Auburn prison in New York State, which used techniques of isolation and silence to encourage prisoners to meditate on their fallen ways and to learn how to work with others. (The Auburn model was imitated in Boston, and thus it is worth noting that Clifford is introduced into *The House of the Seven Gables* after serving approximately thirty years in a Boston prison.) Beaumont and Tocqueville were enormously enthusiastic about the reformatory potential of the new prisons they observed; and in their report, *On the Penitentiary System in the United States*, published in Paris and Philadelphia in 1833, they urged French authorities to undertake penal reform on the U.S. model. Two years later, in 1835, Beaumont published a novel on slavery and race in the United States, *Marie*, and Tocqueville published the first volume of *Democracy in America*.

---

† From G. De Beaumont and A. De Toqueville [sic], *On the Penitentiary System in the United States, and Its Application in France; with an Appendix on Penal Colonies, and Also, Statistical Notes*, trans. and ed. Francis Lieber (Philadelphia: Carey, Lea, & Blanchard, 1833), 20–22, 24–26. Lieber's and Beaumont and Tocqueville's notes have been deleted.

We find in the United States two distinctly separate systems: the system of Auburn and that of Philadelphia.

Sing-Sing, in the State of New York; Wethersfield, in Connecticut; Boston, in Massachusetts; Baltimore, in Maryland; have followed the model of Auburn.

On the other side, Pennsylvania stands quite alone.

The two systems opposed to each other on important points, have, however, a common basis, without which no penitentiary system is possible; this basis is the *isolation* of the prisoners.

Whoever has studied the interior of prisons and the moral state of their inmates, has become convinced that communication between these persons renders their moral reformation impossible, and becomes even for them the inevitable cause of an alarming corruption. This observation, justified by the experience of every day, has become in the United States an almost popular truth; and the publicists who disagree most respecting the way of putting the penitentiary system into practice, fully agree upon this point, that no salutary system can possibly exist without the separation of the criminals.

For a long time it was believed that, in order to remedy the evil caused by the intercourse of prisoners with each other, it would be sufficient to establish in the prison, a certain number of classifications. But after having tried this plan, its insufficiency has been acknowledged. There are similar punishments and crimes called by the same name, but there are no two beings equal in regard to their morals; and every time that convicts are put together, there exists necessarily a fatal influence of some upon others, because, in the association of the wicked, it is not the less guilty who act upon the more criminal, but the more depraved who influence those who are less so.

We must therefore, impossible as it is to classify prisoners, come to a separation of all.

This separation, which prevents the wicked from injuring others, is also favourable to himself.

Thrown into solitude he reflects. Placed alone, in view of his crime, he learns to hate it; and if his soul be not yet surfeited with crime, and thus have lost all taste for any thing better, it is in solitude, where remorse will come to assail him.

Solitude is a severe punishment, but such a punishment is merited by the guilty. * * *

The founders of the Auburn prison acknowledged also the necessity of separating the prisoners, to prevent all intercourse among themselves, and to subject them to the obligation of labour. * * *

In this prison, as well as in those founded upon the same model, the prisoners are locked up in their solitary cells at night only. During day they work together in common workshops, and as they are subjected to the law of rigorous silence, though united, they are yet in fact isolated. Labour in common and in silence forms then the characteristic trait which distinguishes the Auburn system from that of Philadelphia.

Owing to the silence to which the prisoners are condemned, this union of the prisoners, it is asserted, offers no inconvenience, and presents many advantages.

They are united, but no moral connexion exists among them. They see without knowing each other. They are in society without any intercourse; there exists among them neither aversion nor sympathy. The criminal, who contemplates a project of escape, or an attempt against the life of his keepers, does not know in which of his companions he may expect to find assistance. Their union is strictly material, or, to speak more exactly, their bodies are together, but their souls are separated; and it is not the solitude of the body which is important, but that of the mind. At Pittsburg[h], the prisoners, though separated, are not alone, since there exist moral communications among them. At Auburn, they are really isolated, though no wall separates them.

Their union in the work-shops has, therefore, nothing dangerous: it has, on the contrary, it is said, an advantage peculiar to it, that of accustoming the prisoners to obedience.

What is the principal object of punishment in relation to him who suffers it? It is to give him the habits of society, and first to teach him to obey. The Auburn prison has, on this point, its advocates say, a manifest advantage over that of Philadelphia.

Perpetual seclusion in a cell, is an irresistible fact which curbs the prisoner without a struggle, and thus deprives altogether his submission of a moral character; locked up in this narrow space, he has not, properly speaking, to observe a discipline; if he works, it is in order to escape the weariness which overwhelms him: in short, he obeys much less the established discipline than the physical impossibility of acting otherwise.

At Auburn, on the contrary, labour instead of being a comfort to the prisoners, is, in their eyes, a painful task, which they would be glad to get rid of. In observing silence, they are incessantly tempted to violate its law. They have some merit in obeying, because their obedience is no actual *necessity*. It is thus that the Auburn discipline gives to the prisoners the habits of society which they do not obtain in the prisons of Philadelphia.

We see that silence is the principal basis of the Auburn system; it is this silence which establishes that moral separation between all prisoners, that deprives them of all dangerous communications, and only leaves to them those social relations which are inoffensive.

But here we meet with another grave objection against this system; the advocates of the Philadelphia system say, that to pretend to reduce a great number of collected malefactors to absolute silence, is a real chimera; and that this impossibility ruins from its basis, the system of which silence is the only foundation.

We believe that this reproach is much exaggerated. Certainly we cannot admit the existence of a discipline carried to such a degree of perfection, that it guaranties rigorous observation of silence among a great number of assembled individuals, whom their interest and their passions excite to communicate with each other. We may say, however, that if in the prisons of Auburn, Sing-Sing, Boston, and Wethersfield, silence is not always strictly observed, the cases of infraction are so rare that they are of little danger. Admitted as we have been into the interior of these various establishments, and going there at every hour of the day, without being accompanied by any body, visiting by turns the cells, the workshops, the chapel and the yards, we have never been able to surprise a prisoner uttering a single word, and yet we have sometimes spent whole weeks in observing the same prison.

NATHANIEL HAWTHORNE

[Railroads]†

Hawthorne's best-known piece on the relatively new technology of railway transportation is his sketch "The Celestial Rail-road" (1843), but locomotives also have a central place in chapter 17 of *The House of the Seven Gables*. In this journal entry of 1850, Hawthorne describes his railroad journey from Portsmouth, New Hampshire, to Boston via Newcastle, New Hampshire.

Sunday, May 5th, 1850.

I left Portsmouth last Wednesday, at three quarters past 12, by the Concord railroad, which, at Newcastle, unites with the Boston and Maine railroad, about ten miles from Portsmouth. The station at Newcastle is a small wooden building with one railroad passing on one side, and another at another, and the two crossing each other at right angles. At a little distance, stands a black, large, old wooden church, with a square tower, and broken windows, and a great rift through the middle of the roof, all in a dismal stage of ruin and decay. A farm-house of the old style, with a long sloping

† From *The American Notebooks*, ed. Claude M. Simpson (Columbus: Ohio State University Press, 1972), 487–88. Reprinted with permission of the Ohio State University Press.

roof, and as black as the church, stands on the opposite side of the road, with its barns; and these are all the buildings in sight of the rail-road station. On the Concord rail is the train of cars, with the locomotive puffing and blowing off its steam, and making a great bluster in that lonely place; while, along the other railroad, stretches the desolate track, with the withered weeds growing up betwixt the two lines of iron, all so desolate. And anon, you hear a low thunder running along these iron rules; it grows louder; an object is seen afar off, it approaches rapidly, and comes down upon you like fate, swift and inevitably. In a moment, it dashes along in front of the Station-house and comes to a pause; the locomotive hissing and fuming, in its eagerness to go on. How much life has come at once into this lonely place! Four or five long cars, each, perhaps, with fifty people in it; reading newspapers, reading pamphlet novels, chatting, sleeping; all this vision of passing life! A moment passes, while the baggage men are putting on the trunks and packages; then the bell strikes a few times, and away goes the train again; quickly out of sight of those who remain behind, while a solitude of hours again broods over the Station House, which, for an instant, has thus been put in communication with far-off cities, and then has only itself, with the old black, ruinous church, and the black old farm-house, both built years and years ago, before railroads were ever dreamed of. Meantime, the passenger, stepping from the solitary station-house into the train, finds himself in the midst of a new world, all in a moment; he rushes out of the solitude into a village; thence through woods and hills; into a large inland town; along beside the Merrimack, which has overflowed its banks, and eddies along, turbid as a vast mud-puddle, sometimes almost laving the door-step of a house, and with trees standing in the flood, half-way up their trunks. Boys, with newspapers to sell, or apples, lozenges &c; many passengers departing and entering, at each new-station; the more permanent passenger, with his check or ticket stuck in his hatband, where the conductor may see it. A party of girls, playing at ball with a young man; altogether, it is a scene of stirring life, with which a person, who had been waiting long for the train to come by, might find it difficult at once to amalgamate himself.

It is a sombre, brooding day, and begins to rain as the cars pass onward. In a little more than two hours, we find ourselves in Boston, surrounded by eager hackmen.

CRITICISM

Contemporary Responses

The House of the Seven Gables was greeted enthusiastically by most re-viewers, a number of whom saw it as a happier, less morbid novel than *The Scarlet Letter*. Hawthorne himself seemed to share that vision of the novel. Though hardly a best-seller, *The House of the Seven Gables* outsold *The Scarlet Letter* in its first year, compiling sales of 6,710 copies, compared to 6,000 for *The Scarlet Letter*. This section contains five of the approximately thirty known published reviews of *The House of the Seven Gables* plus four more-private responses.

NATHANIEL HAWTHORNE

From Letter to Horatio Bridge, March 15, 1851†

Hawthorne met Horatio Bridge (1806–1893) in the mid-1820s when they were undergraduates at Bowdoin College, and they remained friends up to the time of Hawthorne's death. In 1845 Hawthorne ed-ited, and may have written considerable sections of, the naval officer Bridge's *The Journal of an African Cruiser* (1845). In this letter to Bridge of 1851, Hawthorne offers an early "review" of his upcoming novel.

Lenox, March 15th, 1851.

Dear Bridge,

* * *

The House of the Seven Gables, in my opinion, is better than the Scarlet Letter; but I should not wonder if I had refined upon the principal character[1] a little too much for popular appreciation, nor if the romance of the book should be found somewhat at odds with the humble and familiar scenery in which I invest it. But I feel that portions of it are as good as anything that I can hope to write; and the publisher speaks encouragingly of its success.

* * *

Your friend,
N. H.

† From *The Letters, 1843–1853*, ed. Thomas Woodson, L. Neal Smith, Norman Holmes Pearson (Columbus: Ohio State University Press, 1985), 406.
1. Presumably Holgrave.

HERMAN MELVILLE

Letter to Hawthorne, [April 16,] 1851†

When Herman Melville (1819–1891) met Hawthorne on August 5, 1850, at a picnic in the Berkshires, he believed he had discovered a dark, subversive writer somewhat like himself. In his influential essay "Hawthorne and His Mosses," published in the August 17 and 24, 1850, issues of the *Literary World*, Melville celebrated Hawthorne's "power of blackness." During 1851 Hawthorne and Melville regularly visited with one another while they were living in the western Massachusetts towns of Lenox and Pittsfield, respectively; but by 1853 their friendship had cooled. Hawthorne's letters to Melville have not survived.

                                  Pittsfield, Wednesday morning.
My Dear Hawthorne,—Concerning the young gentleman's shoes, I desire to say that a pair to fit him, of the desired pattern, cannot be had in all Pittsfield,—a fact which sadly impairs that metropolitan pride I formerly took in the capital of Berkshire.[1] Henceforth Pittsfield must hide its head. However, if a pair of *bootees* will at all answer, Pittsfield will be very happy to provide them. Pray mention all this to Mrs. Hawthorne, and command me.

"The House of the Seven Gables: A Romance. By Nathaniel Hawthorne. One vol. 16mo, pp. 344." The contents of this book do not belie its rich, clustering, romantic title. With great enjoyment we spent almost an hour in each separate gable. This book is like a fine old chamber, abundantly, but still judiciously, furnished with precisely that sort of furniture best fitted to furnish it. There are rich hangings, wherein are braided scenes from tragedies! There is old china with rare devices, set out on the carved buffet; there are long and indolent lounges to throw yourself upon; there is an admirable sideboard, plentifully stored with good viands; there is a smell as of old wine in the pantry; and finally, in one corner, there is a dark little black-letter volume in golden clasps, entitled "Hawthorne: A Problem." It has delighted us; it has piqued a reperusal; it has robbed us of a day, and made us a present of a whole year of thoughtfulness; it has bred great exhilaration and exultation with the remembrance that the architect of the Gables resides only

† From *Correspondence: The Writings of Herman Melville, Volume 14*, ed. Lynn Horth (Evanston: Northwestern University Press, 1993), 185–87. Reprinted by permission of the publisher. The dating of the letter was established by Horth; see the textual discussion in *Correspondence*, 184.
1. On April 11, 1851, during one of Melville's visits to the Hawthornes in Lenox, Hawthorne had presented him with an inscribed copy of *House* and had also told him of his difficulties in finding shoes for his five-year-old son, Julian.

six miles off, and not three thousand miles away, in England, say. We think the book, for pleasantness of running interest, surpasses the other works of the author. The curtains are more drawn; the sun comes in now; genialities peep out more. Were we to particularize what has most struck us in the deeper passages, we would point out the scene where Clifford, for a moment, would fain throw himself forth from the window to join the procession; or the scene where the Judge is left seated in his ancestral chair. Clifford is full of an awful truth throughout. He is conceived in the finest, truest spirit. He is no caricature. He is Clifford. And here we would say that, did circumstances permit, we should like nothing better than to devote an elaborate and careful paper to the full consideration and analysis of the purport and significance of what so strongly characterizes all of this author's writings. There is a certain tragic phase of humanity which, in our opinion, was never more powerfully embodied than by Hawthorne. We mean the tragicalness of human thought in its own unbiassed, native, and profounder workings. We think that into no recorded mind has the intense feeling of the visable truth ever entered more deeply than into this man's. By visable truth, we mean the apprehension of the absolute condition of present things as they strike the eye of the man who fears them not, though they do their worst to him,—the man who, like Russia or the British Empire, declares himself a sovereign nature (in himself) amid the powers of heaven, hell, and earth. He may perish; but so long as he exists he insists upon treating with all Powers upon an equal basis. If any of those other Powers choose to withhold certain secrets, let them; that does not impair my sovereignty in myself; that does not make me tributary. And perhaps after all, there is *no* secret. We incline to think the Problem of the Universe is like the Freemason's mighty secret, so terrible to all children. It turns out, at last, to consist in a triangle, a mallet, and an apron,—nothing more! We incline to think that God cannot explain His own secrets, and that He would like a little information upon certain points Himself. We mortals admonish Him as much as He us. But it is this *Being* of the matter; there lies the knot with which we choke ourselves. As soon as you say *Me*, a *God*, a *Nature*, so soon you jump off from your stool and hang from the beam. Yes, that word is the hangman. Take God out of the dictionary, and you would have Him in the street.

There is the grand truth about Nathaniel Hawthorne. He says NO! in thunder; but the Devil himself cannot make him say *yes*. For all men who say *yes*, lie; and all men who say *no*,—why, they are in the happy condition of judicious, unincumbered travellers in Europe; they cross the frontiers into Eternity with nothing but a carpet-bag,—that is to say, the Ego. Whereas those *yes*-gentry, they travel with heaps of baggage, and, damn them! they will never get through the Custom House. What's the reason, Mr. Hawthorne, that in the last stages of metaphysics a fellow always falls to *swearing* so? I could rip an hour. You see, I began with a little criticism extracted for your benefit from the "Pittsfield Secret Review," and here I have landed in Africa.

Walk down one of these mornings and see me. No nonsense; come. Remember me to Mrs. Hawthorne and the children.

H. Melville.

P.S. The marriage of Phoebe with the daguerreotypist is a fine stroke, because of his turning out to be a *Maule*. If you pass Hepzibah's cent-shop, buy me a Jim Crow (fresh) and send it to me by Ned Higgins.

CATHARINE MARIA SEDGWICK

Letter to Mrs. K. S. Minot, 4 May 1851†

Best known for her historical novel *Hope Leslie* (1827), the Massachusetts writer Catharine Maria Sedgwick (1789–1867) achieved renown as a novelist and author of moral tracts. For most of her life, she lived with her mother and father in the Sedgwick family home in Stockbridge, Massachusetts. When the Hawthornes moved to nearby Lenox in 1850, Sedgwick and other members of her family socialized with them on a regular basis. She read *The House of the Seven Gables* shortly after its publication in April 1851, sharing her response in a letter to her niece, Kate Minot.

Your mother, after reading Hawthorne's book [*The House of the Seven Gables*], has most kindly and patiently gone straight through it again in loud reading to your father and me. Your father is not a model listener; ten thousand thoughts of ten thousand things to be done call him off, and would wear out any temper but your mother's. Have you read it? There is marvelous beauty in the diction; a richness and originality of thought that give the stamp of unquestionable genius; a microscopic observation of the external world, and the keenest analysis of character; an elegance and finish that is like the work of a master sculptor—perfect in its artistic details. And yet, to my mind, it is a failure. It fails in the essentials of a work of art; there is not essential dignity in the characters to make them worth the labor spent on them. A low-minded vulgar

† From *Life and Letters of Catharine M. Sedgwick*, ed. Mary E. Dewey (New York: Harper & Brothers, 1871), 328–29.

hypocrite, a weak-minded nervous old maid, and her half-cracked brother, with nothing but beauty, and a blind instinctive love of the beautiful, are the chief characters of the drama. 'Little Phœbe' is the redemption, as far as she goes, of the book—a sweet and perfect flower amidst corruption, barrenness, and decay. The book is an affliction. If affects me like a passage through the wards of an insane asylum, or a visit to specimens of morbid anatomy. It has the unity and simple construction of a Greek tragedy, but without the relief of divine qualities or great events; and the man takes such savage delight in repeating and repeating the raw head and bloody bones of his imagination. There is nothing genial, excepting always little Phœbe, the ideal of a New England, sweet-tempered, 'accomplishing' village girl. I might have liked it better when I was younger, but as we go through the tragedy of life we need elixirs, cordials, and all the kindliest resources of the art of fiction. There is too much force for the subject. It is as if a railroad should be built and a locomotive started to transport skeletons, specimens, and one bird of Paradise!

ANONYMOUS

[Grand Historical Picture]†

This anonymous, untitled review appeared in the "Literary Notices" section of New York's *Harper's New Monthly Magazine*. Because of the relatively large circulation of the magazine, this review was particularly important in publicizing the novel.

Ticknor, Reed, and Fields have issued *The House of the Seven Gables*, a Romance, by NATHANIEL HAWTHORNE, which is strongly marked with the bold and unique characteristics that have given its author such a brilliant position among American novelists. The scene, which is laid in the old Puritanic town of Salem, extends from the period of the witchcraft excitement to the present time, connecting the legends of the ancient superstition with the recent marvels of animal magnetism, and affording full scope for the indulgence of the most weird and sombre fancies. Destitute of the high-wrought manifestations of passion which distinguished the "Scarlet Letter," it is more terrific in its conception, and not less intense in its execution, but exquisitely relieved by charming portraitures of character, and quaint and comic descriptions of social eccentricities. A deep vein of reflection underlies the whole

† From *Harper's New Monthly Magazine*, 2, no. 12 (May 1851): 855–56.

narrative, often rising naturally to the surface, and revealing the strength of the foundation on which the subtle, aerial inventions of the author are erected. His frequent dashes of humor gracefully blend with the monotone of the story, and soften the harsher colors in which he delights to clothe his portentous conceptions. In no former production of his pen, are his unrivalled powers of description displayed to better advantage. The rusty wooden house in Pyncheon-street, with its seven sharp-pointed gables, and its huge clustered chimney—the old elm tree before the door—the grassy yard seen through the lattice fence, with its enormous fertility of burdocks—and the green moss on the slopes of the roof, with the flowers growing aloft in the air in the nook between two of the gables—present a picture to the eye as distinct as if our childhood had been passed in the shadow of the old weather-beaten edifice. Nor are the characters of the story drawn with less sharp and vigorous perspective. They stand out from the canvas as living realities. In spite of the supernatural drapery in which they are enveloped, they have such a genuine expression of flesh and blood, that we can not doubt we have known them all our days. They have the air of old acquaintance—only we wonder how the artist got them to sit for their likenesses. The grouping of these persons is managed with admirable artistic skill. Old Maid Pyncheon, concealing under her verjuice[1] scowl the unutterable tenderness of a sister—her woman-hearted brother, on whose sensitive nature had fallen such a strange blight—sweet and beautiful Phoebe, the noble village-maiden, whose presence is always like that of some shining angel—the dreamy, romantic descendant of the legendary wizard—the bold, bad man of the world, reproduced at intervals in the bloody Colonel, and the unscrupulous Judge—wise old Uncle Venner—and inappeasable Ned Higgins—are all made to occupy the place on the canvas which shows the lights and shades of their character in the most impressive contrast, and contributes to the wonderful vividness and harmony of the grand historical picture. On the whole, we regard "The House of the Seven Gables," though it exhibits no single scenes that may not be matched in depth and pathos by some of Mr. Hawthorne's previous creations, as unsurpassed by any thing he has yet written, in exquisite beauty of finish, in the skillful blending of the tragic and comic, and in the singular life-like reality with which the wildest traditions of the Puritanic age are combined with the every-day incidents of modern society.

1. Acidic, sour.

EVERT AUGUSTUS DUYCKINCK

[Cornelius Agrippa]†

Best known for his editorship of the *Literary World* and the two-volume *Cyclopedia of American Literature* (1855), the New York writer and editor Evert Augustus Duyckinck (1816–1878) was a staunch literary nationalist and enthusiastic promoter of Hawthorne's career. In a letter to Duyckinck of April 27, 1851, Hawthorne expressed his pleasure with Duyckinck's review, though he remarked, "I cannot quite understand why everything that I write takes so melancholy an aspect in your eyes" (*The Letters, 1843–1853* [1985], 421).

You must be in the proper mood and time and place to read Hawthorne, if you would understand him. We think any one would be wrong to make the attempt on a rail-car, or on board a steamboat. It is not a shilling novel that you are purchasing when you buy the House of the Seven Gables, but a book—a book with lights and shades, parts and diversities, upon which you may feed and pasture, not exhausting the whole field at an effort, but returning now and then to uncropped fairy rings and bits of herbage. You may read the book into the small hours beyond midnight, when no sound breaks the silence but the parting of an expiring ember, or the groan of restless mahogany, and you find that the candle burns a longer flame, and that the ghostly visions of the author's page take shape about you. Conscience sits supreme in her seat, the fountains of pity and terror are opened; you look into the depths of the soul, provoked at so painful a sight—but you are strengthened as you gaze; for of that pain comes peace at last, and these shadows you must master by virtuous magic. Nathaniel Hawthorne may be the Cornelius Agrippa[1] to invoke them, but you are the mirror in which they are reflected.

---

† From "The House of the Seven Gables," *Literary World* 8 (April 26, 1851): 334.
1. Heinrich Cornelius Agrippa von Nettesheim (1486–1535), German mystic with an interest in astrology and alchemy. According to legend, he secretly traveled to the New World for demonic purposes.

EDWIN PERCY WHIPPLE

[Hawthorne's Greatest Work]†

A popular critic and lecturer, Edwin Percy Whipple (1819–1886) was a close friend of Hawthorne's publisher, James Fields, and an enthusiastic reader of Hawthorne. He had reviewed *The Scarlet Letter* in the May 1850 issue of the Philadelphia-based *Graham's Magazine*, faulting the novel only for its lack of humor. In a letter to Fields of May 23, 1851, Hawthorne remarked: "Whipple's notices have done more than please me; for they have helped me to see my book" (*The Letters, 1843–1853* [1985], 435).

"The wrong-doing of one generation lives into the successive ones, and, divesting itself of every temporary advantage, becomes a pure and uncontrollable mischief;" this is the leading idea of Hawthorne's new romance, and it is developed with even more than his usual power. The error in "The Scarlet Letter," proceeded from the divorce of its humor from its pathos—the introduction being as genial as Goldsmith or Lamb,[1] and the story which followed being tragic even to ghastliness. In "The House of the Seven Gables," the humor and the pathos are combined, and the whole work is stamped with the individuality of the author's genius, in all its variety of power. The first hundred pages of the volume are masterly in conception and execution, and can challenge comparison, in the singular depth and sweetness of their imaginative humor, with the best writing of the kind in literature. The other portions of the book have not the same force, precision, and certainty of handling, and the insight into character especially, seems at times to follow the processes of clairvoyance more than those of the waking imagination. The consequence is that the movement of the author's mind betrays a slight fitfulness toward the conclusion, and, splendid as is the supernaturally grotesque element which this ideal impatience introduces, it still somewhat departs from the integrity of the original conception, and interferes with the strict unity of the work. The mental nerve which characterizes the first part, slips occasionally into mental nervousness as the author proceeds.

We have been particular in indicating this fault, because the work is of so high a character that it demands, as a right, to be judged by the most exacting requirements of art. Taken as a whole,

---

† From *Graham's Magazine*, 38, no. 6 (June 1851): 467–68. The review appeared in the "Review of New Books" section and is untitled and unsigned.
1. References to the British writers Oliver Goldsmith (1730–1774) and Charles Lamb (1775–1834).

it is Hawthorne's greatest work, and is equally sure of immediate popularity and permanent fame. Considered as a romance, it does not so much interest as fasten and fascinate attention; and this attractiveness in the story is the result of the rare mental powers and moods out of which the story creatively proceeds. Every chapter proves the author to be, not only a master of narrative, a creator of character, an observer of life, and richly gifted with the powers of vital conception and combination, but it also exhibits him as a profound thinker and skillful metaphysician. We do not know but that his eye is more certain in detecting remote spiritual laws and their relations, than in the sure grasp of individual character; and if he ever loses his hold upon persons it is owing to that intensely meditative cast of his mind by which he views persons in their relations to the general laws whose action they illustrate. There is some discord in the present work in the development of character and sequence of events; the dramatic unity is therefore not perfectly preserved; but this cannot be affirmed of the unity of the law. That is always sustained, and if it had been thoroughly embodied, identified, and harmonized with the concrete events and characters, we have little hesitation in asserting that the present volume would be the deepest work of imagination ever produced on the American continent. * * *

The characters of the romance are among the best of Hawthorne's individualizations, and Miss Hepzibah and Phœbe are perhaps his masterpieces of characterization, in the felicity of their conception, their contrast, and their inter-action. Miss Hepzibah Pyncheon, the inhabitant of the gabled house, is compelled at the age of sixty to stoop from her aristocratic isolation from the world, and open a little cent shop, in order that she may provide for the subsistence of an unfortunate brother. The chapters entitled "The Little Shop-Window," "The First Customer," and a "Day Behind the Counter," in which her ludicrous humiliations are described, may be placed beside the best works of the most genial humorists, for their rapid alternations of smiles and tears, and the perfect April weather they make in the heart. The description of the little articles at the shop-window, the bars of soap, the leaden dragoons, the split peas, and the fantastic Jim Crow, "executing his world-renowned dance in gingerbread;" the attempts of the elderly maiden to arrange her articles aright, and the sad destruction she makes among them, crowned by upsetting that tumbler of marbles, "all of which roll different ways, and each individual marble, devil-directed, into the most difficult obscurity it can find;" the nervous irritation of her deportment as she puts her shop in order, the twitches of pride which agonize her breast, as stealing on tiptoe to the window, "as cautiously as if she conceived some bloody-minded villain to be watching behind the elm-tree, with intent to take her life," she stretches out her long, lank arm to put a paper of pearl-buttons, a Jew's harp, or what not, in its destined place, and then strait-way vanishing back into the dusk, "as if the world need never hope for another glimpse of her;" the "ugly and spiteful little din" of the door-bell, announcing her first penny customer; all these, and many more minute details, are instinct with the life of humor, and cheerily illustrate that "entanglement of something mean and triv-ial with whatever is noblest in joy and sorrow," which it is the office of the humorist to represent and idealize.

The character of Phœbe makes the sunshine of the book, and by connecting her so intimately with Miss Hepzibah, a quaint sweet-ness is added to the native graces of her mind and disposition. The "homely witchcraft" with which she brings out the hidden capabili-ties of every thing, is exquisitely exhibited, and poor Uncle Venner's praise of her touches the real secret of her fascination. "I've seen," says that cheery mendicant, "a great deal of the world, not only in people's kitchens and back-yards, but at the street corners, and on the wharves, and in other places where my business calls me; but I'm free to say that I never knew a human creature do her work so much like one of God's angels as this child Phœbe does!" Holgrave, the young gentleman who carries off this pearl of womanhood, ap-pears to us a failure. It is impossible for the reader to like him, and one finds it difficult to conceive how Phœbe herself can like him. The loves scenes accordingly lack love, and a kind of magnetic in-fluence is substituted for affection. The character of Clifford is elaborately drawn, and sustained with much subtle skill, but he oc-cupies perhaps too much space, and lures the author too much into metaphysical analysis and didactic disquisition. Judge Pyncheon is powerfully delineated, and the account of his death is a master-piece of fantastic description. It is needless, perhaps, to say that the characters of the book have, like those in "The Scarlet Letter," a vi-tal relation to each other, and are developed not successively and separately, but mutually, each implying the other by a kind of artis-tic necessity.

The imagination in "The House of the Seven Gables," is perhaps most strikingly exhibited in the power with which the house itself is pervaded with thought, so that every room and gable has a sort of human interest communicated to it, and seems to symbolize the whole life of the Pyncheon family, from the grim colonel, who built it, to that delicate Alice, "the fragrance of whose rich and delightful character lingered about the place where she lived, as a dried rose-bud scents the drawer where it has withered and perished."

In conclusion, we hope to have the pleasure of reviewing a new romance by Hawthorne twice a year at least. We could also hope that if Holgrave continues his contributions to the magazines, that he would send Graham some such story as "Alice Pyncheon," which he tells so charmingly to Phœbe.[2] "The Scarlet Letter," and "The House of the Seven Gables," contain mental qualities which insensibly lead some readers to compare the author to other cherished literary names. Thus we have seen Hawthorne likened for this quality to Goldsmith, and for that to [Washington] Irving, and for still another to Dickens; and some critics have given him the preference over all whom he seems to resemble. But the real cause for congratulation in the appearance of an original genius like Hawthorne, is not that he dethrones any established prince in literature, but that he founds a new principality of his own.

HENRY T. TUCKERMAN

[Sketches of Still-Life]†

The Boston-born writer Henry Theodore Tuckerman (1813–1871) moved to New York in 1845, where he gained a reputation as an essayist and biographer. His essay on Hawthorne in the *Southern Literary Messenger*, which appeared shortly after the publication of *The House of the Seven Gables*, helped secure Hawthorne's national reputation. In a letter to Tuckerman of June 20, 1851, Hawthorne rhapsodized over "your most beautiful article," declaring, "I felt that you saw into my books and understood what I meant" (*The Letters, 1843–1853* [1985], 452).

* * * The scenery, tone and personages of the story [*The House of the Seven Gables*] are imbued with a local authenticity which is not, for an instant, impaired by the imaginative charm of romance. We seem to breathe, as we read, the air and be surrounded by the familiar objects of a New England town. The interior of the House, each article described within it, from the quaint table to the miniature by Malbone;—every product of the old garden, the street-scenes that beguile the eyes of poor Clifford, as he looks out of the arched window, the noble elm and the gingerbread figures at the little shop window—all have the significance that belong to reality when seized upon by art. In these details we have the truth, simplicity and exact imitation of the Flemish painters. So life-like in the minutiae and so picturesque in general effect are these sketches of still-life, that they are daguerreotyped in the reader's

---

2. In 1844 Hawthorne published "Earth's Holocaust" in *Graham's*; it would remain his sole publication in the journal.

† From "Nathaniel Hawthorne," *Southern Literary Messenger* 17 (June 1851): 348–49.

mind, and form a distinct and changeless background, the light and
shade of which give admirable effect to the action of the story: occasional touches of humor, introduced with exquisite tact, relieve
the grave undertone of the narrative and form vivacious and quaint
images which might readily be transferred to canvass—so effectively are they drawn in words; take, for instance, the street-
musician and the Pyncheon fowls, the judge balked of his kiss over
the counter, Phoebe reading to Clifford in the garden, or the old
maid, in her lonely chamber, gazing on the sweet lineaments of her
unfortunate brother. Nor is Hawthorne less successful in those pictures that are drawn exclusively for the mind's eye and are obvious
to sensation rather than the actual vision. Were a New England
Sunday, breakfast, old mansion, easterly storm, or the morning after it clears, ever so well described? The skill in atmosphere we
have noted in his lighter sketches, is also as apparent: around and
within the principal scene of this romance, there hovers an alternating melancholy and brightness which is born of genuine moral
life; no contrasts can be imagined of this kind, more eloquent to a
sympathetic mind, than that between the inward consciousness
and external appearance of Hepzibah or Phoebe and Clifford, or
the Judge. They respectively symbolize the poles of human existence; and are fine studies for the psychologist. Yet this attraction is
subservient to fidelity to local characteristics. Clifford represents,
though in its most tragic imaginable phase, the man of fine organization and true sentiments environed by the material realities of
New England life; his plausible uncle is the type of New England
selfishness, glorified by respectable conformity and wealth; Phoebe
is the ideal of genuine, efficient, yet loving female character in the
same latitude; Uncle Venner, we regard as one of the most fresh,
yet familiar portraits in the book; all denizens of our eastern provincial towns must have known such a philosopher; and Holgrave embodies Yankee acuteness and hardihood redeemed by integrity and
enthusiasm. The contact of these most judiciously selected and
highly characteristic elements, brings out not only many beautiful
revelations of nature, but elucidates interesting truth; magnetism
and socialism are admirably introduced; family tyranny in its most
revolting form, is powerfully exemplified; the distinction between a
mental and a heartfelt interest in another, clearly unfolded; and the
tenacious and hereditary nature of moral evil impressively shadowed forth. The natural refinements of the human heart, the holiness of a ministry of disinterested affection, the gracefulness of the
homeliest services when irradiated by cheerfulness and benevolence, are illustrated with singular beauty. "He," says our author,
speaking of Clifford, "had no right to be a martyr; and, beholding
him so fit to be happy, and so feeble for all other purposes, a gener-

ous, strong and noble spirit would, methinks, have been ready to sacrifice what little enjoyment it might have planned for itself,—*it would have flung down the hopes so paltry in its regard—if thereby the wintry blasts of our rude sphere might come tempered to such a man:*" and elsewhere: "Phoebe's presence made a home about her,—that very sphere which the outcast, the prisoner, the potentate, the wretch beneath mankind, the wretch aside from it, or the wretch above it, instinctively pines after—a home. She was real! Holding her hand, you felt something; a tender something; a substance and a warm one: *and so long as you could feel its grasp, soft as it was, you might be certain that your place was good in the whole sympathetic chain of human nature.* The world was no longer a delusion."

Thus narrowly, yet with reverence, does Hawthorne analyze the delicate traits of human sentiment and character; and open vistas into that beautiful and unexplored world of love and thought, that exists in every human being, though overshadowed by material circumstance and technical duty. This, as we have before said, is his great service; digressing every now and then, from the main drift of his story, he takes evident delight in expatiating on phases of character and general traits of life, or in bringing into strong relief the more latent facts of consciousness. Perhaps the union of the philosophic tendency with the poetic instinct is the great charm of his genius. It is common for American critics to estimate the interest of all writings by their comparative glow, vivacity and rapidity of action: somewhat of the restless temperament and enterprising life of the nation infects its taste: such terms as 'quiet,' 'gentle' and 'tasteful,' are equivocal when applied in this country, to a book; and yet they may envelope the rarest energy of thought and depth of insight as well as earnestness of feeling; these qualities, in reflective minds, are too real to find melo-dramatic development; they move as calmly as summer waves, or glow as noiselessly as the firmament; but not the less grand and mighty is their essence; to realize it, the spirit of contemplation, and the recipient mood of sympathy, must be evoked, for it is not external but moral excitement that is proposed; and we deem one of Hawthorne's most felicitous merits—that of so patiently educing artistic beauty and moral interest from life and nature, without the least sacrifice of intellectual dignity.

The healthy spring of life is typified in Phoebe so freshly as to magnetize the feelings as well as engage the perceptions of the reader; its intellectual phase finds expression in Holgrave, while the state of Clifford, when relieved of the nightmare that oppressed his sensitive temperament, the author justly compares to an Indian-summer of the soul. Across the path of these beings of genuine flesh and blood, who constantly appeal to our most humane sympathies, or rather around their consciousness and history, flits the pale, mystic figure of Alice—whose invisible music and legendary fate overflow with a graceful and attractive superstition—yielding an Ariel-like melody to the more solemn and cheery strains of the whole composition. Among the apt though incidental touches of the picture, the idea of making the music-grinder's monkey an epitome of avarice, the daguerreotype a test of latent character, and the love of the reformer Holgrave for the genially practical Phoebe, win him to conservatism, strike us as remarkably natural yet quite as ingenuous and charming as philosophical. We may add that the same pure, even, unexaggerated and perspicuous style of diction that we have recognized in his previous writing, is maintained in this.

ANONYMOUS

[Sombre Coloring]†

When we had read the first twenty pages of this romance, we felt inclined to dissent from the prevalent opinion of the press, that it was inferior to "The Scarlet Letter." As we proceeded, however, we were forced to acknowledge that our cotemporaries were correct, and that "The House of the Seven Gables" was, as one of the ablest of them characterized it, only another "Twice Told Tale." In short, though superior in the finish of some of its details, the romance, as a whole, is not equal to its predecessor. Nevertheless it is a work of genius. No living American author but Hawthorne could have drawn such a character as Clifford, described such a quaint old house as the Pyncheon Mansion, or imagined such a wild, half unearthly legend as that connected with the wizard's curse. The fault of the book, indeed of all Hawthorne's books, in a moral aspect, is the sombre coloring which pervades them, and which leaves an effect more or less morbid on even healthy minds. The only really loveable character in the book is Phebe [sic], who comes, like a gleam of summer sunshine, to the old house and its legendary horrors. The volume is very elegantly printed.

† From *Peterson's Magazine*, 19 (June 1851): 282–83. Published in Philadelphia, *Peterson's* was a popular women's magazine focusing on art, literature, and fashion.

HARRIET BEECHER STOWE

[A Succession of Rembrandt Pictures]†

Following the phenomenal success of her antislavery novel *Uncle Tom's Cabin* (1852), Harriet Beecher Stowe (1811–1896) went on a tour of the British Isles in 1853, adding a visit to Paris, where, according to her travel narrative of 1854, she found herself meditating on Hawthorne.

One of my favorites [at the Louvre] was Rembrandt. I always did admire the gorgeous and solemn mysteries of his coloring. Rembrandt is like Hawthorne. He chooses simple and everyday objects, and so arranges light and shadow as to give them a sombre richness and a mysterious gloom. The House of the Seven Gables is a succession of Rembrandt pictures, done in words instead of oils. Now, this pleases us, because our life really is a haunted one; the simplest thing in it *is* a mystery, the invisible world always lies round us like a shadow, and therefore this dreamy golden gleam of Rembrandt meets somewhat in our inner consciousness to which it corresponds.

† From *Sunny Memories of Foreign Lands*, 2 vols. (Boston: Phillips, Sampson, and Company, 1854), II.161.

Selections from Classic Studies

ANTHONY TROLLOPE

[A Ghastly Spirit of Drollery]†

The popular British novelist Anthony Trollope (1815–1882) met Hawthorne at a banquet in Boston in 1860. Though he lived in London, he published his 1879 essay on Hawthorne's "genius" in Boston's *North American Review*.

As a novel "The House of the Seven Gables" is very inferior to "The Scarlet Letter." The cause of this inferiority would, I think, be plain to any one who had himself been concerned in the writing of novels. When Hawthorne proposed to himself to write "The Scarlet Letter," the plot of his story was clear to his mind. He wrote the book because he had the story strongly, lucidly manifest to his own imagination. In composing the other he was driven to search for a plot, and to make a story. "The Scarlet Letter" was written because he had it to write, and the other because he had to write it. The novelist will often find himself in the latter position. He has characters to draw, lessons to teach, philosophy perhaps which he wishes to expose, satire to express, humor to scatter abroad. These he can employ gracefully and easily if he have a story to tell. If he have none he must concoct something of a story laboriously, when his lesson, his characters, his philosophy, his satire, and his humor will be less graceful and less easy. All the good things I have named are there in "The House of the Seven Gables"; but they are brought in with less artistic skill, because the author has labored over his plot, and never had it clear to his own mind.

There is a mystery attached to the house. That is a matter of course. A rich man obtained the ground on which it was built by fraud from a poor man, and the poor man's curse falls on the rich man's descendants, and the rich man with his rich descendants are abnormally bad, though very respectable. They not only cheat but

---

† From "The Genius of Nathaniel Hawthorne," *North American Review*, 129, no. 274 (September 1879): 212–15.

murder. The original poor man was hung for witchcraft,—only because he had endeavored to hold his own against the original rich
man. The rich men in consequence die when they come to advanced age, without any apparent cause of death, sitting probably
upright in their chairs, to the great astonishment of the world at
large, and with awful signs of blood about their mouths and shirt-
fronts. And each man as he dies is in the act of perpetrating some
terrible enormity against some poor member of his own family. The
respectable rich man with whom we become personally acquainted
in the story,—for as to some of the important characters we hear of
them only by the records which are given of past times,—begins by
getting a cousin convicted of a murder of which he knew that his
kinsman was not guilty, and is preparing to have the same kinsman
fraudulently and unnecessarily put into a lunatic asylum, when he
succumbs to the fate of his family and dies in his chair, all covered
with blood. The unraveling of these mysteries is vague, and, as I
think, inartistic. The reader is not carried on by any intense interest
in the story itself, and comes at last not much to care whether he
does or does not understand the unraveling. He finds that his interest in the book lies elsewhere,—that he must seek it in the characters, lessons, philosophy, satire, and humor, and not in the plot.
With "The Scarlet Letter" the plot comes first, and the others follow as accessories.

Two or three of the characters here drawn are very good. The
wicked and respectable gentleman who *drees*[1] the doom of his family, and dies in his chair all covered with blood, is one Judge Pyncheon. The persistent, unbending, cruel villainy of this man,—
whose heart is as hard as a millstone, who knows not the meaning of
conscience, to whom money and respectability are everything—was
dear to Hawthorne's heart. He likes to revel in an excess of impossible wickedness, and has done so with the Judge. Though we do not
care much for the mysteries of the Judge's family, we like the Judge
himself, and we like to feel that the author is pouring out his scorn
on the padded respectables of his New England world. No man had
a stronger belief than Hawthorne in the superiority of his own country; no man could be more sarcastic as to the deficiencies of another,—as I had reason to discover in that affair of the peas;[2] but,
nevertheless, he is always throwing out some satire as to the assumed virtues of his own immediate countrymen. It comes from

1. Suffers or endures.
2. May be a compositor's error. At the 1860 banquet attended by Hawthorne and Trollope,
   Trollope praised England as a country that knew what a peach was, whereupon, according to a guest at the banquet, Hawthorne remarked, "I asked an Englishman once who
   was praising their peaches to describe to me exactly what he meant by a peach, and he
   described something very like a cucumber" (quoted in Edwin Haviland Miller, *Salem Is
   My Dwelling Place: A Life of Nathaniel Hawthorne* [1991], 463).

him in little touches as to every incident he handles. In truth, he can not write without satire; and, as in these novels he writes of his own country, his shafts fall necessarily on that.

But the personage we like best in the book is certainly Miss Hepzibah Pyncheon. She is a cousin of the Judge, and has become, by some family arrangement, the life-possessor of the house with seven gables. She is sister also of the man who had been wrongly convicted of murder, and who, when released after a thirty-years' term of imprisonment, comes also to live at the house. Miss Hepzibah, under a peculiarly ill-grained exterior, possesses an affectionate heart and high principles. Driven by poverty, she keeps a shop,— a cent-shop, a term which is no doubt familiar enough in New England, and by which it would be presumed that all her articles were to be bought for a cent each, did it not appear by the story that she dealt also in goods of greater value. She is a lady by birth, and can not keep her cent-shop without some feeling of degradation; but that is preferable to the receiving of charity from that odious cousin the Judge. Her timidity, her affection, her true appreciation of herself, her ugliness, her hopelessness, and general incapacity for everything,—cent-shop-keeping included,—are wonderfully drawn. There are characters in novels who walk about on their feet, who stand upright and move, so that readers can look behind them, as one seems to be able to do in looking at a well-painted figure on the canvas. There are others, again, so wooden that no reader expects to find in them any appearance of movement. They are blocks roughly hewed into some more or less imperfect forms of humanity, which are put into their places and which there lie. Miss Hepzibah is one of the former. The reader sees all round her, and is sure that she is alive,—though she is so incapable.

Then there is her brother Clifford, who was supposed to have committed the murder, and who, in the course of the chronicle, comes home to live with his sister. There are morsels in his story, bits of telling in the description of him, which are charming, but he is not so good as his sister, being less intelligible. Hawthorne himself had not realized the half-fatuous, dreamy, ill-used brother, as he had the sister. In painting a figure it is essential that the artist should himself know the figure he means to paint.

There is yet another Pyncheon,—Phoebe Pyncheon, who comes from a distance, Heaven knows why, to live with her far-away cousin. She is intended as a ray of sunlight,—as was Pearl in "The Scarlet Letter,"—and is more successful. As the old maid Pyncheon is capable of nothing, so is the young maid Pyncheon capable of everything. She is, however, hardly wanted in the story, unless it be that the ray of sunlight was necessary. And there is a young "daguerreotypist,"—as the photographer of the day used to be called,—who falls in love with the ray of sunlight, and marries her at the end; and who is indeed the lineal descendant of the original ill-used poor man who was hung as a witch. There is just one love-scene in the novel, most ghastly in its details; for the young man offers his love, and the girl accepts it, while they are aware that the wicked, respectable old Judge is sitting, all smeared with blood, and dead, in the next room to them. The love-scene, and the hurrying up of the marriage, and all the dollars which they inherit from the wicked Judge, and the "handsome dark-green barouche" prepared for their departure, which is altogether unfitted to the ideas which the reader has formed respecting them, are quite unlike Hawthorne, and would seem almost to have been added by some every-day, beef-and-ale, realistic novelist,[3] into whose hands the unfinished story had unfortunately fallen.

But no one should read "The House of the Seven Gables" for the sake of the story, or neglect to read it because of such faults as I have described. It is for the humor, the satire, and what I may perhaps call the philosophy which permeates it, that its pages should be turned. Its pages may be turned on any day, and under any circumstances. To "The Scarlet Letter" you have got to adhere till you have done with it; but you may take this volume by bits, here and there, now and again, just as you like it. There is a description of a few poultry, melancholy, unproductive birds, running over four or five pages, and written as no one but Hawthorne could have written it. There are a dozen pages or more in which the author pretends to ask why the busy Judge does not move from his chair,—the Judge the while having dree'd his doom and died as he sat. There is a ghastly spirit of drollery about this which would put the reader into full communion with Hawthorne if he had not read a page before, and did not intend to read a page after. To those who can make literary food of such passages as these, "The House of the Seven Gables" may be recommended. To others it will be caviare.

HENRY JAMES

[*The House of the Seven Gables*]†

The novelist Henry James (1843–1916) regarded Hawthorne as a literary genius who was nonetheless limited by the provinciality of

---

3. In a letter of February 11, 1860, to his publisher James T. Fields, Hawthorne remarked, according to Fields, that Trollope's novels were "written on the strength of beef and through the inspiration of ale" (Fields, *Yesterdays with Authors* [1872], 63). Trollope would appear to have read Fields's memoir.
† From *Hawthorne* (London: Macmillan, 1879), 122–26, 129–30.

antebellum New England culture. Published in England in the English Men of Letters series (the only book in the series devoted to an American author), James's *Hawthorne* remains an essential account of Hawthorne's life and art.

The House of the Seven Gables was written at Lenox, among the mountains of Massachusetts, a village nestling, rather loosely, in one of the loveliest corners of New England, to which Hawthorne had betaken himself after the success of *The Scarlet Letter* became conspicuous, in the summer of 1850, and where he occupied for two years an uncomfortable little red house which is now pointed out to the inquiring stranger. The inquiring stranger is now a frequent figure at Lenox, for the place has suffered the process of lionisation. It has become a prosperous watering-place, or at least (as there are no waters), as they say in America, a summer-resort. It is a brilliant and generous landscape, and thirty years ago a man of fancy, desiring to apply himself, might have found both inspiration and tranquility there. Hawthorne found so much of both that he wrote more during his two years of residence at Lenox than at any period of his career. He began with *The House of the Seven Gables*, which was finished in the early part of 1851. This is the longest of his three American novels, it is the most elaborate, and in the judgment of some persons it is the finest. It is a rich, delightful, imaginative work, larger and more various than its companions, and full of all sorts of deep intentions, of interwoven threads of suggestion. But it is not so rounded and complete as *The Scarlet Letter*; it has always seemed to me more like a prologue to a great novel than a great novel itself. I think this is partly owing to the fact that the subject, the *donnée*,[1] as the French say, of the story, does not quite fill it out, and that we get at the same time an impression of certain complicated purposes on the author's part, which seem to reach beyond it. I call it larger and more various than its companions, and it has indeed a greater richness of tone and density of detail. The colour, so to speak, of *The House of the Seven Gables* is admirable. But the story has a sort of expansive quality which never wholly fructifies, and as I lately laid it down, after reading it for the third time, I had a sense of having interested myself in a magnificent fragment. Yet the book has a great fascination, and of all of those of its author's productions which I have read over while writing this sketch, it is perhaps the one that has gained most by re-perusal. If it be true of the others that the pure, natural quality of the imaginative strain is their great merit, this is at least as true of *The House of the Seven Gables*, the charm of which is in a peculiar degree of the kind that we fail to reduce to its grounds—like that of the

1. The given.

sweetness of a piece of music, or the softness of fine September weather. It is vague, indefinable, ineffable; but it is the sort of thing we must always point to in justification of the high claim that we make for Hawthorne. In this case of course its vagueness is a drawback, for it is difficult to point to ethereal beauties; and if the reader whom we have wished to inoculate with our admiration inform[s] us after looking awhile that he perceives nothing in particular, we can only reply that, in effect, the object is a delicate one.

The House of the Seven Gables comes nearer being a picture of contemporary American life than either of its companions; but on this ground it would be a mistake to make a large claim for it. It cannot be too often repeated that Hawthorne was not a realist. He had a high sense of reality—his Note-Books superabundantly testify to it; and fond as he was of jotting down the items that make it up, he never attempted to render exactly or closely the actual facts of the society that surrounded him. I have said—I began by saying—that his pages were full of its spirit, and of a certain reflected light that springs from it; but I was careful to add that the reader must look for his local and national quality between the lines of his writing and in the *indirect* testimony of his tone, his accent, his temper, of his very omissions and suppressions. *The House of the Seven Gables* has, however, more literal actuality than the others, and if it were not too fanciful an account of it, I should say that it renders, to an initiated reader, the impression of a summer afternoon in an elm-shadowed New England town. It leaves upon the mind a vague correspondence to some such reminiscence, and in stirring up the association it renders it delightful. The comparison is to the honour of the New England town, which gains in it more than it bestows. The shadows of the elms, in *The House of the Seven Gables*, are exceptionally dense and cool; the summer afternoon is peculiarly still and beautiful; the atmosphere has a delicious warmth, and the long daylight seems to pause and rest. But the mild provincial quality is there, the mixture of shabbiness and freshness, the paucity of ingredients. The end of an old race—this is the situation that Hawthorne has depicted, and he has been admirably inspired in the choice of the figures in whom he seeks to interest us. They are all figures rather than characters—they are all pictures rather than persons. But if their reality is light and vague, it is sufficient, and it is in harmony with the low relief and dimness of outline of the objects that surround them. They are all types, to the author's mind, of something general, of something that is bound up with the history, at large, of families and individuals, and each of them is the centre of a cluster of those ingenious and meditative musings, rather melancholy, as a general thing, than joyous, which melt into the current and texture of the story and give it a kind of moral richness. A grotesque old spinster, simple, childish, penniless, very humble at heart, but rigidly conscious of her pedigree; an amiable bachelor, of an epicurean temperament and an enfeebled intellect, who has passed twenty years of his life in penal confinement for a crime of which he was unjustly pronounced guilty;[2] a sweet-natured and bright-faced young girl from the country, a poor relation of these two ancient decrepitudes, with whose moral mustiness her modern freshness and soundness are contrasted; a young man still more modern, holding the latest opinions, who has sought his fortune up and down the world, and, though he has not found it, takes a genial and enthusiastic view of the future: these, with two or three remarkable accessory figures, are the persons concerned in the little drama. The drama is a small one, but as Hawthorne does not put it before us for its own superficial sake, for the dry facts of the case, but for something in it which he holds to be symbolic and of large application, something that points a moral and that it beho[o]ves us to remember, the scenes in the rusty wooden house whose gables give its name to the story, have something of the dignity both of history and of tragedy. * * *

* * * Evidently, however, what Hawthorne designed to represent was not the struggle between an old society and a new, for in this case he would have given the old one a better chance; but simply, as I have said, the shrinkage and extinction of a family. This appealed to his imagination; and the idea of long perpetuation and survival always appears to have filled him with a kind of horror and disapproval. Conservative, in a certain degree, as he was himself, and fond of retrospect and quietude and the mellowing influences of time, it is singular how often one encounters in his writings some expression of mistrust of old houses, old institutions, long lines of descent. He was disposed apparently to allow a very moderate measure in these respects, and he condemns the dwelling of the Pyncheons to disappear from the face of the earth because it has been standing a couple of hundred years. In this he was an American of Americans; or rather he was more American than many of his countrymen, who, though they are accustomed to work for the short run rather than the long, have often a lurking esteem for things that show the marks of having lasted. I will add that Holgrave is one of the few figures, among those which Hawthorne created, with regard to which the absence of the realistic mode of treatment is felt as a loss. Holgrave is not sharply enough characterised; he lacks features; he is not an individual, but a type. But my last word about this admirable novel must not be a restrictive

---

2. Clifford spends approximately thirty years in prison.

one. It is a large and generous production, pervaded with that vague hum, that indefinable echo, of the whole multitudinous life of man, which is the real sign of a great work of fiction.

WILLIAM DEAN HOWELLS

[Dim, Forlorn Wraiths]†

The Ohio-born novelist, critic, and editor William Dean Howells (1837–1920) regularly expressed his admiration for Hawthorne. The author of such novels as *The Rise of Silas Lapham* (1885) and *A Hazard of New Fortunes* (1890) and an influential editor at the *Atlantic Monthly* and *Harper's Magazine*, Howells first read Hawthorne in the late 1850s, and in 1860, as he describes in his *Literary Friends and Acquaintance* (1900), called on him to pay homage to his genius. Later in his career, however, Howells began to have second thoughts about the extent of Hawthorne's achievement.

There is, of course, a choice in Hawthorne romances, and I myself prefer "The Blithedale Romance" and "The Scarlet Letter" to "The Marble Faun" and "The House of the Seven Gables." The last, indeed, I have found as nearly tiresome as I could find anything of Hawthorne's. I do not think it is censuring it unjustly to say that it seems the expansion of a short-story motive to the dimensions of a novel; and the slight narrative in which the concept is nursed with whimsical pathos to the limp end, appears sometimes to falter, and alarms the sympathetic reader at other times with the fear of an absolute lapse. The characters all lack the vitality which the author gives the people of his other books. The notion of the hapless Clifford Pyncheon, who was natured for happiness and beauty, but was fated to such a hard and ugly doom, is perhaps too single for the realization of a complete personality; and poor old Hepzibah, his sister, is of scarcely more sufficient material. They move dim, forlorn wraiths before the fancy, and they bring only such proofs of their reality as ghosts seen by others can supply. The careful elaboration with which they are studied seems only to render them more doubtful, and there is not much in the pretty, fresh-hearted little Phœbe Pyncheon, or her lover Holgrave, with all his generous rebellion against the obsession of the present by the past, to render the central figures convincing. Hawthorne could not help giving form to his work, but as nearly as any work of his could be so "The House of the Seven Gables" is straggling. There is at any rate no great womanly presence to pull it powerfully together, and hold it

† From *Heroines of Fiction*, 2 vols. (New York: Harper & Brothers, 1901), I.163–64.

in the beautiful unity characteristic of "The Blithedale Romance" and "The Scarlet Letter." What solidarity it has is in the simple Salem circumstance of the story, where the antique Puritanic atmosphere merges with the modern air in a complexion of perennial provinciality.

D. H. LAWRENCE

[Vacuum Cleaner]†

The English writer David Herbert Lawrence (1885–1930) is best known for such novels as *Sons and Lovers* (1913) and *Lady Chatterley's Lover* (1928). In *Studies in Classic American Literature*, he has appreciative chapters on Hawthorne's *The Scarlet Letter* and *The Blithedale Romance*. These are his complete remarks on *The House of the Seven Gables*.

The House of the Seven Gables has "atmosphere". The passing of the old order of the proud, bearded, black-browed Father: an order which is slowly ousted from life, and lingeringly haunts the old dark places. But comes a new generation to sweep out even the ghosts, with these new vacuum cleaners. No ghost could stand up against a vacuum cleaner.

The new generation is having no ghosts or cobwebs. It is setting up in the photography line, and is just going to make a sound financial thing out of it. For this purpose all old hates and old glooms, that belong to the antique order of Haughty Fathers, all these are swept up in the vacuum cleaner, and the vendetta-born young couple effect a perfect understanding under the black cloth of a camera and prosperity. *Vivat Industria!*

Oh, Nathaniel, you savage ironist! Ugh, how you'd have *hated* it if you'd had nothing but the prosperous, "dear" young couple to write about! If you'd lived to the day when America was nothing but a Main Street.

> The Dark Old Fathers.
> The Beloved Wishy-Washy Sons.
> The Photography Business.
> ? ? ?

---

† From *Studies in Classic American Literature* (1923; rpt. New York: Viking Press, 1964), 104.

F. O. MATTHIESSEN

[Energy of Disease]†

The main theme that Hawthorne evolved from this history of the Pyncheons and the Maules was not the original curse on the house, but the curse that the Pyncheons have continued to bring upon themselves. Clifford may phrase it wildly in his sense of release at the Judge's death: 'What we call real estate—the solid ground to build a house on—is the naked foundation on which nearly all the guilt of this world rests. A man will commit almost any wrong—he will heap up an immense pile of wickedness, as hard as granite, and which will weigh as heavily upon his soul, to eternal ages,—only to build a great gloomy, dark-chambered mansion, for himself to die in, and for his posterity to be miserable in.' But this also corresponds to Hawthorne's view in his preface, a view from which the dominating forces of his country had just begun to diverge most widely with the opening of California: 'the folly of tumbling down an avalanche of ill-gotten gold, or real estate, on the heads of an unfortunate posterity, thereby to maim and crush them, until the accumulated mass shall be scattered abroad in its original atoms.' Hawthorne's objections to the incumbrance of property often ran close to Thoreau's.

What Hawthorne set himself to analyze is this 'energy of disease,' this lust for wealth that has held the dominating Pyncheons in its inflexible grasp. After their original victory, their drive for power had long since shifted its ground, but had retained its form of oppressing the poor, for the present Judge steps forward to seize the property of his feeble cousins Hepzibah and Clifford, with the same cold unscrupulousness that had actuated the original Colonel in his dealings with the Maules. The only variation is that, 'as is customary with the rich, when they aim at the honors of a republic,' he had learned the expediency, which had not been forced upon his freer ancestor, of masking his relentless will beneath a veneer of 'paternal benevolence.' Thus what Hawthorne saw handed down from one generation to another were not—and this paradoxical phrase was marked by Melville—'the big, heavy, solid unrealities' such as gold and hereditary position, but inescapable traits of character.

† From *American Renaissance: Art and Expression in the Age of Emerson and Whitman* (Oxford: Oxford University Press, 1941), 326–27. Copyright © 1941 by Oxford University Press, Inc. Used by permission of Oxford University Press, Inc.

HYATT H. WAGGONER

[Curves, Circles, and Cycles]†

The opening sentences, familiar though they are, are worth quoting:

> Half-way down by a by-street of one of our New England towns stands a rusty wooden house, with seven acutely peaked gables, facing towards various points of the compass, and a huge, clustered chimney in the midst. The street is Pyncheon Street; the house is the old Pyncheon House; and an elm-tree, of wide circumference, rooted before the door, is familiar to every town-born child by the title of the Pyncheon Elm.

In view of what we have discovered of Hawthorne's habit of emphasizing in his descriptions only those details that are most significant, we shall do well to note certain images here. Hawthorne opens his story of the house that, as we later discover, was built by pride and possessed by death on the very day of the housewarming with a description that stresses the darkness and angularity of the structure and the "wide circumference" of the great tree that is said later to "over-shadow" it. A careful reading of the story will disclose no significant feature of structure or texture, image or concept, that is not associated in some way with the suggestions contained in the house and the elm.

The outward appearance of the house, Hawthorne tells us in the sentences immediately following those I have quoted, had always reminded him of a human face. The interior, especially the great chimney in the center, he repeatedly presents in terms of heart imagery. The elm introduced in the second sentence is described more fully later in the first chapter and again in chapter nineteen, where we are once more reminded that it has the shape of a "sphere." It is the source, we learn, of whatever beauty the house possesses, and it makes the house "a part of nature." At the end the few leaves left it by an autumn gale "whisper unintelligible prophecies" as the last of the Pyncheons leave the house forever.

The associations clustered around the house and the elm, and particularly the straight lines and angles of the one and the curves, circles, and cycles of the other, are not equally present everywhere or scattered at random throughout. In the first ten chapters angular images predominate, from their introduction in the title and the

† From *Hawthorne: A Critical Study*, rev. ed. (Cambridge, MA: The Belknap Press of Harvard University Press, 1955, 1963), 162–64. Copyright © 1955, 1963 by the President and Fellows of Harvard College. Reprinted by permission of the publisher.

first sentence through the portrayal of Hepzibah to their last new embodiment in the Pyncheon fowls in the tenth chapter. Meanwhile, however, images of curve and circle, though subordinate, are also present, especially in the several reminders of the shape of the elm, in the introduction of Phoebe, and in the treatment of Clifford's portrait. In the last eleven chapters the action is dominated by the presence of Phoebe and Clifford, both clearly associated with images of curve and circle. When in the last chapter Pyncheon and Maule are united and depart from the house, the theme which has been rendered visible by straight lines and angles is overcome by that embodied in curves, circles, and cycles.

This contrast between two strongly contrasted patterns of imagery, one of which diminishes in frequency and emphasis while the other increases in both, seems to me to lead us to the heart of the novel. The house is both setting and symbol: it is the antagonist in a drama of good and evil. But the elm is taller even than the house, and overshadows it: appropriately enough, it has the last word. Hepzibah, in whose gaunt angularity and frown we see again the features of the house, is in the spotlight in the opening chapters, only to be supplanted by Clifford after his return from prison. As the climax approaches and the two victims of the past make an abortive attempt at flight, it is he who takes command. At the end he too retires into the background while Phoebe and Holgrave lead the way to the new life. The soft lines of Clifford's oval face, the rounded grace of Phoebe, the seasonal-cyclical prophecies of the elm—these replace the rigid angles of the house and of Hepzibah and of the Pyncheon fowls as the revolution of the hands on the face of his watch mock the dead judge's ambitious plans and delusions of permanence.

A. N. KAUL

[The Rising Democracy]†

Maule's curse has the effect, among other things, of making the well of sweet water in the Pyncheon house hard and brackish, and generally of poisoning at the source the life-stream of the Pyncheon generations. His more substantial revenge, however, is that his numerous metaphorical progeny—the lower orders of the rising democracy—take possession of the vast lands originally granted by patent to the Pyncheons' ancestor; and it reaches a triumphant cli-

† From *The American Vision: Actual and Ideal Society in Nineteenth-Century Fiction* (New Haven, CT: Yale University Press, 1963), 191–92.

max when Holgrave, who is more literally Maule's lineal descendant, inherits, together with Phoebe, the Pyncheon estate itself. This story is, in other words, Hawthorne's parable of leveling democracy in America. One notices here again that in his drama of the American past the balancing factor is not the farther past of Europe but the future of America. This is not to say that the democratic development of the early nineteenth century engaged the full range of his sympathies or exhausted for him the whole prospect of possibilities. On the contrary, his attitude toward it is deeply ambivalent. Nor is this ambivalence a matter of hesitating between the Pyncheons and the Maules. It arises from Hawthorne's facing, or rather his not facing enough, the problem of the merged future of the Pyncheons and the Maules—the problem, in other words, of the future of democracy itself.

FREDERICK C. CREWS

[Imperfect Repression]†

*   *   *

Yet in a cryptic way *The House of the Seven Gables* deals extensively with moral and psychological affairs. Its "necromancies," we are told, may one day find their true meaning within "modern psychology" (III, 42).[1] In various ways Hawthorne allows us to see the entire historical, social, and symbolic framework of the romance as pertaining to the question of individual guilt. The focal symbol of the House is endowed from the opening page with "a human countenance" (III, 17), and the struggle for possession of it follows familiar Hawthornian lines. The falsely accused wizard Matthew Maule has not been simply executed by his enemy, Colonel Pyncheon; he has been incorporated into the subsequent life of the House. The new structure "would include the home of the dead and buried wizard, and would thus afford the ghost of the latter a kind of privilege to haunt its new apartments . . ." (III, 21). Like the more strictly figurative "ruined wall" of *The Scarlet Letter*, the Pyncheon estate embodies a mental condition in which an uneasy re-enactment of guilt will be made necessary by the effort to avoid responsibility for that guilt. For all its political and social ramifica-

---

† From "Homely Witchcraft," in *The Sins of the Fathers: Hawthorne's Psychological Themes* (New York: Oxford University Press, 1966), 171–93. Copyright © 1966 by Frederick Crews. Used by permission of Oxford University Press.

1. The parenthetical volume and page references refer to *The Complete Works of Nathaniel Hawthorne*, ed. George Parsons Lathrop, 13 vols. (Boston and New York, 1882–83) [editor's note].

tions, the Maule-Pyncheon antagonism is chiefly a metaphor of imperfect repression.[2]

This imperfect repression is the agent of all the ironic justice in *The House of the Seven Gables*. Every tyrant is psychologically at the mercy of his victim; or, as Hawthorne puts it in his notebook, "All slavery is reciprocal" (*American Notebooks*, p. 107).[3] The rule is first applied to the original Colonel Pyncheon, who dies while inaugurating the House he has built on the executed Matthew Maule's property. It is clear that the Colonel's "curse" of susceptibility to sudden death is nothing other than his guilt toward Maule. The pattern is repeated for Gervayse Pyncheon in the story told by Holgrave; this Pyncheon's greed makes him tacitly co-operate when the second Matthew Maule, supposedly in exchange for a valuable document, takes mesmeric control over his daughter and subsequently causes her death. And if Marks's theory is correct,[4] Jaffrey Pyncheon is similarly enslaved to the oppressed Clifford, who is able to cause Jaffrey's death merely by entering his field of vision. In all these cases it is bad conscience, rather than arbitrary plotting on Hawthorne's part, that has exacted punishment for abuses of power.

It is not possible, however, to say that perfect justice is done. If the authoritarian characters suffer from a secret *malaise* and eventually come to grief, they nevertheless have their full stomachs and public dignity for compensation; revenge is sudden and therefore incomplete. The meek victims, by contrast, are in continual misery (if they survive at all) until the reversal occurs, and even then they retain their internalized sense of persecution. Hepzibah and Clifford, who are presented as figures of infantile innocence, are more pathetic in trying to enjoy their freedom after Jaffrey's death than in their former state of intimidation. "For, what other dungeon is so dark as one's own heart! What jailer so inexorable as one's self!" (III, 204). These sentences, applied to two characters who have done nothing wrong and indeed have been virtually incapable of feeling temptation, may remind us that Hawthorne's focus is not on moral guilt but on a broader phenomenon of psychological tyranny. The very prominence of Hepzibah and Clifford in the plot, along

2. Note, for example, that the hereditary mesmeric power of the Maules, who are said to dominate the Pyncheons in "the topsy-turvy commonwealth of sleep" (III, 42), directly depends on the Pyncheons' continuing bad conscience. Holgrave, the last of the Maules, tells us this (III, 64), and Hawthorne himself speculates "whether each inheritor of the property—conscious of wrong, and failing to rectify it—did not commit anew the great guilt of his ancestor, and incur all its original responsibilities" (III, 34) [Crews's note].
3. Crews's text is *Nathaniel Hawthorne, the American Notebooks*, ed. Randall Stewart (New Haven, CT: Yale University Press, 1932) [editor's note].
4. A reference to Alfred H. Marks, "Who Killed Judge Pyncheon? The Role of the Imagination in *The House of the Seven Gables*," *PMLA*, 71 (1956): 355–69. Earlier in the chapter Crews writes: "As Alfred H. Marks persuasively argues, Hawthorne implies that Jaffrey's mysterious death is caused by the unexpected sight of the 'ghost' of Clifford Pyncheon" (*The Sins of the Fathers*, 177) [editor's note].

with the somewhat ponderous emphasis on the wasting-away of the Pyncheon energies from generation to generation, suggests that impotence rather than guilt may be Hawthorne's true theme.

I mean the term *impotence* in both a social and sexual sense. It is implied that in some way the Pyncheons have become effete by continuing to deny the claims of the vigorous and plebeian Maules. We could say that a failure of adaptation to modern democratic conditions has left the Pyncheons socially and economically powerless. Clearly, however, this failure has a sexual dimension. Not the least of the Maules' secret privileges is to "haunt . . . the chambers into which future bridegrooms were to lead their brides" (III, 21f.)—a fairly direct reference to some interference with normal sexuality. Just as denial of the earthy Maule element in society leads eventually to a loss of social power, so the same denial in emotional nature—symbolized by refusal to intermarry with the Maule line—leads to a loss of sexual power. Hepzibah and Clifford are the embodied result of these denials. * * *

NINA BAYM

[Holgrave]†

* * * If [Holgrave's] radicalism is based on his innocence, and is therefore in error, the error is noble. Radicalism like Holgrave's is inseparable from the kind of spontaneous and impulsive energy he embodies. He is in fact presented as an admirable person, the most unequivocally heroic of Hawthorne's generally weak male characters. He is a courageous, high-principled, idealistic, kind-hearted, self-reliant and sensitive youth, who has "never violated the innermost man," has carried his conscience along with him," who combines "inward strength" with "enthusiasm" and "warmth" and gives a total "appearance of admirable powers" (pp. 177, 180).[1]

* * *

The optimist Holgrave, while recognizing that he operates in a repressive society, refuses to turn his art to twisted purposes. He believes that the world is making strides towards a Utopia where Eros will have a place above ground, and he means to participate in the movement. Art in the interim, as he conceives of it, can have a liberating and constructive effect through its power to expose the truth. His daguerreotypes, taken with the help of the sunlight that

† From "Hawthorne's Holgrave: The Failure of the Artist-Hero," *JEGP*, 69 (1970): 587, 589–90.
1. Page references are to Hawthorne, *The House of the Seven Gables*, ed. William Charvat et al. (Columbus: Ohio State University Press, 1965) [editor's note].

is his friend and ally, show Pyncheon's true nature, illuminating his villainy and identifying him with his persecuting ancestor. His tale of Alice Pyncheon, developed with the help of the moonshine that for Hawthorne always accompanies romance, exposes the depravity of the Maules. Art, thus practiced, can be an agent of progress and reform. The story of Alice Pyncheon demonstrates Holgrave's understanding of his own situation; his refusal to succumb to the opportunity which Phoebe's response gives him demonstrates his moral worthiness. He withstands temptation, and not only Phoebe but art itself is saved by his forbearance.

ERIC J. SUNDQUIST

[Mirror with a Memory]†

The "mirror with a memory" is what Oliver Wendell Holmes called the daguerreotype.[1] We are urged to say that Hawthorne was hardly in need of such an invention, since his mirror of romance continually thronged, much to his horror and delight, with ancestral memories. Hawthorne lived in a thoroughly *speculative* world, haunted by doubles and fathers, fathers and doubles, who stare back at him like a pair of eyes on a canvas, on a page, in a mirror— his own eyes. The camera box used in daguerreotyping is in this respect an uncanny emblem of Hawthorne's art; it is a pair of eyes itself, eyes not one's own that can be used to speculate and represent, used as a tool of art even, perhaps, by a blind man. The mirror of the daguerreotype on the one hand offers the capacity for exact duplication, the means to fix the image in a lasting way; but on the other, it is precisely because the image is lasting and so perfectly a double that the daguerreotype is most unnerving for Hawthorne. Like that "seer, before whose sadly gifted eye" the palatial facade of public character collapses, revealing "the decaying corpse within" (*HG*, 230),[2] the daguerreotype perfects Hawthorne's fantasy of himself as the voyeur who sees all without being implicated in the scene. But Hawthorne *is* implicated in the scene, and to a remarkable extent. The mirror *with* a memory makes the mirror *of* memory lasting: it executes a sign of revenge and conquest, and a reminder of submission to the forms of the past.

† From *Home as Found: Authority and Genealogy in Nineteenth-Century American Literature* (Baltimore: Johns Hopkins University Press, 1979), 141.
1. Quoted in Beaumont Newhall, *The History of Photography from 1839 to the Present Day* (New York: The Museum of Modern Art, 1949), 27 [Sundquist's note].
2. The page reference is to Hawthorne, *The House of the Seven Gables*, ed. William Charvat et al. (Columbus: Ohio State University Press, 1965) [editor's note].

Recent Criticism, 1981–Present

Recent critics have been focusing on the complex historicism of *The House of the Seven Gables*, even as they continue to attend to the novel's aesthetic power and challenges. Three studies in particular have been enormously influential in helping stimulate what could be termed a renaissance of critical interest in Hawthorne's second novel: Michael T. Gilmore's 1981 reading of *The House of the Seven Gables* in connection with the pressures of the literary marketplace, Walter Benn Michael's 1985 examination of the novel in the context of debates on slavery and capitalism, and Gillian Brown's 1990 analysis of the novel with respect to discourses of gender and domesticity. In addition to reprinting these three seminal studies, this section includes five additional critical analyses that look at *The House of the Seven Gables* in relation to the social dynamics of romance (Richard H. Millington), daguerreotypy (Alan Trachtenberg), race (David Anthony), social class (Amy Schrager Lang), and queer interiority (Christopher Castiglia).

MICHAEL T. GILMORE

The Artist and the Marketplace in the House of the Seven Gables†

I

The fairy-tale ending of *The House of the Seven Gables* has not satisfied the novel's modern readers, most of whom have agreed with F. O. Matthiessen that "the reconciliation [of Maule and Pyncheon] is somewhat too lightly made" and that in bestowing the Judge's ill-gotten wealth upon the surviving characters, Hawthorne evidently overlooked his own warnings about the evils of inheritance.[1] William Charvat has suggested that the ending's weakness

---

† From *ELH*, 48:1 (1981): 172–189. Copyright © The Johns Hopkins University Press. Reprinted with permission of The Johns Hopkins University Press. All notes are Gilmore's.

† From *ELH*, 48:1 (1981): 172–189. Copyright © The Johns Hopkins University Press. Reprinted with permission of The Johns Hopkins University Press. All notes are Gilmore's.

1. F. O. Matthiessen, *American Renaissance: Art and Expression in the Age of Emerson and Whitman* (New York: Oxford Univ. Press, 1941), p. 332. For a recent defense of the ending, see Edwin M. Eigner, *The Metaphysical Novel in England and America: Dickens, Bulwer, Hawthorne, Melville* (Berkeley: Univ. of California Press, 1978), pp. 99–109.

348

may stem less from authorial oversight than from the requirements of the marketplace. While noting that Hawthorne himself seems to have shared the popular preference for fiction combining "sunshine and shadow," Charvat points out that he was also alert to "the professional or commercial aspects of his project." Despite the moderate success of *The Scarlet Letter*, he was still hard pressed financially and knew only too well that his reputation for "blackness" (as Melville termed it) was an obstacle to acceptance by the wider public. "We cannot ignore the possibility," adds Charvat, "that Hawthorne, in concluding his book as he did, was yielding to the world's wish that in stories everything should turn out well."[2]

In fact, it seems considerably more than a possibility. The text itself reveals a Hawthorne deeply concerned with his relation to the public and with his priorities as a writer who both craved fame and money and aspired—again in Melville's words—to be a master of "the great Art of Telling the Truth." Melville's famous review of *Mosses from an Old Manse* appeared just as Hawthorne began work on *The House of the Seven Gables*. "In this world of lies," Melville had argued, profound authors had no choice but to become deceivers, to hoodwink the general reader by concealing their meanings.[3] But Hawthorne could not share Melville's apparent equanimity about adopting this strategy. He reacted with pain and dismay when he found himself obliged to employ it in his work-in-progress, and he was unable to suppress his misgivings that in bowing to the marketplace he was compromising his artistic independence and integrity.

II

Hawthorne states in the preface to *The House of the Seven Gables* that the romantic character of his tale consists in its being "a Legend, prolonging itself, from an epoch now gray in the distance, down into our own broad daylight, and bringing along with it some of its legendary mist . . ." (p. 2). He proceeds in the opening chapter to speak of hereditary curses and ghostly powers, but his conception of the legendary is not confined to the paraphernalia of

2. William Charvat, "Introduction," *The House of the Seven Gables*, Centenary Edition of the Works of Nathaniel Hawthorne, ed. William Charvat et. al. (Columbus: Ohio State Univ. Press, 1965), vol. 2, pp. xx–xxii. All citations to *The House of the Seven Gables* will be from this edition; page references will be included in the text. On Hawthorne's relation to the reading public, see also Henry Nash Smith, *Democracy and the Novel: Popular Resistance to Classic American Writers* (New York: Oxford Univ. Press, 1978), pp. 16–34; and Nina Baym, *The Shape of Hawthorne's Career* (Ithaca: Cornell Univ. Press, 1976).

3. Herman Melville, "Hawthorne and His Mosses," in *Moby-Dick*, Norton Critical Edition, ed. Harrison Hayford and Hershel Parker (New York: W. W. Norton and Co., 1967), pp. 542, passim.

gothic romance.[4] He is also referring to that body of knowledge and speculation which is excluded from the officially sanctioned view of things. The legendary encompasses the "rumors," "traditions," and "fables" that necessarily remain clandestine and underground because they express truths too controversial for public utterance. In discussing Colonel Pyncheon's designs on the Maule homestead, Hawthorne observes that "No written record of this dispute is known to be in existence. Our acquaintance with the whole subject is derived chiefly from tradition" (p. 7). Tradition is also his sole authority for intimating a connection between the executed wizard's curse—"God will give him blood to drink"—and the mysterious manner of the Colonel's death. The Colonel's laudatory funeral sermon, "which was printed and is still extant," contains no hint of guilt and retribution. "Tradition—which sometimes brings down truth that history has let slip, but is oftener the wild babble of the time, such as was formerly spoken at the fireside, and now congeals in newspapers—tradition is responsible for all contrary averments" (p. 17). The imputation of troubled consciences to the Colonel's descendants is similarly laid to the town's "traditionary gossips" and to "impressions too vaguely founded to be put on paper" (p. 20).

Despite this last remark, the distinction being made here is not primarily between speech and writing. Hawthorne contrasts spoken words and written ones only insofar as they lend support to the more fundamental distinction between private and public discourse. Criticism of the Pyncheons is more likely to be expressed orally than on paper because the "written record," historical or otherwise, is addressed to the world and dare not impeach the characters of eminent men whom all the world agrees in honoring. The awareness of a potentially unsympathetic audience can be inhibiting to the artist and work against truthfulness in any medium of expression.

This notion is implicit in Hawthorne's discussion of Judge Pyncheon. After noting that no one—neither inscriber of tombstones, nor public speaker, nor writer of history—would venture a word of censure against the Judge, he continues:

> But besides these cold, formal, and empty words of the chisel
> that inscribes, the voice that speaks, and the pen that writes,
> for the public eye and for distant time—and which inevitably
> lose much of their truth and freedom by the fatal conscious-
> ness of so doing—there were traditions about the ancestor,
> and private diurnal gossip about the Judge, remarkably accor-
> dant in their testimony. It is often instructive to take the

4. On Hawthorne's use of the legendary in *The House of the Seven Gables*, see Richard H. Brodhead, *Hawthorne, Melville, and the Novel* (Chicago: Univ. of Chicago Press, 1976), pp. 69–90.

woman's, the private and domestic view, of a public man; nor can anything be more curious than the vast discrepancy between portraits intended for engraving, and the pencil-sketches that pass from hand to hand, behind the original's back (p. 122).

The reference in this passage to loss of truth and freedom has obvious relevance for an author who claims in his preface "a certain latitude" as a writer of romance and who takes as his subject "the truth of the human heart" (p. 1). By extending his observations to the difference between engravings and pencil sketches, moreover, Hawthorne suggests that a major reason for circumspection in addressing the public is the fear of offending potential customers. The inference that the wisdom associated with the legendary is not only guarded and private but unsalable emerges clearly from his description of the Colonel's portrait hanging in the house of the seven gables. With the passage of time, the portrait's superficial coloring has faded and the inward traits of its subject have grown more prominent and striking. Such an effect, Hawthorne notes, is not uncommon in antique paintings: "They acquire a look which an artist (if he have anything like the complaisancy of artists, now-a-days) would never dream of presenting to a patron as his own characteristic expression, but which, nevertheless, we at once recognize as reflecting the unlovely truth of a human soul" (p. 59). In other words, the artist who is determined to express the truth openly in the present will find it impossible to sell his creations.

Perhaps the key word in Hawthorne's description of the contemporary artist is "complaisancy." Whether the prospective buyer is an individual patron or the general public, the artist has to appear accomodating if he wishes to succeed in the marketplace. He cannot afford to be honest because his truth-telling may alienate his audience and deprive him of his livelihood. Although Hawthorne is speaking here of the portrait painter in particular, his analysis applies to anyone involved in the process of exchange. In *The House of the Seven Gables* he comments most directly on the exchange process and the relation of buyer and seller in the chapters devoted to Hepzibah's opening of her cent-shop.

Finding herself practically destitute after a lifetime of patrician indolence, Hepzibah has decided to try her hand at business when the narrative proper opens in contemporary Salem. Although she herself cares little for material comforts, she expects the imminent return of her brother Clifford from jail and refuses to apply for financial assistance to their cousin the Judge, the man she holds responsible for Clifford's long imprisonment. With no other recourse but to support Clifford by her own exertions, she has mustered her

courage to re-open the little shop built into the house by a penurious ancestor and long regarded as an embarrassment by the family.
Hawthorne, in his capacity as "a disembodied listener" (p. 30), follows her protracted preparations for the first day behind the
counter with a mixture of sympathy and satire. She is introduced
sighing at her toilet as she struggles to overcome her reluctance
about facing the world. At least twice she pauses before her toilet
glass in a pathetic attempt to make herself look attractive. Stepping
at last into the passageway, she slowly makes her way through the
house to the shop's entrance and with a sudden effort thrusts herself across the threshold. Her hesitation returns inside the shop
and she nervously sets about rearranging the goods in the window.
Still she hangs back from "the public eye" (p. 39), as if, writes
Hawthorne, she expected to come before the community "like a
disembodied divinity, or enchantress, holding forth her bargains to
the reverential and awe-striken purchaser, in an invisible hand" (p.
40). Unlike Hawthorne himself, however, she is not permitted the
luxury of invisibility: "She was well aware that she must ultimately
come forward, and stand revealed in her proper individuality; but,
like other sensitive persons, she could not bear to be observed in
the gradual process, and chose rather to flash forth on the world's
astonished gaze, at once" (p. 40).

Hepzibah strikingly recalls Hester Prynne standing on the scaffold with her badge of shame. Hawthorne's Puritan adulteress, who
first appears before the reader in the chapter entitled "The Market-
Place," is said to stagger "under the heavy weight of a thousand un-
relenting eyes."[5] As Hepzibah takes her place behind the counter,
she too is tortured "with a sense of overwhelming shame, that
strange and unloving eyes should have the privilege of gazing" at
her (p. 46). In recounting her tribulations, Hawthorne dwells on
the importance of being seen in trade and making a favorable impression. Hepzibah herself feels continued uneasiness over the appearance of the window: "It seemed as if the whole fortune or
failure of her shop might depend on the display of a different set of
articles, or substituting a fairer apple for one which appeared to be
specked" (pp. 46–7). Repeatedly Hawthorne calls attention to the
handicap of her scowl, which results from nearsightedness but has
unfortunately given her the reputation of being ill tempered. When
that shrewd Yankee Dixey passes by the shop, he loudly predicts
that Hepzibah's frown will be her financial undoing. "Make it go!"
he exclaims. "Not a bit of it! Why her face—I've seen it . . . her face
is enough to frighten Old Nick himself, if he had ever so great a

---

5. Nathaniel Hawthorne, *The Scarlet Letter*, Centenary Edition (Columbus: Ohio State
Univ. Press, 1962), vol. 1, p. 46.

mind to trade with her" (p. 47). Overhearing these words, Hepzibah has a painful vision that seems to underscore the futility of her venture. On one side of the street stands her antiquated shop, over which she presides with an offending scowl, and on the other rises a magnificent bazaar, "with a multitude of perfumed and glossy salesmen, smirking, smiling, bowing, and measuring out the goods!" (p. 49). Even the simple-minded Uncle Venner, who offers Hepzibah encouragement along with Benjamin Franklin-like maxims, advocates a beaming countenance as "all-important" to success in business: "Put on a bright face for your customers, and smile pleasantly as you hand them what they ask for! A stale article, if you dip it in a good, warm, sunny smile, will go off better than a fresh one that you've scowled upon!" (p. 66).

As such passages suggest, Hawthorne is using Hepzibah to explore his own ambivalence about courting the public in order to make money. Although she herself is not an artist figure, she resembles her creator both in her history of isolation and her need to earn a living. One thinks immediately of Hawthorne's seclusion for thirteen years after graduating from Bowdoin and his self-designation as "the obscurest man of letters in America."[6] It is no wonder that he gives Hepzibah a Puritan progenitor who was involved in the witchcraft trials like his own ancestor John Hathorne, and who appears in his portrait much as William Hathorne is described in "The Custom-House," clutching a Bible and a sword. As an author who always insisted upon preserving "the inmost Me behind its veil,"[7] Hawthorne would not have found it difficult to appreciate Hepzibah's misgivings about encountering "the public gaze" (p. 35). He would have understood her resentment at the familiar tone adopted by her customers, who "evidently considered themselves not merely her equals but her patrons and superiors" (p. 54). Indeed, he draws an implicit parallel between his writing and the commodities she hopes to sell. Her stock consists primarily of items of food like apples, Indian meal, and gingerbread men, and in the preface he speaks of his book as an object to be eaten, calling it a "dish offered to the Public" (p. 1). And he seems almost as hesitant about getting his narrative under way as she does about opening for business. Just as she pauses apprehensively on the threshold of her shop, so "we are loitering faint-heartedly," says Hawthorne, "on the threshold of our story" (p. 34).

6. Nathaniel Hawthorne, "Preface," *Twice-Told Tales*, Centenary Edition (Columbus: Ohio State Univ. Press, 1974), vol. 9, p. 3.
7. *The Scarlet Letter*, Centenary Edition, p. 7; see also *Mosses from an Old Manse*, Centenary Edition (Columbus: Ohio State Univ. Press, 1974), vol. 10, p. 33: "So far as I am a man of really individual attributes, I veil my face; nor am I, nor have ever been, one of those supremely hospitable people, who serve up their own hearts delicately fried, with brain-sauce, as a tidbit for their beloved public."

Despite his sympathy for her discomfort, Hawthorne is far from
identifying with Hepzibah uncritically. A part of him yearned "to
open an intercourse with the world" and was not above advising his
publisher on how to entrap that "great gull," the general reader.[8]
This part finds her more comical than tragic and strongly disap-
proves of her reluctance to seek her own fortune. Although
Hawthorne himself had difficulty supporting his family by his writing, and lobbied actively for government appointments, in print he
commends the marketplace for fostering self-reliance and expresses
detached amusement at Hepzibah's dreams of being rescued from
trade by a sudden bequest. Too much of a democrat to endorse her
aristocratic pretensions, he agrees with Holgrave that she will discover satisfaction in contributing her mite "to the united struggle of
mankind" (p. 45). Her first sale does in fact bring her an unexpected
sense of accomplishment and dispels many of her fears about commerce with the world. But she lacks both the skill and the temperament to prosper as a saleswoman, and at the end of the day she has
as little to show for "all her painful traffic" (p. 67) as Hawthorne did
after his long apprenticeship as a writer of tales and sketches.

It is through Phoebe rather than Hepzibah herself that Hawthorne expresses his conviction—or more precisely his hope—that
it is possible to be engaged in market relations without suffering a
sense of violation. Phoebe, who has "had a table at a fancy-fair, and
made better sales than anybody," is able to drive a shrewd bargain
relying only on her "native truth and sagacity" (pp. 78–9). Her
practical mind abounds with schemes "whereby the influx of trade
might be increased, and rendered profitable, without a hazardous
outlay of capital" (p. 79). Her smile is unconscious of itself, and
therefore honest and spontaneous; for her it is a simple matter, in
Uncle Venner's phrase, to "put on a bright face for [her] customers." As Hawthorne often states, she has a naturally sunny disposition, and her presence is like "a gleam of sunshine" in the
gloomy old house (p. 80). Hepzibah is quick to acknowledge her superiority as a shopkeeper, and the public shows its agreement by
flocking to the store during the hours when she takes her turn behind the counter.

No doubt Hawthorne wished for comparable good fortune in his
dealings with the public. But he seems to have suspected that his
own sunny smile was not nearly so ready as Phoebe's. And he was
aware of the possibilities for deception in exchange relations, being
based as they are so largely on appearance. There is one character
in particular in *The House of the Seven Gables* who thoroughly ap-

---

8. "Preface," *Twice-Told Tales*, Centenary Edition, p. 6; Hawthorne to James T. Fields, letter of January 15, 1850, quoted by William Charvat. "Introduction," *The Scarlet Letter*,
Centenary Edition, p. xxii, n. 15.

preciates the marketability of a genial countenance, and who incurs the censure that Hawthorne feels toward his own worldly ambition.[9] Although his natural expression is anything but cheerful, Judge Jaffrey Pyncheon has worked up an extraordinary smile for public consumption. The passages describing his sham joviality are remarkable in Hawthorne's writing for their unrelieved hostility and exaggerated irony. In chapter 7, "The Pyncheon of To-day," where he first tries to gain an interview with Clifford, he puts on an especially dazzling face to win the confidence of Hepzibah and Phoebe. As he enters the house, "his smile grew as intense as if he had set his heart on counteracting the whole gloom of the atmosphere . . . by the unassisted light of his countenance" (p. 117). Advancing to greet Hepzibah, he wears a smile "so broad and sultry, that had it been only half as warm as it looked, a trellis of grapes might at once have turned purple under its summer-like exposure" (p. 127). Of course the Judge's sunshiny exterior only masks his darker purposes, and his smile changes to a frown like a thunder cloud when his wishes are opposed. But Jaffrey is too practiced a hypocrite to allow himself to be caught off guard for very long. Hawthorne devotes an entire paragraph to the ingratiating manner with which he covers his departure:

> With a bow to Hepzibah, and a degree of paternal benevolence in his parting nod to Phoebe, the Judge left the shop, and went smiling along the street. As is customary with the rich, when they aim at the honors of a republic, he apologized, as it were, to the people, for his wealth, prosperity, and elevated station, by a free and hearty manner towards those who knew him; putting off the more of his dignity, in due proportion with the humbleness of the man whom he saluted; and thereby proving a haughty consciousness of his advantages, as irrefragably as if he had marched forth, preceded by a troop of lackeys to clear the way. On this particular forenoon, so excessive was the warmth of Judge Pyncheon's kindly aspect, that (such, at least, was the rumor about town) an extra passage of water-carts was found essential, in order to lay the dust occasioned by so much extra sunshine! (pp. 130–31)

The Judge clearly has much in common with the oily, grinning salesmen of Hepzibah's vision. He also bears a marked resemblance to the Italian organ-grinder's monkey, who performs "a bow and scrape" (p. 164) while holding out his palm to receive the public's money.

The Judge has been well rewarded for his assiduous cultivation

9. Marcus Cunliffe suggests that his attacks on the Judge "throw light upon Hawthorne's complicated private defenses against worldly success." See Cunliffe's essay, *"The House of the Seven Gables,"* in *Hawthorne Centenary Essays,* ed. Roy Harvey Pearce (Columbus: Ohio State Univ. Press, 1964), p. 89.

of the public. Whereas Hepzibah's scowl threatens to ruin her, his smile has brought him every imaginable success. He is very rich, enjoys the reputation of a model citizen, and has been showered with public honors, including election to Congress. "Beyond all question," states Hawthorne, he "was a man of eminent respectability. The church acknowledged it; the state acknowledged it. It was denied by nobody" (p. 228). This assessment occurs in chapter 15, "The Scowl and the Smile," where Hawthorne also hints of perceptions more discerning than the world's. In an elaborate metaphor, he compares Jaffrey's public personality to a glittering and sunbathed palace, "which, in the view of other people, and ultimately in his own view, is no other than the man's character, or the man himself" (p. 229). But in some concealed nook of this splendid edifice, inaccessible to public view,

> may lie a corpse, half-decayed, and still decaying, and diffusing its death-scent through the palace! The inhabitant will not be conscious of it, for it has long been his daily breath! Neither will the visitors, for they smell only the rich odors which the master sedulously scatters through the palace. . . . Now and then, perchance, comes in a seer, before whose sadly gifted eye the whole structure melts into thin air, leaving only the hidden nook, the bolted closet, with the cobwebs festooned over its forgotten door, or the deadly hole under the pavement, and the decaying corpse within. Here, then, we are to seek the true emblem of the man's character, and of the deed which gives whatever reality it possesses to his life. And, beneath the show of a marble palace, that pool of stagnant water, foul with many impurities, and, perhaps, tinged with blood,—that secret abomination, above which, possibly, he may say his prayers, without remembering it,—is this man's miserable soul! (p. 230)

In this passage Hawthorne implicitly repudiates any connection between his own art and Jaffrey's manipulation of appearances. Jaffrey is an "artist" of the public, but Hawthorne's seer is an artist of the private, of the legendary. His unflattering vision of the human soul is no more marketable than the antique portrait of the Colonel; he could never hope to present it either to the public or the builder of the palace. Insofar as Hawthorne seeks to portray "the truth of the human heart," he himself is such an artist.

The figure in *The House of the Seven Gables* who most closely approximates this kind of artist is Holgrave, the daguerreotypist and descendant of the wizard. From the moment of their dispossession the Maules have been associated with ghostly powers, poverty, and secrecy. They are said to have outwardly cherished "no malice against individuals or the public, for the wrong which had been done them." Any grievances they may have felt were transmitted "at their own fireside" and "never acted upon, nor openly expressed" (p. 25). Down through the generations they have been marked off from other men by their "character of reserve" and by a self-imposed isolation which has kept them from prospering (p. 26). Holgrave, who appears in the text under the veil of an assumed name, has carried the family traditions into the present. Suspected of practicing the Black Art, he holds views subversive of established authority and generally remains aloof from the society of others. As he tells Phoebe, his impulse is not to bare his heart in public but "to look on, to analyze, to explain matters to myself" (p. 216). Even more so than Hepzibah, he suggests the side of Hawthorne that dominates the prefaces—the Hawthorne who insists on veiling his countenance from the reader's gaze and claims that his seeming intimacies "hide the man, instead of displaying him."[1] He further resembles his creator, who spent a year at Brook Farm, in his association with reformers and "community-men" (p. 84). And he writes stories which he supposedly contributes to periodicals where Hawthorne's own tales have appeared, such as *Graham's Magazine* and Godey's *Magazine and Lady's Book.*

Holgrave, in other words, is like Hawthorne before he wrote *The Scarlet Letter* and became known to the wider public. He obviously has earned little money from his periodical writing, and when Phoebe professes ignorance of his efforts, he exclaims much as the younger Hawthorne might have, "Well, such is literary fame!" (p. 186). The sample of his work reprinted in *The House of the Seven Gables*, "Alice Pyncheon," helps to explain his lack of success with the average reader. Like the larger text of which it forms a part, it tells a story of conflict between the Maules and Pyncheons, but it goes beyond Hawthorne's own narrative in its incautious use of the half-spoken and the legendary. The tale has Matthew Maule openly assert both his right to the house and his power over Alice, thus giving centrality to the very themes of class resentment and psychic mastery that Hawthorne tends to treat with circumspection. In writing it, as Holgrave says, he has essentially followed "wild, chimney-corner legend" (p. 197), and in general he shows neither aptitude nor inclination for an art that will be popular. His daguerreotypes, to borrow the distinction made by Hawthorne, are more like pencil sketches that have to be passed behind the subject's back than portraits suitable for engraving. Holgrave, who realizes this himself, explains to Phoebe that his photographic images bring out "the secret character with a truth that no painter would

1. Nathaniel Hawthorne, "Preface," *The Snow-Image and Uncollected Tales*, Centenary Edition (Columbus: Ohio State Univ. Press, 1974), vol. 11, p. 4.

ever venture upon, even could he detect it. There is at least no flattery in my humble line of art" (p. 91). He then shows her a daguerreotype miniature of the Judge that in the manner of the
Colonel's portrait reveals "the unlovely truth of a human soul." Remarkably enough, according to Holgrave, "the original wears, to the
world's eye . . . an exceedingly pleasant countenance, indicative of
benevolence, openness of heart, sunny good humor, and other
praiseworthy qualities of that cast." The face in the daguerreotype,
however, is "sly, subtle, hard, imperious, and, withal, cold as ice."
The picture's very truthfulness, of course, will make it impossible to
sell; as Holgrave observes, "It is so much the more unfortunate, as
[the original] is a public character of some eminence, and the likeness was intended to be engraved" (p. 92).

While Hawthorne clearly put much of himself into the daguerreotypist, it would be a mistake to exaggerate their similarities.
Rather, as the preface to *The Snow-Image* suggests, one must "look
through the whole range of his fictitious characters, good and evil,
in order to detect any of his essential traits. . . ."[2] The author of *The
House of the Seven Gables* had too much need of money to identify
completely with Holgrave's indifference to popularity. With only his
writing to support himself and his family, he could not afford to despise the commercial advantage of a pleasing exterior. And while he
might sympathize with Hepzibah, it is her cousin the Judge whom
"the world's laudatory voice" has acclaimed and enriched (p. 229).
The conflict between Maule and Pyncheon, Holgrave and Jaffrey, is
accordingly a conflict in Hawthorne's own mind. It reflects the division in his view of the artist as "a man of society" who appeals to
the general reader[3] and as a private teller of truth whose revelations
are unsalable. To gain acceptance with the public, is it necessary to
become a hypocrite like the Judge? Is it possible to depict the truth
of the heart like Holgrave without sacrificing commercial success?
Who is the rightful owner of the house of the seven gables? Of *The
House of the Seven Gables?* What kind of artist is Hawthorne finally
to be?

III

Hawthorne attempts to resolve this dilemma by reconciling Maule
and Pyncheon and writing a book of truth that will attract a popular audience. He proposes to bring the legendary mist into "our
own broad daylight" and to prove that Holgrave's insights are compatible with Phoebe's smile. Along with many of his readers, he had
been troubled by the lack of "cheering light" in *The Scarlet Letter*

2. "Preface," *The Snow-Image and Uncollected Tales*, Centenary Edition, p. 4.
3. "Preface," *Twice-Told Tales*, Centenary Edition, p. 6.

and attributed its popularity primarily to the introductory sketch. The story of Hester and the minister, he had written in "The Custom-House," "wears, to my eye, a stern and sombre aspect; too much ungladdened by genial sunshine; too little relieved by the tender and familiar influences which soften almost every scene of nature and real life, and, undoubtedly, should soften every picture of them."[4] Reviewers, including Hawthorne's favorite critic, E. P. Whipple, agreed. The book was too uniformly gloomy to please the general public.[5] In his second novel, Hawthorne was determined to remedy this commercial failing by alleviating his customary blackness with a liberal use of "genial sunshine."

The finished work does in fact avoid the relentlessly tragic tone of *The Scarlet Letter*. Although the narrative voice sometimes sounds as radical as Holgrave, many passages reveal a penchant for sentiment and fancy. Like the daguerreotypist, Hawthorne questions the integrity of great men and the political system that promotes them. In speaking of Jaffrey's gubernatorial ambitions, for example, he refers to the backroom politicians who "steal from the people, without its knowledge, the power of choosing its own rulers . . . This little knot of subtle schemers will control the convention, and, through it, dictate to the party" (p. 274). But these cynical reflections tend to alternate with heart-warming affirmations worthy of Phoebe. The Hawthorne who writes of the bees sent by God "to gladden our poor Clifford" (p. 148), or who gushes over his young heroine's domesticity, seems less an artist of the legendary than a "pen-and-ink" man addressing "the intellect and sympathies of the multitude."[6] And of course the clearest indication of Hawthorne's wish to effect a compromise between Maule and Pyncheon is the romance of Holgrave and Phoebe. Both characters give up some of their family traits and move toward a common ground. Admitting that his "legend" will never do for a popular audience, the daguerreotypist refrains from exercising the psychic power of the Maules and discovers a new respect for institutions. Phoebe, who has shed some of her sunshine as a result of living in the house, becomes "more womanly, and deep-eyed, in token of a heart that had begun to suspect its depths" (p. 297). Hawthorne's art comes to rest at the dead center of their marriage; in contrast to "Alice Pyncheon," which ends unhappily, the novel itself finds a way to combine salability with knowledge of the heart.

4. *The Scarlet Letter*, Centenary Edition, p. 43; see also Hawthorne to Horatio Bridge, letter of February 4, 1850, quoted by Charvat, "Introduction" to the Centenary Edition of *The Scarlet Letter*, p. xv.
5. Whipple's review is cited in Bertha Faust, *Hawthorne's Contemporaneous Reputation: A Study of Literary Opinion in America and England, 1828–1864* (1939; rpt. New York: Octagon Books, 1968), pp. 71–2.
6. "Rappaccini's Daughter," *Mosses from an Old Manse*, Centenary Edition, p. 91.

Or does it? If, as Hawthorne insisted, the book was "more proper and natural" for him to write than *The Scarlet Letter*,[7] why did he experience difficulty in completing it? According to Charvat, he probably began work in the late summer of 1850, made steady progress, and hoped to finish by November. His publishers, Ticknor, Reed, and Fields, began to advertise "A new Romance by the author of 'The Scarlet Letter' " in the October *Literary World*, and looked forward to having the completed manuscript in their hands by December 1. But Hawthorne slowed down unexpectedly after his rapid start and confessed to James T. Fields on November 29 that the conclusion was giving him particular problems: "It darkens damnably towards the close, but I shall try hard to pour some setting sunshine over it." The effort proved more troublesome and disturbing than Hawthorne anticipated, as is evident from a letter dated ten days later: "My desire and prayer is, to get through with the business already in hand . . . I have been in a Slough of Despond, for some days past—having written so fiercely that I came to a stand still. There are points where a writer gets bewildered, and cannot form any judgment of what he has done, nor tell what to do next." As late as January 12, only two weeks before the completion date given in the preface, he wrote to Fields that he was still "hammering away a little on the roof, and doing up a few odd jobs that were left incomplete." The tinkering continued, Charvat believes, until Hawthorne sent the book to the printers.[8]

There is no way of knowing precisely what changes Hawthorne made to lighten the novel's mood and bring it to "a prosperous close."[9] But hints scattered throughout the final pages support the notion that he was unhappy with his happy ending. At one point he writes that the house continued to diffuse a gloom "which no brightness of the sunshine could dispel" (p. 296); and elsewhere he compares his story to "an owl, bewildered in the daylight" (p. 268). The owl suggests Hepzibah, squinting and frowning in the glare of the public gaze; and Hawthorne used the same word, "bewildered," when he complained of his difficulties with the ending. The comic resolution demanded by his readers, he clearly felt, was violating the logic of his tale and covering up its scowl with an inappropriate smile.

This supposition is also suggested by Hawthorne's treatment of Holgrave in the book's concluding chapters. In chapter 20, "The

7. Hawthorne to Horatio Bridge, letter of July 22, 1851, quoted by Charvat, "Introduction," *The House of the Seven Gables*, Centenary Edition, p. xvi.
8. My account follows Charvat, "Introduction," *The House of the Seven Gables*, Centenary Edition, pp. xv–xxviii. All quotations in this paragraph are from letters to Fields, pp. xxii, xviii.
9. Hawthorne to E. A. Duyckinck, letter of April 27, 1851, quoted by Charvat, "Introduction," *The House of the Seven Gables*, Centenary Edition, p. xxii.

Flower of Eden," the daguerreotypist declares his love for Phoebe and renounces his radicalism. Henceforth he will confine himself "within ancient limits" and even "build a house for another generation" (p. 307). His sudden reversal of character has left most readers unconvinced. But in reality Holgrave shows great reluctance, as Hawthorne notes, "to betake himself within the precincts of common life" (p. 305). He is particularly loath to publicize "the awful secret" (p. 305) of the Judge's death, and the reasons he gives for his hesitation are not very consistent. Supposedly he fears that Clifford's flight will be construed as an admission of guilt, yet he also says that Jaffrey's death, being "attended by none of those suspicious circumstances" which surrounded the uncle's death, will clear Clifford of the earlier crime (p. 304). Phoebe is at a loss to comprehend his indecision. While he keeps putting off the moment of disclosure, she pleads with him not "to hide this thing . . . It is dreadful to keep it so closely in our hearts. Clifford is innocent. God will make it manifest! Let us throw open the doors, and call all the neighborhood to see the truth!" (p. 305). The "truth" in question is the knowledge of the heart, and herein lies the deeper reason for Holgrave's unwillingness to make it known. Jaffrey's body in the house of the seven gables recalls the stately palace with its hidden secret, and the daguerreotypist, who takes a picture of the scene, corresponds to the seer whose "sadly gifted eye" detects the corpse within, "the true emblem" of the man's soul. But this truth, which is also the truth of Hawthorne's art, has been characterized throughout the book as private and unsalable; in revealing it to the public, Holgrave is "inevitably" corrupted "by the fatal consciousness of so doing." His action betrays his calling as an artist of the legendary and is precisely analogous to Hawthorne's contrivance of a happy ending at the expense of narrative consistency. Though the result in both cases may be "Pretty good business," as Dixey puts it (p. 319), Holgrave's reluctance to capitulate is also his creator's.

Hawthorne, to be sure, might have been masking his deeper intentions and inviting an ironic reading that emphasizes the discrepancy between appearance and reality.[1] Melville, it will be remembered, recommended this strategy for the author "too deserving of popularity to be popular,"[2] and in the final chapters Hawthorne tries to make a virtue of necessity by implying that his story's surface is at odds with its inner meaning. When the summer storm subsides the morning after the Judge's death, he points out that the sunshine creates a false impression of the house. "So little faith is due to external appearance, that there was really an inviting

---

1. See William P. Dillingham, "Structure and Theme in *The House of the Seven Gables*," *Nineteenth-Century Fiction*, 14 (1959), 59–70.
2. "Hawthorne and His Mosses," Norton Critical Edition of *Moby-Dick*, p. 536.

aspect over the venerable edifice, conveying an idea that its history must be a decorous and happy one . . ." (p. 285). Several pages later, when the organ-grinder stops to play on Pyncheon street, he continues: "to us, who know the inner heart of the seven gables, as well as its exterior face, there is a ghastly effect in this representation of light popular tunes at its door-step" (p. 294).

Hawthorne's insistence on the disjunction between the house's outward face and its interior is echoed by Holgrave in the book's concluding chapter. As the triumphant party of survivors prepares to take possession of the Judge's country mansion, the daguerreotypist wonders why the dead man did not see fit to embody "so excellent a piece of domestic architecture in stone, rather than in wood. Then, every generation of the family might have altered the interior, to suit its own taste and convenience; while the exterior, through the lapse of years, might have been adding venerableness to its original beauty, thus giving that impression of permanence, which I consider essential to the happiness of any one moment" (pp. 314–15). In one sense this statement represents a compromise between reform and conservatism.[3] Equally important, it advocates a policy of deception with regard to houses, and as such it is also a statement about Hawthorne's art. In the preface he likened the writing of his tale to "building a house, of materials long in use for constructing castles in the air" (p. 3), and of course the title of his novel is *The House of the Seven Gables*.

Hawthorne, then, appears to have agreed with Melville's view of the artist as a con-man; certainly he *wanted* to accept it in order to justify his surrender to the marketplace. But the narrative itself repudiates this strategy as morally reprehensible, and Hawthorne stands condemned for employing it by the value system of his own art. Though appearances may be unreliable in the novel, only one character makes a practice of deliberate deception. Hepzibah's heart is often said to smile while her face is frowning, but she cannot help herself. Hawthorne does the opposite: he smiles while his heart is frowning. In contrast to Phoebe's "natural sunshine" (p. 297), the "warm, sunny smile" he presents to the reader is contrived and artificial. He had to try hard, as he admitted to Fields, to pour sunshine over the tale's darkening close, and in doing so he follows the example of Judge Pyncheon manufacturing a sunny exterior to win the favor of the public. Passages that denounce the villain for hypocrisy became ironically self-accusing when considered in relation to the novel's ending. Indeed, it is as much a struggle for Hawthorne to dispel the gloom of his narrative as it is for the Judge

---

3. See Terence Martin, *Nathaniel Hawthorne* (New York: Twayne Publishers, 1965), pp. 140–1.

to disguise the "black" and "brooding" thunder cloud of his temperament. The acute observer who probably suspected "that the smile on the gentleman's face was a good deal akin to the shine on his boots, and that each must have cost him and his boot-black, respectively, a good deal of hard labor to bring out and preserve them" (p. 117), might have said the same thing about the Judge's creator.

Perhaps even more ironic in this connection is Holgrave's—and Hawthorne's—volte-face on houses. When the daguerreotypist expresses a wish that the exterior of a house might differ from its interior, he unwittingly endorses a scheme of domestic architecture that has been practiced metaphorically by Jaffrey Pyncheon. It seems fitting, therefore, that he should take up residence in the Judge's elegant country-seat rather than in the dwelling built by his ancestor, the house of the seven gables. Moreover, Hawthorne's house of fiction parallels the deceptive edifice of the Judge's being. Since a "devilish scowl would frighten away customers," as Dixey keeps insisting, he imposes a sunbathed conclusion on his narrative to cover up "the fearful secret, hidden within the house" (p. 291). Little wonder that the angry taunting of Jaffrey's corpse in chapter 18, "Governor Pyncheon," has struck many readers as excessive and slightly hysterical. It is not difficult to detect the self-reproach in Hawthorne's outbursts at the dead Judge for seeking profit and worldly honor and for wearing an "odious grin of feigned benignity, insolent in its pretense, and loathsome in its falsehood (p. 282). Compelled by the pressures of the literary marketplace to "put on a bright face" for his readers, Hawthorne had become like the character whom he hated most in all his fiction.

When Holgrave reads Phoebe his story "Alice Pyncheon," and she is overcome by drowsiness, he remarks sarcastically on her "falling asleep at what I hoped the newspaper critics would pronounce a most brilliant, powerful, imaginative, pathetic, and original winding up!" (p. 212). With better reason, Hawthorne entertained a similar hope for the ending of his own story, and the newspaper critics responded by pronouncing *The House of the Seven Gables* a brilliant success, a book, as Whipple put it, in which "the humor and the pathos are combined." "Taken as a whole," Whipple added, "it is Hawthorne's greatest work, and is equally sure of immediate popularity and permanent fame."[4] Although in the long run sales lagged behind *The Scarlet Letter*, the new romance outsold its predecessor in the first year of publication and seemed to justify Hawthorne's decision (as he wrote of Hepzibah) to use "the House of the Seven Gables as the scene of his

4. Whipple's review appeared in *Graham's Magazine*, 38 (June, 1851), 467–8.

commercial speculations" (p. 36). But that decision also seems to have intensified his negative feelings about the marketplace and its corrupting effect both on the writer as a producer and on the work of literature as a commodity. He wrote in the text that "a person of imaginative temperament," happening to pass the house of the seven gables on the morning after the summer storm, "would conceive the mansion to have been the residence of the stubborn old Puritan, Integrity, who, dying in some forgotten generation, had left a blessing in all its rooms and chambers, the efficacy of which was to be seen in the religion, honesty, moderate competence, or upright poverty, and solid happiness, of his descendants, to this day" (pp. 285–86). In an effort to obtain financial security from his writing—what he calls here a "moderate competence"—Hawthorne himself had built a literary mansion very different indeed from that inhabited by "Integrity." When he discovered soon enough that even his concession to the reader would not enable him to support his family, he may have come to feel as Hepzibah did after her first few hours behind the counter: that the enterprise "would prove [his] ruin, in a moral and religious point of view, without contributing very essentially towards even [his] temporal welfare" (p. 55). And while there were no doubt many causes for Hawthorne's "disintegration" as an artist,[5] *The House of the Seven Gables* suggests that his flagging energies may well have been related to his growing alienation from the process of exchange.

WALTER BENN MICHAELS

Romance and Real Estate†

experience hath shewn, that property best answers the purposes
of civil life, especially in commercial countries, when its transfer
and circulation are totally free and unrestrained.
                                    —Blackstone, "Of Title by Alienation,"
                                    Commentaries on the Laws of England

Visiting Salem in 1904, Henry James asked to be shown the "House of the Seven Gables" and was led by his guide to an "object" so "shapeless," so "weak" and "vague," that at first sight he could only murmur "Dear, dear, are you very sure?" In an instant, however,

---

5. See Rudolph Von Abele, *The Death of the Artist: A Study of Hawthorne's Disintegration* (The Hague: Martinus Nijhoff; 1955).
† From *The American Renaissance Reconsidered*, ed. Walter Benn Michaels and Donald E. Pease (Baltimore: The Johns Hopkins University Press, 1985), pp. 156–82. Copyright © 1985 The English Institute. Reprinted with permission of The Johns Hopkins University Press. All notes are Michaels's.

James and the guide ("a dear little harsh, intelligent, sympathetic American boy") had together "thrown off" their sense that the house "wouldn't do at all" by reminding themselves that there was, in general, no necessary "relation between the accomplished thing for . . . art" and "those other quite equivocal things" that may have suggested it, and by noting in particular how Hawthorne's "admirable" novel had so "vividly" forgotten its "origin or reference."[1] Hawthorne would presumably have seen the point of James's response; his own Preface warned readers against trying to "assign an actual locality to the imaginary events" of the narrative, and for the romance as a genre he claimed an essential "latitude" with respect to reference, a latitude not allowed novelists, who aimed at a "very minute fidelity . . . [to] experience."[2] The distinction drawn here between the novel and the romance, between a fundamentally mimetic use of language and one that questions the primacy of reference, has, of course, become canonical in American literary criticism even though (or perhaps just because) its meaning remains so uncertain. Does Hawthorne intend the romance (as some recent critics think) to pose a self-consciously fictional alternative to the social responsibilities of the novel? Or does he intend the romance (as some other even more recent critics think) to provide in its radical fictionality a revolutionary alternative to the social conservativism of the novel?[3] The last paragraph of the Preface suggests that neither of these formulations may be correct.

Looking for the Seven Gables in Salem, Hawthorne says, is a mistake because it "exposes the Romance to an inflexible and exceedingly dangerous species of criticism, by bringing [its] fancy pictures into positive contact with the realities of the moment" (3). The implication seems to be that the romance (unlike the novel) is too fragile to stand comparison with reality, but Hawthorne imme-

---

1. Henry James, The American Scene (Bloomington, Ind., 1968), pp. 270–71.
2. Nathaniel Hawthorne, The House of the Seven Gables, ed. Seymour L. Gross (New York: W. W. Norton, 1967), p. 1. All subsequent references to this work will be cited parenthetically in the text.
3. The texts I have in mind here are Michael Davitt Bell's The Development of American Romance (Chicago, 1980) and an article by Brook Thomas, "The House of the Seven Gables: Reading the Romance of America," PMLA 97 (March 1982):195–211. Thomas contrasts the "freedom of the romance" to the "conservativism of the novel" (196) and suggests that Hawthorne "chose to write romances . . . because they allowed him to stay true to the American tradition of imagining an alternative to the society he inherited" (195–96). Bell sees a similar tension within the romance itself, in an opposition between the "artifice and insincerity of forms" and the "anarchic energy" of the "strange new truths" (xiv) of American life in the mid-nineteenth century.
   In House, this opposition is embodied by the Pyncheons and Holgrave but not, according to Bell, satisfactorily, since the "revolutionary" "alternative to the empty forms of the past" represented by Holgrave and Phoebe seems too "personal" to form "the basis of a new social system" and too transitory to "avoid recapitulating the historical cycle" that created the "repressive formalism" in the first place (182–83). Thomas reads the end in similar terms but somewhat more optimistically, arguing that Hawthorne "seems to have retained a hope for the future," imagining in Phoebe's marriage to Holgrave "a real possibility for a break with the past" (209).

diately goes on to suggest that the difference between the romance and the novel is perhaps less a matter of their relation to reality than of their relation to real estate. He has constructed *The House of the Seven Gables* "by laying out a street that infringes upon nobody's private rights, and appropriating a lot of land which had no visible owner, and building a house, of materials long in use for constructing castles in the air" (3). The romance, then, is to be imagined as a kind of property, or rather as a relation to property. Where the novel may be said to touch the real by expropriating it and so violating someone's "private rights," the romance asserts a property right that does not threaten and so should not be threatened by the property rights of others. The romance, to put it another way, is the text of clear and unobstructed title.

The Money Power

Of course, haunted house stories (like *The House of the Seven Gables*) usually involve some form of anxiety about ownership. Frequently this anxiety concerns actual financial cost. Stephen King, the author of *The Shining*, has put this powerfully in a discussion of the movie *The Amityville Horror*. "What it's about," he says,

> is a young couple who've never owned a house before; Margot Kidder is the first person in her family actually to have owned property. And all these things start to go wrong—and the horrible part is not that they can't get out, but that they're going to *lose the house*. There was some point where things were falling, and the door banging, and rain was coming in, and goop was running down the stairs, and behind me, in the little movie house in Bridgton, this woman, she must have been 60, was in this kind of ecstasy, moaning, "Think of the bills, think of the bills." And that's where the horror of that movie is.[4]

Which is not to say that the financial implications of the haunted house are limited to the actual repair costs of the physical damage

---

But in my reading, the point of the romance is neither to renew the past nor to break with it; it is instead to domesticate the social dislocation of the 1840s and 1850s in a literary form that imagines the past and present as utterly continuous, even identical, and in so doing, attempts to repress the possibility of any change at all. For critics like Bell, *The House of the Seven Gables* fails in the end because Holgrave's "radicalism" succumbs to "conservativism" (184); democracy succumbs to aristocracy, ultimately, the "dangerous" and "subversive" fictionality of the romance succumbs to the "safe and conservative" referentiality of mimesis (14, 18). But what seemed dangerous and subversive to Hawthorne was not so much the "crisis" of reference intrinsic to the romance (Bell calls it a "crisis of belief" [149] and of "correspondence" [153]) as the violently revolutionary power of *mimesis*, the representing form of a market society inimical to the social stability, the individualism, and the rights to property that Hawthorne meant the romance to defend. Thus the novel actually ends triumphantly, with a transformation of "business" into inheritance and mimesis into "fairy-tale."

4. *New York Times Magazine* (11 May, 1980): 44.

done by the ghosts. Think of the plight of the Amityville couple as investors in real estate; having risked everything to get themselves into the spectacularly inflationary market of 1975, they find themselves owning the only house on Long Island whose value is declining. The only one for a few years, anyway, until rising interest rates—as intangible as ghosts but even more powerful—would begin to produce a spectral effect on housing prices everywhere. It may be worth noting that in 1850 Hawthorne was writing at the start of one of the peak periods in nineteenth-century American land speculation, a period in which, according to the agricultural historian Paul Wallace Gates, "touched by the fever of land speculation, excited people throughout the country borrowed to the extent of their credit for such investments."[5]

But the actual price of real estate may not finally be as crucial to the haunted house as the fact of ownership itself and the questions that necessarily accompany that fact: who has title? what legitimates that title? what guarantees it? Again, contemporary examples abound. Because of certain "impediments" on their house, the Lutzes in Amityville never did get clear title although they had what their lawyer called "the best that could be fashioned for their mortgage."[6] And another movie, *Poltergeist*, centers on what is in effect a title dispute between a real estate development company and the corpses who inhabit the bulldozed cemetery the developer builds on. But title disputes have also a more intimate connection to Hawthorne and to *The House of the Seven Gables*. The most prominent and respectable witch brought to trial before Hawthorne's ancestor, the "persecuting" magistrate John Hathorne, was an old woman named Rebecca Nurse, whose family were comparative newcomers to Salem, much resented by the old and increasingly impoverished villagers. The Nurses had bought land from James Allen (land inherited by him from the Endicotts) and were paying for it in twenty yearly installments. In 1692, when Rebecca was accused, they had only "six more years to go before the title was theirs," but the villagers still thought of them as *arrivistes* and continued to call their place "the Allen

---

5. Paul Wallace Gates, "The Role of the Land Speculator in Western Development," in *The Public Lands*, ed. Vernon Carstensen (Madison: University of Wisconsin Press, 1968), p. 352. "The peak years of speculative purchasing," Gates goes on to say, "were 1854 to 1858, when a total of 65,000,000 acres of public domain were disposed of to purchasers or holders of land warrants" (360).

6. Jay Anson, *The Amityville Horror* (New York: Bantam Books, 1978), p. 17. The main obstacle appears to have been that the only heir of the deceased former owners was the son who had murdered them, Ronald. Since Ronald, having killed his parents, was legally barred from inheriting their estate, it is unclear exactly from whom the Lutzes were buying the property. For true horror fans, however, Anson is gratifyingly explicit about who actually ended up owning their "dream house" when the demoralized Lutzes fled to California: "Just to be rid of the place, they signed their interest over to the bank that held the mortgage" (260).

property."[7] Hathorne was fleetingly touched by Rebecca's respectability and by her claim to be "innocent and clear" of the charges against her, but he held her for trial anyway and in the end she was one of the first witches hanged. The day of Rebecca's hanging is remembered by *The House of the Seven Gables* in Maule's curse on the Pyncheons, "God will give you blood to drink"—the dying words of Rebecca's fellow victim, Sarah Good. More importantly, Hawthorne revives the connection between witchcraft and quarrels over property by beginning his narrative with a title dispute. Owner-occupant Matthew Maule, who "with his own toil . . . had hewn out of the primal forest . . . [a] garden-ground and homestead," is dispossessed by the "prominent and powerful" Colonel Pyncheon, "who asserted plausible claims to the proprietorship of this . . . land on the strength of a grant from the legislature" (7). Maule, of course, is executed for witchcraft, while Pyncheon leads the pack of executioners.

In one sense, this reworking of the witch trials is a little misleading; as Hawthorne himself notes, one of the few redeeming qualities of the witch hunters was "the singular indiscrimination with which they persecuted, not merely the poor and aged as in former judicial massacres, but people of all ranks, their own equals, brethren, and wives" (8). But the Pyncheon persecution of the Maules does not follow this model. Indeed, it precisely inverts the pattern described in Boyer and Nissenbaum's extraordinary *Salem Possessed: The Social Origins of Witchcraft*, where the accusers are shown to have been characteristically worse off socially and economically than the accused. Hawthorne does not, however, represent the struggle between Pyncheons and Maules merely as a conflict between the more and less powerful or even in any simple way as a conflict over a piece of land. He presents it instead as a conflict between two different modes of economic activity and in this he not only anticipates recent historians' findings but begins the complicated process of articulating his own defense of property.

The devil in Massachusetts, according to Boyer and Nissenbaum, was "emergent mercantile capitalism."[8] Hawthorne understood the question in terms more appropriate to someone whose political consciousness had been formed during the years of Jacksonian democracy. Maule embodies a Lockean legitimation of property by labor whereas the Pyncheons, with their pretensions to nobility, are something like old-world aristocrats. Except that the pre-Revolutionary fear of a titled aristocracy had, during the Jackson

7. Marion L. Starkey, *The Devil in Massachusetts* (1949; rpt. New York: Anchor Books, 1969), p. 77.
8. Paul Boyer and Stephen Nissenbaum, *Salem Possessed* (Cambridge: Harvard University Press, 1974), p. 209.

years, been replaced by the fear of a "money aristocracy," and Judge
Pyncheon is certainly more capitalist than nobleman. From this
standpoint, the difference between Maule and Pyncheon is less a
difference between bourgeois and aristocrat than between those
whom Jackson called "the agricultural, the mechanical, and the laboring classes" and those whom he called the "money power." And
yet, *The House of the Seven Gables* by no means enacts a Jacksonian confrontation between the "people" and those who sought to
exercise a "despotic sway" over them. Instead the fate of property in
House suggests the appeal of a title based on neither labor nor
wealth and hence free from the risk of appropriation.

"In this republican country," Hawthorne writes, "amid the fluctuating waves of our social life, somebody is always at the drowning-
point" (38). This "tragedy," he thinks, is felt as "deeply . . . as when
an hereditary noble sinks below his order." Or rather, "more deeply;
since with us, rank is the grosser substance of wealth and a splendid establishment, and has no spiritual existence after the death of
these but dies hopelessly along with them." The central point here,
that America is a country where (as a French observer put it)
"material property rapidly disappears,"[9] is, perhaps, less important
than the implied comparison between the impoverished capitalist
and the dispossessed aristocrat. The capitalist who loses everything
loses everything, whereas the nobleman, losing everything material,
retains his nobility, which has a "spiritual existence." This title
cannot be bought or sold; unlike the land you have "hewn out
of the forest," it cannot be stolen either. Aristocracy's claim to land
is unimpaired by the inability to enforce that claim. Indeed, it is, in
a certain sense strengthened, or at least purified, since the assertion of what Blackstone calls the "mere right of property," a right
that stands independent of any right of possession, is the assertion
of a right that is truly inalienable: it cannot be exchanged for anything else, it cannot be taken from you, it cannot even be given
away.

Such a claim to property has from the start its place in *The
House of the Seven Gables*; the Preface's "castles in the air" suggest
in their immateriality a parallel between romance and the property
rights of impoverished aristocrats. And, in the text itself, what
Hawthorne calls the Pyncheons' "impalpable claim" to the rich territory of Waldo County in Maine repeats this structure. Although
the "actual settlers" of this land "would have laughed at the idea" of
the Pyncheons asserting any "right" to it, the effect of their title
on the Pyncheons themselves is to cause "the poorest member of

9. Michel Chevalier, *Society, Manners, and Politics in the United States*, ed. John William
Ward (Ithaca: Cornell University Press, 1961), p. 98.

the race to feel as if he inherited a kind of nobility" (19). This pretension is treated somewhat nervously by Hawthorne's text as a kind of atavistic joke, but the principle on which it is based—title so perfect that it is immunized from expropriation—was by no means completely anachronistic in the 1850s. For example, antislavery polemicists like Harriet Beecher Stowe and William Goodell admitted the comparative superiority of those slave states and societies where, as Goodell put it, slaves are treated as "real estate" in the sense that they are "attached to the soil they cultivate, partaking therewith all the restraints upon voluntary alienation to which the possessor of the *land* is liable, and they cannot be seized or sold by creditors for the satisfaction of the debts of the owner."[1] Of course, it could be argued that this restraint upon alienation should itself be considered a feudal relic, reflecting primarily a nostalgia for the time when land had not yet been transformed into a commodity and thus Pyncheons and slaveholders both could be seen as throwbacks. But, in fact, the notion of inalienable title was central also to one of the most radically progressive social movements of the 1840s and 1850s, the "land for the landless" agitation (opposed by southern slaveholders and northern capitalists both) that culminated in the Homestead Act of 1862.

At the heart of the homestead movement was the conviction that the land should belong to those who worked it and not to the banks and speculators. Attempting to protect themselves from speculation, the most radical reformers urged that homestead land be made inalienable since obviously land that could not be bought or sold could not be speculated upon either. This attempt failed but Congress did, in fact, require that "no land acquired under the provisions of [the Homestead Act] should in any event become liable to the satisfaction of any debt contracted prior to the issuing of the patent."[2] Thus homestead lands, like slaves in Louisiana, represented at least a partial escape from alienability. And, indeed, the desire for such an escape was so strong that Homestead Act propagandists were sometimes willing to sacrifice their Maule-like claim to property through labor for a Pyncheon-like claim to the status of an absentee landlord. In a pamphlet entitled *Vote Yourself a Farm*, the pamphleteer reminds his readers that "if a man have a house and home of his own, though it be a thousand miles off, he is well received in other people's houses; while the homeless wretch is turned away. The *bare right* to a farm, though you should never go

---

1. William Goodell, *The American Slave Code* (1853; rpt. New York: Arno, 1969), p. 65. The central state in question is Louisiana.
2. George M. Stephenson, *The Political History of the Public Lands* (New York: Macmillan Co., 1917), p. 243. For a characteristically helpful discussion of the ideology of homesteading, see Henry Nash Smith, *Virgin Land* (Cambridge: Harvard University Press, 1950), pp. 165–210.

near it, would save you from many an insult. Therefore, Vote your-self a farm."[3] In effect, the Pyncheons have voted themselves a farm, or rather, more powerfully, the bare right to one. Hawthorne himself, figuring the romance as uncontested title and inalienable right, has sought in the escape from reference the power of that bare right. His "castles in the air" of the Preface are equally Hep-zibah Pyncheon's "castles in the air" (65); her "shadowy claims to princely territory." And her "fantasies" of a "gentility" beyond the reach of "commercial speculations" are his claims to a "street that infringes upon nobody's" rights and to "a lot of land" without any "visible owner." Even the map of Waldo that hangs on Hepzibah's kitchen wall images the security of romance's bare right; "gro-tesquely illuminated with pictures of Indians and wild beasts, among which was seen a lion" (33), the map's geography is, Hawthorne says, as "fantastically awry" as its natural history. It is it-self one of those "fancy-pictures" that perish if "brought into con-tact" with reality, an antimimetic map, charting a way out of republican fluctuation and novelistic imitation.

For if the romance seeps out of the Preface and into the text as an impalpable claim to impalpable property, the novel too embodies an ongoing relation to property, in the form of certain "mistakes" provoked by the lies of mimesis. The novel's commercial world con-sists of "magnificent shops" with "immense panes of plate glass," with "gorgeous fixtures," with "vast and complete assortments of merchandize," above all, with "noble mirrors . . . doubling all this wealth by a brightly burnished vista of unrealities" (48). We are un-able to see through these unrealities just as we are unable to see through those other "big, heavy, solid unrealities such as gold, landed estate . . . and public honors" (229). Hawthorne here con-ceives of mass production as a form of mimesis and of the factories that make these stores possible as novels producing the realistically unreal. At the same time, the novel is a figure for appropriation and for those men (like the aristocrat turned capitalist Judge Pyncheon) who "possess vast ability in grasping, and arranging, and appropri-ating to themselves" those unrealities. In fact, the mirror of capital-ism is itself reproduced in such men whose own "character," "when they aim at the honors of a republic" (130) becomes only an "image . . . reflected in the mirror of public opinion" (232). Before the Rev-olution, "the great man of the town was commonly called King" (63); now he must make himself over into a facsimile of the people. They see themselves reflected in him and he, "resolutely taking his idea of himself from what purports to be his image" (232), sees himself reflected in them. Only "loss of property and reputation,"

3. The quotation is in Stephenson, *The Political History of the Public Lands*, pp. 109–10.

Hawthorne says, can end this riot of mimesis and bring about "true self-knowledge."

Judge Pyncheon, who looking within himself sees only a mirror, never seeks such self-knowledge; and the novel, aiming at a "very minute fidelity" to the "ordinary course of man's experience," never seeks it either—its goal is the department store doubling of unrealities. Only the romance, with its dedication to "the truth of the human heart," and, in the text itself, only the daguerreotypist Holgrave can represent the "secret character" behind the mirror and restore appropriated property to its rightful owner. It is, of course, extraordinary that Holgrave who inveighs against all property should come to represent its legitimation, and it is perhaps even more extraordinary that the photograph, almost universally acclaimed in the 1850s as the perfection of mimesis, should come to represent an artistic enterprise hostile to imitation. To understand these reversals, we need to look a little more closely at the technology of imitation and at the social conditions in which that technology and the romance itself were developed.

Holgrave's career, says Hawthorne, was like "a romance on the plan of Gil Blas," except that Gil Blas, "adapted to American society and manners, would cease to be a romance" (176). Although only twenty-one, Holgrave had been (among other things) a schoolmaster, a salesman, and a dentist. His current occupation, daguerreotypist, is, he tells Phoebe, no more "likely to be permanent than any of the preceding ones" (177). According to Hawthorne, such mobility is typical of the "experience of many individuals among us, who think it hardly worth the telling" (176), and certainly too ordinary to be the stuff of romance. Hawthorne exaggerates, of course, but not much. Several recent historians have noted the high degree of geographic mobility in the 1840s and '50s, mostly among young men who, for economic reasons, frequently changed locations and jobs. This phenomenon, according to Robert Doherty, was particularly noticeable in major commercial centers like Salem where it was associated also with increased social hierarchism. In rural agricultural areas, young men tended to stay put and the distribution of property was comparatively even. In towns like Salem, however, "commerce and manufacturing produced great inequalities of wealth,"[4] and over one-third of Salem's population in the fifties consisted of transients. Most of these were propertyless young men whose geographic mobility was produced by hopes of a corresponding economic mobility. Sometimes these hopes were gratified.

---

4. Robert Doherty, *Society and Power* (Amherst: University of Massachusetts Press, 1977), pp. 52–53. "Agriculture," Doherty notes, "produced greater equality, and the only communities approaching equitable distribution of property were low-level, less developed rural hinterlands" (53).

Many men, Doherty suggests, "spent a period of youthful wandering and then settled in at about age 30 and began to accumulate property."[5] Many more, however, "failed to gain even minimal material success." Some of these "propertyless . . . men stayed in town," Doherty writes, some "drifted from place to place, but all were apparent casualties of a social system which denied them property."[6]

The development of such an underclass had obvious social significance, and it suggests also ways in which a career like Holgrave's might not only be inappropriate for romance by virtue of its ordinariness but would even constitute a reproach to the commitment to property on which the romance is based. For a real-life Holgrave in Salem in 1851 stood a three-to-one chance of becoming what Doherty calls a "casualty," never accumulating any property and remaining stuck forever at the bottom of an increasingly stratified society. Hawthorne's Holgrave, needless to say, escapes this fate. Like only a few real-life young men, he rises from "penniless youth to great wealth," and one might perhaps interpret this rise as Hawthorne's ideological intervention on behalf of the openness of American society.

Except that, as we have seen, what made Hawthorne most nervous about American society was precisely its openness, its hospitality to fluctuation.[7] In this respect, the actual economic mobility of life in Salem, the fact that some men rose (according to Doherty, about 23%) and that some men fell (about 13%) would be infinitely more disturbing to Hawthorne than the existence of a permanent class of the propertyless. Inalienable rights can be neither lost nor acquired—how then can we explain Holgrave's happy ending, his sudden rise to property. One clue is that he does not actually earn his wealth, he marries it. Which is not to say that Hawthorne is being ironic about his hero's merits. Just the opposite. The whole point here is that property that has been earned is just as insecure (and, in the end, as illegitimate) as property that has been appropriated by some capitalist trick. Thus, for Hawthorne, the accumulation of property must be remade into an accession to property, and the social meaning of Holgrave's career turns out to be that it is not really a career at all. His period of wandering gives him instead the chance to display a stability of character that provides a

5. Ibid., p. 47.
6. Ibid., p. 49.
7. Hawthorne apparently found the idea of a fixed income as attractive personally as it was socially. James Mellow quotes his sister Ebe: "One odd, but characteristic notion of his was that he should like a competent income that would neither increase nor diminish. I said that it might be well to have it increase, but he replied, 'No, because then it would engross too much of his attention' " (Mellow, *Nathaniel Hawthorne in his Times* [Boston: Houghton Mifflin Co., 1980], p. 94).

kind of psychological legitimation for the fact of ownership: "amid all his personal vicissitudes," Hawthorne writes, Holgrave had "never lost his identity . . . he had never violated the innermost man" (177). Like the romance itself which, despite its apparent freedom from the responsibilities of the novel, "must rigidly subject itself to laws" (1), Holgrave appears "lawless" but in fact follows a "law of his own" (85). Anchoring property not in work but in character, he defuses both the threat posed by the young transients who failed to acquire property (Hawthorne simply legislates them out of existence) and the threat posed by the transients who did acquire property (since he makes that acquisition a function not of social mobility but of the fixed character of the "innermost man"). Apparently a pure product of the "republican" world of fluctuation, Holgrave turns out instead to embody the unchanging truth of romance.

But if Holgrave's career offers Hawthorne the opportunity to transform the social meaning of the new class of landless transients, Holgrave's art, the daguerreotype, hits even closer to home and requires an even more spectacular inversion. The terms of this inversion are quickly apparent in Holgrave's claim that the daguerreotype, despite its apparent preoccupation with "the merest surface," "actually brings out the secret character with a truth that no painter would ever venture upon" (91). It was, of course, far more usual for writers of the forties and fifties to make just the opposite point. The "unrivalled precision" of the daguerreotype and the paper photograph, painters were warned, "renders exact imitation no longer a miracle of crayon or palette; these must now create as well as reflect . . . bring out the soul of the individual and of the landscape, or their achievements will be neglected in favor of the facsimiles obtainable through sunshine and chemistry."[8] For Hawthorne, however, the *daguerreotype* penetrates to the soul, seeing through republican honors to "the man himself."

The triumph of the daguerreotype in *House* is the portraits (Hawthorne's and Holgrave's) of Judge Pyncheon dead. Early daguerreotype portraits were often marred by a certain blurriness; the very oldest surviving portrait (John Draper's picture of his sister Catherine, taken in 1840) was sent to an English photographer accompanied by apologies for the "indistinctness" that results, Draper wrote, from any movement, even "the inevitable motions of the respiratory muscles." But where "inanimate objects are depicted," Draper went on to remark with satisfaction, "the most rigid sharpness can be obtained."[9] Holgrave's job is thus made easier by the

8. The quotation is in Robert Taft, *Photography and the American Scene* (New York: Dover, 1938), pp. 133–34.
9. Ibid., p. 30.

fact that the judge has stopped breathing but the real point here is that the daguerreotype always sees through to the fixed truth behind the fluctuating movements of the "public character." It is as if the subject of a daguerreotype is in some sense already dead, the truth about him fixed by the portrait just as the actual "fact of a man's death," Hawthorne writes in connection with Pyncheon's posthumous reputation, "often seems to give people a truer idea of his character" (310). The daguerreotype, always a representation of death, is also death's representative.

As is the romance. In a passage that anticipates by some forty years Henry James's famous remarks on "the coldness, the thinness, the blankness" of Hawthorne's America, the French journalist Michel Chevalier was struck by the absence in America of those elements that in Europe served, as he put it, to "stir" the "nerves." James would miss the sovereign, the court, little Norman churches; the effect of American life on a "French imagination," he thought, "would probably be appalling."[1] But Chevalier was thrilled not appalled. He did miss what he called the "sensual gratifications"; "wine, women, and the display of princely luxury . . . cards and dice." But, Chevalier says, the American has a way of more than making up for the absence of traditional stimulants; seeking "the strong emotions which he requires to make him feel life," the American "has recourse to business. . . . He launches with delight into the ever-moving sea of speculation. One day, the wave raises him to the clouds . . . the next day he disappears between the crests of the billows. . . . If movement and the quick succession of sensations and ideas constitute life, here one lives a hundredfold more than elsewhere."[2]

If the cold blankness of American life figured for James the difficulty of finding something to represent, that blankness was to Chevalier the setting for a business life of "violent sensations," and to Hawthorne, the violent movements of business were the violence of mimetic representation itself. The world of the "money power," Andrew Jackson warned in his Farewell Address, is "liable to great and sudden fluctuations" which render "property insecure and the wages of labor unsteady and uncertain."[3] "The soil itself, or at least the houses, partake in the universal instability," Chevalier exclaimed.[4] Hawthorne required the romance to fix this instability, to

---

1. Henry James, *Hawthorne* (Ithaca: Cornell University Press, 1967), p. 35.
2. Chevalier, *Society, Manners, and Politics in the United States*, pp. 298–99. Writing in August 1835, Chevalier notes, "Great fortunes, and many of them too, have sprung out of the earth since the spring; others will, perhaps, return to it before the fall. The American does not worry about that. Violent sensations are necessary to stir his vigorous nerves."
3. Andrew Jackson, "Farewell Address," in *American Democracy: A Documentary Record*, ed. J. R. Hollingsworth and B. I. Wiley (New York: Crowell, 1961), p. 374.
4. Chevalier, *Society, Manners, and Politics in the United States*, p. 299.

render property secure. Where representations are unrealities produced by mirrors, the romance represents nothing, not in compensation for the coldness of American life but in opposition to its terrible vitality. Business makes the American "feel life," but that life is a mimetic lie; whereas "death," Hawthorne says, "is so genuine a fact that it excludes falsehood" (310). Celebrating the death—one might better call it the execution—of Judge Pyncheon, the romance joins the witch hunt, the attempt to imagine an escape from capitalism, defending the self against possession, property against appropriation, and choosing death over life.

The Slave Power

The conjunction of death and secure property has its place in another text of 1851, one intended not as a romance but, in its author's words, as a "representation . . . of real incidents, of actions really performed, of words and expressions really uttered."[5] Riding by his slave quarters late at night, Simon Legree hears the singing of a "musical tenor voice": " 'When I can read my title clear / To mansions in the skies' " Uncle Tom sings, " 'I'll bid farewell to every fear / And wipe my weeping eyes.' "[6] Tom is preparing for the martyrdom toward which Legree will soon help him, and his sense of heaven as a "Home" to which he has clear title is barely metaphoric. Slaves, of course, were forbidden to own property but Stowe thought of them as by definition the victims of theft. Slavery, "appropriating one set of human beings to the use and improvement of another" (2:21), robbed a man of himself, and so freedom involved above all the restitution of property. Only in death did the slave's title to himself become "sure"; only in death did Uncle Tom's cabin actually become his.

That freedom in the mid-nineteenth century, the period that C. B. Macpherson has called the "zenith" of "possessive market society,"[7] should be understood as essentially a property relation is not, in itself, surprising, but it does provide in *Uncle Tom's Cabin* some unexpected and little-noted points of emphasis. When, for example, George Shelby frees his slaves, he tells them that their lives will go on pretty much as before but with the "advantage" that, in case of his "getting in debt or dying," they cannot be "taken up and sold" (2:309). The implication here is that Shelby himself would

5. Harriet Beecher Stowe, *The Key to Uncle Tom's Cabin* (New York: Arno, 1969), p. 1. Written in 1853, this book was an extraordinarily successful attempt to defend the veracity of *Uncle Tom's Cabin* by providing massive documentation for the incidents it narrated and the characters it described.
6. Harriet Beecher Stowe, *Uncle Tom's Cabin* (Columbus: Merrill, 1969), 2:246. All subsequent references to this work will be cited parenthetically in the text.
7. C. B. Macpherson, *Possessive Individualism* (New York: Oxford University Press, 1964), p. 272.

never sell them and, in fact, voluntary sales play a comparatively minor role in Stowe's depiction of the evils of slavery. A paragraph from Goodell's *The American Slave Code* helps explain why: "this feature of liability to seizure for the master's debt," Goodell writes,

> is, in many cases, more terrific to the slave than that which subjects him to the master's voluntary sale. The slave may be satisfied that his master is not willing to sell him—that it is not for his interest or convenience to do so. He may be conscious that he is, in a manner, necessary to his master or mistress. . . . He may even confide in their Christian benevolence and moral principle, or promise that they would not sell him. . . . But all this affords him no security or ground of assurance that his master's creditor will not seize him . . . against even his master's entreaties. Such occurrences are too common to be unnoticed or out of mind.[8]

According to Goodell, then, the slave, whose condition consists in being subordinated to the absolute power of his master, may in the end be less vexed by the absoluteness of that power than by its ultimate incompleteness. It is as if the greatest danger to the slave is not his master's power but his impotence. Thus Eliza and little Harry flee the Shelbys because, although they were "kind," they also "were owing money" and were being forced to sell Harry— "they couldn't," she says, "help themselves" (1:128). And when Augustine St. Clare dies, his entire household is overwhelmed not so much by grief as by "terror and consternation" at being left "utterly unprotected" (2:144).

What the slaves fear, of course, is being taken from a kind master to a cruel one; this threat, Goodell thinks, makes them constantly insecure, and the mechanics of this insecurity are the plot mechanism that sells Uncle Tom down the river. But in describing the reaction of St. Clare's slaves to his death, Stowe indirectly points toward a logic of slavery that runs deeper than the difference between good and bad masters, deeper even than the master/slave relation itself. As a matter of course, she notes, the slave is "devoid of rights"; the only "acknowledgment" of his "longings and wants" as a "human and immortal creature" that he ever receives comes to him "through the sovereign and irresponsible will of his master; and when that master is stricken down, nothing remains" (2:144). The point here is not that one man in the power of another may be subjected to the most inhumane cruelties; nor is it the more subtle point that the power of even a humane master dehumanizes the slave. For Stowe, the power of the kind master and the cruel master both can be tolerated since even a Legree, refusing Tom his

8. Goodell, *The American Slave Code*, pp. 65–66.

every want and longing, at least acknowledges those wants by refusing them and thus acknowledges his humanity. Rather, the most
terrifying spectacle slavery has to offer is the spectacle of slaves
without masters. Since the "only possible acknowledgment" of the
slave as a "human and immortal creature" is through his master's
"will," when in debt or in death the master's will is extinguished,
the slave's humanity is extinguished also. The slave without a master stands revealed as nothing more than "a bale of merchandise,"
inhuman testimony to the absolute transformation of a personal relation into a market relation.

Stowe, like most of her contemporaries, customarily understood
slavery as "a relic of a barbarous age";[9] the conflict between the
"aristocratic" "Slave Power" and "republican" "free labor" would
prove "irrepressible," William Seward proclaimed in a tremendously
influential speech,[1] and the supposed "feudalism" of the South was
a northern byword. More recently, Eugene Genovese, reviving the
irrepressible conflict interpretation of the Civil War, has described
the slaveholding planters as the "closest thing to feudal lords imaginable in a nineteenth-century bourgeois republic,"[2] and has argued
that the South was a fundamentally precapitalist society. But, as we
have begun to see, Stowe was basically more horrified by the bourgeois elements of slavery than by the feudal ones. She and Goodell
both were struck by the insecurity of the slave's life and she, in particular, saw that insecurity as the inevitable fate of property in a
free market. Thus she comes to see the evil of slavery not in its re-
version to a barbaric paternalism but in its uncanny way of epito-
mizing the market society to which she herself belongs. Rejecting
the claims of southern apologists that slavery provides a social and
economic refuge from capitalism, Stowe imagines it instead as a
mirror of the social and economic relations coming to the fore in
the bourgeois North.

Hence the slave trade, what she calls the "great Southern slave-
market," dominates her picture of the South and, despite their feudal status, the slaves in her writings share the anxious lives of
Hawthorne's "republican" Northerners—"somebody is always at the
drowning-point." The "fluctuations of hope, and fear, and desire"
(2:245) they experience appear now as transformations of their
market value. Their emotions represent their status as the objects
of speculation. "Nothing is more fluctuating than the value of

9. Stowe, *The Key to Uncle Tom's Cabin,* p. 62.
1. William H. Seward, "The Irrepressible Conflict," in *American Democracy,* pp. 468–69.
   The "experience of mankind," Seward claimed, had "conclusively established" that two
   such "radically different political systems" could never coexist. "They never have permanently existed together in one country," he said, "and they never can."
2. Eugene D. Genovese, *The Political Economy of Slavery* (New York: Random House,
   1967), p. 31.

slaves,"[3] remarks a Virginia legislator in *The Key to Uncle Tom's Cabin*. A recent Louisiana law had reduced their value; the imminent admission to the Union of Texas as a slave state would increase it. The Virginians speak of their "slave-breeding" as a kind of agriculture and of their female slaves as "brood-mares" but Stowe penetrates more deeply into the nature of the commodity by imagining the product without *any* producer. What everybody knows about the "goblin-like" Topsy, that she just "grow'd," is only part of the answer to a series of questions asked her by Miss Ophelia: "Do you know who made you?' "; " 'Tell me where you were born, and who your father and mother were.' " " 'Never was born,' " Topsy replies, " 'never had no father nor mother. . . . I was raised by a speculator' " (2:37). If production in *The House of the Seven Gables* is done with mirrors, production in *Uncle Tom's Cabin* is an equally demonic magic trick, substituting the speculator for the parent and utterly effacing any trace of labor, human or divine.

This replacement of the parent by the speculator assumed an even more lurid countenance when, instead of being separate, the two figures were embodied in the same man, as when a father might sell his daughter. Stowe reproduces a poem by Longfellow called "The Quadroon Girl," in which a planter and slaver bargain in the presence of a beautiful young girl:

> "The soil is barren, the farm is old,"
>   The thoughtful planter said;
> Then looked upon the Slaver's gold,
>   And then upon the maid.
>
> His heart within him was at strife
>   With such accursed gains;
> For he knew whose passions gave her life,
>   Whose blood ran in her veins.
>
> But the voice of nature was too weak;
>   He took the glittering gold!
> Then pale as death grew the maiden's cheek,
>   Her hands as icy cold.
>
> The slaver led her from the door,
>   He led her by the hand,
> To be his slave and paramour
>   In a strange and distant land![4]

Writers like George Fitzhugh defended slavery claiming that it replaced the "false, antagonistic and competitive relations" of liberal

---

3. Stowe, *The Key to Uncle Tom's Cabin*, p. 289.
4. The quotation is in ibid., p. 295.

capitalism with the more natural relations of the family. "Slavery leaves but little of the world without the family,"[5] he wrote in *Cannibals All!*; in a thoroughly paternalist society, all men, black and white, would be related to one another. Writers like Stowe and Longfellow inverted Fitzhugh's defense while preserving its terms. They too were concerned to defend the family against the market but, in their view, slavery only weakened the "voice of nature." It might be appropriate to think of one's children as property but to make that property alienable was to annihilate the family by dissolving nature into contract. "For the sake of a common humanity," Stowe wrote, she hoped that Longfellow's poem described "no common event."[6]

Longfellow's poem is somewhat ludicrous and its effect, perhaps, is to make the danger it imagines seem absurdly remote, in fact no common event. But the transformations worked upon parental and erotic relations by capitalism appear elsewhere in a more penetrating (although in some respects equally lurid) form. Indeed, these transformations, intensified and above all internalized, constitute what I take to be the heart of Hawthorne's concerns in *The House of the Seven Gables*, the chief threat against which the defense of property is mounted. Hence I would like to close by returning to that text and to what might be called its own representation of the quadroon girl.

"If ever there was a lady born" (201), Holgrave tells Phoebe, it was Alice Pyncheon, the daughter of a Pyncheon with aristocratic ambitions who, returning to Salem after a long stay in Europe, fervently hoped to gain "actual possession" of the Waldo territory and, having established himself as a "Lord" or "Earl," to return to England. According to tradition, the only man with access to the deed to Waldo was Matthew Maule, the grandson of the original "wizard," who was rumored still to haunt his old home "against the owner of which he pretended to hold an unsettled claim for ground-rent" (189). Summoned to the house, this young Maule (himself supposed, by the young ladies at least, to have a bewitching eye) demands to see Alice as well as her father. Ushered into his presence, the beautiful girl looks at Maule with unconcealed "admiration," but the "subtile" Maule sees only arrogant indifference in her "artistic approval" of his "comeliness, strength, and energy" (201). Her "admiration" is so open because it is so empty of desire; she looks at him, Maule thinks, as if he were "a brute beast," and he determines to wring from her the "acknowledgment that he was indeed a man." The "business" he has with her father now turns on

5. George Fitzhugh, *Cannibals All!*, in *Ante-Bellum*, ed. Harvey Wish (New York: Capricorn, 1960), p. 129.
6. Stowe, *The Key to Uncle Tom's Cabin*, p. 294.

Alice and on what Hawthorne calls the "contest" between her "un-sullied purity" and the "sinister or evil potency . . . striving to pass her barriers" (203).

Alice is prepared to enter this apparently uneven struggle be-tween "man's might" and "woman's might" because, as she tells her father, no "lady, while true to herself, can have ought to fear from whomsoever or in any circumstances" (202). She knows herself possessed of a "power" that makes "her sphere impenetrable, unless betrayed by treachery within" (203). Hence she allows her father to stand by while Maule, gesturing in the air, puts her into a trance from which Pyncheon, suddenly alarmed, is unable to rouse her. " 'She is mine!' " Maule announces and, when Pyncheon rages against him, Maule asks quietly, " 'Is it my crime, if you have sold your daughter . . . ?' " (206).

Obviously this story repeats in some crucial respects the narra-tive of "The Quadroon Girl," but in pointing to this similarity I do not mean to claim that the bewitching of Alice Pyncheon is an alle-gory of the slave trade. Hawthorne seems to have been largely in-different to the issue of slavery; a few years later, he would urge Charles Sumner to "let slavery alone for a little while" and focus in-stead on the mistreatment of sailors in the merchant marine.[7] I mean instead to see in this story some sense of how deep the no-tion of inalienability could run and especially of how deeply under-mined it could be by conditions closer to home than the slave trade and less exotic than witchcraft. For Alice Pyncheon fancies herself immune to possession (in effect, to appropriation) simply because she feels no desire. She thinks of herself as a kind of impregnable citadel. Desires, like so many Trojan horses, would make her vul-nerable; wanting no one and nothing, she is free from what Haw-thorne, in McCarthyesque fashion, calls "treachery from within," and so impervious to aggression from without. That she in fact suc-cumbs to Matthew Maule does not invalidate her analysis—it only shows that the enemy within need not take the form of felt desire. In their dreams, Hawthorne says, the Pyncheons have always been "no better than bond-servants" (26) to the Maules. Thus, Alice's Pyncheon blood makes her as much an alienable commodity as does the quadroon girl's black blood. And, although *she* feels no de-sire, her father does, "an inordinate desire," Hawthorne calls it, "for measuring his land by miles instead of acres" (208). The bewitch-ing of Alice is here imagined as a business transaction; witches, it turns out, are capitalists by night and (having appropriated her spirit as the Pyncheons did his land), Matthew Maule makes Alice live out her life in unconscious mimicry of the original Salem girls:

7. The quotation is in Mellow, *Nathaniel Hawthorne in His Times*, p. 435.

breaking out, wherever she might be, into "wild laughter" or hysterical tears, suddenly dancing a "jig" or "rigadoon," obeying the every command of "her unseen despot" (209).[8]

"Despot" is a crucial word here; Andrew Jackson described the National Bank as exerting a "despotic sway"[9] over the financial life of the country; Harriet Beecher Stowe called slavery "a system which makes every individual owner an irresponsible despot;"[1] Hawthorne calls Maule, the capitalist wizard, an "unseen despot." The force of the term is in all three cases to represent (internal) conflict as (external) oppression. For example, the point of characterizing the Bank as despotic was to associate it with old-world aristocracy and literally to represent it as un-American. Readers of Jackson's veto message cannot help but be struck by his obsessive concern with "foreign stockholders" in the Bank and with the anonymous threat they pose to "our country." By the same token, Stowe, fearing slavery (if I am right) as an emblem of the market economy, nevertheless thought for many years that the slave problem could be solved by repatriation to Africa, as if exorcising the slaves would rid the South of feudalism and the North of capitalism. Hawthorne too imagines a Maule become a Holgrave, renouncing "mastery" over Phoebe and leaving her "free" out of "reverence for another's individuality" (212). Indeed, the very idea of the romance asserts the possibility of immunity to appropriation in an Alice Pyncheon-like fantasy of strength through purity.

For what does the notion of inalienability entail if not a property right so impenetrable that nothing on the outside can buy it or take it away from you and so pure that nothing on the inside will conspire to sell it or give it away? That no actual possession of land could meet these criteria, we have already seen. What slavery proved to Stowe was that even the possession of one's own body could not be guaranteed against capitalist appropriation. "The slaves often say" (she quotes an "acquaintance") "when cut in the hand or foot, 'Plague on the old foot. . . . It is master's, let him take care of it; nigger don't care if he never get well.' "[2] Even the slave's soul, she thought, could not be kept pure when the "nobler traits of mind and heart" had their own "market value":

---

8. In this connection, it may be worth remembering not only Hawthorne's lifelong fear and dislike of mesmerism but also Stowe's remark that "negroes are singularly susceptible to all that class of influences which produce catalepsy, mesmeric sleep, and partial clairvoyant phenomena" (Stowe, *Key*, p. 46). Mesmerism, as a threat to property, works most easily on those whose title to themselves is least secure, but no one in Hawthorne's world can be entirely safe from the threat of expropriation.

9. Andrew Jackson, "Farewell Address," *American Democracy*, p. 374. See also his "Veto of the Bank Bill," *American Democracy*, pp. 309–21.

1. Stowe, *The Key to Uncle Tom's Cabin*, p. 204.

2. Ibid., p. 22.

Is the slave intelligent?—Good! that raises his price two hundred dollars. Is he conscientious and faithful? Good . . . two hundred dollars more. Is he religious? Does that Holy Spirit of God . . . make that despised form His temple?—Let that also be put down in the estimate of his market value, and the gift of the Holy Ghost shall be sold for money.[3]

Only death offered an escape from this "dreadful commerce." Legree says to George Shelby, who has made him an offer on Uncle Tom's corpse, "I don't sell dead niggers" (2:282).

In Hawthorne's republican world, however, everything is for sale. If not exactly dead niggers, then at least some version of them, like the Jim Crow gingerbread men Hepzibah Pyncheon sells to her first customer. And if not exactly the Holy Spirit, then at least the "spirit" of Alice Pyncheon, held for debt by her father's "ghostly creditors," the Maules. In fact, the whole project of the romance, with its bizarrely utopian and apparently anachronistic criteria for legitimate ownership, had already played a significant, if ironic, role in opening the American land market. The irony, of course, is that Hawthorne and others like him were uncompromisingly opposed to speculation in land. Jackson, for example, reacted against his own early career as a land speculator by defending, in Michael Rogin's words, "original title against actual residents whose long-standing possession was contaminated at the core."[4] But if the goal was purity, the effect on the western frontier was chaos; criteria like Jackson's were so rigorous that they left no man's title secure. Hence, the separation of title from possession, the very condition of romance's attempt to defend against speculation, turned out to be the condition that enabled speculators to flourish. Apparently imagining the terms of a text that would escape republican fluctuation, Hawthorne imagined in fact the terms of the technology that made those fluctuations possible.

The problematic at the heart of this reversal becomes even sharper if we turn from commerce in land to commerce in people. Stowe opposed slavery but she did so, as we have seen, in defense of property. Slaves, she thought, were the victims of theft, their property rights in their own persons had been violated. Attacking southern feudalism, she spoke for free labor and against slave labor. But insofar as her critique of slavery came to be a critique of the "Southern market," it had inevitably to constitute a repudiation of free labor as well. What Stowe most feared was the notion of a

3. Ibid., p. 280.
4. Michael Paul Rogin, *Fathers and Children: Andrew Jackson and the Subjugation of the American Indian* (New York: Alfred A. Knopf, 1976), p. 96. Although he does not explicitly point to the intrinsically self-defeating character of the demand for pure title, Rogin does go on to note that occupancy laws were opposed by "aspiring speculators" as well as by "purists over contractual rights" (p. 97).

market in human attributes and, of course, free labor is just short-hand for a free market in labor. Hence her conception of freedom was itself a product of the economy epitomized for her in the slave trade—free market, free trade, in Blackstone's words, "free and un-constrained" "circulation" of "property."

Hawthorne valued freedom too, as essential to the "individual-ity" he cherished and to the "reverence" for individuality he held highest among the virtues. Matthew Maule leaves Alice Pyncheon's spirit "bowed" down before him; Holgrave demonstrates his own "integrity" by leaving Phoebe hers. But the specter of "treachery within" cannot be so easily laid to rest. For the real question raised by Alice's story is whether "reverence" for "individuality" is not ulti-mately an oxymoron. How should we read what Hawthorne calls Alice's loss of "self-control"? We may read it as a conflict between two forces—the individual self and the market—opposed in princi-ple to one another.[5] In this instance, the market wins, but it need not and, indeed, when Holgrave liberates Phoebe, it does not. Or we may read it as a conflict in which the individual is set against a market that has already gained a foothold within—the Mc-Carthyesque imagination of conspiracy. Here the enemy is still re-garded as fundamentally other but is seen successfully to have infiltrated the sphere of the self—it must be exorcised.

But if we remember that Alice, as a Pyncheon, is already in bondage to the Maules, and if we remember that this fact of her birth seems to her the guarantee of her "self-control," we may be led to a third reading. Here Alice is ultimately betrayed not only by her father's desire but by the very claim to individual identity that made her imagine herself immune to betrayal. Individuality, in this reading, is its own betrayal—the enemy cannot be repulsed by the self or exorcised from the self since the enemy of the self is the self. "Property in the bourgeois sense," C. B. Macpherson has written, "is not only a right to enjoy or use; it is a right to dispose of, to ex-change, to alienate."[6] Property, to be property, must be alienable. We have seen the fate of Hawthorne's attempt to imagine an in-alienable right in land; now we can see the fate of his attempt to imagine an inalienable right in the self. The slave cannot resist her

5. Such a reading is adopted in effect by Michael T. Gilmore who argues that, writing *The House of the Seven Gables*, Hawthorne "was unable to suppress his misgivings that in bowing to the marketplace he was compromising his artistic independence and integrity" ("The Artist and the Marketplace in the House of the Seven Gables," *ELH* 48 [Spring 1981]:172–73. Gilmore's valuable essay seems to me typical of much recent work on the artist in the market in that it calls attention to the importance of the market only to draw ever more firmly the line between the values of that market and the values of art. The point I am urging in this essay is the rather different one that for Hawthorne qualities like independence and integrity (artistic or otherwise) do not exist in opposition to the marketplace but are produced by it and contained within it.
6. Macpherson, *Possessive Individualism*, p. 92.

master because the slave is her master. If from one perspective, this looks like freedom, from another perspective, it looks like just another one of what Stowe called "the vicissitudes of property."

GILLIAN BROWN

From Women's Work and Bodies in
The House of the Seven Gables†

* * *

The Gothic Revival and the Cult of Domesticity

In *The House of the Seven Gables* Hawthorne tells the story of a home business: the narrative begins with Hepzibah Pyncheon "nervously" opening a cent-shop in one of the gables of her ancestral home, a venture which turns out to be a "pretty good business," as one of her neighbors says at the end of the story, when Hepzibah "rides off in her carriage with a couple of hundred thousands" to an "elegant country seat." Shopkeeping ultimately returns Hepzibah to seclusion and wealth, realizing her dream "that some harlequintrick of fate would intervene in her favor." In Hepzibah's version of the American dream, commerce inspires and materializes "her castles in the air," her fantasy of becoming heiress to "unreckonable riches," . . . "so that instead of keeping a cent-shop" . . . "Hepzibah would build a palace."[1]

The romance spun out in this commercial success story allays nervousness about the risks of commerce with a fairy-tale ending of restored wealth and health; the trials of the market are so thoroughly overcome that the reality of free enterprise democracy seems to disappear in the closing scene of retirement to an inherited country estate. That Hawthorne's romance in this sense leaves behind or transcends commerce suggests its resemblance to another artifice of transport from (and within) market society. For this narrative of a woman's removal from commercial nervousness to the social and financial security of a comfortable home also recapitulates the development of bourgeois domesticity in the midnineteenth century: the removal of woman from the realm of pro-

---

† From *Domestic Individualism: Imagining Self in Nineteenth-Century America*, pp. 69–95. Copyright © 1991. Reprinted with permission of The Regents of the University of California. All notes are Brown's; some notes have been condensed for this edition.
1. Nathaniel Hawthorne, *The House of the Seven Gables*, vol. 2 of the Centenary Edition of the *Works of Nathaniel Hawthorne* (Columbus: Ohio State University Press, 1963–), 314–19, 64–65. All subsequent references to this edition of the novel will be noted in parentheses in the text.

duction to an idealized home and, concomitantly, the emergence of
a new individualism identified with this home.

Hawthorne's romanticization of commerce in *The House of the
Seven Gables*, his representation of retail success as a return to
aristocracy, reprises the revivalist gesture that domestic ideology
both generates and exemplifies. In 1820, two-thirds of all the cloth
produced in this country was made by women working in their own
homes. As textile manufactures replaced household production in
successive decades, the memory of household production was retained in the new mass-produced fabric—called "domestic"—and
by the ideology of domesticity, which clothed the individual with a
sense of enduring value in private life. Hence, domesticity, a definition of private space articulated through intrinsic feminine characteristics, emerged as an imaginative reconstruction of a past life
recalled as continuous and sustaining.[2] Forwarding and fostering
the succession of one economic mode by another, the rise of
domestic ideology in nineteenth-century America thematizes as it
sanctions a progressive convertibility. The tautological turn by
which the domestic encapsulates nostalgia for itself works as the
mainspring of a fable of continuity. And the fuel of this romantic
machine is a seemingly inexhaustible one: change itself. From the
phenomenon of economic change, domesticity mines a transformative power by which the past may be reanimated even as it is superseded. It is within this domestic circularity that Hawthorne
discovers a new life for the "circle of gentility" (44), the possibilities
for aristocracy within democracy.

It is in reference to this aristocratic potential of the domestic domain that Emma Hewitt later in the century called her popular
household manual *Queen of the Home*. Hewitt declares: "In this
glorious land where none are royal, all [women] are queens, gov-
erning by the God-given right of womanhood."[3] The aristocratic associations prominent in middle-class domestic ideology signal, not
merely the persistence of aristocratic ideals and middle-class aspirations, but the nostalgic function domesticity serves: its representation of the present in the terms of the past. Thus the
transformation of the House of the Seven Gables from aristocratic
estate to petty shop, described in Hepzibah's descent from "her

---

2. The rise of domesticity and the socioeconomic transformations it accompanied are well
described in Nancy F. Cott, *The Bonds of Womanhood: "Woman's Sphere" in New England, 1780–1835* (New Haven: Yale University Press, 1977), 63–100; the history of
American textile manufacture is traced in Thomas Dublin, *Women at Work: The Transformation of Work and Community in Lowell, Massachusetts, 1826–1860* (New York: Columbia University Press, 1979). A similar description of domesticity's nostalgic function
appears in my essay "Nuclear Domesticity: Sequence and Survival," *Yale Journal of Criticism* 2 (Fall 1988): 179–91.
3. Emma Hewitt, *Queen of the Home: Her Reign from Infancy to Age, from Attic to Cellar*
(Philadelphia: Miller-Megee, 1892).

pedestal of imaginary rank" to "hucksteress of a cent-shop" (38), is a vision of market progress already antiquated in 1851. Hepzibah knows she cannot compete with the "magnificent shops in the cities": "Groceries, toy-shops, dry-goods stores, with their immense panes of plate-glass, their vast and complete assortments of merchandize, in which fortunes had been invested; and those noble mirrors at the farther end of each establishment, doubling all this wealth by a brightly burnished vista of unrealities!" (48). The large retail and department stores which appeared in the 1850s, with their great resources of capital, display, and advertising, eventually replaced both small-town general stores and urban specialty shops.[4] So even the transformation of the House of the Seven Gables is already an anachronism; the belatedness of this accomplishment is underscored by Hawthorne's citation of a precedent for Hepzibah's enterprise in the "petty huckster" Pyncheon ancestor who "bethought himself of no better avenue to wealth than by cutting a shop-door through the side of his ancestral residence" (29).

Hepzibah's shopkeeping thus follows the tradition of the house, a tradition that encompasses the transformation of the "patrician" into the "plebeian" (38), and the rise of the plebeian to proprietor of a "country-seat" (317). In this cyclic narrative, as in the domestic institution of continuity, the past returns. The revivalist energies and effects of domesticity elaborated in *The House of the Seven Gables* are articulated more explicitly in the 1840s and 1850s Gothic Revival vogue in home architecture, popularized in America by the domestic architect and landscape designer Andrew Jackson Downing. Sharing with the cult of domesticity a belief, "above all things under heaven, in the power and influence of the *Individual Home*,"[5] Downing sought to translate domestic rhetoric into a style evocative of home values. Downing believed that the rural Gothic style implemented in England during the 1830s and 1840s, "characterized mainly by pointed gables," "best manifested . . . in every part the presence of cultivated and deep domestic sympathies."[6] Features crucial to the domestic quality of a house included "the chimneys, the windows, and the porch, veranda, or piazza." The identification of these architectural voids as spatial elements of domesticity—"a broad shady veranda suggests ideas of comfort"

4. On the emergence of the department store in the 1850s, see Susan Porter Benson's chapter "The New Kind of Store" in her *Counter Cultures: Saleswomen, Managers, and Customers in American Department Stores* (Urbana: University of Illinois Press, 1986), 12–30; Michael Miller, *The Bon Marché: Bourgeois Culture and the Department Store, 1869–1920* (Princeton: Princeton University Press, 1984).

5. Andrew Jackson Downing, *Rural Essays* (New York: Leavitt and Allen, 1853), 243. This was a posthumous collection of essays and editorials from Downing's periodical *The Horticulturalist*, which appeared in 1846.

6. Andrew Jackson Downing, *Cottage Residences* (1842; rpt. New York: Dover, 1981), 23, and his *The Architecture of Country Houses* (1850; rpt. New York: Dover, 1969), 323.

and bay windows, balconies, and terraces denote "those elegant enjoyments which belong to the habitation of man in a cultivated and
refined state of society"—links the space of interiority with an ideal
of leisure and privacy and ideal of private views and protected access.[7] The American Gothic Revival home retreats from or, like
Hepzibah Pyncheon, transcends the nineteenth-century marketplace, the public realm where "strange and unloving eyes . . . have
the privilege of gazing" (46). Downing conjoined this removal of individuality from the present with the Gothic's romantic suggestions
of the past.

The English Gothic Revivalists who influenced Downing's designs admired the detail work on the Gothic cathedral, identifying
in the irregular components and intricate decorations the mark of
unique artisanship, the lasting effects of the individual. They accordingly developed a domestic architecture that stressed asymmet-
rical designs to emphasize human artisanship and thus to suggest
through picturesque and romantic effects a domain of individuality
in the home. Following Ruskin's view that the Gothic "admits of a
richness of record altogether unlimited," Revivalists sought to preserve a sense of the past, defining home as "a kind of monument"
to human life, work, and experience.[8]

For Ruskin, whose stress on preserving the past dominated the
values of the Gothic Revival in domestic architecture, "there is
sanctity in a good man's house which cannot be renewed in every
tenement that rises on its ruins." Durability and stability in houses
are urged as remedies against "loosely struck" roots in the contemporary landscape—the "pitiful concretions of lime and clay" recently built "upon those thin, tottering, foundationless shells of
splintered wood and imitated stone." Ruskin takes it as "an evil sign
of a people when their houses are built to last for one generation
only." To celebrate a "spirit of honorable, proud, peaceful self-
possession," Ruskin "would have, then, our ordinary dwelling-
houses built to last." And such houses would be monuments to
their builders, museums of their lasting ownership. "This right over
the house, I conceive, belongs to its first builder, and is to be re-
spected by his children; and it would be well that blank stones
should be left in places, to be inscribed with a summary of his life
and its experiences."[9]

It is just this endurance of the past and Gothic-romance exposition of paternal power that both Holgrave and Clifford, the last

7. Downing, *Cottage Residences*, 12–13.
8. John Ruskin, *The Seven Lamps of Architecture* (1848; rpt. New York: Noonday Press,
   1961), 174, 173. This book appeared in an unauthorized edition in New York in 1849; it
   was then issued twenty-five times up to 1894, attesting to the influence of Ruskin on
   American architecture and aesthetics throughout the century.
9. Ruskin, *The Seven Lamps of Architecture*, 170–73.

male descendants of the Maules and Pyncheons, oppose in their critiques of family estates. "There is no such unwholesome atmosphere as that of an old home, rendered poisonous by one's defunct forefathers and relatives," Clifford contends (261). Holgrave welcomes the day "when no man shall build his house for posterity." "If each generation were allowed and expected to build its own houses," he speculates, "that single change, comparatively unimportant in itself, would imply almost every reform which society is now suffering for" (183–84). Observing "the ease of obtaining a house and land, and the ability of almost every industrious citizen to build his own house" in America, Downing advanced an architecture in keeping with Holgrave's ideal.[1] Rejecting Ruskin's preference for the past over the present, Downing appropriated the individualism of English Gothic Revival styles for American values—for the construction of a democratic home as a locus of value and continuity not founded in inheritance. "Placing national feeling and national taste above all others," Downing's "true home" was "not, indeed, the feudal castle, not the baronial hall, but the home of the individual man—the home of that family of equal rights, which continually separates and continually reforms itself in the new world." Like Hawthorne, Downing noted the failure and unsuitability of ancestral estates in America, which were "contrary to the spirit of republican institutions. . . . The just pride of a true American is not in a great hereditary home, but in greater hereditary institutions."[2]

Yet even though Downing inveighed against Pyncheonesque hereditary homes built by the "robbery of the property of another class," he admitted that there was "something wonderfully captivating in the idea of a battlemented castle." The home Downing proposed in place of the castle was "the beautiful, rural, unostentatious, moderate home of the country gentleman." Downing desired "something of the castle in the man," a distinction in individuality.[3] For Downing, aristocratic attributes and democratic values were not incompatible. Democracy offered every individual castles in the air, the opportunity of a kingdom in the domestic domain, apart from democratic struggles. Downing's accommodation for aristocracy within democracy suggests the continuity between Holgrave's radical democratic views and his domestication by Phoebe, who "made the House of the Seven Gables like a home to him" (182).

1. Downing, *The Architecture of Country Houses*, 3.
2. Downing, *The Architecture of Country Houses*, 265, 269, 267, 270. An excellent discussion of Downing's "Americanization" of the English Gothic Revival and of his place in nineteenth-century American architectural history appears in Vincent Scully, *The Shingle and the Stick Style: Architectural Theory and Design from Downing to the Origins of Wright* (New Haven: Yale University Press, 1977), xxiii–lix.
3. Downing, *The Architecture of Country Houses*, 269, 261, 269, 262.

Holgrave's conversion to conservative respect for the "permanence" of a "domestic architecture in stone" reiterates the nostalgic narrative of domestic ideology in which the past is invoked as the rationalization for a new order.[4] The fact that Holgrave can, as it were, have his house and hate it, too, demonstrates the convertibility to continuity that change generates. In other words, the flux of the present, to which Holgrave weds his democratic enthusiasms, is precisely what empowers domestic conversions. The attainment of a democratic home—the property available to the American individual—signifies the establishment of a new system of individual private property. That this new distribution of property entails new forms of inequality is not the point here. What Hawthorne and Downing exhibit is the mechanics of continuity whereby such innovations (and their imbalances) are implemented.

The persistence of aristocratic associations in Downing's American Gothic thus reprises domestic ideology's revivalist performance: the sleight-of-hand whereby progress appears as the reanimated and regenerate past. Downing takes this logic of revivalism even further, to make even the creative processes of domestication disappear. His ethos of retreat and privacy involves not only the removal of the individual from the present world but also the removal of domestic processes, of housework, from the sight of the individual. In order to distinguish the domestic from the economic realm, to create a "counterpoise to the great tendency toward constant changes" in American economic and social life, Downing's house plans obscured every sign of work.[5] He placed the kitchen as far as possible from the parlor, usually in the rear of the house and often in the basement. He designed screens and walls to keep kitchen gardens out of sight. Instead of considering the house as women's workplace, Downing emphasized the primacy of the house's "pleasing effect." In his "ideal of domestic accommodation," he envisions "[e]ach department of the house [as] being complete in itself, and intruding itself but little on the attention of family or guests when it is not required to be visible."[6] This compartmentalization removes labor from the pleasures of domesticity and, more important, from the perspective of domesticity. In Downing's philosophy of domestic architecture, domestic economies recede; the symbolic agency of the home supersedes its work processes. Domesticity in Downing's treatment becomes a

4. For an apposite discussion of how ideology works for the rationalization of capitalism in the expression "A man's home is his castle," see Eve Kosofsky Sedgwick, *Between Men: English Literature and Male Homosocial Desire* (New York: Columbia University Press, 1985), 14–15.
5. Andrew Jackson Downing, *A Treatise on the Theory and Practice of Landscape Gardening* (New York: Wiley and Putnam, 1841), viii.
6. Downing, *Cottage Residences*, 1–3.

nostalgic romance that eliminates any form of industry altogether, imagining an aristocratic republic without the labor that underpins it.

Woman's Work and Ladies' Leisure

The House of the Seven Gables unfolds a similar domestic romance of transformative, invisible labor. In the fulfillment of Hepzibah's fantasy, a family inheritance from the commercial fortune of her cousin Jaffrey eventually transports her to her castle. An incorporation of commercial success into a scenario of restored aristocratic order, this happy ending is assured by a "harlequin-trick" (64), the appearance of the young cousin Phoebe Pyncheon with her "natural magic" (71). Announcing "I am as nice a little saleswoman, as I am a housewife" (78), Phoebe transforms the "squalid and ugly aspect" of trade. Her "homely witchcraft" (72) brings to the labors of shopkeeping and housekeeping "the easy and flexible charm of play" (82). This representation, or disguise, of labor as magic and play spiritualizes housekeeping and shopkeeping, distinguishing them from ordinary human work by their Godlike creative power and ease. The "spiritual quality in Phoebe's activity" effectively eliminates the mundaneness of work, linking her process to that of "God's angels" who "do not toil," "but let their good works grow out of them" (82). So the entry into the House of the Seven Gables of this domestic angel with "her vastly superior gifts as a shop-keeper" (79) proves to be the harbinger of Hepzibah's success. Commutation of commerce into its own antithesis of domestic comfort restores "the aristocratic hucksteress" (79) to her "circle of gentility" (44). This fairy-tale rescue of Hepzibah from "the business of setting up a petty shop" to "earn her own food" (38) images the rise of domesticity and commercial culture as a return to aristocracy. The formation of culture later characterized by Veblen as the culture of conspicuous leisure and consumption is anticipated here in a legend of magical achievement.[7]

The arrival of Phoebe "at the instant of time when the patrician lady is to be transformed into the plebeian woman" signals the preservation of the lady by domestic fiat, the incorporation of ladyship into the domestic domain. "In this republican country, amid the fluctuating waves of our social life, somebody is always at the drowning-point" (38), explains the narrator of *The House of the Seven Gables*. To counter such flux and resuscitate such victims as Hepzibah, one contemporary etiquette guide declared that Americans needed "some standard that knows no fluctuation, no

7. Thorstein Veblen, *The Theory of the Leisure Class* (1899; rpt. New York: New American Library, 1953), 41–80.

caprice."[8] Barbara Welter echoes Hawthorne's description of fluctuations in a free enterprise society: "In a society where values
changed frequently, where fortunes rose and fell with frightening
rapidity, where social and economic mobility provided instability as
well as hope, one thing at least remained the same—a true woman
was a true woman, wherever she was found."[9] The domestic cult of
true womanhood that flourished in popular literature from 1820 to
1860 thus functioned to define a stable identity, a fixity of class
through a character transcending class changes. Domestic femininity served as a fluctuating society's imagination of itself, its deal of
value and inviolability. This is why Hepzibah's boarder, the daguerreotypist Holgrave (whose presence and occupation themselves
indicate the incursion of the social stream of novelties into Hepzibah's long-secluded existence), assures her that it is "better to be
a true woman than a lady" (45). The prerogatives of identity and
continuity once identified with an aristocratic class are now located
in the democratic cult of domesticity: the lady survives in the true
woman.

The aristocratic definitions of the lady and the estate provide
self-insurance: one always has one's place. It is this assurance that
makes the aristocratic fantasy so powerful and so necessary to Hepzibah, that causes her to take such pride in her family's defects and
infirmities. For her, the "native inapplicability . . . of the Pyncheons
to any useful purpose" (77) confirms their particularity and distinction. With her practical skills and gifts, "Phoebe is no Pyncheon,"
in Hepzibah's view, and the older woman cannot help thinking, "[I]f
only she could be a lady, too!" (79). But Phoebe's "patrimony, the
gift of practical arrangement" (71), grants her the faculty of being
"admirably in keeping with herself" (80), the quality of the lady
subsumed under the definition of true womanhood. "Instead of discussing her claim to rank among ladies," the narrator recommends,
"it would be preferable to regard Phoebe as the example of feminine grace and availability combined, in a state of society, if there
were any such, where ladies did not exist. There, it should be
woman's office to move in the midst of practical affairs, and to gild
them all, were it even the scouring of pots and kettles—with an atmosphere of loveliness and joy" (80). This is the romantic ideal
of true womanhood and "the sphere of Phoebe" (80). Phoebe's
sphere, like her angelic assistance in Hepzibah's shop, offers "the
decayed gentlewoman" a more secure ladyship.

In Hepzibah and Phoebe, Hawthorne figures the installation of

8. Caroline Matilda Kirkland, *The Evening Book, or Fireside Talk on Morals and Manners*
(New York: C. Scribner, 1853), 17.
9. Barbara Welter, "The Cult of True Womanhood," in her *Dimity Convictions: The American Woman in the Nineteenth Century* (Athens: Ohio University Press, 1976), 21.

the domestic ideal as a reenactment of a fantasized prior order. Not only do housekeepers appear as ladies in this romance, but housework appears as leisure. The ascension of the Angel in the House romanticizes market history by spiritualizing women's work so that it is dissociated from the physical efforts that signify the human imprint on history. Change itself is thus domesticated in the disembodiment of women's work, in the imagery of women not working. Neither Phoebe nor Hepzibah seems to work: "what precisely was Phoebe's process, we find it impossible to say," the narrator says of her housekeeping (72); the nervous lady "with her habitual sluggishness" (77) cannot work. This appearance of no connection to labor is also characteristic of the domestic ideal of housework, despite its emphasis on prodigious industry. Stowe stressed this facility in her many portraits of successful housekeepers such as Katy Scudder in *The Minister's Wooing*. For such a housekeeper, the more she does, the more ladylike and leisurely she appears:

> She shall scrub floors, wash, bake, and brew, and yet her hands shall be small and white; she shall have no perceptible income, yet always be handsomely dressed; she shall have not a servant in her house, with a dairy to manage, hired man to feed, a boarder or two to care for, unheard-of pickling and preserving to do,—and yet you commonly see her every afternoon sitting at her shady parlor-window behind the lilacs, cool and easy, hemming muslin capstrings, or reading the latest new book.[1]

In this sense the cult of true womanhood (re)produces the lady of leisure by denying the corporeality of women's work.

In this light, Hawthorne's infamous remark on the literary monopoly of "the damned mob of scribbling women" articulates not simply professional jealousy but also his sense of an aesthetic violation: the conspicuousness of exertion, the public sight of women's productivity and corporeality. A mob of scribbling women poses for Hawthorne the question of whether there can be aesthetic creations in the marketplace—not because women cannot write but because they should not *appear* to write. This may be why Hawthorne cast his admiration of Fanny Fern, the author of *Ruth Hall*, in (albeit negative) supernatural terms: "the woman writes as if the Devil were in her."[2] For Hawthorne, a woman's work is ideally never *done*.

The goal of housekeeping is thus its own erasure in leisure. In *The House of the Seven Gables*, this appearance of leisure in house or shop assumes on the one hand a superhuman feminine labor,

1. Stowe, *The Minister's Wooing* (1859; rpt. New York: AMS Press, 1967), 2.
2. *Letters of Hawthorne to William D. Ticknor* (2 vols.; Newark: Carteret, 1910), 1:78.

and on the other a feminine incapacitation. The disappearance or, more precisely, the elision of women's agency in their work facilitates the romanticization of change by denying the connection between women and labor and thus eliminating the process and change that are labor's office. What haunts the House of the Seven Gables, then, is not only the sins of the fathers but also the disembodiments of the present, the ghosts of feminine labor.

The Mesmerized Working Body

Hawthorne's tale is a fable of market labor in which the individual's work, whether shopkeeping or housekeeping or the imaginative labor of story-telling, forms a sphere secure from the processes work signified in the nineteenth century. * * * The idea of work as damaging to the individual pervades nineteenth-century thought; it recurs not only in Marx's exposition of the alienated worker but also in [Catharine] Beecher's worries about the health of housekeepers, in factory novels' descriptions of injured and deformed laborers, and in medical admonitions about the perils of overwork.[3] In *The House of the Seven Gables*, Hawthorne contributes to this colloquy a fiction of safe (protected and protective) labor. The erasures of labor and escapes from commerce performed in Hawthorne's romance and Downing's architecture effectively rescue the body from the publicity of economic processes.

If, for Hawthorne, Phoebe's providential housekeeping serves as a model of imaginative practice and production in which the individual is immunized from the effects of labor (that is, from the vulnerability of her body), then Hepzibah's shopkeeping demonstrates the bodily risks in labor, the ways labor continually exposes and emphasizes the body. For an elderly, poor, genteel spinster in the mid-nineteenth century the economic opportunities were few: sewing, teaching, petty shopkeeping. All of these, in Hawthorne's representation, refer to facts and frailties of Hepzibah's body: "she could not be a seamstress" because of her nearsightedness and "those tremulous fingers of hers," she could not teach school because of the "torpid" state of her heart toward children and the limitations of her memory and learning (38–39). Shopkeeping entails the greatest exposure, the display of herself to the world. What Hepzibah dreads most in opening her shop is the fact "that she must ultimately come forward, and stand revealed in her proper individuality" (40). This is why she tries to imagine a way of performing her

---

3. See, for example, Phelps's prefatory note to *The Silent Partner* (Old Westbury, N. Y.: Feminist Press, 1983), in which she cites the reports of the Massachusetts Bureau of Statistics of Labor on the abuses of the factory system. Specific accounts of the daily endangerments to life and health can be found in the letters of millgirls collected by Thomas Dublin in *From Farm to Factory* (New York: Columbia University Press, 1981).

transactions unseen: "to minister to the wants of the community, unseen, like a disembodied divinity, or enchantress, holding forth her bargains to the reverential and awestricken purchaser, in an invisible hand" (40).

Hawthorne underscores labor's foregrounding of the corporeal in making us "spectators to [Hepzibah's] fate," in dwelling on her "strange contortion of the brow"—"the innocent result of her nearsightedness" mistaken by the world for a scowl—and on the nervous frenzy of "her rigid and rusty frame" "upon its hands and knees" trying to set "her shop in order for the public eye" (33–39). It is as though the conspicuousness to which commerce subjects the woman literally subjects her to the eye, bringing her to her knees.

The subjection to sight enacted and thematized in this cruel scene recalls another public display and humiliation of an aristocratic woman: Alice Pyncheon's mesmeric subjugation by Matthew Maule. Under Maule's power, "a will, most unlike her own, constrained her to do its grotesque and fantastic bidding" (208); upon his command "her spirit passed from beneath her own control," and the proud Alice would suddenly "break into wild laughter" or into tears, or dance "some high-paced jig" more "befitting the brisk lasses at a rustic merry-making" (209). This induced hysteria—the dissociation of will and body accomplished by the mesmerist—exposes the woman in uncharacteristic behaviors, "lost from self-control" (209). The ultimate alien act she performs is a labor for a laborer: she is summoned to wait upon Maule's bride, a laborer's daughter.

In both cases the aristocratic lady is subjugated, but these are not fables of democratic progress or egalitarian justice. Rather, they are horror stories of labor from the aristocrat's point of view. In Hawthorne's horrific imagination and in the aristocrat's horror of the rise of trading and working classes, labor means subjection to a mesmeric power that hystericizes the individual body, undermining the will and compelling certain performances by the individual. Thus Hepzibah's "heart seemed to be attached to the same steel-spring" (49) as the shop-bell that summons her to work. At the sound of the bell, "[t]he maiden lady arose upon her feet, as pale as a ghost at cock-crow; for she was an enslaved spirit, and this the talisman to which she owed obedience" (42). The labor enslaving these ladies reduces their pretensions to aristocratic individuality by accentuating their corporeality and the usages to which it can be put.[4]

---

4. Maria Tatar emphasizes the sexual nature of mesmeric power in this novel, pointing to the attraction the Maule men hold for the Pyncheon women. See her suggestive and informative *Spellbound: Studies on Mesmerism and Literature* (Princeton: Princeton University Press, 1978), esp. 200–217.

Although selling may seem a highly abstract form of labor, removed from the actual bodily endangerment of mill or factory machinery and exempt from the physical and mental exertions of sewing or teaching, in Hawthorne's depiction acts of selling crucially reflect and even magnify the role of the body in commerce. The exchange of goods for money involves an intensification of corporeality: not only is the merchant on display with her goods, her materiality subject to public perusal and indeed a factor in her selling, but she is in touch with each transaction, a contiguity dramatized in Hepzibah's fantasy of making her hand invisible in her transactions and in her practice of drawing on silk gloves before counting her money. But her hand is both visible and available in her shopkeeping; when she takes money, she feels as if "[t]he sordid stain of that copper-coin could never be washed away from her palm" (51). The soiling effect of money is also the theme of stories about Hepzibah's shopkeeping ancestor circulating the fact "that, with his own hands, all beruffled as they were, he used to give change for a shilling, and would turn a half-penny twice over, to make sure that it was a good one" (29). Miserliness, the preoccupation with hoarding and holding money, highlights the role of the hands in trade, the fact of brute physicality in the touch and love of money, and this is also emphasized in Hawthorne's depiction of the grasping hand of the organ-grinder's monkey, noted as well for its "too enormous tail" and "excessive desire."

Though Hawthorne seems to register a revulsion from the corporeal and and the commercial in these examples, the real horror lies in the vision of corporeality as subjugation: like Hepzibah's scowl, the body parts appear to move without volition. The scandalous character of hands in commercial operations derives from their automation, their mechanical and repetitive performances. The monkey, "holding out his small black palm" for money, takes it "with joyless eagerness" and "immediately re-commence[s] a series of pantomimic petitions for more" (164). Similarly, the "petty huckster" Pyncheon is imaged as continually calculating:

> It used to be affirmed, that the dead shopkeeper, in a white wig, a faded velvet coat, an apron at his waist, and his ruffles carefully turned back from his wrists, might be seen through the chinks of the shutters, any night of the year, ransacking his till, or poring over the dingy pages of his day-book. From the look of unutterable woe upon his face, it appeared to be his doom to spend eternity in a vain effort to make his accounts balance. (29)

This story of the shopkeeper's ghost recapitulates another scenario of automatism, the story about a looking glass in the House of the Seven Gables which "was fabled to contain within its depths all the shapes that had ever been reflected there." The story runs "that the posterity of Matthew Maule had some connection with the mystery of the looking-glass, and that—by what appears to have been a sort of mesmeric process—they could make its inner region all alive with the departed Pyncheons; not as they had shown themselves to the world, nor in their better and happier hours, but as doing over and over again some deed of sin, or in the crisis of life's bitterest sorrow" (20–21). The woeful shopkeeper seen at his Sisyphean accounts appears to be under the mesmeric power of the Maules. This power over the Pyncheons seems to operate as a punitive exposure and repetition compulsion; more than an allegory of the psychology of guilt, these stories work to manifest the operations of commerce. What seems crucial in the scenes of repetition the Maules conjure up is not only Hawthorne's moral "that the wrong-doing of one generation lives into the successive ones, and divesting itself of every temporary advantage, becomes a pure and uncontrollable mischief" (2) but the fact that unlawful commerce subjects the Pyncheons to the loss of privacy and self-control all commerce entails. In *The House of the Seven Gables*, it is the poetic justice of commerce to reverse as well as restore fortunes, to undermine as well as underpin self-possession. Thus the shame of the Pyncheons is epitomized in the spectacle of the shopkeeper's subjection to commerce. The manifestation of the dead shopkeeper "ransacking his till" or "poring over" his accounts figures the commercial mechanics of disembodiment and automation, the same mesmerization to which Hepzibah is subjected.

The subjection of body to commerce is foregrounded in still another example of automation, the organ-grinder's "company of little figures, whose sphere and habitation was in the mahogany case of his organ, and whose principle of life was the music, which the Italian made it his business to grind out":

> In all their variety of occupation—the cobbler, the blacksmith, the soldier, the lady with her fan, the toper with his bottle, the milk-maid sitting by her cow—this fortunate little society might truly be said to enjoy a harmonious existence, and to make life literally a dance. The Italian turned a crank; and, behold! every one of these small individuals started into the most curious vivacity. The cobbler wrought upon a shoe; the blacksmith hammered his iron; the soldier waved his glittering blade; the lady raised a tiny breeze with her fan; the jolly toper swigged lustily at his bottle; a scholar opened his book, with eager thirst for knowledge, and turned his head to-and-fro along the page; the milk-maid energetically drained her cow; and a miser counted gold into his strong-box;—all at the same

turning of the crank. Yes; and moved by the self-same impulse, a lover saluted his mistress on her lips! (163)

Yet "the most remarkable aspect" of all this activity "was, that, at the cessation of the music, everybody was petrified at once, from the most extravagant life into a dead torpor" (163). Commerce stills as well as animates process, subjecting human labor to the same conditions to which labor subjects the body. Its intensification of corporeality consists in its power to manipulate the activities through which persons appear more or less in control of their bodies, more or less in possession of their bodies. Like the mesmeric pass, the wave of the hand by which mesmerists directed their subjects, this manipulation displays persons as simultaneously most bodylike, that is, as doing what bodies can usually do—working, hammering, waving, drinking, reading, counting, kissing—and most bodiless, in the sense of being disconnected from the direction of the body. The automated working figures register the double experience of embodiment and disembodiment that commerce generates.

The Interior Exposed

The state of the mesmerized body has become more familiarly associated with hysteria, where the bodily exhibitionism of mesmeric performances becomes more explicit. The spectrum of mesmeric effects Hawthorne describes, running from animation to petrification, reappears in later nineteenth-century classifications of hysterical symptomology. Charcot's famous taxonomy of hysteria detailed the range of hysteric presentations from the seizure—in all its forms, including epileptic fits, acrobatic movements, passionate attitudes, and deliria—to paralysis. Within the seizure itself the static pole of hysteric behavior also recurs in the tableaux of hysteric postures that were photographed and in the momentarily held "grand movements" such as the "arc-en-cercle," a back-bend into which hysterics spontaneously propelled themselves.[5] In the well-known André Pierre Brouillet painting "A Clinical Lesson of Dr. Charcot at the Salpêtrière" (1887), a sketch or engraving of a hysteric in this arched pose occupies the left background. Diagonally opposite from this figure of arrested commotion, the female hysteric supported by Charcot in the right foreground of the painting appears limp and enervated, passively arched backward. This figure was drawn from a fifteen-year-old working-class girl named Blanche

---

5. Jean-Martin Charcot, *Oeuvres Complètes* (Paris: Progrès Médical, 1866), vol. 1, 320–33, 427–34, 436–39; Paul Richer, *Etudes Cliniques sur la Grand Hystérie* (Paris: Delahaye & Lecrosnier, 1885). These works are discussed in George Frederick Drinka's excellent history of *The Birth of Neurosis: Myth, Malady, and the Victorians* (New York: Simon & Schuster, 1984), esp. 74–107.

Wittman who came to the Salpêtrière in 1877 as a nurse and patient. There she became known as the Queen of Hysterics because of "her facility as a hypnotic subject." Noting Wittman's hypnotic state in the painting, Catherine Clément and other feminists have emphasized the theatricality of this clinical exploration, its exhibition of female acrobatics and trances.[6] The resemblance between mesmeric and hysteric performances had led physicians to look for the roots of hysteria in auto-suggestion and to hypnotize hysterics in order to discover and change the influence under which they were acting.[7] Hypnosis, once having illuminated the hysteric's subjection (to her unconscious) by reproducing and objectifying it, became not only a treatment for hysteria but a means of staging it in the clinic or classroom. It is the same ethos of showmanship and publicity that Hawthorne finds unseemly in mesmeric practices.

For Hawthorne, the horror of mesmerism consists in its power to intrude into the "holy of holies," as he wrote to Sophia Peabody before their marriage. Alarmed that Sophia was seeking relief from headaches through mesmeric treatment, Hawthorne urgently protested "that the sacredness of the individual is violated by it." In addition to his fear of this violation by an "intruder" who "would not be thy husband," Hawthorne confides his "repugnance" at the idea of Sophia's "holy name being bruited abroad in connection with these magnetic phenomena."[8] It is the fact that Matthew

6. André Pierre Brouillet, *A Clinical Lesson of Dr. Charcot at the Salpêtrière* (Rare Book Room, Countaway Library of Medicine, Harvard University). A copy of this picture hung in Freud's office and it appropriately reappears as the cover illustration to Charles Bernheimer and Claire Kahane, eds., *In Dora's Case: Freud-Hysteria-Feminism* (New York: Columbia University Press, 1985), and in Elaine Showalter's feminist history of hysteria, *The Female Malady* (New York: Pantheon, 1985), 149. On Blanche Wittman, see Drinka, *The Birth of Neurosis*, 123–51; Catherine Clément, *The Weary Sons of Freud*, trans. Nicole Bell (London: Verso, 1987), 51–55. There is now a vast feminist literature, especially in film studies, treating hysteria as a spectacle. I mention only a few of the most powerful and provocative treatments: Joan Copjec, "Flavit et Dissipati Sunt," *October* 18 (Fall 1981): 21–40; Mary Ann Doane, "Clinical Eyes: The Medical Discourse," in her *The Desire to Desire*, 38–69; Jacqueline Rose, *Sexuality in the Field of Vision* (London: Verso, 1986).

7. Charcot's work on hypnotism and hysteria was available in America beginning in 1879. See, for example, the article he co-authored with Georges Gilles de la Tourette, "Hypnotism in the Hysterical," *Dictionary of Psychological Medicine*, 2 vols., ed. Daniel Hack Tuke (Philadelphia: Blakiston, 1892), 1: 606–10. Hypnotism was also central to other studies of hysteria such as Hippolyte Bernheim, *Hypnotisme, Suggestion; Psychothérapie: Nouvelles Études* (Paris: Doin, 1891), and his *Suggestive Therapeutics*, trans. Christian A. Herter (New York: Putnam, 1889). By the end of the century, Freud and William James, among others, explained mesmeric states as hysterical ones: Sigmund Freud and Joseph Breuer, *Studies in Hysteria 1893–1895*, trans. James Strachey (New York: Basic Books 1957), 215–22; Eugene Taylor, *William James on Exceptional Mental States: The 1896 Lowell Lectures* (Amherst: University of Massachusetts Press, 1984), 35–72. I am suggesting that the association between hysteria and mesmerism was already in place in the 1850s: that the structural similarities of mesmeric and hysteric performances had already long been manifest, and that Hawthorne in *The House of the Seven Gables* represents commerce as homologous with these structures of behavior.

8. Nathaniel Hawthorne, *Love Letters of Nathaniel Hawthorne* (Chicago: Defobs Society, 1997), reprinted in his *The Blithedale Romance*, ed. Seymour Gross and Rosalie Murphy (New York: Norton, 1978), 242–44.

Maule's rapelike possession of Alice Pyncheon must display itself—
the reenactment of the initial violation which publicity entails—
that constitutes the horror of mesmerism in *The House of the Seven
Gables*. Such crimes against Pyncheon women rehearse the exposure of Pyncheon criminality, dramatizing that crime will out because of the penetrability of secrecy, the availability of human
interiority and motivations. Hawthorne's feminization of the Pyncheon subjection to public sight, showing the individual as a body
without a will of her own, underscores this vulnerability of the interior; putting Pyncheon women on exhibition makes clear that no
privacy is inviolate. In *The House of the Seven Gables*, hysterics suffer mainly from public exposure.

Revealed in this exposure is not only "the sacredness of an individual" but the fact of the accessibility of individual interiority. For,
as Hawthorne warned Sophia, it is more than her "own moral and
spiritual being" that she surrenders to "the magnetic lady" (her
mesmerist, Cornelia Park). He objects to "being brought, through
[Sophia's] medium, into such an intimate relation" with the mesmerist. Because Sophia is "part of" Hawthorne, access to her is access to himself.[9] Like the scientific inquiry and experimentation
imaged so threateningly in stories such as "The Birthmark" (1843),
"Rappaccini's Daughter" (1844), and "Ethan Brand" (1851), mesmerism magnifies individual penetrability. Individuality, of course,
is always showing itself; interior states register themselves in objec-
tive correlatives. This is another great theme in Hawthorne's writing: the external manifestations of interior conditions shaping such
tales as "The Minister's Black Veil" (1836), "The Prophetic Pictures" (1837), "The Great Stone Face" (1850), and, obviously, *The
Scarlet Letter*. Not content with allegorical and representational
practices whereby individuality is expressed, Hawthorne's mad scientists and doctors seek to take apart or alter the machinery of
mental or physical processes; they would intervene in the body's ar-
tifactual processes. Mesmerism similarly images the revelation of
how the interior of an individual body works. Even more than
erotic entries and intimacies can be laid bare: the very physiology of
interiority becomes manifest in mesmerism.

Mesmerism, in fact, contributed to the nineteenth-century understanding of mental physiology. Clinical exploration of the mind often
engaged with the claims and methods of mesmerism, called variously mental alchemy, electrical psychology, animal or vital magnetism, supernal theology, somnolism, somnambulism, psycheism,
the science of the soul, spiritual physiology, or simply psychology.[1]

9. Ibid.
1. I draw this list (a partial one) from the 1850s title listings of the publishers Fowler and
   Wells, who had offices in New York, Boston, and Philadelphia.

For the mid-nineteenth century, psychology meant mental processes, which were understood or hypothesized as fundamentally physiological. Thus while on the one hand mesmerism inspired interest in spiritualism, on the other hand it helped illuminate the physiology of the brain and function of the nervous system. Though some medical examinations sought to debunk the metaphysical claims of enthusiasts of mesmerism, the impetus to explain mesmerism was guided more by a spirit of scientific inquiry than one of materialist skepticism. Rationalizing mesmerism illuminated physiological knowledge. Mesmeric phenomena, Dr. Joseph Haddock wrote in 1849, "afford us the means of acquiring a knowledge of the laws and nature of the psychical, or mental, part of our being" and "the means of becoming better acquainted with the more abstruse points in our bodily organization." The knowledge mesmerism makes available is "that every individual has two distinct brains," the cerebrum and the cerebellum. Voluntary nerves and actions arise in the former; involuntary nerves and actions arise in the latter. This standard nineteenth-century account of the nervous system, according to Haddock, explains mesmerism as a variation on the fact "that the brain has an automatic movement of its own." Under a mesmerically induced somnolent state, the cerebral actions of the operator and the subject or subjects are one: "In each person the cerebellum and its system of nerves is in the normal [that is, involuntary] condition, but there is only *one* normal and active cerebrum, namely, that of the mesmeriser or operator." The subjects of the operator "are so intimately, interiorly blended with him, that the absence of their own external cerebral consciousness causes them to feel his cerebral consciousness as their own." Thus, "the idea existing externally in the cerebrum of the mesmeriser, is, when willed by him, perceived by the subject as if existing in his or her own cerebrum."[2] The subject does not even experience his or her own subjection. By this account, the state of normalcy which mesmerism exacerbates is a fluctuation between the voluntary and the involuntary. Mesmerism makes us see the inner workings of the

2. Joseph Haddock, M.D., *Psychology, or the Science of the Soul* (New York: Fowler and Wells, 1850), 8, 18, 56, 41–42, 57–58. The nervous system is now understood to be composed of a four-part brain: the cerebrum, middle brain, cerebellum, and medulla. Voluntary and involuntary nerves are contained in the spinal cord, which is continuous with the lower brain. Some nerves enter and traverse the spinal cord without ever passing into or from the brain: Randolph Lee Clark and Russell W. Cumley, eds., *The Book of Health* (New York: Van Nostrand Reinhold, 1973), 377–83.

On the popularity and influence of mesmerism, see Drinka, *The Birth of Neurosis*, 127–30; R. Laurence Moore, *In Search of White Crows: Spiritualism, Parapsychology, and American Culture* (New York: Oxford University Press, 1977). On the intellectual and political history of mesmerism, see Robert Darnton, *Mesmerism and the End of the Enlightenment in France* (Cambridge: Harvard University Press, 1968). Logie Barrow traces this history through nineteenth-century British society and its importance for labor movements: *Independent Spirits: Spiritualism and English Plebeians, 1850–1910* (London: Routledge & Kegan Paul, 1986).

mind—and the vulnerability these internal processes, like other labors, entail.

The interiority Hawthorne, Downing, and Stowe imagine as transcendent to economic processes appears in the physiology of mesmerism as both similar and sensitive to external events, as a site of engagement with the world. Though Haddock insisted on "the internal operations of the body" as unique, he also characterized them as, "in fact, the anti-types of which the types are found in outward nature."[3] This correspondence between the interior and the exterior predominates in the formulations about mesmerism and the nervous system that emerged in the wake of the invention of the telegraph in 1837. The founder of "the science of magnetism," Franz Mesmer, had in the late eighteenth century postulated the presence of a fluid he called animal magnetism running through the body. In the mid-nineteenth century medical theorists often explained mesmerism by appealing to a more sophisticated paradigm of the nerves as an electrical system. Dr. John Bovee Dods, in the series of lectures he was invited to deliver at the United States Capitol in 1850, declared electricity to be "the connecting link between mind and inert matter." In Dods's view, mesmerism is only a special case of mental functions that work by "electricity, which passes from the brain through the nerves, as so many telegraphic wires, to give motion to the extremities." Disease occurs when "the electricity of the system [is] thrown out of balance," either by "mental impressions" or "physical impression from external nature."[4] It is the force of such impressions, Dods argues, that explains why persons confessed to witchcraft at the Salem trials. On the basis of this model of sympathy between interior and exterior life, physicians introduced electrotherapy as a cure for nervous diseases, including hysteria. It is this link, the potentially oppressive intimacy between the mind and the world, that Hawthorne emphasizes in the Maules' mesmeric manipulation of the Pyncheons and excoriates in Clifford's denunciation of the telegraph as an infringement of "natural rights" to "refuge" (265). Like the other mesmeric powers of commerce, the telegraph threatens an "infinite wrong": no privacy, no relief from whatever we have "fled so far to avoid the sight and thought of" (265).

---

3. Haddock, *Psychology*, 55.
4. Mesmer's theories are published in F. A. Mesmer, *Mesmerism*, trans. George J. Bloch (Los Altos, Calif.: William Kauffmann, 1980); John Bovee Dods, M.D., *The Philosophy of Electrical Psychology, in a Course of Twelve Lectures* (New York: Fowler and Wells, 1850), 54, 58, 72. In the late nineteenth century George M. Beard developed ideas about electricity and the nervous system into a theory of neurasthenia and electrotherapeutics: "The Elements of Electrotherapeutics," *Archives of Electrology and Neurology* 1 (1874): 17–23, 184–94. Beard's best-known work, *American Nervousness: Its Causes and Consequences* (New York: Putnam, 1881), emphasizes the strain socioeconomic conditions imposed on the nerves.

The Domestic Revival: Phoebe's Magic

In *The House of the Seven Gables*, commerce may hold the mesmeric dangers the Pyncheons encounter, but it is also imaged as a revivifying and productive force.[5] Censuring the investigative instrumentality of the telegraph "as regards the detection of bank-robbers and murderers," Clifford alternatively envisions it as a beneficent agent of intimacy:

> An almost spiritual medium, like the electric telegraph, should be consecrated to high, deep, joyful, and holy missions. Lovers, day by day—hour by hour, if so often moved to do it—might send their heart-throbs from Maine to Florida, with some such words as these—"I love you forever!"—"My heart runs over with love!"—"I love you more than I can!"—and, again, at the next message—"I have lived an hour longer, and love you twice as much!" Or, when a good man has departed, his distant friend should be conscious of an electric thrill, as from the world of happy spirits, telling him—"Your dear friend is in bliss!" Or, to an absent husband, should come tidings thus—"An immortal being, of whom you are the father, has this moment come from God!"—and immediately its little voice would seem to have reached so far, and to be echoing his heart. (264–65)

Seen this way, telegraphic communications extend and amplify the body. It is thus the mesmeric force of commerce to reanimate as well as automate the body. The conspicuousness and contiguity to which trade exposes the individual can be gratifying as well as threatening, as Hepzibah discovers in her shopkeeping: she experiences "a thrill of almost youthful enjoyment" in having "put forward her hand to help herself." The coin she touched "had proved a talisman, fragrant with good, and deserving to be set in gold and be worn close to her heart." So much was she affected "both in body and spirit" by its "potent" "efficacy" that "she allowed herself an extra spoonful in her infusion of black tea" (51–52). The new "solidity" (51) Hepzibah experiences expresses a recovery of body effected by commerce.

This possibility of the restoration of body through the magical transformations of commerce is epitomized in the "nice little body" (79) of Phoebe, whose "homely witchcraft" brings out "the hidden capabilities of things" (71) and whose "facile adaptation was at once

---

5. Although the nostalgia promoted by domesticity implies that consumer relations are less familial and familiar than the relations associated with an economy of home production, commerce in *The House of the Seven Gables* is imagined as productive and personal. Recent work by Susan Strasser on personal networks and modes of distribution, redirecting assumptions about the culture of consumption, offers a historical verification of Hawthorne's characterization. See her *Satisfaction Guaranteed*, forthcoming from Vintage Books.

the symptom of perfect health, and its best preservative" (135). Her
true womanhood inheres in this adaptability that does not touch or
temper human essence; a perfect individuality is characterized by a
sound body in any circumstance. So sound is Phoebe's body that her
"homely duties seemed to bloom out of her character; so that labor,
while she dealt with it, had the easy and flexible charm of play" (82).
Her relation to labor reverses its mesmeric power so that she seems
to attract housework "to herself, by the magnetism of innate fitness"
(76). The "potency" of Phoebe's "purifying influence" not only exor-
cises the gloom and "grime and sordidness of the House of the
Seven Gables" (136–37) but also revives her elderly companions:
Clifford "grew youthful, while she sat beside him" (139). "They both
exist by you!" Holgrave tells her. "Whatever health, comfort, and
natural life, exists in the house, is embodied in your person" (216).

Phoebe's beneficent mesmerism images a safe model of labor
within a market economy: the conversionary capacity of commerce
to aid and amplify the individual. Women's work, disembodied, is
reembodied as a rescue mission, and it is in this mission that
Phoebe's housework (like Holgrave's photography, a method of letting the sunshine in) preserves the old order of Hepzibah by graft-
ing it onto the new. Rescue entails repairing imperfections in work,
enabling escapes or recuperations from the accidents of labor. The
reembodiment of women in rescue work explains how "Phoebe's
presence made a home about her" (141). Work itself is repaired in
Hawthorne's romance so that perfect homes can be made by true
women. In keeping with the logic of this reparative labor and re-
constructed life, Hawthorne attributes to Phoebe, the "little figure
of the cheeriest household life" (140), a palpability and physical
presence unique for both its integrity and its reassuring effect.
"Holding her hand, you felt something, a tender something; a substance, and a warm one; and so long as you should feel its grasp,
soft as it was, you might be certain that your place was good in the
whole sympathetic chain of human nature" (141). Whereas the
hands of Hepzibah and her shopkeeping ancestor manifest the operations of capitalist desire—that is, they are the medium through
which trade passes, the automated expressions of a market economy—Phoebe's hand imparts a "natural magic" (71) that animates
objects and revives humanity. "Look where she would, lay her hand
on what she might, the object responded to her consciousness, as if
a moist human heart were in it" (219).

As Phoebe revives the lady, she also reanimates the laborer. As
she restores Hepzibah and Clifford, her marriage restores the family estate to the dispossessed Maules. In Hawthorne's romance of
labor, domestic revivalism amends Ruskin's proposal that we honor
houses as monuments to their founders to suggest that houses me-

morialize the original housebuilder as well—the carpenter. So it is especially fitting that the Pyncheon estate passes to a Maule when Phoebe marries the last Maule, Holgrave, who, like herself, "gave a warmth to everything he laid his hand on" (181). In the ideal housekeeper, "admirably in keeping with herself" (80), Hawthorne figures a labor so perfect it *can* be embodied, because it is perfectly consonant with and thus immune from contingency. Like Phoebe's display of dual talents in house and shop, her marriage highlights the identity of housekeeping with commerce; for in the ability "to bring out the hidden capabilities of things around them" (71), women like Phoebe and artists like Holgrave (he is a photographer, a writer, and a mesmerist) perform transformations and illusions akin to the seemingly magical ways of commerce. It is therefore finally commerce that makes possible a restoration or reconstruction of the body. And it is the commercial production of domestic romance that generates such new forms of individuality as the integrity and interiority of private life exemplified in Downing's homes and Hawthorne's housekeepers. That Hepzibah's "return" to a fantasized prior order is itself a feat of capitalism is made clear in the composition of the country seat to which she removes: it is, as Holgrave somewhat disappointedly notes, a house built of wood, the favored material and construction innovation of Downing in his Americanization of the Gothic Revival. While the ancestral home "belongs to the past, . . . no more to be reanimated in the republic of the new world than the simple faith in the Virgin, which built the mighty cathedrals of the middle ages," Downing maintains that "the true home still remains to us."[6] It remains to us as a result of what Hawthorne calls "pretty good business" (319).

This is not to say that *The House of the Seven Gables* is a manifesto for capitalism and its ethos of changeability, but that it is an imaginative exposition of the beneficent mesmeric potential this transformative economy offers. The romantic architectures of interiority Hawthorne and Downing designed serve to shelter the self from the less attractive effects of this same economy. For Hawthorne, Walter Michaels has recently written, the point of romance, and specifically the point of this novel, is "to domesticate the social dislocation of the 1840s and 1850s in a literary form that imagines the past and present as utterly continuous, even identical, and in doing so, attempts to repress the possibility of any change at all."[7] Yet what gets "repressed" or, more precisely, elided in the institution of continuity depicted in Hawthorne's narrative is not change—indeed, change facilitates the restoration of Hepzibah's

---

6. Downing, *The Architecture of Country Houses*, 269.
7. See Michaels, *The Gold Standard and the Logic of Naturalism*, 88. The political agenda of romance, that is, the question of whether Hawthorne's romance forecloses on demo-

aristocratic lifestyle—but the labor of accommodating and incorporating change, the process of domestication.

The modernization of the Pyncheons and the Maules into a nineteenth-century middle-class family living in a wooden country home depends on and reflects the rise of American bourgeois domesticity. It is the invisible operations of homemaking, what might be called the interior dynamics of romance, that this discussion of *The House of the Seven Gables* has attempted to substantiate. If housekeeping is Hawthorne's analogue for romance, this homely magic thematizes and exemplifies the ethos of changeability which I am arguing that romance reproduces. As we have seen, the appearance of magical housework in *The House of the Seven Gables* replaces and transforms another type of women's work: the mesmerized labors of the Pyncheon ladies. Labor induced by mesmeric fiat, like the labors compelled by economic reverses and social dislocations, takes the form of hysteria in Hawthorne's romance. This all too visible subjection of women is superseded by the elevation of the healthy and healthful housekeeper, whose work is imagined as unseen and incorporeal, and hence immune from any somatic impressions of social disorders. The replacement of the hysterical lady by the true woman represents domesticity as a welcome change that relieves the effects of other changes.

Prior to this replacement, Alice Pyncheon's hysteria reflected the malevolent manipulations through which "the old Pyncheon-house" was attained and maintained (5). In accordance with the mutability of ownership and control that the house epitomizes, hysterical movements and gestures signify a continual subjection to change. The house itself bears the marks of change: the House of the Seven Gables has become in the nineteenth century "a rusty wooden house," the aged and "weather-beaten edifice" from which the Pyncheons finally remove themselves (5). If this image projects the temporality of the newly inherited estate to which the Pyncheons and Holgrave retire, it also implies that the wooden house in which the healthy housekeeper resides may persist as another, more legitimate, long-standing family landmark—stable and solid like "the great elm-tree" known as "the Pyncheon-elm" (5). Indeed,

---

cratic innovation or embraces it, preoccupies recent criticism of *The House of the Seven Gables.* My reading of the inner workings of the romance's transformative operations, foregrounding the women's work which enables Hawthorne's romance of commerce, investigates how this novel encompasses change so as to make it seem tradition. The very configuration of progressivism versus conservatism is thus abrogated here, as Michaels also has argued. The actual operations of change in this romance suggest that the central issue here is the role of women in nineteenth-century social and political transformations: the aesthetics through which a certain profile of political economy emerges. For different views, see Brook Thomas, "*The House of the Seven Gables:* Reading the Romance of America," *PMLA* 97 (March 1982): 195–211; Michael T. Gilmore, *American Literature and the Marketplace* (Chicago: University of Chicago Press, 1985), 96–112.

the seven-gabled wooden house upon which Hawthorne based his romance still stands. Tradition thus endures through transmutation, through the innovations that rehabilitate it.

To further refine Michaels's account: romance, as Hawthorne expounds it, consists in convertibility—the capacity to convert change itself into tradition. That Hawthorne recognized the perfect romance in the rise of the middle-class domestic woman and the individual home she tended is underscored in the novel's final image of Alice Pyncheon "as she floated heavenward from the HOUSE OF THE SEVEN GABLES!" (319). Just as Catharine Beecher envisioned housework as the cure for hysteria, so Hawthorne's romance of Phoebe's magical restoration of Hepzibah restores "joy" (319) to the "mournful" mesmerized lady who "was supposed to haunt the House of the Seven Gables" (83). Under the presiding spirit of domesticity even the ills of the past can be transformed.

RICHARD H. MILLINGTON

[The Triple Beginning of *The House of the Seven Gables*]†

As *The Scarlet Letter* ends, Hawthorne offers us a glimpse of Hester's future. We are to imagine her as a figure of wisdom, offering counsel to a community of perplexed and sorrowful women, the casualties of love. Her bitter experience has at last become a source of authority; the marginal has become central. This vision of Hester anticipates Hawthorne's transformation of his fiction as he moved from *The Scarlet Letter* to *The House of the Seven Gables*. The "hell-fired" intensity of the former book generated in Hawthorne the wish to write something more genial, less gloomy, "a more natural and healthy product of my mind," a work he could feel less "reluctance" about publishing.[1] The lure of the central hinted at in Hester's reward and Hawthorne's remarks is at the heart of *The House of the Seven Gables*'s way of claiming authority, its attempt to reinvent and perform the work of the novelist.

† From *Narrative Form and Cultural Engagement in Hawthorne's Fiction*, pp. 105–114. Copyright © 1992 Princeton University Press. Reprinted by permission of Princeton University Press. All notes are Millington's.

1. This notion of reparation is characteristic of Hawthorne's response to his own novels and—also characteristically—cuts in two directions: the friendliness of *The House* produces the desire to write something with "an extra touch of the devil" in it, and the bitterness of *The Blithedale Romance* in turn produces the intention to be more "genial" the next time out. See *Letters* 2, 312, 421–22, 462, 604. [All page references to Hawthorne's writings in this essay are to the Centenary Edition of the *Works of Nathaniel Hawthorne*, ed. William Charvat et al., 23 vols. (Columbus: Ohio State University Press, 1962–1996)—editor's note.]

The book's ambition to speak from the center of the middle-class culture it addresses has recently attracted readers interested in placing Hawthorne and his work within his historical moment and in defining the ideological force of his fiction. This seems to me precisely the kind of questioning that *The House of the Seven Gables* invites, but most of the readings I have in mind underestimate the extent to which Hawthorne has already performed their task for them. Let me take two influential examples. In *American Romanticism and the Marketplace*, Michael Gilmore reads the book as an allegory of Hawthorne's ambivalence about participating in the literary marketplace. Gilmore's analysis leads finally to an accusation: by giving in to his audience's demand for a happy ending, Hawthorne betrays the dark truths of his art, replicating the hypocrisy that he condemns in Jaffrey Pyncheon. Gilmore gives us a Hawthorne trapped in a simple dichotomy between his real beliefs and his desire for commercial success. Walter Benn Michael's much subtler reading uncovers in Hawthorne's conception of romance a longing for an inalienable right of property, an attempt to escape the knowledge that the self, like any piece of property within capitalism, is subject to appropriation. Both these interpretations derive their éclat from an implicit claim about the limits of Hawthorne's range of vision—as in Gilmore's assumption that Hawthorne's understanding of artistic integrity could not include a complicated engagement in the values of his audience rather than a repudiation of them, and in Michaels's argument that the relation between selfhood and economic relations is being suppressed rather than interrogated.[2] My contention is that such readings miss

2. Michael T. Gilmore, *American Romanticism and the Marketplace* (Chicago: University of Chicago Press, 1986), chap. 5; Walter Benn Michaels, "Romance and Real Estate," in Michaels and Donald E. Pease, eds., *The American Renaissance Reconsidered* (Baltimore: Johns Hopkins University Press, 1985). Other important attempts to place the book ideologically include Kenneth Dauber, *Rediscovering Hawthorne* (Princeton: Princeton University Press, 1977), and Michael Davitt Bell, *The Development of American Romance: The Sacrifice of Relation* (Chicago: University of Chicago Press, 1980). Two writers on Hawthorne who seem to me to see the scope of his designs upon American culture are Brook Thomas and Donald Pease. See Thomas's argument that Hawthorne's romance demystifies cultural authority, revealing it to be a product of historical—and thus revisable—choices rather than "natural" ("*The House of the Seven Gables*: Reading the Romance of America," in *PMLA* 97 [1982]: 195–211). See also his reworking of that essay, which connects the book to the history of property law, chaps. 2 and 3 of *Cross-Examinations of Law and Literature: Cooper, Hawthorne, Stowe, and Melville* (New York: Cambridge University Press, 1987). Though Pease's chapters on Hawthorne in *Visionary Compacts* (Madison: University of Wisconsin Press, 1987) do not include a reading of *The House*, his sense of Hawthorne as engaged in the rescue and reconstruction of communal connection is congenial to the detailed account of the book that I will be offering. Kenneth Dauber's original and important insight about the book—that it is above all an attempt to achieve intimate connection to a community of readers—has been valuable to me, though he pays the odd and unacceptable price of denying Hawthorne any specific ideas about the culture he is connecting to or any investment in the content of his work. My sense of the specificity and force of Hawthorne's engagement with his readers depends to a great extent upon the description of middle-class culture that has emerged from the work of historians of "woman's sphere," and on the account of writing by

the extraordinary way in which an interest in interpreting American culture informs the narrative logic of *The House of the Seven Gables*. * * * One need not naively envision the artist as heroically above or outside ideology to grant Hawthorne something like the intellectual maneuverability—the range of perspective and capacity for analysis—that we think ourselves to possess. I will be arguing that Hawthorne's wish to establish his position at the center of his culture produced neither a straightforward celebration of shared communal values nor even such a celebration betrayed by "deeper" ambivalence, but an investigation of what it means to speak from the center of a community and an attempt to transform that center in the very act of occupying it.

The Play of Voices

The House of the Seven Gables in effect begins three times, assuming each time a new authorial voice and a correspondingly different kind of relation to the reader. In the relation between these beginnings, in the drama of voice enacted in that relation, what will become the work of the novel is at once defined and set in motion. The first of these authorial incarnations speaks the preface. The figure that emerges here—"the Author"—is the writer as public man, and the relation established with the reader is correspondingly circumscribed and correct. We figure corporately, as "the Public" and "the Reader," and the model for our engagement with the book is at once economic and legalistic.[3] With his first sentence the Author encases his relation to the Reader in the formality of a contract—"When a writer calls his work a Romance, it need hardly be observed that he wishes to claim a certain latitude, both as to its fashion and material, which he would not have felt himself entitled to assume, had he professed to be writing a Novel"—and spends the rest of the opening paragraph specifying his rights as a Romancer: this literary form implies, he avers, "a right to present that truth under circumstances, to a great extent, of the writer's own choosing or creation." He goes so far as to fend off an anticipated prosecution for excessive use of the marvelous: "He can hardly be said, however, to commit a literary crime, even if he disregard this caution" (1). The preface, then, conceives of authorship as above all the act of entering a contentious marketplace and suggests that

women offered by literary scholars like Nina Baym and Jane P. Tompkins, whose notion of "cultural work" illuminates Hawthorne's work as well as that of the writers whom the traditional canon of American literature has displaced.

3. The legalism of the narrator's language is noticed by Susan L. Mizruchi in *The Power of Historical Knowledge: Narrating the Past in Hawthorne, James, and Dreiser* (Princeton: Princeton University Press, 1988). Mizruchi's chapter on *The House* offers a valuable account, quite different from my own, of the specific way that Hawthorne's drama of the narrative voice engages antebellum culture. See chap. 3, esp. 103–34.

one had better operate in the literary market as in any other, warily, with full awareness of one's rights and liabilities.

Having established his "immunities" (2), our Author begins to speak less guardedly, specifying—as a trustworthy kind of person to do business with—the particular way he intends to fulfill his end of our literary transaction. As Nina Baym's crucial work on nineteenth-century book reviewing lets us see, the Author follows an itinerary, established in reviews, of public expectations about how novels ought to behave.[4] He will operate within an established range of genres ("Novel," "Romance," "Tale," "Legend") and effects (the "picturesque"). He will, however, offer only a carefully modified assent to other expectations. "Many writers," he notes, "lay very great stress upon some definite moral purpose, at which they profess to aim their works." Though quite able to provide such a moral, he candidly admits his doubt that fiction can claim, "in good faith," to deliver this particular product in the expected way: "A high truth, indeed, fairly, finely, and skillfully wrought out, brightening at every step, and crowning the final development of a work of fiction, may add an artistic glory, but is never any truer, and seldom any more evident, at the last page than at the first" (2–3). In place of such overt moralizing, he offers something more elusive, perhaps riskier: "When romances do really teach anything, or produce any effective operation, it is usually through a far more subtle process than the ostensible one." There is more at stake here than sophistication. Hawthorne-as-public-man is not only giving the literary equivalent of good weight; he is accepting, though on carefully specified, idiosyncratic terms, the ethical role—as a purveyor of moral influence—that his audience demands. Book writing is dramatized as a bargain, in which both author and reader adjust to the desires and expectations of the other.

We thus begin *The House of the Seven Gables* with the drama of the book's own entry into the cultural marketplace that will determine, both ethically and economically, its success. Books, like other products, are subject to the risks of exchange, their claims to "title" and worth valid only if ratified by the public: "He trusts not to be considered as unpardonably offending, by laying out a street that infringes upon nobody's private rights, and appropriating a lot of land which had no visible owner, and building a house, of materials long in use for constructing castles in the air" (3). The scrupulous public voice that advances these claims hints, in the very care with which it conducts this transaction, that it conceives of the world of public interchange as a dangerous place. And in the distance that bolsters its authority, in the exclusion of the private voice, we feel a

---

4. *Novels, Readers, and Reviewers: Responses to Fiction in Antebellum America* (Ithaca: Cornell University Press, 1984), esp. chaps. 8–11.

corresponding constraint as readers, for this preface locks us within a marketplace relation to what we are about to read and to the person that produced it. Hawthorne begins the book, then, by reminding us of the atmosphere of inhibition that the modern marketplace imposes on human connection—the very constriction that we turn to novels to escape.

This lack of intimacy is repaired in the first chapter proper of the book, when we encounter a second authorial voice, an alternative way of conducting the transaction between writer and reader.[5] A much more genial voice welcomes us into the narrative of chapter 1. This version of the writer—let us call him the Historian so as to mark his relation to his materials and his full possession of the story he tells—begins life as an "I," locating the genesis of the book in his private experience—his walks through Salem—and his capacity to respond to the experience of others: "The aspect of the venerable mansion has always affected me like a human countenance, bearing the traces not merely of outward storm and sunshine, but expressive also of the long lapse of mortal life, and the accompanying vicissitudes, that have passed within" (5). His image of the legible countenance establishes a claim to his story quite different from that defended by the preface's Author; his authority is based not on contractual rights but on what he can see and understand. This "I" changes quickly into a "we," invoking the reader not as purchaser but as a member of a community of the thoughtful, the adequately responsive.

Confident of his sympathetic possession of the plenitude of meaning enfolded in the house itself, the Historian openly establishes the authority of his telling by letting us see his version being constructed, by defining his relation to the various versions of the Pyncheon story available to him. He begins his narrative with an act of scrupulous reconstruction, working from two often contradictory sources, an official history associated with a written record and a "tradition" preserved and transmitted by the human voice. This distinction between the authority of the document and the authority of the voice, which will be crucial throughout the book, replays the property dispute between Colonel Pyncheon and Matthew Maule. Maule's claim, based on original occupation and his own labor ("an acre or two of earth, which, with his own toil, he had hewn out of the primeval forest, to be his garden-ground and homestead") is endangered by Colonel Pyncheon's claim, which depends "on the strength of a grant from the legislature" (7). The dispute ends in the triumph of the written; Maule's claim is made

---

5. Kenneth Dauber interestingly suggests that the preface fixes and contains any hostility Hawthorne feels toward the community, thus preserving the novel proper for the establishment of intimacy between him and his readers. *Rediscovering Hawthorne*, 122–24.

moot when he is convicted of witchcraft, and, in an image that suggests being crossed off the human ledger, the authorities "drive the
plough over the little area of his habitation, and obliterate his place
and memory from among men" (7).

The way the narrator makes his way through this dispute is a
guide to the dismantling of illegitimate authority. He is led to distrust the Pyncheon claim because Maule so successfully resisted it
"at a period . . . when personal influence had far more weight than
now" (7), which in turn argues on behalf of the "whispers" that saw
self-interest in the zeal that made Pyncheon so prominent in
Maule's prosecution. He enacts a critical relation to the official version of history, a sophisticated suspicion of the claims of the powerful. Yet these suspicions are tempered by a willingness to toss out
many of the claims of "tradition" as well, "which sometimes brings
down truth that history has let slip, but is oftener the wild babble of
the time, such as was formerly spoken at the fireside, and now congeals in newspapers" (17). This "lettered" narrator's analysis of this
title dispute forges an alliance with the claims of the "voiced"
against the publicly enforced authority of the Pyncheons. Thus we
find our Historian especially alert to the ways in which ideology
works on behalf of the powerful: "There is something so massive,
stable, and almost irresistibly imposing, in the exterior presentment
of established rank and great possessions, that their very existence
seems to give them a right to exist; at least, so excellent a counterfeit of right, that few poor and humble men have moral force
enough to question it, even in their own secret minds" (25). A kind
of counterauthority is achieved—resistant to the official and per-
meable to but open-eyed about the claims of gossip and legend—in
the Historian's exercise of his analytic gifts. It is as though fiction,
with its formal capacity to represent voices, might at last put the
written at the service of the dispossessed.

Yet this narrator does not proceed by analysis alone. When he
moves from the public history he has been reconstructing to the inner experience of its principal characters, he must invoke the constructive, generative powers of the imagination in order to tell his
story:

> For various reasons, however, and from impressions often too
> vaguely founded to be put on paper, the writer cherishes the
> belief that many, if not most, of the successive proprietors of
> this estate, were troubled with doubts as to their moral right to
> hold it. Of their legal tenure, there could be no question; but
> old Matthew Maule, it is to be feared, trode downward from
> his own age to a far later one, planting a heavy footstep, all the
> way, on the conscience of a Pyncheon. If so, we are left to dis-
> pose of the awful query, whether each inheritor of the prop-

erty—conscious of wrong, and failing to rectify it—did not commit anew the great guilt of his ancestor, and incur all its original responsibilities. And supposing such to be the case, would it not be a far truer mode of expression to say, of the Pyncheon family, that they inherited a great misfortune, than the reverse? (20)

Our Historian is engaged here in answering a question of cause that neither orthodox history nor the oral tradition, with its taste for determinism, can compass. Is Pyncheon history the consequence of a series of choices, of newly incurred guilt by appropriation, or an empty and inevitable pattern of repetition? The authority for his claim of ethical freedom is grounded solely in the narrator's capacity for reconstructing Pyncheon moral psychology, perhaps in his belief in moral responsibility itself. What the analytic and the legendary can only identify as pattern, the imaginative recovers as choice.

In this chapter's closing pages, the Historian returns to an image of the house as a plenitude of meaning: "But as for the old structure of our story, its white-oak frame, and its boards, shingles, and crumbling plaster, and even the huge clustered chimney in the midst, seemed to constitute only the least and meanest part of its reality. So much of mankind's varied experience had passed there— so much had been suffered, and something, too, enjoyed—that the very timbers were oozy, as with the moisture of a heart. It was itself like a great human heart, with a life of its own, and full of rich and sombre reminiscences" (27). There is comfort in the fullness of meaning that this image suggests and the promise of stability in our return to it. This narrator conjures up, in his adroit disposal of the authoritarian, in the sympathy through which he recovers the house of the seven gables as a place of connection as well as coercion, and in the openness with which he establishes his own right to tell this story, a world safe enough for the abandonment of the wariness dramatized in the preface. In the wisdom, urbanity, and measuredness of this voice we recognize a familiar figure, the narrator of classic Victorian fiction, in possession, as J. Hillis Miller suggests, of the sum of available communal wisdom.[6] Yet, as the Historian reminds us, his remarks are "preliminary" (26); the "real action of our tale" (6), the narrative proper, has not yet begun. As we shall see, the stability of this voice, its settled wisdom, cannot follow the narrative into the terrain of the "present day" (6). Its mastery belongs only to the historical, the finished; its uninhibitory authority and the sense of communal connection that it confers re-

6. "The Narrator as General Consciousness," in *The Form of Victorian Fiction* (Notre Dame: University of Notre Dame Press, 1968), esp. 62–88.

main only possibilities, hovering at the threshold of the story we are about to enter, a goal rather than a possession.

After the urbanity of the Historian of chapter 1, the voice that opens the present-day narrative seems nearly hysterical. Public without the propriety of the preface's Author, inanely aggressive, this "disembodied listener" introduces us to Hepzibah by ridiculing her, working the exclamation point like a huckster: "Truly! Well, indeed! Who would have thought it! Is all this precious time to be lavished on the matutinal repair and beautifying of an elderly person who never goes abroad—whom nobody ever visits—and from whom, when she shall have done her utmost, it were the best charity to turn one's eyes another way!" (31). When we measure this voice, as we must, against the speaker of the preceding chapter, it comes to seem less a voice than a cultural position, something that is spoken rather than speaks, the dramatization of an unpenetrating unresponsiveness that is one aspect of the public culture the book depicts.

As Richard Brodhead has noticed, this is not the only voice that speaks in this opening chapter: "The cruel humor of this jaunty listener is supplemented by another voice, that of a more omniscient narrator who is privileged to know the interior of Hepzibah's heart and who can thus see her as an object worthy of compassion."[7] Brodhead observes that the chapter moves toward this second perspective—a voice like that belonging to the previous chapter's Historian—arriving finally at an assertion of the significance of everyday life despite the triviality or grotesqueness of its surface. For Brodhead, this oscillation between two opposed voices and perspectives supports a belief in the value of the quotidian by guaranteeing that this claim has been subjected to some skeptical testing, and it moves the reader toward the sympathy that makes the significance of the day-to-day perceptible. I think this drama of voice works in other ways as well, helping us identify what this story is to be a story of, helping us grasp the "real action of our tale" (6). The narrative logic of this chapter and of the book as a whole becomes understandable through the connection between the action performed by the chapter's sole character and the treatment that action receives from the two voices that struggle over its representation.

As we are repeatedly reminded during the course of the chapter, the action it records is as prosaic as can be: down-at-heel aristocrat Hepzibah Pyncheon, forced by financial difficulties to open a cent shop in the family mansion, gets dressed, enters the shop, unbars the door and retreats to the parlor. By this act, she simultaneously

---

7. *Hawthorne, Melville, and the Novel* (Chicago: University of Chicago Press, 1976), 72.

enters the marketplace and the cultural mainstream, feeling this moment as a painful emergence into the public gaze: "She was well aware that she must ultimately come forward, and stand revealed in her proper individuality" (40). The bulk of this chapter is spent not in describing this minimal action but in deciding how it ought to be received. The "disembodied listener," whose voice we have heard ridiculing Hepzibah, focuses relentlessly on her physical appearance and can see only the ludicrous or grotesque aspects of her venture; it can only represent Hepzibah by misrepresenting her. This scoffing voice, in effect, gives expression within the chapter to what terrifies Hepzibah about entering the public gaze, the dangers inherent in being seen and judged—reminding us in the process of what the Author of the preface was defending himself against. It threatens to repel Hepzibah's move toward the center of her culture, to return her to the isolation of her aristocratic fantasies.

What unfolds during the course of the chapter is the dismissal of this voice, its replacement by a more capacious way of seeing and judging that can represent and respond to Hepzibah differently. Or, to put this another way, one might imagine a communal voice educating itself out of blunt-mindedness into perspicacity. This second voice begins by penetrating the off-putting misrepresentation that Hepzibah offers to the world and comes to believe in herself—her nearsighted scowl:

> We must linger, a moment, on this unfortunate expression of poor Hepzibah's brow. Her scowl—as the world, or such part of it as sometimes caught a transitory glimpse of her at the window wickedly persisted in calling it—her scowl had done Miss Hepzibah a very ill-office, in establishing her character as an ill-tempered old maid; nor does it appear improbable, that, by often gazing at herself in a dim looking-glass, and perpetually encountering her own frown within its ghostly sphere, she had been led to interpret the expression almost as unjustly as the world did. . . . But her heart never frowned. It was naturally tender, sensitive, and full of little tremors and palpitations; all of which weaknesses it retained, while her visage was growing so perversely stern, and even fierce. (34)

The narrative voice is reclaiming a true estimate of Hepzibah's character from the shallow but powerful misperception of the community. We should notice, too, that it is reclaiming her *for* the community by revealing what connects her to it despite her aristocratic pretensions: the tender and palpitating heart that links her to the sentimental consensus that holds the community together.

This reclamation of Hepzibah on behalf of the communal is conducted in other ways as well. Most crucially, we come to see her as representative, as culturally valuable despite or even because of her apparent marginality. Under the sympathetic scrutiny of the gentler narrative voice, Hepzibah's significance keeps expanding, and, as it does, the ridiculing voice that opened the chapter begins to apologize for its underestimation of her ("Heaven help our poor old Hepzibah, and forgive us for taking a ludicrous view of her position!"). This narrator begins by placing Hepzibah within the book's historical moment: "For here—and if we fail to impress it suitably upon the reader, it is our own fault, not that of the theme—here is one of the truest points of melancholy interest that occur in ordinary life. It was the final term of what called itself old gentility" (37). This invitation to sympathy yields a sense of her representativeness still more expansive: "In this republican country, amid the fluctuating waves of our social life, somebody is always at the drowning-point. The tragedy is enacted with as continual a repetition as that of a popular drama on a holiday, and, nevertheless, is felt as deeply, perhaps, as when an hereditary noble sinks below his order. More deeply; since, with us, rank is the grosser substance of wealth and a splendid establishment, and has no spiritual existence after the death of these, but dies hopelessly along with them" (38). Hepzibah, then, becomes the occasion for a meditation on the vicissitudes, economic and emotional, of American life. As we have seen, her reluctance to enter the public gaze captures the force of the anxiety that accompanies entering the cultural marketplace—an anxiety implicit in the preface as well and one of the identifying marks of middle-class sensibility—and her decision to open a cent shop is presented as an example of the narrow range of economic possibilities that this culture offers to women.[8] By the end of the chapter this claim of cultural significance has expanded into what might be called the democratization of the tragic, the narrator's claim that the problem of representing Hepzibah, of locating the significant within the trivial, has always attended the discovery of meaning in human experience.

> What tragic dignity, for example, can be wrought into a scene like this! How can we elevate our history of retribution for the sin of long ago, when, as one of our most prominent figures, we are compelled to introduce—not a young and lovely woman, nor even the stately remains of beauty, storm-shattered by affliction—but a gaunt, sallow, rusty-jointed maiden, in a long-waisted silk-gown, and with the strange horror of a turban upon her head! Her visage is not even ugly. It is redeemed from insignificance only by the contraction of her

8. For a valuable account of Hawthorne's insistence on Hepzibah's social representativeness, see Brodhead, *Hawthorne, Melville, and the Novel*, 74–75.

eyebrows into a near-sighted scowl. And, finally, her great life-trial seems to be, that, after sixty years of idleness, she finds it convenient to earn comfortable bread in setting up shop, in a small way. Nevertheless, if we look through all the heroic fortunes of mankind, we shall find this same entanglement of something mean and trivial with whatever is noblest in joy or sorrow. Life is made up of marble and mud. And, without all the deeper trust in a comprehensive sympathy above us, we might hence be led to suspect the insult of a sneer, as well as an immitigable frown, on the iron countenance of fate. What is called poetic insight is the gift of discerning, in this sphere of strangely mingled elements, the beauty and majesty which are compelled to assume a garb so sordid. (41)

The struggle over how to represent Hepzibah ends with her universalization. The act of reseeing Hepzibah that the chapter dramatizes through its vocal combat is, then, a crucial part of what Hawthorne is conceiving as the "action" of the chapter.

What I have described as the triple beginning of *The House of the Seven Gables* should have important consequences for us as interpreters of the book as a whole. To hear the different voices that introduce us to the book, to occupy or resist the various readerly roles—the buyer, the boor, the sympathizer—they assign us, is to become alert to narrative voice as a dramatization of a particular way of participating in a culture. A corollary of such an awareness is the realization that narrative voice within *The House* will be a deployed thing, likely not to represent, in any consistent way, "Hawthorne," or even a single narrative perspective, but a range of available cultural positions and responses and the discourses that articulate them.[9] * * * This understanding of voice solves some of the interpretive problems of *The House of the Seven Gables* by protecting us from condescending to the book by invoking a confused, hypocritical, or ambivalent Hawthorne instead of attending to the kind of cultural analysis his text is performing.

This play of voices helps us understand what is meant when "the real action of our tale" is said to begin in chapter 2, with its move from the historical to the present. This shift from voice to voices suggests that to enter the present is to enter a realm of ideological contest in which ideas of cultural value struggle with one another

9. The great theorist of this way of thinking about voice within novels is M. M. Bakhtin. In "Discourse in the Novel" he argues that the novel as a genre is defined by its permeability to a culture's different voices and by the competition or "dialogue" between them. The "prose artist" is thus to be regarded as a deployer of these voices. *The Dialogic Imagination*, ed. Michael Holquist (Austin: University of Texas Press, 1981), 259–422. One implication of my argument is that Hawthorne, in composing this version of romance, had to do precisely the kind of theorizing about the novel that Bakhtin has made available to us. Susan Mizruchi notes the "dialogic" quality of *The House*'s narrative in *Historical Knowledge*, 39 n. 49.

and no voice can possess authority with the certainty of the Narrator of chapter 1. Our understanding of the "action" of the book we are about to read, then, must expand to include this struggle over the meaning of the emotions, decisions, and movements of the book's characters as well as the events themselves. What this means * * * is that *The House of the Seven Gables* is about the way the culture it addresses works; Hawthorne has invented what might be called the narrative of the cultural system. Thus chapter 2 records as its sole event a change in Hepzibah's cultural position— her move from the margins into the marketplace—and dramatizes a contest over how to understand its meaning for the community she enters. * * * The work done by this invention in narrative form is at once descriptive and ethical, for it sets out not only to understand how this community works but to teach it what it ought to value, to reestablish its moral center.

*   *   *

ALAN TRACHTENBERG

Seeing and Believing: Hawthorne's Reflections on the Daguerreotype in *The House of the Seven Gables*†

1

"I don't much like pictures of that sort—they are so hard and stern; besides dodging away from the eye, and trying to escape altogether. They are conscious of looking very unamiable, I suppose, and therefore hate to be seen. . . . I don't wish to see it any more" (91–92). Phoebe's unease with image effects of the sort produced by daguerreotypes invokes an early moment in the career of photography in America, a moment of shudder, suspicion, and refusal (see also Trachtenberg, "Mirror" and "Photography"). This particular instance occurs in Nathaniel Hawthorne's *The House of the Seven Gables* (1851), a narrative in which daguerreotypes figure consequentially both in the plot and in the literary theory internalized as a major theme within the fiction. For if the narrative launches itself in the preface as an argument on behalf of "Romance" over "Novel," the figurative rhetoric by which Hawthorne embodies that distinction, so crucial to his undertaking, draws on the same daguerrean effects to which Phoebe reacts. Sharing fea-

† From *American Literary History* 9 (1997): 460–481. Reprinted by permission of Oxford University Press. All notes are Trachtenberg's.

tures of both "Novel" and "Romance," of science and magic, of modernity and tradition, the daguerreotype plays a strategic role in the narrative as an emblem of the ambiguity that the tale will affirm as the superior mark of "Romance"—if not exactly "Romance" itself, at least a major narrative resource for defining and apprehending what that term means.

A writer of novels, the "Author" explains in the preface, "is presumed to aim at a very minute fidelity, not merely to the possible, but to the probable and ordinary course of man's experience" (1). Too glaring to miss, the analogy of novel writing to photography seems confirmed by the mimetic intentions of both. But Hawthorne's description of the latitude of the romancer, the allowable deviations from a strictly faithful mimesis, also evoke photography, particularly daguerreotypy: the romancer "may so manage his atmospherical medium as to bring out or mellow the lights and deepen and enrich the shadows of the picture" (1).[1] The literary distinction between two kinds of mimesis—one strictly adherent to an imitation of the probable and the ordinary, the other less constrained and freer to deploy atmospheric effects—corresponds to a distinction already well formulated in theories of photography at the time, between merely mechanical and self-consciously artistic uses of the new medium.[2] While "minute fidelity" seems incontrovertably to associate photography with "Novel," with its recurring imagery of light and mist and shadow, the preface subtlely recruits the daguerreotype for a key role in the definition of "Romance" that the narrative will unfold.

Two sentences are especially important. "The point of view in which this Tale comes under the Romantic definition, lies in the attempt to connect a by-gone time with the very Present that is flitting away from us" (2). The present flits away just as does the picture on the mirrorlike surface of a daguerreotype. But how are we to take "connect," especially in light of the rejection of "very minute fidelity"? Further on the "Author" warns against reading the tale as a too literal picture of an actual place and says that such a

1. Cathy N. Davidson makes a similar observation about the rhetoric of "Romance" in the preface, but where I see Hawthorne as locating the daguerreotype in a suggestively ambiguous site between "Novel" and "Romance," she argues that "Hawthorne adopts a photographic metaphor not to support the realistic novel but to describe the romance" (686). This leads her to argue, without explaining the apparent inconsistency, that "Holgrave's claims for the ultimate truth of the daguerreotype" contrasts with Hawthorne's "enlisting" of the daguerreotype on the side of "Romance" (687). As I try to show, if we recognize the equivocal status of photography already present in the preface, we can avoid what I see as the mistake of taking Holgrave's claims at face value.
2. Richard Rudisill's *Mirror Image: The Influence of Daguerreotype on American Society* (1971) remains the most complete and historically coherent account of intellectual, literary, and popular conceptions of the daguerreotype in the US. Robert Taft's *Photography and the American Scene* provides an indispensable narrative of the appearance of the daguerreotype in America and its commercial development.

reading "exposes the Romance to an inflexible and exceedingly dangerous species of criticism, by bringing his [the author's] fancy-pictures almost into positive contact with the realities of the moment" (3). How are we to understand the difference between dangerous "positive contact" and presumably benign "connect"? We are teased into imagining another mode of fidelity to "Present," to "realities of the moment"—that is, the mode of "Romance," which defines itself not by an absolute difference from "Novel," not by a rejection of mimesis but by the positing of another kind of mimesis, atmospheric, shadowed, faithful to that which flits away: a kind of mimesis that the narrative will apprehend with the help of its ambiguous and problematic daguerreotypes.[3]

A present that flits away, fancy-pictures which might be brought "almost" into "positive contact" with "realit[y]," portraits that dodge the eye and try to escape (to escape detection?)—Hawthorne's figures play nicely on what by 1851 had become a fairly common experience: that apparent trick of the mirrored metallic face of the daguerreotype image, seeming at once here and gone, a positive and a negative, substance and shadow. What one sees, shadow or image, or indeed one's own visage flashed back from the mirrored surface, depends on how one holds the palm-sized cased image, at what angle and in what light. The image materializes before one's eyes as if out of its own shadows. Because of the daguerreotype's peculiar construction, built up, as one recent expert explains, through accumulated surface granules rather than suspended in an emulsion (as in paper prints), what is required for the image to seem legible—or, as they said at the time, to "come to life"—is a specific triangulation of viewer, image, and light.[4]

In the face of such contingency and instability of seeing, no wonder that some like Phoebe felt disconcerted by the experience. Phoebe's outcry and the suggestive language of the preface signal how deeply engaged this narrative is with daguerrean seeing, its ambiguities of affect and, I shall argue, ambivalences of purpose. How are we to understand, for example, the motives and purposes of the novel's ardent daguerreotypist, Holgrave? "I misuse Heaven's blessed sunshine by tracing out human features, through its agency" (46), the young man confesses to Hepzibah. Surely we

3. Although I concur in general with Walter Benn Michaels's argument about the ideological freight carried by the term "Romance" in the text, it is my view that at stake is not mimesis as such but alternative modes of mimesis and that by force of its association (not an absolute one) between "Romance" and the daguerreotype, the former needs to be seen not as antimimetic but something like antipositivist.

4. Susan Barger writes: "In effect, seeing the image is dependent upon the unique viewing geometry made up of viewer, the daguerreotype, and the illumination source" (114). See also M. Susan Barger and William B. White, *The Daguerreotype: Nineteenth-Century Technology and Modern Science* (1991).

want to read "misuse" as coyly self-ironic, a nicely turned dis-
claimer of anything irregular in his craft. Is not his practice of
daguerreotypy a sign of Holgrave's most appealing traits—his experimental bent, his adventuresomeness, his facility with modern
tools? To be sure. But Phoebe personifies the sun's purest rays, and
Holgrave comes close to misusing her; her feminine innocence we
are surely meant to take as the novel's least controvertible value; in
the end it is what saves Holgrave from himself. Our smile at "misuse" fades into a deeper, more shadowed concern when we learn of
Holgrave's secret purpose of revenge against the Pyncheons in
whose house he presently resides. Is he tenant or spy? In any case
he resides in disguise, perhaps even from himself. Might not the
craft he practices in the deep recesses of the old mansion as well as
in his public rooms in the town be viewed as a purposefully atavistic regression to the witchcraft of his ancestors, the original Maules
from whom Colonel Pyncheon, founder of the family, had stolen
the land for his estate and house 200 years earlier?

Etching his text with strokes of ambiguity and dubiety, Hawthorne draws widely on figural terms from the popular discourse of
the daguerreotype circulating in the print culture of the 1840s and
early 1850s (see Trachtenberg, "Mirror" and "Photography"). He
draws on that gothicized discourse not for the sake of local allusions alone but as a vehicle of his deepest intentions in the romance, which are to probe the implications of the new order of
things of which photography serves as the auspicious type. Alternative views of the daguerreotype portrait, of the autoptic process of
apparently unmediated seeing and believing the camera putatively
represents, and of the physiognomic principles of portraits as such
serve the tale's ulterior purposes. To be sure, a narrative more of
picture than action, of tablieux than plot, of gothic device than dialogic interaction, *The House of the Seven Gables* leaves its largest
questions unsettled, its complexities and complications aborted by
the quick fix of a hastily arranged fairy-tale ending in which Holgrave seems to abandon daguerreotypy (this is not clear), along
with his resentment and radical politics (this is clear), for pastoral
squiredom. It is as if, Walter Benn Michaels provocatively suggests,
the daguerreotype of the dead Judge Pyncheon releases them
all from both the burden of a weighty "Past" and the instabilities
of a flitting "Present," frees them altogether from "Novel" to
spend their days within the stone-protected realm of "Romance"
(Michaels 95–101). Whatever authorial purposes account for the
novel's odd ending, it reflects in part on daguerrean visibility, on
photography's cultural work within a society rapidly undergoing
unsettling change toward market-centered urban capitalism. No

wonder Melville found in the narrative an "intense feeling of the visable truth," meaning by that, he wrote to Hawthorne, "the apprehension of the absolute condition of present things as they strike the eye" (124).

2

Hawthorne focuses his inquiry into means and ends of the daguerreotype on the figure of his hero. At present Holgrave lives as an itinerant daguerreotypist, a fact which seems at first marginal to the main action of the narrative, which in summary resembles popular Gothic melodramas: a decaying old house, an ancient crime, a family curse, a thirst for revenge. The story centers on Judge Jaffrey Pyncheon's effort to extract from his cousin Clifford, just released from a lengthy unjust imprisonment, information about a missing family deed to lands in Maine. The Judge had framed Clifford, giving false evidence that convicted his cousin of the murder of their wealthy uncle. Jaffrey's treachery and his greed makes him seem an avatar of the original seventeenth-century Pyncheon, founder of the once magnificent, now decaying House of the Seven Gables. Two descendents whose decrepitude matches that of the ancient house occupy the dwelling: the penurious Hepzibah, whose rather helpless try at selling groceries in a wing of the house opens the action of the novel, and her sadly ruined brother Clifford. They are joined by their sprightly country cousin Phoebe and the ambiguous tenant, the young daguerreotypist with alarmingly radical views on the sinfulness of inherited property and other social conventions. It will emerge that the young man has counterfeited his identity, for he is none other than a descendent of the Matthew Maule from whom the original Pyncheon had wrested the parcel of land on which the house sits. That legalized theft followed Maule's conviction on charges of witchcraft, a false accusation that provoked Maule's wrathful curse from the gallows that the lying, overreaching Pyncheon will drink blood. The stern old man's sudden death in a paroxysm the very day his house was completed (Maule's son Thomas was the chief carpenter) seemed to fulfill Maule's curse, the curse of the dispossessed and the resentful.

By legend the curse persists: virtually every generation has seen a Pyncheon who resembled the hard, unbending founder, even to the point of dying suddenly with a gurgling sound in his throat. The present Judge is the latest avatar and the final one, for Holgrave's camera will show beyond cavil that his death was natural after all, the result of an inherited ailment. The curse lifted, Clifford exonerated, Phoebe and Holgrave married—the entire cast of characters, including the old retainer Uncle Venner, betake themselves to the Judge's country estate, now restored to rightful heirs, the newly wed and redeemed descendents of both Maule and Pyncheon. With harmony between the antagonistic families (a distinctly class antagonism) finally achieved, the story closes happily as Hepzibah, out of the largesse of her newly recovered wealth and social station, dispenses silver coin to the town "urchin."

Like many readers, D. H. Lawrence puzzled over this curious tale of sinful fathers, vengeful sons, and compliant daughters in a bizarrely modern world: "The Dark Old Fathers. The Beloved Wishy-Washy Sons. The Photography Business? ? ?" (104). As far as the plot goes, only the final evidentiary picture of the Judge's death makes a difference, as a kind of messenger from the gods. But Hawthorne has his purposes, slyly insinuated in the daguerrean figures already quoted from the preface. The fixed picture that preserves what flits away had been a popular trope in the photographic trade for more than a decade: "Seize the shadow ere the substance fade." "Fancy-pictures" and "flitting" suggest that Hawthorne in some manner saw his own text as bearing a resemblance to the daguerrean image and its uncanny effects. One recent critic remarks that the narrative itself might be read as a "flickering," apparitional, here-again, gone-again daguerreotype portrait (Davidson 697). The fact that Holgrave is also an author (his name can be read as self-written) carries the suggestion further of a metadiscourse on the art of narrative. Does Holgrave's daguerreotypy serve as a heuristic analogy to Hawthorne's writing of romance?

It is significant in this regard that Holgrave's daguerreotypes appear within a political universe, a world threatened by both past and future, by inherited corruption founded upon illegitimate class privilege, and by the discordant energies of modernity, the railroad, the telegraph, market society. Moreover, associated at once with sorcery through the Maule-eye of Holgrave and with modern mechanical instruments of change, Holgrave's daguerreotypes combine elements of past and present, of tradition and change, of magical and rational systems of knowledge. The narrator situates the products of Holgrave's equivocal craft within a radiating web of implication.

It is noteworthy, then, that the first daguerreotype presented to a viewer in the narrative is a failed image, one that misses its intention: a dour picture of the Judge that so displeases Phoebe that she turns away. The exchange occurs, not incidentally, in the Pyncheon garden near the bubbling waters of Maule's Well. The picture was "intended to be engraved," Holgrave explains, presumably for the

Judge's use in his campaign for governor.[5] What seems to ruin the image is the incorrigible hardness of the Judge's physiognomy:

> Now, the remarkable point is, that the original wears, to the world's eye—and, for aught I know, to his most intimate friends—an exceedingly pleasant countenance, indicative of benevolence, openness of heart, sunny good humor, and other praiseworthy qualities of that cast. The sun, as you see, tells quite another story. . . . Here we have the man, sly, subtle, hard, imperious, and, withal, cold as ice. Look at that eye! Would you like to be at its mercy? At that mouth! Could it ever smile? And yet, if you could only see the benign smile of the original! It is so much the more unfortunate, as he is a public character of some eminence, and the likeness was intended to be engraved. (92)

Holgrave's explanation of the failure, often taken as an unequivocal endorsement on the author's part as well as his hero's, of the new medium, echoes the Enlightenment rationalist ideology embedded within popular commentary on photography. Yet it will prove to be every bit as equivocal as the young Holgrave-Maule himself. "There is a wonderful insight in heaven's broad and simple sunshine," he explains to Phoebe. "While we give it credit only for depicting the merest surface, it actually brings out the secret character with a truth that no painter would ever venture upon, even could he detect it" (91). Knowing that the self-authored Holgrave himself travels under a false sign, that he too harbors a "secret character," is enough warning for us to hold these words at some distance. Is his mention of "secret character," like his present disguised tenancy in the house of his family's dispossession, a tactical move toward his own inherited interest in exposing and destroying the illegitimacy of the Pyncheons? Like the actual pictures he makes—three are mentioned: two portraits of the dubious Judge Pyncheon (one after his death), and another we never see directly, of Uncle Venner, the town's story-teller and down-home philosopher—Holgrave's words about his craft are freighted with implications eventually to be drawn forth.

Other readers have shared D. H. Lawrence's suspicion of something secretive and covert about the novel. "It is . . . full of all sorts of deep intentions . . . certain complicated purposes" (97), remarked Henry James, adding that what Hawthorne evidently "designed to represent was not the struggle between an old society and a new . . . but simply . . . the shrinkage and extinction of a family"

---

5. In *Reading American Photographs* (ch. 1), I discuss the theory and the practice of the public emulatory daguerreotype portrait, especially those "intended to be engraved."

(102). If not "struggle" between the old and new, then at least, as Frank Kermode nicely puts it, the narrative registers "a transition from one structure of society, and one system of belief and knowledge, to another" (429). James notes cogently that the characters "are all figures rather than characters—they are all pictures rather than persons" (99). In the "history of retribution for the sin of long ago" (41), as the narrator describes his tale, Holgrave, who had taken up the daguerrean line "with the careless alacrity of an adventurer" (177), plays a kind of avenging angel, not with a sword but a camera, or better, a certain kind of eye which adapts itself with alacrity (less careless than he admits) to the daguerrean mode of vision. Holgrave's "deep, thoughtful, all-observant eyes" (156), the Maule "family eye" (156) in which "there was now-and-then an expression, not sinister, but questionable" (156), are there to witness the final act of what he conceives as a drama: "Providence . . . sends me only as a privileged and meet spectator" (217). Author, actor, and privileged audience—his role is foretold in the shadowy, teasing way in which the past repeats itself in the world of the narrative. He is the Maule "descendant" whom Hepzibah imagines seeing her fall from lady to hucksteress as "the fulfillment of his worst wishes" (ironically so, for he is also "her only friend") (46). He represents the "posterity of Matthew Maule" who, through "a sort of mesmeric process" can make the "inner region" of the family looking-glass come "all alive with the departed Pyncheons; not as they had shown themselves to the world, nor in their better and happier hours, but as doing over again some deed of sin, or in the crisis of life's bitterest sorrow" (21), as he may indeed have *made* the Judge look in the failed daguerreotype.

"They are all types, to the author's mind," writes James, "of something general, of something that is bound up with the history, at large, of families and individuals" (99). Like each of the principle characters, Holgrave is both himself and not himself, a person and a type, a figure in his own right and a figure in an ancient, repetitive drama. Indeed, the inner life of the plot shapes itself around the need Holgrave feels most acutely to resolve the ambiguity of identity he shares with the Pyncheons: at once themselves and copies of ancient originals "doing over again some deed of sin."

Thus within the drama of the romance Holgrave's often cited words about the sun's "wonderful insight" appear to the reader (if not to Phoebe) as double-edged, covert, shadowed. Can he mean that the sun, sheer material light, does in fact possess an "insight"? Or that he, descendant of the wronged Maules and privy to the ancestral gift of witchcraft (their power to torment bestowed on them by the projected guilt of their oppressors), already knows the "secret" written on the "merest surface" of Judge Pyncheon's self-betraying face and knows craftily how to bring it out? Is the sun aligned with the "Black Arts" Hepzibah affectionately suspects him of (84)?[6] The pedagogy he offers to Phoebe in the garden next to Maule's Well is not so much a lesson in the superiority of photography to painting but on a larger matter related to the "complicated purposes" of the romance: the unreliability of appearances, of representations altogether. Can we believe what we see, the "merest surface" of things and people, crafted surfaces such as paintings, maps, even mirrors, and especially the appearances put on by such public benefactors as the capitalist, politician, and horticulturalist Jaffrey Pyncheon, whose public face is all smiles and benignity? Is there a trustworthy way of seeing through surfaces, interpreting them as signs of something not seen, a "secret character," an invisible writing?

Hawthorne deepens and complicates the issue by raising yet another question about that "character" beneath the Judge's smiling exterior disclosed by the sun, a question about its origins. Is the Judge's character his own, or is it merely a copy of his ancestor's, a replay, like his death, of an inherited infirmity? If he is indeed only a copy of an ancient original, then the "secret" part of his "character" signifies something different from simple hypocrisy or duplicity. The "truth" the sun "brings out" may be hidden from the Judge himself. It lies in his history, a family history of illegitimate class privilege and abrogated power, and particularly of the use of established authority to lend an official seal to the original theft of Maule's land. It is in the Pyncheon interest to keep that origin secret, to repress its threatening truth, and when repression becomes habitual, it produces a secretiveness that no longer understands what it hides or why. What the sun reveals through Holgrave's failed daguerreotype, then, is not the Judge's ineptitude in maintaining an affable facade before the camera but his alienation from his own "character." What the sun reveals, in short, is not just something to be glimpsed beneath a facade, something merely visible, but something to be interpreted. A visibility incomplete in itself, the daguerrean image Holgrave offers to Phoebe's eyes is in search of an explanatory narrative.

3

Near the heart of the plot lies a document, "a folded sheet of parchment" (316) hidden behind the ancestral portrait of the first Pyncheon. "Signed with the hieroglyphics of several Indian sag-

---

6. Associations of daguerreotypy with alchemy abounded in the 1840s and 1850s, for obvious reasons. McLees attributed the origins of the medium to the experiments of "the Alchemic philosophers" (5).

amores," this "ancient deed" (316), which Jaffrey is desperate to lay his hands on, represents the legislative "grant" on which the original Pyncheon based his "claims" against the "right" of Matthew Maule to possess what, "with his own toil, he had hewn out of the primeval forest, to be his garden-ground and homestead" (7). This mere piece of paper, these undecipherable scrawls in a language no one remembers, recall the "recondite documents" (19) Bartleby labors to copy in Melville's "story of Wall Street" (13), or the scraps of paper Ike McCaslin puzzles over in the commissary in Faulkner's "The Bear." Hawthorne represents as an American version of original sin an originating act of ruthless theft the knowledge of which calls into question all constituted authority.[7] What the Judge's "secret character" hides even from himself is the fact that his historical being arises from a crime, his ancestor's deed against "natural right" disguised as a legitimate "claim" in an undecipherable legislative "deed." "Deed"—the conflation of act and word places a lexical pun at the heart of the original sin: the deed (act) of displacing the Lockean "right" to ownership of the products of one's labor with "claims" based upon a cryptic deed (word) written by distant legislators or even more distant sagamores. "Secret character" behind "merest appearance" revives the pun on "deed," signifying at once character as accumulated acts (the Judge's personal sin against Clifford) and character as a written inscription (the Judge's figural reenactment of the first Pyncheon's crime).

Only by restoring this history, which requires a new way of thinking about the relation between self and past, can Holgrave render his daguerreotype of the Judge legible as revelation of hidden truth. The light of the sun alone cannot suffice, contrary to the claims of Holgrave's compeers in the real world of commercial portrait photography. Working photographers proffered visibility as their commodity, the sun their warranty of reliable truth.

In a moral climate in which citizens felt anxious about "character," eager to trust the facades projected in images of men holding public trust yet distrustful of their own eagerness, photographers offered their goods as a social good, a guide to virtue. For was not character readily discernible in the face? And did not the daguerreotype provide the republic with its most foolproof means of discerning character?[8]

---

7. The missing deed, with its inscriptions of Indian "hieroglypics," of course addresses the issue of real estate and "title," which Michaels has shown persuasively informs the narrative and extends the horizon of conflict back to the first transactions between Europeans and native inhabitants, antecedent to the Maule-Pyncheon conflict. Might we not imagine an appropriate decipherment of those hieroglyphics to be a denial of the validity of European concepts of property and ownership altogether? The few references in the text to Indians hint that matters prior to and deeper than the class conflict between the two European families might be at issue in the tale.

8. So thought Marcus Aurelius Root, who wrote that in the power of the face to express inner character, and in the daguerreotype to capture that expression, "lies a valuable secu-

By allowing Holgrave a set of words that seem so in accord with this popular republican ideology of the image, Hawthorne slyly encourages the reader to lower his or her guard. The issue turns on the ambiguity within another key word: "character" as what is true about a person, "character" as an assumed role, such as the public face put on by the Judge, or indeed that performed by the contemporary Maule in his "character" as Holgrave, daguerreotypist. In that drama Holgrave performs both as author and actor: "[I]n this long drama of wrong and retribution, I represent the old wizard" (316). This confession holds the crux of the matter: the conflict between character as a set of moral traits engraved within and visible without, and character as a performed role in a scripted drama. Changing occupations like so many roles, "putting off one exterior, and snatching up another, to be soon shifted for a third," without ever altering the "innermost man" (177), it is Holgrave within whom tension between self and role most overtly plays itself out. At stake is whether he will remain a "type," in the sense of a fore-ordained copy, or become a free historical agent, a self in historical time, free to script his own roles.

Hawthorne formulates Holgrave's inner conflict as that between a commitment to historical or eschatalogical time and represents the conflict as an issue of interpretation. How are we to understand the failed daguerreotype of Judge Pyncheon? Not one of those photographers Walter Benjamin calls "illiterate," who "cannot read his own pictures" (215), Holgrave knows (it is, we might say, his secret knowledge) that the meaning of the daguerreotype cannot rest in the unsupported image alone but only within a particular system of meaning. The system activated by his words to Phoebe is a rather bland but nonetheless distinct version of Christian typology, in which secrets are foreknown by providence. In Hawthorne's half-serious, half-skeptical use of the typological method of interpretation, "secret character" refers to a residue of prophecy uttered in the past: Maule's curse. The face, then, is an inscription which can be known only by reference to something antecedent to itself. The serious side of Hawthorne's typological method says that the secret

---

rity for social order, insuring, as it does, that men shall ultimately be known for what they are" (43–44). The famed Boston daguerreotypist Albert Sands Southworth, sometimes taken by critics as a prototype for Holgrave, offered an interesting variation on this theme, one that veers toward the Hawthornian notion of "Romance." He argued that the power of penetration beneath surfaces belonged not to the mechanical medium but to the "genius" of the true artist. "Conscious of something besides the mere physical, in every object in nature," the true artist will feel "the soul of the subject itself." With these preternatural abilities in play, something emanates *from* the camera as forcefully as the light-borne impressions that enter it. "The whole character of the sitter is to [be] read at first sight." At the same time, "defects are to be separated from natural and possible perfections. . . . Nature is not at all to be represented as it is, but as it ought to be, and might possibly have been" (321–22).

of faces lies in the fact that they are really copies of absent originals. The skeptical side says that the original is not so much an absent figure (the portrait of the ancestral Pyncheon to whom the Judge bears an uncanny resemblance, or the lost deed) but a continuing process, an ongoing history. Judge Pyncheon is either a pure figural reflex of a determining original sin, or a free historical agent responsible for his own badness, his own corruption.

Her shuddering initial reaction to the daguerreotype of the Judge initiates Phoebe into typological explanation. "I know the face," she cries, "for its stern eye has been following me about, all day. It is my Puritan ancestor, who hangs yonder in the parlor" (92). That misidentification is her first lesson; the uncanny resemblance brought out by the daguerreotype points her directly to the typological source of her uncle's "secret character": "It is certainly very like the old portrait" (92). The process begun in the garden continues when Phoebe encounters the Judge face to face; beneath his sunny exterior she recognizes the "hard, stern, relentless look" of "the original of the miniature [the daguerreotype]" (119). As she notes in a recurrence of the uncanny, the "original," the face before her, copies the features of the ancestor whose portrait in its antique, faded condition "brought out" the "indirect character of the man" (58). The ancient portrait strikes her as a "prophecy" (119) of the modern man, and in her "fancies" (124) that in the living Judge "the original Puritan" (120) stood before her, she gives a start (124). Thus, the process of interpretation inaugurated by Holgrave teaches Phoebe a lesson essential to the system of meaning that Hawthorne takes as his object of investigation, one in which material substance of today seems to cast shadows of yesterday.

The process of interpreting the first daguerreotype culminates in the final taking of a likeness, the death portrait that will prove, typologically speaking, that in effect the good Judge had been dead all along, "fixed" as only the dead can be in an unalterable "character": "Death is so genuine a fact that it excludes falsehood, or betrays its emptiness" (310; see Michaels 100–01). For the reading instigated by Holgrave in the garden begins the torturous process of converting the Judge into a scapegoat, to be ritually slain by the camera. On the disclosure of his death everything else depends in this narrative of magical consummations. Both magical and political, Holgrave's reading of the Judge's image, of the Judge himself as an image, dissolves corrupt public authority by disclosing the corpse, the rotten "deed" decaying just behind the elegant facade. Holgrave's is that "sadly gifted eye" whose knowing look "melts into thin air" the "tall and stately edifice" the Judge had constructed for the "public eye" (229). The narrative elaborates this architectural figure. The Judge's self is like a marble palace constructed of "the

big, heavy, solid unrealities" of wealth and power and "public honors," its windows "the most transparent of plate-glass," its dome
open to the sky (229). The architectural figure recalls nothing so
much as one of the era's novel creations, a mercantile shop posing
as a neoclassical palace, while its stateliness recalls the original appearance of the House of the Seven Gables itself: "There is something so massive, stable, and almost irresistibly imposing, in the
exterior presentment of established rank and great possessions, that
their very existence seems to give them a right to exist; at least, so
excellent a counterfeit of right, that few poor and humble men have
moral force enough to question it, even in their secret minds"
(25).[9] The political point of Holgrave's hermeneutics becomes
clear: to penetrate "exterior presentment" in order to disclose the
"counterfeit of right" it claims for itself.

Holgrave's lesson in the reading of the daguerreotype (both typological and historicist) sheds light, moreover, on the role of picturing as such within the texture of the book. The preponderance of
looking, seeing, gazing, scrutinizing—for example, "To know Judge
Pyncheon, was to see him at that moment" (129)—declares the
reading of images (reading in the sense of comprehending the look
of things and persons) as a core issue in the narrative. Often the
verb is made explicit: Clifford "reads" Phoebe, "as he would a sweet
and simple story" (142); Holgrave too "fancied that he could look
through Phoebe, and all around her, and could read her off like a
page of a child's story-book" (182). People stand to each other as
texts, transparently legible or guardedly cryptic. There are texts
within texts, not only figurative storybooks and the "legend" of Alice
Pyncheon composed by Holgrave but a host of pictures: "quaint figures" (11) ornamenting the exterior of the house; "pictures of Indians and wild beasts" . . . "grotesquely illuminat[ing]" (33) the map
of the legendary Pyncheon territories in Maine; "grotesque figures
of man, bird, and beast" painted over the old tea set, "in a world
of their own" (77); and the gingerbread figures of animals and
"the renowned Jim Crow" (50). Some are ephemeral, vanishing as
quickly as they are seen: the "continually shifting apparition of
quaint figures, vanishing too suddenly to be definable," of Maule's
Well (88) and the "brilliant fantasies" that depict the world "in hues
bright as imagination" on the "nothing" surface of Clifford's soap

---

9. Spann quotes an 1846 account of the new A. T. Stewart clothing shop on Broadway:
"The main entrance opens into a rotunda of oblong shape, extending the whole width of
the building, and lighted by a dome seventy feet in circumference. The ceilings and side-
walls are painted in fresco, each panel representing some emblem of commerce. Immediately opposite the main entrance, . . . commences a flight of stairs which lead to a
gallery running around the rotunda. This gallery is for the ladies to promenade upon"
(97). Hawthorne's narrative "connects" with the "Present" in part by drawing figurative
allusions from such self-mirroring, self-referential places of spectacle as the proto—
department stores of the 1840s and their largely female clientele-audience.

bubbles (171). And, of course, there are the most prominent pictures: the ancient portrait of the founding ancestor, the Malbone miniature of Clifford that Hepzibah cherishes, and the daguerreotypes of the Judge. How does one read images of the world, the world deflected into image? The question of visuality as cognition lies athwart the entire narrative.

Indeed, the narrator introduces the larger question at the outset: "The aspect of the venerable mansion has always affected me like a human countenance, bearing the traces not merely of outward storm and sunshine, but expressive, also, of the long lapse of mortal life, and accompanying vicissitudes, that have passed within. Were these to be worthily recounted, they would form a narrative of no small interest and instruction, and possessing, moreover, a certain remarkable unity, which might almost seem the result of artistic arrangement" (5).

Interpretation appears here at the outset not just as a correlation of outer trace and inward life but as "narrative" with its own laws and codes of "arrangement." Here is the method of "Romance" promised in the preface, the method that presumes a relation between outer and inner as inherently ambiguous. Is the narrative true or only a plausible guess, governed equally by the desire for "unity" as by reference to actual fact or document? Indeed, as it proceeds the narrative more and more adduces what it calls "tradition" against "written record," a polarizing of modes of telling that becomes part of a diagrammatic structure of oppositions: on one hand, public records, official, "cold, formal, and empty words" (122); on the other, "the private and domestic view" (122), homely truths, gossip, rumor, chimney-corner tradition. Parallel to this contrast, substantially between writing and speech, is "the vast discrepancy between portraits intended for engraving, and the pencil-sketches that pass from hand to hand, behind the original's back" (122). (Holgrave's daguerreotype, recall, was indeed "intended for engraving," but the measure of its failure was its resemblance to a satiric pencil-sketch view of the Judge). A corresponding opposition in the schema of personae has the Judge, the arch–public figure, set in polar opposition to Uncle Venner, the book's gossip, who mediates between the sphere of women (he makes daily rounds in the town from kitchen to kitchen) and of men: the Judge, who takes "his idea of himself from what purports to be his image, as reflected in the mirror of public opinion" (232), and the Uncle, "the man of patches" (155) whose wardrobe consists of throwaways, "a miscellaneous old gentleman, partly himself, but, in good measure, somebody else" (62).

How are we to understand Holgrave's art of daguerreotypy within this structure of oppositions? The daguerreotype occupies a paradoxical position. The narrative comes down on the side of tradition, gossip, and pencil-sketches, linked through Uncle Venner and Phoebe to an older village culture, a republican culture founded on community and consensus. The old ways survive into and provide a perspective upon a present characterized by two localized but intense images of change: Hepzibah's fantasy of a "panorama, representing the great thoroughfare of a city" (48) and the railroad car vista of Hepzibah and Clifford, during their mad flight from the threatening Judge, of "the world racing past" (256). The latter is more nightmarish and metaphysical, as Clifford discourses crazily in the rattling car on electricity as "an almost spiritual medium" (264), on the blessings of the railroad and the insubstantiality of real estate. The scene is a severe gloss on the deceptively milder "fluctuating waves of our social life" (38) by which the narrator had introduced Hepzibah's reopening of the shop. If that moment of transformation of a patrician into a plebian hints at the upheavals of the Panic of 1837 and its aftermath, the effects of the railroad ride seem momentous: villages "swallowed by an earthquake"; meetinghouse spires "seemed set adrift from their foundations"; the "hills glided away." "Everything was unfixed from its age-long rest, and moving at whirlwind speed" (256). Something even more calamitous awaits the time-stricken couple at "a solitary way-station": an abandoned church "in a dismal state of ruin and decay . . . a great rift through the main-body of the edifice"; a farmhouse black with age, "relics of a wood-pile" near the door (266), gruesome icons of the new mechanical civilization that unfixes everything and bequeaths a wasted godless landscape.

Hepzibah's earlier fantasy in her shop depicts an equally new landscape of modernity but one obverse to the ruinous scene: prosperous mercantile capitalism confidently enjoying its high commercial stage. In place of the riven church, glittering shops; in place of the eye of God, a mirror: "Groceries, toy-shops, dry-goods stores, with their immense panes of plate-glass, their gorgeous fixtures, their vast and complete assortments of merchandize, in which fortunes have been invested; and those noble mirrors at the farther end of each establishment, doubling all this wealth by a brightly burnished vista of unrealities! . . . this splendid bazaar, with a multitude of perfumed and glossy salesmen, smirking, smiling, bowing, and measuring out the goods!" (48). The very figure of Broadway, the fantasy reenacts a world of goods and shoppers doubled by mirrors into unrealities (who can tell the copy from the original?), just as goods double or reduplicate themselves in the guise of their invisible agency, money. The mirror of unrealities leaps out as the apt emblem of commodity culture, the very agent of reproduction, transforming substance into image in a process that itself mirrors the apparent magic whereby money vanishes into goods and re-appears as profit. The mystery of such market transactions arises, as Marx famously pointed out in his formulation of "commodity fetishism" (71–83), by the effacement of all signs of labor by which goods might be recognized and known as the investment of toil. Condensed in Hepzibah's fantasy lies the historical secret of the Judge—not only of his wealth garnered from the "crime" of appro-priation in the capitalist market but his "public character" raised by a trick of mirrors into an edifice resembling a commercial empo-rium disguised as a domed, neoclassical palace. The Judge sees himself only in the mirror of his market self, takes the "unrealities" of doubled wealth as the truth of his being.

Can we doubt Hawthorne's purpose in these alternating views of modern change: a kaleidoscopic view of the old countryside, un-fixed, ruined, deprived of God; a panoramic view of the new city as a marketplace with no perspective outside itself, only an internal mirror doubling its surfaces into "unrealities"? Widely separated in the narrative, the two views form a composite dialectical image less of a "struggle between an old society and a new" than an already accomplished victory of new over old. If the new has no substance, in the old sense of solid reality, the old has no resources, except the resources of "Romance," which imagine the persistence of the older republic of rural virtue in the shadowed regions of the new society.

Recall the ending of the romance: the happy resolution, follow-ing the fortuitous demise of the Judge, of the ancient quarrel be-tween Maule and Pyncheon. Holgrave gives up his Maule eye, quits photography, retires with Phoebe and the others to a country es-tate, a house of stone—the "lapse of years . . . adding venerableness to its original beauty"—while the inhabitants "might have altered the interior" as they wish (314). Withdrawing behind protective walls, the group forms, in Holgrave's anticipatory image, a magic circle against the threat of a political economy that reproduces the world as image-commodities. The happy ending evokes another po-litical economy, transmuted by "Romance" from archaic practice into imaginative value, a critical (even if defenseless and rearguard) perspective upon the new society.

Consider Phoebe, who represents the Pyncheon line melded into the folkways of the old New England countryside. She enters the narrative just as Hepzibah ventures into modernity by opening her shop, as if elicited magically as an antidote to the threatening mir-rored panorama of the city market. Consider the village market Phoebe recreates in her management of the Pyncheon shop. With her first customer, an old woman who "was probably the very last person in town, who still kept the time-honored spinning-wheel in constant revolution" (78), she barters her goods for home-made yarn as the two voices "mingl[e] in one twisted thread of talk" (79). With her "gift of practical arrangement," her "natural magic" (71), she bakes her own goods, such as yeast, beer, cakes, and breads, instinctively following Uncle Venner's old "golden maxims": "Give no credit! . . . Never take. paper-money! Look well to your change! Ring the silver on the four-pound weight! Shove back all English half-pence and base copper-tokens, such as are very plenty about town! At your leisure hours, knit children's woollen socks and mittens! Brew your own yeast, and make your own ginger-beer!" (65–66).

Can it be only a coincidence that Venner's mention of silver and copper links his "golden maxims" surreptitiously to Holgrave's daguerreotypes, images made on silver-plated copper and often "fixed with pure chloride of gold, so that it is impossible that the pictures can fade for ages" (McLees 18)? No matter how oblique, the allusion clarifies brilliantly the paradoxical predicament of the daguerreotype within the text: its association on one side with all the unsettling elements of modernity and, on the other, with traditional modes of figurative cognition and social exchange. Associated with an eye that makes edifices melt away, with forces that unfix, the daguerreotype not only fixes the fleeting image but also fixes it as a "secret character," something solid and definite beneath the Judge's insubstantial surface of smiling munificence. It partakes of the invasive technologies of modern life, the public "gaze" Hepzibah fears, the "eye-witnesses" who report to the Judge on "the secrets of your interior" (236), and represents the black or Maule side of Holgrave's own analytic eye. Yet it is also allied with the solid coin of Venner's maxims against the fluid paper wealth of the Judge, his investments, speculations, membership on corporate boards. If the Judge's edifice of appearances resembles money and what Marx called its all-confounding powers, the daguerreotype redeems paper (or the outmoded, debased copper) into the hard species of silver and gold. If, as popular writers at the time claimed, "character . . . [is] a kind of capital," "like an accumulating fund, constantly increasing in value" (qtd. in Halttunen 47), then Holgrave's silver-plated image drives out false currency and its unrealities.

No wonder, then, that the narrative's third daguerreotype is of none other than Judge Pyncheon's foil, the good Uncle Venner himself. "[A]s a mark of friendship and approbation, he readily consented to afford the young man his countenance in the way of his profession—not metaphorically, be it understood—but literally, by allowing a daguerreotype of his face, so familiar to the town, to be exhibited at the entrance of Holgrave's studio" (157). Here again Hawthorne evokes a common practice of the daguerrean trade, a display of wares to tempt the public into the rooms upstairs. The familiarity of the face would make good bait. But there is a symbolic aspect to the linkage between the young and the old man afforded by the exhibition, heightened all the more by the fact that we never see the actual image. Like the analogy between maxims of gold and silver and the materiality of the daguerreotype, its absence renders Venner's picture all the more potent as a kind of amulet. To grasp the implications of Venner's face as advertised trope for Holgrave's daguerrean practice, we need to look more closely at the old "patched philosopher" and his relevance to the typological theory of character at issue in the narrative.

According to the typological view, characters are not free to choose their destinies; Holgrave must behave as a wizard and Judge Pyncheon as a greedy hypocrite. But Hawthorne allows Holgrave a will to change; he endows him with an inviolable "innermost man." He has nothing to hide, only something hidden within himself he needs to ferret out and overcome. The process of coming to himself, a process enacted in the historical time of the narrative, requires that he exorcise the ghost haunting the house, a ghost in the form of that very typological system that prophesizes Maule to be Maule and Pyncheon Pyncheon and by which Holgrave-Maule must expose and exorcise the corrupt Judge. Jaffrey must die that Holgrave be free. The need is ontological: as long as a representative of the old, tyrannical system of representation lives, the cyclic drama continues. And the camera proves just the right instrument of execution. First, it raises the old legend by revealing the Judge's typological "character" beneath his surface appearance. Second, in the death portrait it turns around and disproves the legend by revealing the death to be of natural causes. In each case the camera's report is meaningful only by interpretation: in the first instance, the old typological account of why the Judge is evil; in the second, a "scientific" account that accords with a view of the Judge as a historical creature, with a view of history as process rather than cycle.

In the end Holgrave abandons the camera, or so we assume, as he enters his estate as a country squire. The modern instrument has served his purpose of a deconstructive politics, of exposure and exorcism. By itself, he has shown, the camera has no theory of character, no independent ideology; it serves the discursive needs of its practitioners and clients. It either provides the compliant mirror images the Judge desires and lives by, or it subverts those images, allowing inner corruption to show through surface displays of virtue. Is there an alternative to these two versions of character—one doomed to repeat the past, the other doomed to live always in the eye of others? An answer lies with "wise Uncle Venner," who presides over the fairy-tale ending, is seen last as the curtain falls, and whose replica exhibited at the entrance to Holgrave's studio holds the key to the daguerreotype's equivocal place in this tale of many equivocations.

Venner condenses an alternative theory of society and character. As "immemorial personage," "patriarch," the "familiar" of the "circle" of families he visits daily, he stands (even too obviously) for continuity, the redemptive folk memory; he is the secular "clergyman," venerable and venerated, whose liturgy is gossip, story, and maxim. He welcomes Holgrave into the storytelling circle as a "familiar." And by exhibiting Venner's image at the entrance to his studio, Holgrave declares his allegiance to continuity, sympathy, communal sustenance, and a theory of character consistent with Venner's "miscellaneous" appearance, his wardrobe of ill-assorted hand-me-downs. "Partly himself, but in good measure, somebody else," Venner is neither entirely self-made (like Holgrave in his adventuring phase) nor other-made (like the Judge). He appears as both a copy and an original, whose patched exterior at once discloses and conceals his inner truth. One can imagine his daguerreotype portrait only as a perfectly equivocal construction; hanging by the door, the portrait declares Holgrave's studio to be, like "Romance" itself, the very place of equivocation, where "merest surfaces" lose their self-sufficiency and seek their meanings in communal narratives, such as Venner's sustaining stories.

To save himself from himself Holgrave must slay the scapegoat, surrogate of the bad father and replace him with a good father, the venerable Venner. Venner saves the young man from the radical implications of his youthful politics, from the dangerous illusion that programmatic politics can effectively shape the tides of change. In the end, a historicist view of history proves too difficult to encompass, the railroad ride of Clifford and Hepzibah too menacing to be sustained. In Hawthorne's method of romance, as James recognized, this point cannot be made in narrative action; it can only be supplied as an authorial observation. Thus, the narrator interpolates a remark regarding Holgrave's revolutionary hatred of the past: "His error lay, in supposing that this age, more than any past or future one, is destined to see the tattered garments of Antiquity exchanged for a new suit, instead of gradually renewing themselves by patchwork" (180). Venner is a walking theory of social change as slow accretion rather than sudden irruption or the imposition of rationalist utopia. He leads the survivors to a recomposed middle landscape, in which the values of an economy based on barter and solid coin are transmuted into values of true exchange among familiars, well protected by solid stone walls. And significantly, some degree of social deference is restored: Hepzibah distributes her largesse, providing Uncle Venner himself a cabin on the edge of the property. Thus the anxiety of visibility is tempered by an imaginary restoration of rank.

The meaning of the ending may lie precisely in its unbelievability, its transformation of an already defeated culture (the republican ideal, associated with Andrew Jackson, of an exchange economy among producers and small shopkeepers in a market free of manipulation by banks) into a permanent value. A lost vision of entrepreneurial, petit bourgeois social relations elevated into a historical impossibility, the dream of a restored "circle": only its impossibility, Hawthorne has us realize, endows the ending with the redemptive power of "Romance." Hawthorne proposes "Romance" as a power to preserve a lost idea of a republic of virtue, at the expense, we must note, of imagining a historical action that might resolve the modern version of the Maule-Pyncheon class conflict. The marriage of Maule and Pyncheon accomplishes what the daguerreotype by itself cannot: it wishes away the nemesis of the modern market, a monied class of investors, speculators, and manipulators.

Hawthorne's view of the daguerreotype seems in the end as equivocal as the political vision of the text as a whole. The popular ideology assumed (or desired) a transparent relation between face and character, between expression and truth. It endowed the mirror image with power to stir emulation, to provide models of visible virtue, to preserve the presence of the missing and the dead ("It is as if the subject of a daguerreotype is in some sense already dead," writes Michaels [100]). In the godless labyrinth of the marketplace, the mirror might serve as a way back toward familiar paths but only within typological narratives in which physiognomy doubles as psychology. Without such narratives, Hawthorne understood, photography threatened to let loose additional ambiguities, confusions between copies and originals. By questioning popular assumptions about the medium, by casting a skeptical eye on the claims of a photographic power independent of self-reflective structures of meaning, Hawthorne represents photography as a new political mode of seeing with unforeseen consequences. Confronting the "visable truth" of his age, in Melville's words, "the absolute condition of present things as they strike the eye," Hawthorne recognizes in the modern engine of visibility a new version of the old challenge of seeing to believing.

Works Cited

Barger, M. Susan. "Robert Cornelius and the Science of Daguerreotypy." Willam F. Stapp et al. *Robert Cornelius: Portraits from the Dawn of Photography: An Exhibition at the National Portrait Gallaery.* . . . Washington: Smithsonian Institution, 1983. 111–128.

Benjamin, Walter. "A Short History of Photography." *Classic Essays on Photography.* Ed. Alan Trachtenberg. New Haven: Leete's Island, 1980.

Davidson, Cathy N. "Photographs of the Dead: Sherman, Daguerre, Hawthorne." *South Atlantic Quarterly* 89 (1990): 667–701.

Halttunen, Karen. *Confidence Men and Painted Women: A Study of Middle-Class Culture in America, 1830–1870.* New Haven: Yale UP, 1982.

Hawthorne, Nathaniel. *The House of the Seven Gables*. Vol. 2 of *The Centenary Edition of the Works of Nathaniel Hawthorne*. Ed. William Charvat et al. Columbus: Ohio State UP, 1965. 20 vols. 1962–88.

James, Henry. *Hawthorne* 1879. Ithaca: Cornell UP, 1967.

Kermode, Frank. "Hawthorne's Modernity." *Partisan Review* 41 (1974): 428–41.

Lawrence, D. H. *Studies in Classic American Literature*. 1923. New York: Viking, 1964.

Marx, Karl. *Capital: A Critique of Political Economy*. Ed. Frederick Engels. Vol. 1. 3rd ed. Trans. Samuel Moore and Edward Aveling. New York: International, 1967. 3 vols.

McLees, James E. *Elements of Photography*. . . . 1855. Rochester: International Museum of Photography at the George Eastman House, 1974.

Melville, Herman. "Bartleby, the Scrivener." *The Piazza Tales and Other Prose Pieces*. 1839–60. Evanston and Chicago: Northwestern UP and the Newberry Library, 1987. 13–45.

———. "To Nathaniel Hawthorne." 16 Apr. 1851. Letter 83 in *The Letters of Herman Melville*. Ed. Merrell R. Davis and William H. Gilman. New Haven: Yale UP, 1960. 123–25.

Michaels, Walter Benn. *The Gold Standard and the Logic of Naturalism*. Berkeley: U of California P, 1987.

Root, Marcus Aurelius. *The Camera and the Pencil: Or, The Heliographic Art*. 1864. Pawlet: Helios, 1971.

Southworth, Albert Sands. "An Address to the National Photographic Association of the United States." *Philadelphia Photographer* Oct. 1871: 320.

Spann, Edward K. *The New Metropolis: New York City, 1840–1857*. New York: Columbia UP, 1981.

Taft, Robert. *Photography and the American Scene: A Social History, 1839–1889*. New York: Macmillan, 1938.

Trachtenberg, Alan. "Mirror in the Marketplace: American Responses to the Daguerreotype." *The Daguerreotype: A Sesquicentennial Celebration*. Ed. John Wood. Iowa City: U of Iowa P, 1989. 60–73.

———. "Photography: The Emergence of a Keyword." *Photography in Nineteenth-Century America*. Ed. Martha A. Sandweiss. New York: Abrams, 1991. 16–47.

———. *Reading American Photographs: Images as History, Mathew Brady to Walker Evans*. New York: Noonday-Hill, 1989.

DAVID ANTHONY

Class, Culture, and the Trouble with White Skin in Hawthorne's *The House of the Seven Gables*†

"What's that you mutter to yourself, Matthew Maule? . . . And what for do you look so black at me?"

"No matter, darkey! . . . Do you think nobody is to look black but yourself?"

—Exchange between Young Matthew Maule and Scipio,
slave of Gervayse Pyncheon, in Hawthorne's *The House of the Seven Gables* (1851)

In May of 1850, while still composing *The House of the Seven Gables* (1851), Nathaniel Hawthorne made a lengthy journal entry

† From *Yale Journal of Criticism*, 12:2 (1999): 249–268. Copyright © Yale University and The Johns Hopkins University Press. Reprinted with permission of The Johns Hopkins University Press. All notes are Anthony's; some notes have been condensed or deleted for this edition.

in which he recounts a visit to the National Theater in Boston for a performance of "Jack the Giant Killer."[1] Hawthorne describes the performance as "somewhat heavy and tedious," but he nevertheless seems to have found the experience intriguing, in particular because of the audience, which he depicts as "more noteworthy than the play." As he explains,

> The theater itself is for the middling and lower classes; and I had not taken my seat in the most aristocratic part of the house, so that I found myself surrounded chiefly by young sailors, Hanover-street shopmen, mechanics and other people of that kidney. It is wonderful the difference that exists in the personal aspect and dress, and no less in the manners, of the people in this quarter of the city, as compared with others. . . . It was a scene of life in the rough. (*American Notebooks*, 501–2, 503)

Going on to describe the shabby dress and uncleanliness of various individuals in the crowd, the heat and over-crowding within the theater itself, and the noise kept up throughout the performance (the audience members "calling to one another from different parts of the house, shouting to the performers and singing the burthens of songs"), Hawthorne makes it clear that cultural consumption of the kind practiced by the lower classes at the theater is all but completely alien to him, in particular because it seems so intimately tied to the visceral, bodily presence of the viewing audience (*American Notebooks*, 502–3).

This is especially evident in his description of two women standing near him, one of whom surprises him by nursing her child in the theater, and the other of whom he finds striking for how dirty and unkempt she appears. The latter of the two is particularly notable to Hawthorne for wearing what he portrays as "the vilest gown—of dirty white cotton, so pervadingly dingy that it was white no longer, as it seemed to me." Hawthorne goes on to say that "she must have had a better dress at home," but he seems unable to shake the image he has of her as excessively unclean (*American Notebooks*, 502). Musing on the differences between the two women, he finally comes to the conclusion that the alleged negative qualities of the dirtier woman may best be attributed to race: she was, he says in a kind of summation, "so dark that I rather suspected her to have a tinge of African blood" (*American Notebooks*, 503).

Coming just a year after the 1849 Astor Place Opera House riot

---

1. Nathaniel Hawthorne, *The American Notebooks*, ed. Claude Simpson, vol. 8 of *The Centenary Edition of the Works of Nathaniel Hawthorne*, ed. William Charvat et al. (Columbus: Ohio State University Press, 1972), 501–3. Subsequent references are to this edition and are cited parenthetically within the text.

in New York, a conflict which crystallized distinctions between
working-class audiences of lowbrow productions such as melodramas or minstrel shows and the city's elite purveyors of highbrow
productions such as the opera, the journal entry is a useful example
of how anxieties over class and gender emerging at mid-century
were sometimes managed by aesthetes such as Hawthorne.[2] The
entry suggests not only that such concerns were being negotiated in
the realm of cultural production and aesthetic "taste," but also that
these differences were often mediated via the third term of racial
blackness. Unsettled by the image of working-class embodiment a
large and "dirty" woman so clearly represents to him, Hawthorne
seems to wish to imagine her difference as the result of "black"
blood. Indeed, the designation even has the effect here of inform-
ing his curiously overdetermined description of her clothing as
"white no longer." Merging the markings of class into the
metaphorical marks of racial difference, Hawthorne seems to be
seeking the means by which to come to terms not only with "shop-
men," "mechanics," and lower-class women, but also with cultural
consumption of the kind practiced by the people in the "rough" of
working-class life in 1850.

Hawthorne's anxieties over differences of class and class embodiment are displayed in a text expressing similar concerns over cultural production, *The House of the Seven Gables*. As Cathy N.
Davidson has suggested,[3] the novel narrates Hawthorne's decided
ambivalence over the new reproductive technologies of mass culture appearing at mid-century, one he had manifested repeatedly in
his journal entries and in some of his early short stories, such as
"Alice Doane's Appeal" (1835) and "Fancy's Showbox" (1837).[4] In

2. The actual riot, in which twenty-two people were killed, was sparked by a rivalry between Edwin Forrest, a working-class "Jacksonian" actor championed by the crowd of
Bowery "b'hoys" who filled the Chatham, Bowery, and other theaters for his melodramas, and George Macready, a British actor whose performance of *Macbeth* conflicted
with Forrest's concurrent version of Shakespeare's play. The best histories of the riot are
Peter Buckley, *To the Opera House: Culture and Society in New York City, 1820–1860*
(New York and London: Oxford University Press, in press); and Lawrence Levine, *High-
brow/Lowbrow: The Emergence of Cultural Hierarchy in America* (Cambridge: Harvard
University Press, 1988).
3. Focusing on the new technologies of photography Hawthorne foregrounds, Davidson
suggests that the novel might be thought of as Hawthorne's meditation on the status of
representational art at mid-century, one which led him to pose difficult and often anxi-
ety-provoking questions not only about distinctions between "high" and "low" art, but
about subjectivity in the age of mechanical reproduction. Cathy N. Davidson, "Photographs of the Dead: Sherman, Daguerre, Hawthorne," *South Atlantic Quarterly* 89:4
(Fall 1990): 696. Subsequent references to this article are cited parenthetically within
the text. For another valuable reading of Hawthorne's negotiation of the emergent forces
of mass culture at mid-century, see Richard Brodhead's discussion of *The Blithedale Romance* in "Veiled Ladies: Toward a History of Antebellum Entertainment," in *Cultures of
Letters* (Chicago and London: University of Chicago Press, 1993), 48–68.
4. In "Alice Doane's Appeal," the unnamed narrator—who, like Hawthorne, has published
stories in *The Token*—has his concerns about his "sluggish and perhaps feeble" pen answered at the tale's end only when he borrows from mass culture the putatively debased

The House of the Seven Gables, this ambivalence is manifested primarily via the "plebeian" artisan and part-time wizard Holgrave, whose name has appeared "on the covers of Graham and Godey," and whose daguerreotypes are part of the mass reproduction of photographic images appearing at mid-century.[5] Tellingly, Holgrave's talents are represented as posing a distinct threat to elite families such as the aristocratic Pyncheons, not only at the level of aesthetic sensibility, but also at the levels of class and gender. In the infamous scene in which Phoebe Pyncheon is mesmerized by listening to Holgrave read a sensational magazine story he has written, for example, we encounter an allegory of reading in antebellum America. Like readers supposedly falling prey to the much-decried enticements of sensation fiction at mid-century (described by one reviewer as "gaping victims" who are "caught and immolated"), Phoebe seems to have been incapacitated less by Holgrave's magical powers than by the pulpy Gothic narrative he reads to her—a condition which renders her vulnerable to the upstart artisan both culturally *and* sexually. Holgrave is thus a fairly radical agent of social disruption: combining an emergent artisan sensibility (one deeply rooted in the working classes) with the new reproductive technologies of mass culture, his real "wizardry" seems to lie in his ability to combine the politics of class struggle with the seductive magic of mass culture.

But if Hawthorne is seeking in *The House of the Seven Gables* to utilize the scene of cultural production as the space in which to negotiate class conflict, he is also in the process of working out what I will describe here as an aesthetics of race. The novel is of course obsessed with the issues of eugenics and degeneration worried over and often sensationalized by reformers such as Catharine Beecher, Horace Greeley and others, with Hawthorne seeking to denounce the insular world of the enfeebled Pyncheon aristocracy and the "pure" "Anglo-Saxon" whiteness they are made to represent.[6] A

---

and manipulative techniques of sensationalism. "Plung[ing] into his imagination for a blacker horror, and a deeper woe," the narrator finally "reach[es] the seldom trodden places of [his listeners'] hearts"; the act wins audience approval, but effaces the moral message he had intended about the wrongs of the New England witchcraft trials. "Alice Doane's Appeal." *Nathaniel Hawthorne: Tales and Sketches*, ed. William Charvat and Roy Harvey Pearce (New York, 1996), 207, 216.

5. Nathaniel Hawthorne, *The House of the Seven Gables* (New York: Penguin Classics, 1986), 25, 186. Subsequent references are to this edition and are cited parenthetically within the text.

6. The Pyncheons are of course neatly paralleled by the degenerated family of hens maintained in the backyard of the House of the Seven Gables, which, "like many a noble race besides, in consequence of too strict a watchfulness to keep it pure," has become "withered" and almost incapable of laying eggs (*Gables*, 89). For contemporary commentary on the perceived threat of upper-class degeneracy at mid-century, see Catharine Beecher, *Letters on Health and Human Happiness* (New York, 1856); and Horace Greeley, "The Discipline and Duties of the Scholar," *Nineteenth Century: A Quarterly Miscellany* 4 (1849).

number of critics have observed that Hawthorne's critique of the Pyncheons founders on a narrative conclusion in which Holgrave is married into the Pyncheon family, an act that appears to regenerate the Pyncheon blood line by absorbing Holgrave's working-class blood and effacing the class *ressentiment* the mysterious artisan offers throughout most of the novel.[7] But such analyses overlook moments of the sort depicted in Hawthorne's description of his suspicion about the "African blood" possessed by the woman in the National Theater—moments which appear at a number of crucial junctures throughout *The House of the Seven Gables*. Indeed, while recent scholarship on the politics of "whiteness" has done much to help us recognize the ways in which, as Toni Morrison so eloquently argues, "Americans choose to talk about themselves through and within a sometimes allegorical, sometimes metaphorical, but always choked representation of an Africanist presence," it remains the case that Hawthorne's works have received virtually no such consideration by critics.[8] In *The House of the Seven Gables*, however, the "Africanist presence" Morrison describes is crucial both for understanding the novel and for understanding how race acted as a crucial third term in negotiations of class and culture during the antebellum period. For what the novel shows is the inextricable relation between representations of white men, such as Holgrave, as they seek to rise both economically and culturally, and the representation, both literal and figurative, of blackness. More specifically, it demonstrates what Amy Schrager Lang describes as a strategy of "displacement" deployed in much of the period's sentimental and sensational fiction, in which anxieties over class struggle—exemplified here in the centuries-long feud between the Pyncheons and Holgrave's ancestors, the Maules—are displaced onto the triangulated third term of racial difference, as a means of obscuring or effacing the realities of class division in the years fol-

---

7. According to Davidson, for example, the ending is "tacked on, like the denouement of the worst kind of melodrama" (691). For a list of critics objecting to the novel's conclusion, see Lawrence Buell, *New England Literary Culture: From Revolution through Renaissance* (Cambridge: Harvard University Press, 1986), 446–47.

8. Toni Morrison, *Playing in the Dark: Whiteness and the Literary Imagination* (Cambridge: Harvard University Press, 1990), 17. Subsequent references are cited parenthetically in the text. Works generally addressing the role of blackness and racial difference in Hawthorne include Jay Grossman, "A is for Abolition? Race, Authorship, The Scarlet Letter," *Textual Practice* 7:1 (Spring 1993): 13–30; and Anna Campbell Brickhouse, "Hawthorne in the Americas: Frances Calderon de la Barca, Octavio Paz, and the Mexican Genealogy of 'Rappacini's Daughter,'" *PMLA* 113:2 (1998): 227–42. Especially helpful to me here in thinking through formations of whiteness in relation to class and categories of blackness have been the following: Eric Lott, *Love and Theft: Blackface Minstrelsy and the American Working Class* (New York and London: Oxford University Press, 1993); David Roediger, *The Wages of Whiteness: Race and the Making of the American Working Class* (London: Verso Press, 1991); Saidiya Hartman, *Scenes of Subjection: Terror, Slavery, and Self-Making in Nineteenth-Century America* (Berkeley: University of California Press, 1997); and Joan Dayan, "Amorous Bondage: Poe, Ladies and Slaves," *American Literature* 66 (June 1994): 239–73.

lowing the social upheaval in Europe in 1848.[9] My suggestion here is that the displacement Lang describes is central not only to the class relations Hawthorne offers in *The House of the Seven Gables*, but also to the vexed relations between mass culture and high culture accompanying class struggle during this period.

Ironically, however, Hawthorne's novel makes it clear that the forms of blackness utilized by Hawthorne in displacing anxieties over class and culture were *themselves* thoroughly mediated *by* mass culture, with stereotyped figures of racial difference providing a myriad of fantasy structures through and within which class difference could be negotiated. Indeed, specifically because of its engagement with various racial (and racist) tropes available within mass culture—from the wide-eyed black servant and the dancing figure of Jim Crow, to the enfeebled "Anglo-Saxon" aristocrat and the white virgin heroine whose "unsullied purity" is violated (*Gables*, 203)—the novel offers a telling example of how literary high culture was tapping into the malleable and frequently unsettling energies and fantasies of race, both "black" and "white," developing during this period within mass culture, in particular as a means of managing anxieties over class conflict and cultural production. *The House of the Seven Gables* reflects an astonishing sensitivity to the contingencies and the blurrings of racial identity during the antebellum period. The text also makes it clear, however, that Hawthorne's anxieties over the categories of class and cultural production were sufficiently powerful to limit his ability to see that the tropes of race he utilized in negotiating these categories were themselves drawn from the repressed, ostensibly illegitimate precincts of mass culture.

The result is that we need to complicate Morrison's reading of the cultural work accomplished by the "Africanist presence" within American fiction. For while figures of blackness often mediate class relations in this novel, the fact is that such figures, lifted from the protean world of mass culture, end up being far less stable or reliable than Morrison suggests. Indeed, rather than acting in the enabling way which Morrison describes—"thoroughly serviceable" and "companionably ego-reinforcing" to white self-presence (*Playing in the Dark*, 8)—the Africanist presence imagined by Hawthorne in *The House of the Seven Gables* repeatedly ends up destabilizing the very social and cultural distinctions it seems to have been deployed to reinforce. These include not only distinctions of high and low culture, but also, and more significantly, the distinctions of surface/depth or interior/exterior so central to the

9. Amy Schrager Lang, "Class and the Strategies of Sympathy," in *The Culture of Sentiment: Race, Gender, and Sentimentality in Nineteenth-Century America*, ed. Shirley Samuels (New York: Oxford University Press, 1992), 130.

maintenance of upper-class white "self-possession." "Black" but also performing blackness, "actual" but also cartoonish and two-dimensional, the black bodies of this novel refuse to adhere to a depth model of the self. Instead, thoroughly mass-mediated, Hawthorne's black bodies provide an excess of signification, the effect of which is to disrupt the effort to displace difference of class and culture onto racial difference. Hawthorne's Gothic romance thus represents a "racial Gothic" in which the ghosts inhabiting the House of the Seven Gables are the uncanny figures of race, themselves derived from mass culture, which have returned to the sphere of highbrow literature to haunt its pages and rewrite the narratives of cultural distinction the novel seeks to offer.

I. "That Jim Crow there in the window": Black Performance, White Tears

Perhaps not surprisingly, racial negotiations of the kind I am describing take place in *The House of the Seven Gables* at moments when categories of class seem most unstable. The first such example comes in the pivotal scene in which Hepzibah Pyncheon makes her initial sale from the cent shop she has established on the side of the House of the Seven Gables. As Gillian Brown has argued, the scene enforces Hepzibah's corporeal "enslavement" to the forces of the financial market with which she and her family are finally forced to make actual physical contact.[1] But it's important to note that the vicissitudes of market embodiment reflected here are both facilitated by and routed through the figure of Jim Crow, who enters the narrative in the form of the Jim Crow gingerbread cookies Hepzibah offers for sale in her newly opened cent shop. Described as "impish figure[s]" who can be seen "executing [their] world-renowned dance" in the cent-shop window, the cookies not only advertise Hepzibah's entrance into the world of retail exchange, they also act as the first goods exchanged between the Pyncheons and the working classes (*Gables*, 51, 36).

Tellingly, the first customer they entice into the shop is Ned Higgins, the son of a working-class laborer whose repeated requests for the cookies eventually force Hepzibah to charge the boy money for the goods. Here is how Hawthorne depicts Hepzibah's first sale:

> The new shopkeeper dropped the first solid result of her commercial enterprise into the till. It was done! The sordid stain of that copper coin could never be washed away from her palm.

1. Gillian Brown, *Domestic Individualism: Imagining Self in Nineteenth-Century America* (Berkeley: University of California Press, 1990), 81–86. For a related discussion of *Gables*, see Walter Benn Michaels, "Romance and Real Estate," *The Gold Standard and the Logic of Naturalism: American Literature at the Turn of the Century* (Berkeley: University of California Press, 1987), 85–113.

The little school-boy, aided by the impish figure of the Negro dancer, had wrought an irreparable ruin. The structure of ancient aristocracy had been demolished by him. (*Gables*, 51)

Described in specifically working-class terms as "dressed rather shabbily . . . in a blue apron, very wide and short trousers, shoes somewhat out at the toes, and a chip-hat" (*Gables*, 49–50), Ned Higgins is a caricature of the working-class corporeality Hepzibah finds so threatening. Indeed, when (a short time after the young boy leaves the shop) Hepzibah waits on a "man in a blue cotton frock" who is "much soiled" and smells of alcohol, it seems clear that we are seeing a grown-up version of the boy as Hawthorne envisions him in future years. Imagined by Hepzibah to be the husband of a "care-wrinkled woman" she has seen earlier, one whom "you at once recognize as worn to death by a brute," the man terrifies Hepzibah, both because of his "brutal" nature and because she imagines he is the overly fertile father of "at least nine children"— all of whom will no doubt turn out like himself, and all of whom will threaten to overrun the degenerated and barren Pyncheon family line (*Gables*, 53).

But Hawthorne's description of Hepzibah's first sale is also telling because "the impish figure of the Negro dancer" mediates her contact with the working-class embodiment represented by customers such as Ned Higgins. This is true on a literal level, in that Jim Crow is the commodity which passes between the classes and who thus "aid[s]" in forcing the Pyncheon family into the material world of retail exchange. But this is also true in the more figural sense that Jim Crow introduces race as a factor in the relations between the two classes. Here this is especially evident, in that Hepzibah is actually marked by her commodity exchange with "the lower classes," the surest sign of which is of course the "sordid stain" she receives from Ned Higgins's coin—a mark which those lucky enough to remain free of such contact manage to avoid (*Gables*, 55). For example, a few moments after Hepzibah experiences her Eden-like "fall" into commerce, she sees a female member of "the idle aristocracy" walking with "ethereal lightness" down the street, and poses the following question to herself: "Must the whole world toil, that the palms of *her* hands may be kept white and delicate?" (*Gables*, 55). The answer of course is "Yes," but what is especially telling here is how issues of class and labor are figured in terms very much like racial markings, with the un-washable "stain" of Ned Higgins's working-class money separating Hepzibah from the "white and delicate" sphere of aristocratic racial purity. Class, in other words, is being made by Hawthorne into a racial issue, a fact which makes blackness a crucial third term in the effort to imagine a distinct difference between working-class whiteness and whiteness of the kind inhabited by the "idle aristocracy."[2]

Hawthorne's use of Jim Crow here echoes a similar figuration of blackness he provides later in the novel. This comes as Clifford Pyncheon watches from a balcony window of the House of the Seven Gables as a young Italian organ-grinder performs on the street in front of the Pyncheon home. Clifford, who is variously described in terms of his "pale" and "yellowing" skin, his "lack of vigor," and his tendency to "burst into a woman's passion of tears," is in many ways a hyperbolic extension of the enfeebled, degenerated male imagined by reformers such as Greeley and Beecher.[3] He is also, however, a figure of the aesthete, whose removal from actual market production Hawthorne seems to find praiseworthy, if impractical. Characterized by qualities of aesthetic appreciation "so refined" they seem to provide him a form of "spiritual" disembodiment (*Gables*, 108), Clifford represents an old-world aesthetic sensibility Hawthorne clearly seeks to mark as incompatible with the modern world of industrialization and mass culture looming close by outside the House of the Seven Gables. This contrast is perhaps best exemplified by Clifford's practice of blowing soap-bubbles from the second-story window, miniature creations Hawthorne de-

---

2. Hawthorne's reliance on a metaphoric slippage between blackness and whiteness in relation to issues of class and labor also informs several of his comments about manual labor in his letters and journal entries from the 1840s and 1850s. This is particularly true of his descriptions of his work as a surveyor in the Salem Custom House, a position which often placed him aboard cargo ships bearing loads of coal. Complaining that his "coal-begrimed visage" or the "sable stains" of his profession give him qualities in common with "chimney sweepers" or with "the black-faced demons in the vessel's hold" (he also describes the longshoremen as looking "like the forgemen in Retsch's Fridolin"), Hawthorne seems drawn to the ways in which the coal dust he encounters provides metaphoric connections between manual labor and the racial markings of blackness—markings which he seems quite willing to ascribe to the white working-class men along Salem's waterfront (*American Notebooks*, 296).

3. The descriptions Hawthorne provides of Clifford's fragile physical and mental condition also echo warnings by antebellum reformers such as John Todd against the evils of masturbation, the ultimate effect of which was thought to be impotence. Advising against the "habit of reverie" as the pathway to "evils which want a name, to convey any conception of their enormity," Todd describes states ranging from nervousness to melancholia and poor memory, all of which speak to Clifford's enfeebled status after his release from jail; John Todd, *The Student's Manual* (1835), 88, 146–47. As Todd and other reformers made clear, the only cure for this disease was heterosexual intercourse within the bounds of marriage. But as Hawthorne explains, Clifford, "who had never quaffed the cup of passionate love[,] . . . knew now that it was too late" (*Gables*, 141)—a fact which highlights the reproductive crisis facing not only the Pyncheon family, but, at least symbolically, upper-class white men in general. For readings of antebellum culture in relation to male moral reformers addressing masturbation, see Vincent J. Bertolini, "Fireside Chastity: The Erotics of Sentimental Bachelorhood in the 1850s," *American Literature* 66 (Dec. 1996): 707–737; and Carroll Smith-Rosenberg, "Sex as Symbol in Victorian Purity: An Ethnohistorical Analysis of Jacksonian America," in *Turning Points: Historical and Sociological Essays on the Family*, ed. John Demos and Sara Spence Boocock, in the supplement of the *American Journal of Sociology* 84 (1978): S212–S247. My thanks to Professor Rosenberg for pointing out to me the connections between Clifford's enfeeblement and the rhetoric of male sexual purity advocated by moral reformers.

scribes in terms which highlight the fleeting nature of the aesthetic Clifford represents. "Little impalpable worlds were those soap-bubbles," Hawthorne explains, "with the big world depicted, in hues as bright as imagination, on the nothing of their surface" (*Gables*, 171). Comprised of an interior logic that the outer world is unable to penetrate without ruining it altogether (in such instances Hawthorne describes the bubble as having "vanished as if it had never been"), the soap bubbles suggest an anti-market aesthetic resistant to reproduction and circulation of the kind taking place in Hepzibah's cent shop (*Gables*, 171).

This fragile aestheticism is precisely what is at issue as Clifford views the Italian organ-grinder. At first it appears that the boy will provide Clifford a picturesque image of life on the streets, in particular because the boy's barrel-organ contains a number of miniature mechanical figures that enact the very kind of utopia Clifford longs for, in which labor is aestheticized. But while the boy's barrel-organ appeals to Clifford's sensibilities, the other attraction he offers does not. This is the monkey that accompanies him, a creature Hawthorne marks by anthropomorphic signs of race, gender, and even sexuality. Described as having a "strangely man-like expression" on his face, "perform[ing] a bow and scrape" for passing pedestrians, and "holding out his small black palm" for money (*Gables*, 164), the monkey is only a thinly veiled caricature of a performative black masculinity, one Hawthorne seems to have expected his readers to recognize. While he does not explicitly "jump Jim Crow," his theatrical "bow and scrape," coupled with his "man-like expression" and his overtly "black" skin, make it clear that Hawthorne is again tapping into the charged images of the performing black male body so ubiquitous throughout antebellum mass culture, in particular within minstrel shows. Indeed, Clifford's location at the second-story balcony window during this performance, looking out for "matter to occupy his eye, and titillate, if not engross, his observation" (*Gables*, 160), makes it easy to read his position as analogous to Hawthorne's own within the National Theater in the summer of 1850, put off and yet fascinated by the working-class crowd around him. The connections between the monkey and the bawdy tropes of minstrelsy are even stronger when one realizes that the monkey is marked by an overdetermined sexuality which his Highland pant suit is literally unable to conceal. Characterized three times in two paragraphs for the "enormous tail" protruding beneath his suit pants (Hawthorne describes it as a "preposterous prolixity . . . too enormous to be decently concealed under his gabardine"), the monkey offers the sort of obscene caricature of black male sexuality so common within the period's minstrel performances. The effect of this on Clifford is dramatic:

having taken a "childish delight" in the Italian boy, he becomes "so shocked" by the "horrible ugliness" of the monkey that he "actually beg[ins] to shed tears" (Gables, 164).

But what is it that Clifford weeps over, exactly? My sense is that his tears are motivated in large part by the vagrant Italian boy who accompanies the monkey. For though the boy receives a sympathetic representation from Hawthorne, the Italian organ-grinder also stands in here for the masses of immigrants pouring into the major cities of the northeast during this period, especially the Italian and Irish (the latter represented rather overtly by Ned Higgins). For example, the metonymical relationship between highly visible street performers such as the organ-grinder and the broad range of ethnic immigrants entering the country at mid-century is something urban reformer Charles Loring Brace makes clear in several of his reflections on Italian street musicians in The Dangerous Classes of New York, a text published in 1872, but which includes essays composed by Brace from 1853 onwards. "They were, without exception, the dirtiest population I had met with," he says of the young boys. "So degraded was their type, and probably so mingled in North Italy with ancient Celtic blood, that their faces could hardly be distinguished from those of Irish poor children—an occasional liquid dark eye only betraying their nationality."[4] Such observations make it clear not only that delineation by category was a crucial component in the construction of racial difference, but also that for many, the immigrant population was often difficult to identify in terms of any single racial category. Accounts such as Brace's thus suggest that Hawthorne's use of a grotesque figure of blackness in relation to the vagrant Italian boy is part of a strategy by which to triangulate anxieties over differences of class and culture, both of which were apparently more difficult to negotiate and contain than was the stock figure of the performing and hyper-sexed black male.

The irony, however, is that the racial stereotypes Hawthorne draws on are themselves derived directly from working-class performances. Here, for example, Hawthorne's cloaked representation of the myth of an overdetermined black male sexuality seems drawn at least in part from the figure of the "black dandy" so often parodied by white minstrel performers during the period, with characters such as "Zip Coon" or "Dandy Jim." Usually depicted in the

---

4. Charles Loring Brace, The Dangerous Classes of New York, and Twenty Years Among Them (New York, 1872), 194. As various chroniclers of urban life in the antebellum northeast made clear, the Italian organ-grinder was a stock figure on the streets of most major cities in the region, organ-grinders' performances usually eliciting a vague social unease characterized by a sentimentalized mix of sympathy, guilt, and disgust. For a similar non-fictional account of street children during this period, see Lydia Maria Child, Letters from New York, 2d ed. (New York, 1845), 95–99.

role of a black male servant taking an absurd pride in his livery out-fit of long tailcoat and loud plaid pants, the black dandy was used to ridicule black male pretensions to class status, and often to par-ody similar pretensions by upwardly mobile white men.[5] But the black dandy also embodied anxieties over white male sexuality. This is perhaps best exemplified in the popular character "Dandy Jim," whose narcissism is neatly conveyed in the 1843 songster, "Dandy Jim, From Carolina," performed by Barney Williams. As the image on the cover of the songsheet makes clear, Dandy Jim, decked out in long tailcoat and cane, is pleasing to no one so much as himself. More telling still, the song lyrics also suggest that the image of himself is one that will multiply endlessly, as do Hepzibah's Jim Crow gingerbread men, throughout antebellum culture—a humor-ous scenario that by the song's end becomes overwhelming for at least one of the song's characters. Near the song's beginning we learn that "Miss Dinah" is so enamored of Dandy Jim that she changes her own name to "Dandy Jim From Carolina"; soon after-ward, she gives birth to a series of babies, each named "Dandy Jim," and each one exactly alike. "The every nigger she has had / Is the very image of ther [sic] dad," the song explains. "The preacher christened eight or nine / Young Dandy Jim from Caroline." But even this nod to Dandy Jim's potency is insufficient indication of his influence. In the closing lines we are told that the parson who has christened the babies is unable to deliver his sermon, in partic-ular because he is unable to clear his mind of Dandy Jim's name, and perhaps of his image as well. The result is that his parishioners are treated to a sermon which consists only of the recitation of the words "Dandy Jim."[6]

Dandy Jim thus tropes the notion of "reproduction" in several ways, both of which would have been chilling to the Pyncheons, if not to Hawthorne himself. For in addition to representing a figure of biological and sexual potency, he also suggests the overwhelming cultural reproduction of images of the black male body—images which, like Hepzibah's commodified Jim Crow gingerbread cookies, contain a threat to the cultural superiority of the aristocracy. The intersection of these concerns is captured in an article which J. S. Dwight reprinted from London in an 1852 issue of his *Journal*

5. As the black male servant Zeke puts it at the opening of Anna Cora Mowatt's 1845 hit play, *Fashion*, "Dere's a coat to take de eyes of all Broadway! Ah Missy, it am de fixin's dat make de natural *born* gemman. A liberry for ever!" Anna Cora Ogden Mowatt, *Fashion* (1845; reprint, New York, 1935), 5. These lines are echoed even more famously by the character Adolph in Stowe's *Uncle Tom's Cabin* (1852), whose habit of dressing himself up in the clothes of his indulgent owner, Augustine St. Clare, is explained away by the putatively humorous fact that "he has, at last, really mistaken himself for his master"; Harriet Beecher Stowe, *Uncle Tom's Cabin, or, Life Among the Lowly* (New York: Pen-guin Classics, 1986), 270.
6. Barney Williams, "Dandy Jim, From Carolina" (New York, 1843).

of Music. Describing a situation similar to that in which Dandy Jim revels, the author of the essay complains that "[t]hey infest our promenades and our concert halls like a colony of beetles. If we avoid their presence in the street or music-room, their names and designations stare us out of countenance from dead walls, boardings, lamp posts, and the interior of omnibuses."[7] Eric Lott suggests that complaints such as this make clear the notion that "[b]lacks were suddenly everywhere—captive countenances paradoxically on the loose, bringing dead walls to life and crowding the omnibuses" (*Love and Theft*, 99). But as Lott also points out, such images were complicated by the fact that many of them depicted working-class white men in blackface. A response such as that printed by Dwight in *The Journal of Music* thus suggests that the problem is not only the insistent representation and presence of blackness (though this seems troubling enough), but also the seizure of the public sphere by lower-class white men. Indeed, it's worth noting that one can't say with any certainty what the monkey's "real" race actually is. Is the monkey a figure for the performances of blackness offered by white men in blackface during the period, or is he a stand-in for an "actual" black man (and if so, is his performance a kind of "blackface" act, or is it something meant to convey his "innately" performative nature)? My sense is that it's impossible to say what kind of blackness we're being prompted to recognize. But the question itself is important, for at least provisionally it suggests that Hawthorne's negotiation of a black Otherness is bound up with the exhaustively stereotyped representations of black men offered within the popular culture of the period; indeed, it may be the case that for Hawthorne there is no distinction between the "real" and the "represented" of racial difference.

Such blurring between the real and the represented of blackness is also manifested somewhat dramatically by Hawthorne in a journal entry from 1838, one suggestively similar to his depiction of the Italian boy's monkey and Hepzibah's Jim Crow cookies. Describing a variety of working-class members of a crowd outside a commencement ceremony at Williams College, he turns to a description of a group of black men who are also part of the crowd. Here is his description of one of the men:

> I saw one old negro, a genuine specimen of the slave-negro, without any of the foppery of the race in our parts; an old fellow with a bag, I suppose of broken victuals, on his shoulders; and his pockets stuffed out at his hips with the like proven-

7. J. S. Dwight, "Negro Minstrelsy in London," *Journal of Music* 1:16 (1852): 62; cited by Lott, *Love and Theft*, 100. Subsequent references to Lott are cited parenthetically within the text.

der—full of grimaces, and ridiculous antics, laughing laughably, yet without affectation—then talking with a strange kind
of pathos, about the whippings he used to get, while he was a
slave—a queer thing of mere feeling, with some glimmering of
sense. (*American Notebooks*, 112)

More direct than his representation of the Italian boy's monkey,
Hawthorne's depiction of the "genuine specimen of the slave-
negro" reflects a cartoon version of black male subjectivity. Here,
this image seems intended to counter concerns of the sort raised by
the black dandy (whose type is referenced in Hawthorne's mention
of black "foppery"). "[L]aughing laughably," with pockets clown-
ishly over-stuffed, and engaged in a stock routine of "ridiculous antics," the man is depicted in terms of a two-dimensional aesthetic
which seems designed to provide Hawthorne with a kind of security
about his own more interior form of white self-possession—one
perhaps challenged by the sometimes raucous festivities of the
working-class members of the crowd at the Williams commencement.[8] Perversely, this form of assurance comes most powerfully in
the "strange kind of pathos" the man is said to display over "the
whippings he used to get." For though on the one hand the description seems to suggest a sympathy extended across lines of race
to one whose feelings might signal an internal—and perhaps
shared—form of suffering and pain, it should more accurately be
read as a sentimentalized and nostalgic return to the plantation
South, perhaps of the sort imagined in "Plantation Melodies" by
Stephen Foster such as "My Old Kentucky Home, Good-Night!"
(1853) or "Massa's In de Cold Ground" (1852)—products of mass
culture in which the representation of the black male body acts as
a reliable space of difference in the efforts of men like Hawthorne
to make their own relations to class and whiteness cohere.[9]

Such moments suggest that the various manifestations of an

8. For a useful discussion of the relation between the constantly repeated image of the
dancing black male body and the racial imaginary of white genteel men such as
Hawthorne, see Maurice Wallace, "The Autochoreography of an Ex-Snow Queen:
Dance, Desire, and the Black Masculine in Melvin Dixon's *Vanishing Rooms*," in *Novel
Gazing*, ed. Eve Kosofsky Sedgwick (Durham: Duke University Press, 1997), 379–400.
As Wallace points out in a discussion of the infamous description Dickens offers in
American Notes (1842) of the minstrel performer William Henry Lane (popularly known
as "Juba"), the dancing, performing body of the black male acts as the site wherein "a
bitter interracial conflict over sex and stereotype" has taken place in the negotiation of
modern masculinity, one pitting white objectification and fetishization versus the potentially decolonizing and "reappropriative power of dance" (381).
9. A similar combination of frivolity and seriousness informs Hawthorne's description of
another black man in the crowd at Williams College: "Then there was another gray old
negro, but of a different stamp, politic, sage, cautious, yet with boldness enough, talking
about the rights of his race, yet so as not to provoke his audience, discoursing of the advantages of living under laws—and the murders that might ensue, in that very assemblage, if there were no laws. In the midst of this deep wisdom, turning off the anger of a
half drunken fellow, by a merry retort, a leap in the air, and a negro's laugh" (*American
Notebooks*, 112).

"Africanist presence" populating *The House of the Seven Gables* are at least potentially unstable as fantasy structures for mediating between the different registers of class and culture Hawthorne sets in motion, in particular because they are so inextricably bound up with the production of mass culture. That much of this mass culture—whether minstrel shows or, as I will discuss in the next section, Holgrave's short stories—was itself produced by the lower classes only complicates all the more the cultural geography Hawthorne seeks to map in his novel. Clifford's tears are thus complex indeed. For, while they are framed as a problem of aesthetic sensibility and projected onto a performative black masculinity, they seem to have been shed for superiorities of class and culture whose fictions are unravelling in the complex representational space of cultural production at mid-century.

II. Reading Holgrave Writing: Mass-Market Mesmerism and Racial Appropriation

A still more complex example of Hawthorne's deployment of blackness in negotiating cultural and class struggle comes in the magazine story Holgrave has authored and which he reads to Phoebe Pyncheon late in the novel. Reproduced in its entirety within *The House of the Seven Gables*, the text-within-a-text provides background to the feud between the Maules, who have been dispossessed of their land, and the Pyncheons, who engineered this displacement by accusing Matthew Maule of practicing witchcraft. Set some forty years after the execution of the founding Maule, the story dramatizes the meeting between Young Matthew Maule, Holgrave's grandfather many times removed, and Gervayse Pyncheon, Phoebe's equally distant uncle. Tellingly, however, the story also provides significant commentary about the ways in which cultural production is bound up with categories not only of class and gender, but of race.

Prior to this reading, Holgrave has already been located on the outskirts of antebellum culture by Hepzibah, who has even "read a paragraph in a penny paper . . . accusing him of making a speech full of wild, disorganizing matter, at a meeting of his banditti-like associates" (*Gables*, 84). But Holgrave also inhabits an important position in terms of cultural production. As he explains to Phoebe upon learning that she has not read any of the fiction he has published,

> Well, such is literary fame! Yes, Miss Phoebe Pyncheon, among the multitude of my marvellous gifts I have that of writing stories; and my name has figured, I can assure you, on the covers of Graham and Godey, making as respectable an appearance,

for aught I could see, as any of the canonized bead-roll with which it is associated. In the humorous line, I am thought to have a very pretty way with me; and as for pathos, I am as provocative of tears as an onion. (*Gables*, 186)

Holgrave's magazine stories occupy space alongside more established writers, but even more importantly, they are manipulative of their readers' affective states. This is reflected not only in Holgrave's ability to produce tears in his readers, but more profoundly when he manages to mesmerize Phoebe by the very act of reading his magazine story to her. Here is how Hawthorne describes the moments immediately following Holgrave's reading:

> Holgrave gazed at her, as he rolled up his manuscript, and recognized an incipient stage of that curious psychological condition, which, as he himself had told Phoebe, he possessed more than an ordinary faculty of producing. A veil was beginning to be muffled about her in which she could behold only him, and live only in his thoughts and emotions. (*Gables*, 211)

What better description of the putatively regressive effects of mass culture during the antebellum period? Fairly clearly, the "drowsiness" Phoebe experiences (*Gables*, 211) is meant to provide a didactic lesson about the powers of mass culture. "I consider myself as having been very attentive," she says, "and, though I don't remember the incidents quite distinctly, yet I have an impression of a vast deal of trouble and calamity,—so, no doubt, the story will prove exceedingly attractive" (*Gables*, 212). Unable to recall the narrative "distinctly" yet judging the story by its sensational qualities of "trouble and calamity," Phoebe makes it clear that to be "very attentive" is for her a passive condition which leaves her vulnerable to the intrusion of the mass culture Holgrave represents. Her mesmerized state might thus be thought of in relation to the benumbed parson in the minstrel song about Dandy Jim; in each case, mass culture has a banalizing effect on the minds of those who encounter it, one that appears to leave its consumers vulnerable to bodily intrusion.

Such concerns over the powers of mass culture are why I find the racial conflicts enacted in Holgrave's story-within-a-story so important. In particular I am interested in the encounter Holgrave's gothic tale narrates between his ancestor Maule and "black Scipio," whom Holgrave describes as one of the black slaves whose "shining, sable face[s]" can be seen "bustling across" the "cheery" windows of the Pyncheon home (*Gables*, 191). The lines which I quote at the outset of this essay represent what I take to be one of the most significant cross-racial exchanges in antebellum literature: "What's that you mutter to yourself, Matthew Maule?" Scipio asks

after delivering a message asking Maule to come see Gervayse Pyncheon, the owner of the House of the Seven Gables. "And what for
do you look so black at me?" But Maule's response—"No matter,
darkey! . . . Do you think nobody is to look black but yourself?"—
has a meaning beyond the straightforward notion of looking angrily
at someone (*Gables*, 188). For Maule is also implying that to "look
black" is to bear the burden of class inferiority and of service in a
way that is racially marked, something about which he is reminded
by the basic—and to Maule highly insulting—fact that Scipio
should even be willing to address him in such a manner. Maule, in
other words, is claiming a position analogical to racial victimage,
one intended to highlight his felt sense of class oppression as he receives a summons to the House of the Seven Gables.

The ensuing visit which Maule makes to the front door of the
Pyncheon home might thus be read as the precursor episode
William Faulkner had in mind when creating the pivotal crisis in
the life of Thomas Sutpen in *Absalom, Absalom!* (1932)—the childhood moment when he is "barred" from the front door of the plantation Big House by the "monkey dressed nigger butler" who tells
him "never to come to that front door again but to go around to the
back."[1] As Hortense Spillers suggests in her reading of this scene,
Sutpen's rejection by the Big House slave forces upon him not only
the shocking recognition that he "has" "race," but, more disturbingly, that class and race are inextricably linked to his sense of
masculinity.[2] In Sutpen's case, this results in a variety of violences,
just as it does in the case of Maule, who, after gaining entrance to
the Pyncheon home, mesmerizes Alice Pyncheon in an action that
looks very much like a rape motivated by his emasculated class status. Pressing a "slow, ponderous, and invisible weight upon the
young maiden," Maule penetrates the spheres of her "unsullied purity," and places her "in a bondage more humiliating, a thousand-
fold, than that which binds its chains around the body" (*Gables*,
204, 203, 208). In what follows, Alice is forced by Maule to perform a variety of demeaning acts for him, including waiting on
Maule's bride the night of his wedding. But the most horrific of
these acts is a stereotypically working-class ethnic dance which
Maule repeatedly commands her to perform. Described as a "high-
paced jig, or hop-skip rigadoon, befitting the brisk lasses at a rustic
merry-making" (*Gables*, 209), the dance links Alice directly to the
sullied bodies of the Irish Ned Higgins and the vagrant Italian boy
outside of Clifford's balcony window, and suggests powerfully that
her mesmerization by Maule has left her tainted by the racialized

1. William Faulkner, *Absalom, Absalom!* (New York: Vintage International, 1986), 187, 188.
2. Hortense Spillers, "Who Cuts the Border?" in *Comparative American Identities*, ed.
Spillers (New York: Routledge, 1991), 10–14.

markings of class difference, much as Maule himself has been tainted by virtue of his working-class status.

Holgrave's Gothic short story thus poses an interpretive challenge. On the one hand, the text seems to enact the strategy of displacement Hawthorne utilizes throughout the novel, with Scipio's "Africanist presence" deployed mainly as a means of introducing race into the encounter between the Maules and the Pyncheons. Barring the door against Maule's entrance, Scipio demarcates the distinctions between upper-class and lower-class white blood so central to the class struggle between the two families; the "shining, sable faces" he and his fellow slaves offer to visitors such as Maule signal, *inter alia*, the "bustling" and "cheery" world of interior white self-possession from which Maule, like the young Thomas Sutpen, is excluded. Simultaneously, the encounter allows Hawthorne to stage Maule (and Maule to stage himself) as racially marked, a fact which seems intended to redirect the very real threat which both he *and* his descendant Holgrave pose into a more easily categorized and thus containable form of Otherness. This form of displacement is played out most dramatically in Alice's untimely and highly sentimentalized death by consumption. A fate brought on when, en route to Maule's wedding, her "gossamer white dress" becomes wet as she "[trod] the muddy sidewalks" of Maule's working-class neighborhood (*Gables*, 209), her death acts as a necessary escape from the racial taint of the lower classes—a fact which, again, suggests the need to displace the violent conflicts of class and culture represented in Holgrave's dangerously mesmeristic magazine story onto the threat of racial tainting.

But Holgrave as Gothic writer might also be thought of as posing a considerable threat, in particular because he seems so canny about racial distinctions of interiority and exteriority (what Young Matthew Maule refers to as the distinction between "looking" and actually "being") which are so troubling to the Pyncheons in their various efforts to maintain the integrity of an upper-class "whiteness." Projecting his antebellum present backward onto his ancestor's colonial past, Holgrave seems here to be deconstructing race as defined by citizen-subjects such as the Pyncheons. For what the exchange between Maule and Scipio once again suggests is that Hawthorne's racial imagination is circumscribed by basic tropes of minstrelsy and racial performance. It may be true that Maule's comment to Scipio about a shared "blackness" is motivated by the theft of his family's property by the Pyncheons, a loss of property symbolized by the "pure and virgin" body of Alice Pyncheon (*Gables*, 200), but his comment also signals a rather profound act of racial *appropriation*. Claiming blackness, Maule appropriates the absolute victimage of this category for its affective resonance; there is simply no more powerful metaphor for pain, abjection, and dis-possession in antebellum culture. Accordingly, in referring to him-self as "black," Maule is in effect blacking himself up in ways not unlike the white performers blacking themselves up to appear as characters such as Dandy Jim. Indeed, Scipio's very name, which is repeated throughout Holgrave's magazine story, is rarely offered without the race-fixing prefix "black" (as in "black Scipio"), a fact which has the double function of taking away what it enforces: Scipio is Other because he is "black," but his "blackness" is appro-priable in ways he is unable to control. Scipio, meanwhile, does not have the option of choosing whether or not to wear the sign of his abjection. And as suggested by the description of Scipio showing the "whites of his eyes" (*Gables*, 192) when Maule arrives at the Pyncheon front door, Scipio too is rendered in terms of a per-formed, minstrelized blackness, one that, like the blackness worn by the Italian boy's minstrel monkey, ends up undermining the no-tion of a stable black "presence" by which to measure white self-possession.

Holgrave's magazine story might thus be thought of as having taken on a life of its own. Rather than being a text which displaces differences of class onto racial difference, Holgrave's text suggests that the representation of race within *The House of the Seven Gables* is somewhat out of control. Nor should this be a surprise: extraordinarily canny about race but also extremely nervous about the intricate relations between race, class, and culture, Hawthorne appears to have found himself reliant upon fantasies of race pro-duced within a mass culture which itself worked consistently (if not always intentionally) to undermine the stability of race as a cate-gory. The result is that Hawthorne's novel, and Holgrave's story along with it, is inscribed within the problematic from which it seeks distance and security. No wonder there is such an odd ten-sion between Hawthorne's novel and Holgrave's story. Like a re-pressed form of cultural knowledge forcing its way to conscious enunciation, Holgrave's story makes its uncanny appearance within *The House of the Seven Gables* in order to tell Hawthorne (and his readers) what Hawthorne does not seem to want to know: that race could not be used as a reliable means of waging conflicts of class and culture, in particular because "race" was itself a fiction fre-quently manipulated by the very people and texts from whom and from which he sought to distance himself.

III. Cultural Vampirism and the End of "Whiteness"

The cultural violences enacted in Holgrave's story suggest that his unexpected actions in the novel's final pages—taking a daguerreotype of the just-deceased Judge Pyncheon and then proposing to the newly monied Phoebe—offer an important final commentary on the relations amongst race, class, and cultural production in *The House of the Seven Gables*. Critics have long pointed out that the marriage effectively ends the feud between the two families, and thus represents a disavowal of the political and imaginative possibilities Hawthorne opened up so suggestively with Holgrave's character. But, and as Cathy Davidson has pointed out, Hawthorne arrived at this scene only after considerable difficulty finishing the novel, a problem which seems to have begun after he wrote the scene in which Holgrave takes his post-mortem image of the dead Judge. Davidson suggests that during this period Hawthorne was facing "his own, direst apprehension about representation," concerns which extend to the ethical politics not only of artistic reproduction but also of subjectivity itself in the age of mechanical technologies such as the daguerreotype ("Photographs," 691).

I find this reading compelling, but I want to suggest what this particular scene might also imply about the connections between class and race I have been describing here. For Holgrave's photographing of the Judge's corpse represents an exchange not at all unlike that which occurs when he incapacitates Phoebe by reading his magazine story to her. Here, however, the transaction is much more violent, as, vampire-like, Holgrave utilizes another form of mass culture—the daguerreotype—in order to steal the Judge's image as "a pictorial record" for his own keeping (*Gables*, 302). "This is death!" exclaims Phoebe when she sees the image produced by Holgrave's creepy handiwork. "Judge Pyncheon dead!" But Holgrave's response makes it clear that Phoebe has experienced a certain, if momentary, confusion over the represented and the actual. "Such as there represented," he says to her, referring to the daguerreotype. "[H]e sits in the next room" (*Gables*, 302). Holgrave is being ironic, but his emphasis on the need to distinguish between the reproduced image of Judge Pyncheon and his actual corpse is telling, for it is a reminder that for many the daguerreotype raised just such questions. Indeed, as early commentators on the new technology of photography often suggested, the photographer was often suspected of having stolen the actual soul of the subject whose image had been taken.[3] I would suggest that Hawthorne participates in this argument, inasmuch as his apparent fascination with forms of mass culture such as the daguerreotype spills over into a certain amount of anxiety. Indeed, this is why the scene at

---

3. As Oliver Wendell Holmes put it in the *Atlantic Monthly* in 1859, the photographer was a "great white hunter" who gathered the images of his quarry like the head and skins of his prey; Oliver Wendell Holmes, "The Stereoscope and the Stereograph," *Atlantic Monthly* (1859): 162, cited by Davidson, 676.

the novel's end, in which Holgrave presses a secret spring which knocks the portrait of Judge Pyncheon "face downward on the floor" of the Pyncheon home, is so significant (*Gables*, 316). The image of the fallen portrait suggests the decline of the elite aesthetic culture Hawthorne alternately mocks and clings to in characters such as Clifford and Alice Pyncheon. Instead, that moment has given way to culture as represented in the arrival of the writer-daguerreotypist Holgrave to the House of the Seven Gables.

But what is it that Holgrave wants with an image of the dead Judge Pyncheon? My suggestion is that a clue to at least a portion of his motivation can be found in the description near the novel's end of the dead Judge, in which Hawthorne turns to an unexpected discussion of the actual pigmentation of the Judge's skin as he sits still upright in his chair in the parlor. As he explains,

> The gloom has not entered from without. . . . The judge's face, indeed, rigid, and *singularly white*, refuses to melt into this universal solvent. . . . Has it yet vanished? No!—yes!—not quite! And there is still the *swarthy whiteness*—we shall venture to marry these *ill-agreeing words*—the *swarthy whiteness* of the Judge's face. The features are all gone. There is only *the paleness* of them left. And how looks it now? There is no window! There is no face! An infinite, inscrutable blackness has annihilated sight! Where is our universe? All crumbled away from us. (*Gables*, 276, emphasis added)

At once playfully overstated and remarkably serious, the passage is perhaps Hawthorne's most profound effort to address the issue of race in the novel. For what he provides here is a last, lingering moment in the history of the "Anglo-Saxon" aristocracy the Pyncheons represent. Moving from "singularly white" to an "ill-agreeing" state of "swarthy whiteness" to a featureless "paleness," Judge Pyncheon's face seems here to be the face of elitist American culture "itself." Increasingly diluted by differences of class and race, that face appears here to reflect a failed last moment in the maintenance of upper-class whiteness.

Holgrave's photographic "vamping" of the Judge might thus be read as a rather radical act of *racial* appropriation. For, while seizing the Judge's "soul," Holgrave should also be thought of as appropriating that which is most dear to those of the Judge's class—the conception of white racial purity which the protective walls of high culture have been erected to protect. It might be said, in other words, that captured on the magically depthless surface of Holgrave's daguerreotype plate is the image of the Pyncheons' lost whiteness "itself," merged rather dramatically now with a document of the mass culture about which, as I have been arguing, Hawthorne himself was so uneasy.

Hawthorne's repeated efforts to displace class difference onto racial difference thus seem to have arrived at something of a dead end near the novel's conclusion. For Holgrave's actions here suggest rather powerfully that race is indeed a fiction, something that can be put on and taken off (or, more disturbingly, appropriated vampirically from unwitting victims). More telling still, Holgrave seems to be indicating that mass culture is the vehicle through which the fictional nature of race is most readily suggested; indeed, in Holgrave's case, mass culture is itself the vehicle through which a kind of racial "theft" might even be pulled off. Perhaps this is what Hawthorne found so unsettling while standing amongst the "Hanover-street shop-men" and "mechanics" at the National Theater in 1850—perhaps he felt that their form of consumption might have a tainting effect on him, one not unlike that which he mocks in representing Hepzibah's horror over the "sordid stain" she receives from her contact with Ned Higgins's "copper-coin." Hawthorne's recourse in his journal entry to a fantasy about "African blood" provides a temporary buffer against such concerns, but in *The House of the Seven Gables*, blackness, plucked from the shape-shifting world of mass culture over which Holgrave presides, turns out to be just as destabilizing a presence as Holgrave himself. The result is that Hawthorne finds himself forced to contain Holgrave in the only way he knows how: by making him more like himself and the other members of the upper middle class who found class decline and racial degeneracy to be related subjects. And this, of course, is accomplished by marrying Holgrave into the Pyncheon family. On the one hand, the marriage suggests the absorption of working-class whiteness into the now refreshed Pyncheon line, and the effacement of class difference altogether. But what is ironic here, of course, is that, in joining the Pyncheon house of culture, Holgrave brings with him the very technologies of mass culture that have acted as agents of racial instability throughout the text. Hawthorne's imagined resolution thus has its nightmarish underbelly. For like a true vampire, Holgrave, once invited across the threshold of his victim's habitation, will never leave. Instead, the House of the Seven Gables (as well as the novel of the same name) will continue to be haunted by the racial, social, and cultural differences that it has sought, generation after generation, to repress and displace—Hawthorne's imagined version of an Africanist presence notwithstanding.

AMY SCHRAGER LANG

From Home, in the Better Sense:
The Model Woman, the Middle Class, and
the Harmony of Interests†

* * *

The problem of *The House of the Seven Gables* is how to make a "home" in the ruins of the House of Pyncheon—how, that is, to release the present from the haunting crimes of class that have entangled Pyncheons and Maules since that "by-gone" age when the aristocratic Colonel Pyncheon, through a combination of "personal influence," "iron will," and legal manipulation, stole the land of the obscure artisan Matthew Maule and called down upon his lineage the curse of choking to death on their own "blood," on their dynastic pretensions. The confusion that leads Clifford Pyncheon to conflate "roof and hearth-stone," terms held to "embody something sacred," and "real estate . . . the broad foundation on which nearly all of the guilt of this world rests"[1] is arguably the confusion the novel aims to resolve. Setting the "private and domestic view" of women against a masculine public one, the truth of "pencil sketches that pass from hand to hand" against the false appearances of "portraits intended for engraving," *The House of the Seven Gables*, like *The Lamplighter*, proposes that the answer to class conflict lies in the purified relations of gender.

That, in any case, is the implication of the novel's notoriously unsatisfactory ending. The marriage of Hawthorne's model woman and her promising young man unwrites the dark history of the Pyncheons and the Maules: the hereditary curse is broken, the crimes of class are transcended, and the energy of a new democratic age is celebrated in the marriage of the versatile and idealistic Holgrave to the competent Phoebe. The fall of the House of Pyncheon is complete, down to the spontaneous destruction of the portrait of its progenitor, and in its place rises a vision of "home." Just as the virtues of domesticity replace the value of property and as conjugal

---

† From *The Syntax of Class: Writing Inequality in Nineteenth-Century American Literature*, pp. 30–41. Copyright © 2003 by Princeton University Press. Reprinted by permission of Princeton University Press. [This reading of Hawthorne's *The House of the Seven Gables* is taken from a larger chapter on class and social reform in *House* and Maria Cummins's popular domestic novel of 1854, *The Lamplighter*. The title phrase *Home, in the Better Sense*, comes from an antebellum reformer, who patronizingly stated about the urban poor, "Homes—in the better sense—they never know" (quoted in Christine Stansell, *City of Women: Sex and Class in New York, 1789–1860* [1987], 202—editor's note.] All following notes are Lang's.

1. Nathaniel Hawthorne, *The House of the Seven Gables* (1851; Columbus: Ohio State University Press, 1965), 263. Hereafter cited parenthetically in the text.

love supplants patrilineage, so the newly constituted Pyncheon-Maule family, harmonizing all interests by its interclass character, will, we are led to believe, sweep away the last vestiges of "ancient prejudice." Lest we doubt this outcome, the newly harmonious relationship of the classes is echoed in the "strain of music" provided by the spirit of "sweet Alice Pyncheon." As the music swells, the new lovers and their antiquated cousins depart the death-ridden mansion to take up residence, "for the present," in the "elegant country-seat" they have conveniently inherited from Jaffrey Pyncheon, the avatar of the family's evil genius.

Other signs, however, are less auspicious: the Pyncheon elm whispers "unintelligible prophecies," and Maule's Well throws up "kaleidoscopic pictures" of the future that only a "gifted eye" can see. The fate of the conjugal family is, as T. Walter Herbert has convincingly shown, ambiguous at best.[2] And so too is the capacity of the unnamed middle class it exemplifies to unwrite the history of class. The trouble with the ending of *The House of the Seven Gables* is voiced by one of those rough "laboring men" whose function throughout is to comment on the Pyncheons' activities: "Well, Dixey . . . what do you think of this? My wife kept a cent-shop . . . and lost five dollars on her outlay. Old Maid Pyncheon has been in trade just about as long and rides off in her carriage with a couple of hundred thousand—reckoning her share, and Clifford's and Phoebe's—and some say twice as much! If you choose to call it luck, it is all very well; but if we are to take it as the will of Providence, why, I can't exactly fathom it!" (318). Of course, "Old Maid Pyncheon" is not "in trade," nor is her newly acquired wealth the product of her labor. Nevertheless, Dixie's friend has a point: the "lower classes," as Hepzibah styles them, seem always to lose on their investments, while the aristocracy, whose demise the novel ostensibly recounts, are fortuitously saved from poverty, not by the "will of Providence" but by patrilineal inheritance. Spoken with bemusement but without "hostility"—that "only real abasement of the poor"—the laborer's aside marks the limits of the social transformation that separates the present from that "by-gone" time when the "aristocracy could venture to be proud, and the low were content to be abased" or at least "kept their resentments within their own breasts" (25).

In the new age of physical and economic mobility, of endlessly fluctuating fortune, rank has lost its saliency. As Holgrave explains to Hepzibah, while urging, with "half-hidden sarcasm," the merits of abandoning the "circle of gentility" and joining instead in "the united struggle of mankind" (45) with "necessity" (44), "these

2. T. Walter Herbert, *Dearest Beloved: The Hawthornes and the Making of the Middle Class* (Berkeley: University of California Press, 1993), chapter 6.

names of gentleman and lady" belong to "the past history of the world" (45). In the present, there are only men and women. The plodding tradesman and the "laborer in his leather jerkin" (12) are no longer remanded to the kitchen. Instead, they, along with the "hard, vulgar, keen, busy, hackneyed New England" women (48) who are their wives, their "urchin" children, the occasional Italian organ-grinder, and the sage but penurious Uncle Venner, rub shoulders with the gentry in the streets and feel free to comment on the affairs of their social betters.

But the new heterogeneity of the once "fashionable quarter" of Pyncheon Street does not mean that distinctions of wealth and power have fallen away. In the democratic present of the novel, "amid the fluctuating waves" that characterize social and economic life, the cunning performance of a false equality by the rich has replaced aristocratic arrogance. The "free and hearty manner" of a Jaffrey Pyncheon toward those more "humble" than himself bespeaks "a haughty consciousness of his advantages, as irrefragably as if he had marched forth, preceded by a troop of lackeys to clear the way" (130). Nevertheless, there is a difference between the old and the new: "hereditary" nobility is gone; "rank," now merely "the grosser substance of wealth and a splendid establishment," has "no spiritual existence after the death of these" (38). But the conventional distinction between the persistence of rank and the transitory character of class contributes in no small way to the laboring man's perplexity. The "public honors" and the political influence wielded by a Jaffrey Pyncheon cannot be bequeathed to his heirs; the "spiritual" substance of his status dies with him. But the actual wealth out of which it grows and to which it contributes, passed on to the next generation, both reifies the divide between rich and poor and ensures its continuance. The performance of social equality that characterizes the new democratic age constitutes a change in form but not substance; it allows the laboring man freely to voice his puzzlement, but it in no way alters the material relationship between himself and the Pyncheons. His family is still out five dollars while theirs inherits a hundred thousand.

Considered from the vantage point of the laboring man, the new social order differs from the old largely by virtue of its greater mystification. Whereas aristocratic privilege and the concomitant language of rank once provided a plausible account of social and economic difference, the persistence of sharp divisions of poverty and wealth into the new democratic age is, as the laboring man makes clear, unfathomable—and, the narrator hints, more dangerous in direct proportion to its inexplicableness. The contemptuous familiarity with which the "lower class" patrons of Hepzibah's cent shop address the impoverished gentlewoman and the hostility it elicits in her—toward them and, paradoxically, toward the idle rich among whom she can no longer count herself—stand as evidence of her absurdly outdated aristocratic pretensions. But, like Holgrave's "half-hidden sarcasm" and Judge Pyncheon's patronizing smile, they also suggest that neither the arrogance of the rich nor the rage of the poor can be safely relegated to the past.

In fact, the staging and restaging of the "crimes" of the Pyncheons and the Maules has the effect of bringing those crimes into the present of the novel, of reminding us not only of the extension of their consequences into the present but of the present potential for their repetition. That is to say, it is not merely guilt that persists into the present but also inequality, and insofar as this is the case, neither the depredations of the rich nor the hostility of the poor can be wholly contained in the past. The Pyncheon "family-mansion," built on the very "spot first covered by the log-built hut of Matthew Maule" (9), in which nearly all the action of the novel, such as it is, takes place, instantiates class conflict both because it gives material form to the expropriation of the land—the "home"—of the Maules and because its siting affords the "ghost" of the dead wizard "a kind of privilege to haunt its . . . apartments" (9). The house of the seven gables is, then, the locus of a conflict between wealth and poverty, prominence and obscurity, that, unresolved and apparently unresolvable,[3] binds generation after generation of Pyncheons and Maules to one another.

Generation after generation of male Pyncheons and Maules, that is: Colonel Pyncheon, who "[wore] out three wives" (123), and the "wizard" Matthew Maule, whose wife is nowhere to be seen; the effete and apparently widowed Gervayse Pyncheon and the virile bachelor carpenter Matthew Maule; Jaffrey Pyncheon, whose wife "got her death-blow in the honey-moon" (123), and the unmarried Holgrave. Like Dimmesdale and Chillingworth in *The Scarlet Letter*, who are united by a hatred that is indistinguishable from love in its "intimacy and heart-knowledge," in its "passionate" need for its object,[4] these men are irrevocably bound together in an endless reenactment and recital of the crimes of their forebears. Each of them both possessed and possessor, they are obsessively involved with one another. Colonel Pyncheon not only occupies the home-site of Matthew Maule, as Maule's ghost occupies his, but engages

---

3. Possible resolutions of the conflict are figured—and thwarted—again and again in the novel. The crime for which Clifford Pyncheon goes to jail originates in the desire of his uncle, to restore the Maules' property and end the curse; similarly, the exchange agreed upon by Gervayse Pyncheon and Matthew Maule generations previously is thwarted ultimately by their methods.

4. For a discussion of Dimmesdale and Chillingworth's relationship, see Lora Romero, *Home Fronts: Domesticity and Its Critics in the Antebellum United States* (Durham: Duke University Press, 1997), chapter 5.

Maule's son as its "architect"; Gervayse and the carpenter Maule conspire together, however uneasily, in the sacrifice of Alice Pyncheon; Holgrave, haunting the House of Pyncheon, presents himself to Phoebe by offering a daguerreotype of Jaffrey Pyncheon and declares his love for her only when Jaffrey is safely dead. I do not mean to imply a homoerotic connection here but rather to propose that male homosociality defines class conflict, that class conflict is offered as an intense form of relationship between men.

Neither the intensity of male entanglement nor the absence of women, as Eve Kosofsky Sedgwick suggests in the course of her exploration of the male-male-female erotic triangle, however, renders women inconsequential to this structure. On the contrary, as Sedgwick has argued, "the status of women, and the whole question of arrangements between genders, is deeply and inescapably inscribed in the structure even of relationships that seem to exclude women—even in male homosocial/homosexual relationships." The "inherent and potentially active structural congruence" between male homosociality and "the structures for maintaining and transmitting patriarchal power,"[5] to which she alludes, demands women for its expression. Illuminating as is Sedgwick's paradigm of a sexual rivalry in which men use a woman as the "conduit" for their keen interest in one another, I want to extend its terms in a direction intimated but not explored by Sedgwick. For the ambiguous status of the woman, as property and as sexual object, suggests her availability as the conduit for a class rivalry that, like sexual competition, binds men to one another. It is not only that the proper circulation of women in lawful alliance, like the "healthy circulation of property," must be accomplished in *The House of the Seven Gables*, as Teresa Goddu has rightly suggested.[6] The relations of inequality between men must be mediated by way of those alliances. Triangulated through the figure of the model woman, the apparently antithetical interests of men of different conditions can be harmonized—but only insofar as that woman's mediatory function vis-à-vis men and the mediatory function of the middle class she serves vis-à-vis extremes of wealth and poverty are collapsed into one.

Logically, then, "Alice Pyncheon," Holgrave's fiction of the laboring man's revenge, occupies a central position in *The House of the Seven Gables*. A powerful cautionary tale, it plays out the unsuccessful negotiation of class interests through a woman whose

5. Eve Kosofsky Sedgwick, *Between Men: English Literature and Male Homosocial Desire* (New York: Columbia University Press, 1985), 25.
6. Teresa Goddu, "The Circulation of Women in *The House of the Seven Gables*," *Studies in the Novel* 22, no. 1 (1991): 119–27.

failure, as woman and therefore as medium, ensures tragedy. It provides, moreover, both an intermediate and an alternative account of the conflict between Pyncheons and Maules. Unlike the "legendary" account of the original conflict offered by the narrator in the prefatory first chapter, the interpolated story of Alice Pyncheon, ironically intended for "Graham or Godey"—women's magazines "programmatically dedicated to advancing the middle class and its values"[7]—is set in the eighteenth century and written by the last descendant of the Maules. Complicating the seventeenth-century story of land theft and wizardry—material and supernatural possession—by introducing sexual possession as the metaphor for these, "Alice Pyncheon" anticipates the importance of Phoebe, its protagonist's nineteenth-century descendant, as the figure of social harmony. In fact, it is precisely in the systematic *correction* of Alice's story that Phoebe's function becomes most clear.

One critical account of this correction proposes that the cross-class sexual attraction between plebeian Matthew Maule and aristocratic Alice Pyncheon, unacceptable in a pre-Revolutionary context, is redeemed in democratic times by the marriage of Holgrave and Phoebe. But Holgrave's fantasy of the revenge of the lower classes is far more complicated than this account suggests. The "bitterness" at "hereditary wrong" that metaphorically turns Matthew Maule's face as "black" as that of Scipio, the "black servant" who delivers Gervayse's summons, is matched by the hauteur with which the "foreign bred" Gervayse, a man of "artificial refinement," receives the "low carpenter-man" from whom he hopes to purchase the secret of the lost deed to Waldo Country that he believes will ensure his fortune. As Holgrave tells it, every detail of the story—from the expensive "English sea-coal" Gervayse burns in his fireplace to his lace ruffles and embroidered vest, his French coffee, his Venetian antiques, and the Claude landscape that adorns his wall—exploits the difference between the Old World and the New to heighten the contrast between the social circumstances of Maule and Pyncheon. The encounter between the carpenter and the would-be "Earl of Waldo"—and Holgrave's fictional account of it—is fraught with class hostility, rendered in the conventional terms of the eighteenth century: bitterly identifying himself as the "grandson of the rightful proprietor of the soil" (194), the "brazen" Matthew Maule refuses to enter the house through the servant's door or to await Gervayse's convenience. Pyncheon, in turn, explains to him, with "haughty composure," that "A gentleman, before seeking intercourse with a person of your station and habits,

7. Nina Baym, *Novels, Readers, and Reviewers: Responses to Fiction in Antebellum America* (Ithaca: Cornell University Press, 1984), 210.

will first consider whether the urgency of the end may compensate for the disagreeableness of the means" (197).

Despite Maule's "stiff" pride and Pyncheon's nonchalant arrogance, despite the hypermasculinity of the one and the effeminacy of the other, the two men strike a bargain: restitution of Maule's land in exchange for information leading to the recovery of the missing deed. Only, however, by means of an alternative exchange of property, through the "clear, crystal medium" of the virginal Alice Pyncheon, can this transaction be consummated. Unlike Phoebe, however, Alice is no model woman, although the "tender capabilities" of her sex are latent in her. She is, on the contrary, a "lady born . . . set apart from the world's vulgar mass by a certain gentle and cold stateliness" (201). Her cool appraisal of the comely Matthew Maule—the "witchcraft" of whose eyes, we are told, has not hitherto escaped the notice of "the petticoated ones" (189)— fuels his hostility and provokes what can only, given its highly sexualized language, be understood as a rape. His "evil potency" breaching the "sphere" of her womanhood, the "barriers" she believes unassailable, Maule, "standing erect" with his carpenter's rule "protrud[ing]" from his pocket, takes "possession" of Alice while her father averts his eyes.

Given the implicit sexual violence of this account, it is not surprising that Alice fails as a medium: her "pure and virgin intelligence" violated, she can provide no clue to the whereabouts of the missing deed. More important, however, the account of Alice's "possession" by Maule, suggesting as it does her unconscious complicity in her own violation, points to her failure as a woman. The "preservative force of womanhood" that should render her "impenetrable" is "betrayed by a treachery within" (203), by the "artistic admiration" (201), at once disdainful and desirous, that provokes Maule to vengeance. That betrayal of self, in turn, manifests itself in precisely the terms familiar from domestic fiction. Alice suffers from a complete loss of "self-control"; "possessed" by Maule, she is lost to herself. To lose "self-control," as novels like *The Lamplighter* make clear, is to lose the quality that most essentially characterizes the true woman and the one that crucially enables her mediatory role.

Alice is in equal parts the victim of the men who exploit her to negotiate an accommodation of their interests—a martyr to her father's desire to measure his land "by miles, instead of acres" (208) and the carpenter's "hereditary resentments" (195)—and of her own fatal willingness to pit "woman's might" against man's. Betrayed by her father and Maule and compromised by her ambiguous interest in the carpenter, she is doomed to live out her days in "humiliating" spiritual bondage and sexual thrall to Matthew

Maule, who claims absolute possession of her—"she is fairly mine" (208)—though he leaves her in the "keeping" of her father. The effect of this possession, of her violation, is to exclude her from the office of woman; "So lost from self-control" is she that she deems it "a sin to marry" (209). But the lack of self-control that renders marriage a "sin" in her eyes is not the only or perhaps even the greatest obstacle to a lawful union: already "possessed" by a man, she is by definition unmarriageable. It makes sense, then, that Alice can be awakened from "her enchanted sleep" (209) only when Maule himself marries and takes legal possession of another woman, thus completing Alice's humiliation. Seduced and abandoned, Alice is released from bondage not to marry but—in the tradition of the eighteenth-century seduction tales it echoes—to die, "penitent of her one earthly sin, and proud no more!" (210). In Holgrave's rendering of her, Alice is, Clarissa-like, the appropriate heroine of her time as likewise is her descendant Phoebe.

In losing the self-control requisite to marriage, what Alice loses is the capacity to make a "home," the capacity most emphatically present in her descendant Phoebe, whose first act on the morning after her fortuitous arrival at the house of the seven gables is to "reclaim" the "waste, cheerless, and dusky chamber" (72) in which she has spent the night. Already possessed of the domestic skill Gerty must acquire just as she already epitomizes middle-class virtue, Phoebe, with "a touch here, and another there" (72), a vase of white roses and a judicious rearrangement of curtains and furniture, transforms the gloomy room into a "kindly and hospitable" one, and what is more, purifies it "of all former evil and sorrow by her sweet breath and happy thoughts" (72). The "process" of Phoebe's domestic art, the narrator tells us, is "impossible" to describe (72), but its effect is to make "a home about her" (141) wherever she goes.

And this is lucky since Phoebe needs a home, although she is no orphan. Displaced by her widowed mother's remarriage, she is nonetheless emphatically her mother's daughter, her "knack" for the domestic, like her skill at gardening and shopkeeping, transmitted entirely through her "mother's blood" (78). No foreign-born exotic but a native daughter of New England, Phoebe is everything Alice is not. Rather than a "born lady," she is the product of an interclass marriage between one of the Pyncheon cousins and a "young woman of no family or property" (24), from whom she "takes everything" (79). Indeed, in the estimation of her cousin Hepzibah, Phoebe is "no Pyncheon," despite her name, precisely as and because she is no "lady" (79). She is, instead, a "woman" and an "angel," "the example of feminine grace and availability combined, in a state of society, if there were any such, where ladies did not exist" (80). As one contemporary British reviewer astutely observed, Phoebe "must stand for the Middle Classes of Society, to whom has been committed by Providence the mission of social reconciliation which, once completed, the disunited are joined."[8]

Exhibiting all the virtues of middle-class femininity, Phoebe is imported directly from the domestic universe of works like *The Lamplighter* into the gothic world of the house of the seven gables just in time to avert the crisis of social classification prompted by her cousin Hepzibah's impoverishment. Phoebe's strategic arrival plays out in narrative form her larger ideological function. Reduced by necessity to engaging in trade, the tragicomic Hepzibah is the type of the "immemorial lady" (38) who feeds on "aristocratic reminiscences" (37) and believes that "a lady's hand soils itself irremediably by doing aught for bread" (37). Driven from her "strict seclusion" (31) into the "world's astonished gaze" (40) as the keeper of a cent shop, Hepzibah is both shamed and baffled to discover that not only the substance but the very terms of her identity have lost their meaning in the new social order. In the "republican country" in which she hopes to eke out a living, the "names of gentleman and lady," as Holgrave informs her, imply not "privilege, but restriction," but labor, he insists, will transform her from a "lady" into what is better, a "true woman" (45). And indeed the first copper coin she puts in the till has a galvanic effect, seeming to demolish in an instant "the structure of ancient aristocracy" (51). But the naturalized language of gender that replaces the ancient distinctions of rank in the new democratic age holds no promise for the antiquated Hepzibah, whose nearsightedness renders the present barely visible. Instead, Phoebe, arriving at the very moment of Hepzibah's putative transformation from "patrician lady" to "plebeian woman," relieves her cousin of the necessity of giving up her aristocratic delusions by taking over the housekeeping and the cent shop and by providing an alternative to both patrician and plebeian.

A Pyncheon without the aristocratic airs of her relatives, a New England housekeeper devoid of vulgarity, Phoebe in her perfect womanhood perfectly mediates between lower and upper classes. And she does so not only symbolically but literally insofar as she moves effortlessly[9] and unselfconsciously between the cent shop, the garden, the street, and the Pyncheon mansion, retaining her own identity intact. "Admirably in keeping with herself, and never

---

8. Quoted from *Tait's Edinburgh Magazine* in Milton R. Stern's introduction to Hawthorne's *The House of the Seven Gables* (New York: Viking Penguin, 1981), xxx.
9. For one reading of effortless labor in *Seven Gables*, see Gillian Brown, *Domestic Individualism: Imagining Self in Nineteenth-Century America* (Berkeley: University of California Press, 1990), chapter 3.

jarr[ing] against surrounding circumstances" (80), Phoebe accomplishes what domestic fiction teaches us only the model woman can: she creates about her "that very sphere which the outcast, the prisoner, the potentate, the wretch beneath mankind, the wretch aside from it, or the wretch above it, instinctively pines after—a home!" (141). Her sympathetic presence harmonizes all differences, assuring everyone from outcast to social pariah to potentate that his "place was good in the whole sympathetic chain of human nature" (141).

In contrast to Alice's aloofness, Phoebe's "poise" reflects a perfect command of the self and protects her from the sexual and spiritual incursions to which Alice falls prey. Recoiling in modesty from Jaffrey Pyncheon's kiss, in which "the man, the sex . . . was entirely too prominent" (118), and unconsciously deflecting Clifford's sexual interest by her innocence, Phoebe is betrayed by no "treachery within." Even when she is mesmerized by Holgrave's tale of Alice Pyncheon—when with "one wave of his hand and a corresponding effort of his will, he could complete his mastery over Phoebe's yet free and virgin spirit" (212)—her "individuality" and the reverence it elicits prevent Holgrave from exercising his power. Phoebe's "individuality" and, as we learn, Holgrave's "integrity" are alike evidence of the unified self that averts disaster. If Phoebe, unlike Alice, suffers no internal division, so too does Holgrave, unlike Matthew Maule, resist the temptation to "acquire empire" over a Pyncheon. Since they are driven neither by arrogance nor by rage, their responses, at this moment, originate neither in history nor in class but in "nature," that is, in gender. Just as Phoebe is utterly at home wherever she is, so Holgrave, despite being "homeless," has "never lost his identity" or "violated the innermost man" (177).

As others have observed, Holgrave bears the characteristics of the propertyless, "self-dependent" young men of the mid–nineteenth century.[1] Proud of his humble origins and full of faith in "man's brightening destiny" and his own "inward strength" (180), Holgrave joins firmness of character to "personal ambition" and generosity of spirit, radical philosophy to "practical experience," "faith" to "infidelity" (181). Restless and unsettled, he is nothing if not another promising young man like Gerty's Willie. "In a country where everything is free to the hand that can grasp it," "the world's prizes" are, if not assured, at least "within his reach" (181).

But if Holgrave is a version of the hardworking and upright Willie Sullivans of domestic fiction, as Phoebe is a version of Gerty, he is nonetheless a far more ambiguous figure. Whereas Willie

---

1. See Walter Benn Michaels, *The Gold Standard and the Logic of Naturalism* (Berkeley: University of California, 1987), 97, and Herbert, *Dearest Beloved*, 100.

straightforwardly strives to recover the social and economic position his family has lost with the death of his father, Holgrave, by
contrast, admits no ambition but that of the social reformer. Asso-
ciating with Fourierists, "community-men and come outers," and
"cross-looking philanthropists," he gives speeches "full of wild and
disorganizing matter" (84). An "enthusiast," as the narrator insists
young men should be, his energies are directed not toward individual success but toward ushering in a "golden era," an end to the
"old, bad way," the "lifeless institutions" of the "rotten Past" (179).
Like other of Hawthorne's young men, Holgrave reveals in his radical reformism a naive rejection of history, a desire to free the present from the domination of the past, to make everything anew. In
the context of Seven Gables this impulse makes a particular kind of
sense, for as the last descendant of Matthew Maule, Holgrave is
the product of a history of exploitation, of a slow decline into obscurity. But the desire to erase the past is in him inextricably and
paradoxically bound to a desire to avenge it; the impulse toward
utopian reform is compromised by the impulse toward revenge.
Thus Holgrave's repudiation of the house of the seven gables as the
quintessential expression of an "odious and abominable Past" (184)
and his decision to reside in it represent not simple perversity,
as Phoebe suspects, but the contradiction at the heart of his radicalism—a contradiction likewise inscribed in his change of name,
undertaken either to free himself of the burden of the Maule-
Pyncheon history or to facilitate his tenancy in the house of the
seven gables. Haunting the House of Pyncheon, Holgrave plays
the role history has bequeathed him even as he calls for an end to
the domination of the present by the past.

In the narrow world of The House of the Seven Gables, the historical conflict between rich and poor devolves into the conflict between Pyncheon and Maule; the persistence of social inequality is
disguised as the ongoing consequence of individual crime. Thus
Holgrave's laudable ambition for social justice, shaped though it
presumably is by his class history, cannot be disentangled from the
desire for private revenge that is the legacy of his family history. His
passionate argument against the permanence of houses, dynastic
and otherwise, is at once a broad argument against inherited wealth
and status and an argument against the Pyncheons' particular
claim to what he legitimately regards as his own inheritance.

Holgrave's unarticulated quarrel with Jaffrey, the heir to the Pyncheon fortune whose daguerreotype he carries, privatizes the problem of social justice and allows for its resolution through the figure
of the model woman. In lieu of the class conflict that binds men
together, the romance's ending offers the heterosexual union of

Maule and Pyncheon, the interclass marriage of Phoebe, who is "no Pyncheon," and Holgrave, who is equally no Maule. Holgrave's restless reformism, his "oscillation," is checked by her "poise," and his world is renovated not by social revolution but by love. Joining Phoebe on her "quiet path," Holgrave trades his utopian dreams for domestic bliss and, of course, in this way achieves them too, at least for himself. The answer to the crimes of history encoded in the decrepit house of the seven gables lies in the prospect of home. Understood in this way, *The House of the Seven Gables*, like *The Lamplighter*, offers home in the better sense—in fact, a home where changes never come, built of stone and conforming to the "peaceful practice of society" (307)—as the site of the harmonious resolution of class difference through gender.

But if the conclusion of *The Lamplighter* leaves in abeyance the question of whether harmony lies in the new world of middle-class domesticity or simply in a reprise of the past, the ending of *The House of the Seven Gables* is even more problematic. Seen one way, the final chapter of *The House of the Seven Gables* simply restores justice of a sort: the Maules get their land back, and the Pyncheons recover their deed. The restitution of one and the discovery of the other lay to rest the crimes of the past. With the death of Jaffrey Pyncheon, the "young giant" of the present is no longer "compelled to waste all his strength in carrying about the corpse of the old giant, his grandfather" (182). History, and with it the conflicting interests of class, comes to an end in a new Eden of love, which, however individual and however transitory, is the only adumbration of utopia in a world renewed at best by "patchwork."

But Holgrave does not simply marry his model woman and regain his land: marriage brings him not only the property the Maules have lost but interest on that property. Through Phoebe, Holgrave inherits Maule's homesite and the house of the seven gables as well as Judge Pyncheon's country estate and his fortune. Just as the new Eden of love is illusory, so too, in *The House of the Seven Gables*, is the perfect harmony of home called into question, not only, as Herbert has argued, because the sanctity of the domestic sphere depends in reality on "womanly dispossession and subordination,"[2] but also because the impulse to "plant a family," to found a dynastic house, is not, as it turns out, peculiar to the Pyncheons but to the wealthy. The conservatism that famously attends Holgrave's accession to property—a conservatism that manifests itself not only in his repudiation of radical reform but in his patriarchal desire to "set out trees, to make fences . . . to build a house for another generation" (307)—is, as the "labouring men" suspect, a luxury of

2. Herbert, *Dearest Beloved*, 105.

class. No longer dispossessed, his promise fulfilled by bequest, Holgrave lays claim to a future in which changes will not come, to a home in the very best sense.

CHRISTOPHER CASTIGLIA

The Marvelous Queer Interiors of
The House of the Seven Gables†

"Marvelous"

The House of the Seven Gables is obsessed with law. In his preface, setting out the distinction between novels and romances, Hawthorne associates the former with realism, in which imagination, denied the possibility of fanciful transformation, becomes enslaved to "the probable and ordinary course of man's existence." Romance, on the contrary, need not "rigidly subject itself to laws," but, demonstrating "a very minute feeling" for "the possible," is able "to mingle the Marvelous" (II: 1) with the probable events of everyday life. "Law" functions here for Hawthorne on several levels. Most immediately, he means "convention," the things "normal" people expect to happen in a "typical" day, life lived, not as a possibility for invention, but within the comfort of predictable pattern. Yet Hawthorne also attaches convention to more recognizable legal constructs, such as contracts: the preface itself takes on a contractual tone, establishing the terms that, if readers agree to them, will enable the romance to be understood and enjoyed. Hawthorne also invokes the legal protection of property, "by laying up a street that infringes upon nobody's private rights, and appropriating a lot of land which had no visible owner, and building a house of materials long in use for constructing castles in the air" (II: 3).[1] In the preface, then, Hawthorne attaches the juridical functions of law (the contractual protection of property rights) to the conventions of everyday life (the predictable life-patterns carried out, presumably, within the privately owned home), both laws represented in

---

† From *The Cambridge Companion to Nathaniel Hawthorne*, ed. Richard H. Millington (New York and Cambridge: Cambridge University Press, 2004), pp. 186–206. Reprinted with the permission of Cambridge University Press. All parenthetical page references are to the Centenary Edition of the *Works of Nathaniel Hawthorne*.
1. On Hawthorne and property law, see Walter Benn Michaels, "Romance and Real Estate," in Walter Benn Michaels and Donald E. Pease, eds., *The American Renaissance Reconsidered: Selected Papers from the English Institute* (Baltimore, MD: Johns Hopkins University Press, 1985), pp. 156–82.

the plot by the officious, grasping, and literal-minded lawyer, Jaffrey Pyncheon.[2]

In *The House of the Seven Gables*, law is not only multiform, but undergoes a historical change over the course of the narrative. Initially, law works upon the outward appearance of things, on the evidentiary basis of which it names a "truth" that will ultimately solve any apparent mystery. By the end of the novel, however, truth resides, not on the outside of things, but in the inner spaces of personality, character, and psyche. As criminality becomes manifest, not in disruptive or violent actions, but in pathologized emotions, affections, and desires, the law, too, takes an inner turn, insisting upon inner orders that are the purview, not of harsh jurists like Judge Pyncheon, but of benevolent reformers like Holgrave, who, at the novel's conclusion, replaces the Judge as the patriarchal head of the House of the Seven Gables. This transfer of power, which I address in the next section of the chapter, symbolizes the triumph, in the decades just before Hawthorne wrote *The House of the Seven Gables*, of reform movements that targeted inner characters over the coercive mandates of external law.

Hawthorne's principal interest—his sympathy, as he might say—is not with the law or its representatives but with those outside the law. Although he claims that the writer of romances "can hardly be said . . . to commit a literary crime" (II: 1), the fate of those who *are* judged to have broken the law—whether the juridical law of private property, the external law of social convention, or the inner law of orderly emotion and proper character—is at the center of *The House of the Seven Gables*. Hawthorne presents such characters as "queer," not in the twentieth-century sense of "homosexual" (although the desires of almost all of these characters fall outside the realm of conventional heterosexuality), but rather in the sense of "deviant." The queer characters of Hawthorne's romance—and almost all the characters are described, at some moment, as queer, although some (Hepzibah, Clifford, Uncle Venner) more consistently than others—deviate not by breaking the law (Clifford has been wrongly imprisoned for murdering his uncle), but by virtue of their excessive and inscrutable emotions, their melancholic devotion to the past, their antisocial reclusiveness, even their lack of control over bodily functions (Jaffrey's "queer and awkward ingurgulation" [II: 124], Hepzibah's near-sighted frown). While authoritative legal and medical theories of the nineteenth century would characterize these behaviors and traits as pathological, predicting their culmination in criminality, misery, illness, and death, they

2. On the contractual nature of Hawthorne's preface, see Fredric Jameson, "Magical Narratives: Romance as Genre," *New Literary History* 7. 1 (1975): 135–63.

enable Hawthorne's characters to sustain hopes and aspirations, however impossible or ill-fated. The mechanisms that allow characters to maintain hope—as he says in describing the romance as a genre, to mingle the marvelous with the mundane—become the basis of what I would call "queer interiority" in the novel, a deviation from the public and inner orders mandated by law. As we will see, queer interiority allows a different form of sociability—what Richard Millington calls "the democratization of the tragic"—to emerge in *The House of the Seven Gables.*[3]

Phrenology, purporting to read bumps on the head as signs of inner character traits such as one's propensity to marry for life, to labor manually, or to dutifully serve one's country, exemplifies the inward turn I am describing in nineteenth-century America. Although we would recognize these traits as outgrowths of social conditioning rather than of biological determination, phrenology insisted on their generation from within the interior of one's body and one's character. If one deviated from virtue—by masturbating, philandering, shirking one's work or one's civic duty—one was not just criminal, but ill, making the regulation of character not coercive, but benevolent (instilling "health" among the citizenry). The social order phrenology imagined therefore came to seem natural, serving the interests of God, not men. At the same time, phrenology opened up the possibility for the very queer excesses it sought to regulate, excesses such as the one Hawthorne places at the heart of romance. In phrenology handbooks, "marvelousness" names the power to see what is not visible in the external world, like ghosts and phantoms (terms Hawthorne frequently uses to describe the existence of his queer characters), but also works of imagination that, like the soap-bubbles Clifford delights in blowing from an upper window of the House, create "Little, impalpable worlds . . . with the big world depicted, in hues bright as imagination, on the nothing of their surface" (ii: 171). The ability to make "brilliant fantasies" (ii: 171) out of nothing might well appear delusional, yet Hawthorne makes it essential to the processes both of art-making and of hopeful world-making.

At the same time, such marvelous creations are also critiques, renderings of the "big world" that, through distortion, show its limitations and cruelties. As such, they challenge the operations of law that normalize only those modes of life that serve the interest of private property and orderly public life. Little wonder, then, that Judge Pyncheon "prided himself on eschewing all airy matter and never mistaking a shadow for a substance" (ii: 118). The

3. Richard H. Millington, *Practicing Romance: Narrative Form and Cultural Engagement in Hawthorne's Fiction* (Princeton, NJ: Princeton University Press, 1992), p. 113.

marvelous—growing from the queer interiors of those who would deviate from normalcy so as to imagine new social configurations, new aspirations, and new democratic interactions—becomes the Other, even the enemy, of the law. When phrenologists analyzed the craniums of the Great Men of the Republic (John Quincy Adams, Daniel Webster, Andrew Jackson), using portraits, death masks, and busts, they found them rich in Enlightenment virtues that make public order possible: common sense, reason, civic responsibility, self-control. Yet to a man, these men were lacking in one trait: marvelousness. What makes them—and the legal structure through which they rule—less than marvelous is their faith in order over excess, of evidence over fantasy, of calculation over imagination. Such hierarchical orderings allowed them to stabilize the establishment and generational perpetuation of private property.[4] Yet the law failed to contain invention, which arises perpetually in *The House of the Seven Gables* to challenge the "common sense" of antebellum America and the rules of property it upheld (in fact, one of the earliest meanings of "queer" is, as Will Fisher has shown, "counterfeit" or "swindle," a betrayal of the orderly transmission of property or economic value).[5] Marvelous hope persists, turning the charge of deviance against those advocates of the law who, like passers-by on Pyncheon Street, delight in bursting bubbles, "perversely gratified, no doubt, when the bubble, with all its pictured earth and sky scene, vanished as if it had never been" (II: 171). But it never vanishes entirely, not while the stuff of romance asserts its marvelous presence, lurking in the queer interiors of *The House of the Seven Gables*. "So much of mankind's varied experience had passed there—so much had been suffered, and something, too, enjoyed—that the very timbers were oozy," Hawthorne writes of the house, "as with the moisture of a heart. It was itself like a great human heart, with a life of its own, and full of rich and sombre reminiscences" (II: 27). Registering the human experiences that make predictable patterns seem flat and inexpressive, the House of the Seven Gables becomes, like the characters who inhabit it, the guardian of queer interiority. Despite the law's desire to make inner life public and orderly, the house always "had secrets to keep" (II: 27).

Outside/in

One of the oddest features of the plot of *The House of the Seven Gables* is that, over two centuries, with the outcome so doubtful, the Pyncheons go on searching for the deed that they believe will

4. Noyse Wheeler, *Phrenological Characters and Talents* (Boston: Dow & Jackson, 1844).
5. Will Fisher, "Queer Money," *English Literary History* 66 (1999): 1–23.

give them legal right to Waldo County in Maine; equally bizarre is the fact that the Maule descendants go on actively frustrating the Pyncheons' efforts to find that deed, despite the fact that Waldo County has long since been farmed out, making the Pyncheons' expectation of a baronic acquisition quixotic, to say the least. Perhaps representatives of both families go on with their customary choreography—the Maules tantalizing the Pyncheons with further mystery, the Pyncheons responding with frenzied study of dubious evidence—because what both parties gain from this dance is more important to them than the land itself. What this dynamic sustains—apart from the drive for material gain—is the legitimacy of law itself, which similarly rests on the dialectic of evidence and mystery, of scrutiny and speculation. Despite their different positions in relation to the law (the Pyncheons generally acting as judges while the Maules serve repeatedly as criminals), both families profit from the legitimacy of law. Both families are wedded to their right to inheritance—of real estate on the part of the Pyncheons, of "secrets" on the part of the Maules—that requites the legal transmission of property across death and generation. The children of both families—Phoebe Pyncheon and Holgrave (a Maule in disguise)—can therefore peacefully wed at the conclusion of the novel. Each family justifying the other's existence through time, the Pyncheons and the Maules create between them a legal world-view—a cosmic search after evidence that will solve timeless and metaphysical "crimes"—that neither family has an interest in bringing to an end.

Hawthorne seems to invite the readers of *The House of the Seven Gables* to share this legalistic world-view, tantalizing us with the possibility of penetrating the secrets of the novel just as the townspeople gaze upon the forbidding exterior of the ancient Pyncheon homestead, which seems to promise so much mystery and musky malevolence within. From the beginning, readers are invited to identify with a host of characters trying to solve some mystery. The formidable Jaffrey Pyncheon seeks to discover the ancient deed, hidden now for almost two centuries. His infirm cousin, Clifford Pyncheon, recently released from prison, strives, like a Transcendental esthete, to discover Ideal Beauty beneath the moth-eaten relics of his ancestral home. Sunny, young Phoebe Pyncheon, come from the country to care for her elderly relatives, attempts to uncover the source of their profound melancholy. Perhaps most of all, Holgrave, a boarder in the Pyncheon home, as a daguerreotypist seeks to bring forth the inner character of his sitters through their posed exteriors, as a mesmerist seeks to bring forth historical secrets repressed in the psyches of his impressionable clients, as a suitor seeks to elicit a confession that Phoebe Pyncheon returns his affection, and as a Fourierian reformer attempts to bring forth the socialistic world order only barely obscured by the materialistic scramblings of the modern age. Around these characters struggling to see what lies just inside (history, the body, crass materiality, inscrutable sadness), we are invited, like the townspeople who continually hover around the Pyncheon home, gossiping about the centuries of strange goings-on within, to muse on the eternal mystery of what makes this odd family tick. It is important to note, though, that not everyone is looking in the same place for the evidence. Some believe the outsides of things are more telling; others look inward.

The faith that external signs will lead to the full revelation of Truth is most essential to the legal structure represented by Judge Pyncheon, one of those "ordinary men to whom forms are of paramount importance" (II: 229). Having arranged "clues" so as to frame his cousin Clifford, who will otherwise inherit the family fortune Jaffrey covets, Judge Pyncheon knows how much the law relies on external signs. His faith that external "facts" will lead, invariably, to hidden "meaning" leads Judge Pyncheon not only to trust in the evidentiary logic he manipulates to Clifford's detriment, but also to his conviction that the deed to the Maine lands, if discovered, will once and for all resolve the Pyncheons' dispute over the rightful ownership of the land. Contracts—which themselves take signatures as signs of good character and good faith—are the lawyer's stock-in-trade, and by insisting that deeds can reverse the course of history, clearing land long settled by independent farmers and returning the Pyncheons to an aristocratic grandeur now democratically distasteful, Judge Pyncheon rationalizes as well his Franklinesque trust that an outward show of good character will disguise a host of inner blemishes.

Such external systems of interpretation support, in turn, a normative social order based upon—and further promoting the interests of—wealth and property. Of the Judge, Hawthorne writes: "you could feel just as certain that he was opulent, as if he had exhibited his bank account" (II: 57). So insistently does the Judge wear his character—and his wealth, the two being one and the same—on his sleeve, that Hawthorne quips, "He would have made a good and massive portrait" (II: 57). Oddly, the Judge's faith in externals and the orders they uphold is seconded by a character with apparently less to gain from that faith, one who shrinks from the Judge at their first meeting: his cousin Phoebe, described by Hawthorne as: "so orderly and so obedient to common rules" (II: 68). "She shocked no canon of taste," Hawthorne insists; "she was admirably in keeping with herself, and never jarred against surrounding circumstances" (II: 80). At the same time, Phoebe's faith that all is what it seems produces its supplemental excess in the form of nagging doubts and suspicions. Watching the Judge in action, Phoebe begins to speculate "whether judges, clergymen, and other characters of that eminent stamp and respectability, could really, in any single instance, be otherwise than just and upright men. A doubt of this nature," Hawthorne concludes, "has a most disturbing influence, and, if shown to be a fact, comes with a fearful and startling effect on minds of the trim, orderly, and limit-loving class" (ii: 131). "But Phoebe, in order to keep the universe in its old place, was fain to smother, in some degree, her own intuitions as to Judge Pyncheon's character" (ii: 131–32), Hawthorne assures his readers. In repressing her own "intuitions," however, Phoebe, who previously prides herself on the utter superficiality of her character, becomes possessed of an unconscious, a broody interiority that makes her subject to the inward-looking law represented by Holgrave, but that also enables her sympathetic attachment to her dark and mysterious cousins.

The Judge, too, is not without his interiority, so much so, in fact, that he makes his outward-gazing law obsolete. Jaffrey not only embodies the shift in law from jurisprudence to social convention, as a reformed rake he also demonstrates the potential rewards for reshaping one's private vices along the lines of representative public virtue. The Judge operates through the public revelation of private shame (the same authority Hawthorne critiques in *The Scarlet Letter*):

> "My dear Cousin," said Judge Pyncheon, with a quietude which he had the power of making more formidable than any violence, "since your brother's return, I have taken the precaution (a highly proper one in the near kinsman and natural guardian of an individual so situated) to have his deportment and habits constantly and carefully overlooked. Your neighbors have been eye-witnesses to whatever has passed in the garden. The butcher, the baker, the fish-monger, some of the customers of your shop, and many a prying old woman, have told me several of the scenes of your interior." (ii: 237)

The Judge functions as a transition between punishment (the imposition of physical force) and discipline (the regulation of "interior" behaviors through the benevolent discourses of health).[6] Having released Clifford from the constraint of the jail, the Judge threatens to confine him, "probably for the remainder of his life, in a public asylum for persons in his unfortunate state of mind" (ii: 236). In doing so, he renders his own juridical control over ex-

---

6. I am building here on the distinction between discipline and punishment made by Michel Foucault in *Discipline and Punish: The Birth of the Prison*, trans. Alan Sheridan (New York: Vintage, 1979).

ternal actions and signs superfluous, replaced, now, by the institutional regulation of private character and inner states.

Hawthorne challenges both forms of regulation, however, by repeatedly showing outward things to be highly unpredictable, unreliable, and manipulatable markers of hidden depths. What Hawthorne states of the Pyncheons' efforts to discover the hidden deed—"Some connecting link had slipt out of the evidence, and could not anywhere be found" (II: 18)—is equally applicable to every effort in the novel to discover truth through external signs. Not only does the evidence leading to the possession of the Maine lands remain elusive, the material existence of the land itself eludes its external representation, "the natural history of the region being as little known as its geography, which was put down so fantastically awry" (II: 33). The "fantastic" (we might say the "marvelous") here queers the legitimate possession of land, just as Hawthorne's romance satirizes the quest for that possession. "There is something so massive, stable, and almost irresistibly imposing, in the exterior presentment of established rank and great possession," Hawthorne writes, "that their very existence seems to give them a right to exist, at least, so excellent a counterfeit of right, that few poor and humble men have moral force enough to question it, even in their secret mind" (II: 25). Showing externals to be, automatically, their own counterfeits, Hawthorne queers property rights—and the external evidence that establishes them—beyond any Pyncheon's power to reclaim.

Hawthorne turns the Judge's body itself into a counterfeit, gleefully needling Jaffrey for his smile, "the sultry, dog-day heat, as it were, of benevolence, which the excellent man diffused out of his great heart into the surrounding atmosphere,—very much like a serpent, which, as a preliminary to fascination, is said to fill the air with his peculiar odor" (II: 119). The snake in this democratic garden is precisely the counterfeit cheer bestowed so promiscuously upon the people, highborn and low, that it becomes a hollow token of fellow-feeling, a parody of the democratic equality of the pursuit of happiness bestowed by the ur-contract, the Constitution. Denying the truth-value of external symbols, Hawthorne uses legal language to condemn the Judge, whose smile "afforded very little evidence of that genuine benignity of soul, whereof it purported to be the outward reflection" (II: 116). The Judge's smile becomes, not what it purports to be on the surface, but the sign of hidden greed and guilt: "As is customary with the rich when they aim at the honors of a republic, he apologized, as it were, to the people, for his wealth, property, and elevated station, by a free and hearty manner towards those who knew him" (II: 130).

The original sin visited on the contemporary inhabitants of the

House of the Seven Gables—Colonel Pyncheon's conviction of Matthew Maule as a witch, resulting in the judge's acquisition of Maule's land holdings—highlights from the beginning the abuses of juridical evidence, arising from a naïve faith that things are as they appear. This originary crime sets in play a tradition of disguise, counterfeit, and swindle, of which judges—the adjudicators of the law—are the worst perpetrators. The solution, for Hawthorne, is not a more truthful alignment of surface and depth, of evidence and criminal "truth," but rather an awareness that surfaces signify only other surfaces: the portrait of Colonel Pyncheon does not give way to the historical personage, but to another text—the deed to the lands in Maine—which, in turn, does not materialize into baronial wealth, but simply into the narrative of the novel itself. Unable to recognize that they inevitably live within a web of surfaces, the characters are driven nearly mad in their desires to break the shell of external signs to reach the kernel of truth within—a process the novel repeatedly figures as "possession." Hawthorne makes this sadistically clear in one of the most bizarre chapters in the novel, "Governor Pyncheon," which describes, in excruciating detail, the atmosphere surrounding Jaffrey's corpse as it sits, undiscovered, in the abandoned house. As it circles the body, facetiously giving it various metaphoric casts and allegorical significances, the narrative voice's macabre delight highlights the materiality of death, rendered ironic by the fact that the Judge, now a lifeless symbol, made his life by insisting upon his power to make externals speak their "truth." In killing off "Governor" Pyncheon, Hawthorne kills off as well the legitimacy of external order over citizens who are more than juridical subjects, and who therefore continually exceed the law's ability to name them in ways that produce shame and guilt for the named, and power and profit for the namer. Judge Pyncheon, "seldom or never looking inward" but "resolutely taking his idea of himself from what purports to be his image as reflected in the mirror of public opinion" (II: 232), makes himself obsolete, capable of producing only "a counterfeit of right" (II: 25).

Having killed off the Judge, however, Hawthorne's trouble with the law begins anew. In representing the Judge's hypocrisy, his "inward criminality" (II: 312) that negates his public self-regulation, Hawthorne orients the reader toward a presumably more recognizably "natural" law based not on external convention but on the inner order of what Harriet Beecher Stowe called "right feeling." Early in the novel, the innocent Phoebe has just learned that the daguerreotypist, Holgrave, associates with "reformers, temperance-lecturers, and all manner of cross-looking philanthropists" (II: 84). " 'But if Mr. Holgrave is a lawless person!' remonstrated Phoebe, a part of whose essence it was, to keep within the limits of law. 'Oh,' said Hepzibah carelessly—for, formal as she was, still, in her life's experience, she had gnashed her teeth against human law—'I suppose he has a law of his own' " (II: 85). Although both women speak of law, neither refers to the legal documents, deeds, and titles typically associated with jurisprudence. Rather, Phoebe means outward conventions, while Hepzibah understands that Holgrave, as a reformer, has an *inner* law, regulating not public behaviors but "deep" emotions (the "confession" he elicits is not of criminal acts, but of love). While Phoebe believes firmly in the mutual dependence of (outward) law and order, Holgrave, who challenges conventions and "acknowledge[s] no law" (II: 84), can remain, insofar as he insists on the inner consistency of "identity" (II: 177), an "orderly young man" (II: 84). If Phoebe's moral system requires the subordination of private anomaly to public order through identification with established norms, Holgrave's renders public rituals of conformity obsolete, since his self-regulating affects internalize the public orders maintained, in Jaffrey's law, by external regulation and censure. Depicting the transformations of "law" from strictures to the regulation of interior states, *The House of the Seven Gables* reveals how civil apparatuses such as domesticity and reform (embodied in the ultimate marriage of Phoebe and Holgrave) led citizens to misrecognize "the social" as an expression of individual and private feeling rather than as a function of labor and profit. In return for their self-regulations, citizens are promised an illusory control, not over the law, but over *the law written in their own natures*.

In addition to being a reformer, Holgrave is a daguerreotypist, a profession that allows him to profit by bringing out his sitters' inner selves: "There is a wonderful insight in heaven's broad and simple sunshine. While we give it credit only for depicting the merest surface, it actually brings out the secret character with a truth that no painter would ever venture upon, even could he detect it" (II: 91). As a daguerreotypist, Holgrave continues the mesmeric tradition of his Maule ancestors, whose "family eye was said to possess strange powers," including that "of exercising an influence over people's dreams" (II: 26). The Maules' power of human interiority is most clear in the narrative of Alice Pyncheon, brought first to humiliating servitude and finally to death by the Maules' mesmeric control over the affective dialectic of desire and shame. Just as Matthew Maule brings forth the insecurity and guilt lurking behind Alice Pyncheon's haughty exterior, so the inner "truth" behind generations of Pyncheon counterfeits is brought forth when the Maules work their magic on the family well, making "its inner region all alive with the departed Pyncheons; not as they had shown themselves to the world, nor in their better and happier hours, but as doing over again some deed or sin, or in the crisis of life's bitter sorrow" (II: 21). While the contemporary Maule, Holgrave, shuns such fabulous displays in favor of technological skill, he too strategically exhorts confessions of affective states. At the conclusion of the novel, Holgrave cements his place as the head of the Pyncheon family by looking into Phoebe and calling forth her feelings: " 'You look into my heart,' replied she, letting her eyes droop. 'You know I love you!' " (II: 307).

When Holgrave gains Phoebe's confession of love and thereby her hand in marriage, the law of inner life produces the commercial success that neither the law of reputation nor legal deeds gained for the Maule descendants. This outcome is hardly surprising, since throughout the romance Holgrave repeatedly advocates the same work ethic one might expect to hear from the Judge. When Hepzibah, forced to open a cent-shop to earn a living, bemoans her fate to Holgrave, the young reformer romanticizes effort for its own sake, not in relation to payoffs in profit or privilege, but of health and civic union: "Henceforth, you will at least have the sense of healthy and natural effort for a purpose, and of lending your strength—be it great or small—to the united struggle of mankind" (II: 45). Hawthorne facetiously echoes this sentiment soon thereafter, attributing labor-for-its-own-sake not just to nature, but to God: "As a general rule," he writes, "Providence seldom vouchsafes to mortals any more than just that degree of encouragement, which suffices to keep them at a reasonable full exertion of their powers" (II: 52). Working not because they fear public scorn but because it is what their healthy nature requires, not for profit but for the inner sense of God's endorsement, the inner law Holgrave represents proves an even more effective force for social order than the external one endorsed by the Judge, since the order Holgrave represents is policed by each citizen in his or her own body. The passing of the law from Jaffrey to Holgrave does not represent an idealized release from the law's repressive coercion, then; "the authorian impulse is not dead," as Millington notes, "but, in analogy to the marketplace, it is becoming more widely distributed."[7] Naturally, then, the Judge's profits pass to the daguerreotypist.

While Holgrave's insistence on inner truth apparently supplants the Judge's reliance on external conventions, Hawthorne suggests the two men are more similar than they initially appear: while Holgrave's conversation with Phoebe "had generally been playful, the impression left on her mind was one of gravity, and, except as his youth modified it, almost sternness" (II: 94). For all his talk about social progress, furthermore, Holgrave does as little to improve the

7. Millington, *Practicing Romance*, p. 149.

material conditions of the poor as does the Judge, preferring not "to help or hinder; but to look on, to analyze, to explain matters to my-self" (II: 216). Hawthorne suggests that reform and conservatism, both serving the interests of middle-class social order, are close kin: "I have a presentiment," Holgrave tells Phoebe, "that, hereafter, it will be my lot to set out trees, to make fences—perhaps, even, in due time, to build a house for another generation—in a word, to conform myself to laws, and the peaceful practice of society" (II: 307). "You find me a conservative already!" (II: 315), Holgrave happily declares.

The shift from outward to inner law has several effects in Ameri-can culture, as *The House of the Seven Gables* demonstrates. Inner law makes the regulation of personal emotion and desire appear not coercive or manipulative but benevolent and self-initiated, trans-forming the experience of the "social" in ways that left citizens iso-lated and without an embodied sense of shared public interest. Inner law, therefore, allows questions properly understood in rela-tion to public institutions to detach from that base, wandering in the citizen's body and beyond it in ways that serve an increasingly mobile economy already national and quickly becoming global. But as Hawthorne suggests by having the "secret character" of the House of the Seven Gables become the subject of gossip among neighbors, tradesmen, and so on, inner life is not located in the in-terior at all, but is the effect of a shared discourse of order seem-ingly divested of the very publicity that is its operational core. Hence, at the conclusion of the novel, the House of the Seven Gables can be abandoned, its interiority produced anew in the Pyn-cheon estate.

Yet some mysteries—some inner riddles—are never "solved" through the public confession of emotional "truth." Why does Phoebe, initially so skeptical about Holgrave, suddenly come to love him? Why does Judge Pyncheon, who surely recognizes the fu-tility of his hope to yet claim the Maine lands, continue to hunt the deed? What is the nature of Hepzibah's attachment to Clifford? These questions—and others that have kept critics coming back to this novel decade after decade—attest to the inability of inner law to ever resolve the unruly, disruptive, and abstruse affective life of citizens into neat and regulated orders. It is in those spaces of *dis*-order that the House of the Seven Gables, and the romance that is its namesake, maintains its secrets and its allure. In those mar-velous spaces, as well, its queerness flourishes.

Queers

What does it mean to say that there are "queers" in *The House of the Seven Gables*?

Hawthorne's romance, to be sure, offers glimpses of what, by the late nineteenth century, would emerge as "homosexual identities." Hepzibah, who refuses to attend church, becoming, in her isolation, a comically bad housewife and an old maid in whom "the love of children had never been quickened" (II: 39), falls far outside nineteenth-century conventions of femininity, which rested on piety and domestic nurturance. If Hepzibah is a "bad" woman, Clifford's "beautiful infirmity of character" (II: 60) comes from his being *too* feminine, as Hepzibah acknowledges in claiming that the town "persecuted his mother in him!" (II: 60). An "old bachelor" of "an eccentric and melancholy turn of mind" (II: 22), possessed of "gentle and voluptuous emotion" (II: 32), Clifford, in his attraction to beauty, his obsession with youth, and his "womanly" sensibilities, is, as Neill Matheson argues, a proto-Wildean aesthete.[8] Insofar as modern homosexual identity gained public intelligibility as an inversion of Victorian gender roles, Clifford and Hepzibah, refusing to hold to their "proper" genders, are arguably among American literature's first homosexual characters.

My interest, though, is not in locating the characters' queerness in sexual identity, since it is precisely their status as fakes, counterfeits, bad copies—subjects who do not embody "natural" identities and whose emotional excesses defy inner order—that makes the characters "queer." I use "queer" here to suggest opacities or excesses within the self that suggest that *all* identities are in essence counterfeits. Judith Butler argues that identity, far from being a static essence that emerges *out from* a person's inner being, is in fact a series of repeated stagings (what Butler calls "performatives") of identity-conventions *on* the body.[9] Performatives posit an original—the "essence" of "who one *really* is"—of which, Butler contends, subjects are always judged to be incomplete or inadequate reproductions. The suspicion that one has not manifested completely the truth of one's identity drives the compulsive enactment of what can never be gotten right: the manifestation, as identity, of an inner truth that, in the end, is never inner at all, but exists in a discursive—and hence social—realm that changes historically, as, therefore, will the "identities" it produces.[1] Phoebe Pyncheon, for instance, in her efforts to align herself perfectly with social norms, recognizes implicitly that her "identity" is a matter of convention, not, as she frequently asserts, of innate "character." At the same time, her awareness of the distance—the never entirely bridgeable

---

8. Neill Matheson, "Clifford's Dim, Unsatisfactory Elegance," unpublished paper, MLA Convention, December, 2000.
9. Judith Butler, "Imitation and Gender Insubordination," in Diana Fuss, ed., *Inside/Out: Lesbian Theories, Gay Theories* (New York: Routledge, 1991), pp. 13–31.
1. *Ibid.*, p. 18.

gap—between "conventions" and the "self" striving to correlate herself with those conventions suggests that Phoebe will repeatedly experience failure. At the same time that Phoebe's efforts to embody convention leave her at a loss (vulnerable to the reformer, Holgrave), those same efforts generate the illusion that identities exist, as originals, prior to the subject's efforts to achieve them. Although Phoebe asserts that conventions have the social force of law, one might well ask who, in her world, lives the "normal" life she strives for? Only her assertions that conventions exist and must be adhered to allow those "laws," or the conventions they supposedly govern, to exist.

Phoebe, to a lesser degree than Clifford and Hepzibah but in ways that allow her to sympathize with them, finds herself a not-quite Pyncheon, a bad copy of the family essence. The reiterative performance of the tense non-alignment of ordinals and (bad) copies is a central plot structure of *The House of the Seven Gables*, played out in repeated ruptures between inheritance and representation. All through the romance, characters comment on the degree to which others do or do not look like "real" Pyncheons. The ur-Pyncheon, in these evaluations, is the founder of the House of the Seven Gables, Colonel Pyncheon, whose disapproving face presides over the inevitable failure of his descendants to measure up to the Pyncheon essence. Hepzibah scowls a bit like her ancestor, but of course she is a woman. Clifford is also too much of a woman, favoring his mother to a degree that leads Hepzibah to exclaim, "He never was a Pyncheon!" (II: 60). Jaffrey claims to see a family resemblance in Phoebe's mouth, but she too resembles her mother too much to really be one of the clan (mothers repeatedly get blamed for disrupting identity, and hence inheritance, in the novel). Even Jaffrey, who most resembles his ancestor, has gesturally transformed his appearance in ways his Puritan forefather would condemn (his too-benevolent smile, for instance, would ill suit the persecutor of witches). Each descendent, in short, is deemed a bad copy of the ancestral original. Yet the determinations of successful or failed "identity" (their identity as Pyncheons) is made through comparison, not with the original ancestor, but with his portrait, itself an interpretation shaped by historically changeable aesthetic conventions. The portrait, that is, is necessarily a counterfeit of its necessarily absent original. It is not coincidental that the deed to the Maine lands, obtained through a foundational act of deception, is hidden behind the portrait; Hawthorne thereby suggests (with his usual allegorical finesse) that behind the assertion of origins one will always find a counterfeit, a false deed. It is precisely identity's status as counterfeit that must be hidden if what is outside (convention) is to appear as if coming from within, for identification to be misunderstood as identity. The Pyncheons' claim to social superiority rests on the assertion of undeviated and un*mediated* inheritance, that all subsequent Pyncheons, being the true reflections of the Pyncheon original, are entitled to the same property willed through a direct line of succession (a line Jaffrey, by framing Clifford and hence circumventing his uncle's will, has already undermined). If the generational transmission of property (including one's principal property, "identity") rests on the truthful representation of a representation, a counterfeit of a fake, however, then the law of inheritance is as deceptive as the Colonel's justice. Put another way, if the original was already a fake, how can Hepzibah and Clifford possibly be bad copies, failed Pyncheons?

That question becomes unaskable—indeed, unthinkable—in the world of the romance precisely because of the social and *legal* authority of those who claim the privilege of sanctioned identity. In declaring his relatives bad copies, the Judge attempts to make them socially invisible, disappeared behind the obscuring walls of the family home. He thereby enacts the form of oppression Butler writes of, working "not merely through acts of overt prohibition, but covertly, through the constitution of viable subjects and through the corollary constitution of a domain of unviable (un)subjects—*abjects*, we might call them—who are neither named nor prohibited within the economy of the law."[2] Refusing to acknowledge, much less regulate, the innate "identity" that resides in the body's interior, Clifford and Hepzibah must repeatedly find themselves abjected. But who does not experience this failure, Hawthorne's romance seems to ask? If Hepzibah and Clifford, who felt "mankind's great and terrible eye on them alone" (II: 169), seem extraordinary in their abjection, Hawthorne hastens to remind the reader that the Pyncheon siblings are exemplary in their discordant identification, "a ruin, a failure, as almost everybody is" (II: 158).

Because they do not make common cause in their abjection, however, Hepzibah and Clifford are kept from asserting their presence, not by prohibition, but by shame, the characteristic state of those without socially sanctioned identities. Hepzibah, when her cent-shop forces her to face the outside world, experiences "overwhelming shame, that strange and unloving eyes should have the privilege of gazing" (II: 46) and later feels "a painful suffusion of shame" (II: 112). When Hepzibah tries to dissuade her brother from going into public, warning him of the townspeople's inevitable judgment, Clifford, whose life has been a series of mortifications, exclaims, "What shame can befall me now?" (II: 113). Shame is a

2. *Ibid.*, p. 20.

potent force, keeping the siblings locked away from the world and thereby preventing them from challenging their cousin's right either to the family wealth (Clifford might assert his innocence in the murder of his uncle) or to public respectability (by publicizing his cheating and lying). In so doing, Clifford and Hepzibah would challenge the laws of normative public order, both by discrediting the Judge's status as representative of public virtue and by showing that *other* forms of identification are possible, forms capable of producing more love, kindness, and creativity than the Judge and his laws ever dreamed of. Because shame operates at the level of emotion and results in self-punishment, it serves the Judge's interests better than any juridical sentence, since his cousins, finding *themselves* lacking and experiencing their punishment not on the outside, where it might elicit sympathy, but on the inside, far from public view, become self-imprisoning subjects. As Hawthorne writes, the couple "could not flee; their jailor had but left the door open, in mockery, and stood behind it, to watch them stealing out. At the threshold, they felt his pitiless gripe upon them. For, what other dungeon is so dark as one's own heart! What jailor so inexorable as one's self!" (II: 169).

While shame works to keep Hepzibah and Clifford—and the challenges they embody—off the streets, it also enables an alternative collective life—a queer sociability—among those sentenced to shame. Creating a world of unpredictable emotions, surprising affinities, and powerful challenges, the errant Pyncheons and their allies turn their failures into an example of what Michael Warner calls the ethics of queer life:

> I call its way of life an ethics not only because it is understood as a better kind of self-relation, but because it is the premise of the special kind of sociability that holds queer culture together. A relation to others, in these contexts, begins in an acknowledgment of all that is most abject and least reputable in oneself. Shame is bedrock. Queers can be abusive, insulting, and vile toward one another, but because abjection is understood to be the shared condition, they also know how to communicate through such camaraderie a moving and unexpected form of generosity.[3]

We can use these terms to understand how an alternative sense of social connection is shaped within the romance by "sympathy," a word widely used in the nineteenth century to describe what we today might call "empathy": the ability of more apparently privileged citizens (those extending sympathy) to acknowledge (at least to

---

3. Michael Warner, *The Trouble With Normal: Sex, Politics, and the Ethics of Queer Life* (New York: The Free Press, 1999), p. 35.

themselves) their own experiences of abjection in order to imaginatively place themselves in the position of the socially wounded.[4]
What sympathy attests to, then, is the ubiquitous experience of
shame, transformed, through sympathy, into a potential enactment
of fellow-feeling. Hawthorne implies as much when he writes that
"Clifford saw, it may be, in the mirror of his deeper consciousness,
that he was an example and representative of that great chaos of
people, whom an inexplicable Providence is continually putting at
cross-purposes with the world" (II: 149). Living at cross-purposes
generates Clifford's and Hepzibah's shame; yet through them
shame becomes re-exteriorized as a social connection, a way of life,
an ethics.

All who share the ethics of Hawthorne's romance—Clifford, Hepzibah, Phoebe, Uncle Venner, and, at least initially, Holgrave, who
possesses "queer and questionable traits" (II: 154)—are at cross-
purposes with the world. Describing the elderly jack-of-all-trades,
for instance, Hawthorne writes that Venner "was commonly regarded as rather deficient, than otherwise, in his wits. In truth, he
had virtually pleaded guilty to the charge, by scarcely aiming at such
success as other men seek, and by taking only that humble and
modest part in the intercourse of life, which belongs to the alleged
deficiency" (II: 61). Casting Venner's social abjection in the language
of legal judgment, Hawthorne not only creates a bond between Clifford and Venner that puts both men at odds with Judge Pyncheon,
he places Venner, like Clifford, outside the "common sense" of his
social world in part because he refuses a coherent identity (those
being associated, by Hawthorne, with the capitalist narratives determining "such success as other men seek"). Venner is "a miscellaneous old gentleman, partly himself, but, in good measure,
something else; patched together, too, of different epochs; an epitome of times and fashions" (II: 62). Rather than condemning Venner for his patchwork persona and consigning him to the shame his
cross-purposeful life would seem to require, Hawthorne credits to it
a rather marvelous counter-wisdom, noting that the old man had "a
vein of something like poetry in him" (II: 61).

Venner's "vein of poetry"—the lifeblood of Hawthorne's queer
ethics—has a transformative power over even the most apparently
"normal" of the Pyncheons. Initially, Phoebe "was not one of those
natures which are most attracted by what is strange and exceptional in human character. The path which would best have suited
her, was the well-worn track of ordinary life; the companions in
whom she would most have delighted, were such as one encounters

---

4. On sympathy in Hawthorne's romances, see Gordon Hutner, *Secrets and Sympathy:
Forms of Disclosure in Hawthorne's Novels* (Athens: University of Georgia Press, 1989).

at every turn" (II: 142–43). Before long, however, Phoebe "grew more thoughtful than heretofore." Finding herself curious about Clifford's past, she "would try to inquire what had been his life" (II: 143). When his history becomes clear to her—partly through what she is told, but also with the help of "her involuntary conjectures," suggesting Phoebe's imagination contains the stuff of gothic cross-purposefulness—"it had no terrible effect upon her" (II: 144). Phoebe's ability to "conjecture" about Clifford—to place herself imaginatively in his shoes—cements her bonds with her outcast cousins, an outcome Phoebe senses from the start of her visit, when she tells Hepzibah, "I really think we may suit one another, much better than you suppose" (II: 74).

The strongest indication of Phoebe's sympathetic bond with her cousins, however, is her adoption of Clifford's characteristic emotional state, "a settled melancholy" (II: 135). "It is perhaps remarkable, considering her temperament," Hawthorne reports, that Phoebe, singing in the evening to Clifford, "oftener chose a strain of pathos than of gaiety" (II: 138). Melancholy, according to Freud, arises from a person's refusal to surrender a lost loved one, object, or ideal, incorporating its qualities into his or her own body, where the anger and ambivalence surrounding loss are experienced as self-revilement.[5] Clifford and Hepzibah clearly fit this pattern: the former struggles with the loss of his youth, while the latter refuses to reconcile herself to her beloved brother's incarceration, both experiencing loss by reviling their own bodies (Hepzibah is ashamed of her unpleasant scowl, while Clifford fantasizes about re-entering society by breaking his body in a self-willed tumble from an upper window). Although Phoebe seems far from this pattern, she too struggles with loss. Recall that when Phoebe first understands that persons of "eminent stamp and respectability, could really, in any single instance, be otherwise than just and upright men," she is "fain to smother, in some degree, her own intuitions" (II: 131–32). Phoebe learns to repress ("smother") the disparity between social custom and her own experiences, thereby constituting a rupture within her understanding of identity. Realizing that the hypocritical Judge Pyncheon might not be "identical" to himself, Phoebe acknowledges the counterfeit nature of those customs upon which she rests her own identity. If that moment of loss risks Phoebe's identity, however, it generates new options for *identification*, not with the public world whose canons of taste she previously upheld, but with the shameful communities created by the socially abject of the House of the Seven Gables. While her desire to identify with the Judge leads her only to failure (he points out to her that she does not look much like a Pyncheon), her embrace of shame—her imaginative sympathy with Clifford and Hepzibah—leads her to melancholic bonds that, if sometimes pensive and pathetic, are also generous, caring, and poetic. Hawthorne shows us, then, that melancholia is not simply nostalgic—a pessimistic longing for a hopelessly lost past—but is productive as well. One might even say that Hawthorne's characters engage melancholy as a "vein of po-etry" that allows them to disavow the sanctioned identities of the public world: Clifford's "griefs were a touch-stone of reality that few feigned emotions could withstand" (II: 146), Hawthorne writes, reversing the usual dichotomy of real/imagined, of genuine/ feigned, usually deployed to Clifford's detriment. At the same time, melancholy allows characters to inscribe in the *present* forms of identification authorized, not by the Pyncheon past, but by the as-sertion of the inevitable loss contained within that past. Using shameful loss to enliven modes of affiliation not yet visible in the "real world," the Pyncheons' melancholy is rather marvelous.

While Clifford and even Phoebe's melancholia are interpretable, other emotions become queer because they are unnameable, even, apparently, by Hawthorne. In this sense, the queerest character in *The House of the Seven Gables* is Hepzibah, whose inner states re-main so elusive that, as Millington rightly notes, the narrative "can only represent [her] by misrepresenting her."[6] Hawthorne refers re-peatedly to her "queer scowl" (II: 50), to "the sad perversity of her scowl" (II: 133), to her "queer and quaint manners" (II: 135), even to her "queer" chickens, who share Hepzibah's "queer, sidelong glances" (II: 89). Hepzibah keeps "the strong passion of her life" in a "secret drawer" (II: 31), never giving it a public name. In that, she is, in this world of confessed inner states, "a queer anomaly" (II: 37). Although her passions are one of the most persistent, if understated, mysteries of the romance, Hepzibah, refusing to acknowledge that she even *has* a "secret," resists the public orders of domestic self-sacrifice and commercial competition. For all its unnameability, Hepzibah's pas-sionate interiority—"the vivid life and reality, assumed by her emo-tions" (II: 66)—becomes, like Clifford's grief, a pointed commentary on the "realities" of the external world, making "all outward occur-rences unsubstantial, like the teasing phantoms of a half-conscious slumber" (II: 66). Although Hawthorne calls Clifford and Hepzibah a "queer couple of ducks" (II: 289), only the latter can reverse the law's demand for confession, ordering the Judge, apropos his motive in persecuting Clifford, "speak it out, at once!" (II: 228).

Hepzibah thus represents what might be the romance's most

6. Millington, *Practicing Romance*, p. 111.

promising insight: the "interior" contains nothing at all, no "essence" to validate the public scrutiny of shameful secrets. If, as Hawthorne claims, "the reader must needs be let into the secret" (II: 28), the secret may turn out to be that there *are* no secrets, at least none that can be brought forth by public law and reconciled with its nominal orders. As Hepzibah defiantly claims in answer to the Judge's demands for her brother's confession, "Clifford has no secret!" (II: 237). In the face of such emptiness, one finds in oneself only one's desire to know, as Hawthorne suggests in one of his first descriptions of the House of the Seven Gables: "As regards its interior life, a large, dim looking-glass used to hang in one of the rooms, and was fabled to contain within its depths all the shapes that had ever been reflected there" (II: 20). In the end *The House of the Seven Gables* shows us what the mirror reveals: the desires of those who would look, the law's dim gaze. Emotions, passions, melancholy all become, in Hawthorne's romance, not interior states, but the external means to a more sustainable, if more provisional, sympathy that is, in turn, the basis of an alternative social affinity. "Mellow, melancholy, yet not mournful," Hawthorne writes, "the tone seemed to gush up out of the deep well of Hepzibah's heart, all steeped in its profoundest emotion. There was a tremor in it, too, that—as all strong emotion is electric—partly communicated itself to Phoebe" (II: 96).

Because emotions became named in antebellum America in part through the binary of public/private (the former being the realm of "masculine" emotions like competitiveness and anger, the latter marking "feminine" emotions like reverence and nurturing affection), the queer community of *The House of the Seven Gables* necessarily flourishes in a space neither private nor public. Every Sunday, Hawthorne relates, his "oddly composed little social party" (II: 155) gathers in the garden, a site that anthropomorphizes the characters' queer transformation of shame into sociability. Made up of "such rank weeds (symbolic of the transmitted vices of society)" (II: 86), the garden becomes, like those who enjoy its at-first-unapparent beauties, a haven from social abjection, where "Nature, elsewhere overwhelmed, and driven out of the dusty town, had here been able to retain a breathing space" (II: 87). Generating a space outside the shameful interior of the house yet making "an interior of verdant seclusion" (II: 145), the garden fosters "the sympathy of this little circle of not unkindly souls" (II: 157).

Just as the garden's "vagrant and lawless plants" (II: 86) bring forth a marvelous sociability, so too the queer passions of its inhabitants bring forth, through what Millington calls "the shared risks of transformative interchange,"[7] not the remorseful self-

7. *Ibid.*, p. 139.

revilements Freud associates with melancholy, but remarkable testimonies of hopefulness and perseverance.[8] Uncle Venner voices the group's characteristic optimism, defiantly claiming, "I'm not going to give up this one scheme of my own, even if I never bring it really to pass" (II: 155–56). Although Hawthorne asserts that croaky voices like Hepzibah's "have put on mourning for dead hopes" (II: 135), the old woman, left for thirty years to long for her brother, keeps alive "in the dungeon of her heart . . . the imprisoned joy, that was afraid to be enfranchised" (II: 102), but which maintains "her undying faith and trust, her fresh remembrance, and continual devotedness" (II: 32). Similarly, "Clifford had willfully hid from himself the consciousness of being stricken in years, and cherished visions of an earthly future still before him, visions, however, too indistinctly drawn to be followed by disappointment" (II: 155). "Individuals, whose affairs have reached an utterly desperate crisis," Hawthorne writes, "almost invariably keep themselves alive with hope, so much the more airily magnificent, as they have the less of solid matter within their grasp, whereof to mould any judicious and moderate expectation of good" (II: 64). This becomes evident in one of the most poignant scenes in the novel. Having sat quietly in his half-somnolent state while his companions socialize in the garden, Clifford suddenly announces, "I want my happiness! . . . Many, many years have I waited for it! It is late! It is late! I want my happiness!" (II: 157).

Ironically, Clifford's happiness is already around him, in the hopeful imagination, the faithful devotion, the caring sympathy—in the queer sociability—of his companions. If the public world is full of citizens who, due to their "judicious . . . expectation of good," are continually confronted by disappointment and shame, if public paradise is lost through the duplicitous snake of sanctioned, but counterfeit, identity, Hawthorne holds out a garden where one can find, in queer inscrutability and unruly passion, what Robert S. Levine has called "the regenerative and redemptive possibilities of reconstituted family."[9] Does the sociability shared by his queer characters, Hawthorne asks, "deserve to be called happiness?" His answer whimsically appropriates the language of counterfeit, not to adjudicate shameful failure, but to reveal the marvelous fantasies that permit the continued life of hope: "Why not? If not the thing itself, it is marvellously like it, and the more so for that ethereal and intangible quality, which causes it all to vanish, at too close an introspection" (II: 158). If Clifford laments to his sister, "We are ghosts!"

---

8. On Hawthorne's hopefulness, see also Brook Thomas, "*The House of the Seven Gables*: Reading the Romance of America," *PMLA* 97. 2 (1982): 195–211.
9. Robert S. Levine, *Conspiracy and Romance: Studies in Brockden Brown, Cooper, Hawthorne, and Melville* (Cambridge: Cambridge University Press, 1989), p. 159.

(II: 169), referring to the civil death that characterizes the socially abject, Hepzibah, for her part, knows all too well that, supported by queer sympathy, "dead people are very apt to come back again!" (II: 76). Finding that they "belong nowhere" (II: 168), Hawthorne's characters show us that happiness is all around us, if only we had their ability to embrace our shame and, recognizing with Clifford how late it is, demand its marvelous outcomes *now*.

Nathaniel Hawthorne:
A Chronology

1804 Born on July 4 in Salem, Massachusetts, the second of three children of Nathaniel and Elizabeth Manning Hathorne. (The "w" was added to the family name by Hawthorne sometime around 1830.)

1808 Hawthorne's father, a sea captain, dies of yellow fever in Surinam. Elizabeth Manning Hathorne and her children move into her parents' home in Salem.

1813 Injures foot while playing ball and is unable to attend school for two years.

1818 Hawthornes move to family property in Raymond, Maine.

1819 Hawthorne returns to Salem to live with his Manning relatives and attend school, while his mother remains in Maine.

1821 Begins Bowdoin College, in Brunswick, Maine; graduates in 1825. While at Bowdoin becomes close friends with Franklin Pierce (who would become the fourteenth president of the United States), Jonathan Cilley, and Horatio Bridge.

1825 Moves to his mother's house in Salem, and lives with his mother and sisters, Elizabeth and Louisa, for the next twelve years. Around this time he begins work on a series of stories, "Seven Tales from My Native Land," and a novel, *Fanshawe*.

1828 Publishes *Fanshawe* anonymously at his own expense, approximately $200. Ashamed of the gothic novel, he burns his own copy and destroys all others that he can find. The novel is not republished until 1876.

1830 Begins publishing tales and sketches in newspapers, magazines, and gift book annuals. He would publish over seventy tales and sketches during the 1830s.

1831 Publishes "My Kinsman, Major Molineaux," "Roger Malvin's Burial," and "The Gentle Boy" in *The Token*, a gift book annual edited by Samuel Goodrich.

1832 Visits New Hampshire and Vermont, and begins work on "The Story Teller," a series of stories linked by an itinerant narrator.

1834 Goodrich decides not to publish "The Story Teller." Portions appear in various periodicals but the overall manuscript has not survived.

1836   Moves to Boston and assumes editorship of the *American Magazine of Useful and Entertaining Knowledge*. The publisher goes bankrupt by June and Hawthorne returns to Salem.

1837   Publishes *Twice-Told Tales*, which receives a laudatory review from his college classmate Henry David Longfellow. He meets Sophia Peabody at the Peabody family home in Salem.

1838   Nearly fights a duel with John O'Sullivan over Salemite Mary Silsbee, and then reconciles with O'Sullivan, the editor of the *Democratic Review*, and begins publishing tales and sketches in his journal. Over the next seven years he would publish two dozen tales and sketches in the notably American literary nationalistic *Democratic Review*.

1839   With the help of his friends, he receives an appointment as salt and coal measurer at the Boston Custom House. Becomes engaged to Sophia Peabody.

1841   Resigns from the Boston Custom House and in April joins the socialistic "utopian" community of Brook Farm in West Roxbury, Massachusetts. Disillusioned with the community, he leaves in November and would eventually sue to recover his initial investment. (He would win the suit but never receive payment.) Publishes the children's books *Grandfather's Chair*, *Famous Old People*, and *Liberty Tree*.

1842   Publishes expanded edition of *Twice-Told Tales*. On July 9 he marries Sophia and moves to the "Old Manse" in Concord, which he rents from the Emerson family. During the more than three years that he lives there, he becomes friends with Ralph Waldo Emerson, Margaret Fuller, and Henry David Thoreau, and also publishes a number of stories, including "The Birth-Mark," "Rappaccini's Daughter," and "The Celestial Rail-road."

1844   Daughter Una born on March 3.

1845   Edits Horatio Bridge's *Journal of an African Cruiser*; moves his family back to Salem to live with his mother and sisters.

1846   Publishes *Mosses from an Old Manse*; son Julian born June 22. With the help of Franklin Pierce, Horatio Bridge, and other friends in the Democratic Party, Hawthorne receives the appointment of surveyor in the Salem Custom House.

1849   Removed from his post as surveyor following the election of the Whig president Zachary Taylor. Mother dies July 31. Hawthorne begins *The Scarlet Letter* later that year, and in "The Custom-House" would take a certain revenge on his Whig adversaries.

1850 Publishes *The Scarlet Letter*. Moves to Lenox, Massachusetts, and becomes friends with Herman Melville, who lives in nearby Pittsfield. Melville's "Hawthorne and His Mosses" is published anonymously in the *Literary World*.

1851 Publishes *The House of the Seven Gables*, *A Wonder-Book for Girls and Boys*, and *The Snow-Image, and Other Twice-told Tales* (December 1851, though dated 1852), along with a new edition of *Twice-Told Tales*. Melville publishes *Moby-Dick* with the dedication: "IN TOKEN OF MY ADMIRATION FOR HIS GENIUS, This Book is Inscribed TO NATHANIEL HAWTHORNE." Daughter Rose born on May 20; moves his family to West Newton, Massachusetts.

1852 Publishes *The Blithedale Romance*, which is based in part on his 1841 experience at Brook Farm, and the campaign biography *The Life of Franklin Pierce*. Purchases Bronson Alcott's former house, "The Wayside," and moves his family to Concord. Death of sister Louisa on July 27 in a Hudson River steamboat accident.

1853 Publishes *Tanglewood Tales*. Appointed U.S. consul at Liverpool by President Franklin Pierce; in July moves his family to England.

1854 Publishes revised edition of *Mosses from an Old Manse*.

1857 Resigns consulship in October.

1858 Hawthornes travel in France and Italy.

1859 Returns to England in June when Una seriously ill, and remains there for a year.

1860 Publishes *The Marble Faun*, which is titled *The Transformation* in England. Returns to The Wayside in Concord.

1862 Publishes "Chiefly about War-Matters" in the July *Atlantic Monthly*, an essay that becomes controversial because of its satirical presentation of Abraham Lincoln. During the Civil War Hawthorne works on drafts of several romances, which he never completes.

1863 Publishes *Our Old Home*, a collection of essays on England, which he dedicates to Franklin Pierce.

1864 Dies in sleep May 19 in Plymouth, New Hampshire, during a carriage trip with his friend Franklin Pierce. Portions of one of his romances in progress, "The Dolliver Romance," appears in the July *Atlantic Monthly*.

Selected Bibliography

NATHANIEL HAWTHORNE'S WRITINGS

Hawthorne, Nathaniel. *The Centenary Edition of the Works of Nathaniel Hawthorne.* Ed. William Charvat et al. 23 vols. Columbus: Ohio State University Press, 1962–96.

BIBLIOGRAPHIES AND COLLECTIONS

American Literary Scholarship: An Annual. Durham: Duke University Press, 1965–present. [Annual bibliographic essay on Hawthorne.]

Callaway, David. "An Annotated Select Bibliography of *The House of the Seven Gables.*" In *Critical Essays on Hawthorne's The House of the Seven Gables* (167–94). Ed. Bernard Rosenthal. New York: G. K. Hall, 1995.

Cohen, B. Bernard, ed. *The Recognition of Nathaniel Hawthorne.* Ann Arbor: University of Michigan Press, 1969.

Crowley, J. Donald. *Hawthorne: The Critical Heritage.* London: Routledge & Kegan Paul, 1970.

Idol, John L. Jr. and Buford Jones, eds. *Nathaniel Hawthorne: The Contemporary Reviews.* New York and Cambridge: Cambridge University Press, 1994.

Millington, Richard, ed. *The Cambridge Companion to Nathaniel Hawthorne.* New York and Cambridge: Cambridge University Press, 2004.

Nathaniel Hawthorne Review. 1986–present. [Annual annotated bibliography on Hawthorne.]

Person, Leland S. "Bibliographic Essay: Hawthorne and History." In *A Historical Guide to Nathaniel Hawthorne* (183–209). Ed. Larry J. Reynolds. New York: Oxford University Press, 2001.

Reynolds, Larry J., ed. *A Historical Guide to Nathaniel Hawthorne.* New York: Oxford University Press, 2001.

Rosenthal, Bernard, ed. *Critical Essays on Hawthorne's The House of the Seven Gables.* New York: G. K. Hall, 1995.

Scharnhorst, Gary, ed. *Nathaniel Hawthorne: An Annotated Bibliography of Commentary and Criticism before 1900.* Metuchen, New Jersey: Scarecrow, 1988.

BIOGRAPHIES

Hawthorne, Julian. *Nathaniel Hawthorne and His Wife: A Biography.* 3rd ed. 2 vols. Boston: James R. Osgood, 1885.

Mellow, James R. *Nathaniel Hawthorne in His Times.* Boston: Houghton Mifflin Co., 1980.

Miller, Edwin Haviland. *Salem Is My Dwelling Place: A Life of Nathaniel Hawthorne.* Iowa City: University of Iowa Press, 1991.

Moore, Margaret B. *The Salem World of Nathaniel Hawthorne.* Columbia: University of Missouri Press, 1998.

Turner, Arlin. *Nathaniel Hawthorne: A Biography*. New York: Oxford University Press, 1980.

Wineapple, Brenda. *Hawthorne: A Life*. New York: Alfred A. Knopf, 2003.

CRITICAL STUDIES

• indicates works included or excerpted in this volume.

• Anthony, David. "Class, Culture, and the Trouble with White Skin in Hawthorne's *The House of the Seven Gables*." *Yale Journal of Criticism* 12 (1999): 249–68.

Arac, Jonathan. *Commissioned Spirits: The Shaping of Social Motion in Dickens, Carlyle, Melville, and Hawthorne*. New Brunswick, NJ: Rutgers University Press, 1979.

• Baym, Nina. "Hawthorne's Holgrave: The Failure of the Artist-Hero." *JEGP* 69 (1970): 584–98.

———. "The Heroine of *The House of the Seven Gables*; or, Who Killed Jaffrey Pyncheon?," *New England Quarterly* 77 (2004): 607–618.

———. *The Shape of Hawthorne's Career*. Ithaca: Cornell University Press, 1976.

Bell, Michael Davitt. *The Development of American Romance: The Sacrifice of Relation*. Chicago: University of Chicago Press, 1980.

———. *Hawthorne and the Historical Romance of New England*. Princeton, NJ: Princeton University Press, 1971.

Bell, Millicent. *Hawthorne's View of the Artist*. New York: State University of New York Press, 1962.

Bellis, Peter. *Writing Revolution: Aesthetics and Politics in Hawthorne, Whitman, and Thoreau*. Athens: University of Georgia Press, 2003.

Berlant, Lauren. *The Anatomy of National Fantasy: Hawthorne, Utopia, and Everyday Life*. Chicago: University of Chicago Press, 1991.

Brodhead, Richard H. *Hawthorne, Melville, and the Novel*. Chicago: University of Chicago Press, 1976.

———. *The School of Hawthorne*. New York: Oxford University Press, 1986.

• Brown, Gillian. *Domestic Individualism: Imagining Self in Nineteenth-Century America*. Berkeley: University of California Press, 1990.

Budick, Emily Miller. *Fiction and Historical Consciousness: The American Romance Tradition*. New Haven, CT: Yale University Press, 1989.

Buell, Lawrence. *New England Literary Culture: From Revolution through Renaissance*. New York and Cambridge: Cambridge University Press, 1986.

Buitenhuis, Peter. *The House of the Seven Gables: Severing Family and Colonial Ties*. Boston: Twayne Publishers, 1993.

Campbell, Charles, "Representing Representation: Body as Figure, Frame, and Text in *The House of the Seven Gables*." *Arizona Quarterly* 47 (1991): 1–26.

• Castiglia, Christopher. "The Marvelous Queer Interiors of *The House of the Seven Gables*." In *The Cambridge Companion to Nathaniel Hawthorne* (186–206). Ed. Richard H. Millington. New York and Cambridge: Cambridge University Press, 2004.

Clark, Robert. *Ideology and Myth in American Fiction, 1823–1852*. London: Macmillan, 1984.

Coale, Samuel Chase. *Mesmerism and Hawthorne: Mediums of American Romance*. Tuscaloosa: University of Alabama Press, 1998.

• Crews, Frederick C. *The Sins of the Fathers: Hawthorne's Psychological Themes*. New York: Oxford University Press, 1966.

Dauber, Kenneth. *Rediscovering Hawthorne*. Princeton, NJ: Princeton University Press, 1977.

Davidson, Cathy N. "Photographs of the Dead: Sherman, Daguerre, Hawthorne." *South Atlantic Quarterly* 89 (1990): 667–701.

Dekker, George. *The American Historical Romance*. New York and Cambridge: Cambridge University Press, 1987.

Dolis, John. *The Style of Hawthorne's Gaze: Regarding Subjectivity*. Tuscaloosa: University of Alabama Press, 1993.

Dryden, Edgar. *Nathaniel Hawthorne: The Poetics of Enchantment*. Ithaca, NY: Cornell University Press, 1977.

Erlich, Gloria C. *Family Themes and Hawthorne's Fiction: The Tenacious Web*. New Brunswick, NJ: Rutgers University Press, 1984.

Fogle, Richard H. *Hawthorne's Fiction: The Light and the Dark*. Norman: University of Oklahoma Press, 1952.

Gallagher, Susan Van Zanten. "A Domestic Reading of *The House of the Seven Gables*." *Studies in the Novel* 21 (1989): 1–13.

Gatta, John. "Progress and Providence in *The House of the Seven Gables*." *American Literature* 50 (1978): 37–48.

• Gilmore, Michael. "The Artist and the Marketplace in the House of the Seven Gables." *ELH* 48 (1981): 172–89.

Gilmore, Paul. *The Genuine Article: Race, Mass Culture, and American Literary Manhood*. Durham, NC: Duke University Press, 2001.

Goddu, Teresa. "The Circulation of Women in *The House of the Seven Gables*." *Studies in the Novel* 23 (1991): 119–127.

Gollin, Rita K. *Nathaniel Hawthorne and the Truth of Dreams*. Baton Rouge: Louisiana State University Press, 1979.

Harris, Kenneth Marc. *Hypocrisy and Self-Deception in Hawthorne's Fiction*. Charlottesville: University Press of Virginia, 1988.

Herbert, T. Walter. *Dearest Beloved: The Hawthornes and the Making of the Middle-Class Family*. Berkeley: University of California Press, 1993.

Hoffman, Daniel. *Form and Fable in American Fiction*. 1961. New York: Oxford University Press, 1965.

• Howells, William Dean. *Heroines of Fiction*, 2 vols. New York: Harper & Brothers, 1901.

Hutner, Gordon. *Secrets and Sympathy: Forms of Disclosure in Hawthorne's Novels*. Athens: University of Georgia Press, 1988.

• James, Henry. *Hawthorne*. London: Macmillan, 1879.

• Kaul, A. N. *The American Vision: Actual and Ideal Society in Nineteenth-Century Fiction*. New Haven, CT: Yale University Press, 1963.

Kermode, Frank. *The Classic: Literary Images of Permanence and Change*. New York: Viking Press, 1975.

Knadler, Stephen. "Hawthorne's Genealogy of Madness: *The House of the Seven Gables* and Disciplinary Individualism." *American Quarterly* 47 (1995): 280–308.

• Lang, Amy Schrager. *The Syntax of Class: Writing Inequality in Nineteenth-Century American Literature*. Princeton, NJ: Princeton University Press, 2003.

• Lawrence, D. H. *Studies in Classic American Literature*. 1923. New York: Viking Press, 1964.

Leverenz, David. *Manhood and the American Renaissance*. Ithaca, NY: Cornell University Press, 1989.

Levin, Harry. *The Power of Blackness: Hawthorne, Poe, Melville*. New York: Alfred A. Knopf, 1958.

Luedtke, Luther S. *Nathaniel Hawthorne and the Romance of the Orient*. Bloomington: Indiana University Press, 1989.

McGill, Meredith L. *American Literature and the Culture of Reprinting, 1834–1853*. Philadelphia: University of Pennsylvania Press, 2003.

McWilliams, John P. Jr. *Hawthorne, Melville, and the American Character: A Looking-Glass Business*. New York and Cambridge: Cambridge University Press, 1984.

Male, Roy R. *Hawthorne's Tragic Vision*. 1957. New York: W. W. Norton & Co., 1964.

Marks, Alfred H. "Who Killed Judge Pyncheon? The Role of the Imagination in *The House of the Seven Gables*." *PMLA* 71 (1956): 355–69.

Martin, Robert K. "Haunted by Jim Crow: Gothic Fictions by Hawthorne and Faulkner." In *American Gothic: New Interventions in a National Narrative* (129–42). Ed. Robert K. Martin and Eric Savoy. Iowa City: University of Iowa Press, 1998.

Martin, Terence. *Nathaniel Hawthorne*. Boston: Twayne Publishers, 1965.

• Matthiessen, F. O. *American Renaissance: Art and Expression in the Age of Emerson and Whitman*. New York: Oxford University Press, 1941.

• Michaels, Walter Benn. "Romance and Real Estate." *The American Renaissance Reconsidered* (156–82). Ed. Walter Benn Michaels and Donald E. Pease. Baltimore: Johns Hopkins University Press, 1984.

• Millington, Richard H. *Narrative Form and Cultural Engagement in Hawthorne's Fiction*. Princeton, NJ: Princeton University Press, 1992.

Mizruchi, Susan L. *The Power of Historical Knowledge: Narrating the Past in Hawthorne, James, and Dreiser*. Princeton, NJ: Princeton University Press, 1988.

Noble, Marianne. "Sentimental Epistemologies in *Uncle Tom's Cabin* and *The House of the Seven Gables*." In *Separate Spheres No More: Gender Convergences in American Literature, 1830–1930* (261–81). Ed. Monika M. Elbert. Tuscaloosa: University of Alabama Press, 2000.

Person, Leland S. Jr. *Aesthetic Headaches: Women and a Masculine Poetics in Poe, Melville, and Hawthorne*. Athens: University of Georgia Press, 1988.

Pfister, Joel. *The Production of Personal Life: Class, Gender, and the Psychological in Hawthorne's Fiction*. Stanford, CA: Stanford University Press, 1991.

Powell, Timothy B. *Ruthless Democracy: A Multicultural Interpretation of the American Renaissance*. Princeton, NJ: Princeton University Press, 2000.

Reynolds, David. *Beneath the American Renaissance: The Subversive Imagination in the Age of Emerson and Melville*. New York: Alfred A. Knopf, 1988.

Schriber, Mary Suzanne. *Gender and the Writer's Imagination: From Cooper to Wharton*. Lexington: University Press of Kentucky, 1987.

Shamir, Milette. "Hawthorne's Romance and the Right to Privacy." *American Quarterly* 49 (1997): 746–79.

Shloss, Carol. *In Visible Light: Photography and the American Writer: 1840–1940*. New York: Oxford University Press, 1987.

Smith, Shawn Michelle. *American Archives: Gender, Race, and Class in Visual Culture*. Princeton, NJ: Princeton University Press, 1999.

Stoehr, Taylor. *Hawthorne's Mad Scientists: Pseudoscience and Social Science in Nineteenth-Century Life and Letters*. Hamden, CT: Archon Books, 1978.

Streeby, Shelley. "Haunted Houses: George Lippard, Nathaniel Hawthorne, and Middle-Class America." *Criticism* 38 (1996): 450–58.

• Sundquist, Eric J. *Home as Found: Authority and Genealogy in Nineteenth-Century American Fiction*. Baltimore: Johns Hopkins University Press, 1979.

Swann, Charles. *Nathaniel Hawthorne: Tradition and Revolution*. New York and Cambridge: Cambridge University Press, 1991.

Tatar, Maria M. *Spellbound: Studies in Mesmerism and Literature*. Princeton, NJ: Princeton University Press, 1978.

Thomas, Brook. *Cross-Examinations of Law and Literature: Cooper, Hawthorne, Stowe, and Melville*. New York and Cambridge: Cambridge University Press, 1987.

Thomas, Ronald R. "Arresting Images in *Bleak House* and *The House of the Seven Gables*." *Novel: A Forum on Fiction* 31 (1997): 87–113.

• Trachtenberg, Alan. "Seeing and Believing: Hawthorne's Reflections on the Daguerreotype in *The House of the Seven Gables*." *American Literary History* 9 (1997): 460–81.

• Trollope, Anthony. "The Genius of Nathaniel Hawthorne." *North American Review* 129, no. 274 (1879): 203–22.

• Waggoner, Hyatt H. *Hawthorne: A Critical Study*. 1955. Rev. ed. Cambridge: Harvard University Press, 1963.

Williams, Susan S. *Confounding Images: Photography and Portraiture in Antebellum American Literature*. Philadelphia: University of Pennsylvania Press, 1997.

TORNADO
BRAIN

CAT PATRICK

PUFFIN BOOKS

PUFFIN BOOKS

An imprint of Penguin Random House LLC, New York

First published in the United States of America by G. P. Putnam's Sons, 2020
Published by Puffin Books, an imprint of Penguin Random House LLC, 2021

Visit us online at penguinrandomhouse.com

THE LIBRARY OF CONGRESS HAS CATALOGED THE G. P. PUTNAM'S SONS EDITION AS FOLLOWS:
Names: Patrick, Cat, author.
Title: Tornado brain / Cat Patrick.
Description: New York: G. P. Putnam's Sons, [2020] | Summary: "A neurodivergent 7th
grader is determined to find her missing best friend before it's too late"
—Provided by publisher.
Identifiers: LCCN 2019048583 (print) | LCCN 2019048584 (ebook) |
ISBN 9781984815316 (hardcover) | ISBN 9781984815323 (ebook)
Subjects: CYAC: Missing children—Fiction. | Best friends—Fiction. | Friendship—
Fiction. | Asperger's syndrome—Fiction. | Attention-deficit hyperactivity disorder—
Fiction. | Sensory disorders—Fiction. | Family life—Washington (State)—Fiction. |
Washington (State)—Fiction.
Classification: LCC PZ7.P2746 Tor 2020 (print) | LCC PZ7.P2746 (ebook) |
DDC [Fic]—dc23
LC record available at https://lccn.loc.gov/2019048583
LC ebook record available at https://lccn.loc.gov/2019048584

Puffin Books ISBN 9781984815330

Printed in the United States of America

Design by Eileen Savage
Text set in Alda OT

10 9 8 7 6 5 4 3 2 1

For the remarkable Adiline M.

What a force of nature you are.

Tornado Brain

prologue

Myth: Tornadoes only move northeast.

PEOPLE USED TO believe that tornadoes only move in one direction—to the northeast—but that's not true. Sometimes they go southwest. Sometimes they touch down and don't go anywhere, getting sucked right back up into the sky. That's disappointing. Sometimes they zig and sometimes they zag. Tornadoes are unpredictable.

If a tornado was in middle school, it might get a lot of weird looks from other kids. Its counselor might call its behavior "unexpected." Its mom might try to get it to move in the same direction as the other tornadoes just to fit in. But maybe the tornado doesn't care about fitting in—even if it means not having a lot of friends.

I can relate because I used to have one friend but now I don't. It's complicated.

I met her during a tornado.

It was the first week of kindergarten. My memories from back then are foggy because I was just a little kid and also my memory is weird, but here's how I think it went. Everyone was at recess and I was circling the outside of the play area alone, thinking of roller coasters because I was obsessed with them then, feeling my way along the chain link because I liked the way my fingers dropped into the spaces between the links and the way my hand smelled like metal afterward. Not a lot of people like that smell.

Sometimes I don't notice things at all and sometimes I notice things too much. That day, I noticed when the wind turbine at the far end of the playground stopped turning. I live in Long Beach, Washington, and it's known for being windy—so windy that there's an international kite festival every August—so when the turbine stopped, it was different. I notice things that are different. The creepy green-gray circular clouds behind the unmoving turbine were different, too. That's called a mesocyclone, which is a word I like.

I don't know if any other kid on the playground saw the twister fall from the funnel cloud that day. I was probably the only one who was looking up instead of playing tetherball or hanging upside down from the monkey bars or something. Being upside down makes my head feel funny.

I watched as the tornado hit the ground and started bumping toward us, tossing things that looked like bugs but were really recycling bins. The emergency system was loud, so I covered my ears. Kids ran inside but I didn't run; I walked . . . in the direction of the tornado. I took my hands off my ears and heard the train sound, far away at first, then louder and louder. The tiny bottom of the tornado got bigger as it collected stuff, pulling up and tossing small trees and even sucking up a utility pole, sending sparks into the sky like fireworks.

I was sucked up, too—by an adult. He grabbed me and started running toward the school. I watched the tornado rip out the far part of the playground fence, which is probably the coolest thing I've ever seen in my life.

"What is wrong with you?" the adult shouted, too close to my ear.

An audiologist once told me that I have better-than-average hearing, so it hurt. If you don't know what an audiologist is, it's a doctor who studies hearing loss and balance issues related to the ears. I don't have either of those things, but still I went to one—along with many other doctors that have *ologist* at the end of their titles.

I cupped my hands over my ears, but I could still hear him shouting: "You need to listen to directions! You could have been killed!"

"It's not my fault," I said. "No one told me any directions."

I bounced along in the teacher's arms, watching the turbine pick up speed until I couldn't see it anymore because it had a tornado wrapped around it like a big tornado hug. The teacher banged through the doors and we were inside the school, running down the hall toward the cafeteria. Without the distraction of the tornado, I noticed his painful grip around my thighs and back. I stiffened and started to slip from his grasp. By the time we made it to the cafeteria, where all the other kids and teachers were hiding under tables, he was holding me only under the arms, my board-straight legs swinging like a pendulum in my flowered capris. My armpits hurt when he finally set me down next to a table in the middle of the room.

"Found her," he said to my teacher. I don't remember her name. I didn't like her very much.

"Come under, Frances," she said. "Sit next to me. It's going to be okay."

"My name is Frankie," I said, crawling under the table. "And I know."

"You gave us a scare, Frankie," she said, stroking my hair. I honestly don't know why people think that's comforting.

"Don't touch me," I snapped, scooting as far away from her as I could get. She looked surprised at first, then frowned and turned to talk to the man who'd carried me.

"I was just watching," I said softly to myself.

"Watching what?" a girl on my right asked. She had braided orange hair with red bows tied at the ends, too many freckles all over her cheeks and forehead, and a terrified expression.

"I saw the tornado!" I said.

"I want my mommy," she said before putting her thumb in her mouth. Now she looked like a baby. "Is it going to get us?" she asked around her thumb, making it harder to understand her. "Will we die? I don't want to die, I want to be a singer. Do you want to hold hands?"

I definitely did not want to touch the hand that she had in her mouth, and I was overwhelmed by her questions.

"What?" I asked, blinking.

"My name is Colette," she answered.

"That's not what I asked."

"What's your name?"

"Frankie."

"I'm scared," she said.

I wasn't feeling scared until the train sound got loud enough to rattle the windows. Then Colette hugged me, and I let her without thinking. Predictably unpredictable, the tornado would turn southwest at the last minute and just miss our school before being whooshed back into the clouds, but of course we didn't know that at the time. I found out later that it was an EF3 on the Enhanced Fujita Scale, which is classified as "intense." I didn't know that then either.

Then I just knew that I was scared, too. I squashed my cheek against Colette's, my arms around her. She was probably the first person other than my family members I'd ever hugged.

"If we don't die, let's be friends," Colette said.

"Okay," I said.

We didn't die, so we were friends.

PART I

Fri-yay

chapter 1

Fact: In some parts of the country,
middle schools have built-in tornado shelters.

COLETTE WENT MISSING on the second Friday in April, almost at the end of seventh grade. It was seven and a half years after the tornado in kindergarten, and Colette and I hadn't been friends anymore for two months.

Before any of us knew she was missing, it was a normal morning. My mom appeared in my doorway at six thirty. Opening my eyes and seeing a person in the doorway made my heart jump.

"I hate it when you do that!" I complained.

"Good morning, Frankie," Mom said in a soothing voice. "Time to get ready for school."

I closed my eyes again.

I'd had trouble falling asleep the night before because I'd been playing something over in my head and when I'm thinking too much at bedtime, my brain doesn't turn off and go to sleep. Plus, I'd forgotten to take the vitamin that helps me sleep. And then I'd woken up twice during the night for no reason, once at two thirty and once at five. It's hard for me to get back to sleep when that happens. Adding it all together, I'd probably had about four hours of sleep.

I rubbed my eyes with my fists, then scooted deeper under the covers, wishing my mom would go away. But I could still smell the scents she'd brought in with her: nice shampoo and disgusting coffee. I pictured a cartoon drawing of coffee-smell pouncing on a cartoon drawing of nice-shampoo-smell. The nice-shampoo-smell fought back and shoved the coffee-smell off, then . . .

"Are you awake, Frankie?" my mom said.

I am now.

Lately, I'd been concentrating on using manners, so I focused on not yelling that I wanted her to leave so I could wake up in peace. *Do not yell,* I told myself, my voice loud in my head. *Do not tell her to get out. Make your voice match hers.*

I opened my eyes and looked at her sideways because I was on my side.

"Hi," I groaned, my tired, grumpy, scratchy voice not sounding like hers at all. She ignored it.

"It's Friday!" Mom said. "Or, since it's your early-release day, should I say, Fri-*yay*?"

We got out of school at 11:25 a.m. on Fridays, so we were

only there for three hours and five minutes, or three class periods—and one of them was homeroom—unless you were an overachiever who'd chosen to take zero period. Zero period is the optional period *before* homeroom and it's way too early for me.

"Uh-huh," I growled, rolling away and pulling the covers over my shoulder. "I'm awake, you can leave now."

"You know the rule," Mom said. "I can't leave until you're upright."

That is the stupidest rule ever! I shouted in my head. It was almost painful not to say it out loud, but I thought about manners and counted to ten and managed not to yell. I threw off my covers and got out of bed, hunched forward, my fists clenched, frowning. But upright.

"There," I said.

"Thank you," my mom said, which bugged me.

I guess I should say right now that I love my mom, so you don't get the wrong idea. She's not mean or anything. I just . . . Things bother me really easily. Or they don't bother me at all. I tend to have extreme feelings one way or the other, not usually in the middle. Maybe that's why I'm sometimes unhappy. I don't know. Anyway.

When my mom finally left, I put on my softest skinny jeans, the ones that I wore at least twice a week. Today, I noticed the seams digging against the sides of my thighs and I hated it, so I changed into a different pair. I pulled on my black hoodie with the thumbholes, testing out the feeling of that for a second, deciding it was okay. The seams of the new pants bugged me, too, so I changed into leggings. They had a hole in the knee but felt okay. I stuck my long fingernail in the hole and made it bigger.

I shoved my unfinished homework into my backpack, then went to brush my teeth. In the mirror, a girl with messy, chin-length hair and too-long bangs, bloodshot brown eyes with dark circles under them, and cracked lips stared back at me. I looked down at my toothbrush: there was a hair on it. I threw it away and leaned over to get a new one out of the cabinet. While I was searching, I found a headband I used to wear all the time when I was younger. I'd never wear it now, but I tried it on, wishing I could text a picture of myself to Colette because I looked hilarious, but I couldn't because we weren't friends anymore. I left the bathroom, dropping the headband on the floor.

I pulled my hood up over my bedhead. From the mini-fridge in my room, I got out the milk, then made myself a bowl of the single brand of cereal I like in the world. I checked my TwisterLvr feed and read about an EF2-category tornado that'd happened in Birmingham, Alabama, the night before. I didn't check my other social media anymore because I didn't want to see all the pictures of Colette and her other friends.

I got my jacket and left. I wanted to ride my favorite

yellow beach cruiser to school, but it wasn't where it was supposed to be, so I had to walk. Only a minute or two into the walk, my phone buzzed in my pocket.

MOM

Do you have your backpack?

I turned around to get it. At the door, Mom held out the pack in one hand and a protein bar in the other. Her dark hair was in a tight bun that looked uncomfortable. I patted the top of my head.

"Don't forget to eat it, please."

"I won't," I said, turning to leave again. She was always reminding me to eat. She didn't remind other people to eat—just me. I guess maybe I needed to be reminded sometimes, but it was still annoying.

"I don't want you to get hangry," she said.

Did you know that the word *hangry* is officially in the dictionary now? It is. I looked it up.

"I'm old enough to know when I need to eat," I complained.

"Yes, at thirteen, you *are* old enough," she said in a way that made me think she was trying to make a point. "Did you brush your teeth?"

"Yes," I said, not totally sure whether I had or not. "Bye."

"Have a great day, Frankie! I love you!"

I made a sound and left again, taking the beach path so I could shout into the wind if I felt like it. I didn't this morning, but I like having options. I like choosing what I get to do because it feels like people are always bossing me around. The only thing is, the beach path takes longer than just walking straight to school. It's like turning the route into an obtuse triangle instead of a line from point A to point B.

Do you know what that is? It's geometry, which I like.

I was late to school so often that the hall monitor didn't blink. I left some books and the uneaten protein bar in my locker, which I don't share with anyone because I don't like when their books touch mine, and left a trail of sand like bread crumbs as I walked down the carpeted hallway to homeroom. The bell rang when I was about halfway to class, and Ms. Garrett didn't say anything when I walked in.

All the other kids were already at their desks, most of them socializing. That's a thing I'm not good at, probably because I don't like *chitchat*—the word itself or the act of doing it.

I sat down at my own private desk island by the window and checked my TwisterLvr account again. Nothing new had happened since the last time I'd checked, which was disappointing.

"Phones away or they're mine," Ms. Garrett said. Some people groaned, but everyone made their phones disappear. Not literally: I don't go to Hogwarts.

Ms. Garrett kept talking: "Let's all work on something productive. That means you too, Anna and Daphne. Marcus! Settle down now."

The room got quiet. Everyone took out homework, because first period is homeroom and that's what you do. I opened *Call of the Wild*, which is about a dog named Buck who lives in the freezing Yukon. Sometimes I specifically don't like books that other people tell me to read, but I liked that one even though reading it wasn't my idea.

This lady—this specialist who was always checking in with me at school—popped her head into the room. Her name is Ms. Faust and she's fine, I guess, except no one else has weird ladies checking up on them, so I pretended not to notice her and eventually she left. Ms. Faust was assigned to me or whatever, so it was her job to check in, but I didn't care. I didn't want her anywhere near me.

I was several chapters into my book when Ms. Garrett put her bony hand on my shoulder, startling me. I cringed and pulled away from her, biting my tongue so I wouldn't say anything she'd think was rude. I didn't want her to call my mom. I touched my opposite shoulder to even myself out, looking down at my notebook and noticing that I'd drawn a few tiny tornadoes while I'd been reading.

"Sorry, Frances," she said, looking embarrassed.

"My name is Frankie," I snapped accidentally. Thankfully, she let it go.

"Again, I apologize. I know you don't like when people touch you, but you didn't answer when I said your name." I strained my neck looking up at her because Ms. Garrett is skyscraper tall (not literally, of course). She kept talking. "Uh, I notice that you're reading your book for English, which is great, but I wanted to make sure you've finished your math homework. We only have a few minutes left in the period and Mr. Hubble asked me to check with you. He said that yesterday, you—"

"It's in my backpack," I interrupted, which wasn't a lie. It *was* in my backpack. It was also unfinished.

"I see," Ms. Garrett said. She tilted her head to the side like my dog does sometimes.

Behind Ms. Garrett, across the room in the regular rows, several kids were watching us. Tess smiled at me with her mouth but not her eyes, a halfway smile, which was confusing; Kai smiled at me with his mouth *and* his eyes, an all-the-way smile, which was confusing in a different way; and Mia didn't smile, just stared, which wasn't confusing in the least. I frowned at all of them and they went back to their classwork.

Ms. Garrett opened her mouth to say something else— maybe to ask to see my homework—but the announcement bell chimed, and the office lady started talking. That was unexpected, because it wasn't announcement day, which is Tuesday. And if we *had* had announcements, they would have been at the beginning of the period, not the end.

"Attention, students and staff," the office lady said. "Please proceed immediately in an orderly fashion to the auditorium for an address from Principal Golden. Thank you."

Ms. Garrett looked at me blankly for a few seconds like she was stunned, but then she told everyone to get up and move toward the auditorium. Kai smiled at me all-the-way again as he left the classroom with his friends. Confused by how I felt about that, I waited until everyone else left, too, and then went into the hall.

I watched Kai walk like he was going to wobble over, laughing so hard his eyes got watery as his friend Dillon told a story about some try-hard tourist who had wiped out at the skate park. Kai had on dark blue skate pants with cargo pockets and checkerboard slip-on sneakers and his shiny black hair looked especially interesting, like he'd been blasted by a huge gust of wind from behind and his hair had gotten stuck. I could see a scab on the back of his arm above his left elbow, which grossed me out.

Their conversation got quieter, then Dillon turned around and looked at me, so I stopped watching Kai and stared at the wall instead.

You should know that most people think Ocean View Middle School looks incredibly strange. About five years ago, when the old school was getting run-down, instead of wrecking it and building something new, they just added on. The front part with the offices, cafeteria, and math and English halls is clean and bright, but the back part with the auditorium and shop and music rooms is dark and smells like old sneakers.

I like to run my hands along walls when I walk because I don't like being surrounded by the other kids since they sometimes accidentally bump me. That's what I was doing when Tess appeared next to me.

Tall and skinny, not as tall as Ms. Garrett, though, she walked sort of bent in on herself like she was trying to be shorter. Her smooth, dark hair was parted on the side, so she had to tuck the hair-curtain behind her right ear to make eye contact. Eye contact made me uncomfortable.

"Did you get in trouble?" she asked quietly, raising her perfectly neat eyebrows. I stared at them: Eyebrows are really weird, actually. They never exactly match. There's always . . .

"Frankie?"

"Huh?"

"I asked if you got in trouble?" Tess repeated.

"For what?"

"For not doing your homework?" She practically whispered it. Tess talked super-quietly, like she didn't want anyone to hear her. I barely could.

"I did my homework," I said, which wasn't a lie. I'd done

some of my homework. And it wasn't really her business in the first place. But I managed not to tell her that. Despite getting hungrier by the second, I was doing okay at manners so far today. I mean, except when I'd snapped at my teacher. But since she hadn't gotten mad, it didn't count.

"Oh, okay," Tess said. "Sorry."

Mia nudged Tess and told her to look at something on her social feed and Tess did and they both giggled—Mia loudly and Tess softly—and I was happy not to be asked any more questions about my homework.

In the auditorium, I followed Tess and Mia down the aisle. Tess was half a head taller than Mia and Mia's butt was half a cheek bigger than Tess's. Tess walked like a normal teenager in her skinny jeans and gray T-shirt with an open sweater that looked like a blanket over it. Mia swayed her hips back and forth in her flowy jumpsuit, making her long, curly blond hair sway, too. They picked a row and I sat behind them on the end by the aisle. I looked around, not seeing where Kai was sitting.

I did notice Ms. Faust smiling at me encouragingly from where she was leaning against the far wall. I wished she'd look at someone else.

"Move over," a mean kid named Alex said, staring down at me. He was always yelling at people—a few times even teachers. I may have big emotions, but not like Alex. "Make room for other people."

"I was here first," I said, my need to sit on the aisle outweighing my desire not to get yelled at by Alex. I really don't like being surrounded. "Here," I said, moving my knees to the left so he could squeeze through.

"Whatever," Alex said, shaking his head and stepping on my foot as he shoved past me.

"Ouch!" I said loudly. He rolled his eyes and didn't apologize. I folded my arms over my chest and slumped down in my chair.

It took a while for all 323 students to sit down. Well, 322 today, but we didn't know that yet. The room felt like being on a beach when an electrical storm is coming, like you could get zapped any minute. That's figurative language—similes and metaphors and stuff. I'm trying to use it more instead of being so literal all the time because people laugh at you when you're literal.

Onstage, Principal Golden held up a hand with her middle and ring finger touching her thumb, the pointer and pinkie sticking straight up: the Quiet Coyote.

"So lame," I heard Alex say loudly. Principal Golden looked right at him in a way I wouldn't want to be looked at by the principal, and he didn't say anything else.

Principal Golden sniffed loudly into the microphone.

"Something has happened," she said, her *p*'s making irritating popping sounds in the mic. "This morning, there has been an incident. We're not sure of the details, but one of our Ocean View students is missing."

I heard the buzzing of the microphone for a couple of seconds before the entire auditorium broke out in whispers.

"Did she say missing?"

"I wonder who it is?"

"What do you think happened?"

My mind started ping-ponging from the idea of a missing student to the missing-kid posters on the bulletin board at I Scream for Ice Cream, where my biological father made me and my sister go when he visited last year even though it was the middle of winter and pouring rain and my sister is lactose intolerant. I shook my head to tune back in to what Principal Golden was saying.

" . . . investigating and we don't know anything more at this time. The police are searching the school and want to speak to select students. Rather than further disrupting this already short school day, the administration has decided to cancel class for the rest of the day. If you ride the bus, please see Mrs. Taylor in the office for instructions on . . ."

Everyone got up at once and started talking except me: I stayed in my seat, waiting for the auditorium to thin out. My row had to exit from the other side because I was blocking my end: even mean Alex went the other way, and I was glad because I didn't want my foot trampled again.

It was 9:40 and I was supposed to be starting second period, English, but instead I was going to go home. My stomach rolled with the weird feeling of change. Change is my enemy.

"She's not answering her phone."

I looked over to see Tess and Mia huddled together in the aisle, whispering to each other. "When's the last time you talked to her?"

"Last night before dinner," Mia said, spinning the ring on her middle finger. "She wasn't in zero period. I thought she slept in."

"That's not like her, though," Tess said, chewing her lip. "Her bag's not in our locker." I leaned forward so I could hear Tess better, wondering if it bugged her that Mia's curls were touching her hand. I brushed my own hand like they'd been touching mine. "Is she home sick?"

They looked at each other, both with big eyes that reminded me of a certain comic book cat, Mia's blue like a sunny day and Tess's green-gray like a cloudy one. Maybe they felt me watching them because they both looked at me at the same time.

"Have you talked to Colette?" Tess asked in her tentative voice.

"Of course I've talked to Colette," I said.

"I mean *recently*," Tess clarified. "Like, did you talk to

Colette yesterday?" Now she was pulling on the lip she'd been biting. It was distracting: I wished she'd leave her lip alone.

"No," I said, just to say something. *No* is an easy response for me.

"This is serious," Mia said, leaning forward like my therapist did sometimes. She lowered her voice. "What if it's her?"

"What if what's her?" I asked.

Mia sighed loudly. "Why are you always so spacey?"

Tess gave her a look, then explained, "Frankie, what we're asking is: What if the missing student is *Colette*?"

I stared at her without saying anything because that idea really didn't make sense to me—since I obviously didn't know at the time that the missing student *was* Colette and since I'd been mostly thinking that it felt strange being told to go home when I'd just gotten to school. This was not my normal routine.

"Come on," Mia said, pulling on Tess's arm, "let's go see if the teachers need help."

chapter 2

Myth: Twin tornadoes are extremely rare.

THE PSYCHIATRIST IS the one who labels you.

My mom picked up clothes and books and papers from
the floor while I lounged on my bed, trying to ignore her,
instead of being at school. I concentrated on not being
annoyed about her touching my stuff because if I exploded,
she'd probably make me go to the psychiatrist again.

Our deal was that if I could keep my anger and other
stuff under control, I could stay off medication. And I really
wanted to stay off medication: it made me sleepy or starving or spacey or bloated or weepy or forgetful or jittery—or
all of the above—depending on which one I was taking. I
was only *on* medication because of the labels—and like I
said, the psychiatrist is the one who labels you.

I got labeled when I was in fourth grade. I'd been

digging through my mom's desk, looking for glue. Instead, I found something that looked like a test—except the questions weren't about math or history or science: they were about behavior.

The directions said to fill in the bubble that fit best. You had to pick whether the statements were not true, sometimes true, often true, or almost always true.

The child wanders aimlessly from one activity to another.
The child has difficulty relating to peers.
The child stares or gazes off into space.
The child gets teased a lot.
The child walks between two people who are talking.
The child offers comfort to others when they are sad.
The child has more difficulty with change than other children.

There were seventy-five statements. None of the bubbles had been filled in yet. My name was at the top of the page.

For a week, I snuck out of bed in the middle of the night to check the drawer and see if the bubbles had been filled in, bringing a notebook with me to write down the words I didn't know so I could look them up in the dictionary. I wanted to know if my mom thought that I never, sometimes, often, or almost always wander aimlessly from one activity to another. If she thought I never, sometimes, often, or almost always have difficulty relating to peers. If I never or always gaze off into space. If I never walk between two people who are talking. If I always get teased a lot.

If the child has more difficulty with change than other children.

I wanted to know what my mom thought of me. But I never found out because one night the bubbles were empty, and the next they were gone. They appeared again in the psychiatrist's office—but no one would show them to me. I remember that I was mad about the bubbles—and also mad because the psychiatrist said labels I didn't understand but looked up on the internet later, like "neurological disorder" and "attention deficit" and "poor executive functioning"— labels that were directed at me! There were all sorts of articles about how parents could "cope with" kids with these problems. Until the labels, I didn't know I was someone my mom had to "cope with." Until the labels, I didn't know I had "problems."

Mad about the bubbles and about not being included in the conversation and about being talked about in a way that felt gross, I had kicked the back of the psychiatrist's desk. That made my mom mad, which made me madder, which made me kick harder. Eventually, I melted out of the chair onto the floor, kicking the back of his desk with full force, over and over and over. My mom and the psychiatrist left until I calmed down, but before they did, I remember my mom crying. I don't like to think about that.

Sometimes I don't remember things at all, and sometimes I remember them too clearly. That's a thing I wish I'd forget.

"Frankie?" my mom asked, back in the present. She was holding a pile of my books and staring at me. I stared back at the reverse-parentheses wrinkles at the top of her nose between her eyebrows. "Did you hear me? I asked if I should call Gabe and make an appointment for you. I'm concerned that you haven't seen him in a while. And with everything going on now, I think it'd be a good idea."

Gabe is my therapist, which is way better than a psychiatrist. Therapists spend more time with you and try to talk to you and give you suggestions. I don't remember that much about the first time I met Gabe, but I do remember that his office was filled with board games and musical instruments and toys, and he talked to me alone, without my mom, and didn't label me or hide bubble worksheets from me. And he let me draw tornadoes while he asked me questions.

"Frankie, are you listening to me?" my mom asked.

"Yes!" I said, taking a deep breath. "But you don't need to call Gabe. I don't need to go to therapy every time some little thing happens." I focused on keeping my voice calm. "I'm fine. Don't worry."

Often, Gabe makes me feel better about things. But

I still didn't want to make an appointment with him. I wanted to prove that I could do it on my own. I didn't want weird Ms. Faust trying to smile at me at school. I wanted to be a normal person who could just live regularly without needing help every other minute.

And I was doing okay—as long as my routine stayed pretty much the same. But then Colette went missing—though I didn't know it was Colette for sure yet—and her current best friends, Tess and Mia, had asked me questions I hadn't exactly answered truthfully and I was home when I should have been in English, so my routine was not the same today.

My mom put down the books and moved super-close to the end of my bed, maybe going to sit on it, and I really didn't want her to. I have a thing about people sitting on my bed, even people I love like my mom.

"This isn't a little thing, Frankie . . ."

Don't sit on my bed, I thought.

"This is a big thing, a missing child."

Don't lean against it like that; it'll make you want to sit!

"Gabe might have some strategies for—"

She sat down.

"Mom! Stop!" I shouted at her, unable to keep my voice level anymore. "The kid is probably dead. We'll all just have to deal with it."

"Frances Vivienne Harper!" Mom gasped.

Whoops.

"I didn't mean that," I said quickly, backpedaling. "I just said that because I'm hungry."

"Get up, then," Mom said, mad, standing and turning toward the door, her knees popping when she moved. I don't know when she'd gotten so creaky. "We're going for a walk and then we'll eat. It's nonnegotiable." Her voice didn't have that nice mom tone to it anymore; it was flat.

"I don't want to go for a walk," I whined. "Can't we just eat lunch? I'm starving."

"You'll be fine," Mom said, still with an angry tone.

Tones are something therapists teach you to try to notice. Gabe calls them "cues." Most people just understand them automatically.

Thinking of that made me think of when I was little and I thought automatic toilets were called *automagic*. On my big list of things to do in life is to write a letter to the people who make the dictionary to see if they'll change it because my word is better. I was thinking about that when my mom raised her voice, which she rarely does.

"Frankie! Get up from that bed!"

"Fine," I said, knowing I was going to get in big trouble if I didn't.

When I stood up, she left. I pulled my puffy vest on over my hoodie, lifted the hood over my head. I couldn't remember when I'd last brushed my hair and there was a huge nest in it. I like my hair—it's really thick and wavy—but I don't like brushing out the nests it makes at all.

I stepped into my red rain boots and tromped out of my room, down the hall, and to the elevator. My mom says the elevators are for the guests—did I mention that we live in an inn?—but I felt like breaking the rules.

Outside, the billowy clouds had parted, and I could see blue sky for miles. It was windy, so I kept my hood up over my head. Wind in my ears is terrible.

Charles, my mom's boyfriend, and our dog, Pirate, were waiting for me in the parking lot, ready to go for a walk on the beach. Charles had on his usual outdoor uniform: work boots, faded jeans, a black T-shirt, a gray windbreaker, and a red beanie with his light brown hair flipping out underneath. When it wasn't topped with a beanie, Charles wore his hair messy, like I did, but his was styled to look that way—with special organic hair products he ordered from Seattle and that my mom teased him about, which usually made him kiss her, which always grossed me out.

I like Charles and used to wonder sometimes if my mom would marry him, but then she didn't so I stopped wondering. My mom isn't the marrying kind: she and my biological father weren't married. Well, I mean, he was married . . . but to someone else. Adults make dumb choices sometimes, but I guess if they hadn't made that dumb choice, I wouldn't exist.

Anyway, my mom and Charles work a lot, so they started this tradition of meeting up at break times for a short walk. Usually, we only have to do it on weekends or when we're off school for teacher work days. I guess they didn't feel like they were seeing me or my sister enough—or asking us enough uncomfortable questions.

"Hey, boss," Charles said, holding out a to-go cup that I knew had hot chocolate in it. His jacket sleeve pulled back when he reached out, showing a peek of the tattoos that covered his entire arm. Arms.

I grunted something as I accepted the cup.

"Say it's mint tea if she asks," Charles instructed, scratching his stubble, and I nodded. My mom doesn't want us having sugar all the time. Well, she doesn't want *me* having it all the time. Or red dye. Or processed foods. "You okay?"

"I'm okay," I said, giving Pirate a rub behind her ear. Her name is Pirate because another dog scratched out her left eye in a fight and she looks like she has a permanent eye patch. It's pretty disgusting, but the rest of her is cute so I try not to look at her eye and love her anyway.

"Did they leave without us?"

"I told them to go ahead," Charles said. "I said we'd catch up."

Charles looked at me sideways like he was trying to figure out my mood, which he does a lot. Sometimes I'm okay with it and sometimes I want to growl at him, which I don't do anymore because Gabe says it's socially unacceptable, but I still think it's a useful way of telling someone to quit it.

It's hard to understand why expressing yourself in growls or just directly saying that you don't like something is bad. Manners seem like wrapping words in cotton balls, and I think it's just easier to say the words without the fluff. I don't have any friends, though, so I'm probably wrong. You probably shouldn't take any of my advice.

We started walking and we didn't say any words for a while—regular ones or cotton-ball ones. The silence made me happy. I missed that about being friends with Colette: she was good at walking without talking without it being weird.

I listened to the sound of Pirate's tags clanking together as we went down the short paved road toward the ocean. They made a little song and I imagined myself dancing, but didn't actually do it.

Soon the pavement turned to sand and my bootheels dug in deeper with every step. I splashed through puddles from a quick rain that had happened earlier, then moved over to the left side of the sandy path to run my hand along the wispy beach grass that came up to my waist.

We got to the point where the grass ends and opens up to the beach, which stretches for miles in both directions. I shaded my eyes so I could see where my mom was: she and my sister were walking at the edge of the tide.

"Some people think the missing kid might be Colette,"

I said to Charles, watching the water. It was choppy today and looked like the waves were siblings fighting with each other. The wind was threatening to pull back my hood, so I yanked the strings tighter. "She wasn't at school today and no one could reach her."

"It's scary, no matter who it is," Charles said.

"Yeah," I said, not sure I really felt scared. I felt more like a mixture of curious and excited, which I'm pretty sure is not the right way to feel when a kid from your school could be in trouble. My emotions don't always work like they're supposed to, and it felt like they were extra off right then because I should have been at school, but I was walking on the beach.

"What if they don't find the kid?" I asked Charles, watching my mom and sister walking, holding hands. I didn't do that with my mom, and it made me feel jealous.

"That would be awful," Charles said, taking Pirate off her leash. She bolted toward the water to chase the seagulls as they searched for lunch of their own. "No matter who it is, it'd be awful."

"Yeah," I said, wondering if I'd really feel awful or if I'd have to pretend to feel awful so everyone wouldn't think I was weird.

Pirate bounded back our way with a huge stick in her mouth, circled Charles, and dropped it near his feet. She waited for him to throw it, then took off again in a flash.

"Hey, Charles?"

"Yeah?"

"I think it's Colette," I said. I just had a feeling.

The truth was, I'd lied to Tess and Mia: I *had* seen Colette the day before. She'd randomly come by my room for the first time since February. We'd had a fight and she'd left. Thinking through the fight was the reason I couldn't fall asleep the night before: it'd stuck with me into the late-night hours. Now I was feeling really confused.

"I hope you're wrong, buddy," Charles said, smiling at me.

Me too, I thought.

"Now what's she doing?" Charles asked, shielding his eyes from the sun and watching Pirate. It looked like she was trying to dig up a crab. "She's going to get pinched again," he said. "I'll be right back."

I nodded and walked over to a log that the ocean hadn't wanted anymore. It had sand packed into the grooves, but it was dry enough to use as a bench. I inspected it for bugs, then sat down, thinking about nothing or everything.

I picked up a stick and wrote *Hi* in the wet sand.

Charles took the stick and wrote in the sand *Hi back*. I hadn't noticed him there again. Then my mom and sister were on their way toward us, and I wondered how much time had gone by while I was spacing out. That happens sometimes.

"What's in the cup?" Mom asked.

"Hot chocolate," I said without thinking. My mom gave Charles a mad-ish look and Charles shrugged.

"No more sugar for you today," Mom said to me, continuing on toward the inn. Charles and Pirate started jogging together in the same direction.

My sister followed them, and as she walked by me, she said, "That sucks for you. She just said she's making chocolate cake for dessert tonight."

"Why are you always so annoying?" I snapped. It was only when I saw the hurt in her eyes that I realized she'd been showing empathy, not rubbing it in.

"Whatever, Frankie," Tess said quietly, shaking her head. "I don't know what's going on with you lately."

She ran off like a gazelle on her long legs and I was left to walk back to the inn alone on my shorter ones.

Oh, did I say that Tess is my sister? Yeah, she is. She's one minute older than me. Yes, that means we're twins. Not identical ones: the fraternal kind.

And yes, my twin sister stole the only friend I'd ever had.

chapter 3

Myth: Tornadoes bring a drop in atmospheric pressure that will make your house explode if your house is closed up.

MY MOM AND Charles live in a cottage behind the inn. Tess and I shared the second bedroom in the cottage until we started middle school. That's when Tess asked Mom if it'd be okay if she started using one of the rooms inside the inn, one of the ones that didn't have a view or anything.

Tess had explained that all of her friends had their own rooms and she needed privacy to work on her art. She wanted to go to art school someday, which I bet she could, except then she'd have to show her drawings to someone and that freaks her out for some reason so maybe not. Anyway, when Tess asked for her own room, I didn't think it was about art: I thought it was about not wanting to share a room with me anymore.

Whatever the reason, Mom and Charles agreed. Mom

set ground rules for Tess, like she could never let anyone in her room without getting permission, and she always had to keep the door bolted at night, and she had to be in her room at nine and stay there all night, and she had to check in with Mom or Charles before going to sleep.

Then I told them that it wasn't fair that Tess got to have a room at the inn and I didn't. Mom probably felt more nervous about letting me do it than Tess—because she trusts Tess more than she trusts me—but she said yes. She made us have connecting rooms, which, honestly, made me feel a lot better because I wasn't sure I'd wanted to move out of the cottage. The whole first year, Tess and I slept with the doors connecting our rooms wide open. Did you know some people think your house will explode if your windows and doors are shut during a tornado? It's not true, but I liked the doors open anyway. Except at the beginning of this school year, Tess started closing hers. And it was weird to have hers closed and mine open, so I started closing mine, too.

I was thinking about how I didn't like closed doors while I watched Tess texting. She had her knees pulled up into the chair and the light from the screen was making her skin look blue. Her thumbs went *tap-tap-tap-tap*, then she waited, biting her thumbnail, for a response.

"Who are you texting?" I asked.

Tess looked up at me sharply, then at Mom's back. Mom

was over by the sink cutting cucumbers into slices for the guest water jugs. The water was running so she hadn't heard me.

"It's a group text," Tess whispered. "Everyone's wondering who the kid is that's missing. Some people got called to the police station."

The water turned off. "Who's in the group text?" I asked.

Mom turned around quickly. "Tess!" she said. "No phones at the table, you know the rule—especially right now, with everything that's going on." She walked over and held out a wet hand for the phone.

Tess frowned at me and handed it over. "Sorry, Mom."

I watched Tess dunk her grilled cheese in her tomato soup and take a bite. She did it so perfectly, not dripping any soup from the bowl to her mouth. My whole body felt aware of the fact that we were at the cottage instead of the cafeteria. I didn't like the alteration in my normal schedule.

"Do you have homework?" Mom asked, not directing the question at either of us. I thought it was weird she was asking about homework, but parents are weird sometimes.

"We didn't have school except for part of first period," I said to her back, leaving a trail of tomato soup like a crime scene on the tablecloth. "How could we have homework?"

"I'm going to work on my portfolio this afternoon," Tess said, probably just to make herself look good since she was mad at me for getting her phone taken away.

"Good for you," I grumbled. Mom turned around and gave me a sharp look.

"Be kind to your sister," she said. "And you'd be smart to work on your big science project. That's a great thing to do today. It'd be a nice distraction."

"That's what I was thinking," Tess said.

"It's not due until May," I protested.

"Yes, but May is only two weeks away, and it's a big undertaking," Mom said. "It'll mean a lot of planning and organization. And you'll want to write and rewrite your assessment to make sure it says exactly what you want it to say." I didn't answer her, because I probably wasn't going to do that and we both knew it, so she asked, "Well, what are you going to do today, then? I want you to find something *productive*. You can't just wander around aimlessly or watch *Tornado Alley* all day."

I rolled my eyes. "Mom, it's *Tornado Ally*. Geez."

"Whatever it's called, you can't spend your whole day watching it," she replied as my brain wandered off.

I'd been watching *Tornado Ally* when Colette knocked on my door the night before. I ignored the first knocks. And the second set. I thought it was a guest knocking on the wrong door, which happens more than you might think. But after the third set of knocks, I flung open the door impatiently.

"Hi, Frankie," Colette said like it was nothing, like she hadn't ignored me since February. She had her bright red hair pulled back in a knot and a big smile on her super-freckled face. She was wearing a blue sweatshirt with a dolphin pattern. The sweatshirt was a little too tight in the waist.

"Hi," I said, going back to my desk.

"I see you're busy," she said, barely stepping into the room. She knew I didn't like people in my space. "I won't stay long, but I was wondering if I could borrow that old notebook? That we used to write in?" I turned in my chair and gave her an annoyed look. She pulled down the hem of her sweatshirt and explained: "I want to copy something."

"No," I said, flipping around to face my computer.

"No?" Colette asked, like she couldn't believe I wouldn't just hand over what she wanted after she hadn't spoken to me for two months.

"No," I said. "You can't have it."

"Come on, Frankie," she said. "I'll take care of it and I'll bring it back. I'll give it to you at school tomorrow."

"No!" I said forcefully, staring at the screen. I could see her reflection in it.

I heard her take a deep breath behind me. "Are you going to do homework at your mom's cottage?"

"None of your business," I said. *Why do you care about my homework?*

"Will you just let me borrow the notebook, please?" Colette asked, sweetness in her voice.

"No!" I shouted.

"Why not?" Colette demanded, anger replacing the sweetness. "It's mine as much as it's yours."

"I lost it," I said quietly, tapping my fingernail on the mouse too softly to make it actually go *click*. My cheeks were growing hot.

"I can tell you're lying," Colette said. "You never look at me when you lie. Why do you have to be like that?"

The little monsters inside that turn up my temperature and make me scream were gathering—and I told myself with my voice on zero that yelling at Colette wouldn't be a good idea because my mom might hear. Or a guest might call the front desk and tell her. Instead, I grabbed my noise-canceling headphones and put them on.

A few seconds later, I felt the door shut hard. It wasn't a slam because Colette wouldn't do that. Only I slam doors, it seems—

"Frankie!" Mom said urgently, pulling me out of my memory. "Please listen to me."

"What?" I asked, blinking, no clue how long she'd been talking to me. "What's happening?"

Tess sighed.

"What?"

She shook her head at me.

"I just got off the phone with the police," Mom said. I hadn't heard her phone ring—I hadn't heard her talking.

I was wondering if my ears were working properly when my mom said, "I'm so sorry, girls, but they told me that the missing girl *is* Colette."

"I knew it," I said flatly.

"No!" Tess wailed over my words, like she hadn't already thought the same thing, tears rushing down her face. "Where do they think she is? Have they checked hospitals? This can't be happening!"

"They don't know anything," Mom said, hugging Tess. She smoothed her hair and wiped her cheeks. "They're trying their hardest to find her. That's why they want her friends to come in and answer some questions. They're hoping it might help."

"When?" Tess whispered.

"Right now."

chapter 4

Fact: Sometimes you can't see a tornado.

MY SISTER AND I stopped having joint birthday parties when we were eleven.

Even though she's not that outgoing, everyone likes Tess. It seems like because she doesn't try to be everyone's friend, they all try harder to be hers. And when it came to our birthday parties, Tess always invited the whole class so no one would feel left out.

Often there would be a theme, like princess or circus or like when we turned eight and my mom let us have Halloween in August. That was Tess's favorite because she loves anything scary and she and Charles made a kid-friendly haunted house in the inn's function room. I hated it. There was this part of the party where Charles, dressed like a zombie, hid behind a door and jumped out when kids came in. It'd made Tess practically pee her pants with laughter, but I'd burst into tears.

Anyway, the parties came with a lot of squealing and stampeding—even from quiet Tess—and usually made me feel like I was watching a noisy kaleidoscope from the corner of a room, depending on which medication they were giving me then.

Medication for someone like me isn't easy. My "challenges," as Gabe calls them, are invisible—just like tornadoes you can't see until they wipe out people's houses in the middle of the night. My mom says my brain is special, but the psychiatrist will tell you that I have several neurological conditions: attention deficit disorder, Asperger's syndrome, and sensory processing disorder. And they aren't as simple as having strep throat and getting antibiotics to treat it. That's why, after the labels, the psychiatrist experimented on me with a bunch of stuff. But nothing ever felt right, and even on medication, I still felt like screaming and crying and generally melting down a lot of the time. Definitely at my birthday parties.

So I stopped having parties. That's why my eleventh birthday was the best one ever.

"If you're not going to have a party, what would you like to do to celebrate your birthday?" my mom asked. "You're turning eleven! And you've had such a great year. There's a lot to celebrate."

It was a Saturday morning and we were all hanging out in the living room of the cottage. Tess was curled up sideways in the big chair, a horror book in front of her face, not really paying attention. Charles wrestled Pirate on the floor, getting dog hair all over his T-shirt for some old rock band I'd never heard of, and Mom and I were on opposite ends of the couch kind of watching whatever movie was playing on whatever channel the TV was on. Everyone was wearing pajama bottoms.

I tossed a pillow in the air and caught it, over and over. I was literally throwing a throw pillow.

"Maybe we could go to the arcade," I said.

Toss. Catch. Toss. Catch. Toss. Catch.

"Okay," Mom said enthusiastically. "We could—"

"Never mind," I interrupted, not wanting her to turn it into a big thing. *Toss. Catch.* "I don't want to go there." I thought a little more, liking the control of planning my very own non-party. "Can I sleep in a tent on the beach?"

Toss. Catch. Toss. Catch.

"Since the beach is technically a road, you can't do that, unfortunately," Charles answered, looking up at me from the floor with his smiling eyes and humongous wild eyebrows. "Sleeping on a road isn't a great idea."

"Ha," I said—not laughing, just saying it—tossing the pillow again. "Can I at least have a fire?"

"Sure," Mom said. I glanced at her and she was watching

me toss the pillow with an expression like that emoji with the perfectly straight mouth, like she wanted to tell me to stop, but knew it would be better not to. Instead, she said, "We can make dinner and s'mores. It'll be great! I could make skewers. You like skewers!" She smiled then; she looked better when she smiled.

"Okay, but I was thinking it'd be a smaller number of people," I said, focusing on the pillow because I knew my mom was going to make a sad-emoji face, and I knew I wouldn't like it. "I just wanted to invite Colette."

"You're not inviting your sister?" Mom asked.

"Are you coming to my party?" Tess asked in a low voice. I guess she had been paying attention after all. I don't know; maybe she always is and just pretends not to be.

"No," I said quickly. Mom was planning to drive Tess and eight friends all the way to Aberdeen to go roller skating, which sounded horrible for at least seven reasons.

"Sorry, Mom, but Frankie's right. It's only fair that I don't go to hers if she's not going to mine," Tess said matter-of-factly.

"But that's . . . ," Mom said, her voice fading away. "You've always . . ." Her voice faded again. She cleared her throat. "The two of you and Colette play together all the time. Are you sure this won't be . . . weird?"

"We don't *play* together," Tess said, her cheeks pink. "We hang out. And it's fine, Mom, really." I think she understood that I placed a lot of value in fairness—and if I wasn't going to her party, then she wasn't going to mine. Fair is fair.

"Well, I'll do something with Tess, then," Mom said. "But you can't light a fire on your own, Frankie. Charles will have to go with you. Or I could, and Tess and Charles could do something?"

"Um . . . ," I said, not hiding a smile. My mom is the worst at starting fires.

"I get it," she said, laughing. "Charles is in charge of the fire."

"That's fine," I said, meaning it. Charles may have been a lawyer before he moved to Long Beach, but he didn't act like it—he acted like a mature kid—so I knew he'd be okay to have around.

On the evening of my non-party, which was the first Saturday after my actual eleventh birthday, Colette, Charles, and I loaded up one of the inn's wagons with firewood, kindling, a lighter, beach blankets, beach chairs, hot dogs, sodas, and stuff to make s'mores. Charles pulled the wagon ahead of us with Pirate circling him like a maniac, seeming as excited to be going to the beach as I was.

We meandered to the right side of the sand path and walked in a line so we could touch the tall beach grass as we went. This car entrance to the beach was closed to protect the razor clam beds from getting crushed. It was illegal to drive onto the beach this way during clam season or to ride a horse over this section of the beach this time of year. Charles was extreme: he wouldn't even let us ride *bikes* through the entrance. Since cars had to drive onto the beach from the north or south entrances, the usual deep tire tracks were filled in by thick, tiny mountains of dry sand.

"What did you do today?" Colette asked.

"I don't know," I said with a shrug. "Nothing."

"Oh," Colette said. "My mom made me go to the grocery store with her and then she took me to the library and I got the next graphic novel in that series I like and then we got smoothies." She paused for a breath. "If you could only have mango or strawberry smoothies for the rest of your life, what would you pick?"

"Mango."

"You didn't think about that very long."

"I hate strawberries."

"If you had to eat strawberries or broccoli for dinner, which one would you choose?" she asked.

"I'd skip dinner," I said, brushing the hair out of my mouth. Colette had her hair pulled up in knots like Mickey Mouse ears, and I maybe should have pulled mine back, too, to keep it out of my mouth, but I hate the feeling of having my ears exposed. And I can't put a hoodie over a ponytail or knot. And hair bands give me headaches.

We'd made it to the medium-dry sand then. I loved looking at the different tracks made by toes and shoe treads and

48

webbed feet and paws, leading around in circles or swirls, a giant game of connect-the-dots between pieces of washed-up seaweed, logs, and shells. I kicked an empty crab claw.

"I brought you a present," Colette said, pausing to take off her flip-flops. "I also brought some music so we can sing if we want to, and two new quiz books."

"I love quizzes," I said. I don't love singing, but I didn't say that.

"I know. This is going to be so fun! My mom said your mom said we could stay out here until ten!"

"I know!" I said, looking toward the water. "It's the best!"

The beach made me feel calm. The tide was low, and the sand near the water was rippled from the waves rolling in and out when the tide had been higher. My eyes got stuck until Colette spoke again.

"What's Tess doing tonight?"

"She went to a movie with our mom," I said flatly. I didn't want her to ask about Tess. Maybe she got that, because she started to run toward where Charles had stopped the wagon and was unloading supplies.

"Let's go!" Colette shouted over her shoulder. Sinking deep into the sand, she looked like she was running in slow motion. Her cheeks were extra pink and her blue eyes were really bright. "It's time to build the fire!"

Just before the sun disappeared that night, Charles used my first phone to take a picture of Colette and me at the water's edge. In the picture, the sky is light blue and peri-winkle at the top. The clouds are gray at the bottom, but coral and gold tipped because of the way the sun's rays are hitting them. Colette and I are silhouettes: one with blowing hair and the other with Mickey Mouse ears. The glassy wet sand reflects the sky and our shadows; we're laughing, the legs of our pants wet from not running fast enough when the waves came in.

That picture of me and Colette at sunset is my favorite picture ever.

I don't have it anymore.

———

THE LONG BEACH Police Station is a squat little box covered entirely in wood shingles, not just on the roof. The worn pieces of wood are nailed in rows on top of rows and faded from the sun—and they look like they'd give you splinters if you ran your hand along them.

The clock on the post cemented to the sidewalk in front of the station said one forty-five, except that it was only one fifteen. I should have been starting my weekend after my early-release morning, but I was here, at the police station.

The clock had been stuck on one forty-five since last summer. It drove me crazy that they didn't fix it. That's an example of how I notice things too much—I couldn't *not* notice, and be bugged by, the stupid clock. It was like a mental hangnail. I think I might get those more than other people, like Tess. She wasn't bugged by the clock.

"Why won't they fix that thing already?" I asked no one in particular.

"Sorry, but how can you be talking about the clock right now when Colette is missing?" Tess asked softly, pulling her sweater tighter around her.

"I'm just saying they should fix it."

Mom held open the door to the police station and I was glad because I didn't want to touch it. I walked through, still stuck on the clock. "It makes no sense that they don't. People need to know what time it is. The *police* need to know what time it is!"

Tess had stopped listening to me.

There were five kids sitting in the chairs lining the wall by the front desk, all of them with one or both parents, except the parents were all sitting in chairs on the opposite wall.

Mia ran over and hugged Tess; she'd saved her a seat. Colette's weird neighbor, Naomi, smiled and waved like she was at some great social event, not about to be questioned by the police. Bryce and Colin were there, of course, since a couple months ago, Colette and Bryce had declared themselves boyfriend-girlfriend and Colin is Bryce's best friend.

People had started calling Colette and Bryce *Brolette*, which is so weird. And it'd been especially weird since

Colette and Bryce had barely ever talked to each other before they'd decided to become a name mash-up.

Sitting next to Colin at the station, on the edge of his chair with his skateboard between his knees, was . . . Kai?

"What are *you* doing here?" I asked before I could get control of the wild horses that sometimes race out of my mouth.

"I . . . uh . . . ," Kai answered, glancing down at the NO HATE JUST SKATE sticker on the top of his board. He looked back at me with his super-dark brown eyes and shrugged.

I resisted a compulsive need to try to touch the tips of his blown-forward black hair or soft-looking skin. I really don't like when people touch me, but when I want to touch things, it's almost painful if I can't.

"That wasn't very nice," my mom whispered harshly as she nudged me toward two open seats on the parent side. I pulled away from her breath in my ear.

"Stop it," I said loudly.

Mom looked embarrassed, but I didn't care much because I was preoccupied by wishing she didn't feel like she had to remind me every time I made a mistake—I almost always already knew—and being mad that she'd whispered in my ear because she should know by now that whispers feel absolutely terrible to me.

I had my finger in my ear, trying to make it feel better,

when two policemen came out and talked to us. I knew one of them: it was Maggie Saunders's dad. He'd spoken at Career Day in fourth grade. He had a round face with an extra chin or two, and I liked him because one time, when he'd caught me cry-laughing while hugging a headstone in the cemetery, he said he wouldn't tell my parents if I promised not to do it again.

I'd never seen the one who wasn't Mr. Saunders before, and he was exactly the opposite of Mr. Saunders. He had humongous muscles and had one of those beard things that wraps all the way around your mouth. I could tell that he was definitely in charge. His name tag said ROLLINS.

"Mia Gilmore?" Officer Rollins asked, and Mia jumped a little. She gave my sister another hug, because they can't do anything without hugging first, which makes me cringe, and then Mia and her mom followed the officers away from our group.

Colin started telling Tess about getting his braces tightened, and Kai answered a question from Naomi about homework, messing with the corner of a sticker on his board deck that was coming up while he talked. When I looked at Bryce, he was staring into space with his light blue eyes. Bryce had never seemed that interesting to me and, as I stared at him staring at nothing, I couldn't understand why Colette would want to pick him to be her first boyfriend.

I wondered if they'd kissed. The thought of kissing a boy completely freaked me out because, I can't be positive, but I'm pretty sure that means someone would touch you.

I don't know why I looked at Kai again right then, but I did. Now he was hunched over, typing on his phone, his mouth open a little in concentration. That's how he sometimes looks when he takes tests, too. Before he caught me watching him, I pulled out my own phone and started reading the latest post on my favorite blog, written by a famous tornado chaser.

Kids and their parents went in, stayed awhile, and left. The police didn't take more than fifteen minutes with each kid, but it felt like forever. Mom went in with Tess and when they came out, Tess's eyes were red and puffy. Tess begged Mom to let her leave without us so she could go to Mia's house and Mom agreed. Finally when I was the last kid in the waiting room, Officer Rollins called my name. My mom and I followed him toward an interview room, but she asked me to wait outside for a few seconds.

"May I speak with you privately first?" Mom asked the officer.

"Of course," he said, and they left me leaning against the wall, listening through a crack in the door.

"I wanted to let you know that Frankie's not neurotypical," my mom began quietly. "She may not answer questions logically or may interrupt when you're speaking. She's very impulsive and she doesn't react well to change, so it's more challenging for her to be here than the other kids. Also, she has SPD, which means that she's very sensitive to touch and may have a big reaction if—"

I tuned out, my cheeks red with embarrassment.

I don't know why I'm the only one whose mom has to warn people in advance.

chapter 5

Fact: The part of the United States
that gets the most destructive tornadoes
is called Tornado Alley.

"HAVE A SEAT, Frances," Officer Rollins said when it was finally my turn in the interview room. My mom sat in the chair closest to the wall. She pulled her frumpy sweatshirt tight around her like she was freezing, but it was hot in the room.

"I wanted to sit there," I said to her, crossing my arms over my chest.

"Be flexible, please," she said.

"I am," I said. "I'm trying." Flexibility is a big deal to her. And to therapists. And, I guess, to people in general. "But can I sit there?"

My mom sighed and moved to the other chair. I bumped her knee and stepped on her toe trying to get around her to sit down in the chair by the wall. "It's too warm," I grumbled, but I stayed put.

"Shall we get started, Frances?" Officer Rollins asked from across the wooden table.

"My name's Frankie," I said, shifting in the hard-back chair with the warm seat. I wished I was at the beach. That's what probably made me ask, "Are you from Long Beach?"

He shook his head. "Tacoma."

"I like Wild Waves," I said.

"Wild Waves is in Federal Way," Officer Rollins said.

"Isn't that close to Tacoma?" I asked. "Like right next to it? Like basically part of it?" He shrugged so I tried again. "I also like the Tacoma zoo."

"Most people do."

"You don't?"

"Well, I'm a grown-up." I thought he was going to give more explanation, so I waited, but he didn't.

"Grown-ups can like zoos."

"Frankie, will you let the man speak?" Mom interrupted. She'd scooted her chair back a little so she was halfway behind me.

I turned around to look at her. "You're creeping me out. Move your chair back up the way it was."

"Don't be bossy," Mom said. "And please remember that Officer Rollins is in charge of this conversation, not you."

"I know he is," I said to my mom. I hoped that she wasn't making a mental list of all the ways I was *not* doing great today—all the reasons to make me start taking medication again. Or at least force me to go talk to Gabe.

She moved her chair forward so she was next to me.

I scanned the corners of the room where the walls met the ceiling. "Is this being recorded?"

My mom sighed.

"Yes," Officer Rollins said.

"Where's the camera?" I asked. My mom cleared her throat, probably trying to remind me to let Officer Rollins talk.

Okay, yes, I talk a lot. Gabe sometimes reminds me not to "monopolize the conversation," which apparently means talking about what you want to talk about and not pausing to listen to what other people want to say—even if you think what they want to say is boring or annoying. It doesn't matter: you still have to do it.

Officer Rollins had his superhuman forearms on the table, and he raised his right one like a drawbridge, pointing up, showing me where the camera was mounted.

"I see it," I said, craning my neck to look at the little dome near the overhead light with a tiny red eye peeking out. "Thanks. That would have bugged me."

"What would have?" Officer Rollins asked, stroking his face fur.

"Looking for the camera," I said. "Better I just know where it is to begin with."

The right corner of Officer Rollins's mouth lifted like it was considering going full-smile but then got tired and defaulted to a frown. His circle beard made it look like he was stuck that way.

I wondered whether he was able to smile. *Is there something wrong with your face? Smiling isn't necessary all the time. Clowns smile too much . . . They're so creepy. Creepy like the Sea Witch. Remember that time we—*

"Is it okay if I ask *you* some questions now?" Officer Rollins asked, interrupting my winding train of thought. I nodded even though, let's be honest, I wanted to ask more about the camera if we were going to talk about anything. "I'll start by saying that you're not in any trouble."

"Why would I be in trouble? Colette's the one missing."

"Yes," he said, smiling for real that time. "And we're trying to find her, which is why we asked all of you in today—to see if you can give us any clues that will help us do that."

"Did you check her phone?" I asked. "Her whole life is on her phone."

"We assume she has her phone with her," Officer Rollins said. "But her phone is off, so we haven't been able to pinpoint her location."

"How about her computer?" I asked. He sighed, and I said, "Okay, you ask the questions."

"Thanks." He checked something in a tan leather notebook in front of him. "So you're one of Colette's best friends, is that right?"

"No."

"No? That's what the other kids said."

My mom shifted in her chair.

"Well, I *used* to be friends with Colette," I clarified, "but we're not friends anymore." Officer Rollins looked at me like he wanted more of an explanation than that, so I kept talking. "When we were younger, Colette and I were best friends . . . and my sister and Colette were friends, too. The three of us hung out together a lot. Then Mia moved here in middle school and joined our group and Tess and Colette both really liked her but I didn't, and then the group changed and I was . . ." I thought about that a second, not knowing what to say. Feeling silly about saying the truth, that I was left behind. "We just stopped being friends. That's all."

Officer Rollins nodded and said, "I get it. I have a fifteen-year-old daughter."

"I'm thirteen."

"I know," he said, smiling. "I'm just saying that I know how these things go."

While he made notes, I noticed that there wasn't a clock in the room. I wondered if that was on purpose, like an interrogation tactic for criminals or something. The room didn't seem very menacing, though: I mean, there was a poster of the beach at sunset.

I daydreamed about building sandcastles with Colette and Tess, racing to stack packed sand bricks as high as we could before the tide came in and swept them away.

"Frankie?" Officer Rollins asked.

"What?" I tuned back in to the conversation. I guess he'd been having it without me.

"I asked: When you were friends, what did Colette like to do?"

"Sing," I answered.

"Oh yeah?"

I nodded. "She secretly wants to be a pop star. She writes songs all the time—or at least she used to." I looked at my mom. "Her parents don't know that, so don't tell them."

Mom smiled at me, and I looked back at Officer Rollins, adding, "She's a pretty good singer."

"That's great information, Frankie. No one else told us that Colette likes to sing." I couldn't help it; I smiled at the praise. He continued, "Do you think that Colette ran away?"

I laughed out loud. "No!" I said. "She's only thirteen! And she's not that brave." Colette couldn't even hug a tombstone.

"But do you think it's *possible* that she ran away? Even remotely?" he asked, looking up at me from his super-messy handwriting. There was no way I could read what it said upside down.

"No," I said. I felt antsy and started swinging my feet.

"We're almost finished," Officer Rollins said, looking down at my feet. He used the end of his pen to skim through his notes. "Just one last question and then you can go, Frankie."

"Okay," I said, glancing at my mom. She gave me an encouraging smile that made me feel like I'd done a reasonable job answering the questions. Then I got the one I didn't want to hear.

"When's the last time you saw Colette?"

No!

I'd decided that lying to the police would be a very bad idea. I'd made a deal with myself that if they asked directly, I'd tell the truth. But now Officer Rollins was looking at me with a question-mark face and it made me really nervous because right after the last time I'd seen Colette, she'd disappeared. And I didn't like feeling like it was even a little bit my fault. Because it absolutely, positively wasn't.

"I saw Colette last night," I blurted out, making Officer Rollins look up at me, surprised.

"What?" my mom said, sitting straighter in her chair. "Why didn't you say anything abou—"

"If you could let Frankie speak, please," Officer Rollins interrupted.

"Sorry," Mom said, "go ahead, Frankie."

"She came to my room at six forty-five."

"I see, and . . . ," Officer Rollins began. Then his words faded and his forehead wrinkled up in confusion. He flipped quickly through the pages in his notebook to find a certain entry. "Do you mean six forty-five in the morning yesterday?"

"Uh . . . no," I said, laughing. "Who would come over that early?"

"You're saying that Colette came to your room at six forty-five in the evening *yesterday*?" I nodded, and he looked at me sternly. "How do you know what time it was?"

"It was right in the middle of *Tornado Ally* and I was annoyed that she was making me miss watching it live." He didn't say anything, so I added, "I don't like watching it recorded and Colette knows that. And it was getting close to homework time, and I'd have to stop watching and leave my room, which made it doubly annoying."

"Why did you have to leave your room to do homework?" Officer Rollins asked. "Did you go to the library?"

I gave my mom a look. "*She* makes me do it at the cottage so she can watch me."

"So I can *help* you," Mom said quietly.

Officer Rollins rubbed his eyes with the palms of his hands and then rubbed his forehead and bald head and I wondered if he'd stop before rubbing his skin off but then he finally stopped. "Frankie, is this some kind of a joke?" he asked.

"What are you talking about?" I asked, not seeing the humor in it at all. I stared at him seriously. Then I got distracted by the number of lines on his forehead. I started counting them: *one, two, three, four . . .*

"Frankie?" He'd raised his eyebrows, making the lines really pronounced. He looked at my mom with an expression that I interpreted as: *I see what you mean.*

I wanted to act normal, but I didn't know what he'd said. "Huh?"

"Will you please try to pay attention?" my mom asked.

"I am!" I snapped.

Officer Rollins took a deep breath. "Frankie, I was saying that someone else said that Colette visited them at precisely six forty-five last evening and stayed for about twenty minutes, and unless Colette is magic, I don't think she could have been in two places at once."

"She's not magic," I said, confused, "and I'm not lying. I know when *Tornado Ally* was posted—you can check on Viewer."

"I'm sorry, are you saying tornado *ally*, or *alley*?" Officer Rollins asked.

"*Ally*, just like I said," I answered. "Like a friend of tornadoes, not Tornado Alley, the place that gets the most tornadoes in the country." I rolled my eyes. "Although all these questions are making me feel like I'm in Tornado Alley . . . and like I need an ally," I joked. No one laughed. I was embarrassed. "I'm telling the truth about when Colette came to my room, too. She was there for like ten minutes. Or fifteen, maybe. The other person has to be lying."

Was it ten? Or more like five? I had no idea, but I wasn't telling him that.

"And you're sure it wasn't more like six thirty when she came by? Because then she could have made it—"

"I'm one hundred percent sure," I interrupted him.

My mom cleared her throat again.

"I wonder if you'd say that if you knew who it was," Officer Rollins said.

"Who is it?" My head was spinning. I was *positive* I'd told him the right time. Why would someone else say Colette had visited them then, too? They were clearly lying! "Tell me who said that."

Officer Rollins closed his notebook and frowned at me. Both adults were quiet for a long time, looking at each other, then at me, then back at each other. Finally my mom shrugged, and Officer Rollins answered the question.

"It was Tess."

chapter 6

Fact: The majority of tornadoes
only last for a few minutes.

I PUSHED THROUGH the doors of the police station and
paused on the sidewalk, my hands balled into fists. A
female officer was going into the building, carrying a big
envelope, and she almost ran into me. I didn't apologize for
stopping abruptly in her path because I was fighting back
angry tears. And I was in the worst possible place to cry:
right on Pacific Avenue. In a story about our town, Pacific
Avenue would have been called Main Street.

My mom had stayed behind to speak with the officer
again privately, frustrating me even more. I turned left and
walked past the mini-carnival, closed until Memorial Day,
to the benches by the fourteen-foot-tall frying pan. The
sign in front of the frying pan will tell you it's from the

1940s and was put there in celebration of the clam festival. I sat down and avoided looking at the tourists getting their pictures taken while pretending to be bacon, which is the least original idea ever.

I tried to talk myself down from ten, because if my mom came out and saw me losing it, that would go on her list of reasons why I should be on medication.

Colette is probably perfectly fine and she'll be home soon, I told myself. *We will all go back to school on Monday and have our normal day and this will just be a weird thing that happened.*

That's self-talk. It's supposed to help, but it didn't. I kicked my heel against the bench a few times, grunting. My face probably looked mad, because when the tourists at the frying pan noticed me, they walked away.

Stop it! I told myself. *Mom's coming out soon.*

I forced myself to stop kicking the bench. I forced my mouth into a fake smile, because sometimes if you do that, you'll accidentally really smile. I didn't, but maybe a weird fake smile looked better than a scowl. I focused on uncurling my fists. Finally I flipped my hands over so my palms were facing up. Someone had told me to do that once—and today, that was the thing that worked. The cool breeze on my palms felt so nice and calming that my fake smile faded to a neutral face and I didn't have to think so much about not kicking the bench: I just didn't do it.

I sniffed and checked my phone. It was 2:50 in the afternoon. Even though it'd felt like longer, my internal freakout had only lasted a few minutes.

I looked across the street at Marsh's Free Museum, which is more of a curiosity gift shop than a museum so I'm not sure why it's called that. The parking lot was crowded because it was starting to get warmer since it was the middle of April, and Marsh's was one of the few things for tourists to do in Long Beach besides hanging out at the beach and taking bacon pictures.

Colette and my sister and I used to go to Marsh's with our piggy banks and buy saltwater taffy and have our fortunes told, then dare each other to look at Jake the Alligator Man for a full minute, which is super-tough because I'm telling you, that half-man, half-alligator thing looks completely gross. I still have some videos of us inside Marsh's saved somewhere. It was part of a game we used to play called dare-or-scare. It was cool.

Thinking of that made my tears dry up.

I wondered if Kai had gone to Marsh's after his interview at the police station; Kai's parents ran the store and they made him help sometimes even though I think that might be illegal. Part of me wanted to go apologize for being rude and part of me felt like he'd probably already gotten over it so what was the point.

"Hi, how are you feeling?" Mom asked carefully when she joined me near the frying pan.

"I'm okay," I said.

"Really?" I didn't like how surprised she looked, but I nodded anyway.

"Well, that's great," Mom said, "because they want you to come back in. Both you and Tess. I just got off the phone with her and she's on her way back. Another officer found something in Colette's locker that they want you to see."

"What?" I asked.

Mom shrugged; the sun blasted into my eyes when I looked up at her. "We'll find out soon," she said. "And I think they want to talk more about when you last saw Colette, too."

"Tess is a liar," I said matter-of-factly. I felt bad about saying it, but it had to be true because I knew I wasn't lying.

"Please don't call your sister names," Mom said, frowning.

Her long, dark brown hair blew up all around her like she was a superhero, and she should have just let it go, but she wrapped it into a lady-knot at the back of her head. Mom, Tess, and I all have the same hair color—except Mom's has some gray in it—but theirs is straight and usually clean and brushed, and mine is curly and usually dirty and wild. That's why I keep it shorter: brushing out snarls is the worst.

"I'm telling the truth," I said, pushing off the bench and walking back toward the police station. Mom followed me. "I know that Colette came to see me at six forty-five. I'm one hundred percent sure that's the right time."

"Frankie, I believe you. But do you think your sister would lie to the police?" Mom asked. "Do you honestly think that?"

"No one would ever think that Tess would lie to the police or do anything wrong," I said, trying to keep my tone of voice steady. "I am the person people would call a liar, no matter what." I blew my bangs out of my eyes; I needed a haircut, but I hated getting them. "I'm telling you the truth."

"I said I believe you," Mom said. "I believe that both of you *believe* you're telling the truth. But one of you must be wrong—by accident, of course."

"Let's just go in," I said. We were outside the police station again.

"We need to wait for Tess," Mom said, leaning to the left so she could see down the street, pulling her sweatshirt tight around her. "She'll be here soon."

"Fine."

———

IN THE SAME interview room as before, Officer Rollins dragged in another chair. Tess sat down in the one by the far wall, hunching forward like she always does, her arms wrapped tightly around herself.

"That's my seat," I said.

"It's not yours," she said quietly, pressing her lips into a line.

"It's the one I sat in before, so it's mine."

"I used this one when Mom and I came in earlier, too. Can't you just sit in the—"

"Tess," Mom said in a low voice.

"What?" Tess asked her quietly. "Can't she just sit in the other chair? This is mortifying."

"Can we get started?" Officer Rollins asked. "There are chairs for everyone."

"Yes, but she's in mine." I pointed at the new chair and said to Tess, "You can use that one."

"So can you?" Tess said like a question. She looked from me to Officer Rollins to Mom. Tess seemed really embarrassed and I didn't like it, but I couldn't stop myself from demanding that she give me the chair by the wall.

Sitting down in the chair that I was standing right next to would have been the easy thing to do. But sometimes I can't make myself do the easy thing.

"I can't sit near the door." My voice was sharper. I started to feel the tightness that happens in my throat before the tears show up. I could feel the scream building in me. Tess needed to *move*.

"You can have my chair," Mom said, getting up.

"You know I can't sit in the middle either." My arms were hanging by my sides, and I flipped my hands so that my palms were facing out, wondering if it'd work again. But it was hot in the room and my head itched and I had to scratch it, so I didn't keep my palms up for long enough.

"Ladies, we really need to get started," Officer Rollins said. He sounded annoyed.

"Tess, please," Mom said to my sister. She sounded desperate. Tears were rolling down my cheeks—I didn't notice them until one dripped into my mouth. I didn't like the warm, salty taste.

Tess stood up, scooted over, and dropped into the new chair with a *thud*, rewrapping her arms around herself and letting her hair fall over half of her face. She had tears in her eyes, too.

I wiped away my own and got into my chair as quickly as I could.

"Now that we're all settled," Officer Rollins said, "I'd like you to both see something we found in Colette's locker." He looked at Tess. "You share the locker with Colette?"

Tess nodded. "What is it?" she asked, sounding scared. It made me feel worse.

"It's a diary," Officer Rollins said.

I tilted my head to the side, picturing Colette taking

some diary with a unicorn on the cover to middle school. "What the heck?" I asked, sniffing because the tears had made my nose run.

"Frankie!" Mom said. "Manners, please."

"It's okay," Officer Rollins said to Mom. Then, looking at me, he said, "It's interesting that you ask that, Frankie, because your name is on it." I opened my eyes wide as he looked at my sister. "Yours too, Tess."

I leaned forward so I could see Tess around Mom. She did the same, the chair incident forgotten. Everyone in my family is used to my emotions.

"He's not talking about—" Tess started to say, but then stopped because she knew that I knew what she meant.

"No way," I said back to her. "It's in my room. In that place."

"I thought so, but then . . ." Her voice trailed off.

"Right?" I said. "How . . ."

"Exactly. And when . . ."

"I know, and . . ." I scrunched up my forehead. "I don't know."

We both looked back at Officer Rollins, who had a confused expression on his face. He cleared his throat. "Okay, then," he said. "I don't know if it's twin language or teen language, but either way, I'm definitely not fluent. Care to elaborate?"

"Huh?" I asked.

"Sorry," Tess said. She apologizes too much. "There's this notebook—"

"Could you speak up a little?" Officer Rollins asked. "I can barely hear you."

"Sorry," Tess said again, a bit louder. "There's this notebook we had when we were younger. Way younger, like in third grade. We wrote in it until the end of elementary school."

I talked over Tess. "None of us were ever in the same class in elementary school, so we wrote notes for each other and left them in a hiding spot in the library. We checked it when it was our class's turn to have library time."

"It was the way we stayed in touch." Tess looked down at her hands, then back at Officer Rollins. "It can't be what you're talking about, though, because Frankie has that notebook at home. And Colette wouldn't take it to school now."

"Did you?" Officer Rollins asked.

"No!" Tess said, her neck red and blotchy.

Officer Rollins bent over and picked up a big puffy envelope near his feet. It was the same envelope I'd seen the woman officer carrying a little while ago. Officer Rollins dumped its contents onto the table. All that was inside was a book inside a plastic baggie. A book that a grown-up might call a diary. The book that Tess, Colette, and I had called—

"Fred!" Tess shouted. "She had Fred!"

Seeing the notebook that Colette had asked me for the night before—the notebook that should have been in my room—was so confusing. I just stared at it for a few seconds, trying to work out how she could have gotten it. Unless it hadn't been in my room in the first place. But then, where had it been? Or unless she'd taken it from my room. But when? Besides eating dinner at the cottage, I hadn't left my room at all.

"Its name is Fred," Officer Rollins said, interrupting my thoughts. "I see."

The reason the diary's name was Fred was because I was a terrible speller when I was younger and I'd been trying to write *friend* on the cover, but I'd forgotten the *i* and the *n*. Thankfully, Tess didn't tell Officer Rollins that humiliating fact about me; instead, she just said, "We liked the name and it was part of our code. Like we'd pass each other in the hallways and whisper, 'Time to meet with Fred,' and none of the other kids would know what we meant."

"I see," Officer Rollins said, removing Fred from the table and putting it back inside the puffy envelope. "This has to go to forensics; I just needed to make sure that the notebook belonged to Colette."

"It belonged to me," I said.

Tess shook her head and said softly, "It belonged to all of us."

"Girls," our mom said sharply, warning us not to fight.

"Sorry," Tess said. I stayed quiet.

"It's okay," Officer Rollins said, smiling at Mom. "We made copies, so you can go through it at home and let us know if you see anything out of the ordinary." He cleared his throat. "It's a long shot, but we're researching every possibility."

"Can we leave?" I asked.

Mom gave me a look.

"In just a minute," Officer Rollins said. "I wanted to ask both of you again: What time did you see Colette last night?" He crossed his arms over his chest and waited.

"Six forty-five," I blurted out.

"What?" Tess asked defensively. "That's when she was in my room. Why would she be in yours?"

"Like she can't come to mine?" I asked back. "Like I have the plague or something?"

"That's not what I meant!" Tess said. "I meant that she ca—"

"Girls!" Mom said again, more serious this time. "Keep your tones down."

"Sorry, Mom," Tess said.

"Yeah, sorry," I mumbled.

I wasn't sorry, though. I was right.

———

MOM LET TESS go off to help Mia make cookies for Colette's parents and flyers to hang up around town, but she made me walk home with her. It was another example of how she treats me like I'm a little kid even though Tess and I are the same age.

She started to ask me questions about the conversation with Officer Rollins, about Fred, about seeing Colette the night before.

"We're not talking about that stuff," I cut her off.

"Then tell me why you seem so angry at your sister lately."

She stole my only friend, I thought, but didn't say, because I wasn't sure if I completely believed it. If anyone had caused a change in our friendship status, it was Mia. But Tess *had* betrayed me, and I ended up friendless. So in a way Tess did steal my only friend—or friends, if you count a sister as a friend—or at least helped it happen. I wasn't about to say all of that to my mom, though: she'd just defend Tess.

"I don't know what you mean," I said instead.

We were walking down Pacific in the opposite direction of the inn. I'd chosen the path, and Mom hadn't said anything. She'd just started walking beside me, carrying my photocopy of Fred.

My hands itched.

"Okay . . . ," Mom said, "then why were you rude to Kai at the station. Did he do something to you?"

That was an easy one. "No," I said. "Kai is nice."

"I thought so," she said. "You two used to be such cute friends. Remember when you made up that language together at summer camp?"

I remembered getting laughed at by the other kids for making up my own language until Kai came over and asked if I would teach it to him, but I didn't say that. I didn't answer at all, and I think Mom understood that she was making me uncomfortable, so she got quiet and we walked in silence the rest of the way down Pacific.

My brain swirled and twisted. *Colette's gone. Why won't she just stop messing around and come back? I should be relaxing right now. Instead, I just left the police station! This is not how the day was supposed to go!*

My head itched. I walked next to my mom, past the kite shop with the blue horizontal siding and the gift shop with the barn-red vertical siding. I scratched my head and counted my steps from one antique streetlight to the next: twenty-two. From that light to the next, I took bigger steps: eighteen. I scratched my head again, noticing that we were almost where I wanted to turn left, so I stepped out between parallel-parked cars to cross. My arm was practically torn from my body when my mom grabbed it and yanked me backward.

"Ouch!" I shouted, pulling myself from her grip as a car horn blared. I flipped around and saw my mom, wide-eyed. "That hurt!" I yelled at her.

"You were almost hit by a car!" she yelled back.

"I saw it!" I shouted, rubbing my sore arm where she'd grabbed it. "I was going to stop."

"It didn't look like it," Mom said in a more normal voice. "Let's go to the crosswalk."

Between us, I hadn't seen the car. But that's not the type of thing you want to admit to your mom if you're trying to stay off medication and out of therapy.

Also, the speed limit is only twenty-five, which is around how fast tornadoes go, so I probably wouldn't have died. I read once that your chances of dying if you're hit by a car going that slowly are only three percent or something. I'm not sure I have that right, though.

Safely across the street, we turned left at Bolstad toward the ocean. Mom didn't say anything when we passed City Hall or the RV Resort; when we walked under the WORLD'S LONGEST BEACH sign and down the long row of beach parking spots.

"Can we take the boardwalk?" she asked. "I don't want to get sand in these shoes."

We were at the big red buoy in the center of the road, almost where the parking stops and the beach begins. You can either go forward out to the sand, turn left and walk the boardwalk, or turn back toward the town. Canada is to the right and Oregon is to the left, if you walk long enough.

I really like walking on the beach and normally would have suggested that my mom just take off her shoes if she didn't want sand in them, but I was so unsettled about all the change, I agreed. And I was glad almost immediately because the hollow *plunk* that the boards made with each of our steps was a beat that calmed me. Walking next to my mom calmed me, too.

"Are you worried about Colette, Frankie?" Mom asked in her soft voice. The wind whistled as it blew in the grass and I could see at least a dozen kites flying over the sand.

"Of course," I said quickly. "Who wouldn't be?"

"I wasn't asking about other people; I was asking about you," she said. "I know the last couple of months have been difficult for you . . ."

"You mean since I lost the only friend I've ever had?"

"I think people's perceptions of things are different," Mom said kindly. "Sometimes people remember things in a negative way while others may remember the experience differently."

"I guess," I said, watching the beach grass ripple like waves; I wished I could run through it and let it tickle my palms. "I don't know how anyone could see it differently, though. Colette made the choice not to be my friend."

"Huh," my mom said. "Is that how Colette would tell the story? That she chose not to be friends with you? Or would she say you got mad and told her you didn't want to hang out with her anymore?"

"By talking about me behind my back, she made the choice," I said. "It's her fault, not mine."

"Oh, Frankie, friendships aren't about fault," Mom said. "They're about forgiveness." She nudged my shoulder with hers; we were nearly the same height and had been since last summer. Tess was way taller. "And they're tough, especially when people grow up and change. You kind of have to keep getting to know your friends all the time. Want to know what other type of relationship is like that?"

"What?" I asked, not minding the conversation.

"Parent-kid relationships," she said. "You guys grow and change all the time and I have to keep trying to get to know the new you."

"I'm the same me," I said. "I haven't changed. Colette has." *Had?* "Mom?" I asked, looking up at her.

"Hmm?"

"What if Colette's dead?"

"Oh, my girl," Mom said, "I don't even want you to think that way. Colette's probably just fine."

Her tone didn't sound convincing.

"I *am* thinking that way, though," I said. "Mom, seriously, what if she's dead?"

Mom looked really sad. "I hope with all my heart that she isn't, for Colette's parents' sake, for Tess's and her other friends' . . . and for yours."

"Me too," I said, because no matter what, that much was true.

chapter 7

Fact: Three types of tornado alerts
are watch, warning, and emergency.

BACK AT HOME after the police station, I felt jumpy, like
during a tornado watch. That's when the weather conditions are right for tornadoes, but the weather people haven't
spotted any funnel clouds yet.

I kept looking out the window, like Colette was just
going to stroll up to the inn with a big smile on her freckled lips. Pacing, with Pirate watching me from the foot of
my bed without lifting her head, I asked Colette a string of
questions aloud.

"Where are you . . . and why was Fred in your locker?
How did you get Fred? And how the heck were you in my
room and Tess's at the same time? Why was Kai at the
police station? . . . Oh, and what's up with your weird boyfriend staring into space?"

Here's a tip about me: I have to have answers. If you tell me a riddle and I can't solve it fast, you just have to tell me the solution. And if you say you'll give me a present later, you might as well give it to me now, because otherwise I'll keep thinking about it like crazy until *later* comes. It's all I'll think about, not wanting to, like how you can't stop touching a hangnail or licking a mouth sore even when it hurts.

So yeah, I have to have answers. The world seems less overwhelming that way.

That's not the greatest way to be, though—at least not if you want to have a lot of friends. People don't always feel comfortable if you just ask them things. That's called "being direct" and most middle school kids I'd encountered so far didn't like it.

Except Kai.

I pulled out my phone and sent him a text. It'd been a long time since we'd texted. The last one I'd sent him was a whole six months earlier.

FRANKIE

Hi 👋 🏆 🍧

KAI

R U eating dessert in a tornado right now?!?

> LOL. No. Wondering why you were at the 🚕 ???

The dots did their dance for longer than I thought they should have, like Kai was really thinking about his answer. I was impatient.

> WELL?

she was at the store

last night

I was wkng

> ????

How should I know

Taking video selfies and stuff

> HUH
>
> Of what

Not talking . . .

Just standing there like a statue and freakin out customers

> 🕐 ?

Sorry-not-sorry was basically my motto.

He sent a crying-laughing emoji with a wave.

One time, Gabe made me practice during one of our therapy sessions. That's an example of how my life is not normal—adults make me *practice* texting. Gabe told me how to look for signs that people were ready to stop a conversation and made me practice ending them. Because otherwise, I'd text people all night long. I mean, if I had anyone to text.

He sent another wave. I wanted to tell him that my previous text rhymed, but that would be continuing the conversation that Kai clearly wanted to end. So I put my phone on my nightstand.

It had been the longest, weirdest Friday ever. And still, dinner wouldn't be for a few hours. I needed something to take my mind off how strange the day had been, so I got the photocopied pages from the police station and started looking through them.

Fred, our notebook or diary or whatever you want to

call it, is about the size of a typical book, but the sheets of paper that Fred was copied onto were bigger, normal pieces of white printer paper. That meant that there was a fat margin between the edge of Fred and the edge of the copy paper—but whoever copied Fred had held him down flat through the process, so part of the person's arm was visible in the margin.

I got distracted and grossed out by the photocopied hairs from the copier's wrist appearing on every page. It took me a few minutes to get over that and start really reading.

When I did, I was embarrassed because stuff I'd thought was important as a third grader felt ridiculous now. The first few notes that Tess, Colette, and I left for each other in the library said things like:

Hi! How are You today?
Hi back! I'm fine how are you ☺
It's cold outside. I don't want to go to recess!
Mr. Ellensburg is so mean!
I wish my mom would let me have a guinea pig!

Most of the messages from Colette and Tess didn't really say much of anything. There were a lot of drawings of kids and tigers and rainbows and dolphins. My messages were more real. One from me to them said:

Emmy hit me in the face with the teltherbal at reces on purpos. Miss French didn't beleeve me that it was on purpos but Emmy laffed about it with her frends and they all made fun of me for crying. She sent me to the nurse since my face is all red. Emmy is mean!

The reply from Tess on the same page said:

She's mean! I'm sorry!

And under that, from Colette:

We beleive you Frankie I'm sorry your face hurts. I told Emmy I'm not going to her birthday party. She said she's having chocolate cupcakes and I said I didn't care because she was mean to my best freind. PS: Tess you're my best freind too.

After a half hour of reading the same type of messages, I decided that there was no way the stuff we'd written in third and fourth grade would help Officer Rollins with anything other than knowing which kids were mean in elementary and that Tess was already starting to be a decent artist.

I got some water from the mini-fridge in my room before continuing with Fred. I knew what was coming: the page about our dare-or-scare game. Chugging my water, I thought back to when we made up the game. It was during winter break in fifth grade and we were bored.

"I'm bored," I had complained to Colette and Tess.

"Me too," Colette complained back.

"Me three," Tess agreed.

We were on Colette's covered front porch, wearing loads of layers, squashed three across in an oversize porch rocker meant for two. It was overcast and too windy to go to the beach.

"We could climb the roof," Colette suggested. Her house is an A-frame; if you don't know what that looks like, imagine a normal two-story house with a triangular roof, then chop off its lower level so the sides of the triangle nearly touch the ground. It looks crazy, like a house that sank into the dirt.

"We did that yesterday," I said.

"I always slide back down," Tess said.

"That's because you don't climb the right way," I told my sister.

"Yes, she does," Colette said, sticking up for Tess. "It was slippery."

"We could do a quiz," I suggested, knowing I was right about climbing.

"Okay," Tess agreed.

"I'm over quizzes," Colette said, which hurt my feelings

a little since she knew I loved them. "Let's put on my mom's makeup!"

Tess's eyes widened, and she sat up straight, smiling. Maybe it was because she was artistic, but she was really good at putting on makeup. She looked at me to see what I thought of the idea.

"No way!" I blurted out. "I can't . . . ," I began, tripping on my words. "The brushes . . . my face . . . it's so . . ."

"It's okay, Frankie," Tess said, disappointed. "She doesn't like the feeling of the makeup on her skin," she told Colette.

"Oh," Colette said.

I felt like I'd let them down, that now I needed to come up with something really great. I considered what the three of us liked to do together. All I could think was that we could make up a game. But not just any game: the best game!

"Let's do truth-or-dare!" I said, jumping off the rocker because honestly I'd been too pinched in there for my liking. But I was on some medication that was keeping me from screaming about it, at least. Except it was the kind that made me feel shaky and hungry, so it still sucked.

I faced my friends. "We can make amazing dares!"

"I love that idea!" Tess said, beaming before her eyes clouded over. "Except we already know all of each other's truths." She bit her fingernail, thinking, then sat up straight with excitement. "How about dare-or-scare?"

Tess loves being scared or scaring people. You might think that's surprising since she's quiet and introverted and apologizes all the time and sometimes seems like she's afraid of the world. But it's a secret way Tess is really brave—braver than me.

"Um . . . ," I began, not into the "scare" idea.

"What do you mean?" Colette asked. She looked intrigued.

"Well, you can either do the dare," Tess said, "or you'll get a scare!" She laughed wickedly.

"I don't want to be scared," I said, flapping my hands. "You know I hate that."

"Then do all the dares." Colette laughed. She put her pointer finger to her mouth, thinking, then said, "Maybe one of the dares will be to hug a tombstone!"

"No!" I said, my eyes wide, my heart racing.

"That would be better than waiting for someone to jump out at you," Tess said. "And besides, you could do it in the daylight." I must have looked terrified, because Tess added, "We can choose a prize for the person who does the most dares."

"What kind of prize?" I asked.

"Taffy," Tess said confidently. Taffy from Marsh's was basically a food group.

"Good idea. Let's start making a list of dares," Colette said.

"Fine," I said, not liking the possibility of visiting the

graveyard but thinking that *I* was going to be the best at dares of all three of us. "I'm going to win and get all of your taffy."

"No, you're not," Tess and Colette said in unison, laughing.

Tess checked the time on the phone she'd gotten for Christmas. "Frankie and I have to be home at five," she said, frowning. "We need to do this fast."

"Hold on," Colette said, jumping up and running inside her house. She was back in seconds with Fred. "We can write the dares down in here."

To my dismay, the first thing Colette wrote was: Hug a tombstone. She nudged me and smiled, telling me I'd be okay. From there, we all shouted ideas, Colette scribbling down the ones that all three of us agreed on: Climb Colette's roof alone. Run your fastest from the inn to the water. Do jumping jacks in the middle of the arcade. And the list went on. We filled a whole page with dares, front and back. It took us so long to make the list that we didn't get to do any dares that day—or, thankfully, scares—but we started the game the next.

Now, in my room, a smile I hadn't even noticed building on my face melted away. Colette and I weren't friends anymore. Tess and I didn't have the same relationship either. They'd both betrayed me.

Sad, I picked up the photocopy of Fred and turned to

the next page, looking forward to going back in time and reading our list of dares. But the next page wasn't about dare-or-scare: it was another note about school. I flipped to the next, and it was doodles, mostly of tornadoes—by me, naturally. I turned all the rest of the pages that Officer Rollins had given me, completely confused. Either he hadn't given me a complete copy of the notebook, or someone had torn out one of the pages.

All I knew was that there was no mention of the dares or scares in my copy of Fred at all.

chapter 8

Myth: You can outrun a tornado.

"CHARLES, I'M BORED," I said, my chin resting on my hand, my elbow on the tall counter of the reception desk. *Bored* is my universal way of saying that I need something different to do, even if I'm not technically *bored*.

"Hmm," Charles said, his eyes on the Rubik's Cube in his hands. As he twisted the annoying puzzle over and around, I looked at the tattoos on his arms: the compass that was also a man's eye whose hair morphed into the ocean with an orca breaching. There wasn't any clear skin from his wrists to beyond his shirtsleeves. Way up on his shoulder, I knew he had a rose for his girlfriend before my mom, who died in a car accident. She's the reason Charles gave up his corporate-lawyer job and moved out to Long Beach, so she's the reason we know him at all, I guess. I was thinking about how much that probably hurt—the tattoos, I mean—when Charles said, "You could sweep the lobby."

"No way," I said.

"Bring in the cushions from the outdoor furniture? It smells like it's going to rain." The main door was propped open and when I took my next breath, I realized Charles was right.

"There are always bugs on the cushions," I said, shivering at the thought.

"Start a new pot of coffee?"

"You sound like Mom."

Charles looked up at me and smiled, the skin around his eyes crinkling. "Maybe she's right that I'm too soft on you and your sister."

"If I do the coffee, is it okay if I go for a bike ride?" I asked.

He looked from me to some guests getting out of their car in the lot; he'd have to check them in soon. He sighed and set aside his Rubik's Cube, then mussed up his own hair.

"I'm okay with fresh air in any capacity," he began, "but today's not a typical day, with Colette missing, and would you look at those clouds? It's going to pour."

"I like riding in the rain."

He scratched his head. "Did you ask your mom?"

"I can't find her," I said. It wasn't necessarily a lie, because I hadn't seen my mom on my way from my room down the hall and down the stairs to the lobby. But I hadn't looked for her either.

"I don't know, Frankie," Charles said, his eyes on the guests, who were loading up a luggage cart. "Do you have your phone with you?"

"Yes," I said, nodding.

"Okay, then you can ride for a half hour," he said, smiling at the guests as they came through the door. "Welcome," he said to them. He looked at me sternly, like a kid pretending to be a grown-up. "Be back in exactly thirty minutes."

"I will!" I called, not doing the coffee, waving behind me. With Charles engrossed in checking in the guests on the computer, I took one of the complimentary beach cruisers that people could use during their stay. He'd probably have said it was okay. Mom might not have. I had to take the green one because my favorite yellow one was still checked out.

I pedaled fast, picturing myself trying to outrun a tornado, looking back over my shoulder a few times on the way toward town, almost seeing it there behind me, just like the one in kindergarten. I imagined it crashing through the new fancy mini-golf course, sending golf balls flying;

bulldozing the theater, making popcorn swirl into the air; and tossing aside the hut where you sign up for horseback rides on the beach.

A horn beeped at me when I paused too long in the middle of an intersection, mesmerized by my imagination. It made me jump and forced me to focus on what was real, the imaginary tornado sucked back into the sky. I quickly rode on, coasting down a few blocks, past the lots of land for sale and two motels. On Bolstad, I turned left toward the ocean.

The dare-or-scare game on my mind, I passed the parking spaces and the buoy, then took another left on the paved bike path that would take me back in the direction of the inn. I was riding in a huge circle. Heavy gray clouds loomed overhead, but no rain fell yet. There was so much going on in my head that I could have ridden all the way to Oregon but there was no way to do that and get back in half an hour.

What I wanted to know was why the dare-or-scare page was missing from Fred. I felt like it meant something. And I didn't understand why or how Colette had had Fred in the first place: I felt like that meant something, too.

I pedaled fast and ducked quickly under the Decapitator, the part of the path that dips under the boardwalk. I passed the inn and kept on going. Houses were to my left, and grassy dunes with the ocean beyond them were to my right.

I didn't want to look left at a specific house for some reason. I didn't dwell on it.

Pedaling, pedaling, pedaling, my mind spun. I'd ridden this path so many times, I probably could have closed my eyes and still known when the curves were coming. I was free to think, think, think of dares.

Do a headstand.
Bark like a dog in the middle of the cafeteria.
Ding-dong-ditch someone's house.
Sing in public.
Stare at something gross for one minute.
Put on makeup without looking in the mirror.
Ask a total stranger for a french fry—and then eat it.

I felt like it was super-important to remember the dares we'd actually done. But no matter how hard I tried, I couldn't remember which we'd done, which had been rejected, and which I was coming up with right then and there. There were so many possible options: think of how many lines are on both sides of a piece of notebook paper!

"Ugh!" I shouted aloud. *I hate my stupid memory!* I shouted in my head, gripping the bike handlebars tight, wishing I knew why Colette had taken Fred, why the dare-or-scare page was missing, and why I was obsessed with remembering the challenges. Shouldn't I have been more concerned about where Colette was than about a stupid notebook and game? I knew I should've, and yet I couldn't stop myself from focusing on the wrong things.

Up ahead, there were two men sitting and smoking on one of the benches along the path. I didn't want to get near them or ride through their smoke cloud, so I stopped the bike hard, skidding, and turned around. I was sweaty and out of breath from pedaling so fast.

The wind was picking up and riding wasn't doing anything to organize my thoughts. I rode back without looking at one of the houses on the right. It made me feel uncomfortable. I didn't dwell on it.

Nearing home, I saw Tess and Mom walking toward the cottage: it must have been dinnertime. Instead of taking the cruiser to the lobby, I left it against the side of the building, then went to meet up with them. I was starving.

———

ON FRIDAYS, MY family makes pizza and plays board games together. Tonight, though, Charles was still working at the front desk, and Tess refused to play anything. She and Mia had taken their cookies to Colette's parents and Tess had been gloomy since she'd gotten back. I felt like there was something wrong with me because I still would have played a game despite maybe being worried about Colette. I don't really know what worry feels like.

We watched a movie instead, something about a girl and a horse. Tess picked it. Mom texted a lot during the movie and got up once to take a call from Colette's mom, which she took in her room with the door closed and which lasted for more than twenty minutes.

When she finally came back, her eyes looked red and puffy. "They still don't know anything," she said.

"Were you crying?" I asked.

"I'm okay," Mom said.

"That's not what I asked."

"I know," Mom said. "Should I make some popcorn?"

My mom's popcorn is the best on the planet, so I said yes and forgot about asking her about crying. We unpaused the movie, and it started raining sideways, the drops tapping on the window like fingertips on a clicky laptop keyboard. I burrowed under a blanket and, with my eyes on the screen, watching the girl with the horse grow up to overcome her challenges, I daydreamed about growing up and becoming a meteorologist or chasing tornadoes or texting through a boring movie or being liked for being nice and funny instead of disliked for being weird.

I daydreamed about Colette knocking on the door to my room and asking for Fred, and me saying yes instead of no. About me asking why she wanted it instead of ignoring her and putting on my headphones. I daydreamed about Colette apologizing about February and inviting me to go do a dare with her—and me agreeing. I daydreamed about winning her taffy but sharing it with her, too.

I daydreamed about Colette being not-missing.

And then I ran through a downpour to bed, and I night-dreamed about her being okay, too.

PART 2

A Bad Saturday

chapter 9

Fact: Tornadoes are born from thunderstorms.

"HEYA, FRANKIE."

"Hi, Teddy," I said to the high schooler behind the counter at the arcade. He was helping someone else, so I had to wait.

Even though my stomach hurt, I was at the arcade right when it opened at ten because going to the arcade was what I always did on Saturdays, and I needed to do what I always did instead of imagining Colette running away or being kidnapped or ripping out the dare-or-scare page from Fred and tearing it up to show me just how much we weren't friends anymore. Except, as mad as I was at her, I couldn't really picture Colette doing something like that.

It was a miracle my mom had let me come today with Colette missing and everything, but she'd been preoccupied by a guest who'd flooded his bathroom.

"Ready?" Teddy asked when it was my turn in line. I stepped forward, not looking at his face: his pimples made me cringe, but I concentrated on not commenting on them. Instead, I looked at the bulletin board on the wall behind Teddy. Colette's school picture stared back at me from a MISSING CHILD poster.

Teddy looked over his shoulder. "Oh hey, that's your friend, right?"

"No," I said. "Can I get my card?"

"What's the password?" he asked.

I rolled my eyes. "The password is 'Give me my card.'" A pain stabbed my lower belly and I wondered if something I'd eaten was making me sick.

"Geez," Teddy said, opening the register and retrieving my preloaded game card. Once a month, my mom put money on it and when it was out, it was out. I left it here so I wouldn't lose it in my bedroom or on the way home or at school or anywhere else I went. Keeping track of things isn't my superpower. "Here you go," he said, handing it over. "Some kid puked by the new shooter, so I'd steer clear of that corner."

"Thanks for the tip," I said, taking the card and turning toward the side of the sprawling space farthest from barf corner.

There were a lot of people there already because Saturday was two-for-one day and people in Long Beach like a deal.

I walked through bodies in the direction of my favorite starting point, Skee-Ball, with my chin awkwardly raised. I have to keep my chin up so that I can't see the carpet in my lower field of vision. It's black with blue swirls and red and yellow psychedelic stars intertwined among the swirls. It's dizzying and is, hands down, the worst thing about the arcade. The flashing lights and noises never bother me, because they're both expected—that's what arcades look and sound like—and because they are constant. But I really hate the carpet.

It's tough walking with your chin up at the arcade because the floor isn't level and twice—near the grabby-claw games and over by the big screens where you slash fruit—the floor either dips or rises, depending on where you're coming from.

Today, I stumbled a little by the grabby claw but made it to the Skee-Ball station without falling. But then someone was on the left-most Skee-Ball game, which is the only one I play, so I had to wait. I felt like there was a thunderstorm brewing inside me I was so impatient.

The player was a little girl who only got the ball into the lowest ring every time, so she should have been done quickly. I stood uncomfortably close to her side—this is what kids do to tell the world *I'm next*, so I had to do it even though it made my thighs feel weak. I whispered for her to hurry up under my breath, and to speed things along,

I picked up the ball for her when she threw it so hard it bounced off the side and onto the dreaded carpet.

I've played Skee-Ball a lot, so I knew when she was almost done with her game. And right then, some other kid—maybe her older brother—and some adult—probably their dad—walked up. When the girl finished her game, the dad swiped the other kid's card and let him go.

"Hey!" I said loudly, the storm inside me building. "It was my turn!"

The dad looked at me, surprised. "Oh, I'm sorry, I didn't see you there. We'll be done in just a few minutes."

I grumbled out loud.

The man looked at me. "The other two lanes are open. You could use one of those?"

"I like this one," I informed him, folding my arms over my chest. "I'll wait."

I screamed at them in my head, trying to ignore the pain in my stomach, until they finally left.

I stepped up to my Skee-Ball lane. Still annoyed about having to wait, I missed the first one, but then every ball I threw went in the tiny top circle. It was my highest score ever.

I went and checked the balance on my card and decided that I could play five more games, so I'd still have enough money on the card next weekend and the following. Thinking of next weekend made me think of Colette, and

I wondered whether she'd be safe back at home by then or whether . . .

I shook my head and went to the riding-motorcycle-race game. There was only one, and thankfully it wasn't taken, so I hopped on and chose the setting where you race through a field. I have to admit that I always picture a tornado bouncing along beside me as I'm racing. One thing on my list of things to do in life is to write the game company that makes it and tell them that the field level would be way better with the addition of a tornado.

I placed third, which was not good enough. I reached forward and slid my card through the reader again. But the screen continued to flash INSERT COINS. I tried the card reader three more times and it didn't work. I knew I'd have to go tell Teddy, but I didn't want to get off the motorcycle because it's a popular game and I just knew some little kid was going to come steal it. Maybe even the Skee-Ball lane thieves. I sat there debating my options for a while, wondering if maybe Teddy would just walk by. He didn't, though. Finally I got up.

"The card reader's broken on the motorcycle game," I told Teddy, facing away from the counter, my eyes on the bright yellow motorcycle. "Can you fix it?"

"I'll have to call the manager," Teddy said. "Card readers are his area."

"But I have to play it!" I protested. "I got third and I need to do better, or I'll be thinking about that the rest of the day!"

"I feel ya," he said. I heard him open the register again. "Here, use these tokens. They'll work."

I turned around and smiled at Teddy. "Thank you!" I said enthusiastically. He looked surprised, like he'd never heard me say that before.

I took the coins and rushed back to the yellow motorcycle, my chin up high to avoid carpet-spotting. Three kids from my school were approaching from the other direction. I grabbed the right handlebar of the motorcycle at the same time that a girl from my science class grabbed the left. Her blond hair was in a high ponytail with a huge polka-dot bow on top that looked really weird.

"I was here first," I said quickly.

"You were not," the girl said, looking me up and down. "Where's Tess?"

I sighed heavily. I'd heard that question about one million times in my life. "Who knows?"

"Really?" the girl asked, her eyes wide, her hand still on the handlebar. "That's surprising. I mean, doesn't she have to like babysit you when you come here?"

"No!" I said loudly. "She doesn't *babysit* me. We're the same age! We're twins!"

"Yeah, but you don't look anything alike," the girl's friend said, frowning at my outfit. She had a huge hair bow, too.

"Duh, we're *fraternal* twins." I tightened my grip on the motorcycle handlebar.

"You just seem . . . younger," the girl from my science class said, smiling in a mean way, making her friends giggle behind her.

"Whatever," I said, but it didn't feel like whatever. My stomach ached and there was a lump growing in my throat. "Just move over, I'm going to play this game."

The girl shrugged, her gaze falling to the seat of the motorcycle as she was turning to leave. "Ew, gross," she said. Her friends leaned in to look and they all grossed out in unison. "Have fun with that!" the girl called over her shoulder at me. Laughing, they walked away.

I looked down at the seat of the motorcycle, rolling the tokens Teddy had given me around in my hand. There was a reddish-brown streak across the seat. I stared at it for a few seconds, my eyebrows furrowed. I wondered if someone else had gotten on the seat without me seeing, but they couldn't have: I'd been watching the whole time. Then I wondered if it'd been there when I'd played the first time . . . and if I had something on my pants. *Gross!*

With my free hand, I brushed the back of my jeans to see if anything felt off. Sure enough, I felt wetness. I looked at my hand, and my fingertips had a faint red tint to them. Immediately, I was angry that someone had spilled something on the seat and left it there for the next person. *I can't believe what some people—*

And then I got it.

There I was, standing in the middle of the arcade, with tons of people there for two-for-one Saturday around me, and *THIS*. As if to say *duh!* the pain in my stomach I'd been experiencing dug in like when a cat doesn't want to be picked up.

I felt the color drain out of my face and turned so my back was to the machine. I looked down at my medium-blue jeans and pulled my sweatshirt down as far as it would go, which was only to my hips.

There aren't bathrooms in the arcade. You can use the outdoor public bathroom or go to one in a restaurant.

What do I do? I thought to myself. *Help! What do I do? Ohmygod, what do I do?*

Tears came to my eyes and my heart sped up. I'd read about all this stuff, and had sat through health class at school, but for some reason, I'd thought it wasn't going to happen to me. I especially hadn't expected it *today*. I dug my nails into my fists, the right fist wrapped around the tokens so tightly they were poking into my skin, too. My breaths were short and fast. A kid at a game next to me looked over, got scared, and ran off. The carpet was swirling. I felt dizzy and hot and helpless, my eyes moving back and forth over the room, searching for anywhere—anywhere!—to hide and think. *Tess would definitely know how to handle this problem without having a breakdown,* I thought. Panicked, I kept looking for a place to go. That's when I saw the door to the laser tag room. Without thinking about it, I darted across the arcade and slipped inside.

The overhead lights were off, but the fluorescent lights were on: bright green and pink and yellow beams told players how to get through the arena. I could hear players up ahead as I made my way down the dark path. I slipped between the partitions and felt my way to a corner that wasn't meant to be part of the game. I slid to the floor and got out my phone.

A memory popped into my head. In fourth grade, a group of girls in my class had coated a soccer ball in mud and thrown it at me at recess because I'd told one of them she looked like my grandma in her new glasses—which had been a fact and which had not been a bad thing, in my opinion. The girl had not agreed. When Colette saw the huge brown stain covering my new shirt and the huge tears in my eyes from being hurt on the outside by the ball and on the inside by the girls, she gave me her sweater. It was a freezing day, but she gave it to me anyway. If we were still friends, if Colette wasn't missing, she'd help.

Slumped in the corner of the laser tag arena, I wiped away tears, debating who to text. It was either Mom or . . . Tess.

FRANKIE

Tess!

I need ur help RIGHT NOW

COME 2 THE ARCADE

She didn't understand what I meant at first.

TESS

Frankie, come on

I don't want to play games

I'm not playing games

I got my YOU KNOW WHAT

What are u talking about?

ARE U SERIOUS

I GOT THAT THING!

u know what I mean right

She'd gotten hers last winter, and I couldn't believe she didn't understand what I was talking about.

> Frankie, will u just say what u mean?
>
> I'm worried about Colette
>
> I seriously don't want to go to the arcade today . . .
>
> maybe next week

> I GOT MY PERIOD!!!!!!!!!!!! !!!!!!!!!!!!!!!!!!!!!!!!!!!!!!!!!!!!

She didn't respond for a few seconds, which felt more like an hour.

> Omg Frankie!
>
> So awesome!

I did *not* think it was awesome in the slightest bit, and I couldn't figure out why Tess or anyone else would think it was. It felt squishy and wet and dirty and crampy and I wanted to teleport myself home and take a shower. And that was saying a lot because I hardly ever wanted to take showers. I didn't say all that to Tess because I just wanted her to stop texting me and get here already.

> Hurry up!!!

I will!

Are you ok?

Yes of course

it's not like I'm dying

Just can't walk out of here

I'm in the laser tag area

HURRY UP

Do u have a sweatshirt to tie around ur waist or something?

I rolled my eyes, because of course I already thought of that, but I hate wearing too many layers, so all I had on under my sweatshirt was a bra.

Walking out of here in a bra is worse than with grossness on my jeans

Whaaaaaa?

Never mind hurry up!!!

Tess did come through for me, getting to the arcade in less time than I thought it would take. She brought a dark sweatshirt that entirely covered my stained jeans and walked her bike alongside mine back to the inn. Plus, she offered to help me when we made it to our rooms. There was no way I was letting anyone get near the bathroom door, and I could read a tampon box perfectly well on my own, but it was nice that she'd offered.

For a second, I forgot that she'd betrayed me a few months ago.

For a second, I had my sister.

chapter 10

Fact: For around twenty-five percent of
tornadoes, you get no emergency warning at all.

"Is everything . . . okay?" Tess asked quietly, glancing down at my replacement outfit: jeans with holes and a gray hoodie, wet at the top from my dripping hair. Tess was in the doorway of her room; I was out in the hallway. "I mean, are you feeling okay?"

"I'm fine," I said, not getting why everyone had to make such a big deal about everything. I like to just handle things and move on. "Here's your sweatshirt." I held it out to her.

"Thanks," she said, walking over and dropping it in the hamper.

"It's not dirty," I said defensively. I'd only had it around my waist for fifteen minutes.

"I wore it riding yesterday," she explained. "It needs to

be washed." She looked at me for a second. "You don't have to stand in the door, you know. You can come in."

I hadn't been in her room recently. It felt strange to step inside.

Tess's room looks exactly like mine—except totally different. We have the same furniture and layout, but her comforter has bright flowers and mine is solid gray. Her walls are covered with inspirational posters and her own drawings of landscapes and people and abstract shapes; mine have pictures of tornadoes from the internet, a map of where the most serious ones have happened, and some sticky notes about things I want to remember. Like passwords and stuff. Her bed is made and, unless someone else snuck in and did it for me, which I hate, mine is not. Her books are on the shelf. Her pencils are sorted by shade in a see-through case. Her clothes are in the closet. Mine . . . aren't.

Tess sat down on the chair by her desk, her left leg folded so she was sitting on her foot. It reminded me of where I'd been sitting in my own room when Colette had been the one near the door two nights ago. Have you ever been to a rodeo when they open the bullpen and the bull charges out? That's what it felt like, only the bull was all the questions I had about Colette and Fred and dare-or-scare bucking around in my brain again.

"Did you notice that the page about dare-or-scare was

missing from the copied pages of Fred?" I asked my sister. "The one with all the dares listed out?"

"Not really," she said, biting her thumbnail.

If Mom were here, she'd tell Tess to stop. Here's a weird thing about us: Tess eats off her nails so there are no white parts showing at all. She always has. I think she does it when she's stressed or maybe she just thinks fingernails are gross. But I don't like having my nails clipped because it feels totally disgusting to me, so my nails are really long. See? Opposites.

"Do you think the police tore it out?" I asked.

Tess looked at me funny. "No, I don't think they'd do that."

"Well, do you think Colette did?"

"I don't know, Frankie, why would she?" Tess seemed to realize she'd been biting her nails and stuck her hands under her thighs.

"Maybe she thought it was embarrassing. Or maybe she ripped it up to be mean to me. Or maybe—"

"What are you talking about?" Tess interrupted. "Colette would never do something *mean* to you on purpose."

"Uh-huh."

"She wouldn't!" Tess said. "Colette has always lov—"

"I want to remember the dares we had listed in Fred," I interrupted loudly. I didn't want to talk about how Colette really would do something mean to me—and had. "Tess, it's *important*."

120

"Why?" Tess asked, chewing her nail again. "You don't think that the dare-or-scare challenge has anything to do with Colette being missing, do you? Because those were just silly dares, like jumping off the dune and landing without falling. They're not—"

"I just want to remember them," I said quietly. "I don't like when I can't remember things." Or maybe it was something more—something nagging at me that I didn't want to tell Tess.

"There were a lot," Tess said, getting up and starting to put away the folded laundry from the pile at the end of her bed. "I don't remember all of them either. It's not just you." I didn't answer, so she added, "Just look at that old Viewer account where we stored the videos."

I smacked myself on the forehead because I hadn't thought of that. Sometimes you can't see the easy answer, even if it's right in front of you. Pulling out my phone, I sank down to the floor and sat, cross-legged, eyes on the screen.

"You can sit in a chair," Tess said.

"Uh-huh," I murmured, not moving as I typed in the address for Viewer, and the password that only Colette, Tess, and I knew. "I haven't been on this account in so long," I said, clicking to open a video. "This is weird."

Tess sat down on the floor next to me and leaned in; I tilted the phone so she could see. She smelled like fruity shampoo. Tess might have been the only person who could sit that close to me without it bugging me—particularly at this point in time, with no medication, limited therapy, and a missing . . . person.

"Look," I said, my voice fading away as we watched a video of sneakers zipping through beach grass past a phone that'd been propped on something. "It doesn't have sound," I observed.

"I don't remember that dare," Tess said quietly. Then, after a few seconds, she asked, "Didn't we make all of the videos together? Why isn't someone holding the camera? Why is it propped up?"

"I don't know," I said to her too-many questions, "but those are Colette's shoes." I'd never owned a pair of vintage white sneakers because the rubber tops make my toes claustrophobic, and Tess's feet are too wide for that brand.

"No, they're not," Tess disagreed.

"Yes, they are," I said. "I'll play it again, look." I started the video over, pausing it when the feet were the closest. "Definitely Colette," I said. "She had on those sneakers Thursday night."

Tess flinched at the mention of the last night we saw Colette. I didn't say anything about the fact that we both thought that Colette had come to our rooms at the same time—and neither did she.

"But this was made two *years* ago, Frankie," Tess said, pointing at the post's date. "It must have been one of the last ones we made. We were probably eleven? Anyway, Colette's taller than her mom now and her feet are huge. She wasn't wearing the same shoes Thursday night as she wore in fifth grade when we did dare-or-scare. They wouldn't fit."

I shrugged, pretty sure that the dirty white sneakers on-screen were the ones I'd stared at when I hadn't wanted to look Colette in the eye two nights before—but sometimes I'm wrong about things. The video *did* say it'd been posted two years ago. Maybe she'd bought a bigger pair of the shoes she'd had in fifth grade.

Or maybe . . .

Something felt off. My stomach hurt—and it wasn't cramps this time. I didn't remember filming the video, but it reminded me of others we'd made. But there were so many that they were all jumbled up in my brain.

I went to another video, the next one in line. This time, the camera climbed someone's porch with whoever was holding it. The person reached out to set down a bunch of flowers in front of the door and I got a glimpse of a dark windbreaker. The person rang the doorbell then turned and ran back down the steps, the camera bouncing and making me feel sick. Then the screen went dark.

"Whose house is that?" I asked.

"Do you remember that one?" Tess asked back. "It looks like the ding-dong-ditch dare?"

I told her I did, but not with flowers, and I couldn't

recognize the house from just the steps, and I started the video again, immediately getting sucked in by the weirdness of it. This one didn't have sound either.

"Frankie! Stop ignoring me. Do you remember this video?" Tess asked, sounding annoyed.

"I answered you."

"No, you didn't!"

Didn't I? I wondered at myself. Sometimes I think I've said things because I hear them so loudly in my head, in my own voice. But I forget to actually say them out of my mouth. Except then I think I did, and that gets confusing for people. And for me.

"No, I don't remember it," I said . . . out loud . . . for sure.

I clicked on the next video. This one was, without a doubt, Colette. It was a video of her profile, her hair pulled back in a knot, wearing a white T-shirt. She was just standing there, not moving, for a full minute. She was inside somewhere, and the video was grainy, like the person holding it hadn't quite focused on Colette's face when they'd started recording. But then I noticed something.

"She's in Marsh's," I said. "See?" I pointed at the blurry shape behind Colette: one of the stuffed dead animals that hang from the ceiling of the store.

"Maybe," Tess said, leaning in closer. "I guess it's possible, but—"

Her phone chimed loudly; it made me jump. I hate phone sounds, so I always keep my phone on silent. Tess leaned away from me so she could get it out of her pocket. The warmth that'd been trapped between our touching arms and legs was released. I shivered.

I stared at the video and wondered if it was the selfie video Kai had told me about yesterday when we'd texted. The one that Colette had taken Thursday night. Except I didn't think that Colette was wearing the same T-shirt in the video that she'd worn to my room. In my room, she'd had on . . . I didn't remember.

Oh, dolphins.

There were only four videos on our account. There should have been way more. Had someone deleted the others? Everything felt off.

"Tess, I really think that Colette might have been doing our dares again."

"It's Mia," Tess said, ignoring me, eyes on her phone. "She's upset because someone drew on one of her flyers. She wants to come over."

"Fine," I said, standing up abruptly, blazing mad. Sometimes I wish my anger would have an emergency system, but it doesn't. Like a tornado showing up without any warning at all, I went from calm to completely annoyed that Tess wasn't listening to me because my gut told me that we should be paying attention to these old videos and she clearly didn't have the same feeling. No one ever listened to what I had to say. "Whatever."

"What's wrong?" Tess asked without looking up from her phone, her dark hair covering half her face, her thumbs flying over the keys.

"Nothing," I said. "I'm leaving."

"Okay, bye," Tess said softly, which sucked. I slammed the door to her room, wishing she had told me to stick around. Wishing she'd have a gut feeling, too; that she'd get obsessed with the missing dare-or-scare page and the videos with me. There were only four videos instead of what should have been about a million. Or at least twenty. I needed to know where the others were—and I wished Tess needed to know, too.

But, as usual, she had better things to do.

chapter 11

Fact: Even though it feels like longer, the average tornado is on the ground for less than ten minutes.

"Is Officer Rollins here?" I asked the lady at the front desk of the police station. I leaned my elbow on the high counter and squashed my cheek against my fist. "I have something to tell him."

It was twelve thirty on Saturday. After I'd left Tess's room, I'd eaten lunch at the cottage with my mom—but I'd pretty much run away after inhaling a sandwich so I wouldn't have to hear more questions about my first period. Didn't she remember her own?

"I'm sorry, Officer Rollins is out, honey," the front desk lady said, her eyes on something behind me.

I turned around to see what she was looking at. As far as I could tell, it was nothing. I hate when people do that. "Made you look" is the worst game ever.

"I can call him for you, if you like?" the lady asked. I didn't answer, so she went ahead and dialed on a black phone on her desk. She talked for a few seconds, then held out the receiver. "Here you go, honey."

I took it and put it to my face, feeling awkward being tethered by a cord to a phone that was tethered to the wall, wondering how many germs might be transferring themselves from the receiver to my cheek right now.

"Hello, Frankie," Officer Rollins said. "Mary says you have something to tell me?"

I felt self-conscious. "Yeah . . . uh . . . so there's a page missing from that notebook you copied for me and Tess, did you notice that?"

"Sorry, Frankie, I can't hear you," Officer Rollins said. There were other voices in the background. "Will you please speak up a little?"

I tried again at volume three. That's more like the volume you need for presenting a report in class, but it was loud wherever Officer Rollins was. Except it sounded like I was yelling in the quiet police station. "The notebook you copied has a page missing from it—unless you didn't give me all of them."

"We gave you all of them," Officer Rollins said. "What was on the missing page?"

"It's a list of dares," I said. "It was part of this game we made up in fifth grade called dare-or-scare."

"I see," Officer Rollins said. "And?"

"And we made videos of us playing the game and put them on a Viewer account and I watched them—well, not those that we made but other ones, maybe newer ones?— because I think Colette was wearing the same shoes in videos that she had on when she came over Thursday night. I mean, I'm not positive, but I think so. They look the same."

The front desk lady was typing something but glancing at me every so often. I turned so my back was to her.

"I see," Officer Rollins said again, his voice sounding like he didn't see.

I thought maybe I hadn't said it right. "The videos say they were added to the account two years ago, but I think they were the same shoes she had on when I saw her, so maybe you could investigate or whatever . . ."

I paused, wondering what I'd hoped he could do with the videos. Now this trip seemed silly and I wondered if Tess had been right not to get obsessed with the videos like I had.

Officer Rollins was quiet, so my brain wandered off like it does sometimes.

I wonder if he's quiet because he's reading my mind, I thought. *That would be a cool superpower. What would I choose as my top five superhero powers? Flying, teleportation—*

"What shoes was she wearing in the videos?" Officer Rollins interrupted my list.

"White sneakers," I said confidently.

"Hmm," Officer Rollins said. I could hear pages turning. "Her parents told us she left the house in flip-flops Thursday night." He paused. "You said the videos are two years old?"

"Well, I mean, that's what the *account* says," I said, "but I think it's wrong."

"But that's what the account says," he repeated.

My face felt hot and I knew it was red; the more people told me I was wrong, the more positive I was that Colette had been wearing white sneakers the night she'd come to ask for Fred and that she'd been wearing the exact same shoes in the videos on Viewer. And that the videos were new and not two years old!

"Maybe her parents remembered wrong," I said.

"Maybe," Officer Rollins said. "People can do that in stressful times like this." Then he added slowly, "They can also make connections that may not be there." I wondered what he meant by that as he kept talking. "Thank you for calling, Frankie. Every tip helps, and I've written down this information and will keep it in mind. Please call me if you think of anything else."

"Okay," I said quietly, feeling like I'd screwed something up, but not knowing what. "Bye."

I handed the receiver back to Mary, the front desk lady,

and turned to leave. I watched my shoes as I walked across the lobby toward the door, spinning about Colette's sneakers, knowing I was right—just knowing it. *Tess doesn't think so,* I thought, *and neither does Officer Rollins. But does Kai? He saw Colette that night, too. I have to go find him and as—*

I slammed right into a wall.

"Ouch!" I shouted, my eyes stinging and watering; I'd hit my nose. Covering my face, I looked up and realized I hadn't hit a wall. Instead, I'd hit a person: the very worst person in town. She's the grouchy old lady who yells at everyone, both people who live in Long Beach and the tourists.

I had run into the Sea Witch.

"Pest!" she snapped in her Russian or Polish or whatever accent, glaring down at me with her glassy gray eyes.

She may have been old, but with a square jaw, shoulders almost as wide as a man's, and a biting tone, she was terrifying. I probably would have yelled at anyone else to *watch out!* but not the Sea Witch.

Stepping away from her, I muttered, "Excuse me," as quietly as Tess talks sometimes, so quietly I don't know if the Sea Witch heard me. We were in the doorway to the police station: her in and me out. My bike was leaning against a planter only a few feet away. I plotted making a run for it.

That's when she grabbed my wrist with her bony fingers. My heart felt like it would jump out of my chest because being touched by her was both scary and terrible at the same time. "You children with no supervision! Running around like you own this place!"

"Let go of me!" I shouted. Mary stood up from her desk and hurried toward us.

The Sea Witch leaned so close to my face that I could smell her sour breath. In a low voice, she said, "You never know what may happen to bad children running around with no parents." She let go of my wrist. "Be careful, you."

I ran to my bike, my heart pounding, breathing hard. It felt like I'd been through something terrifying, like a tornado had ripped through the police station. It was hard to calm down. Checking my phone, I realized I'd only been at the station for ten minutes. When bad things happen, I guess ten minutes can feel like much longer.

———

"Frankie, are you okay?" Kai asked from behind the smaller checkout counter at Marsh's. He had on a navy-blue T-shirt and a yellow beanie pushed back on his head, his wild hair sticking out in front. He was looking at me funny. "You look crazy-pale."

"Oh," I said, sinking my hands into a bin of polished sea glass to try to calm my racing heart. Walking my bike slowly across the street from the police station hadn't helped. I was sweating, too. It was always so hot in Marsh's. "Yeah,

I just . . . Never mind." I didn't want to relive it. I reminded myself why I'd wanted to find Kai in the first place: the videos. "Can we go outside for a minute?"

"Sure," Kai said, nodding. "Gotta tell my mom first. I'll meet you out there."

The fresh air was the best after being inside stuffy Marsh's. I sat on a bench facing the parking lot and the street beyond, my eyes watching the police station like a hawk. *What are you doing there?* I wondered at the Sea Witch. *Did you do something wrong?* I shook my head at myself, thinking that people didn't just walk into the police station if they were the ones who had done something wrong—they were escorted. At least on TV. *But then what were you—*

"I have five minutes," Kai said, making me jump. "Geez, Frankie, is everything all right?"

"I'm fine," I snapped before taking a deep breath and pulling my phone from my pocket. "Anyway, the reason I'm here is . . ." I turned toward him, quickly scrolling to Viewer on my phone. I shoved it in his direction. "Is this the video Colette made when she was here Thursday night?"

Kai took the phone and his eyes widened. "Frankenstein!" I frowned at Kai's latest nickname for me but let him talk. "I totally think it is! Where'd you get this?"

"That's not important." I brushed off his question. "The important thing is that you think it's the video she took."

"Yeah, her hair was pulled back like that."

"Did you notice her shoes?" I asked, hopeful. He shook his head.

"Naw, but that's right where she was standing when she came in," he said, pointing to a black curtain in the background of the video. "She's behind the fortune-teller." He paused, then added, "It's weird, but I think she might have stolen my jacket."

"What?" I asked, looking at him funny.

"Nothing."

I didn't care about Kai's jacket. I thought he'd probably left it at the boardwalk or something. "You're sure about where she was standing?"

"I think so?" Kai said, shrugging.

"No one believes me about Colette making that video on Thursday night," I said.

"Huh," Kai said. "Sorry." He waited a second and then said, "It was weird. Like I said, I wasn't really paying attention because my mom was making me haul boxes around in back when Colette was here. I need to join a club or something so she'll stop making me help out all the time."

As he went on, the Sea Witch popped back into my head. I was bugged by how she'd grabbed my wrist. How she'd told me to be careful. *Be careful of what?*

I forced myself to refocus on the video. It wasn't well-lit or flattering, and it didn't have anything interesting in it. Just Colette. Staring.

Kai's mom popped her head out and told him to please hurry up, the register lines were getting long, then disappeared again.

Kai stood, shoving his hands in his pockets. "I guess it's been five minutes already."

"Hey, will you show me where Colette was standing?"

He looked over his shoulder at the door.

"Really quick?" I pleaded.

"Okay," he said. "Come on."

Kai turned, and I followed him back inside, a double *ding-ding* sounding as we walked through the door. We snaked past the taffy and the ornate collectible dragons, the aisles of plastic toys for kids, and the racks of T-shirts and sweatshirts in every color of the rainbow. On the wood-paneled walls there were heads of dead animals, feathers from dead animals, and framed pictures—of dead animals. They were all for sale, but I didn't know why anyone would ever want to buy them. Marsh's is the weirdest "museum" I've ever seen.

I smeared sweat into my bangs, probably making them look really bad, but I didn't care. I was so focused on stuffed dead animals that I almost ran into Kai when he stopped abruptly. There was a stuffed spider monkey overhead and it looked like it was laughing at me.

"See?" he said, pointing at the back of the fortune-teller machine. He glanced at my bangs but didn't say anything.

"Colette took a selfie video while looking at these tiny license plates with people's names on them?" I asked, more confused than ever. "Why's it always so *hot* in here?"

Kai wasn't sweating despite his beanie. He answered my first question, but not my second.

"Oh, wait. No, she was facing this way," he said, turning around. I copied him, turning around kind of slowly, trying to imagine Colette standing right here.

Then I saw what she'd been looking at and gasped. Kai looked at me, confused. I didn't explain, though; my wheels were spinning faster than anything I could put into words. In five seconds, I'd be back on the beach cruiser, racing toward the inn. All that I said to Kai before bolting out of the store was:

"I know how to find Colette."

———

I KNOCKED ON Tess's bedroom door and when she opened it, I remembered Mia was coming over . . . since Mia was curled up like a cat on Tess's bed, her curly blond hair tied up in a topknot. She had mascara under her eyes like she'd been crying. My eyes got stuck on that for a few seconds; she wears too much makeup. *How much time do you spend doing that every morning? Why would you put on makeup today, if you're so upset that you're just going to cry it off?*

"Hi?" Tess asked, pulling my attention back to her.

"I need to talk to you," I whispered.

"Sorry, I'm kind of busy," she said in a low tone, gesturing at Mia, who was always dramatic. I don't get why Tess and Colette are friends with Mia. I mean, I guess she is student body president, and always coming up with ways to help students, like campaigning for gender-neutral bathrooms and better lunch options. And she volunteers to spend time with old people. But in my opinion, Mia does things to seem nice when really, she's not.

"Just come to my room for two minutes," I said bossily. "It's important."

Tess sighed and told Mia she'd be back in a second, which made Mia sigh. I've noticed that teen girls do a lot of sighing. Cats and dogs also sigh. Pirate is the queen of the dog sighers.

"What's going on?" Tess asked, following me next door to my room, which was unlocked because it always is, which my mom doesn't know. The curtains were billowing in because of a building late-afternoon storm. I turned and faced Tess; she was frowning at the mess all over my floor.

I thought of telling her about running into the Sea Witch, but for some reason, I didn't. Instead . . .

"Colette made the videos Thursday night and she was doing dare-or-scare for sure!" I blurted, the syllables bumping into one another as they fell out of my mouth.

"What?" Tess asked like she hadn't been listening. I

repeated myself—faster and louder and bumpier. Afterward, she asked, "Why do you think that?"

"I went to Marsh's and Kai showed me where Colette stood when she went there Thursday night when she was taking selfies—except she wasn't taking selfies! She was looking at Jake the Alligator Man and taking a video of herself doing it! It's the dare where you had to look at something gross!"

"Wait," Tess said, confused, "you didn't tell me that Colette was in Marsh's."

"Yes, I did," I said, confidently unsure. "Why do you think Kai was at the police station?"

"I don't know, but no, you didn't tell me," Tess said, confidently confident.

"Yes, I did," I insisted. Then quickly I added, so she couldn't get the airspace to disagree again, "The point is that she made a video of herself staring at Jake!"

Tess looked like she was thinking, then said, "That does seem like the dare we made . . ."

"I know!" I said. "That's what I'm telling you!"

She tucked her dark hair behind her ear and started biting her pointer fingernail, her eyebrows pulled together. Her eyes are like a mood ring, and today, they matched the overcast sky. "That's really weird."

"Do you understand what I'm saying?" I asked, starting

to get frustrated. Tess is so soft and delicate about every-thing that sometimes it seems like she's not *there*. I wanted to shake her. "She made the videos we saw on Viewer on Thursday night! We might be able to solve the mystery of where she is if we just figure out—"

"Solve the . . . *mystery*?" Tess interrupted defensively, putting her hands on her hips.

I quickly corrected myself. "I mean we might be able to find her."

Tess let it go, but said instead, "Frankie, the videos say they were added to Viewer two *years* ago."

"I know, that's what Officer Rollins said when I told him. But I think that—"

"You talked to Officer Rollins?" Tess interrupted.

"Will you stop interrupting me!" I shouted at her. She wrapped her long arms around her lanky body and pursed her lips. "I know the dates on the videos are wrong! I have a gut feeling that we need to pay attention to them!"

Tess stared at me for a second, then said quietly, "Frankie, the *police* are looking for her. They know what they're doing. And the dates on the videos aren't wrong."

"Don't you want to just *try*?" I asked. "Don't you want to do something other than sitting around with *Mia*?"

"Why'd you say Mia's name like that?" Tess asked, raising her eyebrows. "She's so nice! What's she ever done to you?"

"Are you serious?!" I shouted.

"Frankie, be quiet," Tess whispered. "One of the guests is going to call the front desk."

I was instantly furious, because Tess knew full well what Mia had done to me. "I don't care!" I screamed right in her face, standing on tiptoe to do it. Then, like a faucet had been turned on, tears gushed from my eyes.

"You are such a jerk," Tess said, stomping out the door but not slamming it, leaving me alone to cry.

I flopped, face-first, onto my bed and put a pillow over my head so I wouldn't get in trouble. Here's an embarrassing thing: the room I live in is double insulated for better soundproofing. My mom tried to have it done without me knowing, but I came home sick from school that day, so I know. Still, I buffered myself with my covers for an extra layer of sound protection because I really didn't want my mom to bring up going back on medication.

I don't need it!

I screamed over and over into the comforter, high-pitched, piercing my own eardrums. When I couldn't scream anymore, I continued to cry. Sometimes when I'm sad, all that my brain will think about is other sad things. It's like it wants to stay in a sad spiral. Today, feeling completely alone and misunderstood, I couldn't help but think about the day in February when Colette and I stopped being friends.

Colette, Tess, Mia, and some other girl in their math class were studying for a test. I came back from collecting shells at the beach and walked into my room, intending to go see if the others were done studying and wanted to hang out. The connecting door between my room and Tess's was open a little, so I could hear their conversation.

"Where's your sister?" Mia asked. I froze in the middle of my room, ears perking up.

"Uh . . . at the beach," Tess answered, her voice preoccupied. I couldn't see her but could picture her in her glasses reading her practice test intently.

"Doesn't she need to study, too?" Mia asked.

No, I thought to myself. *I know how to do geometry.*

"She doesn't really study unless our mom makes her," Tess said. I wanted to creep closer but was afraid the floorboards would creak and announce that I was listening. The door opened and someone else came into Tess's room and I thought: *Great! More people to talk about me!*

"Maybe her tests are just easier," Colette said.

"What do you mean?" some girl I didn't know asked.

"She gets to take them in a special room with just a couple other kids and wear headphones if she wants." Colette was spilling my secrets as if they were nothing, which felt like a slap in the face. And she wasn't even completely telling the truth. I didn't always take tests in different rooms, just sometimes . . . big tests. And I never used the head-phones because gross, who knew how many other kids had smashed their earwax against them?

"Maybe her class is just easier," the other girl said.

I made a face that said: *What the heck? No, it is not!*

I could feel the hotness in my cheeks and waited for Tess to stand up for me, to say that no, my math class was not easier than theirs. That my work was exactly the same. That even if I took a test in a smaller group sometimes, it was still the same test that they got.

I realized I was clenching my fists so tightly that I was digging my nails into my palms. And the conversation didn't stop there.

"Can you imagine Frankie taking this test?" Colette went on. "The question would ask her to calculate the volume of a rectangle and she'd write something about her favorite music. Get it, volume? The way she thinks about things is so random."

"Don't forget about her obsession with tornadoes," Mia said. "She's a total tornado brain."

All the voices that mattered in the world burst into laughter while my heart shattered into pieces. Tears pushed their way out of my eyes and down my hot cheeks; I wiped them away fiercely, so angry and hurt that Colette, my sup-posed best friend, would say those things. That Tess, my own twin sister, wouldn't defend me. Blood was pounding in my ears, making me tune out whatever came next. I needed to leave; I couldn't listen anymore. Silent as a spy on a mission, I left my room and crept away.

The next day was when I stopped taking my medication—without telling my mom at first. And the next week was when I started skipping my appointments with Gabe and hiding from the specialist at school. I wanted to show them all that I was normal just like them.

"I'm normal," I sobbed into my pillow. "I'm normal . . . I'm normal . . . I'm normal . . . I'm normal . . . I'm normal . . . I'm normal . . . I'm normal . . . I'm normal . . . I'm normal . . . I'm normal . . . I'm normal . . . I'm normal . . . I'm normal."

Repeating it didn't help me believe it: it just made the words loop together and sound funny and distract me from my sadness.

And just like that, the tears stopped.

chapter 12

Myth: Green clouds always tell you
that a tornado is forming.

AROUND THREE IN the afternoon, I decided to go out to the beach even though a storm was coming. It wasn't raining yet and the wind would feel nice on my puffy face. I put a windbreaker over my hoodie and left my room, looking sadly at Tess's door from the hallway as I went by.

I crunched across the parking lot, then sank deep into the squishy mountains of sand that made walking feel more like trudging. I didn't mind, though. With the crash of the ocean in my ears, I was immediately calmer and clearer than I'd been when I was cooped up indoors. At the edge of the water, it was windier without the protection of the dunes and my hair covered my face completely until I turned into the wind. There were dark gray clouds looming in the distance, so gray they almost looked green. Or maybe that was my imagination.

Inhaling the sea air, I got out my phone and looked through the four videos on our Viewer account again. It was weird that there were only four. We'd done so many dares—and we'd made videos of everything. With those plus the times Colette or Tess had scared each other (I stuck to dares), we should have had way more videos.

I rewatched the staring-at-Jake video, then the flowers-on-the-porch video. I watched one I hadn't seen before since it was on the second page of the account. It was a video of Colette singing. Her surroundings looked familiar, but I didn't know where she was at first. I wished she'd recorded with sound so I could hear the lyrics.

I made a fresh path of footprints as I watched the videos over and over. When I got to the running-in-beach-grass video the third time, I saw something I hadn't before: whale bones.

From where I was standing, I only had to turn my head to the right to see the whale bones display. Up on a bluff, the wood carvings of mother and baby gray whales were supported at their bellies by metal rods buried in the ground so the whales looked like they were swimming above the sand. The wood versions had replaced an actual whale skeleton when I was a little kid, but everyone still called the new wooden display whale bones. I guess the real skeleton was from a whale that'd washed up on the beach one time. Poor whale.

In the video Colette had made of her running feet, I could see the profile of the mother whale, and the water beyond.

I went over to the highest point of the bluff, then walked around in wide circles, looking at different angles. Behind me to the right, two police officers waded through the brush under the boardwalk, shining flashlights into the space beneath where a person could be hiding . . . or . . . I didn't want to think about that, so I focused on the whale bones.

"This is where the camera was," I murmured to myself, pointing to the ground.

There was a rock the size of a cantaloupe to the left side of the path. I wondered if Colette had put that rock there. I pictured her propping up the camera, hitting record, then running by, filming her feet and everything else the wide-angle caught.

I watched the waves crash, growing feistier with the brewing storm. Every time the sea pulled back, the pipers ran out to try to find food before the tide rolled back in. The seagulls squawked, cars bumped along the sandy roadway, and a family posed for a picture with the irritable ocean as the backdrop.

I tried to imagine Colette here, running past a camera

propped on a rock. I tried not to imagine where Colette was right now, where she'd been all night when everyone else had been sleeping in their warm beds.

You were out alone without friends or parents—just like the Sea Witch warned me about. A chill raced up my spine.

"What are you doing?"

I jumped.

"Don't sneak up on me!" I snapped, folding my arms over my chest. Tess had on a red windbreaker identical to mine. Sometimes our mom got things on sale and bought two of them. I kind of liked when we ended up in the same clothes, but I don't think Tess did.

"Sorry," she said easily. That word was harder for me to say than it seemed to be for her. "What are you doing out here?"

"This is where Colette did the running dare," I said. "Thursday night," I added for emphasis; it was still stinging that Tess didn't believe me. I faced the water and focused on staying calm with the ocean's help. A piece of my hair tickled my nose; I tucked it away. "I can't figure out which dare she was doing—since she was alone, it only showed her feet and the background. Maybe it was the one where you had to jump off the dune."

"I never liked that dare," Tess said. "I always worried I was going to get hurt. Or that you guys would."

You worry about everything, I thought but didn't say.

"Hey, Frankie, I'm not here to fight," Tess said. "I wanted to say sorry for calling you a jerk." She reached out like she was going to touch my shoulder but then didn't. I touched my other shoulder to balance myself out anyway.

"Okay."

"I shouldn't have said it, especially today, when you got your first—"

"Okay!" I cut her off. "I don't want to talk about that. Ever!"

She nodded, then continued. "I'm sorry for another thing, too. When Mia was in my room, we noticed that my clock was set to the wrong time." I stared at the ocean; she went on. "Remember that we just had daylight saving time a few weeks ago?"

"Huh?" I asked. I had no clue what she was talking about. I yanked out a piece of beach grass and started twirling it around my finger. It makes me feel better if my body is doing something, not just standing still.

"My clock," she explained. "I guess I forgot to set it forward when daylight saving time happened because I always just use the alarm on my phone. That's why I said that Colette came to my room at the same time you said she was in yours."

"So I was right," I said quietly.

"Yes, you were right," Tess admitted. "And I'm sorry. For both of those things."

"It's fine," I said. My finger was turning purple from the beach grass wound tightly around it. "It doesn't matter."

"It matters to me when I make mistakes. I mean, I told the police the wrong time. I could have completely messed them up."

"I don't think it was that big of a deal," I said, because now that I wasn't mad at her anymore, I could see that it wasn't. Sure, I wasn't the one who'd made the mistake, but forgetting to change your clock isn't the end of the world. I wanted to say that to Tess, but I didn't because I didn't think she would listen to me.

She was wandering through the grass, looking at the path.

"I did get hurt when I did that dare," Tess said quietly. "I twisted my ankle." Her mood-ring eyes were more green than gray or gold right then.

I nodded, remembering. We'd gone to the arcade earlier that day and played air hockey, then squished into the photo booth like sardines. I still had the picture strip somewhere. I'd made silly faces in all four pictures; Tess had smiled the same way in all of them; and Colette had posed like a model, blowing kisses or baring her shoulder.

"Maybe Colette was doing the dares as a surprise to you or something," I said. "Like as a funny present."

"Frankie, don't get mad at me for saying this, but the videos are old. They're from two years ago. I'm sure she was just messing around back then and we happened to see them now."

"But she made the one in Marsh's Thursday night," I said, breathing deeply to try to keep myself in check. "Kai told me."

"Kai told you that she made *a* video that night, not necessarily *that* video that's on Viewer," Tess said.

"He said her hair was the same," I said.

"She's worn her hair in knots like that since we were little, Frankie," Tess said. "The videos are old."

If your brain twists and turns like mine, it's easy to get confused when people tell you you're definitively wrong. Watching the seagulls struggle to fly in the building wind, I began to question what I was saying. I got out my phone and scrolled through the videos again.

I noticed something about one of them.

"Tess!" I said, turning to face her. "Colette's singing in the gym at school in this one. I didn't recognize where it was at first, but that's where it is, see?" I shoved my phone at her, and she stepped in to look.

"You didn't show me this one," she said, taking my phone and watching. "I wish we could hear what she's singing. I wonder if it's that song—" Tess gasped, making me jump.

"What?" I asked, annoyed at being startled.

"Ohmygod, Frankie, I think you're right!" she said, eyes

wide. "I think you're actually right that she made these videos Thursday night—or at least recently."

I couldn't help myself: I grabbed back the phone to see if I could understand why Tess had flipped the switch from practically telling me I was a liar to agreeing with me so quickly. I stared at the phone, but it looked the same to me.

"She's wearing the scarf she borrowed from me," Tess said.

"So?" I asked.

"So she borrowed it on Thursday night!" Tess said excitedly. "She had to have made this that night!"

"Let's go look at the school!" I said. "Maybe there's a clue that will help us remember more of the dares. I really think that if we figure out what she was doing, we can help find her."

"You're being really . . . you're . . ." Tess began, then paused for a few seconds. "You're doing a nice thing for her, but you and Colette haven't been exactly . . ."

She didn't have to say it; I didn't want her to.

"Just because you think someone sucks doesn't mean you want bad things to happen to them," I said.

Tess nodded slowly.

"Honestly, I think the police are our best hope," she said. "But you were right earlier that trying is better than sitting around stressing out." She smiled a little. "Let's see if the school makes us remember anything else." Ready to go, I started down the path toward the street; she grabbed my arm and I pulled it away, thinking, but not saying, *Don't touch me.* "We're only doing this until dinner, okay? It'll be getting dark after that."

"So?"

"So I don't want to be out in the dark."

That was surprising to hear since Tess had never been afraid of the dark before. In fact, all our lives, she was the one who *wanted* to go out at night.

"Fine by me," I said, feeling unsettled by the change in Tess.

We plodded down the dune.

"Can I tell you a secret?" Tess asked as we trudged through the divots at exactly the same pace. She didn't wait for me to say yes. "Colette came to my room to ask for the scarf, but while she was there, she told me something terrible. Her parents are making her move to Seattle after school gets out. I guess her dad got a new job. She said she doesn't want to go and they got in a big fight about it and she stormed out of the house without telling them where she was going. She was really upset. She asked me to get her some cucumber water to calm her down, but she was gone when I came back."

"Wow," I said.

"You can't tell anyone," Tess said. "Mia doesn't know."

"Why didn't you tell her?" I asked, my chest full in a good way because I had been told something that others hadn't heard.

Tess shrugged. "You know how she is. I mean, she's fun to be around, but she can't keep a secret." She paused. "I told the police, but they already knew because Colette's parents told them about it."

"Tess?"

"Yeah?"

"Maybe Colette really was making you a present with the dare videos," I said. "But not a funny one, more a sentimental one." I hesitated, then added, "More of a goodbye present."

She tucked her hair back. There was a little knot in her hair under her ear like she'd been twisting it. "I guess that's possible," she said quietly. Then, because maybe that possibility stressed her out, she started biting the nail of her middle finger as we walked, in sync, toward school.

chapter 13

Fact: It's possible to have a tornado
and a hurricane at the same time.

TESS AND I stared up at the two-story redbrick building where we spent so much of our time: Ocean View Middle School.

"What time is it?" Tess asked, her arms wrapped around her middle, hunching over. I don't know why some tall girls do that. I wouldn't: I'd stand up straight and touch the ceiling to see how it feels.

"Four fifteen," I said, putting my cell back in my pocket.

"Maybe this is a bad idea. We could get in trouble."

"We won't," I said casually.

"I'm seriously so nervous right now," Tess said, biting her nail. "I feel like I'm going to have a panic attack."

"You won't," I said, because she had never had one.

"How are you not nervous?"

I shrugged. "I don't get nervous."

Sometimes I think that twins get unequal traits, like one gets all of something and the other gets none of it. Tess got all the nervousness and artistic ability and niceness and I got all the . . . I don't know what I got.

Not wanting to think about that, I walked up to the front door of the school and yanked it open.

Tess's eyes widened. "It's unlocked?"

"Some of the teachers work weekends," I said, shrugging again.

"How did you know that?"

"Because of when I did that Saturday kite-making class."

"What if they see us?" Tess asked, looking completely freaked out. I didn't know how someone who loved haunted houses thought going into our school on a Saturday afternoon was so terrifying.

"We could say we forgot a book or something?"

"How did you think of that so quickly?" She was still frozen outside the door.

"I just did," I said impatiently. "Are you coming or not?"

"Ohmygod," Tess whispered as she walked through the door I was holding open. I followed her in. She looked down the hall to the left, then the right. "I don't see anyone."

"Good! Let's go!"

I started walking down the main hall toward the lockers for our grade. The gym where Colette had made the singing-dare video was just beyond our lockers. Tess followed me instead of walking next to me. Once she and Colette tricked me into watching a horror movie where the girl who went last got killed first: I didn't remind Tess of that. She didn't seem in the mood to be scared—any more than she already was. We went by classroom after classroom and they all had their lights off. They weren't dark—just dim—because it was still light out, and they all had windows. The storm clouds had cleared.

"Maybe Principal Golden's here," I said.

"I hope not!" Tess whispered.

"When did you turn into such a scaredy-cat?" I said. This wasn't normal for Tess.

"Shhh!" she whispered. "Be quiet!"

"No one's in the hallway," I said in my regular voice.

"Frankie, stop it!"

"Fine," I groaned, walking in silence for a few minutes. But then, without warning, I became very aware of my socks crowding and tickling my feet inside my shoes; the scratchiness of the tag in my sweatshirt at the back of my neck; the elastic gripping my wrists. There was only one surefire way to get my mind off my grippy, prickly clothing:

To run.

I bolted, pounding my feet hard against the floor all the way down the hall, shaking my wrists as I went. Some person called an occupational therapist had told me to try running once when I was having a supersensory freak-out moment. It worked, so I do it when I can—not in the middle of class or something.

I didn't stop until I reached the beginning of the locker bank. I doubled over and rested my hands on my knees, slowing my breath until Tess caught up.

"Did it work?" she asked.

I stood up straight and nodded once, brushing my bangs out of my eyes.

"Your hair looks cute," Tess said, tilting her head to the side. "The curls are less, uh . . ."

"Frizzy?" I asked, frowning.

She opened her mouth to answer but her phone buzzed and startled us both, making me jump and making her squeal like a mouse. I frowned deeper at being scared, but Tess burst into hysterical laughter because she loves watching other people freak out in fear. I couldn't help but laugh a little, too.

When we calmed down, Tess pulled out her phone and checked it.

"Is it Mom?" I asked, stepping closer to look over her shoulder.

"No, it's Mia," Tess said, reading the text. I moved away quickly while Tess kept talking. "She's back at her house, worrying about Colette. I mean, we all are. I should probably tell her what we think she was do—"

"No!" I shouted. Tess looked at me, surprised. In a lower voice, I said, "Mia's not a part of this. She never was."

When Mia had shown up in the middle of last year, Tess and Colette were fascinated by her mainly because she'd moved here from New York. At least that's what I thought at first. But then Tess and Mia had art class together, and Tess thought Mia's paintings were beautiful and her jokes were hilarious. Mia's big personality is basically the exact opposite of Tess's reserved one—and I guess Tess liked that.

And Colette got obsessed with Mia's stories about riding the subway and seeing celebrities on the street corners and Mia's general coolness. Tess was just friends with her, but Colette seemed to kind of idolize Mia.

But what my sister and my former best friend never noticed while they were friending or idolizing her was that Mia just didn't *get* me. It was obvious. And because of that, our friend group changed.

So much that I wasn't a part of it anymore.

Tess pursed her lips like Mom did sometimes. "I don't understand why you hate her so much."

"I don't get why you *like* her so much." *Especially since she turned Colette into a total backstabber who said terrible things about your sister,* I thought but didn't say.

Tess sighed loudly but put away her phone without replying to Mia's text. She flipped around and went over to her locker. As she was doing the combination, she said, "I don't say bad stuff about *your* friends."

"What friends?" I muttered, wanting to tell her that, by not standing up for me, she'd taken my single friend away. I mean, Tess could have made Colette understand that she'd been wrong. She could have helped Mia get to know me, maybe. Instead, Tess had gone along with the mean stuff Colette and Mia said by not saying anything. Her silence had told them it was okay.

I didn't want to think about that anymore. "Why are you opening your locker?" I asked my sister. "Let's go to the gym."

"Because I want to show you something."

Tess flung open the locker door. I walked over and stood behind her, peering in. It looked like a normal locker—well, normal for Tess and Colette. There was a magnetic mirror stuck to the back of the door surrounded by a bunch of photos taped up with emoji washi tape.

There was a shelf that split the guts of the locker in half and I could tell which part belonged to which girl immediately. On top, the books and binders stood vertically in a row, neatly organized and looking like they were issued yesterday. That was signature Tess. On the bottom, books, loose papers, and tattered folders with drawings all over them were layered in an organized mess, which was Colette in a nutshell.

"Look," Tess said, pointing at the picture collage that covered the entire inside of the locker door.

"What?" I asked.

"Look at the pictures," Tess said.

"What about them?" I asked, not getting what she was saying.

Tess rolled her eyes. "You're in them, Frankie," she said. I took a closer look and she was right: I was in at least a dozen of them.

"What's your point?" I asked, stepping away.

"Just that even though you and Colette were fighting or whatever, she never took down the pictures of you."

I thought about that, and the naturally skeptical side of me said, "That's because she shares a locker with my sister."

Tess ignored that comment, touching a picture of Colette. In it, Colette was smiling huge, jumping off something so her red hair was flying out in all directions. "I hope she's okay."

"Are you crying?" I asked, leaning around to look at her. Her eyes looked like tiny buckets.

"It's just . . . seeing her face," Tess said. "I'm really worried about her, Frankie." Tess looked at me with big, sad eyes and it made my heart pinch. "What if no one finds her?"

"We're going to," I said. "Will you get out a piece of paper and pencil?"

Tess nodded and handed me a notebook with a pen stuck in the spiral. I sat down on the floor, leaning against the wall on the opposite side of the hall, stretching out my legs in front of me. When I did, Tess slid to the floor, too, stretching her legs out like a mirror of mine. The bottoms of our feet were only about a foot apart.

In the notebook, I wrote which dares Colette had done from dare-or-scare recently:

Running off dune dare?
Ding-dong-ditch . . . but with flowers.
Singing in public (gym).
Staring at something gross (Jake).

"We need to remember more of the dares," I said, eyes on the page. "I think it's important. I'll bring this with us." I started to rip out the paper. "And we can write down our notes. Can I borrow the pen?"

I reached across and handed the notebook back to Tess. She looked like she'd been blasted off to space while I was making the list. "What's wrong?" I asked.

"Do you think she killed herself and wants us to find her?"

The words made my heart jump. It felt like too big a thing to say out loud, let alone think about.

"No!" I said. Then, "She better not have!"

"It happens," spacey Tess said. "I read a book about it. You can think someone is completely fine and then they kill themselves. I mean, she *had* gotten into a fight with her parents. She was really upset about the idea of moving to Seattle."

"You should read happier books," I said. Then, rationally, I added, "People kill themselves because they have depression, not because of a single fight."

"How do you know so much about it?"

"I saw a book at Gabe's office once." The conversation was making me feel on edge. I was starting to notice my restrictive clothes again. "Do you think she's depressed?"

"No," Tess admitted. "I don't really know what that means, but I don't think so."

I didn't really either, and I didn't *want* to know. "Stop talking about that."

"Okay," she said, her voice a little more normal.

"Are *you* depressed?" I asked.

"No!" she said strongly, looking at me funny. "Are you?"

"No?" I said like a question, looking at her funny right back. "How do you know if you're depressed?"

I wondered if depression was something you caught like the flu or Ebola and you didn't know you had it until it was too late.

"You're the one who read a book about it!" Tess said.

"I didn't read it cover to cover," I said. "I didn't memorize it! I just flipped through it." Then, "Let's seriously stop talking about this."

"Okay," Tess said. She folded her legs into crisscross applesauce. "But if you ever feel, like, um . . . bad . . . you know you can . . ."

"I know." Awkward pause. "You too."

"I mean because friendships can be—"

"Don't talk about that either." I cut her off, looking back at the paper again. I drew a tornado in the corner, then another one, then another one. Without the notebook under the paper, the pen poked through and made marks on my jeans.

"Let's just get back to dare-or-scare," I said, standing up. "Let's go to the gym and—"

A door slammed with a *boom* at the other end of the main hall. Tess and I both looked toward the sound, then back at each other, eyes wide. She stood up fast.

"Come on," I said in a low voice, pointing toward the gym, which happened to be in the opposite direction of where the sound had come from. "We can go out that way."

We ran down the hall and pushed through the double doors to the gym as quietly as we could, our sneakers squeaking against the shiny floor as we hurried toward the door leading out.

When we were almost there, I turned back to look at the wide-open space. "Where did she make the video?" I asked, pulling out my phone and unlocking it. The screen was still on the singing dare.

"What are you doing?" Tess asked. "Someone's coming; we have to go."

"We will," I said. "Just let me look really quick."

I held my phone out in front of my face and turned in a semicircle, trying to match the backgrounds here to the one in the video.

"She was right over there," I said, pointing. "Under the basket. See, you can see the edge of the poster in the video?"

"Frankie, we have to leave," Tess said, pulling on me.

"Stop!" I said. "I'm trying to concentrate!" But there was no way I could let my brain remember anything when I was being rushed and pulled by Tess. I needed her to be quiet and leave me alone, but she wouldn't. I was starting to get mad. "Stop touching me!"

"Stop yelling at me!" Tess yelled herself. "I'm leaving, and you should, too. We are going to get in trouble, Frankie. This is really stupid!"

"Don't call me stupid!" I shouted, my throat tightening, my cheeks growing hot.

"Ugh!" Tess shouted, frustrated. "I didn't say that!"

"Just leave and go hang out with Mia," I said nastily. "I know that's where you'd rather be."

"I should," Tess said. "At least she doesn't yell at me all the time. I swear, I don't know why you take everything out on me! And you're so mean to Mia for no reason!"

That was it.

I put my phone away and flipped around, hands clenched into fists, the storm rising up from my belly, growing stronger with every vertebra it passed. When it finally reached my mouth, it'd turned into an EF5-caliber issue.

"I hate her!" I screamed, my words echoing off the walls of the huge space. Tess looked like she'd been slapped.

"You have no reason to hate her!" Tess screamed back, looking angrier than I'd ever seen her. We were two storms colliding.

"I have a great reason!" I shouted. "She turned Colette against me! She's a snake and she made Colette one, too. They talked about me behind my back and made fun of me and . . ." I sniffed to try to control the river of tears. "And thanks for standing up for me, by the way! I thought sisters were supposed to be there for each other!"

In a flash, Tess didn't look angry anymore. Instead, she looked shocked, her eyebrows up and her mouth open a little. I turned around and walked toward the door leading outside.

"Wait, Frankie," Tess said, following me. "I don't know what you're talk—"

"Hey, you kids!" the janitor shouted. In normal school hours, he was perfectly harmless. Now he was sweaty, angry, and scary. "You're not supposed to be in here!"

I bolted through the door, and a few seconds later, Tess was outside, too. It was still light out, but the sun was closer to the beach now. The cloudy sky and long shadows gave the town an eerie filter as we ran across the street, through the mini-carnival, down Pacific, past the go-karts and horses, and into the inn's parking lot. The only sounds I could hear were the slaps of our shoes on pavement and the blood pumping in my ears. Pirate was lying under the bench in the covered outdoor area; she raised an eyebrow at me.

"Tell Mom . . . ," I gasped, "I'm sick . . ." I sucked in air. "And I don't want dinner."

I took off running toward the beach. Pirate barked, keeping up with me, her tags going *tink-tink* as she trotted along.

"Wait, Frankie!" Tess called again before I was out of earshot.

I didn't stop: I couldn't be inside. I ran toward the ocean until my feet and pant legs were soaked, and when a huge gust of wind barreled through, I screamed the loudest I ever have in my life.

chapter 14

Fact: Some animals seem to sense when weather disturbances like tornadoes are about to happen.

PIRATE HAD FOLLOWED me. She must have just known I needed a friend. I should have been going to the cottage for dinner, but instead, I walked along the shore with Pirate by my side, then planted myself on a huge log. It was closer to the dune than to the water, which meant it was more sheltered. Pirate lay at my feet and we watched a runner near the surf lean into the wind as she went by almost in slow motion, her hair blown back like she was coming up from underwater.

The waves were so choppy now that the tide was leaving huge, frothy mounds of bubbles on the sand. Then the wind blew the mounds along, and they looked like miniature icebergs. I zoned out, staring at one point, seeing the movement of the waves and the icebergs and the pipers all around in my peripheral vision.

The ocean made me feel calm. It had since the first time I'd seen it. I forget things sometimes, but I haven't forgotten the first time we came here.

Mom picked us up on the last day of preschool with the trunk packed with so much stuff, my artwork and desk supplies had no place to go but under my feet.

"We're going on an adventure!" Mom said when we were buckled up.

"Where are we going?" Tess asked.

"We're going to the beach!" Mom said, but she didn't seem excited. It wasn't sunny out, but she was wearing sunglasses.

"The beach!" I shouted, thinking it'd be like the roped-off sandy area by the small lake near our house. "Yay!"

"When are we coming back?" Tess asked.

"We'll see," Mom said, pulling out of the parking lot. "How would you guys like to watch a show? I put your devices and headphones in the seat pockets."

When we arrived after our five-hour ride, Mom stopped the car under the WORLD'S LONGEST BEACH sign and made us take off our headphones. Normally, I would have protested, but the sight of the ocean was distracting, and if you tell me something is the world's best or longest or tallest something, I get curious.

"Look what we can do!" Mom said before she pushed the gas pedal and drove out onto the sand. "We can drive right on the beach! Isn't this great?"

The drier sand yanked the car back and forth and the bumps made us jump in our seats. Mom rolled down all four windows and the sea air whipped our hair around the car. We made a left onto the packed wet sand and Mom drove along with the waves coming right up to kiss our tires.

"I love it here," I said after only being in Long Beach about five minutes. Already, in preschool, the world felt daunting to me. I could tell right away that the beach would be a place that would make it a little less so.

"I'm scared," Tess said, reaching over and grabbing my hand. "What if we drive under the water?"

"Then we'll meet a narwhal," I said, putting my free hand out of the car to surf on the wind. I loved that feeling.

"Can we go back on the normal road, Mommy?" Tess asked.

"I want to stay on the beach!" I said. "I want to live on the beach."

Mom pulled over and parked the car on the dry sand, so the front windshield was facing away from the ocean and toward a four-story building. It had huge windows looking out toward the water, reflecting it back. Mom turned around and took off her sunglasses. Her eyes were red and tired, but she was smiling.

"You can't live right on the beach, Frankie," she said, "but is that close enough?" She pointed at the building.

"We get to live there?" I asked in disbelief.

Mom nodded. "It's an inn, which is like a hotel. I've been offered a job as the manager. For as long as I work at the inn, we get to live in that little cottage over there." She beamed at us. "Then we can come to the beach every single day."

"Where's Ronan?" Tess asked. "Is he coming, too?"

Ronan was Mom's boyfriend before Charles. I barely remember him: when I think of him, he has a blurry face. I don't think he was very nice to my mom.

"Remember our talk last week?" Mom asked. "Remember what I said about Ronan's mistake and us moving out?"

"Can I go play on the beach?" I interrupted because I didn't want to hear the story again. She said I could, and I went and chased pipers.

Lost in thought about the day we'd arrived, I didn't hear someone come up behind me—but Pirate let me know: her tags *tink-tinked* when she raised her head to look.

"'Sup, Frank and Beans," Kai said. I turned around and looked at him standing there with his skateboard in his hand, still wearing his yellow beanie, the sunset turning his face even more golden than it usually was. I'm not going to lie: it made me feel squishy like a sand mountain.

"Hi," I said.

"Shove over," he said, coming around the log to sit down

with me. I moved as far away as possible without falling onto the sand. "What're you doing out here? My dad's convinced it's going to storm. Hey, Pirate," he said, scratching her head.

"Nothing," I said, because that sounded better than telling him I was recovering from an epic meltdown. "Looks like your mom let you out of the shop."

"Finally," he groaned.

Pirate jumped up on Kai's knees and started licking his face; I liked that he just let her and didn't gross out. Pirate knew not to do that to me because I *would* gross out: I can't help it. Kai just laughed, rubbing her ears with both hands. When he asked, "Who's a good girl?" Pirate smiled at him.

He looked over at me with his nice eyes and good eyebrows. My heartbeat sped up and my hands felt clammy. Maybe I could feel nervous after all! I wanted to tell Tess, but then I remembered I was mad at her.

Kai was still staring at me.

"What?" I asked him, looking back at the ocean so he'd hopefully do the same.

"You didn't write me back earlier," he said. "Did you see my texts?"

"I didn't get any," I said, pulling out my phone, thankful for something to do. After I'd looked at Viewer so many times earlier and not closed the app, the battery on my phone had taken a hit. "It's dead," I said, holding it up as if he could see the tiny battery icon from all the way on the other side of the log. "Why'd you text me?"

"To tell you I remembered something about when Colette came to the store," he said. Pirate settled down on his feet, and Kai kept petting her.

"What did you remember?" I asked excitedly.

"Nothing, just that she asked me where the Sea Witch lives."

I sucked in my breath. "What?" All at once, my body went crazy, my heart jumping hurdles, my neck turning hot, the place where the Sea Witch had grabbed my wrist sending a twinge of pain.

Colette had asked where the Sea Witch lived.

I'd seen the Sea Witch at the police station.

Did the Sea Witch have Colette?

"Why did she want to know *that*?" I managed to ask Kai.

"Dunno," he said super-casually. It made me want to scream and shake him—but then I'd have to touch him.

"She literally asked you for the Sea Witch's address?" I blinked a bunch, as if it would clear up my confusion.

"No, she literally asked for the address of the person with the stuffed animals in their yard," Kai said. "I told her that person was the Sea Witch. *Then* she asked for the Sea Witch's address."

"But why . . ." My mind raced. *Why did . . . what would . . .*

but how... and when...? "Wait." I looked at Kai. "Why did she ask *you* that?"

"Ask me what?" Kai and Pirate were in their own world.

"Why did Colette ask you where the Sea Witch lives?" I shouted. "How the heck do you know that?"

"Whoa, calm your status, Franklin," Kai said good-naturedly. "She buys those weird taxidermy animals my parents sell. She has a collection, I guess. They're too big and heavy for her to take home herself, so she has them delivered." Kai pulled out his phone and scrolled through for a second. Then he showed me a picture of a notecard with a name and address written on it. "See? I sent it to you."

Leaning over to look, I shivered, still phantom-feeling the Sea Witch's fingers wrapped around my wrist. The name on the card said *Mikayla Sievich*.

"See-vich," I murmured, then it hit me. "Is that where she got the nickname? From her last name?"

"I guess so. And because she's such a witch to all the kids in town. She stuck a knife in Dillon's soccer ball once. For real."

"Uh-huh," I said, not totally listening to him. I was too focused on the Sea Witch's warning: *You never know what may happen to bad children running around with no parents.*

Had the Sea Witch done something to Colette?

Kai cleared his throat. "Hey, that sucks that no one else believes you about when Colette made the videos."

"Uh-huh," I said, still more preoccupied by the conversation I was having inside my head.

"I mean, since you can choose the upload date," he said.

My head snapped in his direction. "What?" I shouted. "Why are you just casually telling me all of these important things?!"

"You didn't know that?" he asked.

"No, because you didn't tell me!" I shouted.

He laughed, which might have bugged me if I thought that he was laughing at me in a mean sense. But Kai's not like that.

"Okay!" he said. "So yeah, you can set your upload date to whatever you want. It'll use the current date automatically, or you can change it to anything. Even the future."

"How do you know that? Are you sure?"

"I've done it," he said, nodding. "For the edits that me and Dillon make sometimes of us doing board tricks and stuff."

"But why say a video was uploaded on a different day than when it was?" I seriously could *not* believe that he hadn't told me this until now.

"Dunno why other people would want to," Kai said, "but Dillon has this thing about only posting on our channel on Thursdays. He says, like, people will get more excited to see our board tricks if they have to wait a few days for them." Kai shook his hair out of his eyes and added, "It's lame because we only have seven followers, but whatever. The only problem is if he puts a video on our account with a date from the past, it doesn't hit me up that there's a new video . . . so I don't see it."

"Wait, so you mean that if you make a video on a Friday, you can upload it but change the date to the day before, a Thursday?"

"Yup."

"Or you could upload a video today but change the date to say it was uploaded two years ago?" I asked, trying to understand what Kai was telling me.

"Yup yup," he said.

"And if you did that, people wouldn't get a notification that a new video was uploaded . . . because the date was in the past?"

"You got it," Kai said before cracking up. "Oh man, one time I wiped out *extra* in a video that Dillon posted with a different date. My sister obsessively checks the channel because she has a crush on Dillon, and she saw it and was making fun of me, and I didn't even know what she was talking about to defend myself . . ."

My thoughts were on a Tilt-A-Whirl: changing video-upload dates, Colette making the videos again, Colette asking Kai about the Sea Witch, the Sea Witch being at the police station. The warning.

"I have to find Tess," I said, interrupting whatever Kai

was saying about his epic wipeout. He looked bummed, which I noticed, which I felt proud for noticing, so I forced myself to use the hard word. "Sorry for interrupting you."

"S'okay," Kai said, standing up and brushing the sand off his jeans. "I gotta go anyway; we're going to a movie." He stretched like he'd just gotten up from a nap and looked off to the right, toward the inn. "Oh, hey, you don't need to go far to find your sister. She's coming this way."

Kai and Tess waved at each other, but Kai didn't wait for her to reach the log before he left. I thanked him for the information and tried not to feel sad that he was leaving.

"There you are," Tess said, crunching closer through the sand.

She sat down on the log next to me, but leaving space between us, shivering and pulling her jacket tighter. My log was getting a lot of traffic.

"Frankie, will you please tell me what Colette and Mia did—why you're so mad?" Tess asked.

"I don't want to talk about it," I said quickly. I really didn't, but not because it was painful or because I thought we'd fight again. Well, that stuff, too. But more because I wanted to get all of the other stuff in my brain out of my mouth, so she'd help me figure it out.

Everything except the Sea Witch's warning. For some reason, I wanted to keep that to myself. Maybe I thought it would scare Tess too much—and she was being weird about being scared today. Maybe I thought she'd brush it off like she had with my earlier ideas, when she didn't believe me about Colette making the dare videos recently. Maybe I just wanted to know something that no one else did.

"That's what you've been telling me for months—that you don't want to talk about it," Tess was saying, "but that thing you said in the gym about me not . . . sticking up for you? I don't know what you mean." She paused, then added, "I even called Mia and asked her about it." I looked at her, surprised. "She said she didn't know what I meant, but I . . . I don't know. I feel like she was being weird. Will you please tell me what happened?"

"I'll tell you," I said, and she looked hopeful, "but not right now. Kai told me two things when he was here—and those things are more important than a fight."

"Do you promise we'll talk about it later, though?" Tess asked. And somehow, her caring enough to make me promise made my anger at her stay away. I nodded, and she smiled. "Okay, tell me what Kai said."

chapter 15

Opinion: *The Wizard of Oz* is probably the most popular movie with a tornado in it ever.

"IS IT OKAY if Frankie and I go to a movie after dinner?" Tess asked, looking at Mom with big innocent eyes. She was sitting straight up in her chair and smiling a little, and I made a mental note to practice that posture later. It seemed to be effective, judging by the fact that Mom hadn't immediately said no.

"Together?" Mom asked. She looked at Charles and he shrugged before blowing his nose with a huge honk in a dinner napkin. *Gross.*

"Yes," Tess and I said at the same time.

"It *is* Saturday night," Tess said.

Mom narrowed her eyes at us. "Are you two up to something?"

"We just want to go to a movie," Tess said. Then she

made her tone sound sad. "We just want a distraction. Watching a movie is good for that. There will be other kids there, too."

"That's understandable," Charles chimed in, his nose stuffy. "But because of Colette, it's hard to want to let you two go off on your own at night."

"Stop giving the dog crab," my mom snapped at him, frowning. "It's expensive."

"Sorry, Pirate," Charles said to the beggar by his side. "The lady of the house says you're cut off." He sneezed and I moved my chair away from his.

"We'll be careful," Tess promised. "Can we please go? It's only a few blocks away."

I stayed quiet, letting her handle the negotiations.

"I don't know about this," Mom said, looking at Charles. They stared at each other for like a whole minute, seeming to have a conversation telepathically. Finally Mom sighed and looked at us. "You'll walk there and back together?"

"Yes," Tess and I said in unison.

"And sit together?" Mom asked. "And keep your phones on vibrate?"

We both nodded enthusiastically.

"Which movie are you seeing?" Mom asked.

"The superhero one," Tess said. "It's PG-13."

"You don't like superhero movies," Mom said, eyeing me skeptically.

"This one looks good," I said. *Don't ask me the title. Don't ask me the title!*

"All right, you can go, but text when you get there, and be home by ten thirty," Mom said, giving in.

"The movie might not be over by then," Tess said innocently.

"Fine, eleven," Mom said. "And text when you leave to come home."

"We will," Tess said, nodding.

"Promise," I said.

———

WHEN WE SET out, it was completely dark. I rode behind Tess—in the horror-movie, get-killed-first spot—because she still seemed off about the dark. It wasn't so much that I minded riding in the dark, at least not yet, but I minded the change in Tess. I minded that *she* was afraid.

We rode in the middle of Ocean Beach Boulevard because that's where the lights from the houses on both sides of the streets shone the brightest. There aren't any sidewalks in the residential part of the town, and besides, you can see headlights coming from a mile away.

I followed the blinking light on the back of Tess's bike, talking a lot to keep myself from thinking a lot.

"Is it Seventeenth or Eighteenth?" I called to Tess. It was the third time I'd asked her.

"Eighteenth," Tess answered over her shoulder, her voice higher than usual. "Two more blocks."

"And what are we going to do when we get there?" I asked.

"This was your idea, Frankie," Tess said. "I don't know!"

"We'll just look," I said, trying to make myself feel better. "We can even look from pretty far away if we want."

My stomach did somersaults thinking about riding toward the Sea Witch instead of riding away from her as fast as I could like I wanted to. With every spin of the pedals, I dreaded where we were going more.

In front of me, Tess bumped over a pothole and I dodged it. I kept talking. "Remember when Colette hit that huge pothole that was completely obvious to everyone else but her and she went over her handlebars?"

Tess started laughing, which made me calm down a little. "Ohmygod, yes, she did a full flip in the air. She's the worst bike rider; she's so uncoordinated."

"And that sound she made . . . ," I said, laughing, too. "Yeeeeee-oooow!"

"I forgot about that!" Tess laughed harder. "She's so lucky she landed in grass."

Tess took the right on Eighteenth and I followed, making a wide arc, and the somersaults in my belly were back. Tess slowed down; I almost ran into her back tire, pedaling backward to brake fast since the cruiser didn't have a hand brake.

"Let's leave our bikes here," Tess whispered.

"Good idea," I whispered.

We walked the cruisers over to the side of the road and leaned them against someone's tree. It was low hanging, and I hoped no spiders would drop into my hair.

The big houses on this block were dark: they were probably vacation homes owned by people who didn't live in Long Beach all the time. It felt like they'd been abandoned.

"Maybe we should come back tomorrow," I whispered. My heart was racing and my mouth felt like I'd eaten sand.

"We're already here," Tess said, but she looked like a scared squirrel in a car's headlights. "Let's get it over with."

"Fine," I said. "Let's just go."

Crouched together, walking carefully, we approached a huge house with ten steep steps leading up to a shadowy porch. It didn't look anything like the porch in the ding-dong-ditch dare video, but it looked like a house where a witch would live. The roof jutted up to sharp points and the steps and house itself were solid brick and menacing. The mailbox said *Sievich* in faded, angry handwriting.

"It's not the same house in the video where Colette left the flowers," I whispered to Tess.

"How do you know?" she whispered back.

"Those were wooden steps, not brick. And they were wider."

"You noticed that?" she asked, scooting closer to me. I

shrugged. Sometimes I notice things. Sometimes I don't. It's like I'm always out of sync.

Or at least usually. Gabe tells me not to use "forever" words like *always*. And *forever*. He says they're almost *always* an exaggeration and exaggerations aren't a clear way to speak.

I missed Gabe.

Tess was talking. "Why did Colette want to come here if—"

"Listen," I interrupted. I thought I'd heard something, but when Tess and I stopped talking, there was nothing but the ocean in the distance and a wind chime tinkling on a porch nearby.

"Is that her driveway?" Tess asked, pointing to the gravel alley to the left of the house.

"Probably," I whispered. Tess started walking toward the driveway and I followed automatically because I didn't want to be alone in front of the Sea Witch's house. Of course I noticed that I was in get-killed-first position again. The trees were spooky black silhouettes. "This is a bad idea," I said, tiptoeing behind my sister on the gravel.

"Let me remind you: this was *your* idea," Tess whispered, stopping suddenly when we were all the way down the driveway. "Ohmygod."

"Holy guacamole," I said, blinking in the dim light from the outdoor lamps, taking in the yard. There were animals everywhere—dead, stuffed ones—all looking like they wanted to eat us alive. As I stared at a grizzly bear, something important clicked into place.

I'd been here before—and I remembered why.

I turned toward the porch, which stretched the entire length of this side of the house. It didn't have any furniture, though, like no one ever sat out there, watching the sunset, listening to the waves. This side was covered in gray shingles, not brick, and had more windows than walls—every one of them dark. The house looked like two people with very different faces standing back-to-back: one guarding the street and one watching the ocean.

On this side, the steps up to the porch were wide and wooden. *These* were the steps in Colette's video.

"This was her combo dare!" I whispered to Tess. "Remember? Colette dared us to do something nice *and* daring at the same time. She left taffy that time, but she still did the ding-dong-ditch. You both did it!"

"You did it, too!" Tess said excitedly. "I had no idea it was the Sea Witch's house!"

"Me neither!" I said, horrified at the realization that Colette had come here on Thursday night to redo a dare from our childhood and might have been snatched by a crazy lady. "Do you think she's going to have Colette stuffed like one of her animals?"

"No!" Tess whispered. "Don't say that!"

Tess didn't know about the Sea Witch's warning, and I *definitely* wasn't going to tell her right then, tiptoeing between carcasses of a bobcat and a super-scary-looking bird. The hair on the back of my neck was standing up: a sensation I hated very much.

I looked in the direction of the beach, remembering approaching the house from that way. We'd leave our bikes on the bike path along the dunes and sneak through the huge lawn with little gifts, like pet rocks or taffy. Colette had chosen this house because she felt sorry for whoever lived here among all the dead animals. I wonder if she would have chosen it if she'd known who it belonged to.

"Why did she film this dare again?" Tess asked quietly. "And why the running one—and the singing-in-public one?" She laughed a little. "You wanted to avoid the scare part of dare-or-scare so bad that you were willing to do the singing dare, do you remember?"

I rolled my eyes but didn't answer.

Tess gripped my arm, making me jump. "Maybe she was just doing the dares all three of us did. Maybe she was making the videos as a goodbye present to both of us, Frankie!"

It was a nice thought, but my pessimistic side wouldn't let me believe that Colette had included me in this, especially since I'd yelled at her when she'd asked for Fred.

"I don't think so," I whispered. "Like you just said, I did

every single one of the dares because I didn't want to be scared."

"But I didn't," Tess said. "And Colette didn't. We liked the scares. It wouldn't be that many, honestly. I mean, think about it: All three of us did the dares she made videos of, right? You sang, did this"—she gestured behind her at the house—"jumped off the dune, and stared at Jake, right?"

"Yeah," I said. "I think so."

"So did I—and so did she," Tess said excitedly, her fear temporarily gone from her face. "We just need to figure out what other dares fit."

I was tired, and a feeling of sadness sank into my veins out of nowhere. I looked around the dark landscape and all at once wished I were at home, curled up, scrolling through the TwisterLvr feed like I usually do before bed. "Maybe this whole thing is stupid and neither of us should be here. Maybe I was wrong."

"We need to be here," Tess whispered. "*You* need to be here, not for Colette, but for me. I think you're right about her making the videos Thursday night. I think you're right that figuring out what dares she might have done might help us find her. You're still going to help me, right?" Tess asked, her face close to mine so she could see me in the dark.

I couldn't *not* help my sister, no matter how frightening

the situation was. And honestly, I couldn't not help Colette either. What if she was inside?

"Yeah." I sighed.

"Good," Tess said, nudging me with her shoulder.

I made a little sound that meant *Stop touching me*. We stopped in front of the house, looking up at the porch.

"I wonder if she's home." My eyes rose to the darkened main-floor windows, then to the second floor. "And I wonder what she does with all that space. It's huge."

Are you in there? I asked Colette with my mind. *Should we call the police? But . . . the Sea Witch was at the police station, so obviously they're already onto her. But what if they aren't, and you're trapped?*

I was so confused.

"We need to go up and look in the windows," I said, feeling seasick without even being on a boat.

"Are you serious?" Tess asked. We were gripping each other's arms so tightly that my hand was starting to fall asleep, but I didn't care.

"We have to at least check to see . . ." See what? I didn't know.

"Ohmygod," Tess chattered nervously. "Actually, maybe you're right: this might be the dumbest thing we've ever done. I seriously can't think of anything dumber right now. This is all Colette's fault. If she's not in trouble, I'm going to kill her."

A single porch light was on, hanging right above a big planter with a dead tree in it. The massive porch had nothing on it but a swing with no cushion; it was made of what looked like splintery wood.

"I don't see any clues, do you?" Tess whispered.

"No," I whispered back. "But I can't see much from down here. Maybe there's something in the planter. That's the only place to hide anything."

"I'm scared."

She would have been more scared had she known about the warning.

"It's only five steps," I said, picking up the bravery that Tess had somehow dropped. "We can do it." I pulled my arm from Tess's. "But I can't walk up steps linked like that." I shook my hand a little to get the feeling back. Then I shook it a lot when the pins and needles came.

I looked up at the windows again: they were all still dark.

"I don't think she's home," I said. "Let's look quick and get out of here." I took a deep breath and ran up the steps, like ripping off a Band-Aid.

"Ohmygod," Tess said behind me, then she climbed up, too.

I went straight to the planter and my heart leaped into my throat when I imagined a piece of taffy nestled inside the twisty branches of the dead tree. I jumped.

"What?" Tess whisper-shouted. She was right behind

me, and I really hoped she wasn't considering touching my shoulders. "Why did you jump?"

"I was excited! I thought I saw taffy in the planter. I thought Colette left it."

"Huh?" Tess whispered. "That's weird! Let's get out of here!"

"I'm just going to look to make sure . . . ," I said, peering into the dead branches one more time, to make sure I'd really imagined it. Suddenly there was a face in the long window next to the door, staring at me.

I screamed, then Tess saw her and screamed, and we both raced down the stairs. Like I was being pulled toward the ocean, I started running across the field-size lawn toward the bike path until Tess yelled that we had to get our bikes. Before I rounded the corner toward our bikes, I glanced back at the window.

The face was gone.

chapter 16

Fact: Most tornadoes happen
in the late afternoon.

IT WAS ALMOST ten o'clock—past typical tornado time and, honestly, past our bedtime—when Tess and I walked into the Sand Piper Diner, which was open until midnight on the weekends. I'd never been there that late before. Usually we went on special occasions, like when someone got a good grade on a test—well, when Tess did. I always ordered pumpkin pancakes with blueberries inside.

In the mornings, the patrons are usually regular families, tourist families, or nice older people (meaning not the Sea Witch). That night, there were three packs of rowdy high schoolers in the far corner and a few men who looked like logging truckers scattered around—plus an older couple who seemed to be fighting.

Colette smirked at us from the MISSING CHILD poster

taped to the wall near the cash register. I'd been in line behind her to have my school picture taken that day.

"Here, Frankie, you can use my brush," she'd said after running it through her bright red hair, making it as shiny as her lip gloss.

"Um, no," I'd said, frowning at the brush, thinking of lice and dandruff and other people's skin cells. Catching myself, I'd added, "I mean, no thank you."

Colette had looked hurt anyway.

"Can I use it?" Mia had asked from behind me. "I'm sure it won't make my hair look as good as yours . . ."

They'd smiled at each other, Colette with her freckle-face and Mia with her dimples, and I'd told myself inside that I was wrong for not being the kind of girl who wants to share brushes and lip gloss with her friends.

"It's late," I told Tess now. I looked away from Colette, feeling bad again. One of the high school boys was staring at us. "Maybe we should go home."

"We will," Tess said. "But let's eat first." She looked at me like Mom looks at me, like food will solve all my problems.

"I'm not hungry," I snapped . . . probably because I was hungry. Tess ignored me.

"Sit anywhere you like, girls," the waitress said, passing by the hostess stand with a tray full of food.

"Come on," Tess said, walking toward the booth farthest

away from the high schoolers. I followed Tess with my head down, shoulders forward, a frown on my face.

The waitress came over once she'd dropped off the food she'd been carrying, offering us menus.

"We'll have Tater Tots with ranch and two Cokes, please," Tess said.

"You got it," the waitress said, and she spun around and disappeared. I mean, she didn't literally vanish; she just walked into the kitchen. You're supposed to use metaphors when you tell stories: I don't know why, but people like them better than plain language. Whatever.

I swung my feet under the table and accidentally kicked Tess.

"Ouch," she said. "Will you please keep your feet on your side?"

I rolled my eyes at her but concentrated on not kicking her as I kept swinging my feet.

"What's wrong with you?" Tess whispered, leaning in. "Why are you in a bad mood all of a sudden?"

"I'm not!" I snapped. I was mad about being scared. I was mad that Colette's poster had reminded me of the type of girl I wanted to be—but wasn't. I was mad that we hadn't remembered anything about dare-or-scare. I was mad about Colette being missing and maybe hurt or dead. And, honestly, I was probably hungry. "I'm fine," I added.

"Fine?" Tess asked.

"Fine, I'll tell you, but don't freak out."

"Tell me what?" Tess asked, looking freaked out already.

"I ran into the Sea Witch at the police station earlier and she told me that kids who run around without their parents might get hurt," I blurted out.

Tess stared at me with big eyes. "She said they might get *hurt*?"

I nodded, thinking back. "Or maybe that you never know what will happen to them. Whatever, it was creepy. And she grabbed my wrist."

"Did she hurt you? Do you have a bruise?" Tess asked, looking down at my wrist.

"No, but . . ." Had the Sea Witch grabbed me hard, or just touched me? "That's not the point. The point is that Colette is probably in that crazy lady's house right now!"

The waitress brought the Cokes and Tess thanked her automatically. By the time I said a weak thank-you, she was too far away to hear.

"Maybe . . . ," Tess said about the possibility of Colette being at the Sea Witch's house. She looked confused as she took a sip of Coke. "Maybe we should call the police."

"But she was already *at* the police station!"

Tess nodded. I wished I hadn't told her because her reaction was too calm. And then she just changed the subject.

"We need to figure out what other dares Colette might have been doing—dares that all three of us did."

"No, we don't," I said through gulps of soda. "This is stupid. I can't remember the dares—and with the rest of the videos missing from Viewer, we're never going to remember. All we're doing is putting ourselves in scary situations. We're not going to find her! The police will have to!"

"Don't give up, Frankie," Tess said. "I still think you're right."

"So what?" I asked. "What does being right matter?"

"It matters if it helps find Colette," she said. "And it matters because . . ."

She stopped talking while the waitress set down our Tater Tots. I started eating like I'd never eaten before: I wasn't just hungry, I was starving. I held the Tater Tots with both hands like a squirrel.

"Because what?" I asked with food in my mouth.

"Because you deserve to be right sometimes," Tess said.

I scrunched up my eyebrows at her. I didn't know exactly what she meant, but I felt a lump in my throat that I was pretty sure wasn't a Tater Tot.

"Will you please tell me what happened?" Tess asked quietly. "Between you and Colette?"

The high schoolers erupted with shouts and laughter; one of them had spilled something. I didn't get why it was funny. They were smashed into three booths, but some were kneeling on the bench and turned backward so they could talk to two tables at once. They were leaning on everything, on the back of the booths, the windowsill, the tables. Leaning and laughing, looking so much older than us.

"I'm afraid to go to high school," I whispered, watching them.

"I think it's mostly the same as middle school," Tess whispered. I glanced at her and she was watching them, too, until two of the teenagers started kissing. Tess and I both looked away quickly, me making a grossed-out face and Tess blushing.

"Do you think that Colette has kissed Bryce?" I asked her.

"I know she has," Tess said. "She kissed him at the movies. And again, after school one time."

"Did she say she *liked* it?" I asked.

"I didn't ask her," Tess said. "But if she did it twice, she must have liked it the first time."

I looked back over at the kissing couple. They seemed like they were trying to eat each other's faces off, and the boy's hand was around the girl's body, resting on the lower part of her back. Like, way low. Like the top of her butt.

"Stop staring at them," Tess whispered.

"I'm not *staring*," I said, refocusing on my sister. "Would you let a boy try to eat your face off like that? In public?"

"No!" Tess said, making me feel relieved until she

added, "Not in *public*. But if a boy I liked wanted to kiss me, I'd let him." Her cheeks were bright pink, dotted with tiny freckles—not out-of-control freckles like Colette's, just faint dots the size of marks from a really sharp pencil under Tess's eyes and over the top of her nose.

"Do you like a boy?" I asked, concentrating on making sure my voice was low so I wouldn't embarrass her by letting anyone else hear.

"Sort of," she admitted. Now her mood-ring eyes looked closer to gold.

"Who?" I pressed in a whisper, leaning closer to her.

"Colin," she said, which made her cheeks turn a deeper shade of pink. She meant Bryce's best friend.

"Why do you like *him*?" I asked.

Tess frowned at me. "Why do you like Kai?" It was a whisper, so I knew she wasn't trying to embarrass me, but I still felt embarrassed.

How do you know that? I thought but didn't say, looking around the diner to make sure that no one was paying attention to us.

Tess must have realized I wasn't going to answer. She went back to her original question. "Will you *please* tell me what happened between you and Colette?"

"I don't want to talk about it," I said, angry that she was acting like she didn't remember. I noticed my heartbeat pounding, and the table felt so sticky I wanted to rush to the bathroom to wash my hands. Instead, I wiped them on my clothes.

"You promised you'd tell me," Tess said, tucking her hair behind her ear and looking at me with big eyes. The way she looked, like she had no clue in the world what I could be talking about, really irritated me.

"How can you pretend to be so innocent when you didn't stand up for your own sister?" I asked in a voice louder than I'd meant. Tess's cheeks turned pink again. She dipped her chin.

Instead of telling me to be quiet, though, she asked, "What are you talking about?"

"You just let them laugh at me. I *heard* you." I tried to keep my voice level because we were inside and there were people around. It was like holding on to Pirate's leash when she really, really wants to go in a certain direction.

Tess screwed up her face in confusion. I leaned in and hissed, "Stop acting like you don't know what I'm talking about! You were all in your room, studying for a test. It was you, Colette, Mia, and two other girls."

"Hold on," Tess said calmly, shifting in the booth. "Two other girls? Who?"

"How should I know?"

"We never study with anyone else!" Tess started biting her thumbnail, looking off in the distance like she was thinking really hard. Then she looked back at me quickly. "Do you mean Naomi?"

"Colette's weird neighbor?"

Tess nodded, smiling at me for calling Naomi weird. She really is. She's a close talker, which makes me uncomfortable, and she's always coming up with strange clubs like the "Blue Socks on Tuesdays" club. So yeah, Naomi's weird.

But I guess everyone is, in their own way.

"I have no idea," I said. "I don't know what her voice sounds like. It's not like I have any classes with her or anything."

"That has to be it," Tess said. "She's the only person who's ever come to a study group in my room except Mia and Colette. You know how Mom is about people in our rooms."

"Yeah," I said, never having run into that problem since I don't like people in my room, so I wouldn't ask to invite anyone. Or have anyone to invite anyway.

"Those are the only people who were there. You thought you heard someone else?"

I rolled my eyes, *really* not wanting to have this conversation. But you know how, when you don't want to talk about something, that's all the person you're with wants to talk about?

I grudgingly explained. "You were all studying and then someone asked about why I wasn't studying, and you said because I don't unless Mom makes me—which I do, by the way . . ."

Tess sighed and nodded.

" . . . and the other girl came in and then Colette started talking about how I take tests in a special room and—"

"What?" Tess interrupted, her eyebrows raised.

"And then everyone laughed because I like tornadoes and Mia called me a tornado brain and—"

"WHAT?!" Tess said loudly, not caring who heard her. A few of the high schoolers looked at us for a few seconds before they got bored and went back to their chatter.

"And I snuck away because I didn't want to hear you guys talk about me anymore."

Tess's hand flew to her mouth and her cheeks went red—but she looked mad instead of embarrassed this time. "That's what you've been upset about for, what, like two whole months?"

I nodded. "Wouldn't you be?"

"Of course!" she said. "I just wish you would have *told* me. That's a long time to have hurt feelings!"

"Why did I need to tell you? You were there!"

Tess inhaled and looked up at the ceiling of the diner, then exhaled loudly. "Frankie, do you honestly think that I wouldn't have said anything if I'd been there?"

"But I heard you," I said. "I heard you say that I only study when Mom makes me."

"Yes!" she said. "I said that when I was leaving to go get everyone sodas." She paused and took a big breath. "You thought someone else came *in*. But I went *out*."

"No, that's not what happened," I said, unsure. Or was it just not what I'd *thought* happened?

"Think about it, Frankie," Tess said. "Did you hear my voice after the thing about the studying? Did you hear me *say* anything else? Did you hear me *laugh* at you?" Her eyes welled up with tears. "You didn't! Because I never would!"

"Colette did," I said softly.

"Colette's not your sister. I am." She brushed away her tears as they fell. "I would never do that to you."

"But you're always mad at me," I said. "And you never want to do anything with me."

"You just stopped hanging out with us without any explanation and I thought . . ." She wiped her face again. "I thought you didn't want to do anything with *me*."

"Oh," I said, thinking about that.

The waitress came over. "You two need anything else?"

Tess asked for the check and the waitress pulled it from her apron and dropped it on the edge of the table. She left, and Tess picked up the check, curling the edges of it. She used to rip up paper or napkins or movie tickets or whatever was in her hands. I wondered if she was going to rip up the check.

"I'm so sorry," Tess said.

"It's okay," I said automatically, since that's what you say.

"No, it's not," Tess said. She set down the check and touched my hand across the sticky table. Despite it normally feeling awful to be touched, it felt okay to be touched by her—at least for a second. She must have sensed that because she took her hand away. "They were so rude. And it's one thing from Mia—you know, because you guys have never really been good friends—but from Colette it was . . ."

I nodded. The tears were there again without warning. I wiped my face with my sleeve.

"Let's go home," I said.

Tess didn't argue with me this time. "Okay, Frankie, let's go home."

chapter 17

Opinion: Some people believe that when you
dream about tornadoes, it's because you're
feeling out of control.

"I'M MAKING TEA," I told Tess when we arrived back at the
inn. We were ten minutes late for our eleven o'clock curfew;
we'd had to stop our bikes three times on the way home
from the diner to answer texts from Mom.

"I'm going to tell Mom we're home," Tess said, parking
her bike at the end of the line of loaners near the far wall
of the lobby. She leaned in and whispered, "And make up
something about the movie." She looked uneasy: Tess is a
rule-follower. "Do you want to come with me?"

I shook my head, shifting from one foot to the other. I
didn't want to go back outside where the April night had
turned cold. Inside, the fire was on, making the lobby toasty
warm. "I'm going to take my tea to my room."

No matter what time it is, there's coffee, tea, and

flavored water waiting for guests. Mom likes them to stay hydrated, I guess. Mint tea is something that sometimes helps me calm down, and we're never out of it.

"Okay, see you tomorrow," Tess said sadly. She hesitated at the side door, looking back over her shoulder at me like she wanted to say something. She didn't, though.

I filled a cup with steaming water and added a mint tea bag. I leaned against the wall, waiting for it to steep. I have to do the whole tea-making process down in the lobby because I don't like used tea bags in my room. I don't know why, it's just a thing.

While I waited, my brain played on high speed. I remembered the Sea Witch at the police station—maybe being questioned as a suspect! I thought of her telling me that kids running around without their parents could get in trouble; then, shivering, I thought about her face in the window at her house. I wanted to call Officer Rollins and tell him what she'd said to me. But what if she was really nice to the police and pretended not to know anything and they let her go? And what if she just went home to torture Colette? What if—

"Yo, did you or your sister use Lemonade?" Tyler, the overnight front desk attendant, interrupted my thoughts. He was pulling on his beard—*ick*—and tapping his pen on the counter in time to low music.

I looked at him blankly. "What are you talking about?"

"Lemonade is missing," he said, tugging his beard again. I wished he'd stop that. "Have you seen it?"

I looked at him like he was speaking German. "Huh? What's Lemonade?"

Tyler rolled his eyes at me and pointed over at the row of loaner bikes. "Haven't you ever noticed that they're all named after food? The ones you just brought back are Mint Chip and Black Licorice."

"No, they're not," I said.

But I went over to check. On the back wheel cover of the black bike, in swirly, cursive font, it said *Black Licorice*. Noticing now, I read down the row: the red bike was *Cherry Pie*, the orange was *Marmalade*, and the white one was *Marshmallow*.

"I always thought that was just decoration," I said.

Tyler sighed. "Now that you know it's not," he said, "have you seen Lemonade? The yellow one? No one signed it out."

"I know," I said. "I wanted to use it, but it's gone."

The steeping timer on my phone went off and startled me. Tyler shook his head and put on headphones, telling me that our conversation was over. I removed the tea bag, then added cream, which I like even though it looks kind of gross in the mint tea, and since my mom wasn't watching, I added sugar, too. I got a new spoon to stir everything, then went up to my room.

It was all too much to deal with that night. I vowed to

call the police in the morning and just let them decide what to do about the Sea Witch.

I took off my shoes and walked around piles of clothes and books to my bed. I took a sip of tea and set it on the nightstand, then flopped down, my head on the cool pillow. The window was still open; I listened to nature's sound machine outside. I wanted to check the TwisterLvr feed; I wondered if any tornadoes had happened today. But only for a few seconds, I think, because then I was asleep, somewhere else, a memory inside a dream.

I ran across the huge lawn in front of the Sea Witch's house, stomach muscles sore from laughing. I couldn't see anyone but knew I wasn't alone—I could hear a set of feet running behind me to the right and another to the left. The lawn gave way to longer beach grass: we pounded through, the tallest stalks tickling my palms, before reaching the path where three bikes were waiting for us.

"I'm doing the next dare!" I shouted, breathing heavily through a mischievous smile. "I'm going right now!"

"But it's getting dark!" a voice protested.

"It's dangerous," another agreed.

In my dream, their voices were different and their faces were blurry, but I knew they belonged to Tess and Colette. I just didn't know who was who. I hopped on the yellow bike: Lemonade.

"Wait! Frankie!"

"Don't go tonight!"

"This one is worth *all* of the taffy!" I shouted over my shoulder, curving around the bend in the path and dipping down out of sight. I couldn't see the ocean because of the bluff to my right, but I could hear it. The breeze blew my hair back and I was free to do anything. I could ride forever.

It wasn't quite dark yet, but the clouds made it look like the sun had gone to bed. I could still see the paved path well as it wove through the beach grass and squat little trees poking up here and there. I went by the benches that were put there in memory of someone. I went by the eagle-watching platform that Colette, Tess, and I used to use for a different dare.

"Jump off!" we'd challenge each other.

"Jump higher," we'd scream, and laugh.

In my dream, I rode Lemonade on the bike path until I reached Thirtieth. After a left and a quick right, I rode down Willows Road until it connected with North Head Road, then took another right. I pedaled my hardest, only pausing for breath in the parking lot at Beard's Hollow. I'd gone through Seaview and Ilwaco without noticing: the towns are so close together they're practically on top of each other. I continued up North Head Road because that would be the fastest way to the North Head Lighthouse—the end point of this amazing dare. I knew I'd be to my destination in about fifteen minutes because I'd done it before.

The first few blocks were flat, but then I was careful to stay to the far right on the hilly two-lane road: there wasn't a sidewalk and some parts plunged down to ditches or farther depths. Looking at the dense trees passing by as I pedaled my way up the hill, I swelled with pride. This was *my* dare. I would be the only one to do it!

In the way that dreams fast-forward, mine did, and next I was coasting downhill, where the roadside drops to a wooded ravine. With no cars in sight, I rode straight down the center line, taking my feet off the pedals and feeling like I was flying.

And then I was flying . . . on my bike, over the same route I'd ridden. And then I was back where I'd left my worrying sister and friend. But there was only one person waiting.

"You took Lemonade," she cried. I didn't know whether it was Tess or Colette. I couldn't place her voice and her face wouldn't hold still long enough to be in focus. "You took Lemonade."

"But I'm back now," I said. "Look, I'm back! I did the ultimate dare!"

She wasn't facing me, and it upset me, because I wanted her to be happy for me. And I wanted the other one, Tess or Colette, to be there, too, telling me I had done a good job.

"You took Lemonade," the girl said again.

"But I told you, I'm back!" I shouted at her.

And then her face was in focus—but it wasn't Tess's face. And it wasn't Colette's.

"You took Lemonade," I said to myself. "And you're not back. You're gone."

PART 3

The Rest

chapter 18

Fact: There have been instances of
tornadoes destroying lighthouses.

SUNDAY MORNING, THE real storm came.

Tess and I sat opposite each other at the kitchen table
in the cottage, each with a fleece blanket wrapped around
our shoulders because our PJs had gotten wet running over
from the inn. We were both holding mugs of tea that our
mom had made while we'd waited for the others. I had my
feet up on my chair and my mug rested on my knees, which
was keeping them from jittering. Pirate lay at the foot of
my chair.

The cottage was crowded.

Mom and Officer Rollins sat at the table with us;
Officer Saunders and a policewoman I didn't know sat on
the couch in the living room, which was really the same
room as the kitchen since there wasn't a wall separating

them; and Charles leaned against the kitchen counter with his arms folded across his chest, the orca tattoo on his arm facing out.

The recorder in the middle of the table had a green light illuminated on it. The clock on the microwave said 7:16 a.m. and we'd just finished telling the whole room about dare-or-scare.

It'd been two and a half days since anyone had seen Colette.

Officer Rollins tried to keep it all straight. "So you believe that Colette was making videos Thursday night, and something happened to her when she was filming—and that's why we can't find her?"

"Yes," Tess answered confidently.

"And you also believe that she changed the upload dates on the videos, so it would look like they were older than they are?"

"Yes." Tess nodded.

"Why?"

Tess looked at me, unsure. I shook my head. "We don't know," Tess answered for us.

"But you feel confident that she was re-creating your dare-or-scare game. Is that what you think, too, Frankie?" he asked me.

"I think so?" I said, feeling groggy and frazzled with

most of the police officers in Long Beach stuffed into the tiny cottage.

"And you initially suspected that Colette might be at Mrs. Sievich's residence?"

"Yes," I said, looking down at my hands, feeling stupid. Officer Rollins had already explained that the reason the Sea Witch had gone to the police station was that her property had been vandalized again—I guess it happened sometimes—and officers had gone there to check it out. So they were pretty sure Colette wasn't there. Maybe I felt a little sorry for the Sea Witch. I don't know.

It didn't matter anyway: the dream had made me remember where Colette was for sure—and she wasn't with the stuffed dead animals.

Rollins, as the other officers called him, rubbed his eyes and his forehead, just like he had on Friday. "Frankie, we've been looking for Colette for forty-eight hours straight. We're all exhausted. I don't want to hear that you think she *might* be out there. I need you to tell me *specifically* where you think she is."

Honestly, I thought I'd already said that, but maybe it was just the voice screaming in my head, telling them where to look. Or maybe I felt like I'd told the police because I'd told Tess about my dream, the dream when I remembered the best dare I'd ever come up with.

I took a deep breath, wondering: *What if I'm wrong?* But then I asked myself, *What if I'm right?*

"I think she was trying to do a dare I made up," I began. Everyone in the room was looking at me. Charles nodded, and my mom gave me a reassuring smile, but the way Tess held her chin high like she was holding mine up for me made me feel like it was all going to be all right. "It was around Halloween when I made it up. Tess and Colette had been to three haunted houses already and I knew if I chose to do a scare, they would come up with something terrible. So I had to make the dare really great."

"And?" Officer Rollins asked.

"I dared us to ride to the lighthouse."

My mom gasped.

Tess started biting her thumbnail and the officers in the living room took notes even though the recorder was on in the middle of the table, documenting everything I said.

"It's not that far," I said, turning my mug in my hands. "When I did it, it didn't even take me an hour."

I glanced at my mom, who did not look happy that I'd ridden by myself to the lighthouse. "Did you do it, too?" she whispered to Tess.

Tess looked at me guiltily, then back at Mom. "I told Frankie and Colette that I had, but I lied. I went halfway—but I got scared and turned around."

"I knew it," I muttered.

"Keep going, Frankie," Rollins said.

"Colette doesn't have a bike," I said. He looked at me like he didn't get what I was saying, so I added in explanation, "The yellow bike has been missing from our inn."

"Oh no," Mom murmured, understanding.

"She means that she thinks Colette took a bike from our inn to try the dare," Tess said.

"Yes," I said, nodding, keeping my eyes low.

"Frankie, when you called yesterday, you said there was a whole page of dares in your notebook," Rollins said. "Why would Colette choose this one?"

"I don't know," I admitted. "Tess thought maybe she picked dares that we all did—but Colette never did this one before. I wonder if she picked the hardest ones, or just the ones that were the least . . ."

"Least what?" Mom asked.

"Stupid?" I answered, thinking of the dare where you had to see how many marshmallows you could eat before you threw up.

"Maybe her goal is to do all of them," Tess said quietly. "Maybe she's not finished yet. Maybe she just . . ."

Tess stopped talking and everyone in the room went silent. I don't know why I felt guilty, but I did. Maybe because the dare had been my idea—and now we were sitting around talking with the police and Colette was missing, out there somewhere in the pouring rain.

Thunder rumbled the floor just to make me feel worse.

Officer Rollins looked worriedly out the window, then back at me. "To be clear, do you mean the North Head or Cape Disappointment Lighthouse?"

"Uh-huh," I said.

"Which one," he asked.

"North Head," Tess said.

"Okay, that's good, thank you, Tess," Officer Rollins said. To the other officers in the other room, he said, "That's, what, four miles?"

"More like five, maybe six," said Officer Saunders. He was sitting in my favorite seat on the couch; my thoughts were spinning too fast to care. I felt completely off the rails.

Officer Rollins turned back to me. "And what route did you use, Frankie, when you rode it?"

"Discovery Trail for part of it." I took a breath, knowing my mom wouldn't like the next part. "And North Head Road."

"The bike path?" Officer Rollins asked.

I shook my head no.

"Frankie!" my mom blurted out. "You could have been killed!"

Everyone got silent, probably thinking what I was: I could have been killed but hadn't been—but maybe Colette *had*. The policewoman was typing on her phone faster than a texting teenager.

"You mean Willows to North Head Road?" she asked, her eyes on her phone.

"I guess?" I asked back, because I don't pay attention to streets that much unless I have a reason to.

"Colette could have taken any of the north-south routes," Officer Rollins said to the other officers. "Call Martin from Ilwaco and see if they can spare anyone."

"We need to get the sheriff's office involved, too," the woman officer said.

"They already are," Officer Rollins said. He picked up the recorder and turned it off, then stood up. Seeming to fill the entire kitchen, he said, "We'll need to check around the roadways in both directions in case she reached the lighthouse and turned around—and Discovery Trail, too."

They moved toward the door, pulling their rain gear over their heads, their belts full of stuff, clanking and jangling. "Thank you, girls," Officer Rollins said before shutting the door to the cottage.

Tess hugged me.

I let her.

chapter 19

Fact: Tornadoes that happened before
1950 weren't reliably reported.

"HOW ARE YOU two?" Mom asked later, leaning up against the door frame, looking at us with concern. Tess and I were on the beds we'd slept in forever until we moved into the inn.

Mom went over and sat on Tess's bed. I felt jealous that she wasn't sitting on mine—but I didn't want her to sit on it either. I was confused by that feeling.

"We're fine," I said automatically.

"We're not fine," Tess said. "Did Officer Rollins call?"

Mom shook her head. "Not yet," she said. "I did speak with Colette's mother about an hour ago. The police are still searching. They're trying to move quickly but also be thorough."

"So they're going fast and slow at the same time?" I asked. "That makes no sense."

I looked up at the trio of paper hot-air balloons I'd made with a babysitter once hanging over my bed from hooks on the ceiling. The babysitter had told me to write something inspirational on them. In black marker, one said: *Something inspirational.* In purple marker, another said: *You can do it!* And in green marker, the one closest to me said: *We fly higher than lost balloons.*

"I don't know, Frankie," Mom said. "They're trying their best."

"Okay," I said.

"Do you want pancakes?" she asked us. "I have some blueberries to put in them."

"I want to go back to sleep," Tess said, rolling onto her side, facing the wall. "My eyes sting."

Mom started scratching her back. I was jealous of that, too, even though I can't stand it when she does it to me. It's like I craved and hated the idea of contact at the same time, which made me feel like an alien. Maybe I just wanted to feel like my mom loves me the same as she loves my sister.

"I'm going to the beach," I said, getting up from the too-small bed. I stepped into the rain boots I'd thrown near the bed, but something wasn't right.

"Ugh, I hate these socks!" I crashed down to the floor

and struggled to get the rain boots off so I could readjust my socks. Rain boots are the worst to get off. "Help me!" I shouted at my mom.

"How about some manners?" she asked, walking over to me. I stuck my foot in the air. She trapped my leg between her knees and yanked the left boot off. Then we went through the same process with the right. "Do you want to borrow a pair of my socks?" she asked softly as I grunted and growled at the pair I was wearing.

I was annoyed at her offer. I was annoyed about everything, and I didn't know how to not be.

Finally I got the sock seams lined up on both feet so that they didn't squish my pinkie toes when I put my feet back in the boots.

"There!" I said, standing up and putting my hands on my hips.

"Do you want me to come with you?" Mom asked.

"No," I said. Her face looked hurt, so I added, "I just want to be alone."

"Okay, Frankie, but don't go far—and take your phone. Just in case we hear anything."

I nodded and left the room. The cottage looked empty without all the people in it from earlier: it felt strange. I put on my raincoat over my pajamas, then took an apple from the fruit basket and my phone from the charger. It wasn't pouring anymore—just raining—but still I made sure my phone was deep in my pocket, protected from the water.

I would have taken Pirate with me, but she must have been somewhere with Charles. I missed her clanking tags as I trudged through the sand by myself, eyes on the solid light gray sky. I walked to the closest shelter, which only shelters you against wind, not rain, since it's open at the top.

I was surprised to find a familiar face already there.

"What are you doing here?" I asked.

"Why do you keep saying that to me?" Kai answered. He had a black hoodie up over his hair, which annoyed me because I liked seeing all the weird ways he styled it. I guess it *was* raining.

"I don't mean it in a mean way," I said, kicking the sand. "I'm surprised you're here is all."

"I'm meeting Dillon," he said, and I believed him because his skateboard was next to him, leaning against the bench with the wheels facing out. Also, he had on skate shoes. "We're going to do some tricks off the boardwalk. You can watch if you want."

"You're skating in the rain?" I asked.

"Rain or shine." Kai smiled, but it didn't seem like a real smile, just a polite one. "You should come."

"Thanks, but I'm not in the mood."

"Okay," he said, standing up. He looked at my outfit. "Are you wearing pajamas?"

"So?"

"Nothing," Kai said, stepping away. "Okaybye. Catch you later, Frankincense."

"What does that even mean?" I asked, rolling my eyes.

Kai shrugged. "Something to do with Christmas? You tell me. I'm Buddhist, yo."

"Okay, Mr. Buddhist, aren't you waiting for Dillon to get here?"

"You said you're not in the mood to talk." He pulled his hoodie strings tighter. I really wished he'd let his awesome hair free so I could see what it was doing today.

"No, I didn't. I said I'm not in the mood to watch skateboard tricks."

"Oh."

Kai came back and we both sat on the bench part of the shelter, with about a three-person space between us. Neither of us said anything until it felt so uncomfortable that I had to talk.

"The police were at our house this morning," I blurted out.

"No way," Kai said, his eyes wide, leaning forward on the bench. "Something to do with Colette? What happened?"

The whole story tumbled out of me easily—and with it came tears that I didn't really care about shedding in front of Kai. He didn't make a big deal of it either: he didn't say anything about it at all.

"I remember that dare," Kai said when I finished the part about the officers leaving to search the different paths to see if Colette had been doing the lighthouse dare and had an accident.

"You do?" I asked, surprised.

"Yeah, of course," Kai said. "Don't you remember? I shot the edit for you." I tilted my head sideways; he tried to remind me. "Yeah, your sister was at some camp and Colette was . . . I don't know where she was. But you wanted to do the dare on a certain day because it was sunny out and you were convinced that there was going to be a storm the next day." He laughed a little. "You told me that if no one was there to see it, then no one would believe it happened, and it would be like tornadoes that happened a long time ago but weren't recorded—so I made the edit as proof."

"You *did*?" I asked. "But in my dream, Tess and Colette were there."

"Frankfurter, dreams aren't real." Kai spun one of the wheels on his skateboard.

"Will you ever run out of weird names for me?" I asked, kind of liking the names even though they were so cringey.

Kai shrugged, smiling. He didn't answer me. Instead, he said, "I can't believe you spaced that I was there."

"Yeah, I know," I said.

I thought back for a long time and finally there Kai was, at the blurry edge of my memory, not getting mad when I yelled at him to move out of the way or get closer or hold still. Telling Dillon he was too busy to skate that day. Standing with me in the sun and the rain.

I didn't want to tell him I remembered because I felt like he might think I was lying. Instead, I asked, "Why didn't you ever do the dares with us—or the scares even?"

He smiled, but it seemed like it had some sad in it. "Duh, you guys never asked me to."

Kai looked off in the distance and waved. I turned and saw Dillon standing by the ramp to the boardwalk from the beach. Kai stood and picked up his skateboard. Looking at me, he said, "I always liked helping you, though. It was fun."

He gave a little wave and walked over to where Dillon was standing. I saw him say something to Dillon, then Dillon looked my way. I pulled my feet up under my knees on the bench, wondering if I should go watch them do tricks. But they jumped on their skateboards and took off down the boardwalk while I was weighing the pros and cons. That happens to me a lot: I consider something too long and miss the thing I was considering.

I felt bad.

I felt bad because I did actually want to watch the tricks.

I felt bad because Kai was gone.

I felt bad because I'd never asked him to do a dare.

I felt bad because I'd never noticed that he'd wanted to.

———

FROM THE SHELTER, I saw a police car pull into the parking lot of the inn. I watched two people shapes walk toward the cottage and my heart felt like it was going to break through my rib cage. I ran my fastest back home. I was sure that they'd found Colette—but I didn't know whether they'd found her alive or dead—and my brain was an EF5 tornado.

As I ran, I thought at her:

Why did you go alone?

Did you know you were going to go when you came to my room?

Would you have asked me for help if I hadn't yelled at you?

Why did I ever make up that dare?

It's not my fault.

Why are you so bad at riding a bike?!

Maybe it is my fault.

It's not my fault!

"It's not my fault!!!" I shouted into the wind.

I wondered if anyone heard me.

chapter 20

Fact: The damage path of a tornado
can be more than one mile wide.

TESS WAS SOBBING, folded over, face in a throw pillow on the couch. I couldn't remember the last time Tess had cried like that; I stared at her with my mouth open for a few seconds. I felt like my head was disconnected from my body. I looked down at my muddy feet and struggled out of my boots, getting them to actually come off when I stepped on the heels, thinking that my mom wouldn't want me to track stuff inside. It was a weird thing to be thinking about, but I was in a daze.

I knew Colette must be hurt—or worse. Then I thought of the only time I'd ever seen her hurt before.

It was last year, and we'd walked all the way down the beach to the rocky cove one Sunday afternoon. In some ways, the cove is the best place on the beach because it's sheltered from the wind—so it's nice year-round. Steep black rocks with a forest on top jut up to form a wall that wraps around the sand. Smaller, sharp rocks with barnacles stuck to every surface are either right at the edge of the water, or swimming in it, depending on the tide. The way that the cove was formed, the waves come in from two directions at once, fighting with each other, angry and beautiful. Huge spray kicks up when the fighting waves clash, seagulls watching and snacking on the barnacles like Cheerios.

"My parents keep getting in fights," Colette said, looking out toward the waves. Her red hair was pulled back in a high ponytail and she had on a blue plaid shirt I'd always liked. "I'm afraid they're going to get divorced."

"That sucks," I said, not knowing what else to say.

"Yeah. My mom wants to move."

"No!" I shouted. "You can't!" I thought of how I'd be alone if Colette moved. How I'd have no one to come to the cove with. I thought of myself.

"I know," Colette said. "I'd die."

I started up a pile of barnacle-covered rocks. They weren't steep, but they were jagged. Colette followed me in her flip-flops. When we were at the top, we watched the ocean fight without saying anything.

"Maybe you can live here with us if your parents move," I told her. "You're twelve, you should be able to have a say in where you live."

"My parents don't think so," Colette said.

"You can't leave," I said, feeling desperate.

We'd both been so distracted by the topic that neither of us was paying attention to the water, and soon we were on a tiny island for two. The tide had risen to the point where, if we were to jump off right then, we'd be in water up to our chests—and would potentially be sucked out to sea or battered against the rocks.

"Crap!" Colette shouted, instantly panicking. "We're going to be stuck out here and drown!"

"Calm down," I said, rational. "We just have to wait for the waves to flow out again and jump down. Our feet might get a little wet, but we'll be fine."

She started crying, which shocked me.

I felt brave and ready to handle the situation, which sort of shocked me and sort of didn't. That happens to me sometimes. Sometimes I'm invincible.

"It's going to be okay," I said to her, edging to the side of the rocks. "See? Look, it's already starting to pull back." The water was quickly retreating. "Get ready to jump down to the sand."

"I'm scared," Colette said. I looked around to see if there were any adults just in case we needed help. Two fishermen were on another cluster of rocks. I waved at them, one waved back, and I hoped that reassured Colette that they'd probably help if we called out.

"Come on, jump now!" I jumped, my heels digging deep into the sand when I landed. Colette froze, then a few seconds later took two steps toward the edge. Except one of her flip-flops snagged on the rock. She fell more than jumped off, landing on her hands and knees in the sand and lurching forward so her head hit the next boulder over. Barnacle-covered boulders are sharp.

I reached down and grabbed her hand to help her up. With only one flip-flop and a bleeding forehead, she managed to run behind me to dry sand, chased by the surf the whole way.

When we were safe, we looked at each other and exploded into laughter. One of the fishermen had been keeping an eye on us. He shook his head and turned back toward the water.

"That was awesome," I said.

"No, it wasn't!" Colette said, but she was smiling, so I thought she thought it was awesome, too. People don't always say what they mean.

My mom's voice brought me back to the present. "Frankie?" she asked. "Are you listening?"

The policewoman from earlier was back.

"Is Colette dead?" I asked loudly.

"She's hurt but she's alive," Mom said quickly. She rushed over and put her arm around me. I let her keep it there for a few seconds, then stepped away.

"She's not okay, is she?" I asked, looking at the officer, then at my mom.

"Frankie, I said she's alive," Mom answered. "That's a good thing. She's hurt, yes, but she's alive, thank goodness. I'm going to call her parents and see what they need."

"It's probably best to give them a few hours—" the officer started to say to my mom before I interrupted.

"Where was she?" I asked.

"About a mile from the lighthouse," the officer answered.

Just a mile—a mile is nothing . . . unless it's the width of a tornado. But a mile on a bike is easy.

"Did she finish the dare?" I asked, my voice sounding higher than normal, eyes bouncing back and forth between my mom and the officer.

"Frankie, I hardly think that's relevant right now when—" Mom began.

"Did she finish the dare or not?" I shouted, balling my fists at my side. *Just tell me if she finished the dare or not! I* screamed in my brain. *Tell me if she finished, because if she did, she would have been riding on the more dangerous side of the road—the side with the drop-off into a ravine. She'd be in worse condition if she had finished! I* thought I was screaming out loud, so they'd all understand that I was talking about Colette's health, not some dumb game. But my heart was racing, and my thoughts were spinning. I felt like a human tornado. Some words came out, but some stayed in my head. "Tell me if she finished! Just tell me!"

Tess rose from her place on the couch and wiped her eyes. She looked at me, confused.

"Frankie, the game doesn't matter anymore," she said, probably trying to help. It didn't.

"I don't care about the game!" I shouted.

"Then why do you keep asking if she finished the dare?" Mom asked.

"Ugh!" I shouted at her before stomping my feet several times. Right then, Charles and Pirate came in. Charles looked around the room.

"I saw the police car when we came back from our walk," he said, his face twisted in concern. "What's going on?"

I was still stomping.

"I'll tell you in a minute," Mom said to Charles. "We have a situation here." Then, to me, "Stop that!"

She looked flushed and embarrassed. I desperately wanted to suck it all back in, inside my skin, all the anger and miscommunication and tears. I wanted to vacuum it back up into the sky, like when a tornado changes its mind and returns to the funnel cloud. But it'd already touched down.

"Frankie—" the woman officer began.

I cut her off. "TELL ME IF COLETTE FINISHED THE

DARE!" I screamed at the top of my lungs. "THAT'S ALL I'M ASKING!"

"Whoa," Charles said, holding up his palms. "We need to—"

"Go to your room!" my mom shouted back at me. "You are not allowed to scream at a police officer!"

"But she's allowed to treat me like a baby and not tell me what happened?" I shouted, backing toward the door.

Everyone was standing up now. I thought that the policewoman should have been angry, but instead, she looked like she pitied me, which made it worse.

"Frankie, maybe you just need a second to breathe," Charles said. His eyes had tears in them. "Maybe—"

"Maybe if the police knew how to do their jobs, then Colette wouldn't be hurt right now!" I yelled. "Maybe if they'd found her faster, everything would be okay!"

This made the officer purse her lips, but she didn't say anything.

"I'm so sorry," my mom said. "She tends to get emotion—"

That's all I heard before I slammed the door, leaving without bothering to step back into my boots. I screamed the loudest I could outside, a high-pitched horrible scream that felt like it would break my own eardrums. There was a family walking by and all four of them looked at me, startled.

"Stop looking at me!" I yelled.

The mom took hold of the youngest kid's hand and they all rushed away. I was acting like the type of person who scared little kids, and I couldn't begin to control it.

The wet pebbles and puddles under my socks prevented me from stomping as much as I wanted to, so I screamed again, then leaned over and picked up a rock, throwing it in the direction of the water. It landed with a *thud* in the tall beach grass. The release of the rock had felt good: it'd felt productive. I picked up another rock, this one the size of a golf ball. I cocked my arm back and threw it hard. It thudded louder to the earth. I threw five more rocks of about the same size, each throw more forceful than the last. My shoulder felt like it was going to rip out of the socket, but I was starting to feel a little better.

I saw a spectacular rock near the entryway to the inn: a polished gray rock the size of a large potato. It was much heavier when I picked it up and I knew it'd make the best thud yet. I stepped back so I was close to the building: I would need a running start. My socks were completely soaked, slapping the ground as I walked. I pulled my arm back over my right shoulder, rock in hand, ready to hurl it and all my anger away. But I guess I was *too* close to the building. I was too close, specifically, to the huge pane of glass that my mom calls a "picture window" and that looks to the west from the lobby.

The tip of the rock hit the glass when I pulled my arm back.

The world stood still for a few seconds. Then I heard what sounded like ice popping when lukewarm soda is poured over it. The first shards broke free and huge sheets of glass followed, crashing to the ground around me. Before I knew it, I was an island in a sea of broken glass.

"Mom!" I screamed in a different way, a terrified way. "Help me!" I held my arms close to my body and didn't move. There were tiny pieces of glass all over my pajamas and my socks. "Help, come quick!"

The door to the cottage flew open and my mom came running out with Tess, Charles, and the police officers behind her. When my mom saw the glass, she paused and gasped. I knew she was going to be madder than she'd ever been: I'd probably be grounded for a year. But at first, she didn't look mad: she looked terrified.

She started running again, stopping at the edge of the scene.

"Are you hurt?" she asked. She looked at my shoeless feet, then her eyes moved up to inspect me.

"I don't think so," I said.

"Don't move," she said to me, looking around for something. "I need . . ."

I held still as stone.

"Let me get her," the policewoman said. "I'll carry her over the—"

"I've got it," Charles said, taking a step onto the glass. I think he was going to try to pick me up.

"No," my mom said, grabbing his arm. "She can't . . . you know she doesn't like being touched . . . you'll just make it worse."

Charles winced, probably knowing she was right. It's true that I'd never hugged him and that I shied away from the kind of play fighting he did with Tess, but not because I don't love him or anything. I thought he knew that, but it sure didn't look like he did right then. He looked crushed.

Mom glanced around again, then seemed to decide. She took a step onto the pile of glass herself, and it crunched like tortilla chips under her shoe. She took another step, and another, and another. Then she was in front of me. "Get on my back."

I couldn't jump up for fear I'd miss and slide back down onto a nest of broken glass. My mom bent low and, not wanting it to cut her, I gently shook as much of the glass as I could from my clothes before wrapping my arms tightly around her neck. I practically strangled her when she stood up again with me holding on. I wrapped my legs around her hips and she crunched us both out of the glass.

I started shaking right after she set me down. Now,

apparently, I was a person who vandalized businesses. I started crying again, because I didn't want to be that person. I cried because I was confused by who I was.

"I'm sorry," I whispered to my mom. She'd moved away. She was standing over by the glass debris again in the rain, her hands on her head, staring at the hole that'd been a window. When she looked back at me, covering her mouth, she had tears streaming down her cheeks.

She hadn't heard me apologize.

chapter 21

Fact: The severity of comas is classified on a
number scale, just like tornadoes.

"DID YOU KNOW that according to the Glasgow Coma Scale,
a person with a score of only three or four after twenty-four
hours will most likely die?" I asked.

"No, I didn't know that," Gabe said. "Thanks for telling
me."

It was Monday, the day after the police had found
Colette. Other kids were in school, but Mom hadn't made
me or Tess go—except she *had* made me come to see Gabe.
Gabe and I were in his office over the business that's a tan-
ning salon, a knitting shop, and a coffeehouse in one. I was
sitting in the comfy red chair that Gabe usually sat in, but
I didn't like it very much. Gabe wouldn't let me sit in my
normal spot on the couch—either he wanted to mix things
up to see if I'd freak out about the changes or he just felt like

sitting on the couch. Instead of being mad about it, I tried to focus on my newfound knowledge about comas.

"A person with a score of more than eleven will most likely live," I said. "I don't know what Colette's score is."

I was drawing tornadoes on a notepad, not making eye contact with Gabe.

"You seem to know a lot about comas," Gabe observed.

"Uh-huh," I answered. "A person somewhere in the middle has about a fifty-fifty chance of recov—"

"Frankie," Gabe interrupted.

"What?" I looked at him. He pushed up his black-framed glasses, which weren't as good as his other ones.

"We're running out of time today, and I want to be sure that we're able to talk about you—not just comas," Gabe said. I really didn't like that he'd switched glasses.

"I don't want to talk about me," I said. "I'm fine." I waited a second, biting my tongue, trying not to say what I was thinking. But with everything that'd happened, I couldn't hold things back very well. "I don't like those glasses: they look too . . . blocky. Your blue glasses are better."

"Hmm," Gabe said, leaning forward to take a sip of tea. I liked that he always made me tea and didn't care if I doodled while we talked. "How does Colette being in the hospital make you feel?"

"That's a stupid question," I said, making a big *X* through the last tornado I'd drawn. I glanced up at Gabe to see if his neutral expression had changed when I'd said *stupid*.

"I'm sorry you feel that way," Gabe said, twisting his wedding ring, face still neutral. "Hey, will you make me a deal?"

"Maybe," I said.

"I know you don't want to start taking medication again," Gabe began. I grunted. "But I don't think you're being honest about how you're feeling—and if you're not being honest, then it's harder for me to figure out how to help you."

"Is that a threat?" I asked, my pen scratching around and around on the page.

"Wow, Frankie," Gabe said. "No, it's absolutely not a threat. I'm saying that I understand that you want to make the choice not to take medication—and if that's your choice, then I'm here to help you. But you need to do some work, too. I want you to agree to come here twice a week and do a worksheet in between. You can't blow off our appointments anymore. And you need to try to talk to me about what's happened with Colette. Do you think you can do that?" I shrugged, my eyes on the paper. "Frankie, will you please look at me?"

I looked up at him. Behind the awful glasses, his dark eyes were kind, as usual. Gabe is hard to be mad at or dis-agree with. Do you know adults who aren't like other adults, who just get you more than normal grown-ups? Gabe is one of those.

"What?" I asked.

"Colette's Glasgow Coma Scale score is a five," he said.

"How do you know?"

"Because I know her doctor," he said.

"You're probably not supposed to tell me that," I said. I scratched my head: it itched even though I'd taken a shower that morning.

"Definitely not," Gabe said, "but I know you do better with facts. I know surprises are very challenging for you. This," he said, "is not a surprise you need to have."

"So you're saying she's going to die." I swallowed hard and looked back down at the paper filled with tiny, medium, and huge tornadoes. There were more tornadoes than white space.

The wind blew through the open window and rustled some papers on Gabe's desk. We sat in silence for seventeen ticks of the noisy clock. I pushed my bangs out of my eyes: they were too long.

Colette was going to die, probably.

I stood up because my mom would be here to pick me up any minute. "Bye, Gabe. I'll see you on Thursday."

chapter 22

Myth: People always wake from
comas instantaneously like on TV.

"ARE YOU AWAKE?" Tess asked from her room the next morning. The sun was barely up but I'd been awake awhile.

"Yeah," I said, feeling trapped. I'd slept with my weighted blanket the night before. It'd been comforting at bedtime, but now it was crushing me. I was sweaty, and I struggled as I kicked it off, the superheavy blanket landing on the floor with a *thud*. "Are you?"

"No," she said. No one laughed.

Our connecting doors were open, so I could hear her easily. I pictured her lying halfway off her bed with her hair all crazy.

"Are you going to school?" I asked. Mom had said we didn't have to—that we could take the whole week off if we wanted. It wasn't as great an offer as you might think since no matter where we were, it wouldn't change Colette's situation.

"I'm going," Tess said. "And I have to leave soon, or I'll be late for zero period. We're sculpting today." It didn't sound like she was moving. "Are you?"

"I think so," I said, feeling like school might be better than home. I had an extra hour to think about it since my day wouldn't start until first period.

From my bed, I listened to Tess shuffle around her room, getting ready. She told me goodbye and left, and I finally got up, getting tangled in the weighted blanket on the floor and tripping.

"Stupid blanket!" I said, growling at it.

I ate the only cereal I like in the world with milk from the mini-fridge in my room. I didn't need a jacket because it looked warm outside. I left my room but turned around because I'd forgotten my backpack. I left again, then turned around because I'd forgotten a snack and my mom says I have to take one every day or I'll get hangry.

In the lobby, I asked Charles if I could ride Black Licorice and he said it was okay. I walked the bike outside and put on my helmet while Pirate followed, wagging her tail. When I kicked off and started coasting through the parking lot, Pirate ran next to me, her tags clanking happily. She stopped at the edge of the lot and barked: *goodbye!*

"Have a good day, Pi!" I called over my shoulder.

I rode by the horse corral, the new mini-golf course, and the go-kart track, thinking of Colette, wondering whether she'd be able to do those things again. No one really knew what had happened to her because she hadn't been awake yet to tell them, but Tess thought Colette had been trying to apologize to me by starting up the dare-or-scare game again. Tess thought that Colette had thought that the game was really the only way to show me that she was sorry—because to Colette, dare-or-scare had always been our special thing, just the three of us.

I didn't know what to think about all of that, but I knew about her Glasgow Coma Scale score, which meant that I knew I'd probably never find out what Colette's intentions had been.

I hadn't told Tess about the score, though.

At school, I left Black Licorice in the bike rack without a lock. I stopped by my locker to get a notebook and went to homeroom, feeling the walls as I walked through the school. In my classroom, I sat at my own private desk island by the window and checked the online feed of a brain-injury survivor while the class filled up.

"What's that?" a familiar voice asked over my shoulder.

I angled the screen so that Kai could see it. While he looked at my screen, I checked out his shoes: they were black suede with dark brown accents.

"This girl was in a car accident and the doctors put her

in a coma so that her brain wouldn't swell up." I refocused on my phone and tapped the screen to enlarge a picture of the girl in the hospital: her face was bruised, one eye was swollen shut, and her head was wrapped in gauze. "Now look at her, though." I opened another picture: of the girl in a soccer uniform. "She had to relearn how to talk and walk, but now she can play sports and stuff again."

"Cool," Kai said. His hair was in his face today; he pushed it back and it fell right into his eyes again. "I hope that's how it'll be for Colette."

"Me too," I said.

"My mom said they tried giving Colette hypothermia to try to make her wake up." Kai stepped away from me a little, which I appreciated.

"They froze her?" I asked. "That's terrible."

He made a face. "I know, it sounds like torture. But I guess it can help coma patients wake up or something."

I looked down at my phone screen again. "Colette's not like this girl. Colette went into a coma all by herself. The doctors didn't put her in one."

"Is that better or worse?"

"How should I know?"

Someone hit Kai on the shoulder with a wadded-up piece of paper and he turned around to see who it was. When he saw Dillon laughing across the room, he bent over and threw it back at him.

The bell rang.

"See ya, Frankarama."

Kai smiled a sweet, sad smile at me and went over to his desk in the normal part of the classroom. I still had a desk over there, too, if I wanted it. I just liked the desk island for now.

"Take your seats, please," Ms. Garrett said. "Marcus! It's time to settle down. Everyone, put your phones away and quiet down—that means you too, Tess and Mia. We may only have six weeks left of school, but there's still learning to do."

Six whole weeks left of school: I couldn't believe it was still April. So much had happened since the last time I was in this classroom just four days ago, it felt dizzying.

Like she felt the same way, Tess looked over and held up her hand, a weak high five, or a wave without any movement. Her shoulders were more bent forward than usual, and she looked fragile, like she might break. I waved back, an actual wave, and she smiled, but barely. I wondered if she wished she were at home. I wondered if I did.

Tess looked down at her desk, her dark hair covering her face.

I did my math homework in fifteen minutes because it was totally easy, then got out *Call of the Wild*, hoping to finish reading it before the period ended. I still had to finish a paper on it—I had to *start* a paper on it, actually. But then the phone rang on Ms. Garrett's desk. Everyone looked up at her while she talked to whoever was on the other end.

After she hung up, she looked at *me*.

"Frankie, Principal Golden would like to see you."

"Why?" I asked.

"She didn't say," Ms. Garrett said, pursing her lips and making her face look even more birdlike.

A bunch of kids made noises like *oooh* and *waaaa* and *uh-uhhh*. Some laughed. One—Kai—just looked at me with a worried expression like the one that was probably on my face right then, too.

I hadn't told Kai about the coma scale score either.

"And you too, Tess."

The other kids didn't make any sounds when Tess's name was called.

I left my stuff and took a hall pass from Ms. Garrett. In the hallway, I realized Tess had brought her bag with her. I went back in and got my stuff, causing everyone to turn and stare at me. I wanted to shout at them to leave me alone. But then I noticed Kai's warm smile and it made me feel calmer.

"What do you think is going on?" I asked Tess, back in the hallway.

"It must be something about Colette," she said. "Other-wise why would they call us both?"

We started walking toward the front office, our foot-steps in sync. I wondered if Tess noticed, but didn't ask her because I thought she'd think it was weird that I had. Maybe she wouldn't have. I don't know.

"It has to be about Colette, right?" Tess asked. She bit her pointer fingernail.

"Unless Mom or Charles died or something."

"Ohmygod, Frankie! That's an awful thing to say."

"Okay," I said, wishing I knew as well as Tess did which things would be considered awful—*before* I said them. Frustrated, I thought of some advice Gabe had given me—that people understand you better if you actually talk to them—and so I shared what I was thinking as we passed the classrooms in the English hall. "It's not like I *want* to say awful things, you know."

"I know," Tess said.

"I just say the truth, mostly."

"I know."

"But a lot of people consider the truth to be an awful thing," I said, scrunching up my eyebrows. "Am I supposed to lie? Maybe I'm just bad at lying."

"You're not supposed to *lie* to people," Tess said. "But you're not supposed to say every bit of truth that you think, because some of it is harsh. It comes out as being rude—or insensitive."

I knew all of this from therapy, but it was different hearing it from my sister.

"I don't want to be rude or insensitive."

"Frankie, you're not," she said. I looked down at my shoes. "You're *not*," she said again. "You have a really big heart. And you have a lot of great ideas in your head. But sometimes you just don't have a filter."

"So what's in my big heart and head falls out of my mouth?" I asked, smiling, sort of joking and sort of serious.

Tess smiled back, nodding. "Yeah."

We were outside the main office; Tess stopped, an anxious look on her face. "You know, it makes you who you are, though, and that's good."

I looked away, feeling awkward.

"I'm serious, Frankie," Tess said, touching me on the arm, then taking her hand away quickly. I touched my other arm to balance myself out. "Because you don't have a filter, you spoke up about what you thought had happened to Colette. You spoke up, and it's the reason they found her. She might still be missing right now if you had a filter."

She might be dead anyway, I thought. *Maybe that's why we're being called to see the principal.*

I just thought it, though, because saying it probably would have upset Tess. See? I have a filter . . . sometimes. Maybe it just needs to be changed more than other people's.

IF YOU'VE ONLY seen a hospital on TV, I'm going to be honest with you and tell you that TV is a liar.

The reason Tess and I were called to the office was because Colette's parents were getting desperate and they wanted us to go and try to talk to Colette to see if it'd get a reaction out of her. I guess freezing Colette hadn't worked—I mean, why would it?—and now they wanted to see if hearing familiar voices would help.

"I wonder why they didn't ask Mia to come," I asked Tess as we walked through the hospital doors behind our mom. The doors had slid open automatically, and I wanted to go back out and try it again, but I kept moving. "It smells in here. Gross." I plugged my nose.

"Shh," Tess said. Her face was pale and she looked like she might throw up.

"It's not a library," I said. "The point of us coming here is to talk. I wonder if it will work. And, really, why isn't Mia here? Is she coming, too?"

"I don't know," Tess whispered. "Maybe they didn't ask her because she and Colette haven't been friends for as long."

"So?" I asked.

"So she'd know our voices better," Tess said, looking

around warily. There was an old woman by herself in a wheelchair and she was crying. I looked away.

"That's logical," I said.

Our mom stopped at the information desk and asked which way the ICU was. That stands for "intensive care unit," and I was about to find out that it's exactly where you don't want to be in a hospital.

We went in the direction the information-desk woman had said, down the hall to the left and to the elevator bank at the end. Inside the elevator, Mom pressed the button for floor three and I stared up at the ceiling.

"An elevator would be a terrible place to be in a tornado," I said. "Or in any natural disaster, really."

The elevator doors opened, and it smelled even worse on this floor: like cleaning solution, mashed potatoes, and sickness. "Gross," I said again.

"Frankie, please keep your voice down," Mom said. "People are trying to rest and get well."

I had to try really hard not to point out, again, that a hospital wasn't a library and we'd been specifically asked to come here to talk. I didn't think that I should argue with my mom, though. We walked down the shiny floor to a nurses' station; my mom asked where Colette was. The nurse pointed to wide double doors with push bars in the middle. I followed Mom and Tess through to the ICU.

The room was about half the size of our gymnasium at

school, dim because the windows were all covered, divided into small sections by blue curtains on rods with wheels: movable fabric walls. Each small section had a bed in it. I couldn't see everyone, but I stopped and gaped for a few seconds at the patients lying in the beds I could see until my mom grabbed me by the wrist.

"Don't do that," I said, pulling my wrist away, then wrapping my fingers around my other wrist to even myself out. I followed my mom.

"Please remember to be kind," she whispered.

"I am," I insisted. *Do you think I'm a mean person?* I wondered but didn't ask her. We were rounding a fabric wall and there, in a twin bed on wheels with guardrails on the sides, was Colette. "Yikes," I breathed.

Tess spun around and slumped down so she could slam her face into Mom's shoulder; Mom hugged her tight.

"I know it's heartbreaking to see her like this," Colette's mom said, standing up from one of two chairs against what would have been a wall, if the wall wasn't a blue curtain. Colette got her red hair from her mom, but Colette's mom had a short cut with some gray in it. "Thank you both for coming. We appreciate it so much, and also you helping the police like you did."

"Uh-huh," I said in response, my eyes on Colette, wishing I wasn't looking at what I was looking at. My mom and Colette's mom worked on comforting Tess while I stared.

There were so many weird and terrifying things about the situation. I dug my thumbnails into my pointer, middle, ring, and pinkie fingers, over and over, while I looked.

First, Colette had her eyes closed. You might say, *duh*, but it's not like I'd ever stared at her while she was asleep before. She looked completely different. Open, her eyes would have given me clues about what she was thinking or saying, but closed, they said nothing. I did not like Colette's closed eyes at all.

Pointer, middle, ring, pinkie.

Poke, poke, poke, poke.

Second, there was a tube in her mouth and the outside of it was taped to her cheek—and the tape or the tube or both were pulling the right side of her mouth over in a way that made her look just flat-out creepy.

The others were talking in a whispered huddle. Tess was asking questions I probably wanted to know the answers to, but I didn't try to join their conversation. I went on with my list of horrors.

Third, there was a pole attached to a bag attached to a tube attached to a needle—attached to her arm. That's all I'm going to say about that.

Fourth, the beeping. I like music and the loud noises of crowds don't bug me. But if I'm in a quiet place and there's a noise that cuts through the quiet—something unexpected that's not supposed to be there—it can drive me to the point of screaming.

Beep. Beep. Beep. Beep. Beep.

Stop it, stop it, stop it!

If it stops, she'll be dead. It's monitoring her aliveness.

Beep. Beep. Beep. Beep. Beep.

My annoyance grew and grew, and turned into something that felt more like anger at the beeps. My heartbeat quickened, and my head got hot. I balled my fists and knocked my knuckles against my thighs, purposely out of time with the beeping.

The others were still talking, ignoring me. I knew I couldn't scream in the hospital: I didn't need my mom to tell me that. But I didn't know what to do. Taking a deep breath only sometimes works, but I couldn't do that even if I'd wanted to because I would have been breathing in that *smell*. I searched my brain for other strategies Gabe had taught me. *What was that one? Oh right: Think of a list of things that start with the same letter.* I chose the letter C for Colette. *Camel, car, candy* . . . Each one appeared in my mind at the same beat as the beeps. It was so annoying!

What do I do?

Beep.

I want to leave!

Beep!

Why did you run off and do this to yourself? I screamed at Colette in my mind.

Beeep!!!

And right then, I remembered something.

We were in third grade, I think. There was a school play, *The Three Little Pigs*. I played the role of a lamb and Tess and Colette were both pigs. I'd desperately wanted to be the other pig.

"It's not fair!" I'd cried when I saw the assigned roles posted in the hall. "I don't want to be a lamb! I knew all my lines and I should be a pig!"

"Sorry, Frankie," Tess said. "I wish you were the other pig, too."

Tears shot out of my eyes like sprinklers and I kicked the wall underneath the poster. I kicked it again harder and grunted. Tess's face turned red and she looked around to see who else was watching.

"You're going to get in trouble," Colette warned. "Stop kicking the wall."

I kicked it again, even harder this time. It hurt my toes, but I didn't care. I wailed loudly in the hallway. A teacher would probably come out soon and tell me to go to the principal, and then I'd probably have to work on art and talk about how outbursts at school aren't okay. I didn't want any of those things to happen, but my body did its own thing.

I kicked the wall yet another time.

"Frankie!" Colette said. "Here, look at me." I didn't at first. I couldn't see through my anger.

"Frankie, please!" Tess said, clearly so embarrassed. "You have to stop. Just pay attention to Colette."

"Come on," Colette said. "Look, do this." She dropped her backpack on the floor and was standing with her hands out, palms turned up.

She looked so strange I forgot to be mad for a second. "Are you praying?" I asked. "You look really weird."

Colette laughed. "It kinda looks like it," she said. "But no, I'm turning my palms up. You should try it. When I'm upset, it always makes me feel better."

"It looks stupid," I said.

"Maybe, but it makes me feel better when the air hits my palms," Colette said. "My mom told me to do it. She says it makes you feel more open to possibilities. I don't know what that means, but I like the feel of it anyway."

"You're right," Tess said, copying Colette's palms-up position, "it does feel nice."

"Now you both look stupid," I said. I saw my teacher coming out of the classroom at the far end of the hall, walking purposefully toward us. She looked mad. Tess and Colette both turned around and saw her, too.

"Would you rather look stupid or go to the principal?" Colette asked hurriedly.

"I'd rather be a pig," I said. But then I unballed my fists. I didn't hold my arms up like Colette, but I flipped my hands over at my sides.

"I heard a ruckus out here," my teacher said, frowning at me. "Aren't you supposed to be at recess?"

"We're on our way," Tess said, smiling innocently.

"We were just checking to see who got roles in the play," Colette said.

My teacher looked at me skeptically. "Is everything all right?"

"Everything's fine," Colette answered for me; Tess nodded in agreement. And actually, it was. I didn't feel like kicking the wall anymore: the mad had passed.

When I tuned back in to the ICU, the tube was still in Colette's mouth and the needle was still in her arm. Her eyes were still closed, and the machine was still beeping. But I had my palms up, and I felt calmer.

"Frankie?" Mom asked. "Did you hear me?"

"Huh?" I looked at her; she, Tess, and Colette's mom were all looking at me.

"I said we're going to try this again another day," Mom said. "Tess is upset, and you clearly are, too."

"No, I'm okay," I said, glancing back at Colette. She may have done something really mean to me recently, but she'd done other nice things for me in my life. And she'd been playing dare-or-scare again. And right then, remembering the good things, I thought that maybe Tess was right: I thought Colette had been trying to apologize to me. "I want to try to talk to her."

"You do?" Colette's mom asked. She had tears coming down her freckled cheeks, but she looked happy. "Oh, Frankie, thank you so much."

"If you're staying, then I will, too," Tess said.

"I want to do it alone," I said. Tess frowned, so I added, "Then you can have a turn and I'll wait outside."

"Okay." She didn't look like she felt okay. I don't know if she understood that me wanting to talk to Colette alone didn't mean I didn't want her support. I still did, I just didn't want it right next to me.

A nurse came in to check Colette's beeping monitors and then everyone started to leave. Tess was still sniffling, and I felt bad for her. I also felt bad in general because I wasn't the type of person who cried immediately when they saw a hurt friend. I wished I were more like Tess.

"We'll be sitting in those chairs we passed, right by the elevator, okay, Frankie?" Mom said.

"Okay," I said, still standing in the exact spot I'd been in the whole time, at the foot of Colette's bed.

"Are you sure you're okay?"

I thought of what Colette had told the teacher in the hall that day in third grade. "Everything's fine."

chapter 23

Fact: Swelling in the brain is one of
the things that can cause a coma.

"I THINK YOU'VE been really different since Mia moved here,"
I admitted to Colette. "And you were kind of a jerk that day
when you were studying in Tess's room. Not kind of. You
were a huge jerk. I've been really mad at you since then."

I knew I probably wouldn't have had the guts to say all
that stuff if she'd been awake. I shifted in the chair next to
her bed, trying not to look at her face with the tube taped
to her cheek.

"It's hard to stay mad at someone when they're hurt, so
I'm probably not mad at you anymore, though."

I thought about Colette telling everyone I take tests in
a special room—when I don't even do that all the time. I
thought about her laughing when Mia had called me a
tornado brain—making fun of me. I thought about how I'd

never say something mean about her behind her back, or to her face.

But then, with a sinking feeling in my belly, I remembered that I had.

Colette's parents were always planning day trips to Portland and Seattle and Olympia, dragging her to indie bookstores and tourist traps. Colette hated it because she was never allowed to bring any friends along. At the end of this past January, just a few weeks before she and Mia had teased me during their study group, Colette had gone on one of the day trips with her parents. The Monday afterward, Colette was standing at my locker when I got to school, excited-emoji face, a wrapped box in her hands.

"I got you a present this weekend!" she said, holding the box out in my direction. She had on a bright green sweater that reminded me of spring even though it was the middle of winter. "I found it in a dusty old bookstore. I had to buy it for you: it's perfect! Open it!"

"Okay . . . ," I said, scrunching my eyebrows together, caught off guard by seeing Colette before school when I normally didn't, by the wrong-season color of her sweater, by her giving me a present on a Monday morning. It was all unexpected. And the honest truth is that I was embarrassed to be receiving a gift in the hallway at school: it was making people look at us—at *me*—and I didn't want to be looked at that day. "It's not my birthday."

"I know when your birthday is, silly." Colette shrugged and shoved the box closer toward me. "I got it for you just because. Open it. I promise you'll like it."

I hate being called *silly*. It always translates into *stupid* in my head.

Mad, I said, "I'll open it later." I turned toward my locker, wanting to shove the box inside so people would stop looking at it as they walked by. I did the combination, but it didn't work on the first try, probably because Colette was distracting me.

"Come on, Frankie, open it now," she said, bouncing up and down. "And tell me about your weekend! Did you go to the—"

"I didn't ask you to get me anything," I interrupted, finally managing to open the locker and throwing the box inside. "And you didn't have to bring it to *school*."

My face was hot. Colette hadn't known, but it'd been a bad morning. The medication I'd been taking was making me feel like my head was going to float off into the sky. I hadn't felt like myself at all.

"Here, I'll just tell you what it is," Colette said. "It's this old board game called Tornado Rex. You're going to love it! You play as a hiker trying to get up a hill before a tornado knocks you—"

"Stop talking about it!" I snapped at her. The hallway was crowded and noisy, so not everyone heard me, but some nearby people did. Colette *definitely* did: she looked like I'd hit her. I should have stopped talking, but it wasn't a day when I could control it. "You're always telling me when to do things," I said. "You think you control my schedule! Stop being so bossy!"

The bell rang; we were late for class. Colette's smile had melted.

She looked at me without saying anything for a few seconds, then shook her head. "That's okay, Frankie, you can open it later."

When I was feeling better after school—after the medication had worn off enough to make me feel like my head was reattached—I'd opened the game and tried it out. And Colette had been right: it *was* perfect. I loved it. I'd texted her: thank you and sorry in one. She'd said it was okay.

But a few weeks later she'd laughed when Mia had called me a name, so maybe it wasn't.

"I guess we both made mistakes," I said to Colette, glancing up at her face, then away again. "I'm sorry." I said the hard word to my shoes. "And I'm sorry I was mean when you came to my room the other night."

It hit me that Colette had probably just waited until I'd gone to do homework at my mom's to come in and take Fred: I never lock my door. And then the whole thing made sense. I imagined it all happening like I was there with her.

Colette fought with her parents about moving.

She came to my room, wanting Fred. When I wouldn't give him to her, she waited and took him anyway. Then she left and did the dune dare, but it was too cold, so she came back and asked Tess for a scarf. She knew she'd need it later.

Then she went to Marsh's, but she ditched her dolphin sweatshirt and scarf for that video because it's always so crazy hot in there. Knowing her next dare was outside, with it getting darker and windier, she borrowed Kai's jacket to layer over her other clothes . . . without asking.

She went to the Sea Witch's house. She went to the school. And then she went . . .

"That was a really stupid thing to do," I said to my friend, filled with regret.

I wished I'd put it all together sooner. I wished I could have helped Colette in time. I tried to think of good memories, when we were younger and the dares and scares were just funny and didn't put anyone in the hospital.

"Hey, remember that time that Tess tried to do that dare where we had to jump over the hurdle at the high school, but she just ran right into it?" I asked. "All three of us couldn't stop laughing," I said to Colette. "Remember?"

I pulled my legs up into the chair and crossed them like a pretzel.

"And remember that time when you rode Tess's favorite horse, Prince, and got so mad because he rolled over to scratch on the sand? And your mom was really mad at you for abandoning the ride when she'd already paid for it?"

I drew a tornado swirl with my fingernail on my knee. "And guess what? You know how you did the ding-dong-ditch dare at the Sea Witch's doorstep—and the kindness dare at the same time, which, by the way, was awesome—well, me and Tess went there, and the Sea Witch totally scared us!"

I laughed because it was more funny than scary now.

"And what about that time when . . ."

I went on and on because talking about dare-or-scare with Colette felt good. Talking with Colette about anything felt good, honestly. Even if I was really just talking *to* Colette.

Sometimes I glanced up at her face, only long enough to make sure she wasn't staring at me. She never was—she didn't open her eyes or move a muscle the whole time I was there. But I had a feeling that she could hear me anyway. I had a feeling that even though we'd both messed up, Colette and I were okay—that we were friends again. And I felt like maybe, in her deep, dark coma dreams, she was laughing with me.

———

As I WALKED down the hall to tell Tess it was her turn, a flood of memories came back to me—tons of dares Colette,

Tess, and I had done together. *Eat a plate of spaghetti without a utensil. Strut down the hall at school like a model. Walk into a room of people and yell, "Merry Christmas!" when it's the middle of summer.*

I was in my own world—*our* world—and so distracted I was almost run over by two nurses rushing in the opposite direction.

I didn't wonder where they were going then.

I know now.

chapter 24

Myth: You should take shelter
under a bridge during a tornado.

"SEE YOU NEXT time," Gabe said, smiling, holding his acoustic guitar. He'd played it during our session, which I didn't hate. Another thing I didn't hate? Having sessions with Gabe again. Even when they were weird Sunday sessions like today because my mom was worried about me since they'd buried my best friend the day before.

Outside, my mom waited in her car. She was making me go with her to the outlet mall in Seaside to get summer clothes. I think she just wanted to keep an eye on me, like I was going to freak out or something. Tess was in the back seat with earphones on and a sketchbook on her lap, staring out the window of the car with puffy red eyes.

"How did it go?" Mom asked when I was buckled in,

pulling out of the parking space. Someone was waiting to pull in.

"Fine," I said. I opened one of the granola bars Mom keeps in the glove box for me and took a huge bite. "Where's Charles? I thought he was coming with us."

"Tyler called in sick, so Charles had to work the front desk," Mom said, sounding irritated. "What did you and Gabe talk about?"

"Isn't that supposed to be private?" I asked back, my mouth full. I accidentally bit the inside of my cheek.

"Sorry," Mom said. "I just meant . . ."

She didn't finish her sentence, and I didn't ask her to. That wasn't what I wanted to talk about.

"When are the police going to give us back Lemonade?" I asked instead, touching the bite mark on the inside of my cheek with my tongue.

"The bike?" Mom glanced at me with a surprised look, then turned back to the road. "I don't think they will," she said. "I mean, I think it'll go to the dump. It's . . . broken."

"I want it back." I took another bite of granola bar, carefully chewing on the unbitten side, then looked over my shoulder at Tess, who was still staring out the window instead of drawing or talking to us. "I want it back and I want Charles to fix it. I want it to be my bike, not the inn's."

Mom turned the car left at the gas station, toward Highway 101; the outlet mall was a whole state away, in

Oregon. It'd take us fifty minutes to get there but I was looking forward to driving over the Astoria Bridge, which is really, really long and very cool. It's a flat, floating bridge for part and then it climbs high into the sky so ships can go under it. I was thinking about the bridge when Mom finally answered me.

"Frankie, I don't think it's a good idea for you to be riding around on the bike that . . ."

Sort of killed my friend? I thought, but didn't say, because Gabe was helping me remember to keep my filter on, and that would probably be upsetting to Tess and Mom even though it was the truth.

"It *is* a good idea," I said firmly.

"Why?"

"Because it's a connection to Colette," I said. I looked over at my mom; she had tears in her eyes.

"I guess I can understand that," she said, wiping them away. "You're a wonderful girl, do you know that?"

I wasn't sure why she'd said that, and it made me feel weird, so I ignored it. "So can I have the bike?"

"I can't guarantee anything, but I'll ask the police," Mom said. "Should we turn on some music?"

I found a station I liked and reclined my seat a little, watching the landscape go by. There was a long stretch of thick forest like what Colette had ridden through, as we wound our way toward the bottom of Washington. Then the forest opened up and there was the ocean, blue and beautiful and stretching on forever.

As we crossed the bridge, looking out at the sun reflecting off the teal water, I thought of a conversation I'd had earlier with Gabe. I'd told him that everyone had cried at Colette's funeral yesterday, including the preacher, who was probably pretty used to funerals. The kids from school cried. Tess cried the hardest—just like she'd done every day since Colette had died. But I hadn't cried at all. And it had bothered me, until Gabe said something kind of simple: *Everyone grieves differently.*

In most things in life, I'm the outsider. I'm the different one. Or at least it feels that way. But Gabe had said, "Death is the deal breaker. There is no normal when it comes to grief."

There is no normal. Which means there is no abnormal either.

Today, I grieved by being thankful for cool bridges and that I only had a month left of school, instead of thinking about Colette, because today, thinking about her felt shocking and raw and awful.

Other times I thought of her, though, with her huge smile and sometimes-too-loud laugh; of her model poses in pictures; of the way she'd hurt me; of the way I'd hurt her; of the way she'd accidentally died. And I talked to her. Sometimes I grieved by reading Fred and purposely remembering all the times that Colette and I had shared. All the dares. All the birthdays. All the embarrassing moments. All the *everything*.

My grieving wasn't the same every day. And it wasn't the same as anyone else's way of handling it. It wasn't wrong or right. It wasn't abnormal or normal.

It just was.

chapter 25

Fact: It can take years to
recover from a tornado.

THE FIRST WEEK in June, the night before the last day of
seventh grade, I climbed into bed with my phone, then
checked the TwisterLvr feed for recent tornado activity.
It'd been what I'd done every night before bed for forever,
up until Colette had gone missing. I wanted to get my routine back.

"There was an EF2 near Colorado Springs, Colorado," I
said out loud. "It was only on the ground for a few minutes,
though."

"Huh," Tess said from her bedroom. Our doors were
open, so I heard her pencil clink against the others in the
box when she set it down.

"What are you drawing?" I asked.

"Colette," she answered quietly.

"Are you okay?" I asked. The question felt strange on my lips. I was practicing being empathetic.

"I guess?" she said. I didn't know what I was supposed to say next. I listened to the waves crash for a few seconds, thinking about it. But then Tess said, "I'm sad." I heard the scratch of pencil on paper. I don't know why, but I imagined that she was working on getting Colette's eyes right. "Mom thinks I should go to art camp this summer. It's in Boston and I could stay with Aunt Maureen. Mom says it'd be good for me to get away."

"Do you want to go?" I asked, feeling unsettled about the idea of Tess leaving. She was the only friend I had left. I'd be completely alone. Well, except I'd have Kai.

"I don't know," Tess said. "I don't know anything."

"You know more than I do."

"I don't know if I'll ever feel okay again," she said sadly. "I hope so."

"Me too," I said. "I mean, I hope you feel okay again soon. I hope I do, too."

"You will, Frankie," Tess said.

"We can't know for sure," I said because it was the truth, but Tess got quiet. I wondered if that was the wrong response.

Sometimes I wished that Gabe would just give me a script for life or put a bug in my ear and talk me through everything.

Tess and I both went back to what we were doing. Her

pencil scratched on the page and I scrolled more and read about a tornado in a place called Campinas. I opened my internet app to figure out where that was; the app was still on Viewer from when we'd been looking at the dare-or-scare videos. I tapped the address bar, ready to switch to my search engine, when something caught my attention.

A new video had been added to our Viewer account.

"Tess!" I shouted. "Get in here!"

"What's wrong?" she asked from her bed, clearly not moving.

"I'm serious, come here!"

She sighed loudly, and I heard the art book thunk onto the bed. She clomped in from the other room and stopped next to me. She was wearing her pajamas and her hair was unusually messed up.

"Look!" I said, flipping my phone around so she could see. At first I could tell she didn't notice, because when she did, her wide eyes told me so.

"How did that . . . ," she whispered, grabbing my phone so she could scroll through herself.

I thought about it for a minute.

"She's dead," I said.

"God, Frankie, I know," Tess said, shaking her head at me. "Why do you have to—"

"No, I just mean . . . I'm just thinking," I said. "I just mean that she couldn't have uploaded it."

"Fine."

"Should we watch it?"

I took the phone back. "Of course, but, just a second," I said, thinking furiously. "No one else had the password so . . . she would have had to have started uploading it and then—"

"If she started the upload somewhere there wasn't Wi-Fi," Tess said, "then it would have finished when she got a connection again."

"Like if she started at the lighthouse," I said quietly.

"And didn't make it back to civilization."

We both stared at my phone.

"The upload date is two years ago," I said, pointing at the screen. "She must have changed it again."

"I wish we knew why she kept doing that," Tess said.

"I told you. She did it so we wouldn't see an alert. She probably wanted to surprise us with the videos."

"You never told me that," Tess said. She didn't sound mad, just matter-of-fact. "You told me something about Kai and Dillon and their skateboarding channel."

"Yeah, but . . ." I thought back, trying to remember. I know I'd connected the dots from Kai about why she'd change the dates, understanding that it meant Colette had wanted to keep the videos secret from us. And I thought I'd said that to Tess. But now I couldn't remember doing it.

"Did I tell you that Viewer automatically archives videos

after three years?" I asked. "So our old ones aren't gone forever . . . they're just in the cloud or whatever."

"*I* told *you* that," Tess said, shaking her head.

Tess sat down on my bed next to me, which bothered me, but I didn't make her get off. I figured she wouldn't be there too long. I told myself not to say anything.

Tess leaned closer so she could see the video. I double tapped to start it, neither of us saying anything about how she was alive in this video, and not alive now.

"Turn on your sound," Tess whispered. "She's talking."

"It is on, there's no sound on the videos," I whispered back.

Tess tsked and took the phone from me, messed with it, then handed it back. She rewound the video and hit play, and the sound of Colette's voice startled me.

"How did you do that?" I asked.

"Shhh!" Tess said, and I didn't get mad, because I wanted to hear what Colette was saying in the video, too.

"I want you to know that this dare is terrifying!" Colette said with a laugh. She was on the bike path, holding the camera out from her face. She wasn't wearing a helmet. "Here goes nothing!"

She turned the video on fast motion through her ride. Tess and I were squished together, her biting her nails loudly, me too sucked in by the video to care about Tess's touch or nails or her being on my bed in the first place. I was scared that we'd see Colette go off the road, but instead, in an instant, the fast motion stopped, and Colette was at the lighthouse. She'd made it.

I was letting that thought wash over me when I heard her say, "Frankie, I don't know how you did this like it was nothing—and as a younger kid! You're really brave, my friend." She looked around again. "Okay, that's it for this one."

The video clicked off.

I felt Tess crying next to me, her shoulders shaking and the force of it vibrating my whole bed.

"I'm sorry," I said. "I shouldn't have told you I found it."

"No, it's okay," she said through her tears. "It's good to see her again." Then she asked, wiping her eyes and sniffing, "That's it? There aren't any more?"

"I guess not," I said, scrolling down the page to make sure. "No, that's all."

I scooted over a little to give us both some room. Tess hugged one of my pillows. I didn't want her to, but I didn't say anything because I knew she probably needed the comfort. She wiped her cheeks again with her arm. She was going to get my pillow wet, I knew it. She stared into space, sniffing. I hadn't turned on the lamp, so the room had gotten dark and it made me tired. I scooted close to the wall and leaned back on my other pillow.

"Can I sleep in your room tonight?" she asked. I didn't

answer right away, so Tess said, "It's okay, Frankie, I know you don't like people in your room."

No, I don't.

But you're different.

But you kick!

Also, my space is my space.

But you're so sad.

And I'm sad, too.

The sides of my brain fought for so long that Tess started to get up.

"Wait," I said, not wanting to be mean or insensitive. Wanting to be there for her when she needed me. Wanting to be a friend to my sister.

"It's okay," Tess said again. She looked miserable. "I'll see you in the morning."

I wanted to be someone who could say yes immediately. Who didn't think about how weird it would be to sleep next to another person, even my sister. Other girls had sleepovers—I never did. I wanted to be the girl who had sleepovers.

"Wait, Tess," I said, standing up, thinking of a compromise where someone else wouldn't be in my space—touching my stuff. "Let's sleep in your room."

epilogue

BEFORE SCHOOL ON the first day of eighth grade, I was out on the beach, sitting on a washed-up log while Pirate chased pipers near the water.

I took out my phone and opened Viewer. I purposely hadn't checked it all summer because seeing Colette alive when she wasn't anymore had felt too painful, but I'd promised myself I'd look again before school started, to remember her. School would start in minutes, so I was out of time: I had to look.

I cranked the phone's volume up all the way, feeling stupid that I'd thought there wasn't sound on any of the videos—and thankful that Tess had fixed my phone. With the sound on, I watched the video of the last dare Colette ever did—the ride to the lighthouse—feeling happy when she called me brave. I watched the other videos, too, like her running through the beach grass with the thud of the hollow ground as she ran by, me imagining her jumping off the dune and wondering how far she got before she landed. And then I opened the video where she was singing at school, fast-forwarding past the talking part to the song.

She stood at center court in the gym, singing full volume into a portable microphone she'd had forever. I'd heard her sing before and wasn't shocked by her nice voice.

What she sang, though, that was another story.

Last year, about this time, a bunch of kids from school had set up a bonfire on the beach to celebrate the end of summer. Colette and Tess had forced me to go: I'd wanted to stay in and watch *Tornado Ally*. But they'd bribed me with marshmallows.

Someone had brought a portable speaker and was streaming music. A dad of one of the kids was lurking off to the side in a shelter, looking at his phone. He'd started the fire and had been designated chaperone, I guess.

When Tess, Colette, and I had arrived, we searched for sticks, then put down our blanket and started toasting marshmallows. There were probably twelve or thirteen kids there including us, Mia, Colin, Bryce, and Marcus from homeroom, who was always getting in trouble. That night, we'd all watched as he'd picked up a live crab and chased Mia with it, then gotten scolded by the lurking parent.

Anyway, Kai had been there, too. I'd noticed him through the fire, right when the playlist changed to a song that now I'll probably never forget in my life. You know those songs that feel like they're controlling your emotions? It was one of those.

"You like him, don't you?" Colette had asked, too quietly for anyone else to hear. I'd kept my eyes on Kai, watching him laughing with Dillon about dropping a marshmallow in the sand, daring him to eat it. "Frankie, you do, right?"

I hadn't said anything at first. But something about the song and the warm summer night and the ocean next to me and the stars overhead had made me someone else for a second—someone who could easily identify her emotions.

"Maybe," I'd whispered to Colette. She was the only person I'd ever come close to admitting that to, and that *maybe* had been a big deal to me.

I guess Colette had known it was a big deal, too.

I rewound to the beginning to hear Colette talk.

"Frankie, I have something to say, okay?" She backed away from where she'd propped the phone, stumbling a little on the freshly polished gym floor.

"I'm going to do the dare in a second, but first, I know you're mad at me." Colette looked down at her scuffed white sneakers—I'd been right about those, too. "I'm pretty sure I know why, and I feel really bad about it." She looked up again, her face concerned. "I hope that when you watch these videos of our old dares, you'll see that I'm sorry. It was the best thing I could think to do for you, so you'd know how much I miss our friendship. This weird game you made up was one of my favorite things we ever did together. And I hope seeing it again will make you want to be friends again, because I'm moving soon, and I won't be able to stand it if you're still mad at me."

She looked at the floor and sniffed, then took a deep breath. She tugged down the hem of her T-shirt, tossed her bright red hair over her shoulder, and cleared her throat. She looked around, probably to make sure she was alone.

"Okay, Frankie, this song is for you."

And then she sang my song for Kai.

Even though it was Colette singing and not the real band, it made me feel squishy in the same way that I had last year. And watching Colette sing like she was on a reality show after sneaking into our school, watching her go full-out, I felt braver about school starting. I felt braver about everything. I felt inspired by her.

I wiped away the salty tears that had finally come in their own time, just like Gabe had said they would. I threw the stick Pirate had just dropped at my feet, then I texted Kai.

FRANKIE

Hi

His reply came back quickly.

KAI

Sup!

How was ur summer?

Mostly good

Are you excited for school???

I'm excited to not be at the retirement village anymore

So many old people

I mean they're cool but

My Gpops made me play cards every single day

LOL

So, I was wondering . . .

???

Um . . . ur typing a long time

K now I'm nervous

Frankie?

I might have to call you Frances to get your attention . . .

> Back!

> Pirate wanted me to throw her stick

> NEVER CALL ME FRANCES

LOL, got it

So . . . what's the ???

I took a deep breath.

> I was just going to ask . . .

> Wanna do a dare with me sometime?

It took almost no time at all for him to reply.

YES.

Today

?

My belly and cheeks both felt warm, and I was glad that I was the only person on the beach and that dogs don't care if you're embarrassed.

> Meet later at the frying pan after school . . . 4?

K!!

I sent him a thumbs-up emoji, then he sent a smile emoji back, then even though I wanted to send him fifty more, I put my phone away, thinking Gabe would be proud of me for stopping the conversation.

I didn't know this then since I'm not psychic, but later, Kai would ask me to hold his hand—and I would for a whole minute without freaking out about touching another person, because Kai isn't just any other person. He's Kai. And holding his hand would feel awkward but nice, and less disgusting than I would have imagined.

The reason I could do that is because of change. Change used to be my enemy because I'd thought it was always bad. For sure, there'd been a lot of bad change that'd happened lately. But there'd been a little bit of good change, too: change in me. Sitting on the log, smiling about Kai like my cheeks were going to break, I felt mostly ready to start eighth grade. I felt older. I felt less alone. I felt okay.

And I felt okay that I didn't feel okay about Colette.

I used to try to just deal with things and move on. It's not worth it to think about sad things, like getting teased by kids you don't know. (It's harder when you're being made fun of by kids you do know.) But I used to try to just handle a situation and then forget it if I could. I'm sure Gabe would tell me an official therapy word for that if I asked him.

But Colette . . . Her death was a sad thing I couldn't move on from easily. I didn't know how long losing her would feel like a boulder on my chest—maybe forever. But the thing that made it the tiniest bit better was that now I knew that I hadn't ever really lost her friendship. That made it okay for me to feel not okay—for as long as I needed to.

"I miss you," I said to Colette, hoping the ocean wind would carry my message off to her, wherever she was. I waited a little bit, to see if a message came back. None did, but I still felt like maybe she'd heard me.

I stood up and stretched, ready to go back to the inn to get my backpack for school. Before I called for Pirate, before I started whatever was coming next, I waited just a few seconds longer still. Something felt different about my body: something felt better.

I looked down at my hands and realized that, without knowing it, I'd flipped them over, so the backs of my hands were against my jeans.

Facing the ocean, on the beach where we'd spent so much of our time together, feeling both okay and not okay, I stood as my friend Colette had told me to.

I stood with my palms up.

Author's Note

NEURODIVERGENT IS A newish term for people living with developmental disabilities such as dyslexia, attention deficit hyperactivity disorder (ADHD), Tourette's syndrome, and obsessive-compulsive disorder, and for those on the autism spectrum. I hadn't heard of or used the word until I wrote *Tornado Brain*, despite knowing and loving several people who fall into this category. Instead, I describe them using positive terms like bright, creative, hilarious, curious, and inventive.

That's not always how they describe themselves, though, because living with a developmental disability can make people feel the opposite of bright, inventive, or curious. They can feel stupid, different, weird in a bad way, and disconnected. According to the Centers for Disease Control and Prevention, about one in six of the 74.2 million children in the United States have a developmental disability, so they're not alone—but it doesn't mean they don't feel that way.

My wish is that *Tornado Brain* helps neurodivergent readers feel more connected. Frankie sees the world in a unique way—I hope readers gain a new perspective from her story. And I hope *Tornado Brain* reminds neurotypical readers to practice empathy. Neurodivergence is invisible; reading more books featuring neurodivergent characters is a step toward understanding.

A *Wired* magazine article from 2013 said, "In a world changing faster than ever, honoring and nurturing neurodiversity is civilization's best chance to thrive in an uncertain future."

Civilization's best chance to thrive.

There's nothing stupid about that.

TURN THE PAGE FOR A SNEAK PEEK
OF CAT PATRICK'S LATEST BOOK

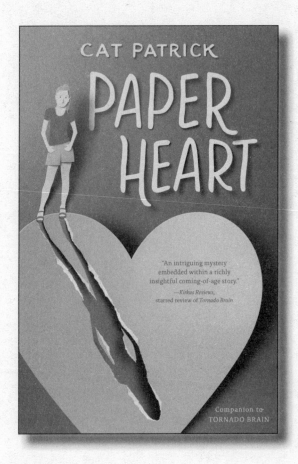

CAT PATRICK

PAPER HEART

"An intriguing mystery
embedded within a richly
insightful coming-of-age story."
—*Kirkus Reviews*,
starred review of *Tornado Brain*

Companion to
TORNADO BRAIN

"WHY ARE YOU calling so early?"

I had the phone on speaker; tears filled my eyes at the sound of my fraternal twin sister's scratchy voice. It wasn't just that it was morning: her voice always sounded like that. It was mesmerizing, even if she was saying . . .

"Seriously, Tess! What's the emergency? Because that's the only reason you should call me before ten."

"Hey, Frankie," I said, hugging my bare knees with my left hand, holding the phone with my right. "Sorry I woke you up."

"You didn't," she said. "You interrupted my daydream."

"Oh. Sorry." I shifted to get more comfortable. Not wanting to wake Kennedy, I'd crept outside to sit on the boulder that was big enough for two. Of course, it was just me on it this morning. I wasn't in the middle, though. I'd left space for Colette.

Stupid. She's gone!

"So, what's up?" Frankie said before a long, drawn-out yawn, all casual, like I was in my room right next to hers at the inn where we lived. Like I wasn't several states away. Like she didn't miss me at all.

"Nothing, I just wanted to say hi to you," I said, deflated. "Mom told me to check in with you guys, and I hadn't had a chance ye—"

"Uh-huh," Frankie interrupted. "Got it."

I heard covers rustling like she was rolling over. I pictured her comforter halfway off her bed; her wavy dark brown hair with a nest in the back; her chocolate eyes with dark circles under them; the floor of her room littered with books, clothes, and papers . . . like usual. The thought made me feel like my insides were melted caramel.

Another call came in: a video call . . . from Frankie.

Sighing, I answered it.

"Hi," I said, smoothing my hair self-consciously since I could see myself now.

A pang of homesickness hit me when Frankie filled the screen. She looked exactly as I'd pictured her. She had on a gray tank top with a blue strap showing underneath, and her bangs were so long, hitting the top of her cheekbones.

Behind her, the window was open, making the sheer white curtain billow in with the breeze.

"I miss home," I said, imagining the smell of the ocean through the screen.

"Yeah," Frankie said. "So, what's up?" she repeated. Frankie wasn't a small-talk kind of person.

"Nothing, I just . . ." *I called because I wish you'd called me. I wish you'd ask me if I'm okay. I know you won't.* "How are you doing?"

"Fine." She stared at herself.

"I mean about Colette," I clarified. It'd been two and a half months since she'd died. The time that'd gone by felt like forever and five minutes at the same time.

"I know, I'm fine."

"You're . . . *fine*?" She sounded like Colette had meant nothing to her, which I knew wasn't true. Still, it was frustrating how, on the outside, Frankie seemed completely normal. "I don't understand why you're not sadder," I admitted without thinking. Often, I filtered what I said to my sister, fearing she'd get upset. Maybe it was the distance that made me feel braver, but today I didn't hold back. "I don't get why I'm the only one who seems to be breaking down."

"You seem fine to me," Frankie said plainly, surprising me by not yelling about what I'd said. "Gabe says everyone grieves in their own way." Gabe was Frankie's therapist. "You cry; I don't. It's not like I don't miss her."

"Okay," I said. "It's just . . ."

Other people might have asked, "Just what?" Frankie didn't.

The conversation wasn't making me feel better, so I decided to switch topics. "Hey, did Colette ever tell you the ghost story about William and Lilah?"

"I hate ghost stories. Why would she tell me one?" Frankie kept her eyebrows natural instead of plucking them, so when she pulled them together, like right now, it was dramatic.

"Nothing, I thought—" A horsefly landed on my knee with its gigantic coal-colored body; I quickly flicked it away before it took a bite. "I told the story to Colette when we were here last summer, and yesterday in a park, I saw someone who reminded me of William."

"Who's William?"

"The guy in the ghost story."

"Is he real?"

"No, Frankie, I made him up," I said, rolling my eyes. "But then I saw someone who looked like how I pictured the guy."

"Cool." My sister was making faces at herself in the camera. She currently had her mouth open as wide as it would go. I could see she needed to floss more.

"It was scary, actually."

"You think everything is scary," Frankie said, hurting

my feelings. "It's weird you like haunted houses and scary books so much when they freak you out."

I don't as much now.

"It was our thing, mine and Colette's," I said.

"Duh." She clenched her jaw and started snarling at the camera like a wolf. Through her teeth, she asked, "What did the guy in the park do?"

"He looked at me in a creepy way and followed me out," I said confidently, even though it was possible he hadn't actually followed me but just left on his own.

"Cool."

Frankie said *cool* a lot. It was almost always a sign she was only half listening. She started alternating exaggerated "ooh" and "aah" faces.

"And he tapped his foot every time I took a step when I went by him. It was so weird. I mean, who does that?"

"Like Colette's soundtrack game," Frankie interrupted.

"What game?" I asked, hugging myself tighter, shivering for no reason. I looked around the prairie; no one was nearby.

"It was really stupid," Frankie said flatly. "It was one of those recess games . . . like jail and jumper."

"I remember those," I said, a creepy feeling spreading through my body. "What was the soundtrack game?" I waited as Frankie contorted her face a few more times. "Frankie! Will you look at me and answer?"

"I can do two things at once," she replied, now admiring her extreme closeup. "One kid walked or ran or hopped around as quietly as they could and someone else tried to make the sounds that matched their movements. The third person was the judge." She looked at the lens for maybe the first time. "See? Stupid. That's why you don't remember it."

"I sort of do," I said, curling deeper into a ball. "But . . . why would the man . . ." It didn't make sense.

Frankie turned the phone so she was upside down. In a monotone voice, she said, "Maybe he's a ghost messenger and Colette's trying to communicate with you."

"Ohmygod, Frankie!" I said, holding the phone out from my face, scared and annoyed at the same time. "That's such a terrible thing to say!"

"No it isn't." She turned the phone again, then set it down so all I could see was the white ceiling. Frankie had put a sticky note up there; I couldn't read what it said. "I'm just kidding."

"It's *not* funny."

"Ghost messengers aren't real. *Ghosts* aren't even real," she said. "I watched a documentary on what happens after we die. Spoiler alert: it's nothing. We just disappear."

The ceiling in Frankie's room didn't notice I suddenly had tears streaming down my face. Neither did my sister, whose volume had gotten faint like she was across the

6

room doing something else. These days, I felt like a balloon with tears instead of helium inside, and the tiniest pinprick would make them leak out.

"Aunt Maureen has breakfast ready," I said, trying to make my voice sound sturdy. "I'd better go. Will you tell Mom I'll call her and Charles later?"

"Uh-huh, yeah," Frankie said. I knew she'd probably forget. "Bye."

She thudded across her bedroom; then I saw her thumb come in close. The call disconnected.

Half an hour later, when breakfast really was ready, my phone buzzed with a new text. The phone stuck to the tablecloth when I picked it up.

FRANKIE

Sorry

I sent back a question mark, then:

TESS

For what?

For making you cry.

I didn't think you noticed

I notice everything

7

> Thanks. I accept

> Accept what?

> Your apology

> That's such a weird thing to say
> I accept
> So frmal
> *formal

> Sorry

It always came back to that. To me being the one to apologize.

Her read receipt told me that she saw my response, but she didn't write back. I left things there, too, not wanting to talk in circles. And her apology had helped.

That doesn't mean I stopped thinking about the seed Frankie had planted in my brain, about Colette trying to contact me. The mean voice shouted in my head that it was a ridiculous thing to consider, but looking back, I see that's when it started. I wonder if things would have gone differently if I'd never called my sister that morning.

Or maybe it all would have happened no matter what.

IN MY DREAM, in the dark, I followed Colette down the cabin steps. She didn't hold on at all; she kept looking back to smile encouragingly at me, and it made me nervous she'd lose her balance, but she didn't.

Her red hair was long and loose around her face, her freckles had multiplied, and she wore a T-shirt that said ASK ME ABOUT THE AFTERLIFE.

She danced and spun and skipped across the thin, worn, multicolor-striped carpeting to the back door of the cabin, the space barely lit by the porch light still on in front. Colette walked into flip-flops, then went outside, me following, the gravel crunching under our feet.

She put her hand up to side-block her mouth: whisper pose.

"I met a boy today," she said at a regular volume. She took her hand away. "He's kind of nerdy but so cute!" She did her signature happy shoulder dance. "He's hung up on his old girlfriend, but if he wasn't, I'd be all, 'I volunteer as tribute!'"

I laughed at Colette's reference to the Hunger Games, a series she'd read so many times the covers of the books were duct-taped to the spines.

"Did your mom give away your copies?" I asked Colette in the dream.

She shrugged. "Not yet, but she will."

"Don't you care?"

Colette didn't answer. Instead, she went over and climbed up the two-person rock. I stared at her as she jumped off into the sagebrush. I bet that scratched her ankles, but she didn't seem to mind. She immediately climbed up again, one knee on the rock first, then all of her.

"The boy I met wants to know why no one saved him," she said, looking ahead of her, not at me. She jumped off, her hair flying straight up, landing with a thud. Laughing bitterly, she climbed back up.

"He's pretty mad about that part. Like, where was his dad? Where were his friends? His stupid girlfriend?"

She jumped off again.

"Why are you doing that?" I asked.

She didn't answer; she only climbed the rock.

"I wonder the same thing: why no one saved me."

"We tried! We tried to figure out where you were, but it was too late!"

Her eyes snapped to mine. They were blank, unfriendly. "Did you, *Tess*?"

Jump.

Climb.

"*Frankie* tried to help me," Colette said. "You just went along with it—but not at first. You didn't even *believe* her at first."

Jump.

Climb.

I felt sick because it was true. Frankie had figured out the clues before I had—and believed them—because she saw things that other people didn't sometimes. That *I* didn't. Colette had been playing the game we'd made up as kids, and Frankie had remembered the details and been able to connect them. Without Frankie doing that, the police might *never* have found Colette.

But it's not like I didn't do other things, like hang up posters and try to be there for Colette's parents. And I helped Frankie when she asked me to. I just didn't figure it out on my own.

Because you're book smart but street stupid, Mean Me said, with me even in dreams.

"You were *both* supposed to be my best friends," Colette said.

Jump.

Climb.

"We are!" I said. "I am," I whispered. "I'll always be your best friend."

Colette looked at me again, with those same empty eyes. "Prove it," she said, stepping to the edge of the rock, her flip-flops hanging over. "If you're my best friend, then save me."

She jumped. But this time the ground opened up like a tunnel to the center of the earth, and instead of falling just three or four feet and landing with a thud in the sagebrush, she was swallowed into the darkness.

"Colette!" I screamed, rushing over to peer down into the pit, unable to see or hear her at all. "Colette! Are you there? Colette! Come back! Colette!" I screamed and screamed and sobbed in my dream.

Then, suddenly, I was awake, Kennedy's hand on my shoulder. I blinked into the darkness, looking for Colette.

"It's okay," Kennedy whispered. "You're okay. You were just dreaming."

I swallowed hard and took a big breath, trying to slow my heartbeat. Kennedy took her hand away, picking up a glass of water on the nightstand. "Here."

I chugged the whole thing, then set down the empty glass.

"Sorry for waking you up," I said.

"Sorry about Colette."

Kennedy flopped back onto her bed, and I rolled over and hugged Woogles, my childhood teddy bear. I spent most of the rest of the night wide awake listening to the noisy crickets—Frankie had been right about them—counting the nails in the logs on the wall, and thinking about the best friend I hadn't been strong enough to save, even in a dream.

Acknowledgments

I<small>F YOU'RE A</small> person who reads acknowledgments, you're my kind of person. Even still, I'll attempt to keep this brief.

Thank you to the team that helped make *Tornado Brain* happen, including Dan Lazar, Cecilia De La Campa, Torie Doherty-Munro, and Alessandra Birch at Writers House; and Stacey Barney, Jen Klonsky, Chandra Wohleber, Caitlin Tutterow, Vanessa DeJesús, and the entire marketing, sales, and publicity machine at G. P. Putnam's Sons. Stacey and Jen, our conference call the day the book landed at Putnam is tucked into my heart for keeps. Thank you, also, to the thoughtful agents and editors around the globe who've connected with Frankie and introduced her to readers far away.

Special thanks to the contributors of several websites for reminding me of tornado facts I learned as a kid or teaching me new ones, including *National Geographic, HowStuffWorks, Scientific American, LiveScience,* and *Weather.com.* To *Superbetter* author Jane McGonigal for introducing me to the idea of turning my palms up to feel less stressed. And to my sister for leaving *Superbetter* on my doorstep precisely when I needed it.

Speaking of sisters, I'd also like to thank my village . . . my siblings and siblings-in-law, parents, aunts and uncles, nieces and nephews, co-parent extraordinaire, century-old grandpa, and the rest of the branches of my family tree—blood or not—in Oregon, California, Wyoming, Colorado, and, of course, Washington.

On the topic of The Evergreen State, I must thank the residents of the town of Long Beach for cultivating such a perfect setting for Frankie's world. Like something a middle schooler might write in a friend's yearbook, "Never change."

You either, Jon. For me, Long Beach equals you. Thank you for introducing me to my happy place and for making it even better, lighting fires in the rain, patiently detangling kites, leading bike tours, committing to reconnaissance missions, and laughing with me when Clue is the most terrifying game on Earth. Thank you for being there through the emotional birth of this book, and always.

And especially, thank you to my daughters. You are, simply, my everything. You inspire me and support me in a way no one else can—L, with your creativity and honesty, and C, with your constant encouragement and editor's eye. This is our book, and it wouldn't have happened without you. I love you both more than you can imagine.

Finally, I want to thank the Frankies out there for striving to thrive in a world that wasn't built with you in mind. Life can be challenging when you think differently. Though it may feel like it sometimes, you are not alone.

Together we can embrace our differences. We can celebrate the creative genius and unique perspectives of people like Frankie instead of trying to shove everyone into the same box. Because if you ask me, if we were all the same, we'd make up a dreadfully boring box.

So thank you, reader, for being uniquely you.

Whatever brand of brain you've got.